WHY SHOULD EVERY CHRISTIAN PRAY FOR AND SUPPORT ISRAEL?

REVEREND NORMA DUNCAN

First Edition

Book

Book Cover Designed by Dennis Foote, Dennis' Computer Graphics.

Printed in the United States of America.

"Scripture taken from the *Amplified Bible, Old Testament*, copyright 1965, 1987 by The Zondervan Corporation. The *Amplified New Testament*, Copyright 1954, 1958, 1987 by the Lockman Foundation. Used by Permission."

ACKNOWLEDGEMENTS

I am especially grateful to my husband, Bill, and my daughter, Deborah Majors, for their editorial assistance and encouragement. This book was made better because of their effort and skills.

Thanks to my typist, Bess Bolen, for making herself so available and for her willing heart.

My gratitude goes out to Gwen Cohen who, after hearing this message on cassette tapes, wrote to us and donated her professional services. She transcribed the message from the tapes and presented it to us in manuscript form, ready for revision. She felt that this message had to be presented to people in written form. God used this wonderful Jewish lady to nudge me into writing this book.

I greatly appreciate my grandson, Joshua Aspinwall, a talented young artist, for the time he spent and the effort he put forth gathering book cover information. His artistic advice and artist's eye were invaluable in the decision-making process. I also appreciate my grandson, Daniel Majors, whose smile and kind words brightened my days and helped me to persevere the four years it took to accomplish the revision of this literary work. I am deeply indebted to Nylene Becker for her trips to the library on my behalf, to Danny Majors, my son-in-law, for utilizing his computer expertise, Deborah, my daughter, Pete and Cynthia Mahon and Nylene for their constant encouragement and for the kind deeds they showed toward me in my time of need and to Ollie Mae Price for the earnest prayers that she prayed for me.

I am deeply indebted to my son, Reverend J. V. Aspinwall, for his willingness to do whatever it took to help me finish this book. He extended overflowing kindness to me during the whole time that I was preparing this work.

INTRODUCTION

When I was asked to write an introduction to *Why Should Every Christian Pray For and Support Israel?* I was eager to be the one to tell you a little about the wonderful lady whose work for God has inspired millions. But before I tell you about her, let me tell you about the work she does. Prior to this book being published and distributed throughout the world, free-of-charge and postpaid, audio-cassette teaching tapes were the medium used to spread the in-depth teachings and expounding of God's Word by His faithful servant, the Reverend Norma Duncan; they too were free-of-charge and postpaid.

We at the Living Word Church of Niceville have received thousands of letters from all over the world reporting the impact God's Word on the tapes has had. From these letters, we have learned that millions of lives have been changed and hundreds of thousands of souls have been saved. We have received word of cases of physical healings attributed to the messages on these tapes, some considered terminal by the medical profession. After learning God's Word from the tapes, people who once harbored deep prejudice and hatred toward Israel and God's people, the Jews, now love Israel and the Jews. Church fellowships have established libraries to house the tapes and spread God's Word in their areas. The tapes are played at crusades throughout East Africa. They are played in churches of all denominations, homes, schools, universities, marketplaces, on the streets and on buses and trains. We have received numerous reports of passers-by falling to their knees in the middle of public streets and marketplaces, and crying out to God as they hear the Truth being broadcast on public address systems and tape players. Hundreds of Pastors, Evangelists and other church workers have written to say that after hearing the inspired information on the tapes, their lives have been changed, and they proclaimed that they have finally heard the Truth.

We in the Living Word Church tape ministry continue to receive letter after letter wanting to know about this woman of God whose teaching of God's Word has transformed their lives. I can tell you that the Reverend Norma Duncan is a remarkable woman who practices what she preaches. She is dedicated and works incessantly to carry out her God-given task. She is unselfish and loyal to the things of God and is faithful and true despite much persecution for teaching the Truth. Her inner beauty outshines even her great physical beauty, and her courage and bravery to battle on in the army of God is inspiring to all who know her.

The Reverend Norma Duncan is not only the founder of a worldwide ministry, but she is also a minister, teacher and author of over 40 books on audio tape. These tapes are now being systematically revised and published in written form. Her work is in many theological colleges and is even in the Christian Embassy in Israel. She has been called by God to shoulder a great work for His name's sake and for His people, the Jews, a task that she carries out with joy and determination. In a world where many ministers lift up themselves and are greedy for gain, Reverend Duncan exalts only God. Knowing that she insists her work be sent out all over the world free-of-charge to all men who request it should give you a glimpse into the righteous character of God's servant. While others seek fame, fortune and an opportunity to express personal opinions and promote themselves, Reverend Duncan is a seeker and expounder of truth, full of zeal and sincerity and is an example to all. I am proud to be not only her daughter and a fellow minister, but also her devoted friend.

In your hands is a great treasure, lovingly and painstakingly prepared over many years by a true minister of God. I rejoiced at the knowledge and wisdom contained in the pages of this book. Words cannot express my deep gratitude toward God and His faithful servant for opening my eyes to such priceless spiritual treasures of a caliber that can only be described as awe-inspiring. The great revelations this book holds made me feel as though I was walking around in the very mind of God.

I've told you a little about the author and I've shared some of the reports we've received, so hang on to your seats and get ready for an unprecedented spiritual adventure which I guarantee you will never forget. You too will be thanking God for this enlightenment and for the dear lady, the Reverend Norma Duncan, God's obedient vessel through whom He sent this incredible information to you. Not only will your eyes be opened to profound truth, but you will be spiritually strengthened, invigorated and refreshed. God be praised!

Deborah Ruth Majors

A GLIMPSE OF WHAT GOD IS ACCOMPLISHING THROUGH THIS TEACHING ON ISRAEL

Numerous people have informed us of how blessed they were by the letters my son, Reverend J. V. Aspinwall, read at the end of the cassette taped series entitled, *Why Should Every Christian Pray For And Support Israel?* So after I had revised that series and put it into book form, I decided that it would be beneficial to leave space for excerpts from some of the many thousands of wonderful letters that we have received from those who have benefited from the Israel teaching.

The following letters will truly bless you. They will bring joy and gladness to your heart and fill your eyes with tears. They will also provide you with a glimpse of what God is accomplishing for His name's sake through the truth in this inspired teaching that you hold in your hands. Furthermore, these letters will show you what can be accomplished for God when thousands of ministers and laymen lay aside denominational barriers in order to promote the truth and to help God vindicate His name.

You will be amazed by the humble, teachable spirits of the men and women who wrote these letters. These wonderful people stand as an example to Christians throughout the world. One man wrote "Many church leaders would learn a valuable lesson in humility from these tapes, *Why Should Every Christian Pray For And Support Israel?"* Along those same lines, I must add that many ministers could also learn a valuable lesson in humility from the contents of the letters that I will soon present.

All I can do is stand in awe as the Holy Spirit moves the truth in this series on Israel through city after city, country after country. God is no respecter of persons. For His name's sake, He offers the truth in this teaching to world leaders and to those who fill the lowliest positions. He offers it to ministers and laymen alike. He offers it to the rich and to the poor. He offers it to the educated and to the uneducated. He offers it to all men, free of charge and postpaid.

Most of the letter excerpts that I will share with you are from men and women living in the country of Kenya, East Africa. I chose Kenya, because as you will soon read for yourself, God has sent revival to Kenya through this teaching on Israel. I believe God has flooded Kenya with the truth on Israel and sent to its people spiritual revival as a reward for a particularly courageous act displayed by Kenya's government. In 1976 Kenya allowed Israel to land and to refuel its planes in Kenya while carrying out a rescue mission in Tempeeka, Uganda. You will recall that Palestinian terrorists had taken 100 hostages and had threatened to kill them if Israel did not meet their demands. Kenya was the only East African country that was willing to allow the soldiers involved in the rescue mission to land and refuel their planes. Thus, God has blessed those who blessed Israel (Kenya) with the greatest gift that He could give the Kenyan people—the truth.

Remember, these letters were written before this series was revised and put in book form, that is, we were still sending out this message via cassette tapes. However, as well as providing you with a glimpse of what God is doing as He moves throughout the world by His Word in this book, the excerpts will also give you an idea of the immense understanding that you are going to receive through the inspired information in this book.

RESPONSES FROM WORLD RULERS AND GOVERNMENT OFFICIALS

1986   Upon receiving the Israel lesson on tape, the PRIME MINISTER OF GRENADA, HERBERT A. BLAIZE, was so impressed that he personally passed them on to radio Grenada.

****

1986 UNITED STATES CONGRESSMAN, EARL HUTTO, REPRESENTATIVE OF FLORIDA, called the taped lesson on Israel, "a wonderful gift." He also said, "Dear Rev. Duncan...I have just finished tape number 1. I wanted you to know that I appreciate very much the opportunity to hear this series of messages and after listening to the first tape, I assure you that I am in complete agreement with you in regard to our need to support Israel. Again, I am grateful to you for sending these tapes to me and others in Congress who have the responsibility of helping the Israeli people in their struggle in the middle east.

****

1986   While in the Senate, THE LATE GOVERNOR, LAWTON CHILES, OF FLORIDA sent a letter of thanks and appreciation for the tapes by Reverend Norma Duncan in which he said, "I am glad to have the benefit of your wisdom on this subject."

****

1986 SENATOR, STROM THURMOND, OF SOUTH CAROLINA wrote: "I am certain that the information it provides will be of beneficial use to me and my staff as relevant matters come before the Senate."

****

1986 CONGRESSMAN, CHALMERS P. WYLIE, OF OHIO wrote: "Thank you for sending me a copy of this lesson. It was most interesting and informative to hear."

****

1986 THE CHANCELLOR OF WEST GERMANY, HELMUT KOHL, replied: "We have taken the tapes to heart."

****

1986 PRIME MINISTER THATCHER'S CORRESPONDENT FROM THE BRITISH FOREIGN OFFICE, after listening to the tapes, called them, "beautifully presented tapes."

****

1986 CORAZON AQUINO, FORMER PRESIDENT OF THE PHILIPPINES, in the middle of a crises in her government, took the time to write a personal letter of thanks and appreciation to Reverend Norma Duncan.

****

OTHER RESPONSES

1986 We were informed by the DIRECTOR OF THE INTERNATIONAL CHRISTIAN EMBASSY IN JERUSALEM, ISRAEL, JOHANN LUCKHOFF, that the lesson on Israel was placed in the library at the Christian Embassy. What a fitting place for such a God-inspired lesson dealing with Israel to be. May all those who enter the Embassy in Jerusalem make good use of this information.

****

LAWRENCE D. WASSER, THE PREVIOUS EXECUTIVE DIRECTOR OF JEWISH NATIONAL FUND, Tampa Office, said that he personally had thoroughly enjoyed the tapes and was making them available to others. He also thanked us for spreading God's word.

****

LETTERS
(EXCERPTS)

DAN-ROES ONGESA—KENYA, EAST AFRICA

Through your compacts (tapes) *Why Should Every Christian Pray For And Support Israel?* approximately 1,893 SOULS WERE CONVERTED.

****

REVEREND FK KOSKI—KENYA, EAST AFRICA

I received your first taped lesson *Why Should Every Christian Pray For And Support Israel?* and how I have been blessed by it. While Norma Duncan was blessed and in tears during the teaching I was crying more. I was so charged by the anointing in the tapes that my head was tight, my eyes swollen and my tears flowed for unspeakable joy. As I listened to the lesson my love for Israel became so extreme that I an unable to find the right words to explain how I felt. If Jesus tarries I will die loving Israel. If Jesus comes I will be caught up loving Israel. I am forced to say that I will love Israel forever and ever for now I know that it is the will of God and I don't care what men say. I am even charged by the Holy Spirit while writing this letter and I want to bless your Senior Minister Norma Duncan for answering the call of God and therefore putting all of us into such a Godly blessing. Praise the Lord. Enclosed are the names and addresses of others who would appreciate this taped lesson.

****

PASTOR JACKSON LUBANGA—KENYA

We are overjoyed with the preaching from your ministry. We are thirsty, thirsty, thirsty for more. I distribute these tapes at all our meetings and crusades. Since you started sending these teachings to me 120,000 SOULS HAVE BEEN CONVERTED through your inspired teaching, which is beyond compare.

****

PASTOR AND MARY BAVUGA—UGANDA

The message entitled *Why Should Every Christian Pray For And Support Israel?* has been spread and is still going forward all over Uganda and we have also started spreading God's Word on the tapes in the countries of Zaire and Rwanda. Ordinary people and church ministers alike are in wonder and are praising the Lord for your teachings.

****

PASTOR MARK GEORGE ONYANGO—KENYA

May the Lord our God bless you mightily for the great work you are doing for the edification of the Church worldwide.

I must testify that your teaching *Why Should Every Christian Pray For And Support Israel?* has brought me to a sharp turning point. I have always considered Israel with negativism, bordering on downright hatred, as a nation that had abused God's election and favor, murdered God's prophets, rejected the Gospel and slaughtered the apostles.

The message in the cassettes showered my heart with such compassion and love for Israel that prayer and support for Israel has become my responsibility and duty.

****

PASTOR N E WILLIAMS—NIGERIA

I am very pleased to express my sincere gratitude and appreciation for the gift of ten taped lesson entitled *Why Should Every Christian Pray For And Support Israel?* I was indeed delighted to get them. I received them with joy and distributed them to those who were waiting for them. They were very excited to get them and after listening to them they all remarked about the beauty of the lesson. I was indeed thankful to you and ever more to God for these taped lessons. I am returning the response card. My returning it is a clear indication that I want to continue receiving these taped lessons from you for it is THROUGH YOUR TEACHINGS THAT GOD IS RAISING UP AND BUILDING UP INFORMED CHRISTIANS IN THIS PART OF THE WORLD.

****

WASHINGTON OLARE—KENYA

Your tapes entitled *Why Should Every Christian Pray For And Support Israel?* did a great work in men's hearts. HUNDREDS OF PEOPLE WERE CONVERTED TO CHRISTIANITY AFTER LISTENING TO THE TAPED LESSON AT A CHURCH SERVICE. I personally presented the tapes to the pastor, so that all people who attended the service could listen to them. The people were shocked by what they heard, and after the service, they came seeking for the tapes.

****

USAF CAPTAIN JIM O'DONNELL—GERMANY

Greetings from Germany. It was a joy to receive your tapes. YOUR TAPED MESSAGES BROUGHT ME TO ACCEPT CHRIST AS MY SAVIOR. Your tapes have opened my heart to God's word after years of Bible study never could or did not. God bless you and all, especially the tape ministry.

****

PASTOR ZACHAYO M. ATONI—KENYA

God enabled me to be in touch with your ministry. I laid hands on your taped cassettes at a crusade in a nearby town. The tapes are entitled *Why Should Every Christian Pray For And Support Israel?* Sincerely speaking, a number of us were spiritually touched by this message. It sheds light on the Jewish nation of which we were ignorant.

May the Lord prosper your ways so that you might produce more messages like this that will cause His flock to walk in white.

I am a pastor/teacher who wishes to receive more messages from your ministry. WE OF THIS WORLD DOWN HERE ARE TREADING ON VERY DANGEROUS GROUND BECAUSE WE DO NOT HAVE ENOUGH LIGHT TO LET OUR LIGHT SHINE. PLEASE, HELP US. THROUGH YOUR GUIDANCE HELP US TO SEE THE LIGHT.

****

FLORENCE O'SEBA—INDIA

I am very much thankful for the cassettes you sent to me. I have enjoyed them a great deal and now I desire to have more. The cassettes have helped me a lot. They have helped me to know more about the Israelites and why we modern-day Christians have to support and pray for Israel. I have so many friends who are interested in listening to these cassettes. MORESO, SOME HAVE BEEN CONVERTED TO CHRISTIANITY THROUGH THESE CASSETTES.

****

JACKIE KWALI—USA

Praise the Lord for having brought you into my life. Your words will be multiplied in Miami. Your tapes give me more and more of the truth as I study. I am thankful to be on your mailing list.

****

MISS SUSAN M. MABOGO—KENYA

I am very grateful for the cassettes you sent to me entitled *Why Should Every Christian Pray For And Support Israel?* May God Almighty continually bless you for this. I have listened to them, and they have not only been a blessing but also a correction to my life. Before I listened to your cassettes, I had unfairly disliked the Israelites. This was because I blamed them for crucifying Jesus Christ and also because I read some of Shakespeare's literature in which the Jews were portrayed as evil-hearted, merciless people. But after listening to your tapes, I realized I was very unfair because, No. 1 It was God's will that Jesus be crucified and the Jews only acted as us Gentiles would have acted at that time and No. 2 I realize that I was following Shakespeare's views of Jews instead of God's view. I disliked them when I had never met a Jew. How unfair. Anyway, YOUR CASSETTES HAVE NOW CHANGED MY DISLIKE FOR JEWS. I NOW LOVE THEM AS CHRISTIANS SHOULD AND I EVER PRAY THAT GOD WILL DELIVER THEM FROM THE HANDS OF THEIR ENEMIES AND BRING THEM PEACE. THANK YOU VERY MUCH FOR SUCH A CORRECTION IN MY LIFE. How blessed you are to be the distributor of the Living Word. May God bless you in all you do to glorify His name. I will always remember to pray for all of you at The Living Word Church of Niceville.

****

ROBERT MAKABI OTWOKI—KENYA

Ref: Information about people turning from Satan to God.

It was just yesterday evening when I saw two men dancing for joy in my friend's house. I WAS SURPRISED TO SEE PEOPLE TURNING FROM EVIL SPIRITS TO THE RIGHT WAY. It was only God's Word on the tapes that you sent to my friend that is turning these people from bad evils to the right way through Christ. I myself am one of those who have turned from evil to the right way. I desire these lessons so that I too can help my friends.

****

ELIAKIM ONGOMA OKIYO—KENYA

The day I received the tapes *Why Should Every Christian Pray For And Support Israel?* I played them to my Bible group. 30 minutes later, I was tongue tied when UPON HEARING THE ISRAEL MESSAGE, THE MAJORITY OF THE PEOPLE FELL DOWN AND WEPT BITTERLY. They asked the Lord to forgive their sins and make them clean and help them to follow God's word on the tapes. My eyes were also opened and I changed a lot and I turned away from my sins. May the Almighty bless this great message of salvation. MORE THAN 100 CAME TO ME IN ONE DAY INQUIRING ABOUT THE LIVING WORD CHURCH OF NICEVILLE'S TAPES.

****

JACOB LAZARO—TANZANIA

The lesson *Why Should Every Christian Pray For And Support Israel?* has made a great change in my life. I heard how the people of Israel treated our Lord Jesus Christ and the way they taunted Him. I hated the Jews so much that all I could speak about them was "they are bad people". NOW THAT I KNOW THE JEWS ARE VERY SPECIAL TO GOD, I REMEMBER THEM IN MY PRAYERS AND I ASK GOD NOT TO LET ME FORGET THEM.

****

CHARLES ODUOR ALOO—KENYA

I'm the leader of the Christian Union, which consists of 64 members. When I was coming home from a seminar, I heard a sermon being played on the train on which I was traveling, entitled *Why Should Every Christian Pray For And Support Israel?* I was so moved by that sermon that when I came to my destination I asked where I could get these tapes full of such teaching for my Christian Union members. I was given your address. If we could receive this taped teaching on Israel to use at the seminar, we would give such thanks and even the <u>angels</u> would say Amen.

****

CHRIS WALYAMA—KENYA

Thank you for the cassette tapes entitled *Why Should Every Christian Pray For And Support Israel?* by Norma Duncan. Our family of six greatly appreciate the tapes. Praise the Lord! When we listened to the message, God started knocking on our hearts. Hence, THEY ALL REPENTED OF THEIR SINS AND GOT SAVED. THEY ALL SHOUTED WITH JOY. Since that day, God's power is really working among us. We gather in our small house sharing God's Word on the tapes. My family appreciates you for preaching to people through the tapes, because they were lost sheep who heard God's voice.

****

MICAH ETABLE ATSULU—KENYA

Greetings from all the members of the Assemblies of God in our church in Kenya. It was a great joy to receive your taped lessons. GOD'S WORD ON THE TAPES CAUSED TWO HUNDRED PEOPLE TO ACCEPT JESUS AS THEIR SAVIOR. that is why I would like the Living Word Church of Niceville to assist me with more of these tapes. I will be grateful to get more taped teachings.

****

REVEREND SILAS ATIENO ONIM—KENYA

Your teachings are helping Christians and the work of God here. They have also been a blessing to me. IN OUR ORGANIZATION WE HAVE SIXTY PASTORS AND EIGHTY PREACHERS THAT NEED THESE TAPED TEACHINGS. We desire to use them in our Bible studies and local churches and in the Bible Institute library.

****

PASTOR DOUGLAS NILANGA NIWIGA—KENYA

I am writing to let you know that I listened to your taped message entitled *Why Should Every Christian Pray For And Support Israel?* What Reverend Norma Duncan taught me through that taped message is a revelation about Israel that remains in my life, along with the burden to teach the Church what I have learned. I can now through this taped lesson offer to Christians the answers to questions that before were too difficult to answer. Your ministry in Africa, and the world as a whole, is a blessed one.

****

HILLARY MAWALMA—KENYA

Ref: Request to be placed on your mailing list. I have just had a chance to listen to your informative teachings, and I must say it is the best religious material that I have ever come across.

****

BEATRICE ADIOMBO—KENYA

The inward power of the Holy Spirit led me to write to you and to let you know that the LIVING WORD ON YOUR TAPES IS BRINGING EVEN THE GREATEST ENEMIES OF THE GOSPEL TO AN EVERLASTING FRIENDSHIP WITH GOD. When we played the tapes entitled *Why Should Every Christian Pray For And Support Israel?*

MANY PEOPLE WERE EAGERLY WILLING TO CHANGE THEIR LIVES AND TO BECOME CHRISTIANS.

****

JERARD AGOMBI ABACK—KENYA

I thank God for having cast His merciful eyes upon me and opening a path of righteousness which would otherwise have remained non-existent to me. I also want to pass my greetings to all those at the LWCN who made this all possible. For a long time I had groped about trying to find the right way. I was confused by the great number of denominations each teaching its own tenants. THEN WHEN I WAS JUST ABOUT ON THE BRINK OF DESPONDENCY THINKING I WOULD NEVER FIND THE ONE WHO HAD THE TRUTH, A FRIEND SENT ME A SET OF YOUR TAPES. TO SAY THAT THE MESSAGE ON THE TAPES DREW ME CLOSER TO CHRIST WOULD NOT DO JUSTICE TO THE SENSATIONAL EXPERIENCE I UNDERWENT BECAUSE IT WAS MUCH MORE THAN THAT. IT WAS THE FEELING ONE EXPERIENCES WHEN SOMETHING HAS BEEN SHROUDED AND UNSOLVABLE FOR YEARS AND THEN THE COVER IS SUDDENLY REMOVED AND ALL THE MYSTERIES GET UNRAVELED. Therefore I feel it wise to clutch at this opportunity to present my application for these tapes so that I will learn more concerning God's Word.

****

MAXINE EILISS—JAMAICA

Thank you for my lesson *Why Should Every Christian Pray For And Support Israel?* I CAN'T STOP PLAYING YOUR LESSON. PLEASE SEND ME SOME MORE. YOUR TEACHING MAKES MY LIFE CHANGE FOR THE BETTER. I FEEL THAT GOD IS SPEAKING DIRECTLY TO ME.

****

PASTOR MOSES KAHENZE—KENYA

Thank you for the tapes. Through the teachings on cassettes we are blessed. WE HAVE MULTIPLIED IN NUMBER IN THE CHURCH AND IN THE PRAYER CELLS.

We have patiently waited for Part 3 of the *True Riches* teaching. You say you are now going to send the teachings in book form....

We are still eagerly waiting for the teachings. The Church is praying for you and this glorious work.

****

AGNES NGARE—KENYA

I am very glad for the way the Lord is using your ministry of distributing cassettes on how to pray for Israel. SINCE YOU STARTED SENDING THE CASSETTES TO ME, I HAVE INTRODUCED IN THE MINISTRY A DEPARTMENT OF AUDIO CASSETTES TEACHINGS BY REVEREND NORMA DUNCAN AND PEOPLE ARE CROWDING INTO THE HALL TO LISTEN. THE WORD IS MOVING, AND PEOPLE MUST BE TAUGHT ABOUT ISRAEL, SO THAT THEY CAN BE IN THE WILL OF GOD. My burden is to raise up intercessors from different denominations and equip them in praying for Israel.

****

KULE F. OPOLLO—UGANDA

To prove how much your tapes help me and others, let me share with you: THREE FRIENDS, ONE CATHOLIC AND TWO MUSLIMS CAME TO THE LORD BECAUSE OF THE MESSAGE ON YOUR TAPES THAT I HAD BORROWED FROM A FRIEND before you sent mine. There are many like these in my home area who have not yet been reached by the good message. Therefore I wish to have more taped lessons. The tapes have helped me a lot in evangelizing. So I hope God will answer my prayers.

****

PASTOR ZACHAYO M. ATONI—KENYA

Dear Beloved Brethren of Niceville, it gives me joy to write to you. We appreciate your work in the tape ministry. Surely this is the needed truth for these last days.

WHEN I SIT DOWN AND HEAR THE TEACHING ON THE TAPES, MY HEART COMES UP WITH PRAISE OF THE WORD OF GOD FROM MY TEACHER, REVEREND NORMA DUNCAN. For, I was waiting to hear from the Living Word Church of Niceville for many months, ever since I wrote to you. WHEN I HEAR THE TAPES I CANNOT HELP BUT SHOUT AMEN AND HALLELUJAH TO EVERY BIT OF TRUTH IN THEM. THIS IS BECAUSE I HAVE BEEN SEARCHING FOR TEACHINGS LIKE THOSE IN THE LIVING WORD CHURCH TAPES. MANY A TIME I HAVE HUNGERED FOR SUCH TRUTH!

IN THE PAST, SOME HAVE COME WITH "A HALF-BAKED TRUTH" THAT APPEARED LIKE TRUTH, BUT THANK GOD, WE NOW HAVE THE WHOLE TRUTH IN KENYA THROUGH THE LIVING WORD CHURCH OF NICEVILLE'S TAPE MINISTRY. WE ARE NOW ABLE TO SEE THE PAST ERRORS OF THOSE TEACHERS AND BRAND THEM FOR WHAT THEY ARE. PEOPLE ARE NOW RETURNING UNDER THE INSPIRATION AND DIRECTION OF THE HOLY GHOST TO THE CHURCH IN KENYA WHERE WE NOW WORSHIP IN SPIRIT AND TRUTH. OUR WORSHIP IS NOW CHRIST JESUS CENTERED. IT IS BASED ON SCRIPTURE. Praise God! We cannot thank you enough dear ones in the Living Word Church of Niceville's ministry in the USA.

****

PASTOR JOHN MBURU—KENYA

I want to express my sincere heartfelt gratitude to God our Heavenly Father for the knowledge and wisdom that He has given to you to teach the truth of the knowledge of God.

I HAVE BEEN LISTENING TO YOUR TEACHINGS ON TAPES....I HAVE NEVER HEARD ANYONE ON EARTH TEACH SUCH GREAT REVELATION AS I HEARD FROM YOU. SURELY IT HAS COME TO BE MY GREATEST INSPIRATION IN MY MINISTRY AND LIFE....

CONTENTS

CONTENTS

Chapter 1

WHY DID GOD CHOOSE
THE JEWISH PEOPLE?

As you read this informative book, you will gain answers to Biblical questions that men have longed to understand throughout the generations. The insight that you will receive will at times stir your emotions, thrill your heart and in some cases even shock you. Even more, your sincere desire to know the pure unadulterated truth regarding the issues that are dealt with in this work will be satisfied. The first question that I will answer is "Why Did God Choose The Jewish People?"

Both Jews and Gentiles have been trying to figure out why God chose the Jews as His own people. Why didn't God choose one of the other nations, nations that were far more attractive and powerful at that time?

The Jews were mere slaves in Egypt. So, why did God choose this unattractive group of people who were to give Him nothing but trouble from the day He brought them out of Egypt? Why did God choose a people who would end up causing Him so much hurt and pain?

It is normal that you would feel puzzled about this issue. After all, even the Scriptures reveal that those Jews whom God delivered from Egypt were an unrighteous, hardheaded, grumbling and complaining bunch of people. They were a people who grieved God the entire forty years they spent in the wilderness. The following verse verifies that truth.

Psalm 95:10 (The Amplified Bible.)

10Forty years long was I grieved and disgusted with that generation, and I said, It is a people that do err in their hearts, and they do not approve, acknowledge, or regard My ways.

Why in the world did God choose such an ungrateful, undeserving, wicked group of people? Why them? Why the Jews?

My friend, the people described in the previous verse do not typify all Jews. Like so many other Scriptures, the people mentioned represented only one generation. They represented the generation of Jews that came out of Egyptian bondage. However, the Jews as a whole were God's chosen people long before He delivered them from Egypt or led them through the wilderness. Furthermore, the Jews were not chosen because they were righteous, different or special. So, the character qualities they exhibited in Psalm 95:10 have absolutely no bearing on this matter.

The fact is, the Jews themselves were not the reason why God chose them as a nation. The Jews had nothing to do with God's choice. Instead, Abraham, righteous Abraham, is the reason they are now God's chosen people. He alone is responsible for God's choice.

God's choice came about because of His love for Abraham and because He had made a solemn pledge with Abraham. God promised that He would bless Abraham and that through his seed (Isaac and Jacob), He would bring forth a people. He also promised He would give this people a portion of land that would remain their possession forever.

Yes, it was because of God's promise to Abraham that the Jews were chosen as God's special people. That fact will become clear as we go through this chapter. To see the promise God made to Abraham, we must study Genesis chapter seventeen. To save space, we will only read a portion of that chapter. I trust that later you will take time to read the rest of it.

> *Genesis 17:1-22 (The Amplified Bible.)*
>
> *1When Abram was ninety-nine years old, the Lord appeared to him and said, I am the Almighty God; walk and live habitually before Me and be perfect (blameless, wholehearted, complete).*
>
> *2And I will make My covenant (solemn pledge) between Me and you and will multiply you exceedingly.*

To help you understand the seriousness of God's pledge to Abraham, let me give you the definition of the word "covenant." This definition is taken from *The American Heritage Dictionary, Second College Edition:*

> **A binding agreement** made by two or more persons or parties; compact....A formal sealed agreement or contract. To promise by a covenant....To enter into a covenant: contract....

In the following verses, verses three and four, you see the pledge that God gave to Abraham. In return, God asked in verse one that Abraham walk before Him in obedience to His commands. Abraham did walk in that manner before God. In fact, he was so obedient that, in Isaiah 41:8, God refers to Abraham as "...*My friend.*" You will recall that Yeshua said in John 15:14, "*You are My friends if you keep on doing the things which I command you to do.*" Obedience made Abraham God's friend.

Abraham walked in trust and obedience before God all the days of his life. Therefore, because Abraham did not break this covenant with God, God was and is required to keep His end of the bargain. Now, it is true that the Israelites did not keep covenant. However, as you saw in verse two, God made His solemn pledge to Abraham, and Abraham did keep covenant. Consequently, God never had an opportunity to get out of the covenant.

It is imperative that you read the next verses very carefully. The information they contain is crucial to the subject that you are presently studying.

3Then Abram fell on his face, and God said to him,

4As for Me, behold, My covenant (solemn pledge) is with you, and you shall be the father of many nations.

It is important that you remember that God's promise was to Abraham alone. In verse four, God addressed Abraham and no one else. God said to Abraham, "...*My covenant (solemn pledge) is with you....*" The reason that point is so vital will become evident as you go through the series. However, right now, try to concentrate on the content of the following verses.

5Nor shall your name any longer be Abram [high, exalted father]; but your name shall be Abraham [father of a multitude], for I have made you the father of many nations.

6And I will make you exceedingly fruitful and I will make nations of you, and kings will come from you.

7And I will establish My covenant between Me and you and your descendants after you throughout their generations for an everlasting, solemn pledge, to be a God to you and to your posterity after you.

As I have repeatedly stated, God's covenant was with Abraham alone; **however, God says in verse seven that He will establish His**

4

covenant between Himself and Abraham and Abraham's descendants. According to *Strong's Exhaustive Concordance of the Bible,* Hebrew and Chaldee Dictionary, the definition of this particular word, "establish," includes the words "to accomplish, perform, make to stand."

Did you notice in verse seven that this was an everlasting promise? God promised Abraham that He would not only be a God to him but also to His covenant descendants forever. My friend, this is why the Jews were chosen. They were chosen because God made an unbreakable promise to Abraham. In verse eight, we see even more of God's sacred pledge to Abraham.

> *8And I will give to you and to your posterity after you the land in which you are a stranger [going from place to place], all the land of Canaan, for an everlasting possession; and I will be their God.*

Because Abraham found favor with God, God made him a promise for the future. Furthermore, as you saw in verse eight, it was because of God's promise to Abraham that the Jews were given a special portion of land, a portion of land that would remain theirs forever. God promised that the land of Canaan would never be taken away and given to another nation. Rather, it would be an everlasting possession to Abraham's covenant descendants.

The land that God promised to Abraham and his descendants is itself very special to God. You see just how special it is to Him in the following verses.

> *Deuteronomy 11:10-12 (The Amplified Bible.)*
>
> *10 For the land which you go in to possess is not like the land of Egypt, from which you came out, where you sowed your seed and watered it with your foot laboriously as in a garden of vegetables.*
>
> *11 But the land which you enter to possess is a land of hills and valleys which drinks water of the rain of the heavens,*
>
> *12 A land for which the Lord your God cares; the eyes of the Lord your God are always upon it from the beginning of the year to the end of the year.*

And now, let us go back to Genesis chapter seventeen. In verses ten through fourteen, you see where God tells Abraham to circumcise all males. This ritual of circumcision would be their reminder of this great promise. It would be a token of the sacred covenant that God had made with Abraham concerning his covenant descendants and their land throughout the generations.

Genesis 17:10-14 (The Amplified Bible.)

10This is My covenant, which you shall keep, between Me and you and your posterity after you: Every male among you shall be circumcised.

11And you shall circumcise the flesh of your foreskin, **and it shall be a token or sign of the covenant (the promise or pledge) between Me and you.**

So, the circumcision was an external observance to remind men of God's covenant with Abraham. God would never forget His promise. However, since men often do forget, God wisely provided them with a reminder. Thereafter, when persecution came and others stole their land, the covenant descendants of Abraham, the Israelites, were able to see their male babies being circumcised and take comfort in what that circumcision represented. Moreover, each time they viewed the circumcision of their own flesh, they remembered God's promise.

For instance, when Rome conquered and temporarily occupied Israel, the Jews' hearts were sustained by what the mark of the covenant represented. Every time the Jews witnessed a circumcision being performed or looked at their own flesh, they were made aware of God's covenant with Abraham. **They were reminded that God was their God who had given them that land, and someday their land would be returned to them.**

12He who is eight days old among you shall be circumcised, every male throughout your generations, whether born in [your] house or bought with [your] money from any foreigner not of your offspring.

13He that is born in your house and he that is bought with your money must be circumcised; and My covenant shall be in your flesh for an everlasting *covenant.*

14And the male who is not circumcised, that soul shall be cut off from his people; he has broken My covenant.

Throughout the years, both Bible scholars and laymen have struggled with the question, "Why did God insist that every male in Abraham's household be circumcised?" In verse nineteen of this same chapter, God told Abraham that He would establish His covenant with

Isaac, not Ishmael. Yet, in Genesis 17:12, God instructed that the sign of God's covenant with Abraham be engraved in Ishmael's flesh. Verse twenty-three of that same chapter informs you that Abraham carried out God's command. According to verse twenty-five of the same chapter, Ishmael was thirteen years old when he was circumcised.

God also instructed that Abraham's servants be circumcised. And we all know that Abraham's servants were not even blood kin. So, why was it necessary for Abraham to circumcise those who were not God's covenant choice?

Let me explain. Since circumcision is only a sign of the covenant between God and Abraham, circumcision does not in itself make the one who undergoes that ritual one of God's chosen people with whom God promised to establish His covenant. No! Before either Ishmael or Abraham's servants were actually circumcised, God had already told Abraham that He would establish His covenant with Isaac, the promised son whom Sarah would conceive and to whom she would give birth. No sign could have in any way changed that fact. However, the sign of the covenant that Abraham had cut into the flesh of Ishmael and all the other males in his household was still useful.

The circumcision would be a reminder to Ishmael and the servants that God had made a covenant with Abraham. It would also remind them that Abraham and Isaac were the ones through whom God would accomplish all that He had promised. The fact that God went to such extremes to make sure that all Abraham's household remembered His covenant with Abraham should have been enough to have caused Ishmael and the servants to do everything in their power to help God carry out His promises. Of course, doing everything in their power would have necessitated that they recognize and support those who were God's covenant choice.

How sad it is that today those true descendants of Ishmael who have been absorbed into the Islamic world do not recognize or support God's chosen covenant people, the Israelites. By putting the sign of the covenant in their forefather Ishmael's flesh, God tried to keep Ishmael and his descendants from going down a path that would pit them against His divine purpose. Yet, despite God's preventive measures, most of Ishmael's descendants insisted on taking the wrong path anyway. Yes, they chose a path that eventually led them to hate and to mistreat God's chosen covenant people rather than respect and support them as God desired that they do.

Now that you know the answer to the question, "Why did God insist that every male in Abraham's household be circumcised?" you are ready to resume your study of Genesis 17:1-22. We will pick up with verse fifteen where God goes on to show Abraham how He will bring about His promise.

> *15And God said to Abraham, As for Sarai your wife, you shall not call her name Sarai; but Sarah [Princess] her name shall be.*
>
> *16And I will bless her and give you a son also by her. Yes, I will bless her, and she shall be a mother of nations; kings of peoples shall come from her.*
>
> *17Then Abraham fell on his face and laughed and said in his heart, Shall a child be born to a man who is a hundred years old? And shall Sarah, who is ninety years old, bear a son?*
>
> *18And [he] said to God, Oh, that Ishmael might live before you!*
>
> ***19But God said, Sarah your wife shall bear you a son indeed, and you shall call his name Isaac [laughter];***

Give careful attention to God's next words:

> ***and I will establish My covenant or solemn pledge with him for an everlasting covenant and with his posterity after him.***

God promised to establish His everlasting covenant with Abraham's descendants through the line of Isaac and his posterity after him. **God did not promise to establish His covenant with Ishmael nor with Ishmael's descendants.** However, Abraham's eldest son Ishmael was not left out. As you know, Ishmael became the father of the Arab nation and was also blessed by God.

> *20And as for Ishmael, I have heard and heeded you:*

Those few words that Abraham spoke in verse eighteen, *"...Oh, that Ishmael might live before you,"* were heard and answered by God. As you continue reading in verse twenty, you see what God gave to Ishmael at Abraham's request.

> *20And as for Ishmael, I have heard and heeded you: behold, I will bless him and will make him fruitful and will multiply him exceedingly; He will be the father of twelve princes, and I will make him a great nation.*

In verse twenty, God promised that Ishmael would become a great nation, and he did. Nevertheless, in verse twenty-one, God was very clear as to whom His solemn pledge, His covenant, would be passed. **God's covenant would be established with Isaac.**

> ^{21}*But My covenant, My promise and pledge, I will establish with Isaac, whom Sarah will bear to you at this season next year.*
> ^{22}*And God stopped talking with him and went up from Abraham.*

After God stopped talking with him, Abraham immediately carried out God's instructions. You are told in verses twenty-three through twenty-seven of this same chapter that every male, including himself, was circumcised. **Thus, the reminder of God's covenant was now in their flesh.**

Once God had made this solemn pledge, this covenant with Abraham, God was committed. He had to keep His word. You see, God does not break covenant. He does not go back on His word. God keeps His promises even to His own hurt just as He told us to do in Psalm fifteen. In Psalm 15:1, David asked God, *"LORD, WHO shall dwell [temporarily] in your tabernacle? Who shall dwell [permanently] in Your holy hill?"* One of the requirements that God gave in answer to David's question is found in verse four of the same Psalm. God answers by saying, he *"...who swears to his own hurt and does not change."*

Since the covenant God made with Abraham was paramount to His choosing the Israelites to be His own special people, let us briefly review some of the numerous aspects of this amazing agreement.

(1) God promised to multiply Abraham exceedingly.

(2) God promised Abraham that he would become the father of many nations.

(3) God promised Abraham that he would be fruitful and that kings would come from him.

(4) God promised to give Abraham a son by his wife, Sarah. That son would be called Isaac.

(5) God promised that He would establish His everlasting covenant with Isaac and Isaac's posterity after him.

(6) God gave Abraham His everlasting solemn pledge that He would be a God to Abraham and his covenant descendants through the line of Isaac forever.

(7) God promised to give Isaac and his covenant descendants the land of Canaan for an everlasting possession.

Gentile Christian, it is because God is so uncompromisingly righteous that we can always trust Him to do what He has promised He would do, even if it means His own hurt. We can have complete faith and confidence in God's word. For, what God has said He will do, He will carry out to the full.

For instance, as we continue to witness God's faithfulness in restoring to Israel every inch of land that He gave to her, we can greatly rejoice. We can allow our faith to increase knowing that our God is a God who keeps His promises. Thus, by returning the land of Israel to those whom He swore it would belong to **forever,** God is gaining the complete trust and confidence of the Gentiles also. Isn't this marvelous! How righteous God is! How wise are His ways!

After God had given His solemn word to Abraham, God's love for Abraham and keeping the promises He had made to him remained uppermost to God. From that point on, almost every recorded act God performed was in some way connected with Abraham and the binding agreement He had made with him including the birth of Isaac, Abraham's son.

Isaac was seventy-five years old when Abraham died. Abraham had had all the time he needed to instruct Isaac in every aspect of the covenant that God had made with him. Isaac had to have known that he was the covenant child with whom God would establish His sacred pledge. Therefore, I am sure it came as no surprise to Isaac when God appeared to him in Genesis 26:3-4. During that appearance, **God assured Isaac that He would establish (perform) with him the oath that He had sworn to his father, Abraham**. Let us read those verses so that you can see that truth for yourself.

Genesis 26:3-4 (The Amplified Bible.)

*3Dwell temporarily in this land, and I will be with you and will favor you with blessings; **for to you and to your descendants I will give all these lands, and I will***

perform the oath which I swore to Abraham your
father.

[4]And I will make your descendants to multiply as the
stars of the heavens, and will give to your posterity all
these lands (kingdoms); and by your Offspring shall all
the nations of the earth be blessed, or by Him bless
themselves,

After reading the previous verses, there can be no doubt that God did establish His covenant with Isaac as He swore He would. However, in that same chapter, there is another very revealing verse which we will also read.

Genesis 26:24 (The Amplified Bible.)

[24]And the Lord appeared to him the same night and
said, I am the God of Abraham your father. Fear not,
for I am with you and will favor you with blessings and
multiply your descendants ***for the sake of My servant***
Abraham.

Did God say He would bless Isaac because Isaac was a Jew? Did He say He would bless Isaac because he was different or special? No! **God said He would bless Isaac and multiply his descendants for the sake of His servant Abraham.**

God had to keep His covenant with Abraham. In this case, God had to keep the portion of His promise mentioned in Genesis 17:19 which reads, "*...Sarah your wife shall bear you a son indeed, and you shall call his name Isaac [laughter]; and I will establish My covenant or solemn pledge with him for an everlasting covenant and with his posterity after him.*"

In Genesis chapter twenty-six, God kept His promise to Abraham and established His covenant with Isaac. His next step was to do the same with Isaac's posterity after him.

Fulfilling His covenant with Abraham was the reason God promised to be with and to bless Isaac. **Furthermore, fulfilling His covenant with Abraham was God's purpose for making specific promises to Isaac's son, Jacob, as he fled from the murderous wrath of his brother, Esau.** That fact will become clear as you read the following text.

Genesis 28:11-15 (The Amplified Bible.)

11And he came to a certain place and stayed there overnight, because the sun was set. Taking one of the stones of the place, he put it under his head and lay down there to sleep.

12And he dreamed that there was a ladder set up on the earth, and the top of it reached to heaven; and the angels of God were ascending and descending on it!

The next verses show beyond doubt that Jacob was indeed the son of Isaac with whom God established His covenant. **Therefore, since Jacob was the forefather of the Israelite nation, these verses provide undeniable Scriptural proof that the Israelites are God's chosen covenant people.**

13And behold, the Lord stood over and beside him and said, I am the Lord, the God of Abraham your father [forefather] and the God of Isaac; I will give to you and to your descendants the land on which you are lying.

14And your offspring shall be as [countless as] the dust or sand of the ground, and you shall spread abroad to the west and the east and the north and the south; and by you and your Offspring shall all the families of the earth be blessed and bless themselves.

15And behold, I am with you and will keep (watch over you with care, take notice of) you wherever you may go, and I will bring you back to this land; for I will not leave you until I have done all of which I have told you.

The knowledge you have just acquired should give you insight into a statement that I made earlier. So, I am going to repeat it. **"After God had given His solemn word to Abraham, God's love for Abraham and keeping the promises He had made to him remained uppermost to God. From that point on, almost every recorded act God performed was in some way connected with Abraham and the binding agreement that He had made with him."** As we progress through this series, you will see that my previous statement is correct.

The bottom line is, God made a binding contract with His friend Abraham. Part of God's agreement was that He would establish His covenant with Abraham's son, Isaac, and his posterity after him. **God did establish His covenant with Isaac. He also established His** covenant with Isaac's posterity through Jacob, Isaac's son, and Jacob's descendants, the Israelites.

The reason God chose the Jewish nation was because He loved their forefathers, beginning with Abraham. He did not choose them because of anything they were or anything they did but simply to keep covenant. **God loved Abraham; God rewarded Abraham. And it was and is because of Abraham that the Jews were and are today God's chosen people.** Because God loved Abraham, He chose his descendants through the line of Isaac and Jacob. Thus, in Deuteronomy 4:37, we read, *"And because He loved your fathers, He chose their descendants after them...."*

God chose the Jews because He loved their forefathers, Abraham, Isaac and Jacob. God chose the Jews in order to keep His binding agreement with Abraham.

Now that you realize that the Jews are really no different than you are, Gentile, now that you realize that they too are just frail human beings, now that you know they were simply a people chosen by God because of Abraham, doesn't this knowledge help you to have more compassion for them? Gentile Christian, don't you now empathize with the Jew? You see, the Jews were chosen to serve God because of Abraham just as we Christians have been chosen to serve God through Jewish Yeshua (Jesus), the Messiah.

My friend, now you know why God chose the Jewish people. He chose them because of their forefather, Abraham. The Lord swore to Abraham that He would establish His everlasting covenant with Isaac and his descendants. Jacob and the Israelites were Isaac's descendants with whom God established His covenant. God also swore that He would be their God, and our righteous God always keeps His word.

Never again will you have to wonder why God chose the Jews to be His own special people. For, thanks be to God, you now know that He chose them because He loved their forefathers Abraham, Isaac and Jacob. He chose them in order to keep the solemn oath that He had sworn to His friend, Abraham.

The question, "Why Did God Choose The Jewish People?" has been fully answered. Therefore, if my providing that answer completed God's purpose for this chapter, I could end chapter one right now. But, I am afraid that answer does not complete God's purpose for this chapter. The fact is, no matter how profound spiritual truth is, truth only has immediate and eternal value when it is applied to a person's life. Therefore, my goal is to leave you with something more than mere head knowledge.

In this particular case, if you now realize and acknowledge that your standpoint on the issue of God's choice is wrong, then applying the truth you have learned to your life will necessitate an attitude change. My aim is to provide you with a glimpse of the advantages of your developing a proper attitude regarding God's choice. I will also furnish you with a brief look at the disadvantages that will result if you fail to change your wrong stand on that issue.

FIRST, LET US CONSIDER SOME OF THE DISADVANTAGES.

(1) If you remain dissatisfied with God's choice, you will really be displaying your dissatisfaction with the Lord. I say that because God is ultimately responsible for choosing the Jews as His own people.

(2) If you continue to imply that God made a mistake when He chose the Jews, you will be diminishing God's wisdom and ability to make the right choice. In your pride, you will be insinuating that you know better than God Almighty.

(3) If you persist in your wrong attitude toward God's chosen people, you will be a hindrance to God fulfilling His purpose on the earth. You will aid God's enemies, including Satan, in their attempt to keep God from honoring His sacred oath to Abraham.

(4) If you continue in the sins of pride and rebellion, you are in spiritual danger. You are in spiritual danger because God's Word warns, *"For rebellion is as the sin of witchcraft, and stubbornness is as idolatry and teraphim (household good luck images)...."* (1 Samuel 15:23.) Also, in the New Testament we read, *"For the wages which sin pays is death...."* (Romans 6:23.)

ON THE OTHER HAND, THE ADVANTAGES OF A RIGHT ATTITUDE IN REGARD TO GOD'S CHOICE ARE MANY.

(1) You will certainly repent of your past wrong attitude regarding God's covenant choice and thus receive God's forgiveness.

(2) You can assure God that you believe He made the right choice when He chose the Jewish people and that you have complete confidence in His decision. You can let God know that you trust Him to do what is best in this area.

(3) You can comfort the Lord by letting Him know that you are aware of His predicament and that you feel for Him. You can show concern and compassion for God's needs by offering to do whatever you can to help Him keep His promise to Abraham.

(4) You can praise the Lord for making such a wise and perfect choice. Plus, you can tell Him how much you admire Him for righteously keeping His covenant at such great personal cost to Himself.

(5) You may have been asking God to use you. Here is your opportunity to be used by God. With the righteous attitude you now have, you have placed yourself in a perfect position to be used. By the time you have finished reading this book, you will have learned exactly how God wants to use you to help Him accomplish His purpose and fulfill His covenant with Abraham, Isaac and Jacob and their descendants, the Israelites.

It is up to you, Christian. Whatever you decide to do is absolutely your own decision. However, my hope and prayer is that you will choose to *"...Repent (think differently; change your mind, regretting your sins and changing your conduct)...."* (Matthew 3:2.)

My hope and prayer is that you will acknowledge and accept with joy God's wise choice. My hope and prayer is that you will open your heart and arms to God's chosen people (the Jews), and from this point on, do all you can to help God fulfill His covenant with Abraham.

The Jewish prophet of God, John the Baptist, said it all in the following verse:

Matthew 3:8 (The Amplified Bible.)

[8]*Bring forth fruit that is consistent with repentance [let your lives prove your change of heart];*

Chapter 2

WHY DID THE JEWS
END UP DWELLING IN EGYPT?

Men often ask the questions: "Since the Jews are God's chosen people, why did God permit them to go into and to remain in Egypt?" and, "How did they end up in slavery there?" In this chapter we will deal mainly with the first question. The second question will be answered in chapter three. However, since the two previous topics are closely related, you will need to keep both questions in mind.

A common explanation given by most teachers for the Jews going into Egypt and remaining there is that the Jews went down to Egypt and resided there as a result of severe famine conditions that existed during that period. Now, it is certainly true that there was a famine at that time. It is also true that the famine had a lot to do with the Jews sojourning in Egypt. However, the previous explanation is extremely shallow and shortsighted. It does not convey true insight into the present subject. Nor does it reveal the real importance of the Jews' entry into Egypt and God's purpose for allowing them to remain there.

The answers we are seeking to the question, "Since the Jews are God's chosen people, why did God permit them to go into and to remain in Egypt?" lie once again in the promises that God made to Abraham, Isaac and Jacob. The following brief summary of the sequence of events that led up to Israel going into Egypt and remaining there will help you to understand my last statement. It will also help you to understand that God simply used the previously mentioned famine conditions as a means to an end, the end being the fulfillment of a particular section of His sacred Abrahamic pledge.

First, we will see in the Scriptures how God told Abraham that his future descendants would dwell temporarily in Egypt. God also warned him that for four hundred years they would be afflicted and oppressed by the Egyptians.

Genesis 15:12-13 (The Amplified Bible.)

12When the sun was setting, a deep sleep overcame Abram, and a horror (a terror, a shuddering fear) of great darkness assailed and oppressed him.

13And [God] said to Abram, Know positively that your descendants will be strangers dwelling as temporary residents in a land that is not theirs [Egypt], and they will be slaves there and will be afflicted and oppressed for 400 years.

Are you beginning to understand the statement I made in chapter one? You will recall that I said, "After God had given His solemn word to Abraham, God's love for Abraham and keeping the promises He had made to him remained uppermost to God. From that point on, almost every recorded act God performed was in some way connected with Abraham and the binding agreement He had made with him." God Himself makes it clear in the previous text that even the Israelites' stay in Egypt was part of God's plan for Abraham's covenant descendants.

It stands to reason that being Abraham's covenant son, Isaac must have known about the prophecy you just read in Genesis 15:13. Therefore, when famine ravaged the land, if Isaac even considered going down to Egypt, I am sure he was delighted when, just prior to God establishing His covenant with him, God intervened and forbade Isaac to enter Egypt.

Genesis 26: 1-2 (The Amplified Bible.)

1AND THERE was a famine in the land, other than the former famine that was in the days of Abraham. And Isaac went to Gerar, to Abimelech king of the Philistines.

2And the Lord appeared to him and said, Do not go down to Egypt; live in the land of which I will tell you.

Like his father before him, Isaac obeyed God's instructions. Genesis 26:6 informs us that he did not go down to Egypt. Instead, he remained in Gerar. Obviously, it was not yet time for God's prophecy in Genesis 15:13 to come to pass. God first had to set the stage for Israel's inevitable entry into Egypt. For, before Abraham's descendants could be allowed to live in Egypt, God had to establish His covenant with Isaac's son, Jacob, and his posterity after him. You see, they were to be the covenant descendants that God foretold would eventually dwell temporarily in Egypt.

You will recall that while Isaac's twin sons were still in their mother's womb, God told Rebekah, *"...the elder shall serve the younger."* (Genesis 25:23.) Later in the series, in a separate chapter, you will learn exactly what God meant by that statement. However, for now, you must focus your attention on the subject at hand which is, "Since the Jews are God's chosen people, why did God permit them to go into and to remain in Egypt?"

Rebekah obviously assumed from God's statement *"...the elder shall serve the younger"* that God intended to establish His covenant with Jacob. Consequently, she aided Jacob in deceptively acquiring Isaac's blessing. Ordinarily, the eldest son, would have received the blessing. But, these circumstances were certainly not the norm.

We are told in Genesis 27:41 that Esau despised Jacob *"...because of the blessing with which his father blessed him...."* In his hatred, Esau made up his mind that when his aged father died, he would kill Jacob. Realizing the danger that Jacob was in, Rebekah persuaded Isaac to send him to her brother Laban's house in Haran.

In chapter one of the present series, you will recall that as Jacob journeyed to his Uncle Laban's house, God appeared to him at Luz (Bethel). **God's purpose for revealing Himself to Jacob as he traveled to Haran was to establish His sacred covenant with Isaac's posterity as He had promised Abraham He would.** Jacob was thus assured by God that he was the one the Lord had chosen to promote the everlasting covenant, the covenant which God had made with Jacob's grandfather Abraham and had established with his father Isaac.

From Bethel, Jacob went to his uncle Laban's house in Haran. He went there with the full intention of someday returning to the land that God promised to give to him and his descendants. However, before Jacob could return to Canaan, he first had to find a wife and begin to produce the covenant offspring that God had promised He would multiply as the stars of the heavens, the offspring that would one day inherit the land of Canaan as their everlasting possession, the offspring that according to God's Word in Genesis 15:13 would first dwell in Egypt and consequently be afflicted and oppressed by the Egyptians for four hundred years.

Jacob was treated badly by his uncle. Laban used, deceived and cheated Jacob. **However, no matter what Laban did, God continued to honor the Abrahamic covenant and the inspired blessing that Isaac had placed upon Jacob.** So despite Laban's dishonesty, Jacob still came out on top. Jacob ended up with both of Laban's daughters as wives, two concubines, eleven sons and almost all of Laban's wealth. For, did not Isaac's blessing in Genesis 27:28-29 include the words, *"...Let everyone be cursed who curses you and favored with blessings who blesses you."*

After twenty years of wearisome labor and mistreatment by Laban, God finally instructed Jacob to return to his native land and to his own people. Jacob obeyed God's commands. Then after Jacob had made peace with his brother Esau, he traveled until he came to Shechem. There he bought the parcel of land that he and his family had encamped on. He called that tiny parcel of the Promised Land El-Elohe-Israel (that is, God, the God of Israel). For God's chosen people, El-Elohe-Israel held great meaning. It symbolized God's promise that one day all the land of Canaan would belong to Jacob's covenant descendants.

Rachel died giving birth to her second son, Benjamin. Jacob mourned for his beloved wife. Nevertheless, he finally had the twelve covenant sons after whom the twelve covenant tribes of Israel were later named. After Rachel's death, Jacob dwelt in Canaan, the land that God promised would someday belong to his posterity. It was not yet time for the Israelites to take possession of the Promised Land. However, it was drawing close to the time when, in order to fulfill God's Word in Genesis 15:13, they would be forced to enter Egypt and set up temporary residence there.

God's promise to Abraham had to be fulfilled in its entirety, and at this point in history, Jacob's son Joseph was the key to God promoting His purpose in that area. To this day, we Christians get very upset when we remember the abominable treatment that Joseph experienced at the hands of his wicked brothers. However, we fail to understand that though God was not responsible for the brothers' jealousy and hatred of Joseph, He was responsible for Joseph being sold to the Ishmaelites and thus carried as a slave into Egypt.

Yes, it was God Himself who sent Joseph into Egypt, not Joseph's brothers. God's reason for sending him there was two fold. First, Joseph's mission was to preserve Abraham's, Isaac's and Jacob's covenant posterity during the famine. Next, Joseph's mission was to win the favor of Pharoah and thus acquire temporary residence in the land of Egypt for Jacob's posterity .

As you know, God had prior knowledge of the impending famine that would soon devastate the land. Consequently, in order to accomplish all that He had promised His friend, Abraham, He had to protect Abraham's covenant descendants. For, God could not keep His unbreakable promise if Abraham's covenant descendants all died of starvation before He accomplished it.

In the following verses, Joseph clearly explains all that I have attempted to relay to you. He assures his brothers that God sent him into

Egypt to ensure the survival of the covenant descendants of Abraham, Isaac and Jacob.

Genesis 45:1-11 (The Amplified Bible.)

1THEN JOSEPH could not restrain himself [any longer] before all those who stood by him, and he called out, Cause every man to go out from me! So no one stood there with Joseph while he made himself known to his brothers.

2And he wept and sobbed aloud, and the Egyptians [who had just left him] heard it, and the household of Pharoah heard about it.

3And Joseph said to his brothers, I am Joseph! Is my father still alive? And his brothers could not reply, for they were distressingly disturbed and dismayed at [the startling realization that they were in] his presence.

4And Joseph said to his brothers, Come near to me, I pray you. And they did so. And he said, I am Joseph your brother, whom you sold into Egypt!

5But now, do not be distressed and disheartened or vexed and angry with yourselves because you sold me here, for God sent me ahead of you to preserve life.

6For these two years the famine has been in the land, and there are still five years more in which there will be neither plowing nor harvest.

7God sent me before you to preserve for you a posterity and to continue a remnant on the earth, to save your lives by a great escape and save for you many survivors.

8So now it was not you who sent me here, but God; and He has made me a father to Pharoah and lord of all his house and ruler over all the land of Egypt.

Verses seven and eight in *The Living Bible* read:

7God has sent me here to keep you and your families alive, so that you will become a great nation.

8Yes, it was God who sent me here, not you! And He has made me a counselor to Pharoah, and manager of this entire nation, ruler of all the land of Egypt.

These Scriptures show beyond doubt that Joseph was acutely aware that God had sent him into Egypt to help Him carry out His promise to Abraham. The Lord had promised Abraham, Isaac and Jacob that they would become a great nation. He could not bring to pass that segment of His binding agreement with Abraham if Jacob's descendants all died of starvation. **So, God made Joseph lord of Pharoah's house and ruler of all Egypt for two reasons:**

(1) To keep His covenant people alive.

(2) To fulfill His solemn pledge to Abraham, Isaac and Jacob regarding their covenant descendants becoming a great nation.

Thus, Joseph sent a message to his father. He encouraged his father to come down to him in Egypt without delay. Joseph warned him that the future held five more years of famine. Verses nine through eleven hold Joseph's message to his father.

> *⁹Hurry and go up to my father and tell him, Your son Joseph says this to you: **God has put me in charge of all Egypt.** Come down to me; do not delay.*
>
> *¹⁰You will live in the land of Goshen, and you will be close to me—you and your children and your grandchildren, your flocks, your herds, and all you have.*
>
> *¹¹And there I will sustain and provide for you, so that you and your household and all that are yours may not come to poverty and want, for there are yet five [more] years of [the scarcity, hunger, and starvation of] famine.*

For generations the Church has overlooked the most significant facts of this whole happening. The Church imagined that a combination of God providing for the Israelites during the famine and the reunion between Jacob and his lost son were the highlights of this incredible story. But, as you now know, God's provision and the father and son reunion, though touching, were secondary. **God's first priority for going to such extremes was to carry out His own purpose (that is, God's first priority for going to such extremes was to keep His solemn oath to Abraham, Isaac and Jacob and make of Jacob's posterity a great nation).**

It is a Scriptural fact that this little band of Israelites, approximately seventy plus the wives of Jacob's sons (Genesis 46:26-27) were not kept alive because of anything they did. **Rather, they survived so that through them God could promote His sacred covenant to Abraham**

and make of them the great nation promised to Abraham, Isaac and Jacob.

Many nations suffered starvation and misery during that particular famine. Yet, the Jews were the only group of people for whom God devised a famine survival plan. That is because they were the only group of people alive with whom He had established His Abrahamic covenant. They were also the only group of people alive through whom He would eventually carry out His solemn oath to Abraham in its entirety.

Egypt benefited greatly from God's famine survival plan. However, that plan had not been devised for Egypt's welfare. Egypt had only been included in God's famine preparations because, as you will soon see, God intended to use Egypt to further His own future purpose regarding the Abrahamic covenant and the Israelites. Keep these truths in mind as you read about Jacob's reaction to the news that Joseph was still alive.

Genesis 45:25-28 (The Amplified Bible.)

25So they went up out of Egypt and came into the land of Canaan to Jacob their father,

26And they said to him, Joseph is still alive! And he is governor over all the land of Egypt! And Jacob's heart began to stop beating and [he almost] fainted, for he did not believe them.

27But when they told him all the words of Joseph which he had said to them, and when he saw the wagons which Joseph had sent to carry him, the spirit of Jacob their father revived [and warmth and life returned].

28And Israel said, It is enough! Joseph my son is still alive. I will go and see him before I die.

These seemingly simple Old Testament Bible stories that we have heard from childhood are as prismatic and precious as beautiful diamonds glistening in the sunlight. For, when these many faceted Bible stories are exposed to the brilliance of added truth, that light is refracted, revealing innumerable levels of understanding that are new and glorious to behold. However, the marvel of it all is that what you have seen to this point is only the beginning of the incredible insight into Biblical happenings that you will receive as the series progresses. So on that note, let us continue our study of why the Jews ended up dwelling in Egypt.

To refresh your memory in regard to God establishing His covenant with Jacob and to make a smooth transition, we will repeat a segment of Scripture that we covered in chapter one.

Genesis 28:11-15 (The Amplified Bible.)

11And he came to a certain place and stayed there overnight, because the sun was set. Taking one of the stones of the place, he put it under his head and lay down there to sleep.

12And he dreamed that there was a ladder set up on the earth, and the top of it reached to heaven; and the angels of God were ascending and descending on it!

13And behold, the Lord stood over and beside him and said, I am the Lord, the God of Abraham your father [forefather] and the God of Isaac; I will give to you and to your descendants the land on which you are lying.

14And your offspring shall be as [countless as] the dust or sand of the ground, and you shall spread abroad to the west and the east and the north and the south; and by you and your Offspring shall all the families of the earth be blessed and bless themselves.

The next verse, verse fifteen, holds information that is extremely important. So, fix your attention on the content of that verse.

15And behold, I am with you and will keep (watch over you with care, take notice of) you wherever you may go, and I will bring you back to this land; for I will not leave you until I have done all of which I have told you.

Once you truly understand the circumstances surrounding God's assurances to Jacob, you realize that verse fifteen could read: I will not leave you and your descendants until you have helped Me carry out My promises to Abraham, to Isaac, and to you.

As you now know, God had already told Abraham in Genesis 15:13 that his descendants would dwell temporarily in Egypt and would be afflicted and oppressed by the Egyptians for four hundred years. **In order for that prophecy to come about, it was first necessary for Abraham's covenant descendants to enter Egypt and to remain there for the specified period**.

Unbeknown to Jacob in Genesis 28:11-15, his future task would be to help God get Abraham's covenant descendants into Egypt. Until Jacob and his descendants fully accomplished their mission, God intended to stick to them like glue. Consequently, at the appropriate time, God went so far as to even accompany Jacob on his journey down to Egypt. In so doing, God kept His word to Abraham. He also kept His word to Jacob in Genesis 28:15, "*...I will not leave you until I have done all of which I have told you.*"

Genesis 46:2-7 sheds even more light on that subject. **For in those verses, we see how God did actually journey down to Egypt with Jacob and his family**.

> *Genesis 46:2-7 (The Amplified Bible.)*
>
> *2And God spoke to Israel in visions of the night, and said, Jacob! Jacob! And he said, Here am I.*
>
> *3And He said, I am God, the God of your father; do not be afraid to go down to Egypt, for I will there make of you a great nation.*
>
> *4I will go down with you to Egypt, and I will also surely bring you [your people Israel] up again; and Joseph will put his hand upon your eyes [when they are to be closed in death].*
>
> *5So Jacob arose and set out from Beersheba, and Israel's sons conveyed their father, their little ones, and their wives in the wagons that Pharoah had sent to carry him.*
>
> *6And they took their cattle and the gains which they had acquired in the land of Canaan and came into Egypt, Jacob and all his offspring with him:*
>
> *7His sons and his sons' sons with him, his daughters and his sons' daughters—all his offspring he brought with him into Egypt.*

With the knowledge of the future that Jacob possessed, it is understandable that even with a personal invitation from Pharoah, he was still skeptical about going into Egypt to live. After all, God had told Jacob's own grandfather Abraham that his covenant descendants would be slaves there, and that they would be afflicted and oppressed by the Egyptians for four hundred years. However, in verses three and four of the previous text, God not only extended comfort to Jacob, but in verse three, He also told him the reason why He wanted him to dwell in Egypt.

God's reason was this: In Egypt He wanted the Israelites to blossom into the great nation that He had promised they would eventually become. Let us read verse three again.

3And He said, I am God, the God of your father; do not be afraid to go down to Egypt, for I will there make of you a great nation.

God said, "...*I will there make of you a great nation*." In other words, God told the Israelites that while they dwelt temporarily in Egypt, He would multiply them until they became the great nation of people that He promised to Abraham, Isaac and Jacob. Thus, unbeknown to the Egyptians, God's plan was to use their land as a place in which to fulfill that part of His sacred covenant. **To put it bluntly, the land of Egypt was chosen by God as a human breeding ground.**

You see, no matter how fruitful the Israelite women were, it would be some years before that small band of people could, by natural reproduction, produce the great nation promised to Abraham, Isaac and Jacob. **They needed time. They also needed a place in which to produce the covenant offspring of Abraham, Isaac and Jacob.**

The end of the matter is: **God required a place in which the future descendants of Abraham could thrive. He decided that that place would be Egypt. Thus God acquired for them, through Joseph, Pharoah's favor and the most fertile strip of land in Egypt.**

Pharoah knew that through Joseph, God had spared him and his people from slow death by famine. He was extremely grateful for God's miraculous intervention. Therefore, because Pharoah was indebted to God, he promised Joseph's family the best of all the land of Egypt, which was Goshen. (Genesis 47:5-6.) God had every detail worked out. The arrangement suited everyone since everyone profited.

(1) God had a place in which His people would have ample time to multiply and become the great nation that He had promised they would be.

(2) The Israelites had everything they needed to flourish numerically and to prosper in every other way.

(3) Pharoah and the Egyptians had an opportunity to show their appreciation to God and Joseph for sparing their lives and their land.

Only the all-wise, all-knowing, uncompromisingly righteous God of Abraham could have masterminded and carried out such a marvelous and totally fair plan. His plan consisted of utilizing the famine to spare the lives of Pharoah and his subjects and to prosper them as payment for the period of time that His chosen people would use their land. His plan also preserved Abraham's, Isaac's and Jacob's covenant descendants, and it provided them with a safe place to propagate in order to bring forth the covenant nation that He promised Abraham, Isaac and Jacob.

During and after the famine, the Israelites dwelt and prospered in the land of Goshen as Pharoah had promised. **And as God had promised, they grew and multiplied exceedingly, steadily producing the great covenant nation that God had promised to Abraham, Isaac and Jacob. Yes, they fulfilled God's purpose for allowing them to dwell in Egypt. They multiplied exceedingly.** See this truth for yourself in the next verse.

Genesis 47:27 (The Amplified Bible.)

*27And Israel dwelt in the land of Egypt, in the country of Goshen; and they gained possessions there **and grew and multiplied exceedingly**.*

Jacob lived in Egypt for seventeen years before he died. During those years, he never forgot God's solemn pledge to Abraham, Isaac and to himself, nor did he forget the reason why His people remained in Egypt. **They were there to multiply. They were there to fulfill the prophecy in Genesis 28:14 and 46:3. They were there to become a great nation. They were there to become as countless as the dust or sand of the ground.**

Even when Jacob was on his deathbed, with Joseph at his side, the first words out of his mouth pertained to God's sacred pledge. Jacob's words are found in the following verses.

Genesis 48:1-4 (The Amplified Bible.)

1SOME TIME after these things occurred, someone told Joseph, Behold, your father is sick. And he took with him his two sons, Manasseh and Ephraim [and went to Goshen].

2When Jacob was told, Your son Joseph has come to you, Israel collected his strength and sat up on the bed.

3And Jacob said to Joseph, God Almighty appeared to me at Luz [Bethel] in the land of Canaan and blessed me

⁴And said to me, Behold, I will make you fruitful and multiply you, and I will make you a multitude of people and will give this land to your descendants after you as an everlasting possession.

Jacob prophesied over and blessed his twelve sons and Joseph's sons. He then charged his family to carry his body back to the Promised Land and to bury him with his grandfather Abraham and Isaac his father.

Before he died, Abraham had purchased a field in the Promised Land to use as a burial place. Abraham and Isaac had been laid to rest in a cave in that field. It was in that very plot that Jacob desired to be buried. Genesis 49:33 then tells us, *"When Jacob had finished commanding his sons, he drew his feet up into the bed and breathed his last and was gathered to his [departed] people."*

Later, with his dying breath, Joseph also remembered God's sacred covenant. He even had the Israelites take an oath regarding his burial. They swore that when Israel's population had reached God's goal and it was time for God to accompany them on their journey to the land that He swore He would give to the covenant descendants of Abraham, Isaac and Jacob, they would take his bones with them and bury them in the Promised Land. **Thus, Joseph died, but the Israelites continued to fulfill God's purpose for their being in Egypt (that is, they continued to multiply).** See this truth in the next verses.

Exodus 1:6-7 (The Amplified Bible.)

⁶Then Joseph died, and all his brothers and all that generation.

⁷But the descendants of Israel were fruitful and increased abundantly; they multiplied and grew exceedingly strong, and the land was full of them.

To this point in time, God's will and purpose for the Israelites living in Egypt had been beautifully accomplished. The Egyptians had kept their agreement with the Israelites, and God's chosen people were multiplying at an incredible rate. As the previous verses divulge, the land of Egypt was literally full of them.

My friend, you now have the answer to the question, "Since the Jews are God's chosen people, why did God permit them to go into and to remain in Egypt?" God permitted them to go into Egypt and

to remain there so that they could help Him carry out His sacred oath to Abraham, Isaac and Jacob. God swore that He would make of them a great nation, and Egypt was chosen by God as the place in which He would perform that part of His binding contract. Yes, God kept His word. He made the Jews fruitful and multiplied them until Egypt was overrun with them. God actually bred and nourished the covenant nation of Israel in the midst of the nation of Egypt.

The Egyptians had, to that point, fulfilled God's expectations to the letter and so had God's chosen people.

Exodus 1:7 (The Amplified Bible.)

[7]*But the descendants of Israel were fruitful and increased abundantly; they multiplied and grew exceedingly strong, and the land was full of them.*

Praise be to our righteous, faithful God! For, He allowed His covenant people to dwell in Egypt in order to make of them the great nation that He had promised to Abraham, Isaac and Jacob. He allowed the Jews to dwell in Egypt in order to keep His sacred Abrahamic covenant.

Chapter 3

WHY DID THE JEWS
END UP IN SLAVERY IN EGYPT?

At the beginning of the previous chapter, I promised I would answer the question, "Why Did The Jews End Up In Slavery In Egypt?" I will now keep that promise. However, it is necessary that I first address the issue of the Jews' transition from free men dwelling contentedly in Egypt to their eventual enslavement by the Egyptians. To help you shift your focus to the latter, we will briefly review some of the highlights covered in chapter two.

(1) It was so important that the Jews dwell in Egypt that God actually accompanied them into Egypt.

(2) God's purpose for allowing His chosen people to dwell in Egypt was to keep the promise He had made to Abraham, Isaac and Jacob. God promised the Jews' forefathers that He would multiply their descendants as the stars of the heavens and make of them a great nation. God chose the land of Egypt in which to accomplish that segment of His binding contract. **God's plan was that His covenant people sojourn in Egypt until they produced the multitude (that is, the nation) of people that He promised to their forefathers.**

(3) To save His people from the effects of an imminent famine and to prepare the way for His people's favorable acceptance by the Egyptians, God sent Joseph before them. Through Joseph, God miraculously spared the Egyptian people from the ravages of famine. Thus, He intentionally filled them with a sense of gratitude and obligation toward God and His servant Joseph.

(4) Unbeknown to the Egyptians, God's blessings and mercy toward them during the famine were really a form of compensation. Those benefits were payment in advance for the period of time that the Jews would use their land to propagate the covenant nation that God promised to Abraham, Isaac and Jacob.

(5) Knowing that he was indebted to God and God's chosen people, Pharoah promised the Israelites the use of the best of the land of Egypt—Goshen. He also promised them the best of all the food in Egypt. Plus, Pharoah instructed them to not worry about any goods they

might be forced to leave behind. He insisted that they would have the best that Egypt could offer.

(6) For a time, God's purpose was fulfilled for the Jews sojourning in Egypt without any complications. He caused them to multiply exceedingly. We will pickup by reading again the last Scripture text in chapter two.

> *Exodus 1:6-7 (The Amplified Bible.)*
>
> *⁶Then Joseph died, and all his brothers and all that generation.*
>
> *⁷But the descendants of Israel were fruitful and increased abundantly; they multiplied and grew exceedingly strong, and the land was full of them.*

Up to this point in time, God's will and purpose for the Israelites living in Egypt had been beautifully accomplished. The Egyptians had kept their agreement with the Israelites, and God's chosen people were multiplying at an incredible rate. As the previous verses divulge, the land of Egypt was literally full of them. However, after Joseph's death, the perfect conditions they enjoyed changed drastically.

In order for me to relay to you the answer of why the previously mentioned perfect conditions changed after Joseph's death, it is necessary that I first impart to you the following eye-opening historical facts. However, I will do my best to be brief, trusting that you will later do your own research into the following matter.

According to the Sixth Edition of *World Civilization* under the heading "The Egyptian Civilization" by Edward McNall Burns, Philip Lee Ralph, Robert E. Lerner and Standish Meacham, while Egypt was in a state of internal chaos, she was invaded by foreigners. The aforementioned internal chaos and foreign invasion lasted for almost two hundred years, from 1786 to 1575 B.C. Under the subheading, "The Invasion of The Hyksos," we read, "About 1750 the land was invaded by the Hyksos" or "Rulers of Foreign Lands...." The Hyksos were a Semitic, war-like people whose military superiority was attributed to their possession of and skill with horses and horse-drawn war chariots.

The next piece of this amazing puzzle is found in *Smith's Bible Dictionary* under the heading "Joseph." Smith reveals that Joseph was probably born about 1746 B.C. Thus, we see that the Hyksos were already in power in Egypt when Joseph was sold by his brothers into slavery. That fact is extremely important because it provides vital answers to questions that men frequently ask.

For example, men have often wondered why, under any circumstances, the Pharaoh of Egypt would have endowed such tremendous power and authority as he did upon a non-Egyptian. You will recall that Joseph was put in command of all the land of Egypt. He was second only to Pharaoh himself.

The answer to the previous query is now evident. For, as you learned, the Pharaoh was himself a non-Egyptian. The foreign rulers had conquered Egypt, and it was a Hyksos who at that time sat upon the throne of Egypt. Thus, it was a Semite Pharaoh who conferred power and authority upon Joseph, the Semite slave.

According to numerous sources, including *Funk and Wagnalls New Encyclopedia* under the heading "Hyksos," "the only detailed ancient account of the Hyksos is in a passage cited by the Jewish historian Flavius Josephus." Mentioned also is the fact that "Evidence from inscriptions and sculpture and pottery remains shows that **these kings adapted themselves to Egyptian customs and took Egyptian names**." *The Zondervan Pictorial Encyclopedia of the Bible,* under the heading "Hyksos," brings out the point that the Hyksos rulers appropriated to themselves Pharonic style including the title, "Son of Re." Hence, we see that these Semite rulers also adopted the Egyptian religion. Like the Pharaohs who had ruled before him, the Hyksos Pharaoh became the focus of Egyptian worship. To himself and the Egyptian people, Pharaoh became the incarnation of the sun god Re, also known as Ra, Amon Ra, Amon and Horus.

In this same source, we read, "...foreigners duly attained to administrative posts (cf. Joseph)...." Thus, we see confirmed the connection between the Semite Hyksos Pharaoh and the Semite slave Joseph. It was evidently a common and acceptable practice at that time for non-Egyptians such as Joseph to be placed in executive governmental positions.

From all available Biblical and historical facts, we must conclude that God raised up the Hyksos in order to use them to help Him carry out His covenant with Abraham, Isaac and Jacob. Joseph's transition from Semite slave to ruler over all the land of Egypt was made easy by the fact that, prior to Joseph's ascension to power, God had already set the stage for His advancement.

While Joseph lived and the Hyksos ruled Egypt, the Israelites fared well. However, after Joseph's death, the favorable conditions that the Israelites had enjoyed to that point in time changed considerably. The next quote from the *The Zondervan Pictorial Bible Dictionary,* under the heading "Hyksos," concurs with my previous statement.

> During their rule, which was more friendly to foreigners than were native Egyptian dynasties, Joseph came to Egypt and rose to be prime minister, bringing his father Jacob's family to dwell in Goshen, near the Hyksos capital at Avaris in the Delta. ...Between 1600 and 1550 B.C. the Hyksos were driven out by a native Egyptian dynasty **unfriendly to foreigners,** and the capital restored to Thebes, its earlier location. **From this time date the misfortunes of Jacob's rapidly increasing descendants, terminating only with their escape from Egypt**.

When in power, the Hyksos had left a portion of Egypt under the rule of the old Egyptian nobility. These Egyptian rulers were required to pay tribute to the Hyksos. It was these same nobles who started the nationalistic revolt against the foreign rulers and ousted the Hyksos from power, driving them out of Egypt. After two hundred years, the native Egyptians were finally rid of all foreign rulers.

It stands to reason that from that time forth, the Egyptians were extremely wary of all foreigners. After all, they had experienced defeat at the hands of foreigners, foreigners who had occupied their land for two hundred years. So, you can see how the Egyptians' hatred of foreigners would have affected their relationship with and treatment of the Israelites.

Moreover, according to Exodus 1:8 in *The Living Bible*, the new native Egyptian king (that is, the king who was responsible for the recorded abuse that the Israelites experienced in Egypt) felt no obligation to the foreigner, Joseph, Joseph's God or Joseph's people. Thus, Pharaoh chose to ignore the past mercy that God had extended toward his nation. He chose to overlook the fact that God had miraculously spared the people of Egypt from the ravages of famine and to disregard the promises that the former Hyksos Pharoah had made to Joseph. Consequently, the second part of God's prophecy in Genesis 15:13 came to pass.

Genesis 15:13 (The Amplified Bible.)

13And [God] said to Abram, Know positively that your descendants will be strangers dwelling as temporary residents in a land that is not theirs [Egypt], and they will be slaves there and will be afflicted and oppressed for 400 years.

As one considers this whole sequence of events, one cannot help but recognize Satan's influence. Yes, it is obvious that Satan was behind all the dastardly deeds that were perpetrated upon the Israelites by the Egyptian people. After all, who would want to see God's purpose in this area frustrated more than God's enemy, the devil. He certainly did not want God's covenant promise to make Abraham a great nation to be accomplished through the fruitfulness of the Israelite people. However, the fact that Satan was at work during that time did not excuse the Egyptians' abominable crimes against God and His chosen people.

I mentioned the Egyptians' crimes against God because, the truth is, God actually suffered the most from Egypt's wicked behavior. You see, because of the previously mentioned two hundred years of foreign rule, the Egyptians came to view Israel's population explosion as a threat to their own safety. Thus, consumed by irrational fear, you might say they went straight for God's jugular vein (that is, His sacred oath to Abraham).

God had made an unbreakable contract with Abraham. In that sacred agreement, God promised He would multiply Abraham exceedingly. He also established His covenant with Isaac and Jacob. Thus, God's reputation was at stake. His agreement with Abraham, Isaac and Jacob had to be kept. Yet, since the Egyptians considered the Israelites to be an internal threat to their own survival, their main objective was to stop the propagation of the descendants of Abraham, Isaac and Jacob at any cost.

The Egyptians used every form of cruelty imaginable to try to put a halt to the reproduction of God's chosen covenant people. However, God had no intention of allowing those ungrateful, promise-breaking people to prevent Him from keeping His promise to Abraham, Isaac and Jacob. **As God had foretold in Genesis 46:3, the Jews would become a great nation, and they would become a great nation in Egypt.**

Thus, the more the Egyptians abused them, the more God caused His people to multiply. Even so, the Israelites' population explosion only served to anger and alarm the Egyptians that much more.

It might seem odd to you that in the previous paragraph I accused the generation of native Egyptians living during that time of defaulting on an agreement that had been made, not by them but by an earlier Hyksos Pharaoh. In order to put your mind at ease regarding that issue, let me assure you that the previously mentioned query will be addressed and satisfactorily answered in subsequent chapters of this book. However, at this time, it is needful that I do not distract you from the issue at hand, which is, "Why Did The Jews End Up In Slavery In Egypt?"

Now that you know how, prior to this incident, foreigners had conquered and ruled Egypt for two hundred years, the following verses will give you insight into the warped mentality of the ruling Pharoah of that period. They will also provide you with a glimpse of the wickedness of his Egyptian subjects. Moreover, they will give you an idea of the severe measures the Egyptians resorted to in order to blot out the covenant descendants of Abraham, Isaac and Jacob.

> *Exodus 1:6-22 (The Amplified Bible.)*
>
> [6]*Then Joseph died, and all his brothers and all that generation.*
>
> [7]*But the descendants of Israel were fruitful and increased abundantly;* ***they multiplied and grew exceedingly strong, and the land was full of them.***
>
> [8]*Now a new king arose over Egypt who did not know Joseph.*

Verse eight in *The Living Bible* reads,

> [8]*Then, eventually, a new king came to the throne of Egypt who felt no obligation to the descendants of Joseph.*
>
> [9]***He said to his people, Behold, the Israelites are too many and too mighty for us [and they outnumber us both in people and in strength].***
>
> [10]***Come, let us deal shrewdly with them, lest they multiply more and, should war befall us, they join our enemies, fight against us, and escape out of the land.***

The Egyptians were terrified that the Israelites, who now outnumbered them, would end up making war against Egypt. Their irrational fears made them feel that they were between a rock and a hard place. On the one hand, the Egyptians felt that if they allowed the Israelites to continue on as they were, they would remain an internal threat. While on the other hand, if they forcibly expelled the Israelites from Egypt, they would then have a nation of people who were greater in number and strength than themselves posing an external threat. Thus, in their shrewdness, the Egyptians contrived a plan that would totally remove both facets of their imagined Israelite threat to Egypt and would, at the same time, allow the Egyptians to capitalize on the available Israelite work force.

> ^{11}*So they set over [the Israelites] taskmasters to afflict and oppress them with [increased] burdens. And [the Israelites] built Pithom and Rameses as store cities for Pharoah.*
>
> ^{12}*But the more [the Egyptians] oppressed them, the more they multipled and expanded, so that [the Egyptians] were vexed and alarmed because of the Israelites.*
>
> ^{13}*And the Egyptians reduced the Israelites to severe slavery.*
>
> ^{14}*They made their lives bitter with hard service in mortar, brick, and all kinds of work in the field. All their service was with harshness and severity.*

Once Pharoah realized that affliction, oppression, harshness, wearisome toil and even severe slavery did not affect the fertility of the Israelite people, he resorted to horrific tactics to try to bring their birth rate under control. He ordered the Hebrew midwives to kill their own peoples' newly born male babies.

This whole devious setup was unmistakably contrived in the pits of hell. It was a plot inspired by the devil to thwart God's will and purpose (that is, to interfere with God carrying out His sacred pledge to Abraham, Isaac and Jacob). **For, on the one hand, we have God causing the Israelites to multiply as the stars of the heavens as He had promised Abraham, Isaac and Jacob He would, while on the other hand, we have Pharoah commanding a segment of God's own covenant people to murder the very offspring that God had sent the Israelites into Egypt to produce.** Thank God that the midwives feared God enough to disregard Pharoah's command.

To verify what I have said to this point, let us read verses fifteen through twenty-one.

Exodus 1:15-21 (The Amplified Bible.)

^{15}*Then the king of Egypt said to the Hebrew midwives, of whom one was named Shiprah and the other Puah,*

^{16}*When you act as midwives to the Hebrew women and see them on the birthstool, if it is a son, you shall kill him; but if it is a daughter, she shall live.*

The main reason Pharoah commanded that only Israelite male babies be destroyed was because he feared that in the future, those male babies would grow into strong men, become fierce warriors and war against Egypt.

^{17}*But the midwives feared God and did not do as the king of Egypt commanded, but let the male babies live.*

^{18}*So the king of Egypt called for the midwives and said to them, Why have you done this thing and allowed the male children to live?*

^{19}*The midwives answered Pharoah, Because the Hebrew women are not like the Egyptian women; they are vigorous and quickly delivered; their babies are born before the midwife comes to them.*

^{20}*So God dealt well with the midwives and the people multiplied and became very strong.*

^{21}*And because the midwives revered and feared God, He made them households [of their own].*

Pharoah's conspiracy to make the midwives of Israel do his murderous dirty work was an utter failure. Instead of his insidious plot diminishing Israel's population, God's people experienced phenomenal growth. As it is written in verse twenty, *"...the people multiplied and became very strong."*

Nevertheless, Pharoah's fearful obsession with the birth rate of the Israelite people persisted. Consequently, he eventually concocted yet another horrendous scheme. This time, he commanded his own subjects to perform the murders that the Israelite midwives refused to do. Can you imagine this? **A whole nation of potential baby killers!**

The Egyptians were even instructed in Hebrew male baby extermination procedures. The depopulation of Abraham's

descendants would be accomplished by drowning. Yes, the tiny, helpless covenant descendants of Abraham, Isaac and Jacob were cast into the merciless waters of the river Nile. Thus, the Nile became the mass grave of the innocence of Israel.

Exodus 1:22 (The Amplified Bible.)

22 Then Pharoah charged all his people, saying, Every son born [to the Hebrews] you shall cast into the river [Nile], but every daughter you shall allow to live.

Oh, the ingratitude and cruelty of the Egyptian people. They repaid God's past kindness by afflicting, oppressing and eventually enslaving His chosen covenant people. They recompensed God's mercy by murdering His beloved people's precious male offspring.

Imagine the heartache the Lord must have endured during that long and awful period. Over and over again, God had to witness the Egyptians drowning His male covenant babies as fast as He could produce them. He had to witness the evil behavior of a people who owed Him so much, a people whose ancestors had only survived the famine because of His kindness. Yes, God had to look on as the Egyptians cast His babies of promise into the dark, cold waters of the river Nile.

My friend, if the insight you now possess into that heartbreaking situation does not cause you to grieve over what God suffered at the hands of the Egyptians, I do not know what it will take to touch your heart. Watching any baby being deliberately drowned like a rat would be traumatic, but these babies were the fulfillment of God's sacred unbreakable promise. And they were being drowned by the very nation of people who owed their survival as a nation to one of the Israelites' former brethren, Joseph.

Another sad point to consider is that the Jews were innocent victims. They had never given the Egyptians reason to suspect them of such treacherous behavior. On the contrary, the Israelites' past and present exemplary conduct should have been all the proof the Egyptians needed to know that they had absolutely no intention of siding with Egypt's enemies or fighting against the Egyptians in the future. If the Israelites had harbored such ambitions, they would have already fought against the Egyptians. For, it is clear that the Israelites outnumbered and were greater in strength than the Egyptians.

Furthermore, the Israelites had no control whatsoever over the population explosion that their race was experiencing. For, as you now

38

know, the Lord Himself was responsible for their fruitfulness. Yet, one cannot fault God for failing to put a halt to the Israelites' fruitfulness in order to keep them out of slavery since He was obligated to cause them to multiply. After all, He had given His solemn oath to Abraham, Isaac and Jacob. God swore to those men that He would multiply their descendants as the stars of the heavens and make of them a great nation. **Furthermore, God told Jacob that his descendants would become that great nation in Egypt**. (Genesis 46:3.) Under such circumstances as I have just described, what else could our uncompromisingly righteous God do but keep His sacred vow to the Israelites' forefathers?

Christian, you now know the answer to the question, "Why Did The Jews End Up In Slavery In Egypt?" **The Jews ended up in slavery because Satan wanted to keep God from fulfilling His sacred promise to Abraham, Isaac, and Jacob, the promise that Abraham's descendants would become a great nation in Egypt. As you now know, Satan played on the unjustified concerns of the Egyptians. Thus, fearing another foreign invasion, the ungrateful ruling Pharoah reneged on the agreement that the earlier Hyksos Pharoah had made with Israel. With one swipe of Egypt's powerful arm, Satan attempted to destroy God's reputation and the covenant nation that God was breeding in the land of Egypt.**

The bottom line is, the Jews were enslaved for simply allowing God to multiply them exceedingly. The Jews were enslaved for allowing God to fulfill His sacred covenant through them. The Jews were enslaved so that God could keep covenant with Abraham, Isaac and Jacob and protect His holy name.

There is yet another aspect of this whole scenario that also needs to be identified. The Jews partly suffered so that you and I might be blessed. For, did not God promise Abraham *"...in you will all the families and kindred of the earth be blessed...."* (Genesis 12:3.) And, did not God also promise Jacob *"...by your offspring shall all the nations of the earth be blessed...."* (Genesis 26:4.) My friend, the Jews had to endure that suffering in Egypt in order for God to be able to eventually bless us Gentiles through the seed of Abraham, Isaac and Jacob, a fact that will be made crystal clear in other chapters of this book.

Certainly, we all gained because of the four hundred years of affliction and oppression that the Jews suffered. We all gained because of the cruel slavery they endured. We all gained because of the terror and grief the Jews experienced by seeing their babies murdered before their eyes. Yes, everything the Jews went through was partly for us. Therefore, we must not exhibit ingratitude and cruelty toward them as Pharoah and the Egyptian people did. We Gentiles must not repay their good deeds by mistreating the very race through whom God has and will continue to bless us.

Oh, my friend, it is time for the Church to express her gratitude to God's chosen covenant people. It is time for us to thank the Jews for sticking in there through thick and thin so that through them all the families of the earth might be blessed. No race of people in the history of the world has ever suffered as they have in order to help God keep His sacred unbreakable promise and thus, protect His reputation. Truly the Jews are to be admired and praised for their endurance.

Chapter 4

WERE THE EGYPTIANS PUNISHED FOR THEIR CRIMES AGAINST THE JEWISH PEOPLE?

It is understandable that after studying the last two chapters you would want an answer to the question, "Were the Egyptians ever punished for their heinous crimes against God and the Jewish people?" That question should and will be addressed in this chapter while the Egyptians' vileness and treachery are still fresh in your mind. The answer to the previous question does, however, necessitate a temporary deviation from the Biblical chronological order of events. Nevertheless, before chapter four is ended, you will possess the answer to the question I just posed. In addition, the information contained in this portion of the series will provide you with insight into terms used in subsequent chapters.

First, I want to draw your attention to God's prediction in Genesis 15:13 that we studied earlier. I also want to remind you that the prophesy did not end in verse thirteen. The following verse (verse fourteen) also contains part of God's future prediction. So, let us read both verses together.

Genesis 15:13-14 (The Amplified Bible.)

13And [God] said to Abram, Know positively that your descendants will be strangers dwelling as temporary residents in a land that is not theirs [Egypt], and they will be slaves there and will be afflicted and oppressed for 400 years.

14But I will bring judgment on that nation whom they will serve, and afterward they will come out with great possessions.

The portion of verse fourteen that we are presently interested in says, *"But I will bring judgment on that nation whom they will serve...."* God foretold that He would execute judgment upon the Egyptians for the four hundred years of tyranny and cruelty that God's people suffered by their hands. To see further evidence of that fact, we will also read the following verse.

Nehemiah 9:10 (The Amplified Bible.)

[10]*You performed signs and wonders against Pharaoh and all his servants and all the people of his land, for You knew that they dealt insolently against the Israelites. And You got for Yourself a name, as it is today.*

The Living Bible reads, "*You displayed great miracles against Pharaoh and his people, for You knew how brutally the Egyptians were treating them....*"

The Egyptian people lifted themselves up in pride, insolence and hatred toward God and everything He stood for. They refused to acknowledge God's past kindness to them. Furthermore, they ruthlessly broke their agreement with God's people. From that point on, their behavior toward the Israelites was barbaric. You will recall, they went so far as to murder the Israelites newborn male babies. They cold-bloodedly drowned them in the river Nile.

The Egyptians repaid God's generosity to them by brutally abusing, enslaving and murdering His chosen people. Consequently, they brought upon their own heads God's curse in Genesis 12:3, "*...I will bless those who bless you and curse him who curses or uses insolent language toward you....*" **To put it bluntly, the Egyptians' punishment was retribution for the four hundred years that they had mistreated God's chosen covenant people.**

God had witnessed every devious plot that the Egyptians contrived to harm His beloved covenant people. He had also witnessed every insidious act and every wrong word that the Egyptians had spoken against His people. It was now time for the Egyptians to reap what they had sown. Yes, it was time for God's warning in Genesis 15:14 to come to pass, "*...I will bring judgment on that nation whom they will serve....*"

Out of what seemed to be an utterly helpless and hopeless situation, God raised up His instrument of judgment, who was of course, Moses. The very decree that threatened the survival of Israel as a race of people became the means to righting every injustice that had been perpetrated upon God's people by the Egyptians.

God not only spared baby Moses from Pharaoh's decree but He used Pharaoh's own daughter to protect, raise and educate Moses in all the wisdom and culture of the Egyptians. Ironically, God had the Egyptians themselves prepare for Him the very vessel He intended to use to pour out His punishment upon all Egypt for their brutal treatment of His covenant people.

Now that you comprehend the Scriptural reasons behind God chastising the Egyptians, we will briefly study the curses (plagues) that God, through Moses, poured out upon them as punishment for their insidious crimes against His people, the Jews.

PLAGUE NO. 1: THE WATERS OF THE NILE TURN TO BLOOD

The first plague that God sent upon the Egyptians involved the waters of the river Nile turning to blood. The following verses give us a glimpse of what the plague of blood entailed.

Exodus 7:14-19 (The Amplified Bible.)

14Then the Lord said to Moses, Pharaoh's heart is hard and stubborn; he refuses to let the people go.

15Go to Pharaoh in the morning; he will be going out to the water; wait for him by the river's brink; and the rod which was turned to a serpent you shall take in your hand.

16And say to him, The Lord, the God of the Hebrews has sent me to you, saying, Let My people go, that they may serve Me in the wilderness; and behold, heretofore you have not listened.

*17Thus says the Lord, In this you shall know, recognize, and understand that I am the Lord: **behold, I will smite with the rod in my hand the waters in the [Nile] River, and they shall be turned to blood.***

Oh, my friend, think about it, the very river in which the tiny, covenant Israelite babies had been drowned turned to blood. The stark realization of the meaning of this judgment is obvious. If the blood of one murdered man (Abel) cried out to God from the ground, how much more would the blood of all those innocent covenant babies whom the Egyptians murdered cry out to God! The river Nile turning to blood showed the Egyptian's guilt. The blood of the innocence of Israel cried out for justice.

The blood did not stay within the confines of the banks of the Nile. No, it spewed into every river, every stream, and every pond of water in

Egypt. It even ended up in the containers used to draw water from the Nile. The blood of those tiny victims cried out for justice, and now justice had arrived. Thus, the bloody waters of the Nile ran like a foreboding messenger throughout Egypt, proclaiming her people's guilt and the start of God's punishment.

> *18The fish in the river shall die, the river shall become foul smelling, and the Egyptians shall loathe to drink from it.*
>
> *19And the Lord said to Moses, Say to Aaron, Take your rod and stretch out your hand over the waters of Egypt, over their streams, rivers, pools, and ponds of water, that they may become blood; and there shall be blood throughout all the land of Egypt, in containers both of wood and of stone.*

During Israel's four hundred years of affliction and oppression, God's covenant babies were not the only Israelites who lost their lives at the hands of the Egyptians. Consequently, the blood (a symbol of Egypt's murderous guilt) was displayed by God throughout all the land of Egypt. Yes, the blood was visible in the waters, and it was also visible on the land. For in verse nineteen, the Lord said, "...*and there shall be blood throughout all the land of Egypt, in containers both of wood and of stone.*"

PLAGUE NO. 2: FROGS

The second plague crawled out of the waters of the Nile and onto the land. Frogs and more frogs covered the land of Egypt. Can you imagine having swarms of slimy, smelly frogs crawling all over your house, all over your food, all over your beds, all over your children and even on your own body?

As we continue to read about God's punishment upon the Egyptian people, try to put yourself in their shoes. Think how you would feel if you were in that same situation. But also, remember the crimes they committed against God and His covenant people. Then ask yourself; Was their punishment to this point in time sufficient? Did the punishment fit the crime?

> *Exodus 8:1-4 (The Amplified Bible.)*
>
> *1THEN THE Lord said to Moses, Go to Pharaoh and say to him, Thus says the Lord, Let My people go, that they may serve Me.*

*²And if you refuse to let them go, behold, **I will smite your entire land with frogs;***

³And the river shall swarm with frogs which shall go up and come into your house, into your bedchamber and on your bed, and into the houses of your servants and upon your people, and into your ovens, your kneading bowls, and your dough.

⁴And the frogs shall come up on you and on your people and all your servants.

God had broadcast the Egyptians' murderous guilt through the watery blood of the Nile and dried blood upon their land. Next, through the frog plague, God had forced the Egyptians to undergo a taste of the discomfort and mental distress and anguish that His people had experienced at their hands for the past four hundred years. Hordes of distasteful, vile frogs crept into every aspect of the Egyptians daily lives. The very presence of those despicable, slimy creatures made their lives unbearable. Just as it had been for the Hebrews under the Egyptians' oppression, so it now was for the Egyptians. For, there was nothing that they could do to alleviate their discomfort.

One shudders at the very thought of that ghastly scene. Everywhere the Egyptians went and everything they did, there were their croaking longlegged tormentors. Even the act of sitting down to weep or to rest was obviously interfered with by those repugnant hordes. For, how could the Egyptians sit down without sitting on the fat, slimy bodies of those frogs and squashing their bowels all over their delicate linen clothing? How could the Egyptians walk through their houses without stepping on the slithering creatures until their intestines oozed between their toes?

Surely their appetites must also have been affected. After all, who would want to eat food after swarms of filthy, smelly frogs had excreted on it. No wonder Psalm 78:45 informs us that the frogs destroyed the Egyptians.

The shoe was on the other foot. The Egyptians who had tormented the Israelites were now being tormented. The Egyptians who had caused the Israelites to undergo mental torture were now suffering severe mental anguish. And as Psalm 105:30 tells us, even Pharaoh did not escape these slimy oppressors. The frogs found their way to his royal chambers also. Yes, Pharaoh, his family and his servants all suffered the same distress, the same mental agony as the rest of the Egyptians. Yet their discomfort had just begun. For many more plagues still lay ahead.

PLAGUES NO. 3 AND 4: BLOODSUCKING INSECTS

The third and fourth plagues were more hideous than the two before. They were more hideous because severe physical pain was continually inflicted upon the Egyptians. Plague three consisted of biting, bloodsucking gnats, and plague four involved bloodsucking gadflies. The physical pain and suffering inflicted by those bloodsucking gnats and flies was recompense for every drop of blood that was extracted from the backs of God's people by the whips of their Egyptian taskmasters. Yes, the Egyptians were paid back for every blow or kick that drew blood, for every bloody nose the Israelites suffered, for every injury that caused their blood to flow.

Exodus 8:16-17 (The Amplified Bible.)

16Then the Lord said to Moses, Say to Aaron, Stretch out your rod and strike the dust of the ground, that it may become biting gnats or mosquitoes throughout all the land of Egypt.

17And they did so; Aaron stretched out his hand with his rod and struck the dust of the earth, and there came biting gnats or mosquitoes on man and beast; all the dust of the land became biting gnats or mosquitoes throughout all the land of Egypt.

Exodus 8:20-24 (The Amplified Bible.)

20Then the Lord said to Moses, Rise up early in the morning and stand before Pharaoh as he comes forth to the water; and say to him, Thus says the Lord, Let My people go, that they may serve Me.

21Else, if you will not let My people go, behold, I will send swarms [of bloodsucking gadflies] upon you, your servants, and your people, and into your houses; and the houses of the Egyptians shall be full of swarms [of bloodsucking gadflies], and also the ground on which they stand.

22But on that day I will sever and set apart the land of Goshen in which My people dwell, that no swarms [of gadflies] shall be there, so that you may know that I am the Lord in the midst of the earth.

23And I will put a division and a sign of deliverance between My people and your people. By tomorrow shall this sign be in evidence.

24And the Lord did so; and there came heavy and oppressive swarms [of bloodsucking gadflies] into the house of Pharaoh and his servants' houses; and in all of Egypt the land was corrupted and ruined by reason of the great invasion [of gadflies].

Psalm 105:31 says, *"He spoke, and there came swarms of beetles and flies and mosquitoes and lice in all their borders."*

Psalm 78:45 says, *"He sent swarms of [venomous] flies among them which devoured them...."*

These verses make it clear that the flies not only sucked the blood of the Egyptians and their animals, but they also pumped poison into their bodies at the same time. Yes, the gnats and blood sucking flies devoured the flesh of the Egyptians and their animals.

Flesh was not all that the flies spoiled. Those flies carried diseases. Did not Exodus 8:24 inform us that "...*in all of Egypt the land was corrupted and ruined by reason of the great invasion of [gadflies]?*" For you see, when the flies died and came in contact with something, that something spoiled. They made even the Egyptian perfume smell putrid. Remember what Ecclesiastes 10:1 says? It says, *"DEAD FLIES cause the ointment of the perfumer to putrefy [and] send forth a vile odor...."*

All four plagues that we have touched on were very severe. However, even combined, they did not compare with the four hundred years of pain and abuse that the Israelites had suffered at the hands of the Egyptians. The punishment still did not fit the crime. Thus, a fifth plague was poured out upon Egypt.

PLAGUE NO. 5: MURRAIN

The fifth plague involved the hand of the Lord falling upon all the livestock of Egypt that were out in the fields. God sent a plague of murrain upon all Egypt's domestic animals. Murrain is a variety of highly infectious diseases that affect domestic animals. Anthrax would fall under the murrain category. And, as you may know, anthrax is very contagious and usually fatal. The next verses reveal what happened to Egypt's livestock.

48

Exodus 9:1-6 (The Amplified Bible.)

¹*THEN THE Lord said to Moses, Go to Pharaoh and tell him, Thus says the Lord God of the Hebrews: Let My people go, that they may serve Me.*

²*If you refuse to let them go and still hold them,*

³*Behold, the hand of the Lord [will fall] upon your livestock which are out in the field, upon the horses, the donkeys, the camels, the herds and the flocks; there shall be a very severe plague.*

⁴*But the Lord shall make a distinction between the livestock of Israel and the livestock of Egypt, and nothing shall die of all that belongs to the Israelites.*

⁵*And the Lord set a time, saying, Tomorrow the Lord will do this thing in the land.*

⁶*And the Lord did that the next day, and all [kinds of] the livestock of Egypt died; but of the livestock of the Israelites not one died.*

You will recall that as compensation for the Israelites' use of Egypt's land, God had allowed Joseph to interpret Pharaoh's dreams. Consequently, during the famine, Pharaoh's storehouses had been full of grain while no one else in Egypt had any food. Thus, Joseph had been able to strike a bargain on behalf of Pharaoh with the inhabitants of Egypt. The bargain was for the Egyptians to give their livestock to Pharaoh in exchange for food. Let us read about that incident in the following verses.

Genesis 47:15-18 (The Amplified Bible.)

¹⁵*And when the money was exhausted in the land of Egypt and in the land of Canaan, all the Egyptians came to Joseph and said, Give us food! Why should we die before your very eyes? For we have no money left.*

¹⁶*Joseph said, Give up your livestock, and I will give you food in exchange for [them] if your money is gone.*

¹⁷*So they brought their livestock to Joseph, and [he] gave them food in exchange for the horses, flocks, cattle of the herds, and the donkeys; and he supplied them with food in exchange for all their livestock that year.*

18When that year was ended, they came to [Joseph] the second year and said to him, We will not hide from my lord [the fact] that our money is spent; my lord also has our herds of livestock; there is nothing left in the sight of my lord but our bodies and our lands.

By giving Pharaoh all the money and livestock in the land, God had more than compensated him for the four hundred years that Israel was to live in Egypt and use his land. However, through the murrain plague, God took back all the livestock in the field. Pharaoh had broken his promise to Joseph, Jacob and the Israelite people. Rather than continuing to let God's people eat of the fat of the land as he had promised he would, Pharaoh afflicted and oppressed them and reduced them to cruel bondage. It is clear that God could not allow Pharaoh or his people to continue to benefit in any way from an agreement that he did not keep.

Notice that in the former paragraph, I accuse the reigning Pharaoh of breaking his agreement with the Israelite people, although, it was an earlier Hyksos Pharaoh who actually made that agreement. My reasons for identifying both the past and present Pharaohs as one and the same person will soon be made clear. Part of the answer to that query will be given in this chapter, while another enlightening segment will be provided later in the series.

You might ask, "But why did the fish, crocodiles and livestock have to suffer and die? Why didn't God confine the plagues to Pharaoh and the Egyptian people?" Let me begin to answer those questions by saying, what greater punishment could the Egyptians have received than to be forced to stand by helplessly while the things they considered sacred died in front of their eyes. Furthermore, what greater humiliation and chastisement could they have been forced to undergo than to be brutally assaulted by their sacred objects of worship.

Since we are at the present time in a study about Israel, I do not want to take the time to go into a lengthy explanation of the animals, insects and fish that were considered sacred by the Egyptians. Rather, let me encourage you to do your own research on that topic. I will simply point out a few pertinent facts that are recorded in *Smith's Bible Dictionary* under the heading "Plagues, The Ten."

Plague No. 1 Blood: The river Nile was one of Egypt's deities. It was adored as a source of life to the agricultural products and the Egyptian people. Plus, certain types of fish and the crocodile that lived in the Nile were considered to be sacred. When God plagued the Nile, everything that lived in it or drank from it suffered.

Plague No. 2 Frogs: The Egyptians viewed frogs as sacred and as objects of worship. Thus, their objects of worship became a horrible oppressive plague.

Plague No. 3 Lice: The land which was worshipped turned into a source of torment. The dust produced the curse. Consequently, the Egyptians incurred religious defilement. Also the air which was worshipped was defiled.

Plague No. 4 Flies: Some feel that these flies were "scarabaus sacer." The scarabaus is a large beetle that is known to attack man. It was considered sacred by the Egyptians. God plagued the Egyptians with the very insects that they revered.

Plague No. 5 Murrain: Cattle were Egyptian deities. They were actually worshipped by them. God sent a plague that killed Egypt's deities.

Now you know why God included in His judgment the animals, fish and insects of Egypt. They were included because they were objects of idolatrous worship. During Joseph's time, God had miraculously intervened in order to spare Egypt from famine and destruction. Therefore, the Egyptians should have known that Joseph's God is the true God. But they refused to acknowledge Him. Instead, they chose to continue to worship their false gods.

It was in the name of their proclaimed false deities that the Egyptians mistreated God's covenant people. Consequently, God used this opportunity to prove to the Egyptian people the absolute powerlessness of their gods. For the people could look at their own difficult circumstances and witness firsthand the fact that their objects of worship were totally helpless to stop or even alleviate the intensity of the plagues or their own personal pain and suffering. Before this chapter ends, I will give you Scriptural proof for what I just said. However, for now, let us concentrate on the plagues that we have not yet touched on.

PLAGUE NO. 6: BOILS

Moses and Aaron were commanded by God to scatter handfuls of ashes from the brickkiln or as the *King James* translation says, *"the furnace."* These ashes were to be scattered toward the heavens in the sight of Pharaoh. *The Amplified Bible* translators were right on target when they chose to use the term *"brickkiln"* in their edition rather than the term *"furnace."* I will explain why after you read the next verses.

Exodus 9:8-11 (The Amplified Bible.)

8The Lord said to Moses and Aaron, Take handfuls of ashes or soot from the brickkiln and let Moses sprinkle them toward the heavens in the sight of Pharaoh.

9And it shall become small dust over all the land of Egypt, and become boils breaking out in sores on man and beast in all the land [occupied by the Egyptians].

10So they took ashes or soot of the kiln and stood before Pharaoh; and Moses threw them toward the sky, and it became boils erupting in sores on man and beast.

11And the magicians could not stand before Moses because of their boils; for the boils were on the magicians and all the Egyptians.

There are numerous points that must be made regarding the plague of boils. But first, let me explain why I said that *The Amplified Bible* translators were right on target when they chose to use the word *"brickkiln"* rather than the term *"furnace."* You can check out the subsequent information in the Hebrew and Chaldee Dictionary of the *Strong's Exhaustive Concordance of the Bible.*

The Hebrew word "kibshan" *("furnace")* found in Exodus 9:8 in the *King James* version of the Bible is from the Hebrew root word "kabash." According to Strong, the definition of the word "kabash" includes "bring into bondage, force, keep under, subdue, bring into subjection." No other Hebrew word which specifies a furnace comes from the root word "kabash." Thus, in this instance, if the Hebrew scholars were to impart to the reader true understanding of the type of furnace mentioned in Exodus 9:8, they had to translate that word *"furnace"* in the manner they did, which was *"brickkiln."* **For you see, that furnace was the brickkiln in which the Israelite slaves were forced to make bricks for the Pharaoh.**

With the information you now have concerning Egyptian idolatry and the brickkiln, you will more quickly comprehend the contents of the next portion of the lesson. For example: the brickkiln represented four hundred years of affliction and oppression. It represented years of slavery and suffering. It represented harsh forced labor in the hot sun, day after day, without one day off to rest and recuperate. It represented the pain of the taskmasters' whips and severe emotional abuse year in and year out. Yes, the brickkiln stood as a horrible monument of the cruel treatment the Israelites had suffered from their merciless Egyptian taskmasters.

God told Moses and Aaron to take handfuls of ash from the brickkiln. Moses was to scatter that ash or soot toward the heavens in the sight of Pharaoh. You might ask: "What was God's purpose for having Moses scatter those ashes from the brickkiln? And, why was it so important that Pharaoh see Moses carry out God's instructions?"

Let us take one question at a time. First the question, "What was God's purpose for having Moses scatter those ashes from the brickkiln?" According to the previous article in *Smith's Bible Dictionary*, scattering ashes was an ancient Egyptian religious rite. The priests of Egypt would scatter the ashes toward the heavens and the sun gods whom they worshipped.

Moses and Aaron simply mimicked the priests. They scattered the ashes toward the heavens as if to invoke the aid of Egypt's sun gods. By their actions they were mocking the Egyptians' false gods. They were mockingly saying to Egypt's false gods: "Come if you can and deliver your followers from the plague of boils that is now poured out upon them. Show us the power that you are supposed to possess. Command your magicians to conjure up a spell that will counteract the plague that the true and only God, the God of Israel, has sent upon all the Egyptians."

The answer to the second question that I posed earlier, "Why was it so important that Pharaoh see Moses carry out God's instructions?" is now obvious. God wanted him to witness the utter impotency of the gods of Egypt. And God had good reason for wanting Pharaoh to realize the helplessness of Egypt's gods.

The Encyclopedia Britannica Micropedia Ready Reference under the heading "Pharaoh" informs us that the people of Egypt believed that Pharaoh himself was a god. They identified Pharaoh with the sky god "Horus" and with the sun gods "Re-Amon and Aton." According to that same source, Pharaoh was believed to have sacred magical powers. Supposedly on the battlefield these magical powers enabled him to slay thousands of the enemy all by himself. He was also supposed to be all-powerful, all-knowing and in complete control of all nature, fertility and even fate. As their god, Pharaoh was also responsible for the Egyptians' financial prosperity and their spiritual well-being.

With the understanding you now have, try to imagine this scene. There stood Pharaoh, supposedly an incarnation of the Egyptian god Horus and also identified with the previously mentioned false sun gods. And there stood Moses and Aaron, ridiculing him by invoking the false gods, Pharaoh (Horus), Re-Amon and Aton, to come to the aid of their Egyptian followers, if they could. It was like Moses and Aaron were tauntingly saying to Pharaoh, "Use now the great magical powers that you are thought to possess. You are supposed to be all-knowing and all-powerful, so come and stop the next plague. Prove before all Egypt that you truly are a god. Show proof, Pharaoh, of your professed magical powers."

Moses knew that Pharaoh was not really a god. Rather, Moses knew he was a fake just as the sun gods, Re-Amon and Aton, were fakes. Like the other gods of Egypt, Pharaoh could not even protect himself from the plagues, never mind his Egyptian subjects or their animals. And that was exactly the point that God wanted to make during the Egyptians' punishment for mistreating His people. God wanted all Egypt to witness the utter impotency of their false gods. He wanted all Egypt to recognize that Pharaoh was not a God. Pharaoh was instead simply a wicked man who was about to experience the same plague of painful boils that every other Egyptian and their beasts would soon experience.

Plus, God had a specific purpose for using the ash from the actual kiln in which Pharaoh had forced the Israelites to make his bricks. God did that so there would be no doubt in anyone's mind as to why Pharaoh, his subjects and their beasts were being punished. **For it was in the name of their god, Pharaoh, that the Egyptians had enslaved and severely mistreated God's covenant people.**

PLAGUE NO. 7: HAIL

The plague of hail was sent mainly to destroy Egypt's vegetation and trees. This would have been particularly devastating to Egypt's economy since according to Exodus 9:31, the barley was in the ear and the flax in bloom. Let us read the description of this particular plague that is provided in God's Word.

Exodus 9:22-26 (The Amplified Bible.)

22The Lord said to Moses, Stretch forth your hand toward the heavens, that there may be hail in all the land of Egypt, upon man and beast, and upon all the vegetation of the field, throughout the land of Egypt.

23Then Moses stretched forth his rod toward the heavens, and the Lord sent thunder and hail, and fire (lightning) ran down to and along the ground, and the Lord rained hail upon the land of Egypt.

24So there was hail and fire flashing continually in the midst of the weighty hail, such as had not been in all the land of Egypt since it became a nation.

25The hail struck down throughout all the land of Egypt everything that was in the field, both man and beast; and the hail beat down all the vegetation of the field and shattered every tree of the field.

26Only in the land of Goshen, where the Israelites were, was there no hail.

Verses thirty-two and thirty-three of the following Psalm provide additional information concerning the destructive hail plague. They shed more light on how every tree in the field was shattered. It seems that the trees broke under the weight of the ice.

Psalm 105:32-33 (The Amplified Bible.)

32He gave them hail for rain, with lightning like flaming fire in their land.

33He smote their vines also and their fig trees and broke the [ice-laden] trees of their borders.

I need to bring certain facts to your attention which involve both plagues seven and eight. Therefore, I will wait to relay that information to you until after we have checked out plague number eight. So, let us do that right now.

PLAGUE NO. 8: LOCUSTS

Exodus 10:12-15 (The Amplified Bible.)

12Then the Lord said to Moses, Stretch out your hand over the land of Egypt for the locusts, that they may come up on the land of Egypt and eat all the vegetation of the land, all that the hail has left.

13And Moses stretched forth his rod over the land of Egypt, and the Lord brought an east wind upon the land all that day and all that night; when it was morning, the east wind brought the locusts.

14And the locusts came up over all the land of Egypt and settled down on the whole country of Egypt, a very dreadful mass of them; never before were there such locusts as these, nor will there ever be again.

15For they covered the whole land, so that the ground was darkened, and they ate every bit of vegetation of the land and all the fruit of the trees which the hail had left; there remained not a green thing of the trees or the plants of the field in all the land of Egypt.

Through the plagues of hail and locusts, God meted out further retribution for Egypt's crimes against His chosen people. God also once again sat in judgment of Egypt's false gods including Egypt's false god, Pharaoh. For remember, as a god, Pharaoh was supposed to be all-powerful. He was thought to have power and control over all nature. Yet he was repeatedly shown to be weak and utterly helpless to stop the barrage of plagues that continued to be poured out upon himself, his people, the animals and now upon all the plant life in Egypt.

Any vegetation or tree that had survived the plague of hail was totally and completely devoured by the locusts. I am sure that when the locusts were finished with Egypt, Egypt's land looked like it had suffered a hundred years of drought and famine. However, this time, Egypt did not have Joseph's aid or God's miraculous stockpile of food to fall back on. She had only God's wrath and punishment for her four hundred years of crimes against Him and His chosen covenant people.

God continued to carry out His sentence against the Egyptian people, their animals, their gods and their plants. **Yes, I said plants**. For you see, even their plants played a role in Egypt's religious life. From *The Zondervan Pictorial Encyclopedia of the Bible* under the heading "Plagues of Egypt" and subheading "The theological significance" I quote:

> It is obvious, however, that **the twenty-two Egyp. provinces each had their respective religious center and totemic animal or plant. It is precisely the attributes of these deities that are involved in the plagues.**

God put His finger on every aspect of Egypt's physical, temporal and religious life. He did not leave one stone unturned. Every religious weakness, every falsity, every sin was exposed and punished. For each evil characteristic had played a role in Egypt's mistreatment of God and God's covenant people. By the time the Lord got through with the Egyptians, I am sure they wished that they had never laid eyes on the Israelites, never mind mistreated them.

PLAGUE NO. 9: DARKNESS

There were numerous reasons for God sending a plague of darkness upon the Egyptians. However, as we learned earlier, God's first priority was to keep His word in regard to His curse falling upon all individuals or nations who abuse His chosen people, *"...I will bless those who bless you [who confer prosperity or happiness upon you] and curse him who curses or uses insolent language toward you...."* (Genesis 12:3.) And of course, there was also God's prediction of His future judgment of Egypt, *"...I will bring judgment on that nation whom they will serve...."* (Genesis 15:14.) Therefore, like all the other plagues, the darkness was punishment for the Egyptians' mistreatment of God's people during the four hundred years they had dwelt in Egypt. The next verses show us exactly what took place during the plague of darkness.

Exodus 10:20-23 (The Amplified Bible.)

20 But the Lord made Pharaoh's heart more strong and obstinate, and he would not let the Israelites go.

21 And the Lord said to Moses, Stretch out your hand toward the heavens, that there may be darkness over the land of Egypt, a darkness which may be felt.

22 So Moses stretched out his hand toward the sky, and for three days a thick darkness was all over the land of Egypt.

23 The Egyptians could not see one another, nor did anyone rise from his place for three days; but all the Israelites had natural light in their dwellings.

As the Egyptians had made prisoners of the Israelites, so God made prisoners of them. They were confined to their own homes. They were forcibly constrained by the plague of darkness. For three days they remained imprisoned in their own homes, unable to see each other, unable to get up and move about, unable to venture over their doorsteps. Verse twenty-three tells us that not one Egyptian rose from his place for three days.

The plague of darkness was also part of God's plan to judge the gods of Egypt. However, there is much more truth to consider in regard to God actually using darkness to punish the Egyptians. It is a known

Biblical fact that if men (including God's own people) will not give to God the glory that is due to Him, acknowledging Him as the true and only God and heeding His voice, He will bring darkness upon them. Plus, if they persist in their pride and stubbornness, that darkness will be superseded by the absolute darkness of death. Biblical evidence to prove what I just said can be seen in the next verses taken from *The Holy Bible, King James Version.*

> *Jeremiah 13:15-16 (King James Version.)*
>
> *15Hear ye, and give ear; be not proud: for the Lord hath spoken,*
>
> *16Give glory to the Lord your God, before he cause darkness, and before your feet stumble upon the dark mountains, and, while ye look for light, he turn it into the shadow of death, and make it gross darkness.*

In the book of Ezekiel, the Lord again mentions darkness in connection with His judgment. Incidentally, the prophetic prediction I just mentioned also involves Egypt. However, it speaks of an entirely different event and time than that which we are presently dealing with. Nevertheless, it does add additional light to the insight you have already received regarding darkness being linked to God's judgment whether that darkness be spiritual or literal. You will understand what I mean when you read the following verses.

> *Ezekiel 30:18-19 (The Amplified Bible.)*
>
> *18At Tehaphnehes also the day shall withdraw itself and be dark when I break there the yokes and dominion of Egypt, and the pride of her power shall come to an end. As for her, a cloud [of calamities] shall cover her and her daughters shall go into captivity.*
>
> *19Thus will I execute judgments and punishments upon Egypt. Then shall they know (understand and realize) that I am the Lord [the Sovereign Ruler, Who calls forth loyalty and obedient service].*

Let us now get back on track and consider how God's plague of darkness once more exposed Pharoah as a bogus god. You will recall that Pharoah was supposed to be the sun god, Re, incarnate (that is, the sun god, Re, in bodily form). He was not only believed to be the god of the solar system, but of all creation. Therefore, Pharoah's subjects obviously pleaded with him to let his solar lightbeams shine upon Egypt so that the plague of darkness would be banished from their land. Of course, their petitions went unheeded. Instead of answered prayer, they received undeniable proof that Pharoah was not the creator who provided light. The sun and the moon did not shed their light at his command. For as it had been in the case of all the former plagues, Pharoah, the false sun god, was totally unable to reverse God's command. Pharoah was incapable of removing the plague of darkness.

All Egypt once again saw Pharoah as he really was, a ridiculously weak counterfeit god. The Egyptians also saw without doubt who the one true God is. For we are informed in Exodus 10:23 that while all Egypt sat in darkness, the true Creator, the God of Israel, provided His people with natural light in all their dwellings. As the Scriptures state, *"The Egyptians could not see one another, nor did anyone rise from his place for three days; but all the Israelites had natural light in their dwellings."*

Not only was Pharaoh shown to be false but everything the Egyptians trusted and believed in was exposed as a lie. Yes, every Egyptian deity and every object of idolatrous worship was shown to be a fabrication. Also keep in mind that the very air that the Egyptians worshipped was to them once again defiled by the plague of darkness. First, the land that was sacred had been darkened by swarms of locusts that in turn devoured the sacred vegetation. Then the plague of darkness filled the air. You might say the idolatrous rug had been abruptly pulled out from under the Egyptians' feet. For they personally witnessed just how ineffective and hollow their gods were. Insurmountable proof of their gods' impotency loomed before them. Yet, even the degree of punishment that they had experienced to that point still did not fit the crime. Hence, the final plague came upon Egypt.

PLAGUE NO. 10: DEATH OF THE FIRSTBORN

Death was poured out upon the Egyptians. The absolute darkness (that is, the gross darkness of death that I mentioned previously as being linked with judgment and punishment) clutched to the midnight garb of the plague of darkness. See this for yourself in the next verses.

Exodus 12:29-33 (The Amplified Bible.)

29 At midnight the Lord slew every firstborn in the land of Egypt, from the firstborn of Pharaoh who sat on his throne to the firstborn of the prisoner in the dungeon, and all the firstborn of the livestock.

30 Pharaoh rose up in the night, he, all his servants, and all the Egyptians; and there was a great cry in

> *Egypt, for there was not a house where there was not one dead.*
>
> *31 He called for Moses and Aaron by night, and said, Rise up, get out from among my people, both you and the Israelites; and go, serve the Lord, as you said.*
>
> *32 Also take your flocks and your herds, as you have said, and be gone! And [ask your God to] bless me also.*
>
> *33 The Egyptians were urgent with the people to depart, that they might send them out of the land in haste; for they said, We are all dead men.*

The tenth plague had to have been more devastating to the Egyptians than all the other nine combined. It is hard to imagine what it must have been like for them. We are told in God's Word that no Egyptian household escaped plague number ten. Verse thirty says, *"...there was not a house where there was not one dead."* Everyone in Egypt was touched by the loss of a father, brother, uncle, child, or other relative. That meant that no one even received or extended to others the usual words of comfort and consolation that provide emotional support during periods of mourning. How could they have comforted others when their own loss and grief was so great. Plus, how could they turn to the gods of Egypt for comfort after those gods had been exposed for the counterfeits that they really were?

You may well ask, "What evil could the Egyptians possibly have done to God or the Israelites during those four hundred years to have deserved this particularly severe punishment (that is, to have caused God to retaliate by slaying all their firstborn)?"

Well, my friend, there is much more involved here than what first meets the eye. **The truth is, God slew all the firstborn in Egypt because, prior to that time, the Egyptians had afflicted, oppressed, enslaved and murdered His firstborn son.** Yes, you read my last words correctly. I said, **"His firstborn son."** I made that statement because God Himself refers to Israel as His firstborn son.

Of course, God is not implying that Israel is His firstborn son in the same sense that Yeshua the Christ is. No! Rather, **Israel is God's firstborn nation.** The Israelites are God's firstborn son in that they were chosen to serve God from among all the peoples of the earth. God gave birth to and nurtured the nation of Israel. Thus, God Himself calls Israel His firstborn son. See this for yourself in the following Scripture.

Exodus 4:19-23 (The Amplified Bible.)

19The Lord said to Moses in Midian, Go back to Egypt; for all the men who were seeking your life [for killing the Egyptian] are dead.

20And Moses took his wife and his sons and set them on donkeys, and he returned to the land of Egypt; and Moses took the rod of God in His hand.

21And the Lord said to Moses, When you return into Egypt, see that you do before Pharaoh all those miracles and wonders which I have put in your hand; but I will make him stubborn and harden his heart, so that he will not let the people go.

22And you shall say to Pharaoh, Thus says the Lord, Israel is My son, even My firstborn.

23And I say to you, Let My son go, that he may serve Me; and if you refuse to let him go, behold, I will slay your son, your firstborn.

Because verse twenty-two is vital to our present study, I am going to repeat it. As you again read God's words, allow God to write them on your heart and mind.

22And you shall say to Pharaoh, Thus says the Lord, Israel is My son, even My firstborn.

I cannot enter into a lengthy study on Israel's birthright at this time. However, so that you will not be left hanging without enough information to comprehend the extent of Egypt's sin or her just punishment, I am going to touch on some Biblical highlights concerning the firstborn.

First, I will share with you a particular section of New Testament Scripture that verifies Israel's sonship. Plus, now that you understand about Israel being God's firstborn son, how much God cares for His son Israel and the pain and humiliation God suffered when His firstborn son was abused, enslaved and murdered by the Egyptians, you will understand why the Jewish apostle Paul said he could wish himself accursed if it would bring the nation of Israel (God's firstborn son) to acknowledge the truth about Yeshua, the Christ. Paul was concerned about God as well as the Jews themselves. He was wanting to relieve God's pain. If Paul had been able, he would have been willing to be accursed so that God could be spared further suffering. The next verses are from *The Revised Standard Version* of the Bible.

Romans 9:1-5 (The Revised Standard Version.)

¹I AM speaking the truth in Christ. I am not lying; my conscience bears me witness in the Holy Spirit,

²That I have great sorrow and increasing anguish in my heart.

³For I could wish that I myself were accursed and cut off from Christ for the sake of my brethren, my kinsmen by race.

⁴They are Israelites, and to them belong the sonship, the glory, the covenants, the giving of the law, the worship, and the promises;

⁵To them belong the patriarchs, and of their race, according to the flesh, is the Christ. God Who is over all be blessed forever. Amen.

Romans 9:4 in *The Revised Standard Version* speaks of the sonship belonging to the Israelites. *The Amplified Bible* says, *"For they are Israelites, and to them belong God's adoption [as a nation]...."*

Throughout the Bible, we are repeatedly made aware that the firstborn son was considered to be exceptional in that his birth order entitled him to special privileges. For example, his birth position automatically made him higher in rank than any of the other male siblings. Furthermore, it was standard procedure that as the firstborn, upon his father's death, he would receive a double portion of the inheritance and take his father's place as head of the household.

God's firstborn son, Israel, is special to God in that the Israelite nation is entitled to certain privileges and is higher in rank than any other nation on the earth. Later in the series, you will be given Scriptural proof of that fact. However, for now, know that the place the firstborn holds in his father's heart goes even beyond rank and privileges. The following Scriptures will give you a good idea of what I mean. So let us begin with the firstborn of Jacob.

Genesis 49:3 (The Amplified Bible.)

³Reuben, you are my firstborn, my might, the beginning (the firstfruits) of my manly strength and vigor; [your birthright gave you] the preeminence in dignity and the preeminence in power.

The Modern Language Bible says, *"...you are my firstborn, my strength and the first issue of my vitality; excellent in dignity, prominent in prowess."*

The Living Bible reads, *"...you are my oldest son, the child of my vigorous youth. You are the head of the list in rank and in honor."*

The Egyptians also laid great value on their firstborn. The contents of the next Scriptures make that fact very clear. So let us get right to the heart of the matter by reading those verses.

Psalm 78:51 (The Amplified Bible.)

51 He smote all the firstborn in Egypt, the chief of their strength in the tents [of the land of the sons] of Ham.

The Modern Language Bible says, *"...He smote all the firstborn in Egypt, the prime of their strength in the tents of Ham."*

The Living Bible simply says, *"...he killed the eldest son in each Egyptian family—he who was the beginning of its strength and joy."*

Oh, my friend, consider the pain and indignities that God had endured during the four hundred years that His firstborn son, Israel, had been mistreated in Egypt. The Egyptians afflicted, oppressed, enslaved and murdered the beginning and prime of His strength and joy, the head of His list in rank and honor. Yes, the Egyptians had abused and held in cruel captivity and even murdered God's beautiful, precious firstborn son.

With the understanding you now possess, let us read again the previous verses in Exodus that pertain to God's firstborn son, Israel.

Exodus 4:22-23 (The Amplified Bible.)

22 And you shall say to Pharaoh, Thus says the Lord, Israel is My son, even My firstborn.

23 And I say to you, Let My son go, that he may serve Me; and if you refuse to let him go, behold, I will slay your son, your firstborn.

Now do you see more clearly why God said in Genesis 15:14 that He would bring judgment upon the nation of Egypt? As I said earlier, the Egyptians had afflicted, oppressed, enslaved and murdered God's firstborn son, Israel. Thus, God meted out just punishment on those wicked people. God killed all their firstborn. They were personally made to feel a measure of the pain, agony, grief and humiliation that their sinful actions had inflicted upon God for the previous four hundred years.

Also, remember what I shared with you earlier. The reason God judged the gods of Egypt was because it was in their name, including their god, Pharaoh (Horus), that the Egyptians had committed their horrendous crimes against God and His chosen covenant people. Think about it. Egypt's god, Pharaoh (Horus), gave the orders to afflict, oppress, enslave and murder God's firstborn son, Israel. Thus, out of Pharaoh's own mouth came the sentence that God would eventually carry out on all the firstborn of Egypt.

Incidentally, if you are wondering why the reigning Pharaoh was punished for his own crimes and the crimes of preceding Pharaohs, it was because all reigning Pharaohs past and present were supposed to be the incarnation of the god Horus (that is, the embodiment of the god Horus in the human form). Hence, it was the same deity, Horus, who was being punished. Plus, in continuing to worship the god Horus, the Egyptians were themselves condoning everything that had been and was being done in his name.

The information in the previous paragraph also provides the answer that I promised regarding why the Pharaoh, who reigned during the outpouring of the ten plagues, was held responsible for breaking an agreement that an earlier Hyksos Pharaoh had made to Joseph and the Israelite people. I repeat, it was because all reigning Pharaohs past and present were supposed to be the incarnation of the god Horus (that is, the imbodiment of the god Horus in human form). Hence, it was the same deity who had made and broken his agreement with Joseph.

Earlier in this chapter, I also promised that I would produce Scriptural proof regarding the Lord judging the gods of Egypt. So now I want to share with you the actual Scripture in which God makes it clear that He did indeed bring judgment upon Egypt's gods as well as the Egyptian people, their animals and their land. I saved that Scripture until now since it also mentions the tenth plague, and I wanted to deal with the plagues consecutively. So let us read that verse without further delay.

Exodus 12:12 (The Amplified Bible.)

*12For I will pass through the land of Egypt this night and will smite all the firstborn in the land of Egypt, both man and beast; **and against all the gods of Egypt I will execute judgment [proving their helplessness]. I am the Lord.***

You now know why God slew all the firstborn of Egypt. It was because Pharaoh and his people had abused and slain God's firstborn son, Israel. However, you might still be wondering why God also slew the firstborn beasts. *Smith's Bible Dictionary* sheds some light on that issue. Smith informs us that by killing all the firstborn of the beasts, God showed the Egyptians that even their sacred temple animals were not exempt from the power and judgment of the true God. Imagine what an impact it must have had on the Egyptians to see the animals that they considered to be deities drop dead in the very temples in which they were worshipped, along with the firstborn of Egypt's idolatrous priests.

PLAGUES CEASE - PUNISHMENT CONTINUES

The ten plagues had finally come to an end. However, God's punishment did not stop at that point. God still had to tie up a few loose ends. For instance, He had to make sure that before they left Egypt, the Israelites received adequate financial compensation for every minute of slave labor that the Egyptians had brutally extracted from them. Consequently, God made the Egyptians, upon request, give to the Israelites all their personal valuables. See this truth in the next verses.

Exodus 12:35-36 (The Amplified Bible.)

35The Israelites did according to the word of Moses; and they [urgently] asked of the Egyptians jewels of silver and of gold, and clothing.

36The Lord gave the people favor in the sight of the Egyptians, so that they gave them what they asked. And they stripped the Egyptians [of those things].

A spiritual and literal battle had taken place in Egypt between the Lord and the gods of the Egyptians and their followers. The Lord had of course won that battle. Thus, the victor took the spoils. Following God's instructions to Moses, the people stripped the Egyptians of their wealth. Hence, Israel was financially reimbursed for her many years of slavery while the land of her defeated foe was spoiled in more ways than one.

Earlier, I commented on the fact that though the ten plagues had ended, Egypt's punishment had not ended. After all, none of the plagues had correlated with the drowning of God's covenant babies. Pharaoh (the false god Horus) was the one who had given the order to drown all God's covenant male babies. Thus, Pharaoh (the false God Horus) would watch helplessly while the true God personally drowned the strongest males of Egypt.

Drowning the strongest males of Egypt was certainly a more difficult task than drowning tiny helpless babies. However, by hardening Pharaoh's heart, God was able to persuade Pharaoh to command all his fighting men to pursue the Israelites into the sea. You know what took place after that. So rather than quoting all of Exodus chapter fourteen, I will instead pick out relevant sections of that chapter, beginning with the following verses.

Exodus 14:5-28 (The Amplified Bible.)

*5It was told the king of Egypt that the people had fled; **and the heart of Pharaoh and of his servants was changed toward the people,** and they said, What is this we have done? We have let Israel go from serving us!*

6And he made ready his chariots and took his army,

7And took 600 chosen chariots and all the other chariots of Egypt, with officers over all of them.

*8**The Lord made hard and strong the heart of Pharaoh king of Egypt, and he pursued the Israelites, for [they] left proudly and defiantly.***

9The Egyptians pursued them, all the horses and chariots of Pharaoh and his horsemen and his army, and overtook them encamped at the [Red] Sea by Pihahiroth, in front of Baal-zephon.

To show you without doubt that an actual battle took place, and that God lured Pharaoh's army into the sea by hardening their hearts, we will read verses fourteen through seventeen. Pay special attention to the first part of verse fourteen, and the first part of verse seventeen.

*14**The Lord will fight for you,** and you shall hold your peace and remain at rest.*

15The Lord said to Moses, Why do you cry to Me? Tell the people of Israel to go forward!

16Lift up your rod and stretch out your hand over the sea and divide it, and the Israelites shall go on dry ground through the midst of the sea.

*17**And I, behold, I will harden (make stubborn and strong) the hearts of the Egyptians, and they shall go [into the sea] after them;** and I will gain honor over Pharaoh and all his host, his chariots, and horsemen.*

Now let us check out the final battle between the one true God, the God of Israel, and Pharaoh (the god Horus) and his army.

> *21 Then Moses stretched out his hand over the sea, and the Lord caused the sea to go back by a strong east wind all that night and made the sea dry land; and the waters were divided.*
>
> *22 And the Israelites went into the midst of the sea on dry ground, the waters being a wall to them on their right hand and on their left.*
>
> *23 The Egyptians pursued and went in after them into the midst of the sea, even all Pharaoh's horses, his chariots, and his horsemen.*

Look closely at the next two verses, for in them you are shown just how personally involved the Lord was in the battle that took place that day. We are told that the Lord looked down through the pillar of fire and cloud and saw all the host of Pharaoh pursuing the Israelites in the midst of the Red Sea. **The Lord then came down to where they were and actually took the wheels off the Egyptian chariots**. Can you picture that scene? God Almighty personally removing those chariot wheels. Another amazing fact is that the Egyptians were aware that the Lord was the One who was fighting against them. They knew that it was the true God who had bound their chariot wheels.

Oh, my friend, God came to demand reprisal for the drowning of His covenant male babies. Just as the Egyptians had deliberately drowned the males of Israel, so God deliberately drowned their males. Plus, the one who had given that order, Pharaoh (the god Horus), stood helplessly watching from the shore while the Lord fought against his army. Yes, the Lord caused the waters to return to their normal flow, and the waves met the Egyptians as they tried to escape. Thus, as the Egyptians had cast God's covenant male babies into the river Nile, so *"...the Lord overthrew the Egyptians and shook them off in the midst of the sea."* Not one man of the Egyptian army survived. All were drowned.

> *24 And in the morning watch the Lord through the pillar of fire and cloud looked down on the host of the Egyptians and discomfited [them],*
>
> *25 And bound (clogged, took off) their chariot wheels, making them drive heavily; and the Egyptians said, Let us flee from the face of Israel, for the Lord fights for them against the Egyptians!*

²⁶Then the Lord said to Moses, Stretch out your hand over the sea, that the waters may come again upon the Egyptians, upon their chariots and horsemen.

²⁷So Moses stretched forth his hand over the sea, and the sea returned to its strength and normal flow when the morning appeared; and the Egyptians fled into it [being met by it]; and the Lord overthrew the Egyptians and shook them off into the midst of the sea.

²⁸The waters returned and covered the chariots, the horsemen, and all the host of Pharaoh that pursued them; not even one of them remained.

Verse twenty-eight says, *"...not even one of them remained."* Can you imagine how Pharaoh (Horus) must have felt as he stood by helplessly watching the Lord drown all those Egyptian males? Surely, at that moment he must have finally understood and felt a measure of the pain that God and His chosen people had felt when he had drowned their male infants.

Now you might still ask, "But, why did the Lord harden Pharaoh's heart so that he would not let the Israelites go and then punish him for not letting them go?" Oh, my friend, Pharaoh not letting God's people go was not the real issue in this matter. Neither was Pharaoh really punished for not letting them go. **Pharaoh, the people of Egypt and Egypt's gods were punished for the four hundred years of crimes that they had committed against God and His people.**

Hardening Pharaoh's heart was simply a strategic maneuver. It was a measure God took to ensure that all the Egyptians and their gods received full punishment for their crimes. And when one considers all the years during which the Egyptians afflicted, oppressed, enslaved and even murdered God's covenant people, one has to applaud the just measures that God took.

Since we have just touched on God hardening Pharaoh's heart, this is a good place to insert even more Biblical information. But first, I want to make something very clear. As we identify the benefits to God and mankind that came out of Egypt's punishment, we must remember that the Egyptians were not punished to provide those benefits. On the contrary, as I have repeatedly stated, they were punished for their four hundred years of wickedness against God and God's covenant people. Any benefits that were derived came about because God in His wisdom brought good out of a bad situation. As God addresses Pharaoh in the following verses, we catch a glimpse of one of the blessings God Himself acquired by hardening Pharaoh's heart and by allowing Pharaoh and his people to live.

Exodus 9:15-16 (The Amplified Bible.)

15For by now I could have put forth My hand and have struck you and your people with pestilence, and you would have been cut off from the earth.

16But for this very purpose have I let you live, that I might show you My power, and that My name may be declared throughout all the earth.

If God's purpose for mankind was to ever be completely accomplished in all the earth, then God first had to make His name known and feared among men. Therefore, Egypt's punishment gave God a perfect opportunity to declare His name and to demonstrate His almighty power.

We know that God was already committed to carrying out His Word in Genesis 12:3, *"...I will bless those who bless you [who confer prosperity or happiness upon you] and curse him who curses or uses insolent language toward you...."* God was also committed to carrying out His prediction in Genesis 15:14, *"...I will bring judgment upon that nation whom they will serve...."* Therefore, the sensible and logical course for God to follow was to carry out Egypt's punishment while at the same time promoting His name. That way many people would benefit from Egypt's chastisement. The power and awesome deeds of the God of Israel who cursed Egypt and the knowledge of Egypt's punishment would be quickly broadcast throughout all the world. Consequently, God's name would be made known in all the nations of the earth.

I said many people would benefit from Egypt's chastisement because the method God chose to declare His name and power was not advantageous to God alone. Rather, God's method brought benefit to all nations or individuals who were and are wise enough to heed God's published warning and recognize His power.

Let me explain: nations or individuals who are smart enough to remember and realize the terrible power that, through His curse, God demonstrated in Egypt will be far less likely to mistreat God's covenant people. Wise men will remember that if they curse or use insolent language toward God's covenant people (the Jews), then as He did with the Egyptians, God will curse them. If God is to keep His word, He has no other choice than to curse those who curse His chosen covenant people.

The knowledge that God provided us with concerning Egypt's punishment and His own awesome power and judgment is knowledge which protects us from the effects of such a terrible curse and brings blessing to our lives. God made His name and power known throughout the earth so that the wise can personally avoid the consequences of His curse. Praise be to the God of Israel who hardened Pharaoh's heart and allowed him and a number of his people to survive the plagues so that His name would be known, and we could be warned and thus escape the same fate that befell the Egyptians. What a merciful, kind and generous God is the God of Israel. He always looks at the overall circumstances and brings good out of every bad situation for everyone involved.

If you look carefully at one of the verses that we studied earlier in this chapter, you can once more actually see written on the pages of God's Word what I have been trying to explain. You can see that the signs and wonders that God performed were to punish Egypt for her abusive and harsh treatment of His people, and that out of that punishment, God got a name for Himself. Let us read again the verse I just mentioned.

Nehemiah 9:10 (The Amplified Bible.)

10You performed signs and wonders against Pharaoh and all his servants and all the people of his land, for You knew that they dealt insolently against the Israelites. And You got for Yourself a name, as it is today.

The Living Bible reads, "You displayed great miracles against Pharaoh and his people, for you knew how brutally the Egyptians were treating them; you have a glorious reputation because of those never-to-be-forgotten deeds."

The Modern Language translation reads, "...so Thou didst cause respect for Thy name, as it is this day."

Oh, my friend, along with the answers to many other queries, you now have the answer to the question, "Were The Egyptians Ever Punished For Their Heinous Crimes Against God And The Jewish People?" Yes, you now know that the Egyptians were severely chastised by God through the ten plagues and other mighty wonders. The consequences Egypt suffered as a result of cursing God's chosen people were phenomenal. Think about it.

(1) **Their gods and sacred objects were shown to be fakes.**

(2) **Their aquatic life was severely depleted.**

(3) **Almost all their livestock was dead.**

(4) **All Egypt's crops, vegetation and fruit trees were destroyed. The land was completely devastated.**

(5) **Every household was mourning the death of at least one loved one.**

(6) **They were stripped of all their treasures.**

(7) **Their population was profoundly diminished.**

Remember, the Israelites were greater in number than the Egyptians. So when the Israelites left, so did Egypt's vast population. Plus, Egypt's firstborn died, Pharaoh's army was drowned at the Red Sea and many of Egypt's inhabitants accompanied the Israelites when they exited Egypt. Without a doubt, Egypt was a ruined nation. <u>Yes, I am sure you will agree with me that the Egyptians were punished for their heinous crimes against God and His chosen people.</u>

You also learned how you yourself can keep from experiencing God's curse. Do not curse or use insolent language toward God's chosen covenant people, and the curse that God poured upon the Egyptians will not be poured upon you.

On the other side of the coin, there are the blessings that are promised to those who bless God's chosen people. Oh, Christian, seek to do God's will. For if you do God's will, you will seek to be blessed rather than cursed.

Chapter 5

WAS THE DELIVERER, MOSES, A FOLLOWER OF GOD BEFORE HE FLED FROM EGYPT?

To this point in the series, many Biblical mysteries that had remained hidden for generations have been unfolded. Yet, the uncovering of those mysteries is but a flicker of light when compared with the brightness of the overall inspired revelation contained in this book. For example, in this chapter you will not only gain the answer to the question, "Was The Deliverer, Moses, A Follower Of God Before He Fled From Egypt?" but you will also see the first recorded instance showing Moses' awareness that he was the long awaited deliverer.

In chapter four, I found it necessary to deviate from the Biblical chronological order of events. However, I assured you that it would be a temporary departure. Also, in that chapter, I briefly touched on the birth of Moses. I stated that out of what seemed to be a hopeless and helpless situation, God raised up a leader who would help Him accomplish His promise to Abraham and deliver His people from Egypt.

To get us back on track and to lay the groundwork for the answer to the previous question, we will cover in more detail the birth, childhood and adulthood of Moses. If studied carefully, the following verses of Scripture provide a great deal of insight into the first forty years of the life of Moses.

Exodus 2:1-15 (The Amplified Bible.)

1NOW [Amraam] a man of the house of Levi [the priestly tribe] went and took as his wife [Jochebed] a daughter of Levi.

2And the woman became pregnant and bore a son; and when she saw that he was [exceedingly] beautiful, she hid him three months.

3And when she could no longer hide him, she took for him an ark or basket made of bulrushes or papyrus [making it watertight by] daubing it with bitumen and pitch. Then she put the child in it and laid it among the rushes by the brink of the river [Nile].

4And his sister [Miriam] stood some distance away to learn what would be done to him.

5Now the daughter of Pharoah came down to bathe at the river, and her maidens walked along the bank; she saw the ark among the rushes and sent her maid to fetch it.

*6When she opened it, she saw the child; and behold, the baby cried. And she took pity on him and said, **This is one of the Hebrews' children!***

It is important to note that in verse six, Pharoah's daughter recognized that the child in the basket was of Hebrew descent. She knew the child had been put upon the waters of the Nile in an attempt to save its life from her own father's edict. The next verses shed a great deal of light on the first years of Moses life. So, fix your attention on them.

7Then his sister said to Pharoah's daughter, Shall I go and call a nurse of the Hebrew women to nurse the child for you?

8Pharoah's daughter said to her, Go. And the girl went and called the child's mother.

*9Then Pharoah's daughter said to her, **Take this child away and nurse it for me, and I will give you your wages.** So the woman took the child and nursed it.*

*10**And the child grew, and she brought him to Pharoah's daughter and he became her son.** And she called him Moses, for she said, Because I drew him out of the water.*

In verse nine, the princess instructed the mother of Moses to *"**take this child away** and nurse it for me."* She did not invite the mother of Moses to come into the palace and look after the babe there. No! She clearly commanded Jochebed to take the child away. Pharoah's daughter even paid Jochebed to feed and nurture her own child.

Verse ten says, *"**And the child grew, and she brought him to Pharoah's daughter and he became her son.**"* Thus, we see that for the first stage of his life, God in his mercy and for His own purpose allowed baby Moses to remain in the loving care of his own mother. Verse ten also makes it clear that the princess did not adopt Moses as her son until after his own mother brought him back to her.

During the years that Jochebed still had possession of her son, she was in a perfect position to teach him spiritual values such as love for and devotion to God, love and compassion for His people, knowledge of the Abrahamic covenant and God's assurances to Abraham. She was also in a position to instill in Moses the fact that as a future prince of Egypt, he would soon be in a position to help his enslaved brethren.

To provide you with further documented evidence for all that I have just said, I have chosen to share with you a quote from *Smith's Bible Dictionary* under the heading "Moses."

> The sister was at hand to recommend a Hebrew nurse, the child's own mother. Here was the first part of Moses training,—**a training at home in the true religion**, in faith in God, in the promises to his nation, in the life of a saint,—**a training which he never forgot,** even amid the splendors and gilded sin of Pharoah's court.

The inspired teachings, teaching about God and God's covenant with Abraham, that Moses received from his parents while living at home flourished in his heart. Those truths became the foundation that God used to frame and build Moses' godly character. Thus, the impact that the training in the true religion had upon his adult life can be seen in the tremendous faith that Moses exhibited. For Moses certainly did not acquire such faith in the true God and His covenant promises from Egypt's heathen priests or from the extensive secular education that he had received in Egypt.

See for yourself, in the following New Testament verses, the quality of the faith that the parents of Moses demonstrated, faith which they in turn instilled in their son. You will then understand why *Smith's Bible Dictionary* boldly stated the previous information.

Hebrews 11:23-25 (The Amplified Bible.)

23[Prompted] by faith Moses, after his birth, was kept concealed for three months by his parents, because they saw how comely the child was; and they were not overawed and terrified by the king's decree.

24[Aroused] by faith Moses, when he had grown to maturity and become great, refused to be called the son of Pharoah's daughter,

25Because he preferred to share the oppression [suffer the hardships] and bear the shame of the people of God rather than to have the fleeting enjoyment of a sinful life.

In the previous verses, Hebrews 11:24-25, you see the first evidence that Moses was a staunch follower of God before his flight from Egypt. You are told in those verses that his faith in the God of Abraham, Isaac and Jacob was so strong and his character so pure, he chose to be known as the son of Israelite slaves rather than be venerated as a member of Egypt's heathen royal family. He preferred to share the suffering, hardships and shame of the people of God rather than enjoy the sinful life offered in Pharoah's court. **Yes, I would say that Hebrews 11:24-25 is adequate proof in itself that Moses was a true follower of God before he fled from Egypt.**

As the Bible scholar, Smith, informs you, Moses never forgot the religious training that he had received while living at home with his Hebrew parents and siblings. However, the writer of The Book of Acts goes a step further. He teaches you that once Jochebed turned Moses over to Pharoah's daughter, the next phase of his training began. In the following New Testament verses, the writer makes it clear that Moses was educated in all the wisdom and culture of the Egyptians.

Acts 7:21-22 (The Amplified Bible.)

21Then when he was exposed [to perish], the daughter of Pharoah rescued him and took him and reared him as her own son.

22So Moses was educated in all the wisdom and culture of the Egyptians, and he was mighty (powerful) in his speech and deeds.

Notice, the writer informs us in verse twenty-two that **Moses was mighty in word and deed.** This does not sound like a man who had a speech impediment as we have been led to believe by many Bible scholars and preachers. Keep this truth in mind, for I will be mentioning it again in a later chapter.

After these brief inferences to his religious and secular education, the Scriptures remain silent for many years regarding the life of Moses. It was not until Moses was forty years old that he is again mentioned. **Yet, the next recorded phase of his life confirms the fact that, contrary to popular belief, Moses was a faithful follower of God and knew he was the deliverer, even before he fled for his life from the**

face of Pharoah. Let us begin to study the first of two Scripture texts which together reveal that truth.

Exodus 2:11-15 (The Amplified Bible.)

11One day, after Moses was grown, it happened that he went out to his brethren and looked at their burdens; and he saw an Egyptian beating a Hebrew, one of [Moses'] brethren.

12He looked this way and that way, and when he saw no one, he killed the Egyptian and hid him in the sand.

13He went out the second day and saw two Hebrew men quarreling and fighting; and he said to the unjust aggressor, Why are you striking your comrade?

14And the man said, Who made you a prince and a judge over us? Do you intend to kill me as you killed the Egyptian? Then Moses was afraid and thought, Surely this thing is known.

15When Pharoah heard of it, he sought to slay Moses. But Moses fled from Pharoah's presence and took refuge in the land of Midian, where he sat down by a well.

To gain more insight into this matter, we must again look to The Book of Acts. There you will see that Moses was indeed keenly aware that he was the God-ordained deliverer of his people before he fled from Pharoah's presence. We will read the following verses from the *Holy Bible*, since in this case, the *King James* translators use wording that is right to the point and easily understood.

Acts 7:22-29 (King James Version.)

22And Moses was learned in all the wisdom of the Egyptians, and was mighty in words and in deeds.

23And when he was full forty years old, it came into his heart to visit his brethren the children of Israel.

24And seeing one of them suffer wrong, he defended him, and avenged him that was oppressed, and smote the Egyptian:

25For he supposed his brethren would have understood how that God by his hand would deliver them: but they understood not.

Contrary to the popular belief that Moses first learned he was the deliverer during the episode of the burning bush, we see in verse twenty-five that Moses was a follower of God and knew he was the deliverer even before he fled from Pharoah's death sentence. Verse twenty-five also lets us know that Moses was himself so convinced that he was the deliverer, he automatically assumed that every other Israelite recognized his divine appointment. *"**For he supposed his brethren would have understood how that God by his hand would deliver them....**"*

Keep in mind the previous truths that you have learned as I now carefully piece together for you the information contained in the last two texts, Exodus 2:11-15 and Acts 7:22-29. To aid you, I will insert additional Biblical insight whenever necessary.

God had given certain assurances to Abraham. God had promised him that after a specific period of time He would deliver the Israelites out of the bondage of Egypt and fulfill His covenant by bringing them back to the Promised Land. Since Moses was the vessel God planned to use to accomplish that phase of the Abrahamic covenant, he had to be fully equipped for his future task. Consequently, Moses received his religious training at home with his family and his secular education later while in the care of his adoptive mother, Pharoah's daughter.

Moses could have chosen to remain in the comfort, security and splendor of Pharoah's palace. Instead, he chose to retain his lowly Hebrew heritage and to fulfill the call that the Lord had placed on his life. Thus, when Moses reached the age of forty, he decided to thoroughly investigate the plight of his people and to assure them that God's deliverance would soon come **at his hand**.

While Moses was surveying the Israelites' situation, he spied an Egyptian brutally beating one of his brethren. Moses foolishly took things into his own hands. He carefully looked around, and when he saw that no one was in sight, he killed that abusive Egyptian. Thus, in the heat of the moment, Moses in ignorance ran ahead of God's schedule and planning. The Biblical fact is, on the one hand, Moses was right on target when it came to realizing his own life's mission. On the other hand, his timing was off and his method was wrong.

As you know, God had foretold that Abraham's descendants would be afflicted and oppressed in Egypt for four hundred years. He also promised that at the end of four hundred years he would bring judgment on the nation of Egypt and afterward cause his people to come out. The problem was that the Israelites had not yet lived in Egypt for four hundred years. Moreover, God had not yet poured out upon the Egyptian nation the foretold judgment after which He promised to deliver His people. Consequently, if Moses had delivered the Israelites from Egypt at that specific time, God's Biblical prophecy would not have come to pass in all its fullness.

Now you might say, "But how can I be sure that the Israelites had not been afflicted and oppressed in Egypt for four hundred years at the time Moses killed the Egyptian?" Well, my friend, a simple computation bears out that fact and proves that my calculation is accurate. So using the following verses, let me share with you how, with God's help, I managed to come up with the correct figure.

Exodus 12:40-41 (The Amplified Bible.)

40Now the time the Israelites dwelt in Egypt was 430 years.

41At the end of the 430 years, even that very day, all the hosts of the Lord went out of Egypt.

Here is a simple mathematical problem that will give you the exact number of years the Israelites had lived in Egypt at the time Moses went to visit his brethren on the particular occasion in question. After fleeing from Egypt, Moses spent forty years in the land of Midian before returning to Egypt. Subtract forty years from four hundred and thirty years to the day that the Israelites dwelt in Egypt and you are left with three hundred and ninety years. Three hundred and ninety years is ten years shy of the prophesied four hundred years. As I said earlier, Moses' timing was off. He was truly the deliverer whom God intended to use to establish His covenant, but he sought to deliver the Israelites ten years too soon.

I also stated that his method was wrong. Moses sought to deliver God's people his way (that is, single-handedly, using brute force), rather than God's way. That fact reveals that though Moses knew he was the deliverer, God had not yet briefed him on the strategy He would use to defeat the Egyptians nor the miraculous role that Moses would play in His overall rescue plan.

Another important point to remember is that when Moses visited his Israelite brethren, he fully expected them to recognize him as the one whom God had raised up to deliver them from bondage. Acts 7:25 in the *King James* translation clearly states, *"For he supposed his brethren would have understood how that God by his hand would deliver them: but they understood not."*

Imagine the shock, disappointment and bewilderment Moses must have experienced upon realizing that the Israelites did not comprehend that he was the one through whom God would fulfill His promise to Abraham and deliver them from the bondage of Egypt. Moses had left Pharoah's palace, turning his back on a life of ease, in order to obey God's call upon his life (that is, in order to help God fulfill His promise to Abraham and rescue his brethren from harsh slavery). Yet, instead of his brethren joyfully accepting him, appreciating his sacrifices and embracing his holy cause, they totally distrusted and rejected him. The following verses taken from the *King James* translation of the Bible provide a glimpse of the utter rejection Moses experienced.

Acts 7:25-29 (King James Version.)

*25For he supposed his brethren would have understood how that God by his hand would deliver them: **but they understood not**.*

I included verse twenty-five because I wanted to make you aware that the Israelites had already rejected Moses as the deliverer before the next recorded incident took place. That fact is extremely important. It is important because it sheds light on the behavior of the man that Moses confronted in the next verses. The response of the abusive Israelite was more than the result of anger over a personal dispute. Rather, the man simply used that already explosive situation to verbally express his mistrust of Moses and his absolute rejection of him as the deliverer.

26And the next day he shewed himself unto them as they strove, and would have set them at one again, saying, Sirs, ye are brethren; why do ye wrong one to another?

*27But he that did his neighbour wrong **thrust him away, saying, Who made thee a ruler and a judge over us?***

*28**Wilt thou kill me, as thou diddest the Egyptian yesterday?***

29Then fled Moses at this saying, and was a stranger in the land of Midian, where he begat two sons.

The fact that the man *"thrust him away"* showed the Israelites' absolute rejection of Moses. The man's words, *"who made thee a ruler and a judge over us?"* showed the Israelites' rejection of Moses as the God-ordained spiritual leader and deliverer of the Israelites. And finally, the man's words, *"wilt thou kill me, as thou diddest the Egyptian yesterday?"* showed the Israelites' mistrust of Moses.

As a follower of God with an awareness that He was the deliverer, Moses had expected the Israelites to open to him their hearts and their arms. But instead, they thrust him from them in total rejection. That one man, in his anger, simply verbalized the feelings of his Israelite brethren as a whole. To them, Moses was just another Egyptian, and they did not like him, believe him or trust him.

One cannot help but feel compassion for Moses. He ended up fleeing from Egypt like an escaped criminal. But I am sure the loss of his princely position, the death sentence that Pharoah had pronounced upon him and even the exile that lay ahead of him did not compare with the inner pain and hurt that he was at that moment experiencing as a result of the ingratitude, hatred and total rejection of his kinsman.

Weary and brokenhearted, Moses ended up in the land of Midian. Nevertheless, at the appropriate time, Moses would accomplish God's plan for his life. He would eventually do what God had raised him up to do. Moses would help God fulfill His covenant with Abraham, Isaac and Jacob. Yes, he would be the instrument God would use to deliver the children of Israel from the bondage of Egypt.

Now you know the answer to the question, "Was The Deliverer, Moses, A Follower Of God Before He Fled From Egypt?" You have seen that Moses was not only a devoted follower of God before he fled from Egypt but that he was also fully aware that he was the long awaited God-ordained deliverer.

Chapter 6

WHY DID GOD DELIVER THE JEWS FROM EGYPT? WHAT WAS THE DELIVERER, MOSES, REALLY LIKE?

During the series, I have carefully plotted out the course. Therefore, you probably realize that like everything else concerning God's dealings with the Israelites, the answer to the question, "Why Did God Deliver The Jews From Egypt?" is closely related to God's covenant with Abraham and His assurances to him. So, I am sure that it will come as no surprise to you to learn that even the Hebrews' liberation from Egypt was a direct result of God's promise to Abraham.

In this chapter, you will receive Biblical proof that God came to the Israelites' rescue in order to keep His promise to His friend. The Lord was compelled to deliver them because of His obligation to Abraham. For as you now know, He could not break covenant. To remind you of the seriousness of God's pledge to Abraham, I will repeat the definition of the word "covenant" taken from *The American Heritage Dictionary, Second College Edition.*

> A binding agreement made by two or more persons or parties: compact....A formal sealed agreement or contract. To promise by a covenant....To enter into a covenant; contract....

It is a known Biblical fact that the Israelites were in bondage in Egypt for generations. Yet, we see in the following verses that, at a particular time in history, God suddenly became actively concerned about their plight.

Exodus 2:23 (The Amplified Bible.)

*23However, after a long time [nearly forty years] the king of Egypt died; and the Israelites were sighing and groaning because of the bondage. They kept crying, **and their cry because of slavery ascended to God**.*

Verse twenty-three clearly states that the Israelites' cry ascended to God because of slavery. But why after four hundred years of cruel treatment by the Egyptians did the Israelites' prayers suddenly have such power with God? Why had God not heard their cries for help prior to that time? We will find our answers in one of the texts that we studied earlier in the series. The text I am referring to is Genesis 15:13, 14, 16. **There God told Abraham that his descendants would be afflicted and oppressed in Egypt for four hundred years.**

Genesis 15:13 (The Amplified Bible.)

[13]And [God] said to Abram, Know positively that your descendants will be strangers dwelling as temporary residents in a land that is not theirs [Egypt], and they will be slaves there and will be afflicted and oppressed for 400 years.

Once again, God had to fulfill His word to Abraham. However, in order for God to keep His word to Abraham, certain things had to take place first.

(1) These people must be Abraham's descendants through the line of Isaac and Jacob.

(2) They must be slaves in Egypt.

(3) They must be afflicted and oppressed in Egypt for four hundred years.

In verse fourteen, God goes on to assure Abraham that when those four hundred years of oppression were accomplished, He would punish the nation of Egypt for their mistreatment of His people, deliver the Israelites from bondage and bring them out of Egypt with great wealth.

[14]But I will bring judgment on that nation whom they will serve, and afterward they will come out with great possessions.

In the first sentence of the following verse, verse sixteen, God goes on to promise Abraham that at a certain point in time, the Israelites would return to Canaan, the Promised Land.

[16]And in the fourth generation they [your descendants] shall come back here [to Canaan] again....

In one of the texts that you read earlier, Exodus 2:23, the end of the previously predicted four hundred years of affliction and oppression was close at hand. The stage was set. Everything was ready. God's word to this point had been fulfilled to the letter. Hence, since their request would now help Him fulfill His purpose and keep His promise to

Abraham, God was finally ready to hear and answer His people's cries for assistance. **Thus, we see that the reason why the Israelites' prayers suddenly had power with God was simply because the timing was right to fulfill God's covenant with Abraham.** On that note, let us again consider the contents of Exodus 2:23, then afterwards, we will continue reading through verse twenty-five.

Exodus 2:23-25 (The Amplified Bible.)

*23However, after a long time [nearly forty years] the king of Egypt died; and the Israelites were sighing and groaning because of the bondage. They kept crying, **and their cry because of slavery ascended to God**.*

In the next verse, verse twenty-four, you will clearly see why *"their cry because of slavery ascended to God"* and why God heard and delivered them. So pay careful attention to every word.

*24And God heard their sighing and groaning **and [earnestly] remembered His covenant with Abraham, with Isaac and with Jacob.***

What does verse twenty-four say that God remembered? **It says God *"remembered His covenant."*** Thus, we clearly see that the reason why God heard the Israelites' cries for assistance at that particular time in history and took action to deliver them was because He had made certain promises and assurances to Abraham, Isaac and Jacob. Those promises not only had to be kept but they had to be carried out exactly as God had foretold. Consequently, timing was crucial.

Since the foretold four hundred years of affliction and oppression were almost accomplished, God had to get these people who were now His people out of Egypt and back to the land that He had told Abraham, Isaac and Jacob they would possess forever. For, at this time, they were certainly not there, were they? Thus, God became concerned and made haste to keep His promise. He became concerned because, as you now know, He had to work within the time frame that He Himself had previously laid out in His own word.

25God saw the Israelites and took knowledge of them and concerned Himself about them [knowing all, understanding, remembering all].

Now you know why the cries of the Israelite slaves ascended to God. You also know why God heard their cries and became concerned over their pathetic plight at that particular time in history. *"Remembering all,"* God set out to ensure that His promise to Abraham was kept and that His plans for their deliverance adhered to His previously foretold time schedule.

The Israelites' prayers were heard, and they were delivered but not because they were better or more superior than any other people of that period. How could the Israelites have been better or more superior than others when they were mere slaves. No! Rather, their deliverance rested solely upon God's promises to Abraham, Isaac and Jacob.

God had made many promises to their forefathers. For example, in Genesis 17:7, God promised Abraham that He would be the God of his posterity after him. Plus, in the verses we read earlier, God promised that after four hundred years of oppression and affliction, He would deliver the Israelites from Egypt and bring them to the Promised Land. **So, because of His covenant with Abraham, God was committed to get these people, people who cried to Him for help, out of bondage and back to the land of Canaan. Furthermore, as I stated previously, He had to accomplish that task within the time frame that He Himself had previously laid out in His own word.**

Immediately, God's plan for rescuing His people from the bondage of Egypt began to take shape. The first item on God's deliverance list was to make contact with the chosen deliverer himself, Moses.

It is at this point that the answer to the second question, "What Was The Deliverer, Moses, Really Like?" begins to come into focus. The character of the deliverer, Moses, is so intertwined with the actual deliverance of God's people that I chose to cover both topics in the same chapter. By doing so, I hope to provide you with a much clearer answer to both questions.

Let us now get back on the subject of God's contact with Moses. We can see with hindsight through the following Scripture that God would accomplish His plan for the deliverance of His people using the very man whom they had already rejected as their ruler and deliverer.

Acts 7:35 (The Amplified Bible.)

[35]It was this very Moses whom they had denied (disowned and rejected), saying, Who made you our ruler (referee) and judge? whom God sent to be a ruler and deliverer and redeemer, by and with the [protecting and helping] hand of the Angel that appeared to him in the bramblebush.

For God to help Moses overcome the damage to his self-esteem that the Israelites' previous distrust and rejection had inflicted upon him was no small task. It is not uncommon for rejection to severely affect a person's attitude and outlook as it did in the case of Moses. You will soon see Scriptural evidence that the rejection that Moses suffered, rejection which we studied about in the previous chapter, so emotionally crippled him that he temporarily set aside his God-given call.

The rejection Moses experienced in Egypt was also partly responsible for him remaining in seclusion in the wilderness for forty years. I say partly responsible because we also know that he did flee from Pharoah's death sentence. However, the fact is that even as an eighty-year-old man, Moses still had not recovered from the effects of the past rejection that he had experienced before leaving Egypt. After all, as you saw in Acts 7:35, the Israelites had completely disowned him. Although Moses still loved God, the Scriptures clearly reveal that his experience with total rejection had taken a devastating toll on his life. Moses had changed from an extremely zealous, outgoing deliverer who, as you learned earlier, was ready to deliver his brethren single-handedly to a quiet, withdrawn shepherd who dreaded the very thought of once again facing his Israelite brethren.

God knew that before Moses would be in any kind of shape to help Him accomplish His future purpose, He had to help Moses get back on his emotional feet. He knew that Moses needed the type of special care and attention that only God in His wisdom could provide. Thus, since Moses was tormented by what he perceived as his own past failures as well as his present inadequacies, God set out to gain Moses' trust and to instill in him the confidence he would need to complete his future mission. God did that by first revealing Himself to Moses in a spectacular display of power. Obviously, God hoped that Moses would realize that he could do all the future things that were required of him through the all powerful Lord who strengthened him—thus, the miraculous episode of the burning bush.

Exodus 3:1-18 (The Amplified Bible.)

1 NOW MOSES kept the flock of Jethro his father-in-law, the priest of Midian; and he led the flock to the back or west side of the wilderness and came to Horeb or Sinai, the mountain of God.

2 The Angel of the Lord appeared to him in a flame of fire out of the midst of a bush; and he looked, and behold, the bush burned with fire, yet was not consumed.

3 And Moses said, I will now turn aside and see this great sight, why the bush is not burned.

4And when the Lord saw that he turned aside to see, God called to him out of the midst of the bush and said, Moses, Moses! And he said, Here am I.

After Moses had obeyed God's instruction and removed his shoes, the Lord identified Himself as the God of his forefathers. God then proceeded to tell Moses how He had heard the cries of the Israelites and had personally come down to deliver them out of the hand of the Egyptians and bring them back to Canaan as He had promised He would.

5God said, Do not come near; put your shoes off your feet, for the place on which you stand is holy ground.

6Also He said, I am the God of your father, the God of Abraham, the God of Isaac, and the God of Jacob. And Moses hid his face, for he was afraid to look at God.

7And the Lord said, I have surely seen the affliction of My people who are in Egypt, and have heard their cry because of their task-masters and oppressors; for I know their sorrows and sufferings and trials.

8And I have come down to deliver them out of the hand and power of the Egyptians and to bring them up out of that land to a land good and large, a land flowing with milk and honey [a land of plenty]—to the place of the Canaanite, the Hittite, the Amorite, the Perizzite, the Hivite, and the Jebusite.

At first glance, one might not notice the marvelous insight contained in the previous verses. One might fail to recognize that God's words and the method He used to present them reveal a glimpse of His great patience, compassion and wisdom.

Let me explain: Forty years prior to the episode of the burning bush, God had witnessed the Israelites' refusal to accept Moses as their ruler and their deliverer. He knew that Moses was suffering from a severe case of rejection and low self-esteem which at that moment rendered him emotionally impotent. Therefore, God was aware that the very last thing Moses needed was to feel that the success or failure of the mission, plus the acceptance or rejection of the Israelites, depended solely on his performance. Thus, in His mercy, God told Moses, "...*I have come down to deliver them out of the hand and power of the Egyptians and to bring them up out of that land to a land good and large, a land flowing with milk and honey....*"

In His compassion for Moses and His great wisdom the Lord skillfully stated that the full responsibility for the mission rested with Him alone. He was the real deliverer. Moses was simply the chosen instrument through whom God would carry out His miraculous plan. God said, *"I have come down to deliver them out of the hand and power of the Egyptians."*

Only after God had assured Moses that he (Moses) was not accountable for the outcome of the mission did He then gently break the news to Moses that he (Moses) must go back to Egypt. I say God gently broke the news to Moses because of the way God put His plan to him in the following verses. First, He reminded Moses of the suffering of his brethren. Then, He reasoned with him.

> *9Now behold, the cry of the Israelites has come to Me, and I have also seen how the Egyptians oppress them.*
>
> *10Come now therefore, and I will send you to Pharoah, that you may bring forth My people, the Israelites, out of Egypt.*

In the next verses, verses eleven and twelve, we see a classic response of a person suffering from rejection and low self-esteem. Moses responded negatively. To put it bluntly, he told God that He had chosen the wrong man for the job. Moses insisted that he was not capable of accomplishing such a task. But God knew better. God knew that Moses was simply dealing with a bad case of inferiority and insecurity. He knew that Moses had voiced those words while in a state of self-depreciation. So God in His wisdom offered moral support. God promised Moses that He would not leave him alone. God would be with him. They would complete the mission together.

> *11And Moses said to God, **Who am I, that I should go to Pharoah and bring the Israelites out of Egypt?***
>
> *12God said, **I will surely be with you**; and this shall be the sign to you that I have sent you: when you have brought the people out of Egypt, you shall serve God on this mountain [Horeb, or Sinai].*

In verse twelve, the Creator, with His supreme understanding of human behavioral characteristics, not only offered Moses a sign, but the sign He offered was itself a vote of confidence. The sign showed Moses that God was so confident that together they could and would complete the mission that He put His own reputation on the line by predicting the victorious outcome.

Remember, I shared with you earlier that it was no small task for God to help Moses rid himself of the emotional baggage he had carried with him out of Egypt? Well, in a moment, you will see that as soon as God relieved one of Moses' fears another pessimistic or skeptical foe immediately popped up. However, as you have seen and will see, one-by-one, God quickly whipped those doubting foes into submission by offering positive solutions to Moses' problems. See what I mean in the next verses.

> *13And Moses said to God, Behold, when I come to the Israelites and say to them, The God of your father has sent me to you, and they say to me, What is His name?* **_What shall I say to them?_**
>
> *14And God said to Moses, I AM WHO I AM and WHAT I AM, and I WILL BE WHAT I WILL BE; and He said,* **_You shall say this to the Israelites: I AM has sent me to you!_**

Verses fifteen through twenty-two are filled with God's instructions and assurances to Moses. However, in verses sixteen through eighteen, God comforts Moses by advising him on how he should approach the elders of Israel. Also, God informs Moses that **this time the elders would believe him and would obey his voice.**

> *16Go, gather the elders of Israel together [the mature teachers and tribal leaders], and say to them, The Lord God of your fathers, the God of Abraham, of Isaac, and of Jacob, appeared to me, saying, I have surely visited you and seen that which is done to you in Egypt;*
>
> *17And I have declared that I will bring you up out of the affliction of Egypt to the land of the Canaanite, the Hittite, the Amorite, the Perizzite, the Hivite, and the Jebusite, to a land flowing with milk and honey.*
>
> *18And [the elders] shall believe and obey your voice; and you shall go, you and the elders of Israel, to the king of Egypt and you shall say to him, The Lord, the God of the Hebrews, has met with us; and now let us go, we beseech you, three days' journey into the wilderness, that we may sacrifice to the Lord our God.*

Despite God's comfort and assurances, Moses again responded with negativity. He would not let go of his past hurt. He could not yet deal with the thought of subjecting himself to more of the same rejection.

Put yourself in Moses' shoes. Moses had expected the Israelites to accept him and follow him the first time. Yet, when he had tried to help them, they refused to even listen to him. They had neither believed nor obeyed him. They cast him away, totally disowning him. Moses had fled Egypt a lonely, broken man, disowned by his own people and disowned and hunted by the Egyptians. Thus, in the following verse, it is Moses' past rejection that again speaks out.

Exodus 4:1 (The Amplified Bible.)

*¹AND MOSES answered, **But behold, they will not believe me or listen to and obey my voice; for they will say, The Lord has not appeared to you.***

For the third time, God offered Moses comfort and moral support in word and deed. He again tried to build up Moses' confidence. He sought to stir up Moses' trust and faith in Him (God) by performing more incredible miracles. We see in verses two through nine how God turned Moses' rod into a serpent and then back into a rod. He even made Moses' hand leprous and then healed it. Plus, God assured Moses that when he got to Egypt, He would make water turn to blood on dry land. Yet, all this still did not pull Moses out of his state of self-depreciation. Moses continued to emotionally beat himself to a pulp.

Moses even expressed doubt in his own ability to verbally communicate. Here we have an extremely educated man of his day, a man whom Acts 7:22 informs us was mighty in speech and in deeds, trying to convince God that he is not articulate enough to be his spokesperson.

According to *Strong's Exhaustive Concordance of the Bible*, in the Greek language, this particular word "mighty" in Acts 7:22 means powerful or capable. Yet, in an effort to belittle his own God-given capabilities and oratory skills, Moses actually inferred that he was slow of speech. According to the previous source, by using the term "slow" in the derogative way Moses used it, he was as much as implying that he was stupid regarding verbal communication skills.

Oh, the mercy and compassion that God expressed toward Moses that day when, for the fourth time, God comforted him, extending moral support not only in immediate word but also in promised deed. For, the Lord promised that He would teach Moses what to say and how to say it.

Exodus 4:10-20 (The Amplified Bible.)

*¹⁰And Moses said to the Lord, **O Lord, I am not eloquent or a man of words,** neither before nor since You have spoken to Your servant; **for I am slow of speech** and have a heavy and awkward tongue.*

¹¹And the Lord said to him, Who has made man's mouth? Or who makes the dumb, or the deaf, or the seeing, or the blind? Is it not I, the Lord?

*¹²Now therefore go, **and I will be with your mouth and will teach you what you shall say.***

To this point, the Lord had exhibited extreme patience and longsuffering toward Moses. God needed Moses to help Him keep His promise to Abraham. So, for that reason, God had bent over backwards to help him. God had worked to build up Moses' confidence, shown him great miracles, relieved his unnecessary fears and anxieties and made him specific promises. However, when, after all this extraordinary divine help, Moses still insisted that he was not capable of such a task and that God should get someone else to do the job, God became furious. Yet, who could blame God for feeling angry under such circumstances. Read for yourself what happened in the following verses.

> *13And he said, __Oh, my Lord, I pray You, send by the hand of [some other] whom You will [send].__*
> *14Then the anger of the Lord blazed against Moses ....*

My friend, the character trait that Moses exhibited in this instance was not humility as some would have you believe. No! True humility does not express itself in an unwillingness to trust and obey God. True humility would not infer that the all knowing, all wise God was mistaken in His judgment or that He had made a bad or foolish choice. Mary, the mother of Yeshua, exhibited true humility when in Luke 1:38 she said, *"...Behold, I am the handmaiden of the Lord; __let it be done to me according to what you have said....__"*

No! Moses did not demonstrate true humility in this instance. Rather, he exhibited a lack of faith and trust in God's ability to choose the correct instrument to help Him accomplish His plan. The result of Moses' continued self-depreciation had brought him close to the point of sin.

There is a footnote for Exodus 3:11 in *The Amplified Bible.* In that footnote is evidence that the Bible scholar F. B. Meyer caught a glimpse of what you have been given in great detail in this portion of the series. I think you will find that footnote interesting.

> There was something more than humility here; there was a tone of self-depreciation **which was inconsistent with a true faith in God's selection and appointment**. Surely it is God's business to choose His special instruments; **and when we are persuaded that we are in the line of His purpose, we have no right to question the wisdom of His appointment. To do so is to depreciate His wisdom or to doubt**

**His power and willingness to be come
all that is necessary to complete our
need**. (F.B. Meyer, *Moses, the Servant
of God*).

After Moses' last comment, God no longer pampered him. Rather than additional pampering, God saw that Moses needed a firm hand. Of course, God was right. It is obvious that Moses realized he had gone too far, and he stood corrected. I say this because he did not utter a single word after God became angry with him. From that point on, God did the talking, and the gist of His words were these: Your brother is coming out to meet you. I will tell you what to say, and you will tell him what to say; he will speak for you. Take your rod with you; you will need it to do the miracles and all that I have commanded you to do. God's method worked; Moses did not argue. Instead, he went home, got his family and, accompanied by God, departed for Egypt.

> *14Then the anger of the Lord blazed against Moses; He said, Is there not Aaron your brother, the Levite? I know he can speak well. Also, he is coming out to meet you, and when he sees you, he will be overjoyed.*
>
> *15You must speak to him and put the words in his mouth; and I will be with your mouth and with his mouth and will teach you what you shall do.*
>
> *16He shall speak for you to the people, acting as a mouthpiece for you, and you shall be as God to him.*
>
> *17And you shall take this rod in your hand with which you shall work the signs [that prove I sent you].*
>
> *18And Moses went away and, returning to Jethro his father-in-law, said to him, Let me go back, I pray you, to my relatives in Egypt to see whether they are still alive. And Jethro said to Moses, Go in peace.*
>
> *19The Lord said to Moses in Midian, Go back to Egypt; for all the men who were seeking your life [for killing the Egyptian] are dead.*
>
> *20And Moses took his wife and his sons and set them on donkeys, and he returned to the land of Egypt; and Moses took the rod of God in his hand.*

It is obvious that God was still in the process of molding Moses' character even as he journeyed with him to Egypt. I say it is obvious because in the following verses, we see another glimmer of Moses' character as it was at that time. Moses had failed to carry out a vital command of God. He had failed to circumcise his own son. Moses had put the wishes of his wife before the commands of God. In doing so, Moses had sinned. His disobedience had not only displeased God and put the mission in jeopardy, but it had also put his own son in spiritual danger. You will recall that God had warned Abraham in Genesis 17:14 that any male who is not circumcised would be cut off from his people (destroyed), and would not inherit the covenant promises.

Here was Moses on his way to help God establish His sacred Abrahamic covenant when he had not even put the sign of the covenant in the flesh of his own son. Moses deliberately disobeyed God. Consequently, God had to show Moses that He would not tolerate such sin. On that occasion, God brought Moses about as close to death as one can get without actually dying. Moreover, God would have actually killed him had Moses not repented. As a result of his sin, Moses became so ill that his wife had to perform their son's circumcision for him.

I think you should read about that incident for yourself, so that you too will understand the importance of your own obedience to God's commands. Also, you need to be aware of what the man, Moses, was really like before God reshaped his character. Why? Because, understanding what he was like before and after will give you a new respect for the man, Moses. It will also make you appreciate God even more knowing how He patiently worked with Moses and what He went through with Moses in order to keep His promises to Abraham, Isaac and Jacob.

Exodus 4:24-26 (The Amplified Bible.)

24Along the way at a [resting-] place, the Lord met [Moses] and sought to kill him [made him acutely and almost fatally ill].

25[Now apparently he had failed to circumcise one of his sons, his wife being opposed to it; but seeing his life in such danger] Zipporah took a flint knife and cut off the foreskin of her son and cast it to touch [Moses'] feet, and said, Surely a husband of blood you are to me!

26When He let [Moses] alone [to recover], Zipporah said, a husband of blood are you because of the circumcision.

The *Amplified Bible* provides a footnote for the previous verse, verse twenty-five. As you read it, notice that the words of the Bible scholars mentioned confirm what I am teaching.

> He who is on his way to liberate the people of the circumcision has in Midian even neglected to circumcise his

> second son Eliezer (J.P. Lange, *A Commentary*). It was necessary that at this stage of Moses' experience he should learn that God is in earnest when He speaks, and will assuredly perform all that He has threatened (J.G.Murphy, *A Commentary on the Book of Exodus*).

Moses recovered from his close call with death. However, during that frightening experience, he had learned a valuable lesson. He learned and would remember that God requires absolute obedience to His commands. **Thus, Moses was almost ready to help God fulfill His promise to Abraham and to deliver the children of the covenant from the bondage of Egypt.**

While God had been at work preparing Moses for the great task of delivering His people, the Israelites were still in cruel bondage. They had absolutely no idea what God had been doing or was doing behind the scenes. So, since as far as they were concerned, no change had as yet taken place, they automatically assumed that God had not heard and answered their cries for assistance.

Viewing the previous overall situation with hindsight is like observing a bumblebee in flight. For example, there are times when the bee seems to be literally suspended in air. To the natural eye, he appears to be motionless. It is only when the bee darts forward that one becomes aware that he was in flight the whole time. One simply could not detect his movement.

So it is with God and His people. To the Israelites' natural eye, it looked like God was not moving on their behalf. However, the whole time, unbeknown to them, God was moving. **God was actually at work preparing the very vessel through whom He intended to keep His promises to their forefathers and deliver them from the bondage of Egypt.** The problem was, they just could not see what God was doing behind the scenes. It was not until Moses appeared, carrying God's message of deliverance (the bee darted forward), that the Israelites finally realized that God had heard and miraculously answered their prayers.

Furthermore, as God had promised Moses, the Israelites actually accepted the fact that God had sent Moses to them. This time, they not only believed Moses, but they were so grateful that God had heard and answered them, they even bowed their heads and worshipped the Lord. See this for yourself in the next verses.

Exodus 4:29-31 (The Amplified Bible.)

²⁹*Moses and Aaron went and gathered together [in Egypt] all the elders of the Israelites.*

³⁰*Aaron spoke all the words which the Lord had spoken to Moses, and did the signs in the sight of the people.*

³¹*And the people believed; and when they heard that the Lord had visited the Israelites, and that He had looked [in compassion] upon their affliction, they bowed their heads and worshiped.*

The next chapter, Exodus chapter five, informs you of Pharoah's response during and after Moses' and Aaron's first confrontation with him. If you are familiar with that particular story, you will recall how Pharoah refused to obey God's commands. He would not let God's people go into the wilderness to make sacrifice to the Lord their God. Pharoah was so rebellious that he punished the Israelites for even asking for time off to worship their God.

That punishment came in the form of a demand. The demand was that the Israelites perform an impossible task. Pharoah commanded that they make bricks without the usual necessary supply of straw. Although Pharoah deprived the Israelites of the straw, he still insisted that their daily quota of bricks not be diminished. Thus, God's people were scattered throughout all Egypt, forced to gather short stubble instead of straw. Then, when they could not meet their usual tally of bricks because of the short supply of straw, the Israelite foremen were brutally beaten by their Egyptian taskmasters.

The foremen took their case to Pharoah, explaining to him how the Egyptians were forcing them to make bricks without straw and how they were beating them because they could not meet the expected quota. But, since Pharoah was initially responsible for that unfair rule, he showed them no mercy. Instead, he accused them of being lazy and idle. He insisted that the reason they wanted time off to go and make sacrifices to their God was because they had too much time on their hands. Thus, Pharoah's cruel work order remained intact. There would be no straw provided, and the quota would not be lessened one iota.

So that I can present to you additional information that pertains to Moses' rejection problem, we will read about the incident that happened right after the foremen's previously mentioned appointment with Pharoah.

Exodus 5:19-23 (The Amplified Bible.)

19And the Hebrew foremen saw that they were in an evil situation when it was said, You shall not diminish in the least your full daily quota of bricks.

Can you imagine what took place when, after leaving Pharoah's presence with the previous distressing judgment weighing heavy on their minds, the Hebrew foremen bumped into Moses and Aaron on the road? If you imagined the worst, you are right. The Hebrew foremen railed at Moses and Aaron. The next verses give you an idea of how they verbally blamed Moses and Aaron for their present miserable plight

20And the foremen met Moses and Aaron, who were standing in the way as they came forth from Pharoah.

21And the foremen said to them, The Lord look upon you and judge, because you have made us a rotten stench to be detested by Pharoah and his servants and have put a sword in their hand to slay us.

How do you think Moses responded to the Israelites latest barrage of rejection and blame? Do you think Moses finally exhibited faith and trust in God? Well, I am afraid he did not. Would you believe he reverted right back to his previous state of doubt and self-deprecation. Just as the foremen had wrongfully accused and scolded him, so Moses wrongfully accused and scolded God. He questioned God's method and motives. He again questioned God's choice. And in verse twenty-two, he as much as said to God, "I told you so." See this truth for yourself in the following verses.

22Then Moses turned again to the Lord and said, <u>O Lord, why have You dealt evil to this people? Why did You ever send me?</u>

23For since I came to Pharoah to speak in Your name, he has done evil to this people, <u>neither have You delivered Your people at all.</u>

At this stage in the game, God could not allow Moses' attitude to interfere with His keeping His solemn pledge to Abraham. So God responded to Moses' questions and doubts by telling him what He was now going to do and why. He told Moses that He was now ready to deal with Pharoah. He then got down to the heart of the matter, explaining once again His reason for being involved in that situation in the first place.

God reminded Moses that He would Himself personally carry out His promises to Abraham, Isaac and Jacob and consequently

96

establish His covenant with their descendants, the Israelites. Hence, as God had promised their forefathers, He would be their God, He would deliver them from the bondage of Egypt, and He would bring them to the Promised Land (Canaan). In the following verses, we again see the Biblical answer to the question, "Why Did God Deliver The Jews From Egypt?" **We see that God delivered the Jews from Egypt in order to keep His promises to Abraham, Isaac and Jacob.**

Exodus 6:2-8 (The Amplified Bible.)

2And God said to Moses, I am the Lord.

3I appeared to Abraham, to Isaac, and to Jacob as God Almighty [El-Shaddai], but by My name the Lord [Yahweh—the redemptive name of God] I did not make Myself known to them [in acts and great miracles].

4I have also established My covenant with them to give them the land of Canaan, the land of their temporary residence in which they were strangers.

5I have also heard the groaning of the Israelites whom the Egyptians have enslaved; and I have [earnestly] remembered My covenant [with Abraham, Isaac, and Jacob].

6Accordingly, say to the Israelites, I am the Lord, and I will bring you out from under the burdens of the Egyptians, and I will free you from their bondage, and I will rescue you with an outstretched arm [with special and vigorous action] and by mighty acts of judgment.

7And I will take you to Me for a people, and I will be to you a God; and you shall know that it is I, the Lord your God, Who brings you out from under the burdens of the Egyptians.

8And I will bring you into the land concerning which I lifted up My hand and swore that I would give it to Abraham, Isaac, and Jacob; and I will give it to you for a heritage. I am the Lord [you have the pledge of My changeless omnipotence and faithfulness].

In the previous verses, the Lord Himself answered the question, "Why Did God Deliver The Jews From Egypt?" **God explained that He did it in order to keep His solemn pledge to Abraham, Isaac and Jacob.** In those same verses, God also promised certain actions He would take in order to keep His covenant with Abraham, Isaac and Jacob.

(1) He would free the Israelites from their bondage in Egypt.

(2) He would rescue them with special and vigorous actions and mighty acts of judgment.

(3) He would be their God.

(4) He would deliver them from Egypt and bring them to Canaan (the Promised Land).

God had sworn to Abraham, Isaac and Jacob that He would do all those things, and God wanted the Israelites to know that He was about to fulfill His sacred covenant. However, when Moses relayed God's last message to the covenant descendants of Abraham, they refused to listen to and heed Moses' voice. Thus, Moses returned to God feeling dejected, disillusioned and disappointed.

For a moment, let us consider God's side of this issue. God had a multitude of problems to deal with, and He was getting no cooperation from either the Israelites or Moses. On the one hand, He had the Israelites who wanted instant deliverance. And, because they had been so mistreated by the Egyptians, they had difficulty trusting anyone or anything. On the other hand, He had Moses with his questionings, his accusations, his negativity, his lack of faith and trust in God's ability to choose the right vessel and make the right decisions and his low self-esteem. Plus, on top of all that, God had the responsibility of punishing and conquering the Egyptians and their gods and fulfilling His covenant with Abraham in its entirety, including getting these people, His people, out of Egypt and back to the Promised Land.

The last thing God needed was for Moses to start moaning and complaining again about his inability to do the job. Yet that is exactly what Moses did. Instead of giving God a little support and comfort, Moses insisted that God's plan was not going to work since He had chosen an incompetent vessel to carry it out. Read the next verses for yourself and you will see what I mean.

Exodus 6:9-12 (The Amplified Bible.)

9Moses told this to the Israelites, but they refused to listen to Moses because of their impatience and anguish of spirit and because of their cruel bondage.

10The Lord said to Moses,

11Go in, tell Pharoah king of Egypt to let the Israelites go out of his land.

12But Moses said to the Lord, Behold [my own people] the Israelites have not listened to me; how then shall Pharoah give heed to me, who am of deficient and impeded speech?

From the time Moses came face to face with God, he had failed to exhibit the character of humility. God, on the other hand, had displayed great humility throughout their relationship. For example, even during the previously mentioned situation in Exodus 6:9-12, God manifested true humility. It takes a great deal of humility to keep your word to a friend (Abraham) at the expense of your own hurt, and that is exactly what God did when He disregarded Moses' last remarks.

God intended to keep His pledge to Abraham at any cost to Himself. So, since Moses was the key to keeping that promise, God humbly ignored Moses' insulting comments in order to push forward His deliverance plan. In addition to His willingness to overlook Moses' disrespectful statement, God once again changed His method of dealing with Moses. This time, He took Moses into His confidence. God laid out His plans for dealing with Pharoah before him. He assured Moses that the battle strategy He was using was absolutely necessary since He had to accomplish certain aspects of His plan **before** the Israelites could leave Egypt. God's plan and His reason for carrying it out exactly as He did at that point went something like this:

(1) Moses would go to Pharoah and present God's command.

(2) God would harden Pharoah's heart so that he would not listen to Moses.

(3) Pharoah's refusal to obey would leave the way open for God to fulfill the promises He had previously made to Abraham in Genesis 15:13-14 which included: *"But I will bring judgment on that nation whom they will serve, and afterward they will come out...."*

Oh, my friend, do you see the righteousness in what God was doing? So that He could keep His word to Abraham, God had to meet His previous stipulations in Genesis 15:13-14 exactly as He had stated that He would. Thus, in order to fulfill His word in its entirety, God had to punish the Egyptians **before** the Israelites could leave their land. Consequently, He could not provide instant deliverance for His people. **The bottom line is: Every single thing God did during that whole affair, right down to the order of events, revolved around His promises to Abraham.**

As you read the following verses, try to picture God as the Supreme Commander relaying His battle strategy to His top general because that is exactly what was taking place. Trained as a prince of Egypt, Moses would have completely understood the necessity for wartime strategy. He would have recognized that God's plan was uncompromisingly righteous and extremely wise. And last but not least, he would have realized the need for him to align himself with God's plan, since under the given circumstances, God's way was the best and only way to handle that situation.

Exodus 7:1-6 (The Amplified Bible.)

1THE LORD said to Moses, Behold, I make you as God to Pharoah [to declare My will and purpose to him]; and Aaron your brother shall be your prophet.

2You shall speak all that I command you, and Aaron your brother shall tell Pharoah to let the Israelites go out of his land.

3And I will make Pharoah's heart stubborn and hard, and multiply My signs, My wonders, and miracles in the land of Egypt.

4But Pharoah will not listen to you, and I will lay My hand upon Egypt and bring forth My hosts, My people the Israelites, out of the land of Egypt by great acts of judgment.

5The Egyptians shall know that I am the Lord when I stretch forth My hand upon Egypt and bring out the Israelites from among them.

6And Moses and Aaron did so, as the Lord commanded them.

Obviously, God's last approach in dealing with Moses' problems worked. Moses fell right in line with God's orders. His attitude changed completely. Suddenly, his faith rose up, crowding out all previous doubts and fears. Thus, Moses, God's mighty general, went forth with the Lord to punish and conquer Israel's foes (the Egyptians and their false gods) and consequently, to bring about God's promises to Abraham, Isaac and Jacob.

God's patience, humility, faithfulness and righteousness had finally paid off. Sometimes, we tend to overlook the fact that God, not Moses, was the real hero in the deliverance of the Israelites from Egypt. The Lord underwent much pain to keep His sacred promise to Abraham. God's willingness to endure severe difficulties in order to painstakingly prepare Moses and use him to bring the Israelites out of the bondage of Egypt and back to the Land of Promise stands as a monument to His holy, faithful character.

By the time God got through refining Moses' life, God had gained a truly faithful, loyal friend. God had taken a life that had been emotionally broken into many pieces and when He had finished putting all the pieces back together again, Moses was spiritually stronger than he had ever been. Self-depreciation turned into true humility. Doubt and skepticism turned into faith. Fear turned into courage and boldness. **Furthermore, to this very day, the whole world knows that God truly did make a wise choice when He picked Moses to help Him keep His promises to Abraham, Isaac and Jacob.**

As the Lord had commanded, the now courageous prophet of God, Moses, and his brother, Aaron, confronted Pharoah for the second time. **With Moses' help, God would deliver the Israelites from the bondage of Egypt and bring them back to the land of Canaan so that His sacred covenant with Abraham would be fulfilled.**

After all your years of searching, Christian, you finally understand why God delivered the Jews from Egypt. Never again will you have to wonder why God miraculously rescued the Hebrew children from Pharoah's oppression. For, you now know beyond doubt that <u>God delivered the Jews in order to keep His covenant with His righteous friend, Abraham.</u>

You also received insight into what the deliverer, Moses, was really like. The knowledge you gained should have given you new respect for the man, Moses. For, you are now aware that he had to overcome many character flaws in order to become the mighty vessel of God whom God's people today greatly admire and look up to.

Most of all, you have been given deeper insight into the holy character of God. Surely our God is to be praised. We have overwhelming proof that He is faithful. His word is to be trusted. <u>Blessed be the Lord our God, for He delivered the Israelites out of the bondage of Egypt exactly as He promised Abraham, Isaac and Jacob that He would.</u>

Chapter 7

WHAT WAS GOD'S PURPOSE FOR TRANSFORMING AARON'S ROD INTO A SERPENT?

In chapter four, we studied in detail every miracle and mighty act of judgment that God performed in Egypt, except one. The miracle we did not cover involved Aaron's rod changing into a serpent.

Throughout the years, the miracle of the serpent has continued to puzzle the Church. Whenever God's people read the Scripture describing that particular phenomenon, numerous questions begin to surface. One of those questions is, "Why did God choose to use a serpent in His miracle?" Rest assured, the answer to that question, along with many other answers to specific queries, will be provided in this portion of the series.

The main reason the miracle in question has remained so open to controversy is because most people feel uncomfortable with the idea that God even used a serpent in His miracle at all. These people experience discomfort because, with good reason, they associate the serpent with Satan.

On more than one occasion, the Scriptures depict Satan as a serpent. For example, in Genesis 3:1, the Scriptures reveal that while in the form of a serpent, Satan tempted Eve. Consequently, mankind fell into sin. Then, of course, there is the well-known verse in Revelation in which Satan is actually identified as *"that old serpent."* Since I quoted from the *Holy Bible, King James Version*, let us read the last reference from that translation.

Revelation 12:9 (King James Version.)

9And __the great dragon__ was cast out, __that old serpent,__ __called the Devil, and Satan,__ which deceiveth the whole world: he was cast out into the earth, and his angels were cast out with him.

Yeshua was aware that men associated the serpent with Satan. He knew the sacred Scriptures. It was because of His absolute knowledge of the Scriptures that in Matthew 23:33 He referred to the wicked religious leaders of His day as *"__You serpents! You spawn of Vipers!__"*

Yeshua attributed those titles of Satan to Israel's religious leaders because, at that time, they were exhibiting the wicked character of Satan.

However, the opposite side of the coin is quite different. There are passages of Scripture in which the term *"serpent"* denotes specific characteristics that God's people are encouraged to acquire. For instance, in Matthew 10:16, Yeshua instructed His own disciples to be wise as serpents. Other Scriptures, such as Isaiah 14:29, refer to righteous men as serpents. In that particular text, God's Word alluded to Israel's righteous King Hezakiah as a serpent.

In verses such as Deuteronomy 32:24, God warns His own people that if they sin, He will send serpents to punish them. The book of Numbers provides us with an actual instance when the Israelites did sin, and God did send the promised fiery serpents among them. However, under God's instructions, Moses erected a serpent made of bronze, and that bronze serpent was used by God as an instrument of healing for those who had sinned. See this happening for yourself in the subsequent verses.

Numbers 21:6-9 (The Amplified Bible.)

⁶Then the Lord sent <u>fiery (burning) serpents</u> among the people; and they bit the people, and many Israelites died.

⁷And the people came to Moses, and said, We have sinned, for we have spoken against the Lord and against you; pray to the Lord, that He may take away the serpents from us. So Moses prayed for the people.

⁸And the Lord said to Moses, Make <u>a fiery serpent</u> [of bronze] and set it on a pole; and everyone who is bitten, when he looks at it, shall live.

⁹And Moses made a serpent of bronze and put it on a pole, and if a serpent had bitten any man, when he looked to the serpent of bronze [attentively, expectantly, with a steady and absorbing gaze], he lived.

You will recall that Yeshua compared His own crucifixion to the previous serpent episode. His exact words are written in the following verses.

John 3:14-15 (The Amplified Bible.)

¹⁴And just as Moses lifted up <u>the serpent</u> in the desert [on a pole], so must [so it is necessary that] the Son of Man be lifted up [on the cross],

¹⁵In order that everyone who believes in Him [who cleaves to Him, trusts Him, and relies on Him] may not perish, but have eternal life and [actually] live forever!

By now, it should be clear to you that in God's Word the serpent signifies both good and evil. It represents both the righteous and the unrighteous. The serpent is used on the one hand to punish and to inflict pain and death and on the other hand, symbolically, to provide physical and spiritual healing and life. The bottom line is that the serpent, like every other creature, was created by God Almighty. Therefore, God has and will continue to use the serpent in whatever capacity He sees fit.

Hopefully, the information I just presented will have helped to remove any reservations you may have had concerning God's use of a serpent in the miracle in Pharaoh's court. I guarantee you that once you learn God's purpose for employing the serpent in His miracle, you will see the incredible wisdom of His choice

There is another facet of Moses' miracle that arouses curiosity in most Christians. Since Moses performed a supernatural miracle of God, Christians wonder how the magicians of Egypt were able to duplicate it? Who or what was their source of power?

Some Christians are of the opinion that Pharoah's magicians had no power source. They feel that they simply practiced deceptive illusions. If that had been the case, I am afraid Aaron's rod would have had a difficult time swallowing those illusions. No! I think we need to lay aside men's assumptions and opinions and instead, stick strictly to Biblical facts. Otherwise, we may get caught up in the ridiculous.

Scriptural evidence indicates that the magicians could certainly have performed duplicate miracles by Satan's power. However, as we investigate that avenue, it is important to keep in mind that Satan's power is limited. Only with God's permission is Satan allowed to use miraculous power. For example, the Lord allowed Satan to perform numerous miracles during righteous Job's ordeal.

For a moment, let us consider a few of those supernatural feats that Satan executed. In Job 1:16, Satan caused fire to fall from heaven. That fire burned up Job's sheep. Then in Job 1:18-19, Satan miraculously conjured up a whirlwind which killed all Job's sons and daughters. And let us not forget how, in Job 2:7, Satan caused painful boils to break out all over Job's body.

My friend, there is no denying that when it suits God's purpose, Satan is indeed capable of performing miracles. The book of Revelation even furnishes us with a preview of his future miraculous escapades. **In Revelation 12:9, you saw that the dragon is "...*that old serpent, called the devil and Satan....*"** Keeping that fact in mind, let us checkout what God's Word tells us about the devil and the awesome power he will one day be allowed to bestow upon some of his followers.

Revelation 13:1-4 (The Amplified Bible)

1[AS] I stood on the sandy beach, I saw a beast coming up out of the sea with ten horns and seven heads. On his horns he had ten royal crowns (diadems) and blasphemous titles (names) on his heads.

*2And the beast that I saw resembled a leopard, but his feet were like those of a bear and his mouth was like that of a lion. **And to him the dragon gave his [own] might and power and his [own] throne and great dominion.***

3And one of his heads seemed to have a deadly wound. But his death stroke was healed; and the whole earth went after the beast in amazement and admiration.

*4**They fell down and paid homage to the dragon, because he had bestowed on the beast all his dominion and authority**; they also praised and worshiped the beast, exclaiming, Who is a match for the beast, and, Who can make war against him?*

In this same chapter, we see a second example of the power that the dragon, Satan, will be allowed to possess in the future.

Revelation 13:11-14 (The Amplified Bible.)

*11Then I saw another beast rising up out of the land [itself]; he had two horns like a lamb, and he spoke (roared) like **a dragon**.*

12He exerts all the power and right of control of the former beast in his presence, and causes the earth and those who dwell upon it to exalt and deify the first beast, whose deadly wound was healed, and to worship him.

13__He performs great signs (startling miracles), even making fire fall from the sky to the earth in men's sight.__

14And because of the signs (miracles) which he is allowed to perform in the presence of the [first] beast, he deceives those who inhabit the earth, commanding them to erect a statue (an image) in the likeness of the beast who was wounded by the [small] sword and still lives.

After reading the previous information, I am sure you will agree that the questions, "Since Moses performed a supernatural miracle, how were the magicians of Egypt able to duplicate it?" and "Who or what was their source of power?" have been adequately answered. __The magicians of Egypt were able to emulate that miracle, because, with God's permission, Satan was their source of power__.

The only thing left for us to do before I begin to answer the question, "Why did God choose to use a serpent in His miracle?" is to read the Biblical account of that mighty act of God. So let us do that.

Exodus 7:6-13 (The Amplified Bible.)

6And Moses and Aaron did so, as the Lord commanded them.

7Now Moses was 80 years old and Aaron 83 years old when they spoke to Pharoah.

8And the Lord said to Moses and Aaron,

9When Pharoah says to you, Prove [your authority] by a miracle, then tell Aaron, throw your rod down before Pharoah, that it may become a serpent.

*10So Moses and Aaron went to Pharoah and did as the Lord had commanded; **Aaron threw down his rod before Pharoah and his servants, and it became a serpent.***

11Then Pharoah called for the wise men [skilled in magic and divination] and the sorcerers (wizards and jugglers). And they also, these magicians of Egypt, did similar things with their enchantments and secret arts.

12For they cast down every man his rod and they became serpents; but Aaron's rod swallowed up their rods.

13But Pharoah's heart was hardened and stubborn and he would not listen to them, just as the Lord had said.

Moses' character had almost overnight undergone a spiritual metamorphosis. He had shed his attitude of self-depreciation, self-doubt and questioning. He now stood before Pharoah, an eighty-year-old spiritual giant, bold and fearless and full of faith in God. Truly, the Lord had molded a misshapen lump of clay into a beautiful vessel through whom He would accomplish His covenant with Abraham.

The now transformed Moses would represent God Himself. He would be the instrument God would use to bring the promised judgment upon Pharoah and his subjects for their cruel treatment of God's people. You will soon see that the miracle described in the verses we just read was actually a preview and a forewarning of that judgment which was soon to come upon all Egypt.

It is time now for me to answer the question, "Why did God choose to use a serpent in His miracle?" **The answer to that question is that, in this instance, <u>God chose to use a serpent because the serpent was known and accepted as the symbol of Pharoah's supreme power.</u>**

Most likely, you have seen an Egyptian uraeus on display in a museum or portrayed in Egyptian artwork or while watching a film. The definition of the word "uraeus" in *The American Heritage Dictionary, Second College Edition* reads as such:

> The figure of the sacred serpent, depicted on the headdress of ancient Egyptian rulers and deities as an emblem of sovereignty....

In chapter four, you learned that Pharoah (the god Horus) was thought to be all-powerful, all-knowing and in complete control of all nature, fertility and even fate. As their god, Pharoah was responsible for the Egyptians' financial prosperity and their spiritual well-being. He was also believed to be endowed with magical powers.

That same source, *The New Encyclopedia Britannica Micropedia Ready Reference*, under the heading "Pharaoh," tells us that Pharoah's uraeus (the serpent on his crown) supposedly "spat flames at his enemies." Remember, he was falsely accredited with the power to be able to single-handedly trample thousands of the enemy on the battlefield. So, after joining the facts about the uraeus with all the information you received in chapter four, it should come as no surprise to you when I tell you that according to *Smith's Bible Dictionary*, under the heading "Serpent," the serpent was worshipped by the Egyptians.

The time has come for me to connect together all the pieces of this amazing puzzle. Since, only then will you truly comprehend the awesome spiritual significance of the events that took place during Moses' second confrontation with Pharoah.

One of the pieces of the puzzle is seen in Exodus 7:1 in the *Holy Bible, King James Version*. There God said to Moses, "...***I have made thee a god to Pharoah: and Aaron thy brother shall be thy prophet.***" In a few moments, you will realize the great importance of those words. You will see what a vital role that statement played in God's overall strategy.

Moses, a judge of Israel who was as God's representative and spokesperson about to pass God's judgment upon all Egypt and their gods, was in the true Biblical sense of the word *"**a god**."* Yeshua Himself, when speaking to the religious leaders of Israel in John 10:34, referred to them as *"gods."* Yeshua said, *"Is it not written in your law,* ***I said, ye are gods?***" I think it will help you if you also read the following verses, for they reveal why Yeshua referred to the religious leaders of Israel as *"gods."*

Psalm 82:1-8 (The Amplified Bible.)

*[1] GOD STANDS in the assembly [of the representatives] of God; in the midst of the magistrates or judges **He gives judgment [as] among the gods.***

Verse one in the *Holy Bible, King James Version* reads, "***GOD standeth in the congregation of the mighty; he judgeth among the gods.***"

[2] How long will you [magistrates or judges] judge unjustly and show partiality to the wicked? Selah [pause, and calmly think of that]!

3Do justice to the weak (poor) and fatherless; maintain the rights of the afflicted and needy.

4Deliver the poor and needy; rescue them out of the hand of the wicked.

5[The magistrates and judges] know not, neither will they understand; they walk on in the darkness [of complacent satisfaction]; all the foundations of the earth [the fundamental principles upon which rests the administration of justice] are shaking.

6I said, <u>You are gods</u> [since you judge on My behalf, as My representatives]; indeed, all of you are children of the Most High.

7But you shall die as men and fall as one of the princes.

8Arise, O God, judge the earth! For to You belong all the nations.

As you can see in God's Word, people who are in a position to speak for God or to pass judgment in God's stead are representing the Lord. Therefore, those people are referred to in the Scriptures as *"gods"* (that is, *"gods"* with a small g). *"<u>I said, You are gods [since you judge on My behalf, as My representatives]</u>."* Remember, one of the Ten Commandments expressly states, *"Thou shalt have no other gods <u>before</u> Me."* (Exodus 20:3.) The Lord was compelled to insert the word *"<u>before</u>"* in that command, because He Himself had already designated His true representatives as *"gods."*

God's representatives **are not**, I repeat, **are not** to be worshipped. To do so would be to commit the deadly sin of idolatry. The Israelites did not worship Moses. Neither did they put the god, Moses, **before** the Lord. For, like God's representatives today, Moses was simply a man like any other man. Nevertheless, since such men and women are endowed with the power to represent the Lord on earth, for the Lord's sake, they are to be greatly regarded and treated with deep reverence and respect.

With the knowledge you now possess, you will understand that when I speak of the god, Moses, I am referring to him strictly in the Biblical sense. On the other hand, when I speak of the god, Horus, I am speaking of the false god, Pharoah. I have amplified the previous point because I do not want you to misconstrue or misinterpret my words when I refer to either of those men as gods.

Now, let us get down to the core of the matter. As you know, God's first priority was to keep His promises to Abraham, Isaac and Jacob. **One of those promises involved bringing judgment upon the Egyptians and their gods for their abhorrent treatment of the Israelites**. The best way I know to describe God's judgment strategy is to compare it to a gigantic power game, a power game in which the deck was already stacked against Israel's enemies.

The playing field covered all the land of Egypt. The players were God Almighty and the evil god of this world, Satan. The pieces through whom the players wielded power were the god Moses and his prophet Aaron on the one side and the god Pharoah and his magicians on the other side. The pawns (those who had no personal power) were the Israelites and the Egyptians.

God had purposely made the pieces equal (that is, since the Egyptians considered Pharoah to be a god, the Lord raised up a worthy opponent, the god Moses). Furthermore, since God knew that His rival, Satan, lacked the necessary power needed to adequately participate in the game, God gave him a handicap (that is, an advantage to equalize his chances of succeeding). Satan was allotted a certain amount of miraculous power. That supply of power was not only used by his followers to duplicate Moses' serpent miracle but we are told in Exodus 7:22 that, like Moses, the magicians also turned water to blood. Plus, in Exodus 8:6-7, again like Moses, the magicians caused frogs to come up onto the land.

However, as I said earlier, Satan's power is strictly limited to what God allows. Unbeknown to Satan, God had given him only enough power to accomplish God's purpose regarding Egypt's punishment. Consequently, the magicians were able to play off the miracle of the serpent and to miraculously intensify two of the supernatural plagues that God had already poured out. But unlike Moses, they were not able to halt or so much as ease the plagues. They could not even heal themselves of the painful boils on their own bodies.

Consider the stupidity of the way the magicians used the miraculous power that Satan had invested in them. Egypt's water supply had turned to blood. So, what did the magicians do to ease the people's discomfort? They made more water turn to blood. Moreover, Moses plagued Egypt with frogs. So again, what did the magicians do to help the people? They caused more frogs to come up onto the land. The end result was that rather than relieving the Egyptians' suffering, they added to it. So, under such circumstances, I do not think the people of Egypt would have been too impressed with the magicians miracles, do you?

All the magicians really succeeded in doing through their miracles was to make themselves look stupid and to prove to everyone that God, not Pharoah, was all-powerful. Plus, for a time, the magicians actually helped God harden Pharoah's heart. Thus, they assisted the Lord in carrying out His promised judgment of Egypt and her gods.

Because the Egyptians viewed the serpent as the symbol of Pharoah's power, the Lord chose to use the serpent in His first move of the power game. God turned Aaron's rod into a serpent to prove to all Egypt and their gods that **He**, not Pharoah, is all-powerful. Furthermore, as you will soon see, the Lord's opening move proclaimed His promised judgment upon the Egyptians and their gods.

On that dreadful day, the god Moses and the god Horus stood pitted against each other. Truth, light and righteousness looked straight into the face of deception, darkness and wickedness. The spiritual battle had begun. The demons must have shivered in terror upon realizing that the foundation of Satan's Egyptian domain was about to crumble. For, unlike the magicians of Egypt, they had to have known that the power Satan had invested in the god Pharoah and his magicians was no match for the power of the Lord that the god Moses would soon display.

As God had commanded, the god Moses instructed Aaron his prophet to throw his rod down before the god Pharoah (Horus). Those Egyptians who were present in Pharoah's court that day must have been totally shocked by the sight of Aaron's rod changing into a serpent. They had to have drawn back in fear and awe. How confused they must have felt to see an Israelite cause a rod to turn into a sacred serpent, the symbol of the god Pharoah's power and sovereignty and to them an object of worship.

It is no wonder that the god Horus (Pharoah) immediately sent for his wise men and sorcerers. He had to save face. After all, another god had, by a miracle, displayed the symbol of His own supreme power, power that the god Pharoah claimed solely for himself. Thus, Egypt's wise men and sorcerers ran to Pharoah's aid. They too had power. They too would make their rods turn into serpents.

Exodus 7:10-12 (The Amplified Bible.)

*10So Moses and Aaron went to Pharoah and did as the Lord had commanded; **Aaron threw down his rod before Pharoah and his servants, and it became a serpent**.*

11Then Pharoah called for the wise men [skilled in magic and divination] and the sorcerers (wizards and jugglers). And they also, these magicians of Egypt, did similar things with their enchantments and secret arts.

12For they cast down every man his rod and they became serpents; but Aaron's rod swallowed up their rods.

2 Timothy 3:8-9 furnishes us with the names of two of Pharoah's magicians. They are Jannes and Jambres. Plus, by comparing certain evil men of his day to Jannes and Jambres, Paul also provides us with a good description of the type of men Pharoah's magicians were. They were rebellious in that they resisted the truth that Moses relayed to them. Also, the *King James Version* applies to them the word *"reprobate."* In *The American Heritage Dictionary, Second College Edition,* the word reprobate is defined:

> A morally unprincipled person. One who is predestined to damnation.... Rejected by God and without hope of salvation....

From the previous report, we catch a glimpse of the utterly evil spirits that the god Moses confronted that day. The magicians of Egypt were the image of their master, the devil, in both character and deed. They were so deluded that they actually thought they could match, if not surpass, the miracle of the serpent that Moses performed. And for a moment, it seemed to all who were present that Pharoah's magicians were right, for through them Satan made his first move of the contest. The magicians duplicated Moses' miracle. However, instead of producing one serpent from one rod as Moses had done, all the magicians threw down their rods, and all their rods became serpents. Thus, the solitary effect of Moses' serpent no longer inspired such awe, since it was outnumbered and surrounded by the sacred serpents of the god Horus.

The power game was intensifying. Everyone present was holding their breath, wondering what Moses' next move would be. To the outward eye, it appeared that Moses was trapped. His serpent was surrounded by the magicians' serpents.

However, God was in no way defeated. Rather, the whole time, the Lord had been skillfully setting up Satan for the big fall. Everything was proceeding according to the Lord's plan. Moses was positioned exactly as God had placed him, and the next move was the Lord's.

Suddenly, Aaron's rod opened its mouth and lunged forward. It then swallowed up all the magicians' rods.

Exodus 7:12 (The Amplified Bible.)

*12For they cast down every man his rod and they became serpents; **but Aaron's rod swallowed up their rods.***

God had won that first round of the power game, and as the victor, He had also made an awesome statement.

(1) God had shown that **He**, not Satan, not Pharoah, not the magicians, **but He, the Lord God Almighty, was all-powerful and all-wise**.

(2) The Lord had shown that Satan's representative, the god Pharoah, was no match for His representative, the god Moses.

(3) The Lord had given to Satan, to Pharoah and to the Egyptians as a whole, a warning of what was about to happen. **The preview of God's judgment was that just as Moses' rod had swallowed up the rods of the magicians so the Lord would swallow up (that is, destroy) the nation of Egypt and their gods.** Yes, the Lord would destroy the nation that for four hundred years had cruelly afflicted and oppressed His beloved covenant people and opposed His purpose. God's curse would be poured out upon all Egypt and their gods, *"...I will bless those who bless you [who confer prosperity or happiness upon you] and curse him who curses or uses insolent language toward you...."* (Genesis 12:3.)

The cost of abusing God's covenant people would be the total destruction of Egypt. God would destroy Egypt's water, Egypt's aquatic life, Egypt's comfort, Egypt's prosperity, Egypt's health, Egypt's livestock, Egypt's crops, trees and vegetation, Egypt's land, Egypt's air, Egypt's firstborn, and Egypt's gods (that is, everything that the Egyptians worshipped or considered to be sacred).

God's judgment started with Moses debasing the magicians' sacred serpents. In so doing, he also debased Pharoah's power since the serpent was the symbol of that power. That day, Moses had begun to literally accomplish the work that he had symbolically acted out during the episode of the burning bush. He had picked up a serpent by the tail, and that serpent was powerless to harm him. Let us read the following text, and then I will explain in more detail.

Exodus 4:1-4 (The Amplified Bible.)

[1]*AND MOSES answered, But behold, they will not believe me or listen to and obey my voice; for they will say, The Lord has not appeared to you.*

[2]*And the Lord said to him, What is that in your hand? And he said, A rod.*

[3]*And He said, Cast it on the ground. And he did so and it became a serpent [the symbol of royal and divine power worn on the crown of the Pharaohs]; and Moses fled from before it.*

[4]*And the Lord said to Moses, Put forth your hand and take it by the tail. And he stretched out his hand and caught it, and it became a rod in his hand.*

Notice in verse three that even *The Amplified Bible* translators show you what that serpent represented. **The serpent was** *"the symbol of royal and divine power worn on the crown of the Pharaohs."* So, it is quite possible that Moses was more startled by what the serpent represented than he was by the creature itself. After all, he had been raised in the Pharoah's palace. He had been taught from childhood that the serpent spat flames of fire at Pharaoh's enemies. Consequently, since by that time, Moses was himself classed as an enemy of Pharoah, he may have fled to get out of reach of those imaginary flames.

Remember, that particular serpent miracle took place at the burning bush. It happened before Moses underwent his spiritual metamorphosis. At that time, Moses not only lacked self-confidence but he also lacked faith and trust in God. It took his witnessing a miraculous burning bush that was not consumed and hearing the literal voice of God before Moses had enough courage to obey God's instruction to pick up the snake by the tail. However, he did it, and when he did, it once again turned into a rod.

For a moment, let us consider Moses' rod. The rod plays an important role in this whole scenario. Under the heading "rod" in *The Zondervan Pictorial Encyclopedia of the Bible*, we read:

> The rod also became **the symbol of authority and rule** prevalent in Bible use. "Moses took the rod of God." (Exodus 4:20); and he and Aaron wrought numerous miracles with rods.... The rod as a symbol of God's anger and

chastisement occurs in numerous passages....

There are other references to Moses' rod in the previously mentioned article. However, I chose to share with you only the portion of that article which offers a measure of insight into our present topic. My intention is to equip you with enough understanding to enable you to fully receive the following truth. To set the stage of comprehension, we will read Exodus 4:20. That verse shows you beyond doubt that the rod Moses had in his possession when he encountered the Lord at the burning bush became *"the rod of God."*

Exodus 4:20 (The Amplified Bible.)

20*And Moses took his wife and his sons and set them on donkeys, and he returned to the land of Egypt;* **and Moses took the rod of God in his hand.**

As the serpent was the symbol of Pharoah's power, so the rod of Moses was the symbol of God's power. God had invested His awesome power and authority in Moses, and Moses' rod (the rod of God) represented that God given power and authority. **The bottom line is that Moses' rod had become a scepter.**

During the occurrence of the burning bush, the Lord had a specific purpose for causing the symbol of Pharoah's power (the serpent) to miraculously appear. He also had a purpose for ordering Moses to pick up the serpent by the tail. God was showing Moses who was really in control. Moses picked up a dangerous serpent by the tail (a serpent that represented Pharoah's power), and it did not harm him. It did not harm him because it could not harm him. God showed Moses that next to the Lord, Pharoah was powerless.

When the serpent became a rod at the burning bush, God was simply displaying His power over Pharoah. He was assuring Moses that compared to Him, the Pharoah was weak, ineffective, helpless and powerless. **God caused the serpent, the symbol of Pharoah's power, to disappear and to be replaced with the symbol of God's authority and power, the rod of God**. When meditating upon God's supreme power in the following verses, righteous Job said it all.

Job 12:16-25 (The Amplified Bible.)

16*With Him are might and wisdom;* **the deceived and the deceiver are His [and in His power].**

17He leads [great and scheming] counselors away stripped and barefoot and makes the judges fools [in human estimation, by overthrowing their plans].

18He looses the fetters [ordered] by kings and has [the] waistcloth [of a slave] bound about their [own] loins.

19He leads away priests as spoil, and men firmly seated He overturns.

20He deprives of speech those who are trusted and takes away the discernment and discretion of the aged.

21He pours contempt on princes and loosens the belt of the strong [disabling them, bringing low the pride of the learned].

22He uncovers deep things out of darkness and brings into light black gloom and the shadow of death.

23He makes nations great, and He destroys them; He enlarges nations [and then straitens and shrinks them again], and leads them [away captive].

24He takes away understanding from the leaders of the people of the land and of the earth, and causes them to wander in a wilderness where there is no path.

25They grope in the dark without light, and He makes them to stagger and wander like a drunken man.

You will recall that during the episode of the burning bush when Moses was afraid that the people would not believe that the Lord had appeared to him, the Lord instructed him to perform before them the same miracle involving the serpent and the rod. Of course, the Israelites would have been aware of the significance of that miracle. To them that miracle was more than just a rod changing into a serpent and then back into a rod. There was a message for the Israelites in that miracle. **That message was: Do not fear Pharoah. He can do you no more harm. He is powerless to fight your God. The all-powerful Lord God Almighty is about to destroy him.**

Earlier, we studied about Moses' confrontation with Pharoah and his magicians. We carefully checked out the miracle of the serpent that was performed before Pharoah's eyes. So with the information you now have, I am sure you understand what I meant when I told you, "That day, Moses had begun to literally accomplish the work that he had symbolically acted out during the episode of the burning bush. He had picked up a serpent by its tail and the serpent was powerless to harm him."

God had given Moses power and authority to trample underfoot Egypt's serpents (that is, to trample underfoot the enemies of the Lord and the enemies of the Lord's people). Neither Satan, nor Egypt's false gods, nor Pharoah's magicians could overcome or even come close to matching the incredible supernatural power that God had invested in His representative, Moses. During that round of the power game, all God's enemies were, in essence, conquered by the mighty rod of God.

God's predicted judgment of Egypt and their gods began that day. Moses' rod swallowing the magicians' rods signaled to all that the Egyptians would be stripped of their power and severely punished for their mistreatment of God's covenant people, the Jews. **God's promises to Abraham would be fulfilled in their entirety.**

Now you know the answer to the question, "What Was God's Purpose For Transforming Aaron's Rod Into A Serpent?" **You also know to what extremes God will go in order to keep His covenant with Abraham, Isaac and Jacob and to punish all those who mistreat His chosen covenant people.**

God's Word continues to cry out a warning to all men. That warning is that He will bless those who bless Israel and curse those who curse her. Egypt was cursed. Earlier, we studied the plagues that God poured out upon Egypt as a result of God's curse. Egypt was swallowed up (destroyed) by the rod of God (that is, Egypt was destroyed by the supreme power of God Almighty).

Chapter 8

WHY DID MOSES
HAVE POWER WITH GOD?

Let us examine another event in Jewish history in which God's covenant with Abraham played a tremendous role. The episode I am referring to involved Moses and the Israelites. It took place at Mount Sinai (or Horeb) after the Israelites' glorious exodus from Egypt.

While Moses was on Mount Sinai receiving the Ten Commandments from God, the wicked Israelites were playing the harlot. They were actually bowing down and offering sacrifices to an idol, a golden calf. To make matters worse, it was Aaron, the brother of Moses, who had shaped and made the golden calf for them.

We all love to tell of the power that Moses had with God. We often recount how, when Moses prayed, God answered. Yet, under such appalling conditions as those described in the former paragraph, why did Moses still have power with God concerning these people? Why did God continue to hear and answer the prayers Moses prayed on their behalf? As you will soon see, it was once again God's covenant with Abraham that gave Moses power with God and stayed the hand of the Lord from destroying that evil group of people.

The only reason the descendants of those wicked Israelites still exist today is because of God's promise to His devoted friend, Abraham. For though the Israelites deserved to die, God spared them in order to keep His solemn pledge to Abraham. You see, God had to protect His own name; He had to protect His reputation. God could not break His promise for all the world to see. If He had done so, it would have caused the nations to misunderstand His intentions and fail to trust Him from that point on.

For verification of these facts, we will again turn to our only reliable source of truth, the Bible.

Exodus 32:7-14 (The Amplified Bible.)

*7The Lord said to Moses, Go down, for **your** people, whom **you** brought out of the land of Egypt, have corrupted themselves;*

In verse seven, God is so disgusted with the Israelites' idolatrous behavior that He tells Moses, "...*your* people, whom *you* brought out of the land of Egypt, have corrupted themselves." The Hebrews were so wicked that the Lord wanted to disown them. God continues to voice His grievance in the following verses.

> 8*They have turned aside quickly out of the way which I commanded them; they have made them a molten calf and have worshiped it and sacrificed to it, and said, These are your gods, O Israel, that brought you up out of the land of Egypt!*

No wonder God wanted to disown that rebellious, wicked bunch of people. No wonder God wanted to wipe them off the face of the earth, to utterly destroy them.

> 9*And the Lord said to Moses, I have seen this people, and behold, it is a stiff-necked people;*
> 10*Now therefore let Me alone, that My wrath may burn hot against them and that I may destroy them; but I will make of you a great nation.*

God wanted to get rid of every one of Abraham's descendants, except for Moses. He wanted to start all over again from scratch. However, the Lord had promised Abraham, Isaac and Jacob many things, and He had to keep His promises. In addition to this, there stood Moses with total trust and confidence that God would keep His promises without wavering one iota from His Word.

By now you may be asking, **"But why could God not destroy that corrupt bunch of people and raise up more descendants of Abraham through his righteous servant, Moses?"** The answer to your question is in Genesis 15:13-16. We studied that portion of Scripture earlier, but it is necessary that we read it again since those verses contain insight into our present topic.

> Genesis 15:13, 14, 16: (The Amplified Bible.)
>
> 13*And [God] said to Abram, Know positively that your descendants will be strangers dwelling as temporary residents in a land that is not theirs [Egypt], and will be slaves there and will be afflicted and oppressed for 400 years.*

14But I will bring judgment on that nation whom they will serve, and afterward they will come out with great possessions.

16And in the fourth generation they [your descendants] shall come back here [to Canaan] again, for the iniquity of the Amorites is not yet full and complete.

In these verses, God told Abraham that His covenant descendants would be enslaved in Egypt, and the Egyptians would afflict and oppress them for four hundred years. He also told Abraham how He would judge Egypt for her wicked treatment of His people. Plus, **He assured Abraham that in the fourth generation, He would rescue these slaves, bring them out of Egypt and cause them to go back to the Promised Land, Canaan.**

Moses did not fit this bill. To keep this promise, God had to use Abraham's descendants who were oppressed, afflicted and enslaved in Egypt. We all know that Moses was never oppressed or enslaved in Egypt. Moses had not been afflicted. On the contrary, Moses was raised as Egyptian royalty. He had been accepted and reared as the son of Pharoah's daughter. His position as a prince of Egypt afforded Moses a life of ease and opulence. Moreover, he received the best education available. No! God could not fulfill His words in Genesis 15:13,14,16 with Moses alone. As rotten as these Israelites were, God still needed them to help Him carry out His promises to Abraham.

Let us take up now where we left off in Exodus 32:11-14. Moses reminded God that because He loved Abraham, Isaac and Jacob, He chose these people. He reminded God that they were **His** people, and He could not disown them. He reminded God that because He loved their forefathers, **He** was the One who brought Abraham's, Isaac's and Jacob's descendants out of Egypt, and He must not destroy them.

Moses went further. He cautioned God. Moses warned God that if He destroyed this people, everyone would be left with the wrong impression. Everyone would be left with the impression that He destroyed Abraham's descendants and broke His covenant with Abraham, Isaac and Jacob because it was too hard for the God of Israel to keep His promises. He told God, "Lord, the nations will believe that You brought these people out of Egypt only to do them harm."

Exodus 32:11-14 (The Amplified Bible.)

*11 But Moses besought the Lord his God, and said, Lord, why does Your wrath blaze hot against **Your** people, whom **You** have brought forth out of the land of Egypt with great power and a mighty hand?*

12 Why should the Egyptians say, For evil He brought them forth, to slay them in the mountains and consume them from the face of the earth? Turn from Your fierce wrath, and change Your mind concerning this evil against Your people.

Not only did Moses want God to keep His promise, but the main reason behind his wanting this promise kept was to protect God's reputation. Consequently, Moses' immediate reaction and righteous thinking saved God's reputation as well as the children of Israel.

See for yourself in verse thirteen what caused God to hear and heed Moses and thus change His mind. See for yourself that which gave Moses power with God. **God's holy name, God's reputation, was at stake. Therefore God's promise to Abraham, Isaac and Jacob had to be kept.**

13 [Earnestly] remember Abraham, Isaac, and Israel, your servants, to whom You swore by Your own Self and said to them, I will multiply your seed as the stars of the heavens, and all this land that I have spoken of will I give to your seed, and they shall inherit it forever.

In essence, Moses simply said, "Lord, you promised Abraham, Isaac and Jacob that You would multiply their seed as the stars. These people are the result of Your promise. You also told them that these descendants of theirs would inherit that special piece of land You keep telling us about. Lord, all the Egyptians and other nations are watching to see if Your word is good. They are watching to see if You keep covenant. So, if You fail to keep Your promise, Your reputation will be ruined. Lord, You must not destroy this people in Your anger even though they deserve to die. **Your reputation, Your name must come first." Thus, because of God's covenant with Abraham, Isaac and Jacob, God's hand was stayed. For, God had to protect his reputation.**

*14 Then the Lord turned from the evil which He had thought to do to **His** people.*

Did you notice in the previous verse that the Jews are once again called *"His people"*? They are *"His people"* **because He promised Abraham, Isaac and Jacob that He would be their God**.

It is quite clear that God's covenant promise to Abraham, Isaac and Jacob was the main factor in this event. Moses had power with God because he put God in remembrance of that sacred promise. By doing so, he turned away God's anger. Moses knew that God would keep His promise. **He knew God would keep His promise to protect His own holy name**. Also, He would keep it out of love for Abraham, Isaac and Jacob.

You have just received the answers to two questions.

(1) Why did Moses have power with God?

(2) Under such appalling conditions as we previously studied, why did Moses still have power with God concerning the wicked Israelites?

However, there is yet another incredible revelation to be gleaned from the contents of the last text, Exodus 32:12. For generations Christians, including learned Bible scholars, have been unable to comprehend the true meaning of the words Moses directed toward the Lord in that verse. In ignorance, many Christians refuse to even accept Moses' statement. They insist that Moses' words could not possibly apply to God. However, with the insight into God's covenant with Abraham that you now have, you will soon realize that Moses' words very definitely applied to the Lord.

The words of Moses that I am referring to are found in the last sentence of the following verse. So pay close attention.

Exodus 32:12 (The Amplified Bible.)

*12Why should the Egyptians say, For evil He brought them forth, to slay them in the mountains and consume them from the face of the earth? **Turn from Your fierce wrath**, and change Your mind concerning **this evil** against Your people.*

I repeat, *"Turn from Your fierce wrath, and change Your mind concerning **this evil** against Your people."*

Moses' words sound very harsh for a man to use when addressing the all-righteous God, God Almighty. If one does not comprehend the correct meaning of this particular word, *"evil,"* or the underlying reason behind Moses' statement, one would incorrectly feel that Moses was downright disrespectful. After all, he accused God of planning evil against His people. Moses went so far as to exhort God Almighty to change His mind concerning the evil intentions He had toward the Israelites. I think it will help you if you also read the previous verse from *The Living Bible.*

Exodus 32:12 *(The Living Bible.)*

12*Do you want the Egyptians to say, 'God tricked them into coming to the mountains so that he could slay them, destroying them from off the face of the earth'? Turn back from your fierce wrath. Turn away from this terrible evil you are planning against your people!*

Why did Moses consider the evil God planned against Israel to be so terribly wrong that he dared to rebuke the Lord? We know that the Israelites deserved to die. They had sinned a great sin against God by breaking His commands and worshipping an idol (a golden calf). By the standards of God's own Word, they deserved to be stoned to death. Yet, here was Moses rebuking the Lord for even entertaining the thought of destroying them.

My friend, the reason why the evil that God planned against Israel was not acceptable was because He had made an unbreakable covenant with Abraham. Since Abraham had faithfully performed His role in the covenant, it would have been unthinkable for the Lord to fail to carry out His end of the contract. **The evil that God planned against His people was not in itself wrong. They deserved to die. However, if God had destroyed Israel, He would have been guilty of breaking His solemn oath to His faithful friend, Abraham, and that would have been totally unacceptable. Breaking covenant would have been a different type of evil than the evil God planned against Israel. It would have been morally wrong, and God could not permit Himself to be associated with such unrighteousness.**

You see, God creates physical evil (calamity) to punish the wicked. But moral evil proceeds from men. Albeit, as I said earlier, if God had broken His word to Abraham, His action would also have been morally wrong. You will understand what I just said when you read the following verse in the 1965 edition of *The Amplified Bible.*

Isaiah 45:7 (The Amplified Bible.)

⁷I form the light and create darkness; I make peace [national well-being]. Moral evil proceeds from the will of men, but physical evil proceeds from the will of God], and I create [physical] evil—calamity; I am the Lord who does all these things.

God found Himself between a rock and a hard place. On the one hand, He had the idolatrous, sinful descendants of Abraham who deserved death. On the other hand, He had the binding contract that He had made with their forefathers which Moses insisted that He keep for the sake of His own reputation. Thus, recognizing that two wrongs do not make a right, the righteous Lord of all the earth adhered to Moses' counsel. He humbly changed His mind and attitude. **Because destroying these covenant descendants of Abraham would have been morally wrong, the Lord turned from the evil (calamity) that He had planned against His people.** See this truth for yourself in the following verse.

Exodus 32:14 (The Amplified Bible.)

¹⁴Then the Lord turned from the evil which He had thought to do to His people.

God had purposely bound Himself by the solemn pledge he made with Abraham. He had left Himself no way of escape. Being able to view the past with hindsight enables you to see that fact. It enables you to see that the only way the descendants of Abraham, Isaac and Jacob could have survived God's righteous judgment was because of the unbreakable Abrahamic covenant. Had it not been for God's solemn oath to Abraham and the fact that breaking it would have been morally wrong and would have ruined His own good name, God would have completely destroyed the Jewish nation.

Think about it! If God had broken His promise and had consumed the descendants of Abraham, Isaac and Jacob from the face of the earth, His evil against Israel would have resulted in far reaching severe repercussions.

(1) His reputation would have been ruined.

(2) From then on, no one would have trusted the Word of God.

(3) God would have proved to be an unfaithful friend to righteous Abraham. He would have been known as a covenant breaker.

124

(4) His will and purpose upon the earth would have been frustrated. The devil would have been the victor.

(5) Every nation on earth would have been derogatively affected. The nations' future opportunity for salvation and blessing would have been destroyed along with Abraham's descendants. For, God had promised Abraham "...*in you will all the families and kindred of the earth be blessed....*"

It is evident that God had purposely bound Himself with an unbreakable covenant so that He could not, under any circumstances, destroy the descendants of Abraham, Isaac and Jacob. God's unbreakable contract with Abraham was the tool God used to protect Himself from His own righteous indignation. In His wisdom, God knew that each time He would find Himself between a rock and a hard place, someone like Moses would be there to remind Him of His unbreakable covenant with Abraham, Isaac and Jacob. Thus, for His name's sake, He would be forced to keep His word.

With the added insight you now have, read again the verses that describe God's dilemma and His righteous conclusion to that dilemma. And as you read, notice the role that the Abrahamic covenant played in God changing His mind.

Exodus 32:9-14 (The Amplified Bible.)

9And the Lord said to Moses, I have seen this people, and behold, it is a stiff-necked people;

10Now therefore let Me alone, that My wrath may burn hot against them and that I may destroy them; but I will make of you a great nation.

11But Moses besought the Lord his God, and said, Lord, why does Your wrath burn hot against Your people, whom You have brought forth out of the land of Egypt with great power and a mighty hand?

12Why should the Egyptians say, For evil He brought them forth, to slay them in the mountains and consume them from the face of the earth? Turn from Your fierce wrath, and change Your mind concerning this evil against Your people.

13[Earnestly] remember Abraham, Isaac, and Israel, Your servants, to whom You swore by Your own self and said to them, I will multiply Your seed as the stars of the heavens, and all this land that I have spoken of will I give to Your seed, and they shall inherit it forever.

14Then the Lord turned from the evil which He had thought to do to His people.

What a wonderful righteous God we serve! We serve a God who will keep His promise even when it directly affects and hurts him. He spared this multitude of people who had humiliated him. He spared a people who had broken His heart, a people who were rebellious and disobedient, a people who were grumblers and complainers, evil and corrupt. And He did it in order to keep a promise He had made to a man, to one righteous man. God went on suffering this humiliation and hurt generation after generation for a two-fold reason. **He did it to keep His covenant promise which would eventually benefit all mankind and to protect His holy name**. What a God! What a Savior!

You now know why Moses had power with God. **Moses had power with God, because he put the Lord in remembrance of His sacred unbreakable covenant with Abraham, Isaac and Jacob.**

Chapter 9
Part One

WHY DOES GOD LOVE
THE JEWISH PEOPLE?

God's love for the Jewish people is a known Scriptural fact. Throughout the Bible, the reader is continually informed about God's love for Israel. When speaking of His love for the Israelites, the Lord often comes across like a husband expressing his deep love for and faithfulness and devotion to his wife. At other times, He sounds like a mother doting over her beloved children. Indeed, when one studies God's Word with an open heart, there is no denying God's love for the Jews, the lineal descendants of Abraham, Isaac and Jacob. Furthermore, as you will see in the succeeding verse, **God's love for them will never diminish or fail—it is everlasting.**

> *Jeremiah 31:3 (The Amplified Bible.)*
>
> *3The Lord appeared from of old to me [Israel], saying,*
> ***Yes, I have loved you with an everlasting love;***
> *therefore with loving-kindness have I drawn you and continued My faithfulness to you.*

God's *"everlasting love"* for Israel has many beautiful facets. Each of these facets expresses specific areas of the larger more complex *"everlasting love"* mentioned in Jeremiah 31:3. Included in God's everlasting love are such aspects as loving-kindness, steadfast love, tender mercies and numerous others. Moreover, each of these aspects has its own array of love qualities. Therefore, because God's everlasting love puts forth so many different budding branches, it is important to remember that each facet of God's love is simply an expression of His overall *"everlasting love"* for Israel.

You saw two of the many manifestations of God's *"everlasting love"* for Israel in Jeremiah 31:3. In that verse, God Himself tells Israel, *"...I have loved you with an everlasting love; therefore with loving-kindness have I drawn you and continued my faithfulness to you."* By inserting the conjunctive adverb *"therefore"* in verse three, thus joining the two main clauses, God clearly states that His *"loving-kindness"* and *"faithfulness"* are automatically manifested toward the Israelites as a result of His *"everlasting love"* for them. As I

128

pointed out earlier, loving-kindness is one of the manifold expressions of God's everlasting love.

This word *"loving-kindness"* is an eye opener in itself. According to *Strong's Exhaustive Concordance of the Bible,* "Hebrew and Chaldee Dictionary," the definition of the word *"loving-kindness"* includes: favor, kindness, mercy, and pity.

Another aspect of God's *"everlasting love"* for Israel that shows up frequently in the Scriptures is *"steadfastness"* or *"steadfast love."* The *American Heritage Dictionary, Second College Edition* defines the word steadfast: Fixed or unchanging....Firmly loyal or constant.

In just two word definitions of the many facets of God's *"everlasting love,"* you have been given a glimpse of the enormity and intensity of the amazing *"everlasting love"* that God has for His chosen covenant people. You have seen that God's kindness, favor, mercy and pity toward Israel are absolutely unchanging. They will endure through good times and bad times. They will remain forever. **For, in Jeremiah 31:3, God Himself proclaims that He loves Israel *"with an everlasting love."***

Now you might say, "How can God love these people with an 'everlasting love' when they have been, and in many cases still are, rebellious, hardhearted and sinful? After learning about God's covenant with Abraham, Isaac and Jacob, I finally understand why God has put up with the Jews' sinful behavior all these years. But I will never understand why He continues to love them like He does."

I realize that at this moment, God's *"everlasting love"* for Israel seems to you to be an unfathomable puzzle. But, the only reason why you have difficulty solving that puzzle is because you do not yet have the necessary Biblical facts needed to complete it. However, in a moment, you will be provided with the most crucial piece of that love puzzle. This key puzzle piece will show you exactly why God loves and will continue to love the Jewish people, no matter what.

My friend, you are about to see Scriptural evidence which proves that, like everything else involving God's ceaseless relationship with the Jewish people, **God's unshakable love for them is completely dependent on the covenant He made and established with their forefathers. In the following verse, you will see that God is actually sworn by His solemn covenant oath to love the Israelites with a**

steadfast (fixed, unchanging, firmly loyal) love. And as you know, God never breaks His sacred promises.

Deuteronomy 7:12 (The Amplified Bible.)

*12And if you hearken to these precepts and keep and do them, **the Lord your God will keep with you the covenant and the steadfast love which He swore to your fathers.***

I have kept my promise. I have provided you with the most crucial piece of the love puzzle, **the most crucial piece being God's sworn covenant oath to Abraham, Isaac and Jacob mentioned in the previous verse.** Therefore, since you now comprehend that God's love for Israel is part of His unbreakable sacred covenant with Abraham, Isaac and Jacob, you should have no difficulty fitting together the remaining pieces of the puzzle. So, on that note, I will repeat the portion of Deuteronomy 7:12 that is relevant to the point I just made. Moses told the Israelites, *"...the Lord your God will keep with you **the covenant and the steadfast love which He swore to your fathers."***

There is no way around it. Regardless of the circumstances, God is committed to keeping His solemn covenant which includes loving the Jewish people **forever.** And that, my friend, is why even though they are not always deserving of His love, God continues to extend to them His kindness, favor, mercy, pity and all the other attributes that fall under the heading of His sworn *"everlasting love"* for Israel.

You are now acutely aware of the role that the sacred Abrahamic covenant plays in this matter. Therefore, there should no longer be any doubt in your mind as to why God loves and will continue to love the Jewish people. **God swore to Abraham, Isaac and Jacob that He would love their covenant descendants forever, and God always keeps His sacred promises.** God has proven time and time again that He faithfully keeps His word even to His own hurt.

Earlier, I assured you that once you had the main piece of the love puzzle (meaning, once you had understanding of God's Abrahamic covenant love oath), all the other pieces would quickly fit into place. Well, one of those revealing puzzle pieces is that God's *"everlasting love"* for the Israelites neither has nor ever had anything to do with their being worthy or deserving of that love. For, as you now know, God's boundless love for Israel rests solely upon His binding covenant with Abraham, Isaac and Jacob. God swore that He would love the covenant descendants of Abraham, Isaac, and Jacob (the Israelites) with *"**an everlasting love,"*** and God will perform to the full all that He has promised. And that, my friend, is why despite the Jews' past wicked behavior and in some cases their present rebelliousness and hardheartedness, God still continues to love them with a steadfast (fixed, unchanging firmly loyal or constant) love.

Moses' words in Deuteronomy 7:6-13 will guide you toward even deeper Scriptural insight into God's extraordinary covenant love for Israel. So, stay alert as one by one I connect additional pieces of the picture to this amazing Biblical puzzle.

As you read the following verses, please take note of how closely God's covenant choice and love are tied together. For, I promise you that before you get to the end of this chapter, you will realize how totally linked they are to each other. **God's covenant choice and His everlasting covenant love are inseparable in that they are identified in the Scriptures as being essentially one and the same.**

> *Deuteronomy 7:6-13 (The Amplified Bible.)*
>
> *⁶For you are a holy and set apart people to the Lord your God; **the Lord your God has chosen you** to be a special people to Himself out of all the peoples on the face of the earth.*
>
> *⁷**The Lord did not set His love upon you and choose you** because you were more in number than any other people, for you were the fewest of all people.*

Truly, the prophet Moses shows you in the previous verses that God's covenant love and choice are intrinsically one. In verse six, Moses told the Israelites, "*...the Lord your God has **chosen you**....*" Then, continuing with the same thought, in verse seven, he explained to them that God did not choose them because of their great number.

The truth I want to point out is that in verse seven when Moses again referred to God's choice, he deliberately included God's love. He said, *"**The Lord did not set His love upon you and choose you** because...."* Moses intentionally included God's love because as you now know, God's covenant love was reserved for His chosen people with whom He established His sacred Abrahamic covenant. God's covenant love was automatically bestowed upon Israel along with His covenant choice in order to keep His solemn unbreakable oath to Abraham, Isaac and Jacob. For, Moses said in Deuteronomy 7:12, "*...the Lord your God will keep*

with you __the covenant and the steadfast love which He swore to your__
__fathers__."

Deuteronomy 7:7 contains yet another incredible puzzle piece. So,
pay attention as you read that verse again.

> *7The Lord did not set His love upon you and choose*
> *you because you were more in number than any other*
> *people, __for you were the fewest of all people.__*

Through Moses, God tells His people that He did not set His love
upon them and choose them because of their great number.   He
reminds the Israelites that He chose them and loved them when they
were *"__the fewest of all people.__"*

After reading verse seven, it is only natural that you would want to
know just how and when God did set His love upon and choose the
Israelites.   Therefore, in order that I might share with you the answer to
this query, we will resume our study of the remaining six verses of
Deuteronomy 7:6-13 in part two of this chapter.

You must first understand the truth that Moses relayed in
Deuteronomy 7:7 if you are to obtain the answer to the question, "How
and when did God set His love upon and choose the Israelites?"
However, in order to understand the content of that verse, you must keep
in mind the following reality.   Despite the fact that like Jacob, both
Abraham and Isaac were God's chosen covenant people, neither of them
were Israelites.   On the contrary, their covenant descendant Jacob, who
was the sole founder of the Israelite nation, was the very first Israelite.
You will recall that the nation of Israel was even named after Jacob.

The previous information is extremely important because it forces
you to acknowledge the truth that before Jacob there were no Israelites
for God to love and choose.   __Consequently, God had to have set His__
__everlasting covenant love upon Israel by choosing their forefather__
__Jacob__.   More Scriptural confirmation of the truth that God set His love
upon and chose Israel by choosing Jacob will be provided later in this
chapter.

There are times when every Bible student finds it hard to incorporate
certain pieces of the Scriptural puzzle into the broader Biblical aspect of
things.   For instance, one of those hard to fit segments of the overall
Scriptural picture is the portion which reveals exactly when and where
God chose Jacob.   If, as I did for many years, you try to cram that piece

of the picture into a space where it does not belong, you will inevitably run into problems.

Inaccurately placed pieces of the puzzle will not only detract from your overall view of the beauty of the complete Scriptural picture, but they will also cause you to end up with a surplus of left over, conflicting puzzle pieces that do not fit into any of the remaining spaces.

The end result is that you will have to admit that you have wrongly placed one or more of the puzzle pieces, or go through the rest of your life without ever truly solving that particular Scriptural query. From then on, one Scripture will conflict with another. They will conflict simply because vital pieces have been positioned incorrectly. Worst of all, until those improperly fitted puzzle pieces are removed and inserted in the appropriate spaces, they will continue to hamper your advancement and growth in the knowledge of God's Word and rob you of insight into His overall plan and purpose.

Earlier, I shared with you how in the past, like many other Christians, I had attempted to force into the wrong space a specific piece of the overall Scriptural puzzle. The puzzle piece I am referring to shows exactly when and where God chose Jacob. The wrong space, into which I had insisted on forcefully inserting that information, was Genesis 25:23. You will recall that in the formerly mentioned verse, God informed Rebekah, *"...the elder shall serve the younger."* At that time, I was convinced that Genesis 25:23 revealed the exact moment when God chose Jacob. However, I eventually discovered that my calculation was off by many years.

Let me offer you Scriptural proof as to why my positioning of the puzzle piece mentioned in the former paragraph was incorrect. Through Moses, God told the Israelites in Deuteronomy 7:7 that He did not set His love upon them and choose them because of their great number. **He reminded the Israelites that He loved them and chose them when they were _"the fewest of all people."_** *"The fewest of all people"* was one of the pieces of the puzzle that I was unable to connect. You see, since I had crammed the previously mentioned puzzle piece into the wrong space, the entire picture was thrown out of sync. I was left with a whole pile of puzzle pieces that I could no longer find corresponding places for.

I will now take a moment to explain why Genesis 25:23 cannot accommodate the puzzle piece mentioned in the former paragraph, *"...you were the fewest of all people."* We are told in Genesis 25:21-23 that Jacob and Esau were twins. Consequently, they both shared the same womb. Furthermore, God told their mother, Rebekah, that in her womb were the founders of two entirely different nations.

Now, if Rebekah had carried one child, if the founder of only one nation had been in her womb, then the previously mentioned puzzle piece would not have distorted the picture so completely. However, under such circumstances as the Scriptures describe, how could the founder of Israel, Jacob (one man), have been fewer than the founder of Edom, Esau (one man)? In order for the Israelites to have been the fewest of all people, they had to have been the least in number of all people. Yet, as you can see for yourself, in this instance, Jacob and Esau each totaled one founder of one completely different nation. Outside of the two yet unborn babies, no other Israelite or Edomite existed at that time. So as you can see, **the Scriptures themselves confirm that the Israelites were not the fewest of all people when their founder, Jacob, was still in his mother's womb**. Therefore, God could not have set His love upon and chosen Jacob and consequently Jacob's descendants at that time.

Now, it is obvious that since God is all-knowing, He knew before the twins were even conceived the one to whom He would eventually appear and with whom He would establish His covenant. Yes, our all-knowing God knew that He would eventually establish His covenant with Jacob and consequently Jacob's descendants, the Israelites. However, Moses' statement *"for you were the fewest of all people"* makes it equally obvious that God did not set His covenant love upon and choose Jacob and his seed, the Israelites, at that particular time.

You are about to see in the following verses that when God spoke to Rebekah, He did not even address the issue of His covenant with Abraham and Isaac. God definitely made a prediction in those verses, but He did not make a covenant choice. What I mean by my last statement (God did not make a covenant choice) is that God did not identify the one with whom He would eventually establish His covenant. The fact is that when God spoke to Rebekah in Genesis 25:21-23, His prediction in that case had nothing to do with the Abrahamic covenant. Read the Lord's words to Rebekah for yourself and you will see that what I have said is absolutely factual. You will see that the Abrahamic covenant is not mentioned at all in God's statement.

Genesis 25:21-23 (The Amplified Bible.)

21And Isaac prayed much to the Lord for his wife because she was unable to bear children; and the Lord granted his prayer, and Rebekah his wife became pregnant.

22[Two] children struggled together within her; and she said, If it is so [that the Lord has heard our prayer], why am I like this? And she went to inquire of the Lord.

23The Lord said to her, [The founders of] two nations are in your womb, and the separation of two peoples has begun in your body; the one people shall be stronger than the other, and the elder shall serve the younger.

There is absolutely no mention in the former verses of God's covenant love or God's covenant choice or any of God's covenant promises or God's covenant, period. Rather, in verse twenty-three, God predicted future events that would involve both nations that were in Rebekah's womb (Edom and Israel).

In chapter ten of this book, I will cover in detail the fulfillment of God's prophecy in Genesis 25:23. At that time, you will receive undeniable Scriptural confirmation of the truth that I just shared with you. You will see that the prediction God made in verse twenty-three concerned the God-ordained positions that both of the nations in Rebekah's womb would one day temporarily fill. You will also learn exactly what God's forecast concerning those two nations entailed. However, since I know that your questions on that topic will be answered in the next chapter, I will not at this time divulge any more information on the subject of God's prediction in Genesis 25:23.

The questions that you need to focus your attention on at the present time are these: Since it is now evident that God did not set His love upon and choose Jacob and his descendants when Jacob was in his mother's womb, then just when did God set His love upon Jacob and choose him and his seed? When were the Israelites *"the fewest of all people"*?

The answers to the questions in the former paragraph are provided in the following text in the *Holy Bible, King James Version.* In those verses you will see the exact moment when God set His love upon and chose Jacob and consequently His descendants, the Israelites. For, you will actually read the statement God Himself made when, in order to keep His sworn oath to Abraham and Isaac, He established His sacred covenant with Jacob.

Genesis 28:10-15 (King James Version.)

10And Jacob went out from Beersheba, and went toward Haran.

11And he lighted upon a certain place, and tarried there all night, because the sun was set; and he took of the stones of that place, and put them for his pillows, and lay down in that place to sleep.

12And he dreamed, and behold a ladder set up on the earth, and the top of it reached to heaven: and behold the angels of God ascending and descending on it.

13And, behold, the Lord stood above it, and said, I am the Lord God of Abraham thy father, and the God of Isaac: the land whereon thou liest, to thee will I give it, and to thy seed;

14And thy seed shall be as the dust of the earth, and thou shalt spread abroad to the west, and to the east, and to the north, and to the south: and in thee and in thy seed shall all the families of the earth be blessed.

15And, behold, I am with thee, and will keep thee in all places whither thou goest, and will bring thee again into this land; for I will not leave thee, until I have done that which I have spoken to thee of.

My friend, this was when God established His covenant with Jacob and in so doing set His covenant love upon and chose him and his future descendants, the Israelites. For, as you saw in verses thirteen and fourteen of the previous text, with His own mouth, **God promised to give to Jacob and his future seed, the Israelites, all that He had sworn by covenant to Abraham and Isaac.** And, as Moses later told the Israelites in Deuteronomy 7:12, *"...the Lord your God will keep with you the covenant and the steadfast love which He swore to your fathers."*

By loving and choosing Jacob, God automatically extended His love and choice to his descendants, the Israelites. For, the Israelites were Jacob's future covenant seed that God specifically identified and included in the previous verses, Genesis 28:13-14. They were the beneficiaries of all God's covenant promises, including God's covenant love. Yes, God showed His love for and choice of the whole nation of Israel when He established His covenant with and thus loved and chose the first Israelite (Jacob), the forefather and founder of the Israelite nation. as he traveled to Haran.

136

As you saw in Genesis 28:13-15, when God audibly chose and loved Jacob and his future seed, the Israelites truly were *"the fewest of all people."* For, by that time, Jacob's twin brother, Esau, had a number of wives and children. He had already begun to propagate the predicted nation of Edom. While on the other hand, when God chose Jacob by establishing His Abrahamic covenant with him as he journeyed to Haran, Jacob had no wives and no children. Without a doubt, when God set His love upon Jacob and chose him, the Israelites were indeed *"the fewest of all people."* For, at that time, the only Israelite that existed on the face of the earth was Israel's founder, Jacob.

My friend, you cannot get any fewer than one person. However, though at that time, the Israelites truly were *"the fewest of all people,"* Jacob, their founder, had God's Abrahamic covenant promise that his descendants (the Israelites) would be *"...as [countless as] the dust or sand of the ground...."* **In addition, as God's covenant choice, Jacob and his future descendants, the Israelites, automatically possessed God's sacred Abrahamic covenant promise of *"everlasting love."***

You now understand that God's covenant choice and His sworn *"everlasting love"* for Israel are essentially one and the same. You also know exactly when and where God set His love upon and chose Jacob and his descendants, the Israelites. Moreover, you know when the Israelites were the fewest of all people. God set His love upon and chose Jacob and his future descendants when He established His covenant with Jacob as he traveled to Haran—Genesis 28:13-15. For without a doubt, at that time, the Israelites were indeed the fewest of all people. Furthermore, you know that God established His covenant with Jacob and consequently loved and chose Jacob and his descendants in order to keep His sworn oath to Abraham and Isaac.

It is now time for me to keep my earlier promise and present additional Scriptural confirmation of two former points that I made. The previously mentioned confirmation will encompass:

(1) The truth regarding God setting His love upon and choosing the Israelites through their forefather Jacob.

(2) The fact that God's covenant love and His covenant choice are essentially one and the same.

You are about to see Biblical evidence which proves that God's covenant love and His covenant choice are so intrinsically one that, in

His communication between Himself and the Israelites, God's own words acknowledge the interchangability of those two terms.

In the following text, you will see for yourself in the Scriptures where God specifically addressed the Israelites informing them that by His choosing Jacob over Esau, they, as Jacob's covenant descendants, automatically gained His (God's) promise of *"everlasting love."* **Yes, you will see that God's covenant choice and God's everlasting covenant love are so innately intertwined that when God referred to His covenant choice in the subsequent verses, He actually used the word *"loved"* in the place of the word chose.**

Malachi 1:1-2 (The Amplified Bible.)

*¹THE BURDEN or oracle (the thing to be lifted up) of **the word of the Lord to Israel** by Malachi [My messenger].*

*²**I have loved you**, says the Lord. Yet you say, **How and in what way have You loved us?** Was not Esau Jacob's brother? says the Lord; **yet I loved Jacob (Israel)**,*

I want you to read again the previous verses, plus a segment of verse three, from *The Living Bible*. The reason I am only using a portion of verse three is because I will be covering these same verses in more detail in a later chapter. Therefore, I will share with you only the portion of verse three that is needed to confirm the truth regarding God's love and choice being interchangeable.

Malachi 1:1-3 (The Living Bible.)

*¹Here is **the Lord's message to Israel**, given through the prophet Malachi:*

*²,³"**I have loved you very deeply**," says the Lord. But you retort, "Really? **When was this?**" And the Lord replies, "**I showed my love for you by loving your father, Jacob. I didn't need to. I even rejected his very own brother, Esau....**"*

God rejected Esau by choosing Jacob as he traveled to Haran. However, God did not mention His choosing Jacob. Instead, in verse three, God interchanged the word choosing with the word *"loving."*

The question is, "When and where did God show His love for (that is, set His love upon) the Israelites?" And, the answer to that question is that God chose and showed His love for Israel when He chose and loved their founder, Jacob. God chose and showed His love for Israel when He kept His word to Abraham and Isaac and established His covenant with Jacob as he traveled to Haran—Genesis 28:10-15.

Can it be any clearer? In Malachi 1:1-3, the Israelites asked God, "How and when did You love us?" In answer to their question, God pointed them to the moment when He had previously made known His covenant choice, the moment when He had established His Abrahamic covenant with Jacob. God replied, "I showed My love for you by loving (that is, by choosing) your forefather, Jacob, over Esau." He then emphasized the fact that He did not have to love Jacob (that is, He did not have to choose Jacob), but He did. And when He did, He inevitably made them, as Jacob's descendants, the recipients of His covenant love.

My friend, you now know that the exact moment when God set His love upon and chose the Israelites was when, in Genesis 28:13-14, He established His Abrahamic covenant with the first Israelite, Jacob, the founder of the nation of Israel.

You also comprehend the Biblical fact that God's covenant choice and His everlasting covenant love are an intrinsic, inseparable part of each other . So, based on that same Biblical premise, let us briefly trace God's promise of everlasting covenant love from its original source all the way to the Israelite nation.

God made and established His covenant with His chosen vessel, Abraham. And as you now know, when God made Abraham His covenant choice, Abraham automatically became the recipient of God's everlasting covenant love (that is, God set His love upon Him).

The second in line to inherit God's sworn *"everlasting love"* was Abraham's son, Isaac. You saw in chapter one of this work that God kept His promise to Abraham and thus established His Abrahamic covenant with and thereby set His sworn *"everlasting love"* upon Isaac.

Now, Ishmael was also Abraham's son. Yet, as you saw earlier in the series, the Scriptures make it crystal clear that Ishmael was not God's covenant choice. Therefore, God did not set His everlasting covenant love upon Ishmael. Nor did God set His covenant love upon Ishmael's descendants.

Next, we have Jacob whose covenant call we have just covered. Though Jacob and Esau were twin brothers, God chose to establish His covenant with and thus set His covenant love upon only one of them. God chose (that is, God set His covenant love upon) Jacob, the founder of the Israelite nation as he traveled to Haran—Genesis 28:13-14.

In choosing (that is, in loving) Jacob, his descendants, the Israelites, became the automatic beneficiaries of God's everlasting covenant choice and love. For, through them, God intended to promote the sacred covenant which He had made with Abraham, Isaac and Jacob.

As you will learn before this series is over, God's *"everlasting love"* for Israel will continue to be extremely instrumental in the fulfillment of the binding covenant that God made with Abraham and the completion of God's purpose for mankind as a whole.

You now possess the answer to the question, "Why Does God Love The Jewish People?" **You know that in order to carry out His own purpose on the earth, God swore by oath that He would love forever the lineal descendants of Abraham, Isaac and Jacob. And God cannot and will not ever break His sacred binding oath.**

Chapter 9
Part Two

WHY DOES GOD LOVE
THE JEWISH PEOPLE?

In chapter nine, part one, you received the answer to the question, "Why Does God Love The Jewish People?" You saw in the Scriptures that God's love for the Jewish people neither had nor has anything to do with any bad or good works that they have done. Rather, God's love for the Jewish people rests solely on the covenant and steadfast love that He swore to their forefathers. God promised to love the Jewish people forever, and God will keep His legally binding oath even to His own hurt.

With the previous question answered and with the added insight into God's *"everlasting love"* that you now possess, you should find the remaining verses of Deuteronomy 7:6-13 quite enlightening. You will recall that we studied the first two verses and part of verse eight of this text in chapter nine, part one of this work. Therefore, to refresh your memory, I have again included those verses in the following reference.

> *Deuteronomy 7:6-13 (The Amplified Bible.)*
>
> *⁶For you are a holy and set-apart people to the Lord your God; the Lord your God has chosen you to be a special people to Himself out of all the peoples on the face of the earth.*
>
> *⁷The Lord did not set His love upon you and choose you because you were more in number than any other people, for you were the fewest of all people.*
>
> *⁸But because the Lord loves you and because He would keep the oath which He had sworn to your fathers, the Lord has brought you out with a mighty hand and redeemed you out of the house of bondage, from the hand of Pharaoh king of Egypt.*

In verses six and seven, Moses told the Israelites that the Lord did not love them and choose them because they were numerically attractive. On the contrary, God loved them when they were *"...the fewest of all people."* You now know when, where and why God loved and chose the Israelites. You also know when they were *"the fewest of all people."* All the previously mentioned queries were covered and fully explained in chapter nine, part one of this series.

In verse eight, Moses informed the Israelites that it was because God loved them and because He would keep the promises He made to their forefathers that the Lord brought them out of Egypt with a mighty hand and redeemed them from out of the house of bondage, from the hand of Pharaoh. Remember that when Moses spoke these words, Jacob and his descendants, the Israelites, had already been chosen. Consequently, they possessed God's everlasting love before He delivered them from Egypt. Thus, Moses could boldly state that it was because God loved them and because He would keep His oath to Abraham, Isaac and Jacob that God brought them out of the bondage of Egypt.

As you read verse nine, notice again how inseparable are the Abrahamic covenant and God's steadfast love and mercy.

> *9Know, recognize, and understand therefore that the Lord your God, **He is God, the faithful God, <u>Who keeps covenant and steadfast love and mercy</u>** with those who love Him and keep His commandments, to a thousand generations,*

In verse nine, Moses instructed the covenant descendants of Abraham, Isaac and Jacob to consider the faithfulness of the God they served. He reminded them that their forefathers fulfilled their part of the sacred Abrahamic covenant by obeying God's commands. As a result of their forefathers' obedience to God's commands, God was able to keep His promises to their forefathers and they (the Israelites) were the proof that God kept and continues to keep His solemn word.

In verse ten, Moses went on to inform the Israelites that when men hate God and show their hatred by breaking covenant with Him and disobeying His commands, it is then a different story. God will not put up with deliberate disobedience. He will eventually destroy those who disobey His commands and refuse to repent (that is, those who refuse to change their mind, attitude and conduct and align their lives with God's Word). Had Abraham disobeyed God's commands, God would not have kept with him His covenant and *"steadfast love"* which was eventually extended to the Israelites through Isaac and Jacob. Abraham's obedience was crucial to the advancement and fulfillment of the covenant God made with him.

10And repays those who hate Him to their face, by destroying them; He will not be slack to him who hates Him, but will requite him to his face

After warning the Israelites of the punishment that awaited them if they disobeyed God's commands, Moses told the Israelites that their compliance with God's commands would ensure that God would keep with them the covenant and steadfast love promised to their forefathers. The condition God stipulated was absolutely fair, since at Horeb (or Sinai) they had, of their own volition, entered into a blood covenant between themselves and God. The Israelites' role in that solemn agreement was to keep their promise and obey all God's commands. So, it was not unreasonable for God to insist that they keep their word and obey His commandments.

By now, you are probably aware that whenever I interject additional information into an existing topic (in this case, the Horeb covenant), I have good reason for doing so. In this instance, my aim is to equip you with the knowledge you need to more fully comprehend the following verses. I want you to understand that when God instructed the Israelites to obey His commands, He was actually instructing them to keep the covenant (that is, the agreement) that they themselves had made with Him at Horeb. I also want you to understand that the blessings listed in verse thirteen are partly the result of both the previously mentioned covenants (that is, part of them belong to the Abrahamic covenant, and the rest belong to the Horeb covenant). As you read the following verses, it will soon become apparent to you why I felt the necessity to insert the previous information concerning the Horeb covenant.

11You shall therefore keep and do the instruction, laws, and precepts which I command you this day.

12And if you hearken to these precepts and keep and do them, the Lord your God will keep with you the covenant and the steadfast love which He swore to your fathers.

13And He will love you, bless you, and multiply you; He will also bless the fruit of your body and the fruit of your land, your grain, your new wine, and your oil, the increase of your cattle and the young of your flock in the land which He swore to your fathers to give you.

So that you can quickly grasp the point that I am making, I will take a moment to divide God's blessings in verse thirteen into two separate groups. Those blessings that come under the heading of the Abrahamic covenant are God's promise to love and multiply the covenant descendants of Abraham Isaac and Jacob and to give them the land of Canaan as an everlasting inheritance. The blessings that fall under the heading of the Horeb covenant are God's promise of abundant harvests and an increase of livestock in the Land of Promise. The Horeb blessings are for the purpose of equipping the Israelites with everything they need to help God carry out His promises to their forefathers.

The Scriptures reveal that God carefully chooses the most advantageous, most excellent blessings for the Israelites. Yes, God makes sure that His chosen covenant people receive the very best. There are a number of reasons why God is so generous with the Israelites. And, of course, one of those reasons is because He loves them with an *"everlasting love."* I chose to read the next text from *The Living Bible* because the translators of that version do an excellent job of communicating the truth I just mentioned.

> Psalm 47:4 *(The Living Bible.)*
>
> [4]*and will personally select his choicest blessings for his Jewish people—the very best for those he loves.*

It should now be obvious to you why the Jews, as a whole, are so prosperous. They are prosperous because God selects the very best for them. And, God selects the best for them, because He loves them with an everlasting love. However, God has an underlying objective for selecting the choicest blessings for His covenant people. Let me explain. The wealth God did and does allow His chosen people to accumulate is given to them for a specific purpose. God gives the Israelites power to get wealth so that He might through them promote the covenant which He swore to their forefathers, Abraham, Isaac and Jacob. See this for yourself in the following verses.

> Deuteronomy 8:17-18 *(The Amplified Bible.)*
>
> [17]*And beware lest you say in your [mind and] heart, My power and the might of my hand have gotten me this wealth.*
>
> [18]*But you shall [earnestly] remember the Lord your God, for it is He Who gives you power to get wealth, that He may establish His covenant which He swore to your fathers, as it is this day.*

Everything that God gives to Israel, even Israel's power to get wealth, He gives in order to promote His covenant which He swore to Abraham. Isaac and Jacob.

The information you just received regarding God's everlasting love for Israel and the blessings that God's love entails is probably already whirling in your mind. Numerous questions are no doubt forming to which you desire immediate answers. **You may be wondering why, since God loves the Jews with an everlasting love, He has, at intermittent periods throughout history, allowed them to be subjected to great suffering. You may also be wondering why God has at times permitted His beloved people to be persecuted and abhorrently abused by the gentile nations.**

In the next portion of this chapter, I will answer the questions that are contained in the former paragraph. As I do, you will again realize why earlier I found it necessary to interject information into the present topic that pertains to the Horeb covenant (that is, information that pertains to the Israelites solemn promise to obey all God's commands). The commands the Israelites promised by covenant to obey at Horeb (or Sinai) were given to them by God. However, because God's laws were delivered to them by Moses, they became known as "the Law of Moses, Moses' Law" or "the Law."

Chapters twenty-seven and twenty-eight of the book of Deuteronomy provide a more detailed account of the blessings God promised to Israel if she kept her part of the Horeb agreement and obeyed His commands. However, contained in that same portion of Scripture is a list of curses, curses which the Lord warned would come upon Israel if she refused to keep the Horeb covenant and disobeyed His laws.

If you take time to read the previously mentioned chapters in Deuteronomy, you will immediately recognize why, throughout history, Israel's suffering has been so frequent and intense and why periodically the nations have been allowed to temporarily persecute, abuse and conquer God's chosen nation.

The bottom line is that though there are exceptions to this rule, exceptions which you will learn about later in this series, much of Israel's suffering has been the consequence of her own sinful behavior. During such periods of deserved punishment, Israel actually experienced the horrors of the curses that God foretold would come upon her if she broke the covenant that she made with Him at Horeb and disobeyed His laws.

My friend, it makes sense that the Israelites could not have experienced God's blessings and curses at the same time. To have done so would have been impossible, since the curses automatically counteract the blessings. No, the Israelites could not have experienced God's blessings and curses at the same time. Israel either dwelt contentedly on the Promised Land in the spiritual and temporal peace and prosperity that comes through internal and external righteousness, or she temporarily became spiritually and materially impoverished, and was persecuted, and laid waste by the nations.

By her own actions, Israel herself chose blessings or curses. If she chose to keep her agreement with God and obey His commands, she experienced the promised Horeb covenant blessings and enabled God to keep with her the covenant and steadfast love which He swore to her forefathers. If she chose to break the Horeb contract and to sin against God by breaking His commands and refusing to repent, she experienced the foretold Horeb curses. Thus, if her choice was the latter, the curses inevitably nullified the Horeb blessings. The curses also temporarily restrained God from promoting His Abrahamic covenant and from publicly demonstrating His *"steadfast love"* toward Israel via the choicest blessings mentioned in *The Living Bible*, Psalm 47:4.

The conditions stipulated in the Horeb covenant served a two-fold purpose. They provided God with an avenue to discipline His beloved people when they broke their agreement and deliberately and habitually sinned. They also gave God the right to **temporarily** drive the Israelites off the land that He promised would remain theirs forever.

However, the severe effects of the prophesied curses that followed such sinful episodes did not mean that God no longer loved the descendants of Abraham, Isaac and Jacob. Nor did those effects mean that God had backed out of His unbreakable promises to their forefathers concerning the Israelites. God's covenant and His promise of *"everlasting love"* are to the descendants of Abraham, Isaac and Jacob as a whole. They are not dependent on one particular generation or individual. Therefore, when a specific generation of Israelites chose to break the covenant they had made with God at Horeb, their sinful, unrepentant actions did not automatically exclude succeeding generations of Israelites from obtaining the promises of the Abrahamic covenant or the blessings of the Horeb covenant.

It is true that when a certain generation of Israelites broke the Horeb covenant, committed the sin of idolatry and refused to repent, they forfeited the Horeb blessings. They also temporarily restrained God from visibly keeping with them the Abrahamic covenant and from showing obvious evidence of His steadfast love and mercy which He swore to their forefathers. However, under such circumstances as I have just described, God patiently waited until a more receptive future generation of Jews came along. Once He found a receptive generation, He faithfully resumed pouring out the Horeb blessings. He also kept with that generation the Abrahamic covenant and again visibly demonstrated the steadfast love and mercy which He swore to Abraham, Isaac and Jacob.

An example of what I just said can be seen in God's dealings with the Israelites during their wilderness experience. You will remember that those who came out of Egypt committed great sin, including the sin of idolatry. Therefore, they did not get to enjoy either the blessings of the Horeb covenant or the promises and blessings of the Abrahamic covenant. For instance, they did not get to enter into or to profit by the prosperity of the Promised Land. However, another generation of Israelites (their own children) did get to enjoy the fruit of the Abrahamic covenant promises and visibly experience God's steadfast love and mercy. They also reaped all the blessings of the covenant that their fathers had made with God at Horeb.

God promised to love the descendants of Abraham, Isaac and Jacob with an *"everlasting love."* But that did not include His blessing those descendants who broke covenant with Him, committed sin and afterwards refused to repent. When the Jews refused to abide by the covenant they made with God at Horeb, they themselves tied God's hands and prevented Him from visibly demonstrating His everlasting love through His promised blessings. For, as you know, God cannot reward sinful behavior. You yourself saw earlier in Deuteronomy 7:10 how Moses clearly told the Israelites that God *"repays those who hate Him to their face, by destroying them; He will not be slack to him who hates Him, but will requite him to his face."*

Maybe this next scenario will help you to understand how it all works. It will show you how God's everlasting love for Israel remains the same through good times and bad. Imagine a man standing on the edge of a cliff. As long as he recognizes the law of gravity and is careful, he will remain safe. If he leans too far forward, the law of gravity will cause him to lose his footing and fall to his death. He will not fall because gravity changed. No! He will fall because he broke the rule regarding safety and the law of gravity prevailed.

So it is with God's *"everlasting love"* for Israel. When the Israelites kept the Horeb agreement and obeyed God's laws, they remained safe in God's covenant love and reaped all the benefits of both the Horeb and

Abrahamic covenants. When they refused to obey God's commands and committed the sin of idolatry, they removed themselves from both the Horeb blessings and the protection of God's Abrahamic covenant love. Thus, they were destroyed (cursed). However, in such cases, God's *"everlasting love"* for Israel did not change. God's love remained the same. The Israelites simply failed to abide by the rules that pertain to God's covenant love.

My friend, you now have the answer as to why, though God loves the Jews with an everlasting love, throughout history when they sinned greatly, He intermittently allowed them to be subjected to severe suffering. And, you know why He periodically permitted His beloved people to be persecuted, abused and **temporarily** conquered by Gentile nations. You now know that they suffered such hardships because of the foretold Horeb curses, curses which were poured out upon them as a consequence of their own sinful behavior. **However, you also know that during those periods of chastisement, God never stopped loving His chosen people. For, God swore to their forefathers that He would love Israel with an everlasting love, and God will keep His sacred promise even to His own hurt.**

God's faithfulness to the Abrahamic covenant, including His promise of *"everlasting love,"* never did nor ever will change. No matter what Israel is or what she does, God's love remains the same. To give you an idea of just how complete God's love toward Israel is and how faithful He is to the promises He made to Abraham, Isaac and Jacob, I want to share with you a very revealing verse of Scripture.

As you read God's words spoken by the prophet Hosea, consider the faithfulness of the God you serve. Consider the fact that though God hates the sins that the Israelites periodically commit against Him, especially the sin of idolatry, He still faithfully demonstrates His devoted *"everlasting love"* toward them and with *"loving-kindness"* draws them to Himself.

Hosea 3:1 (The Amplified Bible.)

*[1]THEN SAID the Lord to me, Go again, love [the same] woman [Gomer] who is beloved of a paramour and is an adulteress, **even as the Lord loves the children of Israel, though they turn to other Gods and love cakes of raisins [used in the sacrificial feasts in idol worship].***

I ask you, does God's Word in the previous verse even insinuate that God stops loving the Israelites when they reject Him and commit horrendous sins against Him, even the sin of idolatry? No! It does not! Rather, it proves the opposite. It proves that God's love for Israel is truly steadfast (that is, God's love for Israel is truly "...fixed or unchanging...firmly loyal or constant...." *(The American Heritage Dictionary, Second College Edition.)* It proves that God's love for His chosen people is not dependent upon anything they do or fail to do. God swore that He would love Israel forever, and God remains faithful to His word. For His own name's sake, His love for Israel cannot and must not waver.

If you are wondering why God would purposely and knowingly bind Himself to the Abrahamic contract, a contract from which He would find no permanent relief or escape, a contract that would subject Him to continual anguish, pain, humiliation and embarrassment, then give careful consideration to the following explanation.

(1) If the righteous God of Abraham, Isaac and Jacob had not bound Himself to an unbreakable contract with Israel's forefathers, He could never have restrained Himself from completely destroying the nation of Israel for her idolatrous sins. Proof of that fact can be seen in one of the incidents that you studied earlier in this series. I am referring to the time when Moses managed to change God's plan to destroy the Israelites from off the face of the earth by reminding Him of His legally binding agreement with Abraham, Isaac, and Jacob.

(2) If our uncompromisingly righteous God had not sworn His *"everlasting love"* for Israel, He could never have continued to extend to the Israelites His forgiveness, mercy, pity and favor each time they broke the Horeb agreement and committed idolatry.

(3) If our holy God had not bound Himself by an unbreakable everlasting contract to love Israel forever, He would not have been able to suffer the humiliation and embarrassment of having to repeatedly take back His unfaithful, adulterous wife (Israel).

(4) If God had not fettered Himself to the legally binding Abrahamic covenant, His plan for all mankind could never have become a reality. For, as you now know, God's plan was to bless (that is, to save) all the nations of the earth through Abraham, Isaac, Jacob and Jacob's covenant descendants, the Israelites.

To bring the previous truth closer to home, I will add one more sentence. If God had not willingly and knowingly bound Himself to the unbreakable Abrahamic covenant, then gentile, you and I would never have had an opportunity to be saved from sin.

Later in the series, I will be covering much of the previous information in greater detail. However, until then, I am sure that the preceding brief explanation will temporarily suffice and will provide you with food for thought as you continue the present study concerning God's *"everlasting love"* for Israel.

With the previous information fresh in your mind, let us read again our main text. As you do, carefully weigh its content in the light of the knowledge that you now possess.

Jeremiah 31:3 (The Amplified Bible.)

3 The Lord appeared from of old to me [Israel], saying, Yes, I have loved you with an everlasting love; therefore with loving-kindness have I drawn you and have continued My faithfulness to you.

You now have insight into God's loving-kindness. But, what about the other aspect of God's everlasting love that is mentioned in the previous verse? What about **God's *"faithfulness"***? For a moment, let us consider this wondrous quality called *"faithfulness,"* and let us learn how it applies to Israel. For, then you will understand that when God speaks of His *"faithfulness"* in the context of Jeremiah 31:3, He is referring to His unswerving loyalty to the covenant and steadfast love which He swore to Abraham, Isaac and Jacob. He is referring to His faithfulness to His promise to extend loving-kindness to their covenant descendants, the Israelites. Yes, He is referring to His faithfulness in keeping His solemn oath.

It is because the Israelites know that God will remain faithful to all that He promised to their forefathers that they confidently believe that when they repent, God will forgive their sins. Yes, they have faith that God will extend to them His promised loving-kindness (that is, His favor, mercy and pity). They also believe that, under the previous conditions (repentance), God will move on their behalf even though they do not deserve His help or mercy. They are aware that God has bound Himself with His own unbreakable sacred oath, and He will thus keep His promise even to His own hurt. **For instance, in the following** verses, **King David implores God to have mercy upon him and to blot out his sins according to His** *"steadfast love,"* **His** *"mercy"* **and His** *"loving-kindness."*

> *Psalm 51:1-2 (The Amplified Bible.)*
>
> [1] *HAVE MERCY upon me, O God, according to Your steadfast love; according to the multitude of Your tender mercy and loving-kindness blot out my transgressions.*
> [2] *Wash me thoroughly [and repeatedly] from my iniquity and guilt and cleanse me and make me wholly pure from my sin!"*

Those same verses in the *Holy Bible, King James* translation read as such:

> [1] *HAVE mercy upon me, O God, according to Thy loving-kindness: according unto the multitude of Thy tender mercies blot out my transgressions.*
> [2] *Wash me thoroughly from mine iniquity, and cleanse me from my sin.*

My friend, do you now understand why, throughout the Psalms, David, when imploring God to forgive His sins, continually employs such terms as *"loving-kindness, mercy, tender mercies,"* and so on. The fact is that whenever David uses such words, he is simply reminding God of His obligation to keep His covenant promises to Abraham, Isaac and Jacob. He is requesting that God extend to him, as a lineal descendant of Jacob, His *"steadfast love"* and therefore show him the promised favor, mercy and pity.

David understood the Abrahamic covenant loving-kindness of the Lord. Therefore, like Moses, he knew the God-ordained buttons he must press in order to get his prayers answered. Whether his need entailed forgiveness, deliverance from his enemies, vindication, or any other legitimate crisis, David knew that as a lineal descendant of Abraham, Isaac and Jacob, the key to getting his prayers heard and answered was to put God in remembrance of His sacred oath to his forefathers. For then, God had no other choice but to act.

God was compelled to keep His word to David's forefathers and consequently to extend to David His *"everlasting love"* which includes *"loving-kindness"* (that is, *"kindness, favor, tender mercies and pity"*). You see. David. like all other lineal descendants of Abraham, Isaac and

Jacob, was a recipient of the numerous benefits God promised to his forefathers. And, as you now know, those benefits include God's sworn *"everlasting love"* and everything that the Abrahamic covenant love entails. David's next words confirm all that I have just said.

Psalm 25:6-7 (The Amplified Bible.)

^6*Remember, O Lord, Your tender mercy and loving-kindness; for they have been ever from of old.*

^7*Remember not the sins (the lapses, and frailties) of my youth or my transgressions; according to Your mercy and stead-fast love remember me, for Your goodness' sake, O Lord.*

David knew exactly what he had to do in order to force God to move on his behalf. You just saw a good example of David's prayer skills in verse six. In that verse, he reminded God of the sacred covenant oath He made to his forefathers. And, despite David's past sins, as a covenant descendant of Abraham, Isaac and Jacob, he still expected God to faithfully keep that promise and to extend to him the needed facets of His *"everlasting love"* (that is, the promised *"loving-kindness, favor, tender mercies and pity"* and so forth).

David never asked God to deal with him according to what he deserved. David was too wise to make such a stupid request. He was completely aware that he did not in any way deserve God's *"favor, mercy and pity."* Therefore, David asked God to deal with him according to the promised *"loving-kindness"* which He swore to his forefathers.

Psalm 119:124 (The Amplified Bible.)

^124*Deal with Your servant according to Your mercy and loving-kindness, and teach me Your statutes.*

You have just seen how David, a covenant descendant of Abraham, Isaac, and Jacob, reminded God to exercise His sworn loving-kindness on his behalf. You will now see an example of how David used that same method of prayer when requesting deliverance from his enemies. As you read, notice again how, like every other Israelite, David is totally dependent on God's faithfulness to His unbreakable Abrahamic covenant promises.

Psalm 69:13-16 (The Amplified Bible.)

¹³*But as for me, my prayer is to You, O Lord. At an acceptable and opportune time, <u>**O God, in the multitude of your mercy and the abundance of your loving-kindness hear me, and in the truth and faithfulness of your salvation answer me.**</u>*

¹⁴*Rescue me out of the mire, and let me not sink; let me be delivered from those who hate me and from out of the deep waters.*

¹⁵*Let not the flood waters overflow and overwhelm me, neither let the deep swallow me up nor the [dug] pit [with water perhaps in the bottom] close its mouth over me.*

¹⁶<u>***Hear and answer me, O Lord, for your loving-kindness is sweet and comforting; according to your plenteous tender mercy and steadfast love turn to me.***</u>

With the added insight into God's unbreakable Abrahamic covenant and steadfast love that you now have, can you finally understand the confidence with which David prayed? David knew that God would confirm His *"everlasting love"* toward him since God was sworn by His own solemn oath to do so. Therefore, in the following verse, with complete optimism and assurance, David boasts of God's faithfulness to dispatch His promised loving-kindness.

Psalm 42:8 (The Amplified Bible.)

⁸<u>*Yet the Lord will command His loving-kindness*</u> *in the daytime, and in the night His song shall be with me, a prayer to the God of my life.*

You may ask, "But where will God command His promised *'loving-kindness'* to go?" Let me answer your question by showing you an actual instance in the Bible where David, as a covenant, lineal descendant of Abraham, Isaac and Jacob, rightfully prayed that God would cause His *"loving-kindness"* to come <u>to him.</u>

Psalm 119:41 (The Amplified Bible.)

⁴¹*Let Your mercy and loving-kindness come also <u>to me,</u> O Lord, even Your salvation according to Your promise;*

Psalm 119:76-77 (The Amplified Bible.)

⁷⁶Let, I pray You, Your merciful kindness and steadfast love be for my comfort, according to Your promise to Your servant.

⁷⁷Let Your tender mercy and loving-kindness come to me that I may live, for Your law is my delight!

Does it now make sense to you why David liked to sing about God's *"loving-kindness"* (that is, God's *"kindness, favor, mercy and pity"*)? Does it also make sense why he liked to sing about God's *"faithfulness"*? David liked to extol God's loving-kindness and God's faithfulness to the covenant He made with Abraham, Isaac and Jacob because those promises are the lifeline of the Jewish people, and David was a Jew. Look what David sang in Psalm 92:1-2 in *The Modern Language Bible.*

Psalm 92:1-2 (The Modern Language Bible.)

¹IT IS good to give thanks to the Lord, to sing praises to Thy name, O Most High,

²To proclaim Thy loving-kindness in the morning and Thy faithfulness into the night.

Everything in David's life revolved around God's unbreakable covenant and the binding promise of *"everlasting love"* that God had made to his forefathers. As you saw earlier in Psalm 69:13, even the right to have his prayers heard by God involved David's reliance on God's promised *"everlasting love"* and all its many beautiful facets. See this truth again in the following text taken from the *Holy Bible, King James* translation.

Psalm 119:149 (King James Version.)

¹⁴⁹Hear my voice according unto thy loving-kindness: O Lord, quicken me according to thy judgment.

As you will see in the next verses, **David depended on God's "faithfulness" in continuing to pour out His promised "loving-kindness" even to the extent of His very life and health.** We will read again from the *Holy Bible, King James Version.*

Psalm 119:159 (King James Version.)

¹⁵⁹Consider how I love thy precepts: quicken me, O Lord, according to thy loving-kindness.

Let us check out a few more of David's prayers which confirm the truth you learned in the previous verse. In the following three texts, **we have David asking God to preserve his life because of God's promised** *"steadfast love."*

Psalm 119:88 *(The Amplified Bible.)*

88 **According to Your steadfast love give life to me;** *then I will keep the testimony of Your mouth [hearing, receiving, loving and obeying it].*

Psalm 119:116 *(The Amplified Bible.)*

116 **Uphold me according to Your promise, that I may live;** *and let me not be put to shame in my hope!*

Psalm 119:154 *(The Amplified Bible.)*

154 **Plead my cause and redeem me; revive me and give me life according to Your word.**

In the succeeding text, the Psalmist sought to help his Jewish brethren understand the greatness, importance and beauty of God's mercy and loving-kindness that endures forever. He devoted Psalm 107 to that end. Then, in the last verse of that same Psalm, he assured his Jewish brethren that if they were wise and would observe all that he had shared with them in his Psalm, they too would gain understanding of the mercy and loving-kindness of the Lord.

Psalm 107:43 *(King James Version.)*

43 *Whoso is wise, and will observe these things, even they shall understand the loving-kindness of the Lord.*

Upon receiving the Psalmist's previous inspired instruction, it is no wonder that when Old Testament Jewish men worshipped in the temple of God, they meditated intently on God's *"loving-kindness."* For they knew beyond doubt that God would faithfully keep His solemn covenant pledge to their forefathers. Yes, they knew that, for the sake of His sacred oath, God would encompass the descendants of Abraham, Isaac and Jacob with *"favor, mercy and pity."* Look with me in the *Holy Bible, King James* translation. There you will read how, when they worshipped in the temple, David and those with him meditated on **God's everlasting** *"loving-kindness"* **toward the Jewish nation.**

Psalm 48:9 (King James Version.)

⁹We have thought of thy loving-kindness, O God, in the midst of thy temple.

Of course, righteous Old Testament believers were well aware that if the Israelites were to really comprehend the loving-kindness that God promised to Abraham, Isaac and Jacob, they had to do more than just meditate on it. **Yes, they knew that before they could fully understand and experience the visible evidence of God's Abrahamic *"loving-kindness,"* they must do as Moses instructed in Deuteronomy 7:11-12. They must keep the covenant that they themselves had made with God at Horeb and observe all that God commanded.**

In the following verse, David describes the kind of life the Israelites could expect to live if they faithfully kept the Horeb covenant and obeyed God's commands. It would be a life in which God's Abrahamic *"steadfast love"* would be fully realized.

Psalm 25:10 (The Amplified Bible.)

¹⁰All the paths of the Lord are mercy and steadfast love, even truth and faithfulness are they <u>for those who keep His covenant and His testimonies.</u>

Throughout the Bible, the Jewish people relied on God's promised *"everlasting love"* and all its facets for their spiritual and literal survival. Each time they found themselves in difficult circumstances, even when their trouble was the result of their own sins, they eventually cried out to God, begging Him to remember His promised *"loving-kindness."* And of course, God always came to their rescue.

An example of the Jews' dependence upon God's promised *"loving-kindness"* is evident in the Biblical records of their captivity in Babylon. You will recall that God sent His people into exile in Babylon as punishment for their abominable sins. The curse that Moses had foretold in Deuteronomy 11:26-28 fell upon Israel and it temporarily overshadowed the blessings of the Horeb covenant as well as the visible expression of God's promised everlasting Abrahamic covenant love.

However, when the prophesied seventy years of punishment and exile was completed, the prophet Daniel interceded in prayer on Israel's behalf. He beseeched the Lord to keep His promise of *"mercy"* and *"loving-kindness"* and thus faithfully extend forgiveness and deliverance toward the covenant descendants of Abraham. Isaac and

Jacob. Daniel made it clear that he was not presenting his petition because he felt that they deserved God's help but rather because of God's binding covenant oath to their forefathers.

My friend, in the following verses you will see the secret of Daniel's power with God. Yes, you will see why God heard and answered the intercessory prayer of His servant Daniel. You will realize that God heard and answered Daniel's prayers in order to keep His covenant and steadfast love which He swore to Abraham, Isaac and Jacob.

> *Daniel 9:18-19 (The Amplified Bible.)*
>
> *18O my God, incline Your ear and hear; open Your eyes and look at our desolations and the city which is called by Your name; for we do not present our supplications before You for our own righteousness and justice, but for Your great mercy and loving-kindness.*
>
> *19O Lord, hear! O Lord, forgive! O Lord, give heed and act! Do not delay, for Your own sake, O my God, because Your city and Your people are called by Your name.*

God keeping His word to Abraham, Isaac and Jacob is so important to Him that He put His faithfulness to His word even above His own name. For generations, God allowed His name (His reputation) to be profaned and dragged through the mud in order to keep His promises to Abraham, Isaac and Jacob. When the Israelites deserved to be destroyed for their sin, God put His word to their forefathers before His own emotions and had mercy on them.

> *Psalm 138:2-4 (The Amplified Bible.)*
>
> *2I will worship toward Your holy temple and praise Your name for Your loving-kindness and for Your truth and faithfulness; for You have exalted above all else Your name and Your word and You have magnified Your word above all Your name!*
>
> *3In the day when I called, You answered me; and You strengthened me with strength (might and inflexibility to temptation) in my inner self.*
>
> *4All the kings of the land shall give You credit and praise You, O Lord, for they have heard of the promises of Your mouth [which were fulfilled].*

Verse four of the previous text speaks of all the kings of the earth giving God credit for keeping His promises. However, the Scriptures go a step further. They actually identify a particular ruler who did recognize that God had kept His covenant promises to Israel regarding His *"steadfast love."* That ruler was the queen of Sheba. **While visiting King Solomon, the queen told him that it was because of God's *"everlasting love"* for the Israelites that God had blessed them with such a wise king.**

I Kings 10:9 (The Amplified Bible.)

*⁹Blessed be the Lord your God, Who delighted in you and set you on the throne of Israel! **Because the Lord loved Israel forever, He made you king to execute justice and righteousness.***

As David said in Psalm 138:4, *"All the kings of the land shall give You credit and praise You, O Lord, **for they have heard of the promises of Your mouth [which were fulfilled].***"

Let all the kings and the people of the earth praise the Lord! Let rulers and their subjects recognize that God Almighty is uncompromisingly righteous in character. He is a God of integrity and *"faithfulness."* Let all the earth proclaim their confidence and trust in the word of the Lord. For, despite the number of times that the Israelites deeply hurt and angered Him, God still kept with them the covenant and steadfast love which He swore to Abraham, Isaac and Jacob. Yes, God placed keeping His word, and thus pouring out His *"mercy"* and *"loving-kindness"* upon their descendants, even above His own name. And because God was so faithful, King David could sing His praises with conviction, and so can we.

From now on, when you read David's songs applauding God for His *"mercy"* and *"loving-kindness"* that endure forever, you will know exactly what David is referring to. **Yes, you will know that he is speaking of the everlasting covenant love that God promised to the lineal descendants of Abraham, Isaac and Jacob.** In the following verses, David is repeatedly giving God the credit He deserves for faithfully keeping His covenant promises to Abraham, Isaac and Jacob.

Psalm 136:1-26 (The Amplified Bible.)

*¹O give thanks to the Lord, for He is good; **for His mercy and loving-kindness endure forever.***

*²O give thanks to the God of Gods, **for His mercy and loving-kindness endure forever.***

^{3}O give thanks to the Lord of lords, *for His mercy and loving-kindness endure forever—*

^{4}To Him Who alone does great wonders, *for His mercy and loving-kindness endure forever;*

^{5}To Him Who by wisdom and understanding made the heavens, *for His mercy and loving-kindness endure forever;*

^{6}To Him Who stretched out the earth upon the waters, *for His mercy and loving-kindness endure forever;*

^{7}To Him Who made the great lights, *for His mercy and loving-kindness endure forever—*

^{8}The sun to rule over the day, *for His mercy and loving-kindness endure forever;*

^{9}The moon and stars to rule by night, *for His mercy and loving-kindness endure forever;*

^{10}To Him Who smote Egypt in their firstborn, *for His mercy and loving-kindness endure forever;*

^{11}And brought out Israel from among them, *for His mercy and loving-kindness endure forever;*

^{12}With a strong hand and with an outstretched arm, *for His mercy and loving-kindness endure forever;*

^{13}To Him Who divided the Red Sea into parts, *for His mercy and loving-kindness endure forever;*

^{14}And made Israel to pass through the midst of it, *for His mercy and loving-kindness endure forever;*

^{15}But shook off and overthrew Pharaoh and his host into the Red Sea, *for His mercy and loving-kindness endure forever;*

^{16}To Him Who led His people through the wilderness, *for His mercy and loving-kindness endure forever;*

^{17}To Him who smote great kings, *for His mercy and loving-kindness endure forever;*

^{18}And slew famous kings, *for His mercy and loving-kindness endure forever—*

^{19}Sihon king of the Amorites, *for His mercy and loving-kindness endure forever;*

^{20}And Og king of Bashan, *for His mercy and loving-kindness endure forever;*

*21And gave their land as a heritage, for **His mercy and loving-kindness** endure forever;*

*22Even a heritage to Israel His servant, for **His mercy and loving-kindness** endure forever;*

*23To Him Who [earnestly] remembered us in our low estate and imprinted us [on His heart], for **His mercy and loving-kindness** endure forever;*

*24And rescued us from our enemies, for **His mercy and loving-kindness** endure forever;*

*25To Him Who gives food to all flesh, for **His mercy and loving-kindness** endure forever;*

*26O give thanks to the God of heaven, for **His mercy and loving-kindness** endure forever!*

From this time forth, every time you study Scripture that mentions God's *"mercy and loving-kindness"* that *"endure forever,"* you will know what God's written Word is referring to. Every time you read a Psalm that speaks of God's *"forgiveness, kindness, favor, tender mercies, faithfulness"* or any of the other aspects of God's *"everlasting love,"* you will have insight into the Psalmist's words. Every time you meditate on the prayer lives of the great intercessors of the Bible, intercessors such as Moses and Daniel, you will know how they managed to get God's attention and acquire for Israel God's forgiveness even though the Israelites did not deserve God's mercy or pity. **Yes, you now possess the key of knowledge that unlocks the truth regarding God's *"everlasting love"* for Israel. The key is God's covenant and steadfast love which He swore to Abraham, Isaac and Jacob.**

You now know the answer to the question, "Why Does God Love The Jewish People?" God loves and will continue to love the Jewish people because of the unbreakable *"covenant and steadfast love"* which He swore to their forefathers.

My friend, if you embrace and apply to your life the truth that you have received in parts one and two of this chapter, it will make you free. Yes, the truth you now have will free you from men's sinful, lying doctrines and from your own previous ignorance regarding this matter.

From now on, when men insist that God no longer loves the Jewish people, you will recognize that they are telling lies. You will also know that men are teaching false doctrine whenever they insist that God is no longer obligated to the Jewish people. For, you now

know that God's obligation to the Jewish people is everlasting. God must and will faithfully continue to keep with them the covenant and the steadfast love which He swore to their forefathers, Abraham, Isaac and Jacob.

I am sure that the previous inspired information regarding God's *"everlasting love"* for the Jewish people has filled your heart with a new sense of awe, respect and admiration for the God of Abraham, Isaac and Jacob. However, God's desire is that the truth you have learned will accomplish more than just stir up your emotions. God's desire is that it will change forever the way you view and the way you treat God's beloved covenant people, the Jews.

Since you now know that God's love for the Jews is eternal, won't you purpose in your heart to love them too? For in doing so, you will not only bring God deep joy and comfort but you will also bring upon yourself God's blessing that is recorded in Genesis 12:3, *"I will bless those who bless you...."*

Chapter 10

WHY DID GOD SAY HE
LOVED JACOB AND HATED ESAU?

You now possess the truth regarding the fact that God's love for Israel is an intrinsic part of the Abrahamic covenant. Therefore, you are in a perfect position to be able to comprehend another incredible revelation.

For generations, the most renowned Christian teachers and Bible scholars have endeavored to correctly analyze and accurately divide the Word of truth in Romans 9:12-13. Yet, regardless of their attempts to rightly handle and skillfully teach those verses, they have failed to adequately explain the meaning of God's statements, *"The elder shall serve the younger,"* and *"Jacob have I loved, but Esau have I hated."* Today, however, by the aid of the Holy Spirit, you shall finally have true insight into both those statements of God.

On that exciting note, let us begin by reading the verses of Scripture that I mentioned in the former paragraph. We will read them from the *Holy Bible, King James Version.*

> *Romans 9:12-13 (King James Version.)*
>
> *12It was said unto her, The elder shall serve the younger.*
> *13As it is written, Jacob have I loved, **but Esau have I hated.***

Men's wrong or inadequate interpretations of Romans 9:12-13 have left many in the Church feeling that God was unfairly partial or even prejudiced in His dealings with Jacob and Esau. They have been led to believe that God loved the child Jacob and hated the child Esau while they were still in their mother's womb. If you are one of those misinformed people, after you have received the correct interpretation of Romans 9:12-13, you will be able to discard such unsettling, preconceived, spiritually harmful ideas.

Your studying the subject of God's love for Jacob and his descendants, the Israelites, in the previous chapter gives you a significant edge as you enter into the present teaching. Among other truths, you learned that God did not set His love upon Jacob and his descendants nor make His covenant choice known when the twins were in their mother's womb but rather when Jacob was grown and on his way to Haran. The prediction God made while the twins were in their mother's womb was not a forecast of who the covenant child would be, but rather, it was a forecast of an event that would involve the **future descendants** of both unborn children. Absolute Scriptural confirmation of that truth will be provided later in this chapter.

You also learned that God setting His love upon and choosing Jacob and his descendants as Jacob traveled to Haran had nothing whatsoever to do with their being worthy or deserving of that covenant love (that is, that covenant choice). Rather, God loving and choosing Jacob and the Israelites, as Jacob traveled to Haran, was solely the result of God's own need to fulfill His word and keep the covenant and steadfast love which He had sworn to Abraham and Isaac.

As chapter ten progresses, you will receive undeniable Scriptural proof that God did not hate Esau the unborn child. You will also be supplied with additional verification of the fact that God did not make His prediction in Genesis 25:23, *"...the elder shall serve the younger,"* because He thought that Jacob the individual was better, more likable or more righteous than Esau the individual. You will realize that God's statements did not reflect partiality in any way and that God certainly was not prejudiced. For, you will be given additional confirmation that God's statement, *"...the elder shall serve the younger,"* did not pertain to the unborn twins as individuals at all.

The truth is that because of men's ignorance of Paul's writings in Romans 9:12-13, for generations, God has been falsely accused of showing unfair favoritism toward one of Rebekah's unborn twins and undeserved hatred toward the other. So it is high time that someone set the record straight and gave God's people an opportunity to adjust their wrong thinking and to discard the underlying assumptions that have become so deeply entrenched in their minds. Therefore, I will lay out the Scriptural evidence so that you will finally have a chance to see the truth on this matter and joyfully submit to God's Word.

As I have pointed out over and over again, it is true that before the twins were born, God foretold in Genesis 25:23 that the elder would serve the younger. However, as you will soon see in the Scriptures, unlike those who practice prejudice, God's prediction in that verse was not antagonistic in design or effect. Neither was God's judgment unreasonable or formed without knowledge or without careful examination of all the facts. And last but not least, God's prediction was not based on irrational suspicion, bias or hatred of the unborn child,

Esau. All the previous descriptions fit the dictionary definition of the word "prejudice."

Yes, you will soon be made aware that God's actions did not fit the previous definition of one who is prejudiced. Prejudice is an extremely harsh word which is totally inaccurate when used to describe God's righteous judgment or prediction in this matter. Associating the word "prejudice" with God's forecast in Genesis 25:23, "...*the elder shall serve the younger,*" borders on the ridiculous.

On the other hand, the Biblical evidence proving God's innocence regarding the previously mentioned accusations is extensive. For example, later in this chapter you will see that God's prediction in Genesis 25:23, "...*the elder shall serve the younger,*" was righteous in that it showed a glimpse of God's future justice upon wicked people who would dare to blatantly insult Him and attempt to interfere with Him fulfilling His sworn oath to Abraham and Isaac.

It is extremely important that further proof of God's innocence be presented and that the truth regarding His innocence be established in order to refute men's erroneous charges and insinuations that God was guilty of unfair partiality or prejudice in predicting that the elder would serve the younger and in making His statement later, "...*I loved Jacob, and I hated Esau....*" You see, God's reputation is at stake here. Therefore, it is only right that His name be completely exonerated of all presumed wrongdoing in these areas.

In order to carry out the task described in the former paragraph, it is necessary that we again study three of the texts that we covered in chapter nine of this work. You will recall that in chapter nine, I shared with you that we would do exactly that. You must keep in mind, however, that we will be examining only a small portion of the overwhelming evidence which verifies God's innocence.

First, let us deal with the often asked questions: "Since both brothers were Isaac's sons, why did God set His love upon and choose to establish His covenant with Jacob as he traveled to Haran? Why was it even necessary for God to choose between the two brothers at all? If, as you say, God was not unfairly partial or prejudiced, why could He not have fulfilled His sworn covenant oath to Abraham and Isaac by using both brothers in a covenant capacity?" The answer to the previous questions can be clearly seen in the verses that we will read next from the *Holy Bible, King James Version.*

Genesis 25:21-23 (King James Version.)

²¹*And Isaac intreated the Lord for his wife, because she was barren: and the Lord was intreated of him, and Rebekah his wife conceived.*

²²*And the children struggled together within her; and she said, If it be so, why am I thus? And she went to enquire of the Lord.*

²³*And the Lord said unto her, <u>Two nations are in thy womb, and two manner of people shall be separated from thy bowels; and the one people shall be stronger than the other people; and the elder shall serve the younger.</u>*

Notice in verse twenty-three that **two nations** were in Rebekah's womb. Notice also that the separation of those two peoples (the Israelites and the Edomites) had already begun before the twins were born. Verse twenty-two informs you that the founders of those two nations actually struggled together in the womb. Therefore, since only one nation could inherit the Promised Land, how could God choose both of Isaac's sons?

It stands to reason that God could not have two totally separate, opposing peoples claiming title to the same piece of land. Under such circumstances one nation would have been continually fighting with the other. It would have been total chaos. No! God's way was the best way. God's way was the righteous way. In order to keep the covenant and steadfast love that He had sworn to Abraham and Isaac, God established His covenant with one of those two equally undeserving leaders of nations as he journeyed to Haran. And, for His own reasons, the one God chose was Jacob.

Considering the previous point, I do not think anyone can find fault with God's judgment in this matter, do you? Neither do I think that anyone can accuse God of being unfair or prejudiced in any way. Truthfully, I do not know of anyone else who could have handled that situation as well as God did. He did an excellent job. After all, Abraham and his nephew Lot could not even dwell together peaceably on the same grazing plains without their servants fighting and squabbling among themselves. So, how could two opposing nations own the same piece of land without continually bickering and fighting and hindering God's purpose? God had to make a choice between those two nations, and He made His choice known as Jacob traveled to Haran. It is as simple as that.

I am sure you will agree that I have adequately answered the questions: Since both brothers were Isaac's sons, why was it even necessary for God to choose between them at all? If, as you say, God was not unfairly partial or prejudiced, why did He not fulfill His sworn oath to Abraham and Isaac by using both brothers in a covenant capacity? **The answer, in part, is that two opposing nations were in Rebekah's womb, and both those nations could not own and live peaceably on the same piece of land.**

When one looks closely at the content of Genesis 25:21-23, it becomes evident that when the Lord made His statement in verse twenty-three, *"...the elder shall serve the younger,"* He was referring to the two nations that were in Rebekah's womb **and not** to the individual children.

The Lord told Rebekah, **"*Two nations* are in thy womb, and *two manner of people* shall be separated from thy bowels...."** Still referring to the same two nations, the Lord predicted, *"...**and the one people** shall be stronger than **the other people;** and the elder shall serve the younger."*

There can be no doubt that God's prediction in Genesis 25:23 identified the fact that the older nation, Edom (the descendants of Esau), would serve the younger nation, Israel (the descendants of Jacob). As you can see with your own eyes in the previously mentioned verse, God absolutely was not referring to the twins themselves. Instead, He was referring to the nations of Edom and Israel.

In order to clear God's name of the false accusations that have been heaped upon it because of men's misinterpretations and misrepresentations of Paul's quotation in Romans 9:12, *"It was said unto her, The elder shall serve the younger,"* I cannot allow this opportunity to pass without once again impressing upon your mind that God did not show partiality to one unborn twin over the other. How can anyone insist that God was partial to one twin over the other since the twins were still in their mother's womb when God made His prediction in Genesis 25:23? Furthermore, how can anyone insist that God exhibited partiality when His prediction was not meant for either of the unborn twins personally? As you now know, God spoke of two nations. He did not speak of two individuals. And, later in the series, you will see in the Scriptures exactly what God's prediction entailed.

My friend, you now know why it was crucial that God establish His covenant with only one of Isaac's twin sons. You have also received additional Scriptural confirmation that God's prediction in

Genesis 25:23 involved the descendants of Jacob and Esau **and not** the twins themselves. God foretold that the nation of Edom (the older nation) would serve Israel (the younger nation).

Now that you understand one of the main reasons why it was absolutely essential that God choose between Isaac's two sons, you are ready to proceed to the next point. So, to refresh your memory, let us once again read Paul's words in the following verse from the *Holy Bible, King James Version.*

> *Romans 9:13 (King James Version.)*
>
> *13As it is written, Jacob have I loved,* **but Esau have I hated.**

You will recall that God eventually changed Jacob's name to Israel. From that point on, God referred to the descendants of Abraham, Isaac and Jacob as Jacob or Israel. On the other hand, Esau's descendants were known as Esau, Edomites, Edom, Mount Seir or by their Greek name, Edumea. Genesis 36:8 in *The Amplified Bible* reads, *"So Esau dwelt in the hill country of Seir; **Esau is Edom**."* The importance of the previous information will become clear as the series progresses.

Before you read the next verses, I want to emphasize three important facts.

(1) Paul's reference to Jacob and Esau in Romans 9:13, *"Jacob have I loved, but Esau have I hated,"* was borrowed from Old Testament Scripture, to be precise Malachi 1:1-5.

(2) As it was in Genesis 25:23, God's words in Malachi 1:1-5 (which by the way, were not recorded until approximately four hundred and fifty years before Yeshua's birth) again included the future descendants of Jacob (Israel) and Esau (Edom) rather than just the two brothers.

(3) God's words in the first two verses of Malachi chapter one were intended to remind Israel of the everlasting covenant love that God had extended to them through their forefather, Jacob.

We will now briefly study all five of the previously mentioned verses.

Malachi 1:1-5 (The Amplified Bible.)

¹THE BURDEN or oracle (the thing to be lifted up) of **the word of the Lord to Israel** *by Malachi [My messenger].*

As I said earlier, God's words in Malachi 1:1-5 were directed toward the nation of Israel. To verify that fact, in verse one, Malachi states, **This is** *"...the word of the Lord to Israel...."*

Now let us read verse two of our present text.

²I have loved you, says the Lord. Yet you say, How and in what way have You loved us? Was not Esau Jacob's brother? says the Lord; yet I loved Jacob (Israel),

Upon careful examination of the contents of the previous verses, one realizes that they hold tremendous insight. For, as you learned in chapter nine, God clearly informed the Israelites that in choosing and thus setting His love upon their forefather, Jacob, He indirectly chose and set His love upon them. Moreover, since God chose to establish His covenant with Jacob, the Israelites automatically became the recipients of the covenant and steadfast love that God had sworn to their forefathers.

To keep things in perspective, you must call up yet another truth that you studied earlier in the series. I am referring to the fact that neither Jacob nor his descendants were worthy of God's covenant choice or God's steadfast love. On the contrary, God chose them, loved them and established His covenant with them as Jacob traveled to Haran in order to keep the oath which He had sworn to Abraham and Isaac. Therefore, it stands to reason that since God did not feel that Jacob and His descendants were any more worthy or deserving of His covenant choice and love than Esau and his descendants, God's choice could not have had its roots in prejudice. The very notion that it did is silly. For, we are dealing with two sons who were of the same parents, race and religion and who were both equally unworthy and undeserving of God's covenant choice.

Being able to view the whole scenario with hindsight, the apostle Paul was acutely aware that like God's choice of Jacob and his descendants as Jacob traveled to Haran, God's earlier prediction in Genesis 25:23 (that is, God's prediction that the nation of Edom would serve the nation of Israel) was not based on prejudice. For, in the very next text that you will read, when referring to the previously mentioned forecast, Paul leaves no doubt of the fact that God's prediction in

Genesis 25:23 had nothing to do with one founder being more worthy or deserving than the other.

You already know why one of the unborn founders could not have been more worthy than the other. You know that neither founder had anything to do with God's announcement in Genesis 25:23, *"...the elder shall serve the younger,"* for, God made His prediction before the founders of either Edom or Israel were born. Moreover, God deliberately made His forecast to Rebekah before the twins were born so that there would be no doubt in anyone's mind that His prediction was not based on partiality or prejudice, but rather, **it was based on God's own need to further His own future purpose**. Read Paul's words from the *Holy Bible, King James Version.*

> *Romans 9:10-12 (King James Version.)*
>
> *10And not only this; but when Rebecca also had conceived by one, even by our father Isaac;*
>
> *11(For the children being not yet born, neither having done any good or evil, **that the purpose of God** according to election might stand, not of works, but of him that calleth;)*
>
> *12It was said unto her, The elder shall serve the younger.*

Notice in verses eleven and twelve that Paul's whole emphasis is on God making His statement *"The elder shall serve the younger"* in order to further carry out His own purpose of election. Consider what God's purpose of election involves. It involves God fulfilling His sacred promises to Abraham and thus accomplishing His will upon the earth. God foretold that the nation of Israel would one day rule over the nation of Edom so that He could fulfill His predictions and His promises to Abraham through the nation with whom He would later establish His covenant.

Paul also stated in verse eleven that God's announcement to Rebekah regarding the two nations in her womb had nothing whatsoever to do with any good work that Israel's founder, Jacob, had so far done or any evil work that Edom's founder, Esau, had so far done. How could any good or evil work done by either founder of those nations have had any bearing on God's prediction when God had foretold that future situation before either child was born? The truth is, as I said earlier and as the apostle Paul reiterated, God made His prediction that the descendants of one twin would be in servitude to the descendants of the other in order further to carry out His own purpose and not because of any good or evil work that either of the unborn founders of those two nations had so far done.

Paul's words in verse eleven regarding God making His prediction in Genesis 25:23 in order to promote His own purpose are entirely Scriptural. As a matter of fact, hundreds of years earlier, the prophet Isaiah had made that same point. Isaiah even went a step further. He let it be known that **all** God's forecasts and His fulfillment of them are intended to further God's own purpose and desires. See this truth for yourself in the following text.

Isaiah 46:9-10 (The Amplified Bible.)

9[Earnestly] remember the former things, [which I did] of old; for I am God, and there is no one else; I am God, and there is none like Me,

10Declaring the end and the result from the beginning, and from ancient times the things that are not yet done, saying, My counsel shall stand, and I will do all My pleasure and purpose.

God predicts the future to show that His counsel will stand no matter what. Men have nothing whatsoever to do with it. God will bring to pass all that He has spoken. For, He alone can forecast what will be in the future and then make His predictions come true. And, God makes His predictions so that neither boastful men nor graven images can take credit for that which He alone has done. Read in the next verses in *The Amplified Bible* what the Lord Himself says on this matter.

Isaiah 48:3-8 (The Amplified Bible.)

3 I have declared from the beginning the former things [which happened in times past to Israel]; they went forth from My mouth and I made them known; then suddenly I did them, and they came to pass [says the Lord].

4 Because I knew that you were obstinate, and your neck was an iron sinew and your brow was brass,

5 Therefore I have declared things to come to you from of old; before they came to pass I announced them to you, so that you could not say, My idol has done them, and my graven image and my molten image have commanded them.

6 You have heard [these things foretold], now you see this fulfillment. And will you not bear witness to it? I show you specified new things from this time forth, even hidden things [kept in reserve] which you have not known.

7 They are created now [called into being by the prophetic word], and not long ago; and before today you have never heard of them, lest you should say, Behold, I knew them!

8 Yes, you have never heard, yes, you have never known; yes, from of old your ear has not been opened. For I, the Lord, knew that you, O house of Israel, dealt very treacherously; you were called a transgressor and a rebel [in revolt] from your birth.

Surely God's Word speaks for itself, fully explaining that as it is with all God's other predictions, God's forecast in Genesis 25:23 that the nation of Edom would serve the nation of Israel had nothing to do with partiality or prejudice. God's disclosure in that verse was made in order to further carry out His own purpose and desire regarding His covenant with Abraham and Isaac. Neither of the unborn twins in Rebekah's womb had anything to do with God's prediction. Without a doubt, God's inspired Word in Isaiah 46:9-10 and Isaiah 48:3-8 puts that argument to rest.

You are now in possession of even more insight into God's statement in Malachi 1:2, *"I have loved you, says the Lord. Yet you say, How and in what way have You loved us? Was not Esau Jacob's brother? says the Lord; yet I loved Jacob (Israel)."* However, you may still be wrestling with other issues that pertain to God's previous statement in Malachi. You might be thinking, "Yes, I do now have more understanding as to why God said He loved Jacob (Israel). Nevertheless, God loving Jacob and his descendants still does not explain His statement in Malachi 1:3, *'I have hated Esau.'* I need to know exactly what God meant by those words. I need to know why God hated Esau."

The best way I know to begin to explain God's statement, **"I have hated Esau..."** is to once again refer you to the *Holy Bible, King James Version*. We will read Malachi 1:2-5 from that translation. The importance of temporarily using the *King James Version* is to keep you from being unnecessarily distracted by the additional aids provided by *The Amplified Bible* translators.

> *Malachi 1:2-5 (King James Version.)*
>
> *2I have loved you, saith the Lord. Yet ye say, Wherein hast thou loved us? Was not Esau Jacob's brother? saith the Lord: yet I loved Jacob,*

Earlier, I reminded you of three points to keep in mind while you again study Malachi 1:1-5. One of those three points was that God's words in Malachi 1:1-5 included the future descendants of Jacob and Esau rather than just the two brothers. In verse two, God's words pertained to Jacob, the individual, and Esau, the individual, only in the sense that God was trying to convey to the Israelites that in choosing and thus loving their forefather, Jacob, as he traveled to Haran, He had inevitably chosen and loved them. **However, in verses three through five, God switches His attention to the descendants of Esau.**

If you are to correctly understand the true contents of Malachi 1:1-5, it is imperative that you comprehend my last statement regarding God turning the focus of His comments toward the **descendants** of Esau in the last three verses of that text. Absolute proof of what I just said regarding God transferring His comments toward the **descendants** of Esau can be seen in Malachi 1:3-5. For, as you study those verses, **you will then realize that God never did to Esau the things mentioned in those three verses. However, as you will soon see in the Scriptures, God did do those things to Esau's descendants.**

Remembering that in the next verses of Malachi chapter one, God is speaking of Esau's descendants whom He actually addresses by the names **Esau** and **Edom**; let us continue reading.

> *3And I hated Esau, and laid his mountains and his heritage waste for the dragons of the wilderness.*
>
> *4Whereas Edom saith, We are impoverished, but we will return and build the desolate places; thus saith the Lord of hosts, They shall build, but I will throw down; and they shall call them, The border of wickedness, and, The people against whom the Lord hath indignation for ever.*
>
> *5And your eyes shall see, and ye shall say, The Lord will be magnified from the border of Israel.*

As I said earlier, God never hated nor did He remain angry forever with Esau, the individual. Neither did God punish the twin, Esau, in the manner described in the previous three verses. No! No! No! **It was the descendants of Esau (Edom) whom God hated and punished so severely, not Esau the individual.**

Now that you comprehend that in Malachi 1:3-5 God is referring to Esau's descendants, you are ready to learn exactly what the descendants of Esau did to deserve God's hatred and to incur God's never ending wrath. You will then know beyond a doubt that God's hatred was directed toward the nation Esau founded **and not** toward Esau, the unborn baby. **I repeat, God did not hate Esau, the individual. God hated Esau, the nation.** Furthermore, you are about to see Scriptural evidence which proves that God's hatred of the nation of Edom is absolutely justified.

I will now clarify my previous statement regarding God's hatred of Edom being justified. I will also provide additional Scripture to further confirm the truth that it was Esau's descendants and not Esau the child whom God hated. I will place the previously mentioned Scriptural evidence before you piece by piece. You can rest assured that when I have finished presenting all the following facts, there will be no doubt remaining in your mind as to why God stated that He hated Esau (that is, why God stated that He hated the nation of Edom). For you will fully realize that God's hatred was indeed justified.

In order to provide you with an overall view of events, I refer you to an earlier period in history. We will begin at the point in time when, with his mother's approval and aid, Jacob deceptively acquired the eldest son's blessing from his father, Isaac. Under normal circumstances, tribal tradition would have required that Esau receive Isaac's blessing. However, these were not normal circumstances.

Pay close attention as you read the words that Isaac pronounced over Jacob from the *Holy Bible, King James Version*. For, the first piece of promised evidence is within the contents of the previously mentioned blessing.

Genesis 27:28-29 (King James Version.)

28 Therefore God give thee of the dew of heaven, and the fatness of the earth, and plenty of corn and wine:

[29]Let people serve thee, and nations bow down to thee: **be lord over thy brethren, and let thy mother's sons bow down to thee**: *cursed be every one that curseth thee, and blessed be he that blesseth thee.*

Part of the inspired prophetic blessing that Isaac conferred upon his son, Jacob, was *"...**be lord over thy brethren, and let thy mother's sons bow down to thee....**"* However, there is no Biblical record of Esau, the individual, ever bowing down to his brother Jacob. On the other hand, we are informed in Genesis 33:3-8 that on one occasion Jacob did bow down before Esau, calling him *"...my lord."* So, do those recorded Biblical facts mean that Isaac's prophecy never came to pass? No! Of course not! You see, Isaac was not speaking about Jacob, the individual, being lord over his twin brother, Esau. Nor was he speaking about Esau, the individual, bowing down to his twin, Jacob. Rather, as the Lord did in Genesis 25:23, Isaac was referring to Esau's descendants. Isaac was foretelling how in the future Esau's descendants (the Edomites) would bow down in servitude before Jacob's descendants (the Israelites). **Isaac was prophesying that the time would come when the Israelites would rule over the Edomites.**

You now possess a fuller understanding of what Jacob's blessing did and did not entail. However, Esau also received a blessing from his father, Isaac. So, let us shift our attention to the substance of the blessing that Esau acquired.

Genesis 27:37-40 (King James Version.)

[37]And Isaac answered and said unto Esau, **Behold, I have made him thy lord, and all his brethren have I given to him for servants**; *and with corn and wine have I sustained him: and what shall I do now unto thee, my son?*

[38]And Esau said unto his father, Hast thou but one blessing, my father? bless me, even me also, O my father. And Esau lifted up his voice, and wept.

[39]And Isaac his father answered and said unto him, Behold, thy dwelling shall be the fatness of the earth, and of the dew of heaven from above;

*[40]***And by thy sword shalt thou live, and shalt serve thy brother; and it shall come to pass when thou shalt have the dominion, that thou shalt break his yoke from off thy neck.**

The first point to notice is seen in verse forty. Isaac prophesied, "...***by thy sword shalt thou live***...." Isaac was informing his son Esau that his future descendants would live by destroying and plundering other peoples. It is imperative that you retain that truth, because you will need to call it up later in the lesson.

The second point to be aware of is that in the previously mentioned verse, verse forty, Isaac prophesied that Esau (the nation of Edom) would serve his brother Jacob (the nation of Israel). Furthermore, he told Esau that the day would eventually come when the nation of Edom would possess the power to free itself from that yoke of servitude.

Once again, I remind you that Esau, the individual, was never bound in servitude to Jacob. Therefore, Esau never needed the prophesied power to free himself from a yoke that he never wore. **However, later in the lesson, you will learn that Esau's descendants, the Edomites, completely fulfilled Isaac's inspired prophecy.**

By now you understand that both of Isaac's blessings simply confirmed the words that God had previously spoken to Rebecca in Genesis 25:23. So as you again read verse twenty-three, keep in mind that God is referring to the descendants of Esau and Jacob, not the unborn babies. To aid you, I have again accented God's words in verse twenty-three which emphasize that fact. We will read from the *Holy Bible, King James Version*.

> *Genesis 25:23 (King James Version.)*
>
> *23And the Lord said unto her, **Two nations** are in thy womb, and **two manner of people** shall be separated from thy bowels; **and the one people shall be stronger than the other people, and the elder shall serve the younger.***

Not only was God Himself the first to foretell that in the due course of time the nation of Edom would end up being in servitude to Israel, but in doing so, God again proved that He had foreknowledge of all future events that pertained to those two nations. Before either founder of those nations was born, our all-knowing God knew which one of the twins was the founder of His chosen covenant nation (Israel). He also knew which one of the twins was the founder of the Edomite nation, the nation which would eventually end up serving His chosen people. However, God did not establish His Abrahamic covenant with Jacob and his decendants at that time. As you saw earlier in the series, God set His love upon the Israelites and made His covenant choice known to Jacob when he was grown and on his way to Haran.

Esau's descendants, the Edomites, turned out to be an evil bunch of people. Consequently, it was partly because of the wicked deeds that they perpetrated upon God's covenant people, Israel, that God came to hate them, destroy them and make them no promise of future mercy. Any good Bible encyclopedia or Bible dictionary will back up what I just said regarding the Edomites' wickedness, their eventual destruction and God making no allowances for their forgiveness.

One particular incident which reveals the type of wicked behavior that characterizes the Edomites and which is partly responsible for God's hatred of that nation is recorded in the book of Numbers. The incident I am referring to took place soon after God's people had exited Egypt. That fact alone made the whole episode extremely sad since the Israelites were still unsettled and therefore must have felt extremely vulnerable.

Esau's descendants on the other hand, were by then firmly established as a nation in the land of Edom (or Mount Seir). They were ruled by a monarchical form of government. Thus, it was to the king of Edom that the Israelites presented their petition for safe passage through Edomite territory.

Keep in mind that the Edomites and Israelites were related to each other. They had the same forefathers, namely Abraham and Isaac. The Edomites were also aware of Israel's four hundred years of affliction and oppression and their miraculous deliverance from Egypt by the hand of God. It was because of those two points that the Israelites naturally assumed that the Edomites would respond kindly to their needy plight, grant their request and mercifully extend to them safe passage through their land. But as you will read in the subsequent verses, neither kindness nor mercy was what Israel received at their hands.

Numbers 20:14-21 (The Amplified Bible.)

14 ***And Moses sent messengers from Kadesh to the King of Edom****, saying, Thus says your kinsman Israel: You know all the adversity and birth pangs that have come upon us [as a nation]:*

15How our fathers went down to Egypt; we dwelt there a long time, and the Egyptians dealt evilly with us and our fathers.

16But when we cried to the Lord, He heard us and sent an angel and brought us forth out of Egypt. Now behold, we are in Kadesh, a city on your country's edge.

17Let us pass, I pray you, through your country. We will not pass through field or vineyard, or drink of the water of the wells. We will go along the king's highway; we will not turn aside to the right hand or to the left until we have passed your borders.

18But Edom said to him, You shall not go through, lest I come out against you with the sword.

19And the Israelites said to him, We will go by the highway, and if I and my livestock drink of your water, I will pay for it. Only let me pass through on foot, nothing else.

20But Edom said, You shall not go through. And Edom came out against Israel with many people and a strong hand.

21Thus Edom refused to give Israel passage through his territory, so Israel turned away from him.

Had their hearts been right, the Edomites could have used their strategic advantage for good. They could have used their position to advance God's purpose for selecting the Israelites. However, in their hatred of Israel, they chose to oppose God's will and purpose by blocking the Israelites' access to the Promised Land. They cared nothing for the spiritual aspect of the situation. Neither did they give any thought to the consequences of their sinful actions. To put it bluntly, they exhibited the same character defects that their forefather and founder, Esau, had displayed.

You will recall that Esau lived only for the present. He proved that he cared nothing for spiritual things when he impulsively and thoughtlessly sold his birthright for a bowl of lentil stew. By so doing, Esau relinquished his position as future spiritual head of the household.

Likewise by their actions, Esau's descendants considered God's sacred Abrahamic covenant and God's chosen covenant people as being insignificant compared to the momentary gratification that the immediate situation afforded them. You see, they were so absorbed in their hatred of Israel that they took more pleasure in slighting and injuring the Israelites than they did in doing right and pleasing the God of their forefathers, Abraham and Esau. They had cultivated animosity, hate and anger until their all-consuming hatred had turned them into unmerciful, irrational brutes and put them in opposition to God and His word.

You will recall that part of God's prediction regarding Esau (Edom) and Jacob (Israel) in Genesis 25:23 reads, "...*the one people shall be stronger than the other people...*" Numbers 20:14-21 reveals that the nation of Edom was indeed stronger than the nation of Israel. Verse twenty of that text reads, "...*And Edom came out against Israel with many people and **a strong hand.**"*

Since the Israelites were not a war-like people and were therefore no threat to Edom, there was absolutely no excuse for Edom's hostile and aggressive behavior. At that time, the descendants of Esau had an opportunity to use their superior strength to defend and aid God's chosen people and in doing so promote God's will and purpose on the earth. However, they chose instead to do the opposite. They sinned against God and God's chosen people, Israel. The Edomites chose to use their strength in a totally derogative manner. They used their physical might to oppose God's will and purpose.

To this point, you have only seen a glimpse of why, in Malachi 1:3-5, God stated that He hated the descendants of Esau, that He would destroy them, and that He would never cease being angry with them. Therefore, in order to provide you with a broader view of God's reasons for making such statements, we will continue to briefly trace Edom's treacherous behavior throughout the annals of Bible history.

It was approximately four hundred years after Edom's abusive confrontation with Israel before Esau's descendants are again mentioned in the Bible. Nevertheless, the following text leaves no doubt that those four hundred years had not in the least changed Edom's attitude toward Israel. Edom remained Israel's staunch enemy. Thus, in an effort to put a stop to Edom's continual raiding of the Promised Land, King Saul went out to do battle with Esau's descendants.

I Samuel 14:47-48 (The Amplified Bible.)

*47When Saul took over the kingdom of Israel, he fought against all his enemies on every side: Moab, the Ammonites, **Edom,** the kings of Zobah, and the Philistines. Wherever he turned, he made it worse for them.*

180

⁴⁸He did valiantly and smote the Amalekites, and delivered Israel out of the hands of those who plundered them.

Notice the highlighted portions of the previous verses. As well as accentuating the word *"Edom,"* I also accented the portion that reads, *"He did valiantly and smote the Amalekites, and delivered Israel out of the hands of those who plundered them."* I stressed those points because they are the fulfillment of part of the inspired prophetic blessing that Isaac placed upon Esau in Genesis 27:40.

There is a footnote for Genesis 27:41 in *The Amplified Bible* which informs us that **the Amalekites (mentioned in I Samuel 14:48) were also descendants of Esau**. As a matter of fact, if you read Genesis 36:16, you will see that Amalek was the grandson of Esau and one of the tribal chiefs of Edom. My next point will show you why that information is so important to the present study.

You will recall that part of the prophetic blessing that Isaac gave to Esau was that Esau's descendants would live by destroying and plundering other nations. Isaac predicted, *"And by thy sword shalt thou live...."* (Genesis 27:40, *King James Version.*) I Samuel 14:47-48 leaves no doubt that Isaac's prophecy did come true. Not only did Esau's descendants live by the sword, but they even plundered God's own chosen nation, Israel. Sadly, the Edomites' actions again proved that they cared nothing for God's name or God's solemn Abrahamic oath or God's chosen covenant people. They were wicked through and through. Furthermore, they were totally absorbed in their hatred of God's chosen covenant people, Israel.

Most Bible scholars agree that the Edomites' hatred of the Israelites stemmed from the conflict that arose between the founders of both their nations (that is, the founders, Jacob and Esau). However, Bible teachers have failed to educate the Church regarding the fact that the Edomites' hatred of Israel was totally unfounded. Therefore, let me take a few moments to correct their unintentional yet harmful neglect by showing you that there was no rational basis for Edom's anger and hostility toward Israel.

(1) Neither Esau nor his descendants were deprived of their intended position because Jacob ended up with the eldest brother's blessing. For, as you now know, the predicted roles that Edom and Israel were destined to perform during a certain specified future period had been foretold

before the founders of either nation were born. God had informed Rebecca, "...*the elder shall serve the younger.*" Therefore, there was absolutely no way that those roles could have been reversed. Neither the Edomites nor the Israelites had any control over God's decision. The choice was God's alone. Edom would be in servitude to Israel "...*in order further to carry out God's purpose of selection.*" (Romans 9:11, *The Amplified Bible.*) Since the twins were yet unborn and had done no good or evil, in this instance, the emphasis should be on God's **purpose** of selection (that is, God's purpose for selecting one nation to serve and the other to be served) rather than who He selected. And as you now know, God's **purpose** for selecting Israel to be served by the nation of Edom was to promote His Abrahamic covenant through the nation of Israel. Therefore, when blessing his son Esau, Isaac was compelled by the spirit of God to prophetically confirm God's prediction in Genesis 25:23. In this case, in order to carry out God's future purpose, both nations were selected. One nation was called to serve and the other was called to be served.

The fact is that since Edom's founder was "*the elder,*" the Edomites could never have swapped places with the Israelites. They could never have altered their fate regarding the servitude issue. In Genesis 25:23 God had predicted exactly how the future would turn out and no man could have undone that which God had foretold. In order further to carry out His own purpose, God had stated, "...*the elder shall serve the younger.*" So as you can see, neither Esau nor his descendants, the Edomites, had anything stolen from them as a result of Jacob's actions. Therefore, they had absolutely no reason to be angry with his descendants, the Israelites.

(2) If the Edomites' cycle of hatred was perpetrated upon the Israelites because of Esau's hatred of Jacob mentioned in Genesis 27:41, then again, their hatred was unjustified. You see, Esau's anger was really the result of his dissatisfaction with the contents of the prophetic blessing that Isaac had placed upon him. Esau blamed Jacob for the servitude that Isaac had prophetically pronounced upon his descendants (Edom). Esau did not want his future descendants bowing down in servitude to his brother's future descendants. However, again, Esau's hatred of Jacob was unjustified. For Isaac was simply confirming that which God had already told to Rebecca before the twins were even born, "...*the elder shall serve the younger.*"

Even if Esau had made it back in time to receive the eldest son's blessing, Isaac's words over him would have been completely different than those inspired words which he spoke over Jacob. The bottom line is that one way or the other, the same result would have been achieved. You see, things had to turn out just as they did because, before the twins were born, God had already foretold how things would be. And, God always speaks the truth.

With the insight you now possess, read carefully Esau's angry words in the *Holy Bible, King James Version.* Then you will understand all that I have said regarding Esau's anger resulting from his displeasure with the prophetic announcement of servitude that Isaac had pronounced upon his descendants, the nation of Edom.

Genesis 27:41 (King James Version.)

41And Esau hated Jacob because of the blessing wherewith his father blessed him: and Esau said in his heart, The days of mourning for my father are at hand; then will I slay my brother Jacob.

(3) Jacob and Esau eventually made peace. They wept on each other's shoulders. When, after their reunion the two brothers again parted, there was absolutely no animosity, hostility or problems of any kind between them. Each had apparently accepted the foretold God-ordained roles that their future descendants would play in God's overall plan. Therefore, since no bad feelings existed between the two brothers, there remained no hostility or hatred to kindle the Edomites' fiery family feud. The fact is that even later when Esau moved away from Jacob and Canaan, his decision to leave the Promised Land was not based on nor the result of sibling strife. Rather, Esau's departure from Canaan was based solely on his own need to provide adequate grazing land for his animals. See this for yourself in the following text.

Genesis 36:6-8 (The Amplified Bible.

6Now Esau took his wives, his sons, his daughters, and all the members of his household, his cattle, all his beasts, and all his possessions which he had obtained in the land of Canaan, and he went into a land away from his brother Jacob.

7For their great flocks and herds and possessions [which they had collected] made it impossible for them to dwell together; the land in which they were strangers could not support them because of their livestock.

8So Esau dwelt in the hill country of Seir; Esau is Edom.

The Edomites had obviously contrived reasons to hate Israel out of the wicked imaginations of their own hearts. Thus, we are forced to assume it was really the truth God had spoken to Rebekah and that Isaac later prophetically confirmed that they really hated. Under no circumstances were the Edomites willing to subject themselves to God's will in the area of their being subservient to Israel. However, the innocent Israelites were the ones who took the thrashing for Edom's discontentment with God's word. The Edomites sinfully took out their anger, frustration and dissatisfaction with God's prediction on His innocent chosen covenant people. Yet, however twisted their rationale, the Edomites convinced themselves that they had every reason to continue to hate and harass God's chosen people.

In time, by the hand of God, David did acquire for Israel temporary relief from Edom's hostility. That relief came through the fulfillment of God's word to Rebekah and segments of the inspired prophetic blessings that Isaac had given to Jacob and Esau.

(1) God informed Rebekah in Genesis 25:23, *"...the elder shall serve the younger."*

(2) Isaac confirmed God's word to Rebekah in his blessing upon Jacob in Genesis 27:29, *"...be lord over thy brethren, and let thy mother's sons bow down to thee...."*

(3) Again, Isaac confirmed God's word to Rebekah in Genesis 27:37 when he said to Esau, *"Behold, I have made him thy lord, and all his brethren have I given to him for servants;"* and also in Genesis 27:40, *"And by thy sword shalt thou live, and shalt serve thy brother."*

Esau's descendants were destined to serve Jacob's descendants. Thus, God's prediction eventually came to pass through King David. The Edomites became the servants of the Israelites, ushering in the previously mentioned temporary period of relief from Edom's harassment and hostilities that Israel so desperately needed.

> *II Samuel 8:13-14 (The Amplified Bible.)*
>
> [13] *David won renown. When he returned he slew 18,000 Edomites in the Valley of Salt.*
>
> [14] *He put garrisons throughout all Edom, __and all the Edomites became his servants__. And the Lord preserved and gave victory to [him] wherever he went.*

The Edomite thorn in Israel's flesh had been pulled out. However, God's intervention in that situation involved more than Israel's personal comfort and security. It involved God carrying out His purpose of election. The nation of Israel had been chosen to promote God's covenant with Abraham. And, God had made it known to Rebekah that the Edomites would be used to help Israel accomplish His purpose in that area. And that, my friend, is why God predicted, *"...the elder shall serve the younger."*

The Zondervan Pictorial Encyclopedia of the Bible under the heading "Edom" gives you insight into exactly how the nation of Edom fit into God's plan at the time of their subjugation. They not only fulfilled God's word to Rebekah and Isaac's prophetic blessings over his two sons, but they also had a part in fulfilling God's word to King Solomon regarding the material wealth that God promised to give to him.

> **The subjugation of Edom** marked an important stage of economic growth of the kingdom under Solomon, for not merely did he secure control of the rich caravan trade by this means, but also made possible the exploitation of the copper and iron mines of the territory....

I think the previous brief excerpt proves that David's conquering Edom and subsequently bringing the Edomites into the prophesied servitude (II Samuel 8:14) played a much larger role in God's overall plan than merely providing Israel with a measure of relief. And that is why once God had used the Edomites' forced labor to further carry out His purpose of election (that is, to promote His Abrahamic covenant through His chosen people, the Israelites), the final section of Isaac's prophetic blessing concerning Esau's descendants came true. You will recall that Isaac prophesied over Esau, *"...it shall come to pass when thou shalt have the dominion, that thou shalt break his yoke from off thy neck."* (Genesis 27:40.) In the following text, you will see that in time the yoke of servitude which Israel had placed upon Edom's neck was indeed broken.

II Kings 8:20-22 (The Amplified Bible.)

20In his days, Edom revolted from the rule of Judah and set up a king over themselves.

21So Jehoram [of Judah] went over to Zair with all his chariots. He and his chariot commanders rose up by night and slew the Edomites who had surrounded them; and [escaping] his army fled home.

22So Edom revolted from the rule of Judah to this day. Then Libnah revolted at the same time.

II Kings 8:22 is proof that Isaac's blessing in Genesis 27:40 did indeed come true. As prophesied, Esau's descendants broke the yoke of servitude that Israel had put upon their neck. However, after they were free, Edom's hatred of Israel persisted. The descendants of Esau took pleasure in taking advantage of Israel's suffering. They waited for opportunities to shed the blood of God's people, choosing times of calamity. They actually enjoyed watching Israel's humiliation and pain. A glimpse of Edom's mistreatment of Israel can be seen in the following text. We will read the first eleven verses of that text from *The Living Bible.*

If you want to see what the face of real prejudice looks like, then fix your attention on the evil character of Edom (also known as Mount Seir). **You will then understand why God hated Esau (Edom) and why He swore that He would never stop being angry with that nation.**

Ezekiel 35:1-15 (The Living Bible.)

1Again a message came from the Lord. He said:

2Son of dust, face toward Mount Seir and prophesy against the people saying;

3The Lord God says: I am against you and I will smash you with my fist and utterly destroy you.

4,5Because you hate my people Israel, I will demolish your cities and make you desolate, and then you shall know I am the Lord. You butchered my people when they were helpless, when I had punished them for all their sins.

6As I live, the Lord God says, since you enjoy blood so much, I will give you a blood bath—your turn has come!

7I will utterly wipe out the people of Mount Seir, killing off all those who try to escape and all those who return.

8I will fill your mountains with the dead—your hills, your valleys and your rivers will be filled with those the sword has killed.

9Never again will you revive. You will be abandoned forever; your cities will never be rebuilt. Then you shall know I am the Lord.

10__For you said, 'Both Israel and Judah shall be mine. We will take possession of them. What do we care that God is there!'__

11Therefore as I live, the Lord God says, __I will pay back your angry deeds with mine—I will punish you for all your acts of envy and of hate.__ And I will honor my name in Israel by what I do to you.

Consider the Edomites' heinous crimes against Israel that are recorded in the previous verses.

Verses four and five inform you that Mount Seir (the Edomites) hated God's people so much that they butchered the Israelites when they were helpless.

Verse six lets you know that the Edomites enjoyed spilling the blood of God's covenant people.

Verse ten tells you that the Edomites actually boasted how they would steal the Promised Land, the land that God had sworn by Himself would belong to Israel forever, and keep it for themselves.

Verse eleven shows you why God stated in Malachi 1:3 that He hated Esau (that is, why God stated that He hated the nation that Esau founded). In verse eleven, **God foretold that He would repay the Edomites' wickedness by treating them in exactly the same way that they had treated Israel. Thus, because the Edomites hated Israel, God hated them. Moreover, because the Edomites' anger toward Israel was unending, so God's anger toward Edom is also unending. Yes, God hated Esau (Edom) in the same way that Edom had hated His chosen people.**

Because the contents of verse eleven is so important, let us also read that verse from *The Amplified Bible*.

*11Therefore, as I live, says the Lord God, **I will deal with you according to the anger and envy you showed because of your enmity for them,** and I will make Myself known among them [as He Who will judge and punish] when I judge and punish you.*

Verse eleven in *The New International Version* reads:

*11Therefore as surely as I live, declares the Sovereign Lord, **I will treat you in accordance with the anger and jealousy you showed in your hatred of them...***

You might well ask, "But, why was God's hatred against Edom so severe? I realize that the Edomites did horrible things to Israel but for that matter, so did Israel's other neighbors. Yet God never said He hated them. Neither did God say that He would never stop being angry with any of the other nations that surrounded Israel."

My friend, when you read verses ten and eleven together, you quickly realize that the Edomites' sin against Israel was not God's only reason for hating and destroying their nation. It was also the Edomites' sin against God Himself that made them God's hated foe and thus made them abhorrent in His sight. You see, the Edomites knew that God actually dwelt among His covenant people. And yet, they still made their wicked plans to destroy God's special people and to take possession of God's Holy Land (God's dwelling place).

Read again verses ten and eleven for yourself and you will see the Edomites' sin against God Almighty and God's promised recompense for their arrogant and blasphemous behavior.

Ezekiel 35:10-11 (The Living Bible.)

*10"For you said, 'Both Israel and Judah shall be mine. We will take possession of them. **What do we care that God is there!'***
11Therefore as I live, the Lord God says, I will pay back your angry deeds with mine—I will punish you for all your acts of envy and of hate. And I will honor my name in Israel by what I do to you.

In Ezekiel 35:10-11, God leaves no doubt as to why He hated these despicable, blasphemous people, the Edomites. God gives further clarification of His reasons for hating Edom in the next four verses of Ezekiel chapter thirty-five. There, God's Word shows you that in hating Israel, Edom automatically hated God too. For, as you know, God had established His covenant with the Israelites. He had set them apart for His own purpose. God needed the elect (the Israelites) to help Him keep the promises that He had sworn to Abraham, Isaac and Jacob. Moreover, God loved the Israelites with an everlasting love. **Thus, Edom's hatred and abusive words against Israel were really directed toward God. And worst of all, with his mouth Edom deliberately blasphemed God Almighty.**

Ezekiel 35:12-14 (The Amplified Bible.)

12And you shalt know, understand, and realize that I am the Lord [the Sovereign Ruler, Who calls forth loyalty and obedient service], and that I have heard all your revilings and scornful speeches that you have uttered against the mountains of Israel, saying, They are laid waste and desolate; they are given to us to devour.

13Thus you have boasted and magnified yourselves against Me with your mouth, multiplying your words against Me: I have heard it.

14Thus says the Lord God; While the whole earth rejoices, I will make you a waste and desolation.

Can there be any doubt as to why God hated the descendants of Esau? They not only spoke evil against Israel, but they also blasphemed God Almighty. They boasted great words against Him. They even threatened to steal the land that God had sworn by a solemn covenant to give to Israel forever. The Edomites (Mount Seir) stood in opposition to God's word and God's will and purpose being carried out on the earth. They openly exhibited hatred for God and everything He stood for. And that is why God hated them. **God did not hate the unborn twin Esau. No! God hated his evil, blasphemous, disrespectful, greedy, detestable descendants.**

God hated the Edomites so much that He foretold that just as they had rejoiced over Israel's ruin, so, He would rejoice over their horrible fate. Furthermore, God predicted that the whole world would rejoice with Him over their deserved destruction. All Edom rejoiced over Israel's calamity and ruin. Thus, all the world would rejoice over Edom's ruin. To show you what I mean, let us read verses fourteen and fifteen from *The Living Bible*.

Ezekiel 35:14-15 (The Living Bible.)

14The whole world will rejoice when I make you desolate.

15You rejoiced at Israel's fearful fate. Now I will rejoice at yours! You will be wiped out, O people of Mount Seir and all who live in Edom! And then you will know I am the Lord!

When you consider what the Edomites did to God's name, God's chosen covenant people, God's land and even the Holy City of God, Jerusalem, you can understand why the Lord made reference to all peoples rejoicing at their destruction.

Another Bible reference that vividly describes Edom's monstrous behavior is the whole book of Obadiah. We will read only a part of the prophet Obadiah's inspired clarification of events from *The Amplified Bible.* However, I hope that you will take the time later to read the whole book of Obadiah.

Obadiah 1:10-14 (The Amplified Bible.)

10For the violence you did against your brother Jacob, shame shall cover you, and you shall be cut off forever.

Notice that God said to the whole nation of Edom, *"For the violence you did against your brother Jacob...."* Once again, God was referring to Esau's descendants (the nation of Edom) and the violence that they had committed against Jacob's descendants (the nation of Israel). Jacob, the twin, had died long before the previously mentioned violence against His descendants had taken place. So, it is obvious that God was not speaking of the Edomites doing violence to Jacob. No! As I have already stated, God was referring to the violence that Esau's descendants did against the nation that Jacob founded.

11On the day that you stood aloof [from your brother Jacob]—on the day that strangers took captive his forces and carried off his wealth, and foreigners entered into his gates and cast lots for Jerusalem—you were even as one of them.

12But you should not have gloated over your brother's day, the day when his misfortune came and he was made a stranger; you should not have rejoiced over the sons of Judah in the day of their ruin; you should not have spoken arrogantly in the day of their distress.

13You should not have entered the gate of My people in the day of their calamity and ruin; yes, you should not have looked [with delight] on their misery in the day of their calamity and ruin, and not have reached after their army and their possessions in the day of their calamity and ruin.

14And you should not have stood at the crossway to cut off those of Judah who escaped, neither should you have delivered up those [of Judah] who remained in the day of distress.

Are you aware that Esau's descendants, the Edomites, even delighted in seeing God's Holy City, Jerusalem, leveled to the ground? Did you know that they verbally yelled out that desire when Jerusalem was invaded by her other enemies? I know your heart will be saddened and appalled as you read David's words in the next verses.

Psalm 137:7 (The Amplified Bible.)

7Remember, O Lord, against the Edomites, that they said in the day of Jerusalem's fall, Down, down to the ground with her!

You should now understand why, when speaking of Edom's punishment, God said in Ezekiel 35:9, *The Living Bible*, "*Never again will you revive. You will be abandoned forever; your cities will never be rebuilt....*" In Ezekiel 35:11, God had warned that He would do to Edom what she did to His chosen people, Israel. And God always keeps His word. The Edomites had said, tear down Jerusalem to the ground. So, God paid them back by throwing Edom to the ground.

Is it any wonder that God said He hated Esau (Edom) and that He would never cease to be angry with the Edomites? Is it any wonder that God made Edom no promise of mercy for the end of time? And, is it any wonder that God's punishment of Edom was so extreme and adamantly final? No! It is not!

The next two texts describe the punishment that Edom received. God's prophetic description is explicit and easy to understand. It needs no amplification. So read the following details for yourself, and as you do, keep in mind the terrible blasphemies and atrocities that Edom committed against God and His chosen covenant people. These reports are taken from *The Living Bible*.

Isaiah 34:5-17 (The Living Bible.)

5And when my sword has finished its work in the heavens, then watch, for it will fall upon Edom, the people I have doomed.

⁶*The sword of the Lord is sated with blood; it is gorged with flesh as though used for slaying lambs and goats for sacrifice. For the Lord will slay a great sacrifice in Edom and make a mighty slaughter there.*

⁷*The strongest will perish, young boys and veterans too. The land will be soaked with blood, and the soil made rich with fat.*

⁸***For it is the day of vengeance, the year of recompense for what Edom has done to Israel.***

⁹*The streams of Edom will be filled with burning pitch, and the ground will be covered with fire.*

¹⁰*This judgment on Edom will never end. Its smoke will rise up forever. The land will lie deserted from generation to generation; no one will live there anymore.*

¹¹*There the hawks and porcupines will live, and owls and ravens. **For God will observe that land and find it worthy of destruction. He will test its nobles and find them worthy of death.***

¹²***It will be called "The Land of Nothing,"*** *and its princes soon will all be gone.*

¹³*Thorns will overrun the palaces, and nettles will grow in its forts, and it will become the haunt of jackals and a home for ostriches.*

¹⁴*The wild animals of the desert will mingle there with wolves and hyenas. Their howls will fill the night. There the night-monsters will scream at each other, and the demons will come there to rest.*

¹⁵*There the owl will make her nest and lay her eggs and hatch her young and nestle them beneath her wings, and the kites will come, each one with its mate.*

As you read the next text, **keep in mind that Bozrah was a city in Edom.**

Jeremiah 49:7-22 (The Living Bible.)

⁷*The Lord of Hosts says: Where are all your wise men of days gone by? Is there not one left in all of Teman?*

⁸*Flee to the remotest part of the desert, O people of Dedan; for when I punish **Edom**, I will punish you!*

9,10Those who gather grapes leave a few for the poor, and even thieves don't take everything, but I will strip bare __the land of Esau__, and there will be no place to hide. Her children, her brothers, her neighbors—all will be destroyed—and she herself will perish too.

11(But I will preserve your fatherless children who remain, and let your widows depend upon me.)

12The Lord said to Edom: If the innocent must suffer, how much more must you! You shall not go unpunished! You must drink this cup of judgment!

13__For I have sworn by my own name, says the Lord, that Bozrah shall become heaps of ruins, cursed and mocked; and her cities shall be eternal wastes.__

14I have heard this message from the Lord: He has sent a messenger to call the nations to form a coalition against Edom and destroy her.

15I will make her weak among the nations and despised by all, says the Lord.

16You have been fooled by your fame and your pride, living there in the mountains of Petra, in the clefts of the rocks. But though you live among the peaks with the eagles, I will bring you down, says the Lord.

17__The fate of Edom will be horrible; all who go by will be appalled, and gasp at the sight.__

18Your cities will become as silent as Sodom and Gomorrah and their neighboring towns, says the Lord. No one will live there anymore.

19I will send against them one who will come like a lion from the wilds of Jordan stalking the sheep in the fold. Suddenly Edom shall be destroyed, and I will appoint over the Edomites the person of my choice. For who is like me and who can call me to account?

20What shepherd can defy me? Take note: The Lord will certainly do this to Edom and also the People of Teman—even little children will be dragged away as slaves! It will be a shocking thing to see.

21The earth shakes with the noise of Edom's fall; the cry of the people is heard as far away as the Red Sea.

*²²The one who will come will fly as swift as a vulture
and will spread his wings against Bozrah. Then the
courage of the mightiest warriors will disappear like
that of women in labor.*

There is an enlightening footnote for Jeremiah 49:13 in *The
Amplified Bible*. It reads as such:

> How except by divine inspiration could
> the prophets have foretold that Edom's
> desolation would be perpetual? After
> 2,500 years the statement is so literally
> true that in the land of Edom, where
> millions once lived, there are only a few
> people barely existing, and the land is in
> ruins. For there was no prophecy that
> Edom would recover "in the latter days"
> (Jer. 48:47), as was predicted for Moab
> and Ammon, but Edom's desolation
> was to be lasting. The short book of
> Obadiah presents an interesting further
> clarification of God's reason for this
> exceptional treatment of Edom....

Surely there can be no doubt remaining in your mind as to why God
stated that He hated Esau (that is, why God stated that He hated the
descendants of Esau). And surely you agree with me that God's hatred
was justified even as His never ending anger is completely justified.

Oh, my friend, open your spiritual eyes and see the truth. For just as
surely as the Scriptures reveal why God loves the descendants of Jacob
(Israel), so they also reveal why He hated the wicked descendants of
Esau (Edom). God did not show unfair favoritism nor was He
prejudiced in His dealings with the twin sons of Isaac. When the twins
were in their mother's womb, God simply made a prediction that the
descendants of one twin would serve the descendants of the other in
order to further His own will and purpose on the earth. Furthermore,
God did not show partiality or prejudice in making His choice known to
Jacob as he traveled to Haran. God's motives were pure. He simply
wanted to keep covenant with Abraham and Isaac. So, in order to keep
His word, He established His covenant with one of Isaac's undeserving
twin sons. Yes, God loved and chose Jacob.

Because you have the inspired Scriptures, you are able to see with
hindsight the wisdom of God's prediction to Rebekah that the nation of

Edom would serve the nation of Israel. You are also able to see with hindsight God's wisdom in making His covenant choice known to Jacob as he journeyed to Haran. Whereas, it was with foresight that God made His prediction to Rebekah that the Edomites would serve the Israelites. It was also with foresight that God later made known His covenant choice to Jacob as he traveled to Haran.

Though at times the descendants of Jacob have done very wickedly, your being able to view Bible history with hindsight should convince you that the Israelites were still the better candidate to help God keep His promises to Abraham and thus fulfill His plan for all mankind. On the other hand, the Edomites' character, which God later revealed on the pages of His Word, makes it clear to any intelligent reader that the Edomite nation was not the best prospect for the job. After all, you saw for yourself in the previous Scriptures that Edom's disposition would not have aided God in fulfilling His overall plan. Rather, the Edomites would have worked to try to defeat God's will and purpose just as surely as they did in those recorded instances that you studied earlier.

I ask you, my friend, with the knowledge you now possess, if you were in God's shoes and you yourself were faced with making the same decision that God was faced with, which nation would you choose to help you accomplish your purpose for all mankind? Would you choose Edom or Israel? You would of course choose Israel. For, despite Israel's failings and the fact that like Edom, Israel was unworthy and undeserving of God's covenant love and choice, with your foreknowledge, you would know that Israel was still the better candidate for the job.

God's reasons for predicting that Esau's descendants would be in servitude to Jacob's descendants should now be crystal clear to you. Before the twins were born, God predicted that Esau (that is, the nation of Edom) would serve Jacob (Israel) in order to further His own purpose. Furthermore, God made that prediction because He did not want the descendants of either nation trying to take credit for what He would bring to pass. (Isaiah 46:9-10, Isaiah 48:3-8.) Thus, as I said earlier, unlike those who practice prejudice, God's decision that Edom would serve Israel was not antagonistic in design or effect. On the contrary, God's judgment was reasonable. Yes, His judgment was formed with knowledge and made only after careful examination of all the facts.

God's prediction was undoubtedly righteous and undeniably wise. We should praise God for making and fulfilling such an intelligent, logical, practical, thoughtful and merciful prediction. Yes, we should praise God for making a prediction that would inevitably help to clear His name, fulfill His promise to Abraham and eventually benefit all mankind. Praise be to our all-knowing, all-wise, wonderful God! Praise Him because His reasons (that is, His motives behind His prediction to Rebekah) were altogether good and right.

You now have insight into God's purpose for loving and choosing the founder of the Israelite nation and his descendants, the Israelites, as Jacob traveled to Haran. God's objective was to fulfill His solemn oath to His friend, Abraham. God did not hate Esau or his descendants when He chose and set His love upon Jacob and his descendants. God never hated Esau the individual. Furthermore, it was hundreds of years after Esau's death that God developed hatred for the nation that Esau had founded (that is, for Edom).

You were also given a glimpse of God's reasons behind His earlier prediction to Rebekah in Genesis 25:23. It is obvious that God considered all the facts. He took into consideration the future characters of both nations struggling in Rebekah's womb. And, though at that point, neither nation was any more worthy or deserving than the other, knowing all things, God saw that as difficult as it would be, He could better accomplish His future purpose for all mankind by predicting that Esau's descendants would serve Jacob's descendants rather than the other way around. God simply predicted that He would bring some good out of a bad situation.

As I said earlier, we are able to see the wisdom of God's prediction to Rebekah with hindsight whereas God, being all-knowing, made His prediction using foresight. For, though neither the Edomites nor the Israelites had to that point done any evil or good works to bring about God's prediction, God knew what the future held. He knew that Esau's descendants would turn out to be a cruel, rebellious, wicked people.

Last but not least, you now understand why God made the statement, "*I hated Esau....*" In Deuteronomy 7:10, Moses said that God "*repays those who hate Him to their face, by destroying them; He will not be slack to Him who hates Him, but will requite him to his face.*" God kept His Word in Deuteronomy 7:10. He repaid to the Edomites' face the same hatred and conduct that they had expressed toward Him by hating His chosen people, rejoicing in their calamity, shedding their blood, making plans to steal their land and experiencing delight over the fall of Jerusalem. Most of all, God repaid them for their blasphemy and hatred against Him and their attempts to defeat His purpose and desire for all mankind.

The end result was that the wickedness and devastation that, in their hatred, the Edomites planned for Israel was turned back upon their own heads. God repaid Edom tit for tat, deed for deed, hatred for hatred. God continued His punishment until the nation of Edom was utterly destroyed, never to rise again.

After seeing a glimpse of Edom's wicked character, would you rather God have chosen and loved the Edomite nation instead of the nation of Israel? Of course you would not! The Edomites were wicked through and through. Did you know that the wicked deeds of Esau's descendants are even recorded in the gospels? For example, King Herod the Great was one of Esau's descendants. He was the son of an Edumean (that is, he was the son of an Edomite). Edumea is Greek for Edom.

You will recall that it was King Herod who murdered, in Bethlehem, all Israelite infants two years old and under. Yes, it was an Edomite, a descendant of Esau, whom Satan used to try to murder the Messiah. It was a wicked Edomite whom Satan used in His attempt to kill Yeshua before He could reach adulthood and accomplish that which He had come to earth to do.

After the Romans destroyed Jerusalem in 70 AD, all traces of the Edomites disappeared. Thus, God's words in Jeremiah 49:21-22 in *The Living Bible* came to pass. *"The earth shakes with the noise of Edom's fall; the cry of the people is heard as far away as the Red Sea. 22The one who will come will fly as swift as a vulture and will spread his wings against Bozrah.* ___Then the courage of the mightiest warriors will disappear like that of women in labor.___*"* Truly, the peoples of the earth should not mourn over Edom's fate. Rather, as God foretold that men would do when He destroyed the nation of Edom (Ezekiel 35:14-15), we too should rejoice. We should rejoice over the fact that God's righteous justice prevailed, and His word was fulfilled. Moreover, we should learn a valuable lesson. We should learn that those who hurt God's covenant people hurt the apple of God's eye.

On that note, it seems right to me that I bring this portion of the series to a close with a word of comfort and warning. In chapter nine, you saw that for the sake of their forefathers, God loves the Jewish people with an everlasting love. However, God's love for the Jewish people does not mean that God does not have the capacity to also love you and me. Did not Yeshua Himself say in John 3:16, *King James Version*, *"For God so loved **the world**, that He gave His only begotten Son, that **whosoever** believeth in Him should not perish, but have everlasting life."*

Nevertheless, as you have seen recorded in the Bible, because of His promise to Abraham, God loves the Jewish people with a fixed or unchanging love. So my friend, do not be like the wicked descendants of Esau and thus incur God's curse. Do not do harm to God's covenant people. And, do not support those who try to harm Israel or those who try to lay claim to the land that God swore would belong to Israel forever. For the sake of the Lord's name and for your own future good, learn to love and support God's chosen people, the descendants of Abraham, Isaac and Jacob. Then, you will be truly blessed. For did not God say in Genesis 12:3, *"I will bless those who bless you [who confer prosperity or happiness upon you] and curse him who curses or uses insolent language toward you...."*

Edom was cursed. But my friend, if you are righteous and wise, you will make up your mind to be blessed.

Chapter 11

WHY DID GOD CHOOSE ABRAHAM?

"How much better it is to get skillful and godly Wisdom than gold! And to get understanding is to be chosen rather than silver." (Proverbs 16:16, The Amplified Bible.)

The preceding ten chapters of this book contain an abundance of the two godly qualities mentioned in the previous verse, Proverbs 16:16. They contain priceless treasures of wisdom and understanding. However, the treasury door is still wide open. So, I encourage you to stay alert as you again pass through it. For you must do your best to get the remaining wisdom and understanding that God has provided for you in this series, wisdom and understanding that is better than gold and silver.

Among many other truths, you now understand why God chose the Jewish people. You know that God chose them in order to keep His promises to Abraham, Isaac and Jacob. Yet, you may still ask, "Yes, I now know why God chose Abraham's descendants, **but why in the world did God choose Abraham in the first place? And why did God make His sacred covenant with Abraham?"**

By calling up portions of the prior chapters and combining that knowledge with the information you will receive in this portion of the series, you will certainly obtain the answer to the previous questions. You will learn exactly why God chose Abraham. You will also learn why God made His sacred covenant with Abraham. However, in order for you to acquire the first building block of understanding on that subject, you must journey with me back in history to the time when God created Adam and Eve and placed them in the Garden of Eden.

As a result of my last statement, I am sure that many questions have formed in your mind. Some of those questions might be, **"I believe that God created man, but can you tell me exactly why God created him?** Was man created to care for the animals that God had also created, animals over which man was given dominion? Was man created to be the caretaker of the Garden of Eden?" No my friend, man was not created to do either of those things. Man was created for one purpose and one purpose only. **Man was created to obey God's commandments**.

Thank God that the true purpose of man's existence is clearly outlined in the sacred Scriptures. And, thank God that you can read that inspired definition for yourself. You can know the truth. After you have read the next verse of Scripture, no one will ever again be able to deceive you on that issue. You will know beyond doubt that men were created to keep God's commandments.

Ecclesiastes 12:13 (The Amplified Bible.)

13All has been heard; the end of the matter is: **Fear God and keep His commandments, for this is the whole of man [the full, original purpose of his creation, the object of God's providence, the root of character, the foundation of all happiness, the adjustment to all inharmonious circumstances and conditions under the sun] and the whole [duty] for every man.**

I do not think God could have made the content of that verse in Ecclesiastes any clearer, do you? **The full original purpose of man's creation is to fear God and keep His commandments**. Man could not have been created to fill a greater or more glorious role. He was made solely for God's good pleasure, satisfaction and delight. The whole purpose for his existence is to serve and to please his Creator by keeping God's commands.

When Satan deceived Eve into breaking God's commands, he not only caused man to fall into sin, he also robbed mankind of the ability, power and desire to perform the purpose for their existence. From that moment on, men floundered about like fish out of water. They were spiritually helpless. They were powerless to consistently do right. Mankind could no longer function in the capacity that they had been created to fill.

Now that you are aware that men were created for the sole purpose of keeping God's commands, you have a better idea as to the extent of men's fall from their duty to God. Since, according to I John 3:4, sin is the breaking of God's law (that is, sin is the breaking of God's commands), men ended up doing the exact opposite of what they were created to do. Consequently, they no longer desired to work for God's good pleasure, satisfaction and delight. Instead, they chose to do their own will and pleasure which inevitably resulted in spiritual catastrophe. To put it bluntly, man was ruined. He was spiritually impoverished. Man was completely under Satan's control.

To the outward eye, man's future looked totally hopeless. However, there is no hopelessness with God. In His great wisdom, the Lord had foreseen the previous happening. Therefore, prior to man's fall, He had set in motion an emergency plan, a plan that would eventually restore man to his original spiritual position. A glimpse of God's restoration strategy is revealed in His warning to Satan after man's fall.

Genesis 3:14-15 (The Amplified Bible.)

14And the Lord God said to the serpent, Because you have done this, you are cursed above all [domestic] animals and above every [wild] living thing of the field; upon your belly you shall go, and you shall eat dust [and what it contains] all the days of your life.

15And I will put enmity between you and the woman, and between your offspring and her Offspring; He will bruise and tread your head underfoot, and you will lie in wait and bruise His heel. [Galatians 4:4.]

Bible scholars agree that in verse fifteen God was referring to the Anointed One, the promised Messiah, whom I Peter 1:20 tells us was chosen and ordained to conquer Satan before the foundation of the world. In addition, *The Amplified Bible* translators have provided you with a footnote for Genesis 3:15. That footnote reads as such:

> Christ fulfills through His victory over Satan the wonderful promise here spoken. See also Isa. 9:6; Matt. 1:23; Luke 1:31; Rom. 16:20; Gal. 4:4; Rev. 12:17.

God foretold in Genesis 3:15 that the Christ would be born of a woman and that He would conquer man's enemy, the devil. Messiah would bruise and tread Satan's head underfoot. After which, He would restore man to his former standing with God. Yes, the promised Messiah would free men from sin. Furthermore, He would give men the ability, power and desire to overcome and conquer sin and thus remain free. Free to do what? Men would remain free to work for God's good pleasure, satisfaction and delight. They would remain free to do what Ecclesiastes 12:13 informs you that men were originally created to do— free to *"...fear God and keep His commandments...."*

The following New Testament reference verifies my last statement. It proves beyond doubt that the Messiah's mission was to undo the evil works that Satan had done. You have already seen in God's Word what Satan's evil works were. He deceived men into breaking God's commands. By doing so, Satan robbed men of the ability, power and desire to accomplish the function that they had been created to perform. Thus, the Messiah's mission was to destroy (that is, to undo) those evil works of Satan by returning to men the power and desire to once again do what they were created to do.

I John 3:8 (The Amplified Bible.)

8[But] he who commits sin [who practices evildoing] is of the devil [takes his character from the evil one], for the devil has sinned (violated the divine law) from the beginning. ***The reason the Son of God was made manifest (visible) was to undo (destroy, loosen, and dissolve) the works the devil [has done].***

As I said earlier, Yeshua's mission was to destroy the previously mentioned works of the devil and thus equip men to once again do what they were created to do. Yeshua accomplished His mission. Through His death, He provided everything men need to be free from sin and to consistently keep God's commands. The following verse gives you a glimpse of the power, ability and desire to do right that Yeshua extended to mankind.

Philippians 2:13 (The Amplified Bible.)

13[Not in your own strength] for it is God Who is all the while effectually at work in you [energizing and creating in you the power and desire], both to will and to work for His good pleasure and satisfaction and delight.

Let us get back on track now. The translators of *The Amplified Bible* have inserted an additional reference at the end of Genesis 3:15. They point you to Galatians 4:4. As you read Galatians 4:4, you will again see that I am right on target regarding the content of Genesis 3:15 referring to the Messiah.

Galatians 4:4 (The Amplified Bible.)

4But when the proper time had fully come, God sent His Son, born of a woman, born subject to [the regulations of] the Law,

By now, I am sure you comprehend that the Messiah was the foundation of the emergency plan that God had in place prior to man's fall, the emergency plan that God first revealed in Genesis 3:15. Only the all-powerful, all-knowing, all-righteous and compassionate one true

God was capable of designing and implementing such an awesome, selfless plan.

God knew that it would take Him thousands of years to complete such a complicated program. He also knew that the consistent application of His strategy, spanning over those thousands of years, would exact from Him, the draftsman, an unfathomable degree of patience, endurance and suffering. Nevertheless, after He had carefully examined all the facts, God determined that the end result would be worth the tremendous sacrifices that He knew He would be forced to make. I say that because, as you know, God did follow through with His restoration plan despite its negative aspects that affected Him personally.

One of the previously mentioned negative aspects that affected God over the long haul was the grief He continually experienced because of man's sin and rebellion. For example, imagine the anguish God must have suffered before and during Noah's time. You will recall that men became so wicked that God had no choice but to flood the earth and destroy them.

Yet, even after God had admitted that He was sorry He had ever created mankind, He still refused to abort His restoration plan. God spared righteous Noah and his family. He allowed a remnant of eight people to survive the flood in order that they might help Him bring to pass His Word in Genesis 3:15. For, since God had foretold in the previously mentioned verse that the Messiah would be born of a woman, it was necessary that He keep a remnant of the human race intact in order to fulfill that prophecy.

The new beginning that men enjoyed after the flood did not change their sinful hearts. As men multiplied, they continued to pursue every sort of evil. It was not long before the whole earth was again filled with idolatry, murder and corruption. Yet, despite men's wickedness, God refused to give up the fight. In Genesis 3:15, He had foretold that the Messiah would be born a human being in order to conquer Satan and thus return to men the power they needed to accomplish all that God had originally created them to do, and God had no intention of retracting His word. So what did God do? He simply shifted to the next phase of His restoration plan.

The main feature of the second stage of God's plan involved a covenant. And since a covenant is a binding contract between two or more persons, God needed a man with whom He could make that agreement.

Finding the right man to fill the previously mentioned role had to have been a tremendous undertaking in itself. I say that because God had to find a man who could meet His covenant partnership prerequisite. The man God searched for had to possess certain character qualities. For instance, he had to be someone with enough courage and moral character to uphold his end of the bargain. For, if at any time during his lifetime that man failed to fulfill his role in the agreement, the contract would automatically become invalid. Consequently, God would be loosed from all obligation, and the completion of His restoration goal would be set back. So, to a large degree, the first part of the covenant stage of God's plan would be dependent on the man with whom He chose to make the agreement.

Earlier in the series, you saw an example of why the completion of the second portion of God's plan would have been in jeopardy if God had not bound Himself by an unbreakable contract. You saw that being tied to the Abrahamic covenant was protection, not only for His chosen people, but also, for God, Himself.

You will recall that the chosen people rebelliously broke the covenant that they had made with God at Horeb. The Israelites sinned against God by deliberately disobeying His commands. They went so far as to commit the sin of idolatry. They prostrated themselves before a golden calf. God was so outraged by His peoples' wicked behavior that the only thing that kept Him from eradicating them was His obligation to the Abrahamic covenant. For, if God had destroyed Abraham's covenant descendants, men would have accused Him of reneging on His sworn contract with Abraham, and His reputation would have been ruined.

There was, however, another advantage to God being bound by an unbreakable covenant. Let me explain. You now know that God had to fulfill His prophecy in Genesis 3:15. You also know that the Israelites were chosen to help Him carry out His prophetic warning in that verse. They were to be a holy nation, a nation set apart for God's purpose. Through their seed (that is, through the seed of Abraham, Isaac and Jacob), the promised Messiah would one day be born, bruise and tread Satan's head underfoot, enable mankind to do what they had been created to do and thus completely fulfill God's warning to Satan. Therefore, God being obligated to perform His part of a binding contract gave Him added incentive to spare the nation of people that He needed to help Him carry out His warning in Genesis 3:15.

The promised Messiah was to be the key to man's salvation. He was to be the key to men eventually being restored to their original spiritual position. And as I have repeatedly declared, God had to keep the covenant race alive so that, at the appropriate time, the Messiah could take on their seed and thus fulfill His Word in Genesis 3:15.

Considering all the previous facts, it stands to reason that in order for God to have furthered the covenant stage of His restoration plan, He definitely needed a special kind of man with whom He could make the previously mentioned agreement. God needed a man who would trust Him implicitly. Most of all, He needed a man who possessed mature, living faith (that is, a man who would not only have faith in God's word but who would obey it).

God found such a man. The man was Abram, later called Abraham. God immediately put Abraham to the test to see if he really would believe and obey His commands. That test involved total trust, sacrifice and obedience. God instructed Abraham to leave his own country, his relatives and his father's house, and go to a strange land which He promised to show him.

God assured Abraham that if he obeyed His commands, He would greatly bless him. God also promised that through Abraham all the families of the earth would be blessed. Of course, God was speaking about the peoples of the earth being blessed through the promised Messiah, the Messiah who would come through Abraham's covenant seed (that is, through the seed of Abraham, Isaac and Jacob), the Israelites.

It took a tremendous amount of living faith for Abraham to believe and to act upon all that God had commanded and promised, but he did. Abraham passed his first test with flying colors. He combined obedience to God's commands with his faith. Leaving every thing behind except his wife, his nephew Lot, his servants and his belongings, he set off for the Promised Land.

God must have been overjoyed with the way Abraham responded to His commands. He had finally found a man who would trust and obey Him, a man who would help Him fulfill His prophecy in Genesis 3:15, a man who would help Him carry out His restoration plan, a man who would be the father of the covenant nation through whom the promised Messiah would come, a man who would enter into a sacred covenant with Him and faithfully keep his end of the agreement.

The fact is that if God was going to help men recognize and once again perform the full original purpose for their existence, He had to have a man such as Abraham. God had to have a man with enough stamina to do what was right in God's sight. He had to have a man who was absolutely trustworthy, a man who would faithfully keep covenant. For, only then would God be able to bring to pass all that He had promised him in that covenant. And as you learned earlier, those covenant promises were meant to eventually bless (save) all mankind.

God made His choice. God chose Abraham. God felt assured that He could trust Abraham to help Him carry out His restoration plan. However, if Abraham had failed his first test, if he had refused to carry out God's instructions to leave Ur of the Chaldeans, God would not have made His covenant with him. For as you know, God had to have a faithful man (that is, God had to have a man who would be completely faithful to His commands).

Abraham did not let God down. He victoriously passed his test. Thus, when God saw how truly faithful Abraham was to His commands, He proceeded with His restoration plan. Without a doubt, it was Abraham's obedience that made it possible for God to eventually enter into an unbreakable covenant with him. See this for yourself in *The Living Bible*, paying special attention to the highlighted portion of verse eight.

> *Nehemiah 9:7-8 (The Living Bible.)*
>
> *7"You are the Lord God who chose Abram and brought him from Ur of the Chaldeans and renamed him Abraham.*
>
> *8When he was faithful to you, you made a contract with him to forever give him and his descendants the land of the Canaanites, Hittites, Amorites, Perizzites, Jebusites, and Girgashites; and now you have done what you promised, for you are always true to your word.*

Nehemiah 9:8 confirms the fact that it was only after God was convinced that Abraham could be trusted to faithfully carry out His instructions that He entered into a sacred covenant with him. The reason why Abraham's obedience to God's commands was crucial to God's restoration plan is because his obedience assured the validity of the sacred contract that God had made with him. The fact is that obeying God's commands was Abraham's sole responsibility in the covenant. The next verses which are taken from *The Living Bible* leave no doubt as to Abraham's covenant role.

Genesis 17:1-2 (The Living Bible.)

¹When Abram was ninety-nine years old, God appeared to him and told him, "I am the Almighty; <u>obey me</u> and live as you should.

²,³,⁴I will prepare a contract between us, guaranteeing to make you into a mighty nation. In fact you shall be the father of not only one nation, but a multitude of nations!" Abram fell face downward in the dust as God talked with him.

The *Holy Bible, King James Version* says, *"...<u>**I am the Almighty God; walk before Me, and be thou perfect. And I will make My covenant between Me and thee**</u>...."* Abraham immediately began to fulfill his part of the contract. His next act of obedience was to obey God's instructions in verses nine through fourteen of the same chapter. As God had commanded, Abraham circumcised every male in his camp. Before you study the next segment of this work, I strongly recommend that you take the time to read for yourself God's instructions in Genesis 17:9-14. You may also want to read Abraham's obedient response to God's commands. (Genesis 17:23-27.)

Inasmuch as you now have insight into the content of Genesis 3:15, and since I just brought up the subject of circumcision, I want to take a few moments to impart food for thought regarding the external ritual of circumcision.

You are already aware that circumcision is a token or sign of the covenant that God made with Abraham. But have you ever wondered why God chose that particular ritual as the external sign of the Abrahamic covenant? Why did God decide to put the sign of His covenant in the foreskin of man's flesh? Why did He not insist that the external reminder of the covenant be put in a more exposed part of the body so that it would be visible to all? Why did God choose to put the sign of His covenant with Abraham in the most private part of man's body?

My friend, with the knowledge you now have, there is only one answer that makes sense. So I will take a few moments to impart that answer. You will recall that in Genesis 3:15, God told Satan that the Messiah would be born a human being. That same verse in the *Holy Bible, King James Version* reads, *"And I will put enmity between thee* *and the woman, and between thy seed and **her seed;** it shall bruise thy head, and thou shalt bruise his heel."*

As a result of God's prediction in Genesis 3:15 that the Messiah would be born a human being, Isaiah foretold that a virgin would conceive and bear the promised Messiah. (Isaiah 7:14.) That virgin would of course be a covenant descendant of Abraham through the line of Isaac and Jacob. The following verse provides New Testament verification for what I just shared with you regarding the Messiah taking on Himself the seed of Abraham. Read that truth for yourself from both the *Holy Bible, King James Version* and *The Living Bible.*

Hebrews 2:16 (King James Version.)

¹⁶*For verily he took not on him the nature of angels;* **_but he took on him the seed of Abraham._**

Hebrews 2:16 (The Living Bible.)

¹⁶*We all know he did not come as an angel but as a human being—yes, a Jew.*

Since the Messiah was destined to be born a human being, it made perfect sense for God to put the sign of the covenant in the human organ that is responsible for propagating humankind. Furthermore, since the Jews were the covenant seed of Abraham through whom the promised Messiah would eventually be born, it made even more sense for God to include the external ritual of circumcision in the Mosaic Law. For, the Mosaic ritual of circumcision guaranteed that the sign of the covenant would be engraved in the foreskin of every male organ that would have a part in continuing to propagate the actual covenant race through whom the Messiah would come.

There is no other external part of the male body, other than the male organ of copulation, that has anything to do with propagating human kind. Think about it! Do the male's arms, legs or feet have anything to do with the propagation of human kind? Do the male's eyes, ears or nose have anything to do with the propagation of human kind? No! A thousand times no! As I previously stated, only the male organ of copulation has anything to do with the propagation of human kind.

Briefly, the plan was that with their organ of copulation, each covenant Israelite male would continue to plant the holy covenant seed of Abraham. In order to fulfill Genesis 3:15 and God's covenant with Abraham, the Messiah would eventually take on the seed of Abraham, Isaac and Jacob (that is, He would be born a human being and a Jew).

He would conquer Satan and thus return to men the power and desire they needed to fulfill the full original purpose of their creation. He would bring blessing (salvation) to all the peoples of the earth.

I am sure you will agree that, considering all the facts, there was no more logical or better external place on man's body for God to put the sign of the covenant than in the foreskin of the male's organ of copulation. For, the male organ of copulation would be the instrument that would be used to plant the holy, covenant seed of Abraham, Isaac, and Jacob, the covenant race through whom the promised Messiah would come.

God commanded that the external ritual of circumcision be performed on every eight-day-old covenant male descendant of Abraham, Isaac and Jacob. Thus, each time God's instruction was executed and a Jewish male baby cried out in discomfort as his foreskin was severed, the fulfillment of Genesis 3:15 and the Abrahamic covenant were proclaimed. At the same time, each newly circumcised male infant proclaimed that with his organ of copulation, he would continue to propagate the covenant seed of Abraham through whom the promised Messiah would be born, conquer Satan and restore all the peoples of the earth to their original spiritual state.

My friend, you now know why God chose to put the sign of the covenant in the foreskin of the male descendants of Abraham, Isaac and Jacob. You also know why God chose Abraham. God chose Abraham to help Him fulfill His Word in Genesis 3:15. God planned to accomplish His word by entering into an unbreakable contract (covenant) with Abraham and by using him to propagate the holy covenant nation through whom the promised Messiah would one day come as a human being. God chose Abraham to help Him fulfill His word and to aid Him in the restoration of mankind.

Even with the insight that you now possess regarding God's purpose for choosing Abraham, you may still have questions about that issue. You might say, "I am extremely grateful for the marvelous insight and understanding that I have already received concerning why God chose and made His covenant with Abraham. However, if there is more Biblical evidence available on that subject, I would certainly like to have it."

I am happy to inform you that additional Biblical evidence pertaining to the previous matter does exist. For example, in the following text, God Himself reveals yet another facet of Abraham's mission. God actually comes right out and tells you that He chose Abraham so that Abraham would teach his descendants to obey God's commands. You already know that men observing God's commands is the full original purpose of their creation. Hence, Abraham was called to help men make an effort to do what they were created to do.

Genesis 18:17-19 (The Amplified Bible.)

17And the Lord said, shall I hide from Abraham [My friend and servant] what I am going to do,

18Since Abraham shall surely become a great and mighty nation, and all the nations of the earth shall be blessed through him and shall bless themselves by him?

19For I have known (chosen, acknowledged) him [as My own], so that he may teach and command his children and the sons of his house after him to keep the way of the Lord and to do what is just and righteous, so that the Lord may bring Abraham what He has promised him.

Verse eighteen of the previous text provides confirmation of the former study regarding circumcision. It shows you that Abraham was indeed chosen to propagate the great nation of people through whom the Messiah would come, the nation of people through whom all the families of the earth would be blessed (that is, saved).

In verse nineteen, God states the other reason why He chose Abraham. **God chose Abraham so that he might train his descendants to begin to perform the full original purpose of their creation. He chose Abraham so that Abraham might teach his children to obey God's commands.** (Ecclesiastes 12:13.) By so doing, Abraham would enable God to keep the covenant promises that He had made to him, promises that would eventually fulfill God's Word in Genesis 3:15 and thus bring about God's will for the restoration of mankind.

In a little while, I will present documented evidence that proves that Abraham was faithful in accomplishing the purpose for which God chose him. Then you will know that Abraham did his best to train his children to observe all that God had commanded.

As part of their training, Abraham set a consistently righteous example before his children. Unquestionably, he obeyed God's commands. However, the day came when God put Abraham to the ultimate test. God commanded that Abraham offer up his own son as a burnt offering.

It is hard to imagine the emotional trauma that Abraham must have experienced as a result of God's command. For he knew that if he failed to obey that command and refused to take the life of his only covenant son, the sacred contract between himself and God would be canceled. Moreover, he knew that there was much more at stake than his son's life or his own loss. Abraham was aware that the future restoration of mankind depended on his faithfulness to his role in the sacred covenant. So as you can see, Abraham's test involved much more than men have realized. It involved the future blessing (that is, the future salvation) of all the peoples of the earth.

Abraham was also aware that God needed Isaac to propagate the great covenant nation through whom all the peoples of the earth would eventually be blessed. Moreover, he believed that God would keep the covenant promises that He had made to him. Abraham was convinced that if he obeyed God's command and took Isaac's life, God would raise up Isaac from the dead in order to keep His Word in Genesis 17:19. For, in that verse, God promised to establish His covenant with Isaac and his posterity after him, and God could not promote that segment of His covenant with a heap of ashes.

We are often overcome with wonder when we meditate on the faith and obedience that Abraham exhibited on the previous occasion. Yet, we fail to realize that Isaac displayed an equal amount of those same qualities. **Abraham had trained his son so well that Isaac was willing to allow himself to be sacrificed. Yes, he was willing to die in order to carry out God's instructions.**

Now you might say, "Since Isaac was only a child, did he really have a choice in the matter?" My friend, at the time in question, Isaac was not a small child. He was perhaps twenty-five years old when God commanded Abraham to offer him as a sacrifice. Therefore, Isaac had to have been a willing sacrifice.

Earlier I told you that I would present documented evidence to the effect that Abraham did an excellent job of training his children to obey God's commands. That promised evidence is that Abraham's son, Isaac, made a conscious decision to lay down his life in order to obey God's commands. Read the following footnote for Genesis 22:9 in *The Amplified Bible* and you will understand what I mean. As you do, bear in mind that the contents of Genesis 22:9 read, *"When they came to the place of which God had told him, **Abraham built an altar there; then he*** *laid the wood in order and bound Isaac his son and laid him on the altar on the wood."*

> Isaac, who was perhaps twenty-five years old (according to the ancient historian Josephus), shared his father's confidence in God's promise. Was not his very existence the result of God keeping His word? (Gen. 27:15-17.)

Could any other father have done a better job of training their son to trust and obey God than Abraham did? I do not think so. In total trust and obedience to God's commands, Isaac placed his life completely in God's hands. Thus, Abraham raised his knife to slay a willing sacrifice. However, just before Abraham could cut Isaac's throat, God stopped him. Of course, God never had any intention of allowing Abraham to kill his only covenant son. God was simply testing Abraham. He wanted to find out if Abraham would trust and obey Him no matter what He asked of him.

When God saw that Abraham believed His covenant promises so completely and obeyed His commands no matter what it cost him personally, God was absolutely convinced that He had chosen the right man with whom to make His sacred covenant. For after the previous incident, God knew beyond doubt that Abraham would continue to keep his end of the agreement. Thus, the Lord went on to swear by Himself that He would faithfully keep every covenant promise that He had made to Abraham.

Genesis 22:15-18 (The Amplified Bible.)

15The Angel of the Lord called to Abraham from heaven a second time

*16And said, **I have sworn by Myself, says the Lord,** that since you have done this and have not withheld [from Me] or begrudged [giving Me] your son, your only son,*

17In blessing I will bless you and in multiplying I will multiply your descendants like the stars of the heavens and like the sand on the seashore. And your Seed (Heir) will possess the gate of His enemies,

*18And in your Seed [Christ]shall all the nations of the earth be blessed and [by Him] bless themselves, **because you have heard and obeyed My voice.***

There was nothing that God could not ask of Abraham, not even the life of his own son. Abraham was totally committed to carrying out God's instructions. In obedience to God's commands, he had left his father's house; he had propagated the covenant seed (Isaac) through whom the Messiah would come; he had trained his children to obey everything that God had commanded; and he brought to the altar as an offering his own son, Isaac. Abraham joined works of obedience to his faith, thus making his faith alive and active. It was that combination of faith backed up with obedience to God's word (that is, obedience to God's commands) that caused God to account Abraham's living faith (that is, Abraham's faith and obedience) as righteousness.

As you read the next text, keep in mind that in this particular case when James speaks about works, he is referring to works of obedience to God's commands. **For example, in this instance, Abraham's works consisted of his obedience to God's commands regarding sacrificing his own son.**

James 2:17-26 (The Amplified Bible.)

17So also faith, if it does not have works (deeds and actions of obedience to back it up), by itself is destitute of power (inoperative, dead).

18But someone will say [to you then], You [say you] have faith, and I have [good] works. Now you show me your [alleged] faith apart from any [good] works [if you can], and I by [good] works [of obedience] will show you my faith.

19You believe that God is one; you do well. So do the demons believe and shudder [in terror and horror such as make a man's hair stand on end and contract the surface of his skin]!

20Are you willing to be shown [proof], you foolish (unproductive, spiritually deficient) fellow, that faith apart from [good] works is inactive and ineffective and worthless?

21Was not our forefather Abraham [shown to be] justified (made acceptable to God) by [his] works when he brought to the altar as an offering his [own] son Isaac?

22You see that [his] faith was cooperating with his works, and [his] faith was completed and reached its supreme expression [when he implemented it] by [good] works.

23And [so] the Scripture was fulfilled that says, Abraham believed in (adhered to, trusted in, and relied on) God, and this was accounted to him as righteousness (as conformity to God's will in thought and deed), and he was called God's friend.

24You see that a man is justified (pronounced righteous before God) through what he does and not alone through faith [through works of obedience as well as by what he believes].

25So also with Rahab the harlot—was she not shown to be justified (pronounced righteous before God) by [good] deeds when she took in the scouts (spies) and sent them away by a different route?

26For as the human body apart from the spirit is lifeless, so faith apart from [its] works of obedience is also dead.

Because Abraham obeyed all that God had commanded, even to the degree of being willing to take his own son's life, God was in turn able to keep with him the promises He had made. God later confirmed that very fact to Abraham's obedient covenant son, Isaac.

Genesis 26:1-5 (The Amplified Bible.)

1AND THERE was a famine in the land, other than the former famine that was in the days of Abraham. And Isaac went to Gerar, to Abimelech king of the Philistines.

2And the Lord appeared to him and said, Do not go down to Egypt; live in the land of which I will tell you.

3Dwell temporarily in this land, and I will be with you and will favor you with blessings; for to you and to your descendants I will give all these lands, and I will perform the oath which I swore to Abraham your father.

4And I will make your descendants to multiply as the stars of the heavens, and will give to your posterity all these lands (kingdoms); and by your Offspring shall all the nations of the earth be blessed, or by Him bless themselves.

⁵For Abraham listened to and obeyed My voice and kept My charge, My commands, My statutes, and My laws.

Abraham fulfilled God's purpose for his life. He obeyed God's commands, and he also taught his family to observe them. In doing so, righteous Abraham won amazing blessings for all mankind. Because Abraham fulfilled God's purpose for choosing him, all men now have an opportunity to be eternally blessed (that is, all men now have an opportunity to be saved from sin and to be free from Satan's power).

Genesis 28:14 (The Amplified Bible.)

¹⁴And your offspring shall be as [countless as] the dust or sand of the ground, and you shall spread abroad to the west and the east and the north and the south; and by you and your Offspring shall all the families of the earth be blessed and bless themselves.

Truly, Abraham's seed (Isaac, Jacob, and the Israelite nation) has been a source of great blessing to all the peoples of the earth. And every one of those blessings are the result of God's faithfulness to His word, His restoration plan and the faithfulness of the obedient man whom God chose to help Him carry out that plan.

It is important to note that the promised Messiah, Yeshua, never changed the focus of God's restoration plan. And that is why after His resurrection, Yeshua instructed His disciples, in Matthew 28:16-20, to go and teach men to obey God's commands. Yeshua wanted men to fulfill God's purpose for creating them. He wanted men to *"fear God and keep His commandments."* (Ecclesiastes 12:13.)

Yeshua had every right to expect men to do what they were created to do. He had every right to expect men to keep God's commands. After all, Yeshua had given His life to fulfill the prophesy made in Genesis 3:15. Through His death and resurrection, He bruised and trampled Satan's head underfoot and in so doing, He destroyed Satan's power over mankind.

Yeshua now has all power in heaven and on earth. Therefore, since Satan no longer has control of the human race, men are now free to carry out the full original purpose of their creation. They are free to obey all God's laws (that is, they are free to obey all God's commandments).

If you are wondering how Yeshua's death enabled men to be free from sin and Satan's power, then pay attention to the following brief explanation. You will recall that God made a covenant with the Israelites at Horeb. That covenant was sealed with sacrificial animal blood. As you learned earlier, nothing was wrong with the Horeb covenant in itself. It was a good agreement between God and His chosen people. No! The problem was not with that particular agreement. The problem was that when the Horeb covenant was made, Satan still had power over mankind. Consequently, the Israelites were not able to keep the Horeb agreement. They did not possess either the power or the desire needed to consistently obey God's commands.

Obviously, God's restoration plan did not include keeping His people permanently tied to a covenant that they were not equipped to keep. Frankly, the Horeb covenant was a temporary aid. It was intended to last only until God could bring into being the everlasting new covenant promised in Jeremiah 31:33-34.

When the time came for God to make His new covenant with men, God took upon Himself the seed of Abraham. Hence, as God had foretold in Genesis 3:15, the Messiah (that is, *"Immanuel [God with us]*,*"* Yeshua) was born a human being—a Jew.

At the young age of thirty-three, in obedience to God, Yeshua willingly laid down His life in order to acquire for men the promised new covenant and to seal that covenant with His own blood. That is why we Christians continue to speak so highly of and to sing praises about the blood of Yeshua.

Unlike the ritualistic animal blood, the holy blood of Yeshua made the new covenant a binding **everlasting** contract. Thus, God's promises in that binding contract have ultimately freed men from Satan's power and equipped them to once again perform the full original purpose of their creation. Read the contents of the blood-sealed new covenant in the following verses, and see for yourself God's sacred binding promises.

Hebrews 10:16-17 (The Amplified Bible.)

16This is the agreement (testament, covenant) that I will set up and conclude with them after those days, says the Lord: I will imprint My laws upon their hearts, and I will inscribe them on their minds (on their inmost thoughts and understanding),

*¹⁷He then goes on to say, **And their sins and their lawbreaking I will remember no more.***

As you can see, the blood-sealed new covenant contains specific promises of God. It contains God's promise to give you understanding of His laws (commandments) and the power you need to obey them. Your role in the new covenant is to utilize that power to learn and obey those laws. God also promises to forgive your past sins. Your role in the new covenant is to repent of your past sins so that you can receive that promised forgiveness.

Since you now have forgiveness from your past sins and since you also have the power to learn and obey God's commands, Satan no longer has any hold on you. His power over you has been destroyed. Thus, since Yeshua has endowed you with the previously mentioned overcoming new covenant power, you do not have to sin anymore (that is, you do not have to go on breaking God's commands). The truth is that if you are a genuine believer, in order for you to sin, you have to literally volunteer to break God's commands.

My friend, I thank God that you have grace! However, I do not thank God for grace because you cannot stop sinning. No! I thank God for the grace that stands in for you until you finally come to the realization that you do not have to sin by breaking God's commands. I thank God that grace abounds for you until you are spiritually intelligent enough to utilize the awesome, overcoming power that God has invested in you, power to bruise and trample Satan's head underfoot as your God and Savior did, power to learn and obey God's laws, power to be free from sin (that is, free from breaking God's laws), power to be free from men's wrong doctrines, power to perform the full original purpose of your creation. (Ecclesiastes 12:13.)

Listen Christian, for you to dare to insist that after Christ's death you still do not have enough power to stop sinning is to insist that Yeshua's blood was shed in vain and that God has failed to keep His blood-sealed new covenant promises. Therefore, I must address that issue. Throughout this series, you have seen Scriptural proof that God keeps His word even to His own hurt. So think carefully. If God keeps the Abrahamic covenant that was sealed with animal blood, and, if God keeps the Horeb covenant that was sealed with animal blood, how much more will He keep the new covenant that He sealed with His own blood?

We know beyond doubt that God is faithful to His promises. So, it is obvious that the problem is not with the new covenant. Rather, the problem lies with those people who say they belong to God and yet keep on sinning as though the new covenant does not exist.

The Jewish apostle John conveys the same truth that I am teaching. So, pay close attention to the content of the next two Scriptural quotes. The first one is taken from the *Holy Bible, King James Version.*

1 John 3:3-6 (King James Version.)

3 And every man that hath this hope in him purifieth himself, even as he is pure.

4 Whosoever committeth sin transgresseth also the law: for sin is the transgression of the law.

5 And ye know that he was manifested to take away our sins; and in him is no sin.

6 Whosoever abideth in him sinneth not: whosoever sinneth hath not seen him, neither known him.

To make sure that you fully comprehend the awesome truth that John is relaying to you in the previous text, let us also read his inspired words from *The Living Bible* translation.

1 John 3:3-9 (The Living Bible.)

3 And everyone who really believes this will try to stay pure because Christ is pure.

4 But those who keep on sinning are against God, for every sin is done against the will of God.

5 And you know that he became a man so that he could take away our sins, and that there is no sin in him, no missing of God's will at any time in any way.

6 So if we stay close to him, obedient to him, we won't be sinning either; but as for those who keep on sinning, they should realize this: They sin because they have never really known him or become his.

7 Oh, dear children, don't let anyone deceive you about this: if you are constantly doing what is good, it is because you are good, even as he is.

8 But if you keep on sinning, it shows that you belong to Satan, who since he first began to sin has kept steadily at it. But the Son of God came to destroy these works of the devil.

9The person who has been born into God's family does not make a practice of sinning, because now God's life is in him; so he can't keep on sinning, for this new life has been born into him and controls him—he has been born again.

The Jewish apostle, John, speaks truth. So Christian, do not let ignorant men or the devil deceive you any longer. John tells you in verse four that if you keep on sinning, you are against God. John also tells you in verse six that if you keep sinning, you sin because you do not know God—you do not belong to Him. John insists in verse eight that your disobedient actions prove that you still belong to Satan.

You are now equipped with the information you need to more fully understand the following text. Earlier, I stated that Yeshua never changed the focus of God's restoration plan. Rather, Yeshua furnished everything men needed to fulfill the original purpose of their creation. And that is why, in the subsequent verses, Yeshua instructed His disciples to go and teach men to obey God's commands (that is, to go and teach men to *"fear God and keep His commandments"*— Ecclesiastes 12:13). As we briefly study the contents of the next five verses, I will do my best to explain any points that are relevant to the present subject.

Matthew 28:16-20 (The Amplified Bible.)

16Now the eleven disciples went to Galilee, to the mountain to which Jesus had directed and made appointment with them.

*17And when they saw Him, **they fell down and worshiped Him;** but some doubted.*

The previous incident took place after Yeshua's resurrection from the dead. In verse seventeen, Matthew tells you that on that occasion, Yeshua's disciples fell down and worshipped Him. Why did those Jewish men worship Yeshua? They worshipped Him, because according to Isaiah 7:14, Yeshua is *"Immanuel [God with us]."* For that same reason, when Yeshua again appeared to His disciples after His resurrection, it is recorded in John 20:28 that the Jewish apostle, Thomas, called Yeshua *"My Lord and my God!"*

Let us now read verses eighteen through twenty of Matthew twenty-eight. With the insight you now possess, you should quickly understand the truth that Yeshua is relaying to you in those verses.

18Jesus approached and, breaking the silence, said to them, All authority (all power of rule) in heaven and on earth has been given to Me.

Yeshua stated, *"All authority (all power of rule) in heaven and on earth has been **given** to Me."* If you check the word *"given"* in the *Strong's Exhaustive Concordance of the Bible*, Greek Dictionary of the New Testament, you will realize that *"given"* is only one of a variety of words that Bible translators could have inserted in verse eighteen. An alternate word could have been *"yielded"*, since *"yielded"* is included in the definition of the Greek word didomi.

Consider how verse eighteen would read if Bible translators had chosen to use the word *"yielded"* rather than *"given"*. It would read, *"All authority (all power of rule) in heaven and on earth has been yielded to Me."*

In this case, *"yielded"* is an extremely appropriate word. It is appropriate because when Christ died, sealing the new covenant with His own blood and was afterward resurrected, Satan had to yield (that is, he had to give up) his power over man to the victor, Yeshua. Thus, Yeshua truly did possess all power in heaven and on earth.

In a moment, you will be reading the rest of Yeshua's statement. However, before you do, I want to bring something else to your attention. In Matthew 28:19, Yeshua continues His statement with the words, *"Go then..."* or as the *King James Version* says, *"Go ye therefore...."* The previous point is extremely important. It is important because it proves that the commission the disciples received came about as a result of the power that had been yielded to Yeshua. I will explain in more detail after you read the actual commission.

19Go then and make disciples of all the nations, baptizing them into the name of the Father and of the Son and of the Holy Spirit,

20Teaching them to observe everything that I have commanded you, and behold, I am with you all the days (perpetually, uniformly, and on every occasion), to the [very] close and consummation of the age.

Did you notice the way Yeshua phrased the contents of the commission? He did not tell the apostles to teach everything God commanded. No! He specifically instructed them to teach men **to observe (that is, to teach men to obey)** everything that God had commanded. You see, by obeying all that God had commanded, men would automatically fulfill the full original purpose of their creation. Men would keep all God's commandments. (Ecclesiastes 12:13.)

Briefly, let me fill in the gaps and sum up the content of Yeshua's statement in verses eighteen through twenty of the previous text.

Yeshua *("Immanuel [God with us]")* came to earth as a human being in order to trample Satan's head (power) underfoot. Christ's aim was to remove from Satan the power he had over the entire human race and thus enable men to stop sinning and to again perform the original purpose of their creation.

A fierce spiritual battle had raged between the Lord and His adversary, the devil, but praise be to God, the Lord prevailed over Satan. Yeshua completely accomplished His earthly mission. By obediently laying down His human life, He acquired a new covenant and sealed it with His own blood. Moreover, on the third day, He arose from the grave as the Old Testament prophets had foretold. By His previous acts, the Lord conquered both sin and death.

Satan was forced to submit to the victor, Jewish Yeshua. On Satan's part, submission required that he yield to Yeshua the control that he had previously wielded over mankind. Under such circumstances, Satan had no other choice but to relinquish that power. After all, Yeshua had won a binding new covenant between God and men, a covenant that He had purchased and sealed with His own blood. In the new covenant, God promised to write His laws on His peoples' hearts and minds so that they would know them and obey them. He also promised to forgive their sins. Therefore, from that point on, there was no way that Satan could have kept or can keep God's people from fulfilling the full original purpose of their creation.

Oh, my friend, I think it is obvious that Yeshua never changed the focus of God's restoration plan. On the contrary, as God the Father, He was, like Abraham, willing to take the life of His own Son to fulfill it. As God the Son, He was like Isaac, willing to lay down His life to fulfill it. Yeshua was not only willing but in obedience to God, He actually laid down His life. However, also like Abraham and Isaac, Yeshua knew that God would raise Him from the dead in order to fulfill His Word in Psalm 16:10. And praise be to God, He did.

I am sure you will agree that along with many other queries, I have adequately answered the question, "Yes, I now know why God chose

Abraham's descendants, but why in the world did God choose Abraham in the first place?" However, since there are so many facets to that answer, let me end this chapter with a brief review of those points.

(1) Abraham was chosen to help God fulfill His Word in Genesis 3:15 (that is, to propagate the covenant seed through whom the Messiah would come, conquer Satan and spiritually restore mankind).

(2) Abraham was chosen by God to help men begin their long and trying journey back to the original purpose of their creation. He was chosen to obey God's commands and to teach his children to do the same.

(3) Abraham was chosen by God to enter into a covenant with God, a covenant that was intended to bring about eternal blessings (that is, eternal salvation) for all mankind.

What a plan! What a God! Praise be to the God of Abraham, Isaac and Jacob!

Chapter 12

HOW DID ISRAEL FIT
INTO GOD'S RESTORATION PLAN?

Abraham had accomplished every aspect of his God-ordained mission, a mission that is described in the foregoing chapter. He had walked in obedience to God's commands all the days of his life and had taught his children to do the same. In doing so, Abraham had not only enabled God to bring him all that He had promised, but his obedience had also allowed God to advance to the next stage of His restoration plan. You will recall that the ultimate goal of God's plan was to fulfill His prediction in Genesis 3:15, *"And I will put enmity between you and the woman, and between your offspring and her Offspring; He will bruise and tread your head underfoot, and you will lie in wait and bruise His heel. [Galatians 4:4.]"* Yes, the ultimate goal of God's plan was to fulfill Genesis 3:15, conquer Satan and restore men to the full original purpose of their creation described in the following text.

> *Ecclesiastes 12:13 (The Amplified Bible.)*
>
> *13All has been heard; the end of the matter is:* **Fear God [revere and worship Him, knowing that He is] and keep His commandments, for this is the whole of man [the full, original purpose of his creation**, *the object of God's providence, the root of character, the foundation of all happiness, the adjustment to all inharmonious circumstances and conditions under the sun] and the whole [duty] for every man.*

Upon reviewing the Biblical facts in the previous paragraph, you are probably thinking, "After studying chapter eleven of this book, I can certainly see how Abraham assisted God in carrying out His restoration plan. **However, I still do not understand how the covenant descendants of Abraham, Isaac and Jacob aided God in reinstating men to their original spiritual position.**"

My friend, the Israelites were given a specific job to accomplish on the earth. Israel's mission consisted of numerous responsibilities, all of which were crucial to God's overall plan. To give you an idea of the broadness of the scope of Israel's God-given commission, I will briefly touch on some of her main duties. As we cover several aspects of Israel's many faceted mission, please make every effort to concentrate on the subject at hand. Do not allow yourself to get side tracked by pursuing avenues of thought that have nothing to do with the topic that is under examination. Rather, try to focus your attention on Israel's role in God's restoration plan.

ISRAEL'S JOB DESCRIPTION, DUTY NO. 1: PRODUCE THE PROMISED COVENANT NATION.

Israel's first assignment was to produce the great covenant nation that God had promised to Abraham, Isaac and Jacob. (Genesis 12:13, 26:3, 46:3.) Genesis 3:15 had to be fulfilled. Therefore, Israel was chosen by God to be the nation through whom the Messiah would come and crush Satan's power and restore mankind to their original spiritual position. In earlier chapters of this series, you learned exactly how God accomplished the propagation phase of His restoration plan. So, it is not necessary for me to go into a lengthy explanation of that subject. Instead, I will simply review some of the highlights of those former chapters.

You will recall that as part of His strategy, God forced Jacob and his family to enter into Egypt and to temporarily dwell there. Egypt was chosen by God to become a human breeding ground for the propagation of God's covenant nation. Albeit, Satan interfered with God's plan. He attempted to put a stop to the Israelites' phenomenal population growth. You will remember that Satan was behind Pharoah's horrific edict—ordering the murder of all newborn Israelite male babies.

Now that you have insight into God's warning to Satan in Genesis 3:15 (that is, now that you know that Satan was aware of how God intended to bring his control over mankind to an end), you can see even more clearly why Satan was concerned about the Israelites' high birth rate. You can also comprehend why he went to such extremes to try to put a halt to their population explosion. Satan knew that God's covenant people, the Israelites, were destined to be the nation through whom the Messiah would eventually come. He also knew that the success of the procreation segment of God's plan held serious future consequences for him.

Israel paid a tremendous cost in order to become the great nation that God promised to Abraham. For over four hundred years the Israelites multiplied in Egypt, and throughout most of that time, they were afflicted and oppressed. Eventually, they were enslaved, and during their enslavement, their male babies were murdered by the Egyptians.

I am sure you will agree that Israel sacrificed a great deal to do God's will and thus fulfill her role in His restoration plan. Yet, despite all the hardships she faced, Israel accomplished her first assignment. And, because she succeeded in producing the promised covenant nation, all men now benefit from her past suffering, perseverance and eventual triumph.

ISRAEL'S JOB DESCRIPTION, DUTY NO. 2: EXALT AND MAKE KNOWN GOD'S NAME.

The covenant nation of Israel was assigned to exalt God's name and to prepare the way for its acknowledgment by all the nations.

> *Isaiah 63:11-14 (The Amplified Bible.)*
>
> *11 Then His people [seriously] remembered the days of old, of Moses and his people [and they said], Where is He Who brought [our fathers] up out of the [Red] Sea, with [Moses and the other] shepherds of His flock? Where is He Who put His Holy Spirit within their midst,*
>
> *12 Who caused His glorious arm to go at the right hand of Moses, dividing the waters before them, **to make for Himself an everlasting name,***
>
> *13 Who led them through the depths, like a horse in the wilderness, so that they did not stumble?*
>
> *14 Like the cattle that go down into the valley [to find better pasturage, refuge, and rest], the Spirit of the Lord caused them to rest. **So did You lead Your people [Lord] to make for Yourself a beautiful and glorious name [to prepare the way for the acknowledgment of Your name by all nations].***

What a marvelous mission God entrusted to the nation of Israel. She was called to show forth God's power and greatness. She was appointed to bring acclaim to God's name before all the other nations. And just how did Israel accomplish that particular task? She accomplished it by simply being the nation through whom God fulfilled His covenant promises and through whom God exhibited His awesome power and mighty works.

In Egypt, God executed many miraculous acts of judgment and awesome exhibitions of power. After Israel's exit from Egypt, He performed the amazing feat of dividing the Red Sea. In all of those incredible happenings and many others, Israel was the chosen instrument through whom God achieved success. Yes, through the descendants of

Abraham, Isaac and Jacob, God miraculously gained the reputation that He sought. As the previous verse states, the God of Israel led His people out of Egypt to the Promised Land **to make for Himself "...*a beautiful and glorious name [to prepare the way for the acknowledgment"* of His name *"by all nations"].***

ISRAEL'S JOB DESCRIPTION, DUTY NO. 3: TRAVEL TO AND POSSESS THE PROMISED LAND.

After the Israelites had completed the first two stages of their God-ordained mission, they were immediately compelled to perform another difficult task. They were required to travel from Egypt to Canaan, the Promised Land, and to take possession of it.

Sadly, the generation of Israelites who came out of Egypt did not fulfill that duty. They lacked faith in God's ability to deliver the occupants of Canaan into their hands. Consequently, because of their unbelief (that is, because they lacked faith and obedience to God's commandments), they never got to enter the Promised Land. Instead, it was their children who eventually inherited the land of Canaan and completed the portion of God's restoration plan that we are presently studying. Yes, it was their children who in faith and obedience to God's commands conquered the people of Canaan and inhabited the land where the promised Messiah would one day be born of a woman, tread Satan's head underfoot and free mankind from Satan's control.

ISRAEL'S JOB DESCRIPTION, DUTY NO. 4: WATCHMAN AND PROPHET.

Israel's fourth assignment was every bit as amazing as the three that we have already covered. Ephraim (Israel) was called and commissioned to be a watchman with God and a prophet to the nations.

Hosea 9:8 (The Amplified Bible.)

[8]*Ephraim was [intended to be] a watchman with my God [and a prophet to the surrounding nations]....*

As a prophet to the surrounding nations, Israel's first responsibility was to set a righteous example before the Gentiles. Israel was to accomplish that duty by keeping the vow she had made before God at Horeb and obeying God's commandments.

Also, Israel's job as a prophet made her God's spokesman. Israel was intended to be a righteous mouthpiece through whom God's utterances would be made known to the Gentiles. She was intended to be an instrument through whom God would eventually reveal His perfect will to all men. God's plan included Israel predicting and recording future events, events that would affect all mankind. It is because the prophet, Israel, fulfilled the previous aspect of her mission that today we have God's spoken Word recorded in the sacred Scriptures.

As a watchman with God, Israel's responsibilities were to observe the times, patiently wait for the promised Messiah and at the appropriate time, give distinct warnings of the Messiah's approach and arrival.

Thank God that some Jews, Jews such as John the Baptist and the Lord's disciples, did remain faithful to their God-given call and commission of watchman with God and prophet to the nations. For as you will see later, because of their faithfulness, all men have been and are given an opportunity to know God's will and to be saved from sin.

ISRAEL'S JOB DESCRIPTION, DUTY NO. 5: A HOLY PRIESTLY NATION.

The fact that God had previously predicted that the promised Messiah would take on the covenant seed of Abraham, Isaac and Jacob, *"In you will all the families and kindred of the earth be blessed..."* (Genesis 12:3, 26:4, and 28:14), made it essential that the nation of Israel be consecrated and set apart for God's service. The following verse describes that very crucial element of God's restoration plan. For it clearly explains that **the covenant nation of Israel was called to be to God a kingdom of priests, a holy nation.**

Exodus 19:6 (The Amplified Bible.)

6And you shall be to Me a kingdom of priests, a holy nation [consecrated, set apart to the worship of God]. These are the words you shall speak to the Israelites.

The Israelites were called to be, **to God,** a kingdom of priests. And, since God is holy, He required that those who ministered to Him also be holy. Now, you might wonder what it means for a nation to be considered as holy. Well, in the succeeding verse, Yeshua Himself explains that a man becomes holy by the truth (that is, a man becomes holy by learning and obeying God's commands). Apply Yeshua's definition of the word *"holy"* to the nation of Israel, and you will have your answer regarding what it means for a nation to be holy. You will also understand what God requires of those who minister to Him.

John 17:17 (The Amplified Bible.)

17Sanctify them [purify, consecrate, separate them for Yourself, make them holy] by the Truth; Your Word is Truth.

John 17:17 in *The Living Bible* reads:

17Make them pure and holy through teaching them your words of truth.

God considered the Israelites to be holy when they made every effort to do what they were created to do. He considered them to be a holy nation when they kept the Horeb covenant. He considered them to be a holy nation when they feared God and obeyed His commandments. The following verse is yet another Scriptural verification of the previously stated fact.

Deuteronomy 28:9 (The Amplified Bible.)

9The Lord will establish you as a people holy to Himself, as He has sworn to you, if you keep the commandments of the Lord your God and walk in His ways.

While we understand God's need for holiness, it is important to note that God did take into consideration the fact that mankind was at that time still held captive by sin. Indeed, in fulfillment of His promised Abrahamic covenant mercy and loving-kindness, God generously made provision for those times when the Israelites would fail to be holy (that is, those times when they would fail to keep the Horeb covenant and would sin by breaking His commands). I am sure that you are already aware that this provision was bestowed upon the nation of Israel in the form of the external ritualistic animal sacrifices. God promised that He would forgive His peoples' sins when they truly repented and offered the appropriate animal sacrifices.

To bring your focus back to this brief study of what constitutes a holy nation and to confirm the previous truth that holiness consists in obeying God's commands, we will read the verses before and after Exodus 19:6. As you read, fix your attention on the highlighted portions of those verses, especially verses five and six. For, those two verses contain God's prerequisite for a holy priestly nation.

Exodus 19:3-8 (The Amplified Bible.)

*3And Moses went up to God, and the Lord called to him out of the mountain, **Say this to the house of Jacob and tell the Israelites;***

4You have seen what I did to the Egyptians, and how I bore you on eagles' wings and brought you to Myself.

*5Now therefore, **if you will obey My voice in truth and keep My covenant,** then you shall be My own peculiar possession and treasure from among and above all peoples; for all the earth is Mine.*

*6**And you shall be to Me a kingdom of priests, a holy nation [consecrated, set apart to the worship of God].** These are the words you shall speak to the Israelites.*

God required that the nation of Israel be holy by devoting themselves to the duty that men were originally created to perform. He required that the Israelites be holy by keeping the covenant that they made with Him at Horeb and obeying His commands. Moreover, in the next verses, you are given proof that keeping God's commands is exactly what the Israelites promised to do. Yes, the Israelites agreed to obey **all** God's commands.

7So Moses called for the elders of the people and told them all these words which the Lord commanded him.

*8And all the people answered together, and said, **All that the Lord has spoken we will do.** And Moses reported the words of the people to the Lord.*

Another reason why it is absolutely essential that God's priestly nation obey His commands and live holy lives is because it is a priest's job to show God's people in what way their lives are wrong. A priest's responsibility is to teach men what is right and wrong by the standards of God's Word. So, it stands to reason that it does no good for priests to fulfill this obligation if they themselves fail to do right (that is, if they themselves fail to obey God's instructions). It is a proven fact that wicked priests do more harm than good. You see, by their disobedient actions, they encourage those in their charge to imitate their unrighteous, hypocritical behavior.

The next reference divulges the truth regarding the necessity for priests to obey God's commands and thereby set an exemplary example before God's people.

Ezekiel 44:23-24 (The Amplified Bible.)

23 The priests shall teach My people the difference between the holy and the common or profane, and cause them to distinguish between the unclean and the clean.

24 And in a controversy they shall act as judges, and they shall judge according to My judgments; <u>and they shall keep My laws and My statutes in all My appointed feasts, and they shall keep My Sabbaths holy.</u>

The Living Bible reads as such:

23 <u>He shall teach my people the difference between what is holy and what is secular, what is right and what is wrong.</u>

24. They will serve as judges to resolve any disagreements among my people. Their decisions must be based upon my laws. <u>And the priests themselves shall obey my rules and regulations</u> at all the sacred festivals, and they shall see to it that the Sabbath is kept a sacred day.

God required that the Israelites do one thing and one thing only. As I have repeatedly stated, He required that they make every effort to fulfill the original purpose of their creation. He required that they fear Him and keep His commandments. Since God's covenant people were intended to be priests to God, their obedience to God's laws was of great importance to Him. To see Biblical evidence that obedience was the only requirement that God ever made on His holy, priestly nation, read the following two verses, noting the highlighted sections.

Deuteronomy 10:12-13 (The Amplified Bible.)

12 <u>And now, Israel, what does the Lord your God require of you but [reverently] to fear the Lord your God,</u> [that is] to walk in all His ways, and to love Him, and to serve the Lord your God with all your [mind and] heart and with your entire being.

13 <u>To keep the commandments of the Lord and His statutes which I command you today for your good?</u>

God expected the Israelite nation to meet His conditions in Ecclesiastes 12:13. God demanded that His people make every effort to fear Him and keep His commandments. And to find out whether the

Israelites would or would not meet His righteous requirement, God thoroughly tested them. As a matter of fact, the whole forty years they spent in the wilderness turned out to be one big test. Indeed, their entire difficult wilderness experience (that is, each individual obstacle they faced in the wilderness) gave God an opportunity to find out if they would keep His commands or not. Moreover, every instruction God gave them during that period served the same purpose.

Confirmation of all that I have just stated is evident in the following two texts. In the first example, God instructed His people to gather only a one day supply of manna at a time. He specifically gave that instruction so He could observe their reaction to His command as well as the conclusion that they eventually reached. For, as I said, God's main objective was to see if they would or would not obey His stipulated commands.

Exodus 16:4 (The Amplified Bible.)

⁴Then the Lord said to Moses, Behold, I will rain bread from the heavens for you; and the people shall go out and gather a day's portion every day, that I may prove them, whether they will walk in My law or not.

The second example relays the same truth as the previous one. It again brings out God's motive for subjecting the Israelites to such rigorous testing in the wilderness. God wanted to observe the Israelites' behavior. **He wanted to find out if they would or would not fulfill their holy priestly role and obey His commands.**

Deuteronomy 8:1-2 (The Amplified Bible.)

¹ALL THE commandments which I command you this day you shall be watchful to do, that you may live and multiply and go in and possess the land which the Lord swore to give to your fathers.

²And you shall [earnestly] remember all the way which the Lord your God led you these forty years in the wilderness, to humble you and to prove you, to know what was in your [mind and] heart, whether you would keep His commandments or not.

It is a Biblically established fact that the Israelites accepted the conditions of their priestly position prior to their being set apart for God's service. Their assent is clearly recorded in one of the verses that we read previously, Exodus 19:8. The Israelites' exact words of acceptance were, *"All that the Lord has spoken we will do."*

As a result of them agreeing to uphold God's priestly conditions, the Israelites were appointed as priests to God Himself. Notice the highlighted portion of yet another verse that we covered earlier. For it leaves no doubt that **the Israelites were indeed called to be priests to Almighty God Himself.**

Exodus 19:6 (The Amplified Bible.)

6And you shall be __to Me__ a kingdom of priests, a holy nation [consecrated, set apart to the worship of God]. These are the words you shall speak to the Israelites.

I cannot conclude Israel's Job Description, Duty No. 5 without first emphasizing the fact that God never withdrew Israel's priestly charge. The Israelites' appointed position has not nor ever will be canceled out. Israel will always be a chosen race and a royal priesthood. That is why God's design for the Jewish nation remained the same after Christ's death and resurrection. Furthermore, that is why even today, the Israelites are priests to the King of Kings and Lord of Lords. To see New Testament proof of that fact, study the next Scriptures carefully.

I Peter 2:9 (The Amplified Bible.)

9__But you are a chosen race, a royal priesthood, a dedicated nation,__ [God's] own purchased, special people, that you may set forth the wonderful deeds and display the virtues and perfections of Him Who called you out of darkness into His marvelous light. [Exodus 19:5,6.]

Notice that *The Amplified Bible* translators provide you with an additional reference for the previous verse. That reference is Exodus 19:5-6. And my friend, you already know that Exodus 19:5-6 contains the identity of the chosen race, the royal priesthood whom the Jewish apostle is referring to in I Peter 2:9. Yes, in Exodus 19:5-6, God Himself identifies the lineal descendants of Abraham, Isaac and Jacob as His holy, priestly nation.

Do not be fooled Christian Gentile. **Peter is not addressing Gentiles in I Peter 2:9. On the contrary, Peter is addressing Jewish believers.** Moreover, Peter's oration to the Jews makes perfect sense since according to Galatians 2:7, he was an apostle (special messenger) to those of the circumcision (that is, to the lineal descendants of Abraham, Isaac and Jacob). To obtain further Scriptural evidence that proves that the contents of Peter's letter was addressed to Jewish believers, you only have to read the first verse of his epistle. So, let us do that right now.

I Peter 1:1 (The Amplified Bible.)

[1]*PETER, AN apostle (a special messenger) of Jesus Christ, [writing]* **to the elect exiles of the dispersion scattered (sowed) abroad** *in Pontus, Galatia, Cappadocia, Asia, and Bithynia,*

When Peter wrote this letter, the Jews were the exiles who were scattered throughout the world. We Gentiles did not fit Peter's description. Most Bible scholars agree that Peter's letter was indeed intended for Jewish believers. For example, in *Smith's Bible Dictionary* under the heading "5500 Questions and Answers on the Holy Bible," subheading "Patient Suffering (I Peter 1:1)," we read:

> To whom did Peter address his epistle?—To the same **dispersed Jews** as James.

Since in the previous quote, the Bible scholar, Smith, refers to Peter addressing the same dispersed Jews as James, I think it would be wise to read about that situation in James' letter.

James 1:1 (The Amplified Bible.)

[1]*JAMES, A servant of God and of the Lord Jesus Christ,* **to the twelve tribes scattered abroad [among the Gentiles in the dispersion]:** *Greetings (rejoice)!*

Surely there is no doubt remaining as to the fact that in his first letter, the apostle Peter was addressing Jewish believers. However, there is yet another portion of Peter's letter that again makes that truth crystal clear. In the following verse, you will see additional evidence that Peter's letter was directed specifically toward Jewish believers.

I Peter 2:12 (The Amplified Bible.)

[12]**Conduct yourselves properly (honorably, righteously) among the Gentiles,** *so that, although they may slander you as evildoers, [yet] they may by witnessing your good deeds [come to] glorify God in the day of inspection [when God shall look upon you wanderers as a pastor or shepherd looks over his flock].*

A person cannot be both a Jew and a Gentile. Jews are Jews, and Gentiles are non-Jews. Therefore, it is obvious that when in

I Peter 2:12, the Jewish apostle Peter instructed a certain group of people to watch their behavior when they were among the Gentiles, the group he was addressing had to have been Jews. The evidence pointing to that fact is overwhelming. For instance, in the epistle of Peter that we are presently examining, the apostle provides even more confirmation of that same truth. As you read Peter's words, pay attention to the highlighted portion.

I Peter 3:6 (The Amplified Bible.)

*6It was thus that Sarah obeyed Abraham [following his guidance and acknowledging his headship over her by] calling him lord (master, leader, authority). **And you are now her true daughters** if you do right and let nothing terrify you [not giving way to hysterical fears or letting anxieties unnerve you].*

I ask you, would Peter have called Gentile Christians *"true daughters"* of Abraham's wife, Sarah? No, of course not. However, he most certainly would have addressed Jewish believers by that title (that is, those believers who were the lineal descendants of Abraham, Isaac and Jacob).

When one combines all the previous evidence, there can be no doubt that, in I Peter 2:9, Peter is referring to Jewish believers. Think about it! Did not God Himself say to the Israelites in Exodus 19:6, *"You shall be to me a kingdom of priests, a holy nation...."* Gentile Christian, for God's name's sake, you should shout for joy over the fact that Peter shows you that God's will has been and is being done on earth, and that through the Messiah, the Jews are gradually becoming the holy priestly nation that He always intended them to be.

Before you study Israel's next Job Description Duty, I want you to read again Peter's words in 1 Peter 2:9. For, you are now equipped to read his words with understanding. Yes, you now comprehend that in this verse, the apostle Peter is addressing Jewish believers. He is addressing the chosen covenant race, the royal priesthood.

I Peter 2:9 (The Amplified Bible.)

9But you are a chosen race, a royal priesthood, a dedicated nation, [God's] own purchased, special people, that you may set forth the wonderful deeds and display the virtues and perfections of Him Who called you out of darkness into His marvelous light.

ISRAEL'S JOB DESCRIPTION, DUTY NO. 6: A LIGHT TO THE NATIONS.

Israel's Job Description No. 6 is described by the Lord Himself in Isaiah 49:6.

Isaiah 49:6 (The Amplified Bible.)

*⁶He says, It is too light a thing that you should be My servant to raise up the tribes of Jacob and to restore the survivors [of the judgments] of Israel; **I will also give you for a light to the nations, that My salvation may extend to the end of the earth.***

The Israelites' God-ordained position as priest to God equipped them for their future role of *"a light to the nations."* I say that because God demanded strict obedience to His commands from His priestly nation. And, the only way God's covenant people could illuminate the paths of the Lord for the Gentiles was through their obedience to God's Word and by exhibiting God's character in their own lives (that is, by exhibiting God's moral excellence, righteousness and goodness in their own character).

God always wanted His chosen people to demonstrate to the Gentile nations how a nation under God's laws and protection lives and flourishes. He wanted the Gentiles to be able to look at the nation of Israel and see a true example of righteousness. He wanted the Gentile nations to stand in awe as they witnessed Israel's joy, peace, contentment and spiritual prosperity, prosperity that comes through internal and external righteousness. God wanted Israel's exemplary conduct to incite the Gentiles to praise and glorify God and to eventually help the Gentile nations to come to know Him.

When Yeshua walked the earth, He continually reminded His fellow Jews of God's Word in Isaiah 49:6. He exhorted them to rise up and fulfill their God-ordained mission and to begin to be the light of the world that God had always intended them to be. Yeshua implored His Jewish brethren to let their light shine so brightly that men (the Gentile nations) could not help but notice their good works of obedience to God's commands. He assured the Israelites that if they exhibited God's righteous character, they would most definitely cause the Gentiles to glorify God. See this truth for yourself in the *Holy Bible, King James Version.*

236

Matthew 5:14-16 (King James Version.)

*14**Ye are the light of the world**. A city that is set on an hill cannot be hid.*

15Neither do men light a candle, and put it under a bushel, but on a candlestick; and it giveth light unto all that are in the house.

*16**Let your light so shine before men, that they may see your good works, and glorify your Father which is in heaven.***

You must keep in mind that God did not send Yeshua to the Gentile nations. Yeshua stated that fact Himself in Matthew 15:24 when He said, *"I was sent **only** to the lost sheep of the house of Israel."* God sent the Messiah (Yeshua) to the Jews. The Messiah then commissioned the Jews to carry the light of His truth to the Gentiles.

Recognizing the previous truth is extremely important, especially when you study the gospels. For example, when you have understanding of that truth, texts such as Matthew 5:14-16 take on new dimensions. For, you then comprehend that the contents of those verses were originally intended for the Jews. They were intended for the people whom God chose to be a light to the Gentile nations. God's exact words to Israel in Isaiah 49:6 were, *"...I will also give you for a light to the nations, that my salvation may extend to the end of the earth."*

The Jewish apostles, Paul and Barnabas, took their job as light bearers very seriously. The following verses show you just how serious they were about completing their God-ordained mission in Isaiah 49:6 and Matthew 5:14-16. Yes, the Jewish apostles of Yeshua radiated light to all the nations. As the Lord had commanded, they let their light shine so that men (the Gentiles) saw their good works of obedience to God's Word and glorified and thanked God for the Word of God. Read the following text and you will see what I mean.

Acts 13:44-49 (The Amplified Bible.)

44The next Sabbath almost the entire city gathered together to hear the Word of God [concerning the attainment through Christ of salvation in the kingdom of God].

45But when the Jews saw the crowds, filled with envy and jealousy they contradicted what was said by Paul and talked abusively [reviling and slandering him].

46And Paul and Barnabas spoke out plainly and boldly, saying, It was necessary that God's message [concerning salvation through Christ] should be spoken to you first. But since you thrust it from you, you pass this judgment on yourselves that you are unworthy of eternal life and out of your own mouth you will be judged. [Now] behold, we turn to the Gentiles (the heathen).

47For so the Lord has charged us, saying, I have set you to be a light for the Gentiles, (the heathen), that you may bring [eternal] salvation to the uttermost parts of the earth.

48And when the Gentiles heard this, they rejoiced and glorified (praised and gave thanks for) the Word of God; and as many as were destined (appointed and ordained) to eternal life believed (adhered to, trusted in, and relied on Jesus as the Christ and their Savior).

49And so the Word of the Lord [concerning eternal salvation through Christ] scattered and spread throughout the whole region.

Now that you understand that in I Peter 2:9, Peter was addressing Jewish believers and that part of the Jews' mission is to be a light to the nations, you will have even greater insight into the following Scripture.

I Peter 2:9 (The Amplified Bible.)

9But you are a chosen race, a royal priesthood, a dedicated nation, [God's] own purchased, special people, that you may set forth the wonderful deeds and display the virtues and perfections of Him Who called you out of darkness into His marvelous light.

ISRAEL'S JOB DESCRIPTION, DUTY NO. 7: MESSENGERS OF TRUTH.

The covenant descendants of Abraham, Isaac and Jacob were designed to be *"a light to the nations"* in word and deed. They were designed to be God's messengers of truth. This Job Description Duty is substantiated in the next verses taken from *The Living Bible.*

Isaiah 42:19 (The Living Bible.)

19Who in all the world is as blind as my own people, who are designed to be my messengers of truth? Who is so blind as my "dedicated one," the "Servant of the Lord"?

It is not necessary for me to go into a detailed explanation of how the Israelites carried out their designed commission and became God's messengers of truth. For earlier, in Acts 13:44-49, you saw a good example of the Jews' faithfulness to their mission. That good example was exhibited by Paul and Barnabas. The fact is that because Jews such as Paul and Barnabas faithfully performed their God-ordained role of messengers of truth, God's Word has spread throughout the world. Consequently, the Gentile nations were given an opportunity to know the truth of God's Word. They were also given an opportunity to know the promised Messiah, Jewish Yeshua (Jesus). Thus, like the Gentiles in Acts 13:38, for almost 2,000 years, men throughout the world have rejoiced, glorified, praised and given thanks for the Word of God.

ISRAEL'S JOB DESCRIPTION, DUTY NO. 8: WITNESSES.

Israel's Job Description, Duty No. 8 is revealed in the following text.

Acts 1:8 (The Amplified Bible.)

*8But you shall receive power (ability, efficiency, and might) when the Holy Spirit has come upon you, and you shall be **My witnesses** in Jerusalem and all Judea and Samaria and to the ends (the very bounds) of the earth.*

It is important that you understand that in Acts 1:8, Yeshua was again addressing Jews. However, He was not addressing all Jews. And, He most certainly was not addressing any Gentiles.

The problem is that most Christians today do not understand the true definition of the word "witness" that Yeshua used in Acts 1:8. They do not comprehend the fact that Yeshua was telling His **Jewish** disciples that they were going to fulfill God's Word and be **eye**witnesses of His miracles, death and resurrection to the ends of the earth. If you consider what an eyewitness is, it makes sense that only certain Jews could possibly have been His messengers of truth in the capacity of eyewitnesses. Furthermore, only certain Jews could possibly have been a light to the world in the area of eyewitnesses. So, let me reaffirm my previous statement that Yeshua was not speaking to Gentiles in Acts 1:8. He was not even speaking to all Jews. He was instead addressing and commissioning a select group of Jews.

We Gentiles must be willing to put things in their proper perspective, or we will never be able to attain true understanding of

God's Word. How can we ever really praise God for fulfilling His Word and for carrying out every detail of His great salvation plan if we insist on appropriating for ourselves promises and positions that rightfully belong to God's Abrahamic covenant people?

God has the right to use whoever He chooses to carry out His salvation plan. In this case He chose a select group of people from the nation that He designed to fulfill the role of messengers of truth. He chose those who were designated beforehand to be eyewitnesses of His death and resurrection. In the next verses, you will see for yourself that certain of His Jewish disciples were indeed called to be eyewitnesses (that is, they were chosen to bear witness to His miracles, death, and resurrection). As you read the following Scripture, keep in mind that those eyewitnesses consisted of Jews who had been designated beforehand by God as witnesses. Also, keep in mind that **only those Jews who saw Him and ate and drank with Him after His resurrection were appointed as eyewitnesses**.

> *Acts 10:37-42 (The Amplified Bible.)*
>
> *37The [same] message which was proclaimed throughout all Judea, starting from Galilee after the baptism preached by John—*
>
> *38How God anointed and consecrated Jesus of Nazareth with the [Holy] Spirit and with strength and ability and power; how He went about doing good and, in particular, curing all who were harassed and oppressed by [the power of] the devil, for God was with Him.*
>
> *39And we are [eye and ear] witnesses of everything that He did both in the land of the Jews and in Jerusalem. And [yet] they put Him out of the way (murdered Him) by hanging Him on a tree;*
>
> *40But God raised Him to life on the third day and caused Him to be manifest (to be plainly seen),*
>
> *41Not by all the people but to us who were chosen (designated) beforehand by God as witnesses, who ate and drank with Him after He arose from the dead.*
>
> *42And He charged us to preach to the people and to bear solemn testimony that He is the God-appointed and God-ordained Judge of the living and the dead.*

It makes sense that only those Jewish disciples who walked with the Lord during His time on earth and to whom He revealed Himself after

His resurrection could possibly have been His eyewitnesses. According to *The American Heritage Dictionary*, Second College Edition, an eyewitness is "...a person who has personally seen someone or something and can bear witness to the fact."

Neither Christian Jews nor Christian Gentiles today are witnesses in this sense of the word since they did not bear witness to anything Christ did or said. No one who is alive today saw the miracles that Christ performed. No one living today bore witness to the Lord's death or saw Him after He was resurrected from the grave. As a matter of fact, not many Jews who were alive at that time were privileged to see Him after His resurrection. Only those Jews who the Lord had chosen beforehand to be His eyewitnesses actually got to see Him after His resurrection. One of the Lord's main reasons for revealing Himself at that time to that select group of Jewish disciples and for allowing them to eat and drink with Him was to equip them to be eyewitnesses of His resurrection. You saw that very truth in Acts 10:39-41. To refresh your memory, let us read those verses again.

> *Acts 10:39-41 (The Amplified Bible.)*
>
> ³⁹***And we are [eye and ear] witnesses of everything that He did both in the land of the Jews and in Jerusalem.*** *And [yet] they put Him out of the way (murdered Him) by hanging Him on a tree;*
>
> ⁴⁰*But God raised Him to life on the third day and caused Him to be manifest (to be plainly seen),*
>
> ⁴¹***Not by all the people but to us who were chosen (designated) beforehand by God as witnesses, who ate and drank with Him after He arose from the dead.***

Those Jewish disciples who were chosen to be the Lord's witnesses realized the importance of their mission. It was the **eye**witness facet of their calling that drove them to fill the vacant position that Judas Iscariot had left open.

> *Acts 1:21-22 (The Amplified Bible.)*
>
> ²¹*So one of the [other] men who have accompanied us [apostles] during all the time that the Lord Jesus went in and out among us,*
>
> ²²*From the baptism of John at the outset until the day when He was taken up from among us—**one of these men must join with us and become a witness to testify to His resurrection.***

On the day of Pentecost, Peter carried out the Lord's command in Acts 1:8. He stood before the people of Israel and bore solemn eyewitness testimony of Christ's miracles, death and resurrection. I trust that you will take time and read this whole chapter for yourself. I will share only those verses needed to make my point.

Acts 2:22-32 (The Amplified Bible.)

22You men of Israel, listen to what I have to say: Jesus of Nazareth, a Man accredited and pointed out and shown forth and commended and attested to you by God by the mighty works and [the power of performing] wonders and signs which God worked through Him [right] in your midst, as you yourselves know—

23This Jesus, when delivered up according to the definite and fixed purpose and settled plan and foreknowledge of God, you crucified and put out of the way [killing Him] by the hands of lawless and wicked men.

24[But] God raised Him up, liberating Him from the pangs of death, seeing that it was not possible for Him to continue to be controlled or retained by it.

25For David says in regard to Him, I saw the Lord constantly before me, for He is at my right hand that I may not be shaken or overthrown or cast down [from my secure and happy state].

26Therefore my heart rejoiced and my tongue exulted exceedingly; moreover, my flesh also will dwell in hope [will encamp, pitch its tent, and dwell in hope in anticipation of the resurrection].

27For You will not abandon my soul, leaving it helpless in Hades (the state of departed spirits), nor let Your Holy One know decay or see destruction [of the body after death].

28You have made known to me the ways of life; You will enrapture me [diffusing my soul with joy] with and in Your presence.

29Brethren, it is permitted me to tell you confidently and with freedom concerning the patriarch David that he both died and was buried, and his tomb is with us to this day.

30Being however a prophet, and knowing that God had sealed to him with an oath that He would set one of his descendants on his throne,

31He, foreseeing this, spoke [by foreknowledge] of the resurrection of the Christ (the Messiah) that He was not deserted [in death] and left in Hades (the state of departed spirits), nor did His body know decay or see destruction.

*32This Jesus God raised up, **and of that all we [His disciples] are witnesses.***

Another verse of Scripture that verifies the truth regarding what it means for a man to be one of the witnesses mentioned in Acts 1:8 is Acts 3:15. In that verse, Peter again makes the point that the disciples are the Lord's eyewitness.

Acts 3:15 (The Amplified Bible.)

*15But you killed the very Source (the Author) of life, Whom God raised from the dead. **To this we are witnesses.***

The apostle Paul was himself a Jew, and yet, he had no difficulty understanding or accepting the fact that he **was not** one of Yeshua's appointed witnesses mentioned in Acts 1:8. Therefore, when he preached about Christ's death and resurrection in the synagogue in Antioch, he made it clear to all that only those Jews to whom the Lord appeared after His resurrection were Yeshua's chosen witnesses. See this for yourself in the following verses.

Acts 13:28-31 (The Amplified Bible.)

28And although they could find no cause deserving death with which to charge Him, yet they asked Pilate to have Him executed and put out of the way.

29And when they had finished and fulfilled everything that was written about Him, they took Him down from the tree and laid Him in a tomb.

30But God raised Him from the dead.

*31And for many days He appeared to those who came up with Him from Galilee to Jerusalem, **and they are His witnesses to the people.***

Paul was definitely a witness for the Lord. However, like us, he was only able to bear witness to that which he had personally seen and heard.

And, as you know, Paul had not walked with the Lord during His time on earth. He had not seen the miracles that the Lord had performed. He had not seen nor did he eat and drink with the Lord after His resurrection. Furthermore, Paul was not among those whom the Lord had appointed to be His witnesses in Acts 1:8. You saw that truth for yourself in Acts 13:31. In that verse, Paul himself identified those particular witnesses as those to whom the Lord appeared after His resurrection and who came up with Yeshua from Galilee to Jerusalem.

Read the next verses and see for yourself how Paul, like us, could only bear witness to those things which he had seen with his own eyes and heard with his own ears. As Ananias told him, Paul would bear witness to his own salvation experience and everything that he had seen and heard. However, this in no way meant that he was designated beforehand by God to be an eyewitness of the Lord's life, death and resurrection.

Acts 22:12-15 (The Amplified Bible.)

12 And one Ananias, a devout man according to the Law, well spoken of by all the Jews who resided there,

13 Came to see me, and standing by my side said to me, Brother Saul, look up and receive back your sight. And in that very instant I [recovered my sight and] looking up saw him.

14 And he said, The God of our forefathers has destined and appointed you to come progressively to know His will [to perceive, to recognize more strongly and clearly, and to become better and more intimately acquainted with His will], and to see the Righteous One (Jesus Christ, the Messiah), and to hear a voice from His [own] mouth and a message from His [own] lips;

15 For you will be His witness unto all men of everything that you have seen and heard.

Peter, unlike Paul, was most definitely among those appointed witnesses in Acts 1:8. Therefore, Peter and the other eyewitnesses continued to drum home the point that they were the Lord's eyewitnesses of His miracles, death and resurrection to their fellow Jews. To see this truth in the Scriptures, take a few moments and read Acts 5:29-32, 4:33, and 1 Peter 5:1.

John, who was also one of the Lord's eyewitnesses mentioned in Acts 1:8, writes the following words regarding that sacred appointment.

244

1 John 1:1-2 (The Amplified Bible.)

*1[WE ARE writing] about the Word of Life [in] Him Who existed from the beginning, **Whom we have heard, Whom we have seen with our [own] eyes, Whom we have gazed upon [for ourselves] and have touched with our [own] hands.***

*2And the Life [an aspect of His being] was revealed (made manifest, demonstrated), and saw **[as eye witnesses]** and are testifying to and declare to you the Life, the eternal Life [in Him] Who already existed with the Father **and Who [actually] was made visible (was revealed) to us [His followers].***

Surely, those Jews who were designated beforehand by God to be the eyewitnesses mentioned in Acts 1:8 did carry out and fulfill the Lord's instructions and prediction. They were endued with power from on high as the Lord had predicted. Moreover, through that promised power, they bore eyewitness testimony of the Lord's miracles, death and resurrection until the day that they were martyred because of their witness.

Whether we realize it or not, we Gentiles are deeply indebted to the Jewish people. This brief exposition of just a few facets of Israel's great commission proves that fact. For even though Israel often strayed from her God-ordained mission, the truth remains that God did manage to accomplish and is still accomplishing His will through His blessed chosen people, Israel.

(1) Israel did produce the promised covenant nation of people through whom the Messiah came and destroyed Satan's power over mankind. Israel underwent great suffering in Egypt in order that we Gentiles could receive the promised blessings.

(2) Israel did prepare the way for the acknowledgment of God's name. And because she did accomplish her mission, you and I have knowledge of many of the mighty works that God performed in Egypt and throughout history. Furthermore, every true Christian Gentile does now acknowledge God's name.

(3) Israel did travel to and possess the Promised Land in which the Messiah was born, conquered Satan and freed mankind from Satan's

control. So again, through Israel's hardships and sufferings, all mankind has been blessed.

(4) Israel did eventually carry out her duty as God's watchman and prophet to the nations. The Israelites waited patiently for the Messiah. And just remember, when the Lord (the Messiah) finally did arrive, His mother was Jewish, His brethren were Jewish, His disciples were Jewish, and many in Israel believed on Him. Furthermore, because of those Jews who did fulfill their mission as watchman and prophet, all men now have an opportunity to know God's will for mankind and be saved.

(5) Israel did become God's holy, priestly nation. For though the Israelites as a whole often failed the Lord, God always preserved a remnant of faithful Jews who obeyed His Word and lived holy lives. That remnant of holy priests did preserve for all men the written Word of God. Moreover, as I Peter 2:9 informs us, a remnant of faithful Jewish believers did *"set forth the wonderful deeds and display the virtues and perfections"* of the Lord.

(6) As you saw in Acts 13:44-49, the Israelites did eventually fulfill their role of light bearers to the nations. And, because of Jewish believers such as the apostles Paul and Barnabas, we Gentiles are now able to acknowledge the Israelites' good and faithful deeds (that is, the Israelites' works of obedience to God's commands) and thus glorify the God of Abraham, Isaac and Jacob.

(7) All men know that the Israelites did perform their commission regarding their being messengers of truth. After all, it was to Jewish believers that Yeshua gave the great commission in Matthew 28:16-20. Thus, it was Jewish believers who spread the gospel and taught the Gentiles about Yeshua (Jesus) and the truth of God's Word. Had it not been for the Jews carrying out their God-ordained commission, we Gentiles would still be in spiritual darkness. So, we Gentiles must not ever forget that Christianity is Jewish in every sense of the word. Therefore, upon accepting Yeshua as Savior, Gentiles are converted to the Jewish religion (that is, shoots from a wild olive tree, are grafted into Abraham's tree). (Romans 11:17.)

(8) Last but not least, the offspring of Jacob did perform their God-ordained role as eyewitnesses to Christ's miracles, death and resurrection.

Thank God for His chosen people, the descendants of Abraham, Isaac and Jacob. Thank God that they brought God's blessings to the Gentile nations of the world. **There is no doubt that Israel certainly** did aid God in His restoration plan. The evidence of that fact can be seen throughout the sacred Scriptures. Living proof that Israel carried out her part in God's restoration plan can also be seen in the life of every truly born again Christian who is obedient to God's commands. So I say again, we Gentile Christians are deeply indebted to the Jews, and it is high time that we let our gratitude be known.

Chapter 13

WHAT WAS THE NUMBER ONE PRIORITY OF THE MESSIAH'S BIRTH?

Most people who are alive today have heard of the Jewish Messiah, Yeshua (Jesus). Yeshua lived on the earth as a human for only thirty-three years. However, His life and teachings have had such an impact on mankind that even today His birth is the standard by which men measure time itself (B.C. and A.D.).

Every Christian proclaims the truth that Yeshua came to earth to bring the gift of salvation to all men. However, are you personally aware that man's salvation was not His number one priority? My last question may have startled you. In your surprise, you may have thought, "How could anything have been more important than men's souls? If man's salvation was not Yeshua's first priority for coming to this earth in the form of a man, what in the world was His number one priority?"

My friend, does it seem unreasonable to you that **the honor of the Lord God Almighty** was Yeshua's first priority rather than men's sinful souls? In this chapter, you will see Scriptural evidence which proves that the main purpose for Christ's birth was multi-faceted and, every one of those aspects involved God's welfare. **Yes, you will see that Yeshua was born to protect God's name. He was born to protect God's honor and reputation by fulfilling God's recorded predictions and judgments and by keeping the promises that God made to Abraham**.

In order for me to effectively present the previously promised Scriptural evidence, I need to briefly cover a number of critical Biblical points beginning with an episode that took place in the Garden of Eden. I am referring to man's dreadful fall from righteousness to sin. It is also necessary that you once again draw from the information contained in chapters one through twelve of this series. For example, you will recall that in Genesis 3:15, God warned Satan that the Messiah would be born a human being, trample Satan's head underfoot and thus free mankind from Satan's control.

Now you might say, "Earlier in the series, you produced Scriptural evidence which explained why God did not destroy the idolatrous nation of Israel at Mt. Sinai. You proved that though the Israelites deserved to die, God spared them in order to keep the Abrahamic covenant and thus protect His own name. However, it is hard to understand why prior to that incident, God also spared Adam and Eve, since in their case no such covenant existed. Furthermore, unlike Israel, if God had destroyed Adam and Eve, the nations would not have misunderstood His intentions or lost confidence in Him because at that time there were no nations. Adam and Eve were the only humans on planet Earth. So, since liquidating those two humans would not have produced any serious consequences for His name, why didn't God simply destroy His then defective creation and start all over again?"

Let me share with you a few of the reasons why God chose to spare mankind.

(1) God **Almighty** could not have allowed His adversary, the devil, or anyone else to defeat His purpose for creating mankind.

(2) It is true that at that time no other humans existed. Therefore, no human would have witnessed the destruction of Adam and Eve or misunderstood God's intentions or lost confidence in Him. However, there most certainly would have been a vast multitude of other eyewitnesses. The whole spirit world would have either been present during man's destruction or would have eventually learned about that happening. Angels, seraphim and cherubim would have been among that untold number of potential eyewitnesses. Consequently, if God had admitted defeat and failure by destroying His creation, His reputation would most certainly have been at risk.

Let me give you an example of how God's reputation would have been marred if He had destroyed His human creation. From the point of man's destruction, God could never have made a statement such as the one He made in Genesis 18:14, *King James Version,* **"Is any thing too hard for the Lord?"** Furthermore, Yeshua, *"Immanuel [God with us],"* could not have made the claim that He did in Matthew 19:26, *"With men this is impossible; **but with God all things are possible.**"*

As you have just seen, if the incident in the Garden of Eden had not been properly handled, God's reputation would have been seriously injured. In the eyes of that great company of angelic eyewitnesses, God's previous statement would have gone from "With God **all things** are possible" to "With God **most things** are possible."

God could not have taken the chance of allowing any of those would be eyewitnesses to have perceived Him as anything less than what He truly was **Almighty**. Neither could the merciful, compassionate Creator have let anyone go away with the mistaken impression that He had created two humans and then destroyed them after Eve had been treacherously deceived by man's enemy, the devil. For under such circumstances, some angelic beings may have concluded that the Almighty, all-wise God had destroyed man because it was too hard for Him to come up with a solution that would have enabled future humans to be free of sin and Satan's control and allowed them to once again perform the purpose of their creation. Such a conclusion would have left God's enemy, Satan, looking like the victor.

Bear in mind that like men, angels were created with a free will. So just because they were angels did not mean that they would agree with God's decision, think well of Him or even serve Him. Remember, a number of angels chose to rebel against God and side with God's enemy, the devil. Those rebellious beings are identified in the Bible as fallen angels.

God could not have risked anyone being left with a wrong impression concerning His **almighty power,** His **wisdom** or His **uncompromisingly righteous character.** No matter what the cost, He had to prove to everyone that *"with God all things are possible."* Thus, a glimpse of God's restoration plan for mankind became known to all with God's prediction to Satan in Genesis 3:15. God foretold that the Messiah would be born of a woman, trample Satan's head underfoot and consequently free men from Satan's control. The day would come when men would once again be enabled to do all that God had originally created them to do. Yes, in God's time, men would again be free to consistently fear God and keep His commandments.

From the moment the almighty, all-wise, righteous judge of all the earth had verbalized His prediction in Genesis 3:15, He was obligated to keep His Word. God had orally bound Himself to fulfill the previous prophecy and He had done it before men and the whole spirit world.

On the one hand, because Eve had been wickedly deceived into breaking God's commands, **God would prove to all that He truly is a compassionate and merciful God with whom all things are possible**. He would spare men and at great cost to Himself, He would eventually return them to their original spiritual position. On the other hand, no one had deceived or tempted Satan. Therefore, since Satan had made a conscious choice to deliberately sin and had deliberately deceived the human race into following his wicked conduct, **God would prove to all that He will not tolerate men or angels rebelliously opposing His will and purpose or willfully and deliberately disobeying His commands**. He would eventually strip Satan of all power and completely destroy him.

In the meantime, however, God intended to use Satan as a dishonorable vessel. Ironically, in the previous capacity, God would force Satan to unwittingly play an important role in the restoration of mankind. Satan had deceived man into breaking God's commands. Therefore, before God destroyed him, He intended to make Satan an unwitting tool to test man's faith. By using Satan in this role, God knows the exact point in time when each man's faith is transformed into living faith (that is, faith combined with obedience to God's commands). (James 2:17-26.) For Old Testament verification of my last statement, read the Book of Job. For New Testament confirmation, see 1 Peter 5:8-10.

Earlier, you learned that in order to further His restoration plan, God had to make sure that the human race survived. Therefore, despite men's deplorable sinful state, God allowed them to remain alive generation after generation. Yes, even though men's wickedness deeply grieved and offended Him personally, God still caused them to exist in order that He might fulfill His Word in Genesis 3:15 and thereby protect His reputation. You will remember that in a former chapter, **we studied the incident of Noah and the flood so as to show God's mercy for His own name's sake (that is, for the sake of His own reputation).**

Eventually, God found a man through whom He could accomplish His purpose on the earth. The man was Abraham. In a nutshell, God chose Abraham to help Him carry out His Word in Genesis 3:15, to teach his children to begin to do what they were created to do (obey God's commands) and to make with him a sacred, binding covenant. The Abrahamic covenant was intended to help God fulfill His Word in Genesis 3:15. For, included in that contract was a promise of future salvation for all mankind.

God chose to establish His covenant with Abraham's descendants, Isaac, Jacob and Jacob's posterity, the Israelites. In Egypt, the Lord raised up a great covenant nation (Israel) through whom the promised Messiah would be born. Afterward, as promised, God delivered the Israelites from the bondage of Egypt, commissioned them and gave them His laws. He also gave to the Israelites the land of Canaan for an everlasting possession. God's intention was that the Messiah would be born a Jew in the Promised Land in order to fulfill Genesis 3:15 and His Abrahamic covenant promises and thus protect His holy name.

From that point on, all the Israelites had to do in order to please God and meet His one requirement was to obey His commands and then sit back and patiently wait for the arrival of the promised Messiah. For, as you know, the Messiah was to take on the seed of Abraham, Isaac and

Jacob. The Messiah was to be born a Jew, conquer Satan, and consequently free men to once again perform their whole duty to God. In order to protect God's name, the Messiah would fulfill God's Word in Genesis 3:15 and God's covenant promises. It is clear that God had laid hold on (that is, chosen) Israel to help Him carry out His restoration plan for His own name's sake.

Throughout the ages, God continued to raise up holy prophets in Israel. The prophets' duties were numerous. However, at this time, we are going to concentrate on only one area of the prophets' mission—prophecy. To help you identify segments of the prophet's predictions that are most relevant to the present topic, I have continued to highlight certain portions of Scripture.

God's prophets continually foretold the Messiah's first and second coming. Nothing remained hidden or obscure. Everything, including the Messiah's birth, death, resurrection, second coming and His future judgment upon both mankind and the devil is recorded in the sacred Scriptures.

To show you what I meant when I said everything about the Messiah's coming is recorded in detail in the Scriptures, I will give you a brief outline of the prophesied events of His birth and their fulfillment. For, in tracing those events, you will receive the Biblical evidence that I promised regarding the Messiah's first priority for being born a human being.

You will see beyond doubt that the Messiah's first priority was indeed to protect God's holy name by fulfilling God's Word in Genesis 3:15 and God's covenant promises to Abraham, Isaac and Jacob. For, the all-righteous God could not permit Himself to become known as one who failed to fulfill His predictions and warnings. Neither could He permit Himself to become known as a covenant breaker. God's honor and His reputation were at stake. Thus, the Messiah's first priority was to glorify God by fulfilling His Word.

Let us now briefly study the Old Testament prophesies which involve the Messiah's birth and their fulfillment.

Isaiah foretold that a prophet would go before the Messiah to prepare the way for Him. The following verses hold Isaiah's prophecy.

Isaiah 40:3-5 (The Amplified Bible.)

3A voice of one who cries: Prepare in the wilderness the way of the Lord [clear away the obstacles]; make straight and smooth in the desert a highway for our God!

4Every valley shall be lifted and filled up, and every mountain and hill shall be made low; and the crooked and uneven shall be made straight and level, and the rough places a plain.

5And the glory (majesty and splendor) of the Lord shall be revealed, and all flesh shall see it together; for the mouth of the Lord has spoken it.

To accomplish what was spoken by Isaiah, the angel of the Lord appeared to a certain Jewish priest in Israel named Zacharias [or Zachariah]. The angel told the priest that he and his aged barren wife would have a child. He went on to tell Zacharias that his future son was chosen to fulfill the prophets' inspired prediction in Isaiah 40:3. **Yes, the angel told Zacharias that his son would be the forerunner of the soon to come Messiah, the Anointed One**. I think you will grasp better the fulfillment of Isaiah's previous prophecy by reading those recorded details for yourself in the *Holy Bible, King James Version.*

Luke 1:5-25 (King James Version.)

*5THERE was in the days of Herod, the king of Judea, **a certain priest named Zacharias [or Zachariah]**, of the course of Abia: and his wife was of the daughters of Aaron, and her name was Elisabeth.*

6And they were both righteous before God, walking in all the commandments and ordinances of the Lord blameless.

7And they had no child, because that Elisabeth was barren, and they both were now well stricken in years.

8And it came to pass, that while he executed the priest's office before God in the order of his course,

9According to the custom of the priest's office, his lot was to burn incense when he went into the temple of the Lord.

10And the whole multitude of the people were praying without at the time of incense.

11And there appeared unto him an angel of the Lord standing on the right side of the altar of incense.

12And when Zacharias saw him, he was troubled, and fear fell upon him.

13But the angel said unto him, Fear not, Zacharias: for thy prayer is heard; and thy wife Elisabeth shall bear thee a son, and thou shalt call his name John [Jewish name Yohanan].

14And thou shalt have joy and gladness; and many shall rejoice at his birth.

15For he shall be great in the sight of the Lord, and shall drink neither wine nor strong drink; and he shall be filled with the Holy Ghost, even from his mother's womb.

16And many of the children of Israel shall he turn to the Lord their God.

17And he shall go before him [Messiah] in the spirit and power of Elias, to turn the hearts of the fathers to the children, and the disobedient to the wisdom of the just; to make ready a people prepared for the Lord.

18And Zacharias said unto the angel, Whereby shall I know this? for I am an old man and my wife well stricken in years.

19And the angel answering said unto him, I am Gabriel, that stand in the presence of God; and am sent to speak unto thee, and to shew thee these glad tidings.

20And behold, thou shalt be dumb, and not able to speak, until the day that these things shall be performed, because thou believest not my words, which shall be fulfilled in their season.

21And the people waited for Zacharias, and marvelled that he tarried so long in the temple.

22And when he came out, he could not speak unto them: and they perceived that he had seen a vision in the temple: for he beckoned unto them, and remained speechless.

23And it came to pass, that, as soon as the days of his ministration were accomplished, he departed to his own house.

254

24And after those days his wife Elisabeth conceived,
and hid herself five months, saying,

25Thus hath the Lord dealt with me in the days wherein
he looked on me, to take away my reproach among men.

God's prophet, Isaiah, not only prophesied about the forerunner of the anointed One, but he also foretold in detail the events surrounding the Messiah's birth. Isaiah prophesied that the Messiah would be born a human being—a child. He pronounced the Messiah's gender—a son. Isaiah even proclaimed Messiah's deity. He described Him as "**The mighty God**" and "**The everlasting Father.**" We will read Isaiah's prophesy from the *Holy Bible, King James Version.*

Isaiah 9:6 (King James Version.)

*6For unto us **a child** is born, unto us **a son** is given: and the government shall be upon His shoulder: and his name shall be called Wonderful, Counsellor, **The mighty God, The everlasting Father**, The Prince of Peace.*

In the following verse, Isaiah again speaks of the Messiah's divinity. Isaiah told Israel that the Messiah would be *"Immanuel [God with us]."* **The prophet informed Israel that the Messiah would be God Himself incarnate (that is, God embodied in human form). Thus, God made it clear that He would Himself carry out the most difficult part of His restoration plan. God would Himself fulfill His Word in Genesis 3:15 and His covenant promise to Abraham in Genesis 12:3, "...*in you will all the families and kindred of the earth be blessed....*"** In the same inspired prediction, Isaiah also told the Jews what the sign of Messiah's coming would be. **The sign would be that an unmarried woman who was a virgin would conceive and bear the Christ, the anointed One.**

Isaiah 7:14 (The Amplified Bible.)

14Therefore the Lord Himself shall give you a sign: Behold, the young woman who is unmarried and a virgin shall conceive and bear a son, and shall call His name Immanuel [God with us].

To again fulfill God's Word in Genesis 3:15, God's sacred covenant with Abraham and Isaiah's prophecy, the Angel of the Lord visited the unmarried Jewish virgin of whom Isaiah had prophesied. The virgin's name was Mary (Jewish name Miriam, from Hebrew Miryam). Mary was of the tribe of Judah and of the line of David. Let us read now what took place during the angel's visit with Mary. We will continue reading from the *Holy Bible, King James Version*.

Luke 1:26-38 (King James Version.)

26And in the sixth month the angel Gabriel was sent from God unto a city of Galilee, named Nazareth,

27To a virgin espoused to a man whose name was Joseph, of the house of David; and the virgin's name was Mary [Miriam].

28And the angel came in unto her, and said, Hail, thou that art highly favoured, the Lord is with thee: blessed art thou among women.

29And when she saw him, she was troubled at his saying, and cast in her mind what manner of salutation this should be.

30And the angel said unto her, Fear not, Mary [Miriam]: for thou hast found favour with God.

31And, behold, thou shalt conceive in thy womb, and bring forth a son, and shalt call his name JESUS [YESHUA].

32He shall be great, and shall be called the Son of the Highest: and the Lord God shall give unto him the throne of his father David:

33And he shall reign over the house of Jacob for ever; and of his kingdom there shall be no end.

34Then said Mary unto the angel, How shall this be, seeing I know not a man?

35And the angel answered and said unto her, The Holy Ghost shall come upon thee, and the power of the Highest shall overshadow thee: therefore also that holy thing which shall be born of thee shall be called the Son of God.

36And, behold, thy cousin Elisabeth, she hath also conceived a son in her old age: and this is the sixth month with her, who was called barren.

37For with God nothing shall be impossible.

38And Mary said, Behold the handmaid of the Lord; be it unto me according to thy word. And the angel departed from her.

If you continue reading in Luke chapter one, you will be reminded of how the virgin Mary, who was by then pregnant with the Christ child, traveled to a city of Judah to visit Zacharias the priest and Elizabeth, his wife. When Mary arrived at the couples' home, the Holy Spirit spoke through both pregnant women, divulging many beautiful truths. The most important revelation was voiced by Mary herself. **She revealed that the Messiah would be born in fulfillment of God's covenant with Abraham, Isaac and Jacob**. As you read Mary's words, keep in mind that the Abrahamic covenant, with its mercy and loving-kindness, came into being so that God might fulfill His Word in Genesis 3:15 and protect His reputation.

Luke 1:54-56 (King James Version.)

54He has helped His servant Israel, in remembrance of His mercy;
55As he spake to our fathers, to Abraham, and to his seed forever.
56And Mary abode with her about three months, and returned to her own house.

Verses fifty-four and fifty-five in *The Amplified Bible* read as such:

*54He has laid hold on His servant Israel [to help him, to espouse his cause], **in remembrance of His mercy,***
*55**Even as He promised to our forefathers, to Abraham and to his descendants forever.***

God could not have made Mary's inspired words any clearer. Mary proclaimed that God had laid hold of the Israelites (that is, chosen them) to espouse His cause by producing the nation through whom the Messiah would come and bless all the nations. Yes, God had chosen the Israelite, Mary, a descendant of Abraham, Isaac and Jacob to help Him fulfill His Word in Genesis 3:15 and the Abrahamic covenant, and in so doing, to help Him protect His holy name. Praise be to our righteous, faithful God! For just as He predicted, the Messiah would be born a human being—a Jew of the house of David.

When Mary's betrothed, Joseph, learned that she was with child, he intended to put her away quietly. However, the Angel of the Lord appeared to him in a dream. The angel explained to Joseph that the unborn child was a product of the Holy Spirit and, he should not be afraid to marry Mary. Hence, Joseph took the pregnant virgin to be his wife.

Matthew 1:18-25 (King James Version.)

18Now the birth of Jesus Christ was on this wise: When as his mother Mary was espoused to Joseph, before they came together, she was found with child of the Holy Ghost.

19Then Joseph, her husband, being a just man, and not willing to make her a publick example, was minded to put her away privily.

20But while he thought on these things, behold, the angel of the Lord appeared unto him in a dream, saying, Joseph, thou son of David, fear not to take unto thee Mary thy wife: for that which is conceived in her is of the Holy Ghost.

21And she shall bring forth a son, and thou shalt call His name JESUS [YESHUA]: for He shall save His people from their sins.

22Now all this was done, that it might be fulfilled which was spoken of the Lord by the prophet, saying,

23Behold, a virgin shall be with child, and shall bring forth a son, and they shall call His name Emmanuel, which being interpreted is, <u>God with us.</u>

24Then Joseph being raised from sleep did as the angel of the Lord had bidden him, and took unto him his wife:

25And knew her not till she had brought forth her firstborn son: and he called His name Jesus [YESHUA].

Mary was still pregnant with the Christ child when her relative Elizabeth gave birth to John, the prophesied forerunner of the anointed One. During Mary's stay with Elizabeth, Zacharias the priest, had been unable to communicate orally with her. For, you will recall that he had been struck dumb by the angel Gabriel as punishment for his unbelief.

However, once Zachariah's wife gave birth to the forerunner of the promised Messiah, the priest's mouth was opened as the angel had promised. The next verses describe events as they took place. This time, we will return to our main source of reference, *The Amplified Bible*.

> *Luke 1:57-66 (The Amplified Bible.)*
>
> [57]*Now the time that Elizabeth should be delivered came, and she gave birth to a son.*
>
> [58]*And her neighbors and relatives heard that the Lord had shown great mercy on her, and they rejoiced with her.*
>
> [59]*And it occurred that on the eighth day, when they came to circumcise the child, they were intending to call him Zachariah after his father,*
>
> [60]*But his mother answered, Not so! But he shall be called John [Yohanan].*
>
> [61]*And they said to her, None of your relatives is called by that name.*
>
> [62]*And they inquired with signs to his father [as to] what he wanted to have him called.*
>
> [63]***Then Zachariah asked for a writing tablet and wrote, his name is John [Yohanan].*** *And they were all astonished.*
>
> [64]*And at once his mouth was opened and his tongue loosed, and he began to speak, blessing and praising and thanking God.*
>
> [65]*And awe and reverential fear came on all their neighbors; and all these things were discussed throughout the hill country of Judea.*
>
> [66]*And all who heard them laid them up in their hearts, saying, Whatever will this little boy be then? For the hand of the Lord was [so evidently] with him [protecting and aiding him].*

The priest's mouth was opened so that the Holy Ghost could speak through him. The next verses contain the words that this holy priest of Israel prophesied concerning the soon to be born anointed child, Yeshua, the child who, for God's name's sake, was to be born in direct fulfillment of God's Word in Genesis 3:15 and God's sacred Abrahamic covenant promises.

Luke 1:67-73 (The Amplified Bible.)

67Now Zachariah his [John's] father was filled with and controlled by the Holy Spirit and prophesied, saying,

68Blessed (praised and extolled and thanked) be the Lord, the God of Israel, because he has come and brought deliverance and redemption to His people!

69And He has raised up a Horn of salvation [a mighty and valiant Helper, the Author of salvation] for us in the house of David His servant—

70This is as He promised by the mouth of His holy prophets from the most ancient times [in the memory of man]—

71That we should have deliverance and be saved from our enemies and from the hand of all who detest and pursue us with hatred;

Look carefully at the next two verses, for they prove that Yeshua was born in direct fulfillment of the covenant God made with Abraham, Isaac and Jacob. As you learned earlier in the series, God had to keep His sacred covenant promises at any cost in order to protect His own reputation (that is, His holy name). Thus, Christ was actually born for the Lord's name's sake. See this Biblical fact for yourself in the following segment of Zachariah's prophecy. See why Yeshua was born.

72To make true and show the mercy and compassion and kindness [promised] to our forefathers and to remember and carry out His holy covenant [to bless, which is all the more sacred becaue it is made by God Himself],

73That covenant He sealed by oath to our forefather Abraham:

In the previous verses, you are informed that the Messiah was born to fulfill God's promise of everlasting covenant love for Israel which He swore to Abraham, Isaac and Jacob. You learned in an earlier chapter that God's love for His chosen people is part of the covenant and that His love has many facets. It includes the mercy, compassion and kindness mentioned in verse seventy-two. **In that same verse, you also see proof that Yeshua was born to carry out the promises in the Abrahamic covenant, promises which God swore by Himself that He would keep.**

260

My friend, the Holy Ghost Himself relays these truths to you on the pages of God's Word. The Holy Ghost comes right out and tells you that the Messiah (Yeshua) was born to fulfill God's sacred covenant with Abraham, Isaac and Jacob, including His promise of everlasting love. What better way could God have proved His everlasting love for Israel and His faithfulness to His Word than to come to earth in the form of a male Jewish baby and, Himself, fulfill the promises that He had made to their forefathers regarding them.

You must keep in mind, however, that God's prediction in Genesis 3:15 existed long before the Abrahamic covenant. As you learned earlier, God entered into the binding covenant with Abraham in order to ensure the fulfillment of His statement in Genesis 3:15. For, in that verse, God had foretold that He would accomplish certain feats. To protect His reputation, God therefore had to follow through and keep His Word. Otherwise, both men and angels would have lost respect for God's Word and from then on, they would have been unable to confidently trust Him.

Yet, it was the necessary fulfillment of Genesis 3:15 that totally confused the Jewish people. You see, the Jews failed to understand that the Messiah would make two prophesied visits to earth. During the Messiah's first visit, He would defeat Israel's **spiritual** enemies and bring salvation to all men as God had foretold in Genesis 3:15, the Abrahamic covenant and through His holy prophets. Albeit, as it was also prophesied, during His second visit to earth, the Messiah would defeat and punish Israel's **human** enemies.

Of all the enemies that Israel ever had, Satan and his army of fallen angels were by far the worst. In the first place, Satan was initially responsible for all the suffering that Israel had ever experienced. In addition, Satan wielded more control over Israel than any earthly nation ever had or ever could. He rendered God's people, and for that matter all mankind, powerless to do what they were created to do. He kept them in spiritual bondage.

It stands to reason that the Messiah conquering Israel's human enemies without first defeating her spiritual foes would have been futile. For after being delivered from her human enemies, Israel would still have been completely under the control of her spiritual enemies (Satan and his army of fallen angels). Consequently, under those circumstances the horrible cycle of helplessness, sin and suffering would have continued.

It is also obvious that obtaining deliverance from the hands of their human foes, without first being delivered from sin and Satan's control, would not have enabled the Israelites to serve God fearlessly in holiness and righteousness within God's presence all the days of their lives as the prophets had foretold. (Luke 1:74-75.) Only when they acquired deliverance from **all** their enemies who detested them and pursued them with hatred, both human and spiritual, could they truly enjoy internal and external peace.

When one considers the whole picture, one has to applaud God's absolute wisdom, His uncompromisingly righteous character and His absolute faithfulness to His Word. For, as God had foretold, the Messiah, *"Immanuel [God with us],"* was born a human being. Yes, Yeshua was the Horn of **Salvation**, who, as the prophets had foretold, was raised up in the house of David. **He was raised up to fulfill Genesis 3:15 and the portion of the Abrahamic covenant that includes salvation for all the nations. However, most of all, He was raised up to protect God's holy name.**

The conclusion is that the Messiah, *"Immanuel [God with us],"* came to earth the first time as a man in order to make spiritual warfare with and to conquer Satan, the enemy of man's soul. However, when He comes to earth the second time, He will complete all the remaining inspired prophesies that pertain to Him. Yes, when the Messiah returns to earth, He will eliminate all Israel's human foes. Thus, Israel will finally be delivered from **all** her enemies, both spiritual and physical.

Pay close attention as you again read the words of the Jewish priest, Zechariah, from *The Amplified Bible.* For, he reveals much of what I just shared with you.

> *Luke 1:67-75 (The Amplified Bible.)*
>
> *67Now Zachariah his [John's] father was filled with and controlled by the Holy Spirit and prophesied, saying,*
>
> *68Blessed (praised and extoled and thanked) be the Lord, the God of Israel, because he has come and brought deliverance and redemption to His people!*
>
> *69And He has raised up a Horn of salvation [a mighty and valiant Helper, the Author of salvation] for us in the house of David His servant—*

*70This is as He promised by the mouth of His holy
prophets from the most ancient times [in the memory
of man]—*

*71That we should have deliverance and be saved from
our enemies and from the hand of all who detest and
pursue us with hatred.*

*72To make true and show the mercy and compassion
and kindness [promised] to our forefathers and to
remember and carry out His holy covenant [to bless,
which is all the more sacred because it is made by God
Himself],*

*73That covenant He sealed by oath to our forefather
Abraham:*

*74To grant us that we, being delivered from the hand
of our foes, might serve Him fearlessly*

*75In holiness (divine consecration) and righteousness
[in accordance with the everlasting principles of right]
within His presence all the days of our lives.*

The previous verses, verses seventy-four and seventy-five, show
you that the Messiah was born to fulfill God's Word in Genesis 3:15
and thus restore man to the original purpose of his creation. The
Messiah was also born to keep the promises that God made to
Abraham, Isaac and Jacob, mentioned in verses seventy-two and
seventy-three. Most importantly, He was born to protect God's
name.

Notwithstanding, since the salvation of all the families and kindred
of the earth is included in God's Word in Genesis 3:15 and in the
covenant promises, then of course, the salvation of mankind was indeed
an important factor of Christ's birth. **It just was not His top priority**.
Rightfully, protecting God's name by fulfilling God's Word was the
Messiah's top priority. To the Christ, man's salvation was a prelude to
the glorification of God's name. Did not Yeshua Himself relay that
same truth in the following verses?

John 17:1, 4 (The Amplified Bible.)

*1WHEN JESUS had spoken these things, He lifted up
His eyes to heaven and said, Father, the hour has come.
Glorify and exalt and honor and magnify Your Son, so
that Your Son may glorify and extol and honor and
magnify You.*

4I have glorified You down here on the earth by completing the work that You gave to Me to do.

Yeshua clearly tells you in verse one that He was about to die for the honor of God. He asked God to honor Him, only, so that He could honor and exalt God's name. In verse four, Yeshua shows you how He honored God on the earth. He did it by completing the work that God gave Him to do. And what was that work? His work was fulfilling God's Word in Genesis 3:15, keeping the Abrahamic covenant promise regarding man's salvation and bringing to pass all that the prophets predicted that pertained to Him.

Keeping the former information in mind, read once again the Abrahamic covenant promise of salvation for all the Gentile nations.

Genesis 12:2-3 (The Amplified Bible.)

2And I will make of you a great nation, and I will bless you [with abundant increase of favors] and make your name famous and distinguished, and you will be a blessing [dispensing good to others].

3And I will bless those who bless you [who confer prosperity or happiness upon you] and curse him who curses or uses insolent language toward you; in you will all the families and kindred of the earth be blessed [and by you they will bless themselves].

Genesis 18:18 (The Amplified Bible.)

18Since Abraham shall surely become a great and mighty nation, and all the nations of the earth shall be blessed through him and shall bless themselves by him?

The previous Abrahamic covenant promise of salvation for all men should enable you to more fully understand why the Jewish apostle Paul said what he did in the following text.

Galatians 3:8 (The Amplified Bible.)

8And the Scripture, foreseeing that God would justify (declare righteous, put in right standing with Himself) the Gentiles in consequence of faith, proclaimed the Gospel [foretelling the glad tidings of a Savior long beforehand] to Abraham in the promise, saying, In you shall all the nations [of the earth] be blessed.

264

God fulfilled the previous portion of the Abrahamic covenant, *"In you shall all the nations [of the earth] be blessed,"* when, as the priest Zachariah prophesied in Luke 1:74-75, through the Messiah's death, He redeemed men, the Jew first and then the Gentile. He redeemed men by fulfilling Genesis 3:15 and thus making it possible for them to be free from sin and the devil's power. For only then could men serve God fearlessly in holiness all the days of their lives. After all, being free from earthly enemies does not make a man holy or righteous. However, being free from man's spiritual enemy, the devil, and from filthy sin (that is, the breaking of God's commands) does enable a man to be holy and righteous all the days of his life. Yes, through His death, Yeshua freed men to obey God's commands and, in doing so, enabled them to once again do what they were originally created to do.

You now understand more fully why Christ was born. **He was born to fulfill God's Word in Genesis 3:15, God's covenant promises to Abraham, Isaac and Jacob and the prophets predictions and thus protect the honor of God's holy name.** To refresh your memory of that fact, let us read again Zachariah's words in the following two verses.

Luke 1:72-75 (The Amplified Bible.)

72 To make true and show the mercy and compassion and kindness [promised] to our forefathers and to remember and carry out His holy covenant, [to bless, which is all the more sacred because it is made by God Himself],

73 That covenant He sealed by oath to our forefather Abraham:

74 To grant us that we being delivered out of the hand of our foes, might serve him fearlessly,

75 In holiness (divine consecration) and righteousness [in accordance with the everlasting principles of right] within His presence all the days of our lives.

I am sure you will agree that I have answered the questions, "How could anything be more important than the saving of men's souls? If man's salvation was not God's first priority for coming to this earth in the form of a man, then what in the world was His number one priority?"

The number one priority of the Messiah's birth was multi-fold. It included fulfilling God's Word in Genesis 3:15, keeping God's covenant promises to Abraham, Isaac and Jacob, and most importantly, protecting the honor of God's holy name. After learning in the first twelve chapters of this book about all the pain, grief and frustration God went through in order to keep His Word in Genesis 3:15 and His covenant with Abraham, surely you will concede that Yeshua's first priority was absolutely fair and righteous. <u>For what could possibly be more important than God's predictions and judgments being fulfilled and God's sacred covenant promises being kept in order to protect the honor of God's holy name?</u>

Before we continue, let me relay to you yet another vital truth. Men have racked their brains trying to figure out why *"Immanuel [God with us]"* came to earth as a human being and gave His life for undeserving mankind. We Gentile Christians have always been especially sensitive of the fact that we are not worthy to reap the benefits of such an extraordinary sacrificial feat. Deep in man's heart there has always been the nagging question, "Why was Christ willing to suffer such an agonizing death for rotten, undeserving sinners like us who, for the most part, do not even appreciate His sacrifices? It just does not make sense." No, my friend, it does not make sense. Only the truth makes sense. And you now know the truth.

You know that Christ's number one priority for being born and for laying down His life was to fulfill God's Word and thus protect God's holy name. What is more, from the moment you truly realized that truth, you started to perceive past, present and future events in a totally different light. And like your Lord, protecting the honor of God's name is now your number one priority also.

There is a footnote for James 1:27 in *The Amplified Bible* that explains your new informed attitude concerning God's name. That footnote is an excerpt from Robert Jamieson, A. R. Fausset and David Brown, *A Commentary on the Old and New Testaments.*

> Religion in its rise interests us about ourselves; in its progress, about our fellow creatures; **in its highest stage, about the honor of God.**

If you truly comprehend the previously mentioned number one priority and if you are therefore deeply concerned about God's honor (that is, you are deeply concerned about God's name), then let me show you how you will personally view past, present and future Biblical events from this point on.

(1) God made His prediction in Genesis 3:15 in order to fulfill His will and purpose and thus protect His holy name.

(2) God spared Noah and his family in order to fulfill His Word in Genesis 3:15 and thus protect His holy name.

(3) God chose and loved Abraham and made with him a binding covenant in order to fulfill His Word in Genesis 3:15 and thus protect His holy name.

(4) God chose Isaac and his son Jacob in order to fulfill His Word in Genesis 3:15 and His covenant with Abraham and thus protect His holy name.

(5) God chose and loved the descendants of Abraham, Isaac and Jacob (the Jews) in order to fulfill His Word in Genesis 3:15 and the Abrahamic covenant and thus protect His holy name.

(6) God caused Israel to become a great nation in order to fulfill His Word in Genesis 3:15 and the Abrahamic covenant and thus protect His holy name.

(7) God delivered the Jews from the bondage of Egypt with wondrous miracles and mighty acts of judgment in order to fulfill His Word in Genesis 3:15 and the Abrahamic covenant and thus protect His holy name.

(8) God spared idolatrous Israel, even though she deserved to die, in order to fulfill His Word in Genesis 3:15 and the Abrahamic covenant and thus protect His holy name.

(9) God gave Israel the Promised Land as an everlasting possession in order to fulfill His Word in Genesis 3:15 and the Abrahamic covenant and thus protect His holy name.

(10) Yeshua was born a human being in order to fulfill God's Word in Genesis 3:15 and the Abrahamic covenant and thus protect God's holy name.

(11) Yeshua gave His life on Calvary to free the Israelites from sin and Satan's control and bring salvation to all the Gentile nations in order to fulfill God's Word in Genesis 3:15 and the Abrahamic covenant and thus protect God's holy name.

Everything,—everything,—everything that Christ did, suffered or accomplished on earth was to fulfill God's Word and thus protect God's name (that is, everything Christ did, suffered or accomplished on earth was to glorify God's name). Never again will you have to try to fathom why Yeshua was born or why He was willing to die for sinners. You now have the answer to both those questions. **You know that Yeshua was born and died for undeserving sinners in order to fulfill God's prediction in Genesis 3:15 and God's sacred covenant promises to Abraham and thus protect the honor of God's holy name.**

Now that you understand what the first priority was for the Messiah's birth, I am sure you will also view the following events from a different, more enlightened perspective. So, let us continue with our investigation of the Messianic predictions of God's holy prophets.

Even the geographical location of the Messiah's birth was pinpointed by the prophet Micah. God's prophet Micah foretold that *"Immanuel [God with us],"* would be born in Israel in the little town of David, Bethlehem.

> *Micah 5:2 (The Amplified Bible.)*
>
> *2But you, **Bethlehem Ephratah,** you are little to be among the clans of Judah; [yet] out of you shall One come forth for Me Who is to be Ruler in Israel, **Whose goings forth have been from of old, from ancient days (eternity).***

I again direct you to the Gospel of Luke. For in the following verses, Luke recorded the fulfillment of Micah's previous prophecy. As you read, continue to keep in mind that God caused all the Biblical prophesies to come true in order to keep His Word in Genesis 3:15 and His covenant with Abraham and thus protect and bring honor to His holy name. This time, we will utilize the *Holy Bible, King James Version.*

> *Luke 2:1-6 (King James Version.)*
>
> *1And it came to pass in those days, that there went out a decree from Caesar Augustus, that all the world should be taxed.*
>
> *2(And this taxing was first made when Cyrenius was governor of Syria.)*
>
> *3And all went to be taxed, everyone into his own city.*

4And Joseph also went up from Galilee, out of the city of Nazareth, into Judaea, <u>unto the city of David, which is called Bethlehem;</u> (because he was of the house and lineage of David:)

5To be taxed with Mary his espoused wife, being great with child.

6And so it was, that, while they were there, the days were accomplished that she should be delivered.

The Messiah, whose goings forth according to Micah 5:2 have been from eternity, was born in Bethlehem as Micah had predicted. And, as Isaiah had foretold, as it was during His entire lifetime, there was no royal, kingly pomp surrounding the Messiah's birth. No costly apparel draped His tiny body. Outwardly, there was nothing about this holy child, *"[Immanuel God with us],"* that would have caused men to desire Him. See this for yourself in the following verse taken from *The Amplified Bible.*

Isaiah 53:2 (The Amplified Bible.)

*2For [the Servant of God] grew up before Him like a tender plant, and like a root out of dry ground; **He has no form or comeliness [royal, kingly pomp], that we should look at Him, and no beauty that we should desire Him.***

Again, see for yourself on the pages of God's Word the prophesied humble conditions of the Messiah's birth that came to pass in the little town of Bethlehem. For you will then agree with Isaiah that there was certainly no royal pomp connected with His arrival on this planet. For the sake of His reputation, God humbly came in the form of a human child to fulfill His Word in Genesis 3:15 and His sacred covenant with Abraham. Yet, when it came time for the King of the Universe to be born, there was not made available for Him even a tiny corner in the local inn.

Luke 2:6-7 (The Amplified Bible.)

6And while they were there, the time came for her delivery,

7And she gave birth to her Son, her Firstborn; and she wrapped Him in swaddling clothes and laid Him in a manger, because there was no room or place for them in the inn.

The Christ child (the Messiah) was finally born. However, there were many prophesied events that still had to be fulfilled. For example, in the following verse, the prophet Isaiah clearly foretold another very important happening.

Isaiah 60:7 (King James Version.)

*7All the flocks of **Kedar** shall be gathered together unto thee, **the rams of Nebaioth shall minister unto thee**: they shall come up with acceptance on mine altar, and I will glorify the house of my glory.*

To bring about Isaiah's prophecy in the previous verse, an angel of the Lord appeared to nomad shepherds of Kedar and Nebaioth (that is, an angel appeared to the descendants of Ishmael) who were guarding their flocks at night. The term "rams" in Hebrew refers to the "strong men" (the shepherds) of Kedar and Nebaioth. *Smith's Bible Dictionary* under the heading "Kedar" reads:

> Kedar, the second in order of the sons of Ishmael, Gen. 25:13; I Chron. 1:29, and the name of a great tribe of Arabs settled on the northwest of the peninsula **and on the confines of Palestine**.... They appear also to have been, like the wandering tribes of the present day, "archers" and "mighty men." Isa. 21:17; comp. Ps. 120.5. That they also settled in villages or towns we find from Isaiah. Isa. 42:11. The tribe seems to have been one of the most conspicuous of all the Ishmaelite tribes, and hence the rabbins call the Arabians universally by his name.

According to this same source under the heading "Nebaioth," Nebaioth was the first son of Ishmael and was also the father of a pastoral tribe *"the rams of Nebaioth,"* mentioned in Isaiah 60:7. The tribe of Nebaioth wandered in the desert in search of pasturage for their flocks until they eventually came to Kedar.

The fact that Kedar (the descendants of the second son of Ishmael) settled on the border of Palestine is very important. It is evidence that it would not have been unusual for the shepherds of Kedar and Nebaioth to have been feeding their flocks on the border of Palestine when the angel appeared to them. This is especially true since the Angel of the Lord had appeared to Hagar in Genesis 16:7-12 and had informed her that Ishmael's descendants would dwell on the borders of all his kinsmen.

The next verses contain the fulfillment of Isaiah 60:7. As you read about this incident, keep in mind that God made His Word in Isaiah 60:7 come true in order to fulfill His prediction in Genesis 3:15 and His sacred covenant with Abraham. For, God's first priority was to remain faithful to His Word in order to protect His own name.

> *Luke 2:8-20 (King James Version.)*
>
> *8And there were in the same country shepherds abiding in the field, keeping watch over their flock by night.*
>
> *9And, lo, the angel of the Lord came upon them, and the glory of the Lord shone round about them: and they were sore afraid.*

According to Strong's "Greek Dictionary of the New Testament," the term *"country"* used in verse eight can also be interpreted *"coast."* The second definition for the word *"coast"* in *The American Heritage Dictionary,* Second College Edition reads, "the frontier or border of a country."

If you give careful attention to the angel's words in the next verse, you will realize that the Abrahamic covenant is again mentioned. For the angel explains that the good tidings which he came to bring would be **"to all people."** And, as you know, God's covenant with Abraham in Genesis 12:3 states *"...**in you will all the families and kindred of the earth be blessed**...."* How fitting it is that the Gentile descendants of Abraham's eldest son, Ishmael, were eyewitnesses to the arrival of the promised Jewish Messiah. How marvelous it is that in fulfillment of Isaiah 60:7, Ishmael's descendants actually ministered to the holy child, Yeshua. I say it is fitting and marvelous because like all the other nations, the Arab nation (the descendants of Ishmael) would have an opportunity to be blessed (saved) through that promised holy Jewish child, the Savior of the world, the Savior to whom they did minister.

> *10And the angel said unto them, Fear not: for, behold, I bring you good tidings of great joy, **which shall be to all people.***
>
> *11**For unto you is born this day in the city of David a Saviour, which is Christ the Lord.***

12And this shall be a sign unto you; Ye shall find the babe wrapped in swaddling clothes, lying in a manger.

Before you continue reading, there is yet another prophecy that you should be aware of. You will recall that in Isaiah 9:6, the prophet foretold that the Messiah would be called the *"Prince of Peace."* In the following prophecy, Isaiah is again the instrument through whom God foretold these wonderful tidings of peace.

Isaiah 57:19 (King James Version.)

19I create the fruit of the lips; __Peace, peace to him that is far off, and to him that is near,__ saith the Lord; and I will heal him.

Now that you have more insight into the angel's visit with the shepherds and you are enlightened as to whom the shepherds really were, we will pick up reading where we left off in Luke chapter two. Pay particular attention to verse fourteen of the following text. For, in that verse, you will see the fulfillment of Isaiah's prophecy in Isaiah 57:19.

12And this shall be a sign unto you; Ye shall find the babe wrapped in swaddling clothes, lying in a manger.

13And suddenly there was with the angel a multitude of the heavenly host praising God, and saying,

14Glory to God in the highest, __and on earth peace, good will toward men.__

15And it came to pass, as the angels were gone away from them into heaven, __the shepherds said one to another, Let us now go even unto Bethlehem, and see this thing which is come to pass, which the Lord hath made known unto us.__

16And they came with haste, and found Mary, and Joseph, and the babe lying in a manger.

17And when they had seen it, they made known abroad the saying which was told them concerning this child.

18And all they that heard it wondered at those things which were told them by the shepherds.

19but Mary kept all these things, and pondered them in her heart.

272

20And the shepherds returned, glorifying and praising God for all the things that they had heard and seen, as it was told unto them.

As we continue to track the occurrences surrounding the Messiah's birth, we must not overlook the fact that like all male Jewish babies, Yeshua was circumcised when He was eight days old. His circumcision is recorded in Luke 2:21.

The reason we must not overlook the Messiah's circumcision is because the circumcision was the external sign of the Abrahamic covenant. Furthermore, since Yeshua was the promised Messiah who had been born a man in order to fulfill the Abrahamic covenant, it was important that He also obey God's circumcision command. After all, as you learned earlier in the series, He was the fulfillment of circumcision. He was the promised Messiah who had taken on the seed of Abraham.

The next recorded event took place when the days of Mary's purification, according to the Law of Moses, were accomplished. Mary and Joseph brought the Christ child to the temple in Jerusalem to present Him to the Lord and to offer the required sacrifice. We will pick up in the following verse.

Luke 2:25-33 (King James Version.)

25And, behold, there was a man in Jerusalem, whose name was Simeon; <u>and the same man was just and devout</u>, waiting for the consolation of Israel: and the Holy Ghost was upon him.
26<u>And it was revealed unto him by the Holy Ghost, that he should not see death, before he had seen the Lord's Christ.</u>

As you read the next verses, consider the words that were spoken by the righteous Jewish man, Simeon. For his words also speak of God's Word in Genesis 3:15 and God's covenant promises.

27And he came by the Spirit into the temple: and when the parents brought in the child Jesus, to do for him after the custom of the law,

28Then took he him [Yeshua] up in his arms, and blessed God, and said,

29Lord, now lettest thou thy servant depart in peace, according to thy word:

30For mine eyes have seen thy salvation,

31Which thou hast prepared before the face of all people;

32A light to lighten the Gentiles, and the glory of thy people Israel.

33And Joseph and his mother marvelled at those things which were spoken of him.

Simeon spoke the truth regarding the baby, Yeshua, being the promised Messiah and Savior. The truth Simeon spoke was confirmed by the Jewish prophetess, Anna. We are told in the Scriptures that Anna was a widow who was very old and that she never left the temple courts. Day and night she remained at the temple praying and fasting. However, when the prophetess, Anna, heard Simeon proclaiming the baby Yeshua to be the promised Messiah, she confirmed his words in the following verse of that same chapter.

Luke 2:38 (King James Version.)

38And she coming in that instant gave thanks likewise unto the Lord, and spake of him [Yeshua] to all them that looked for redemption in Jerusalem.

Yeshua was approximately two years old when the fulfillment of yet another of Isaiah's prophesies came true. As Isaiah foretold, men traveled to Jerusalem from the east, bringing gifts to the Messiah, *"Immanuel [God with us]."* We will read Isaiah's prediction from *The Amplified Bible.*

Isaiah 60:6 (The Amplified Bible.)

6A multitude of camels [from the eastern trading tribes] shall cover you [Jerusalem], the young camels of Midian and Ephah; all the men from Sheba [who once came to trade] shall come, bringing gold and frankincense and proclaiming the praises of the Lord.

Most of the Church teaches that there were three wise men. However, if you search the Scriptures, you will find no mention of the numeral three in connection with the Magi (that is, the wise men). Christian, it is time to lay aside men's traditions. It is time to follow truth rather than fiction. As you just saw in Isaiah 60:6, the Magi traveled to Jerusalem in a caravan. Therefore, the Magi had to have been many in number.

When the Magi arrived in Jerusalem, they told how they had seen the new king's star in the east and had come to worship Him. Thus, the phenomenon prophesied by Balaam in the following verse came to pass.

Numbers 24:17 (King James Version.)

*17I shall see Him, but not now: I shall behold Him, but not nigh: **there shall come a Star out of Jacob,** and a Sceptre shall rise out of Israel, and shall smite the corners of Moab and destroy all the children of Sheth.*

The Amplified Bible translators provide a footnote for the previous verse from J. P. Lange, *A Commentary.* I will share with you a portion of that footnote. However, I trust you will take time to read the entire article.

> The star which the wise men from the
> East saw, and which led them in the
> way to the newborn 'King of the Jews,'
> refers clearly to the prophecy of Balaam
> (Matthew 2:1,2.)

The following verses show the fulfillment of both Isaiah 60:6 and Numbers 24:17. So, I think it will be beneficial if you simply read Matthew's account of that happening for yourself. However, I will continue to insert valuable insight as we proceed.

Matthew 2:1-8 (King James Version.)

*1NOW when Jesus was born in Bethlehem of Judaea in the days of Herod the king, **behold, there came wise men from the east to Jerusalem,***

*2**Saying, where is he that is born King of the Jews? for we have seen his star in the east, and are come to worship him.***

3When Herod the king had heard these things, he was troubled. and all Jerusalem with him.

⁴And when he had gathered all the chief priests and scribes of the people together, he demanded of them where Christ should be born.

⁵And they said unto him, In Bethlehem of Judaea: for thus it is written by the prophet,

⁶And thou Bethlehem, in the land of Juda, art not the least among the princes of Juda: for out of thee shall come a Governor, that shall rule my people Israel.

⁷Then Herod, when he had privily called the wise men, enquired of them diligently what time the star appeared.

⁸And he sent them to Bethlehem, and said, Go and search diligently for the young child; and when ye have found him, bring me word again, that I may come and worship him also.

Matthew reveals in verse three that not only King Herod, but all Jerusalem was troubled by the appearance of the Magi and the Magis' proclaimed reason for visiting Jerusalem. Have you ever wondered why the presence of the Magi caused such a disturbance in Jerusalem? Have you ever wondered why the presence of the Magi or their mission gave Herod reason to believe that his throne was threatened by the innocent child whom they sought? Well, I think you will understand why, once you possess the incredible historical input that I am about to impart to you. The promised information can be found in *The Zondervan Pictorial Encyclopedia of the Bible* under the heading "Magi."

Space is limited, so I can only sketch for you a brief outline of the data contained in the previous source of reference. However, I trust that you will try to acquire a copy of this Bible encyclopedia and read the article in its entirety.

The Zondervan Pictorial Encyclopedia of the Bible informs us that King Cyrus the Great, conqueror and ruler of the Persian empire acknowledged the Magi as the supreme priestly caste of the empire. They were also advisors to the King. King Xerxes, son of Darius, a successor of Cyrus, consulted the Magi when planning his strategy for his invasion of Greece. In the mid-third century BC, the Magi were incorporated into the constitutional government of the empire and given considerable privilege by their Parthian overlords. The magian Zoroastrianism was reinstated as the state religion.

One of the most amazing historical facts recorded in this informative article reveals that **it was the Magis' job to choose and if necessary**

depose the kings of the empire. Think of it! The Magi were actually responsible for making or breaking kings. So, since Palestine had once been part of the Persian empire, it is no wonder that their presence posed a problem for King Herod. Let me read to you a section of the previously mentioned article.

> A constitutional council, known as the Megistanes, was instituted whose duty was to assist in the election (and, if need be, the deposition) of the monarch; and to serve as his advisors in governing the nation. **The magian hierarchy was accorded the senior position in this council....**

Even when other countries had deserted the Magi religion, in Persia proper, the Magi were still accorded their traditional veneration. And according to that same source, some of Persia's kings may themselves have been Magi.

The day came when the Persians and the Magi overthrew Parthian rule. Consequently, the Magi were again granted the highest religious and governmental powers. Amazingly the Magi still maintained that power when the Jewish Messiah was born.

With the information you now have, can you imagine the astonishment that all Jerusalem must have experienced at the sudden appearance of the Magi? **And, can you visualize the shock and fear that must have been revealed on King Herod's face upon realizing that a group of Persian king makers had entered Jerusalem? For "king makers" is exactly how** *The Zondervan Pictorial Encyclopedia of the Bible* describes them.

> ...It was, therefore, a group of Persian-Parthian king makers who entered Jerusalem in the latter days of the reign of Herod.

To make matters worse, the time was ripe for a Parthian invasion. Thus, Herod must have been petrified. Let me pick out a few pertinent segments of the previous article and you will understand what I mean.

> At the time of the birth of Christ (probably C. 4 B.C.), Herod was certainly close to his last illness. Augustus was also aged; and Rome,

since the retirement of Tiberius, was without any experienced military commander. Pro-Parthian Armenia was fomenting revolt against Rome (a revolt that was successfully accomplished within two years). The time was ripe for another Parthian invasion of the buffer provinces, except for the fact that Parthia itself was racked by internal dissension. **Phraates IV, the unpopular and aging king, had once been deposed, and it was not improbable that the Pers. Magi were already involved in the political maneuvering requisite to choosing his successor.** It is possible that the Magi might have taken advantage of the King's lack of popularity to further their own interests with the establishment of a new dynasty which could have been implemented only if a sufficiently strong contender could be found. At this point in time it was entirely possible that the Messianic prophesies of the O T, culminating in the writings of Daniel, one of their own chief Magians, was of profound motivating significance. The promise of divinely-imposed world dominion at the hands of a Jewish monarch was more than acceptable to them. Their own Pers. and Medro-Pers. history was studded with Jewish nobles, ministers and counsellors; and in the great Achaemenid days some of the kings themselves were apparently partly of Jewish blood.

Oh, my friend, think of the terror and awe that the appearance of the Magi must have provoked when they entered Jerusalem. The next portion of the previous article says it all.

In Jerusalem the sudden appearance of the Magi, prob. traveling in force with all imaginable oriental pomp, and accompanied by adequate cavalry escort to ensure their safe penetration of Rom. territory, certainly alarmed Herod and the populace of Jerusalem, as is recorded by Matthew. It would seem as if these Magi were attempting to perpetrate a border incident which could bring swift reprisal from Parthian armies. Their request of Herod regarding Him who "has been born King of the Jews" (Matt. 2:2), was a calculated insult to him who had contrived and bribed his way into that office.

You now have insight into the reason why all Jerusalem was troubled by the appearance of the Magi and by their inquiry of *"Where is He who has been born King of the Jews?"* (Matthew 2:2.) It is obvious that three wise men did not cause such a stir. I am afraid the three wise men are mere fiction. It is ridiculous to think that all Jerusalem would be in an uproar over the arrival of three ordinary foreigners. No! **Jerusalem was in an uproar, because the king-makers entered Jerusalem in full force and pomp as described in the previous article.**

Can you now understand Herod's purpose for gathering together the chief priests and the scribes? His main objective for congregating all the learned men of Israel was to have them pinpoint for him in the Scriptures the actual place of the Messiah's birth. Unaware of his wicked plot to kill the Messiah, the priests and the scribes immediately assured Herod that according to Micah 5:2, the Anointed One would be born in Bethlehem.

Herod secretly met with the Magi in order to extract from them information about the star that they had seen. Herod's intention was to use that information to find out the approximate age of the Christ child. You see, his plan was to murder the child whom he mistakenly believed threatened his throne.

After questioning them, the old king directed the Magi to Bethlehem. He requested that when they found the child, they should let him know where the child was so that he too could go and worship him. However, we know that Herod had no intention of worshipping the infant Jewish Messiah. No! Herod had something entirely different in mind. He planned to remove what he perceived to be a threat to his throne. He planned to murder the Anointed One, the Christ child.

The Magi left Jerusalem and traveled to Bethlehem. Amazingly, the star that they had seen in its rising in the east appeared and went before them. The star led them right to the place in Bethlehem where the holy Jewish child was. Full of joy, the wise men went into the house where the child and His mother were. There, they fell down before the young child Messiah and worshipped Him. They also presented the anointed One with precious gifts of gold, frankincense and myrrh. **Thus Isaiah's words in Isaiah 60:6 were fulfilled, for, the Magi had visited Jerusalem before they arrived at Bethlehem with their gifts**.

Matthew 2:7-12 (King James Version.)

7Then Herod, when he had privily called the wise men, enquired of them diligently what time the star appeared.

8And he sent them to Bethlehem, and said, Go and search diligently for the young child; and when ye have found him, bring me word again, that I may come and worship him also.

9When they had heard the king, they departed; and, lo, the star, which they saw in the east, went before them, till it came and stood over where the young child was.

10When they saw the star, they rejoiced with exceeding great joy.

11And when they were come into the house, they saw the young child with Mary his mother, and fell down, and worshipped him: and when they had opened their treasures, they presented unto him gifts; gold, and frankincense, and myrrh.

12And being warned of God in a dream that they should not return to Herod, they departed into their own country another way.

After the Magi had gone, the angel of the Lord appeared to Joseph in a dream, telling him to take the Christ child and His mother and flee from Bethlehem. The angel of the Lord instructed Joseph to go to Egypt, for Herod intended to search for the Christ child in order to destroy Him. The following verse describes what happened next in fulfillment of a particular prediction given by the prophet Jeremiah. You will see Jeremiah's prophecy a little later.

> *Matthew 2:16 (The Amplified Bible.)*
>
> *16Then Herod, when he realized that he had been misled by the wise men, was furiously enraged, **and he sent and put to death all the male children in Bethlehem and in all that territory who were two years old and under**, reckoning according to the date which he had investigated diligently and had learned exactly from the wise men.*

Now my friend, you know who was behind Herod's dastardly deed. Satan of course! Yes, Satan knew that everything God had foretold in Genesis 3:15 was beginning to come to pass. the Messiah had been born in Bethlehem as the prophets had foretold, and Satan was scared out of his wits. He knew that Yeshua was the promised Messiah who would one day crush his head and destroy his power over mankind. So what did Satan do? He used a ruthless tyrant, a tyrant who, like himself, did not want to relinquish the power and control over men that he had gained. Yes, Satan used wicked King Herod to try to murder *"Immanuel [God with us]"* and defeat God's plan.

Jeremiah's prophecy, which I mentioned earlier, came true. Rachel wept for her children. Rachel's name was mentioned in Jeremiah's prophecy because her tomb was in Bethlehem, the place where the slaughter of innocent Jewish children was prophesied to take place.

> *Jeremiah 31:15 (King James Version.)*
>
> *15Thus says the Lord: A voice was heard in Ramah, lamentation, and bitter weeping; Rachel weeping for her children refused to be comforted for her children, because they were not.*

As I mentioned earlier, prior to the slaughter of the innocent in Bethlehem, Mary and Joseph had been warned by an angel of the Lord to take the Christ child and flee to Egypt which they did. Yet, even that trip to Egypt and their eventual return to Israel was prophesied by God's prophets.

> *Hosea 11:1 (The Amplified Bible.)*
>
> *1WHEN ISRAEL was a child, then I loved him **and called My son out of Egypt.***

Bible prophesies foretelling the circumstances surrounding Yeshua's birth are so numerous that space does not permit me to present all of them at this time. I have, however, kept my word. I provided you with a brief outline of the prophesied events of the Messiah's birth.

I also promised that I would answer the question, "How could anything be more important than the saving of men's souls? If man's salvation was not Yeshua's (God's) first priority for coming to this earth in the form of a man, then, what in the world was His number one priority?" I feel that I have more than adequately answered both questions. I have proved to you through the Scriptures that the most important purpose for Christ's birth was to fulfill God's Word in Genesis 3:15, keep the promises God made to Abraham and thus protect the honor of God's name.

Christian, wake up! Should not God's Word being fulfilled and His promises being kept have taken priority over men's sinful souls? Should not God's reputation have taken priority over mankind who profaned it? For once Christian, can you not put God's rights and God's needs before your own welfare? Can you not make God's honor your first priority?

It was imperative that you saw the truth for yourself on the pages of God's Word. For now you finally have true insight into God's will and purpose on this issue. **You finally understand that the number one priority of the Messiah's birth was to fulfill God's Word in Genesis 3:15 and the sacred covenant that God made with Abraham, Isaac and Jacob and thus protect the honor of God's holy name.**

Chapter 14
Part One

WHY DID THE JEWS FAIL
TO RECOGNIZE THE MESSIAH?

The Bible contains a mountain of inspired predictions regarding the promised Messiah. In chapter thirteen, we studied a number of those forecasts. We specifically concentrated on the Biblical predictions which foretold the circumstances surrounding the Messiah's birth.

Once one becomes aware of the enormous quantity of prophetic data on the previously mentioned subject, one cannot help but wonder why the Jews had and still have difficulty recognizing the promised Messiah. Neither can one help but wonder why they were and are unable to differentiate between the Messiah's first and second Biblically prophesied visits to earth.

There is another dilemma that, if one is not informed, is also hard to fathom. I am referring to the Jews' shortsightedness regarding God fulfilling His Word in Genesis 3:15 and the Abrahamic covenant. After all, the Scriptures specifically foretold that the Messiah would come as a human being and that He would conquer Satan. Furthermore, God clearly promised Abraham that in him all the nations of the earth would be blessed (that is, saved).

We know that the Jews continually cried out to God, begging Him to send the Messiah and to remember His promises to Abraham. Yet, when God brought to pass His Word in Genesis 3:15 and the Messiah was born in Bethlehem as Micah had predicted, the Jews as a whole were oblivious to the fulfillment of that Scripture. Also, when God performed His covenant promise to bless the nations (that is, to bring salvation to the nations) through the seed of Abraham, Isaac and Jacob, the Jews failed to believe that the Messiah had even been born, never mind the fact that He had fulfilled a segment of the Abrahamic covenant.

To this day, the Jews, as a nation, do not accept Yeshua as the Christ, the Anointed One. So, the question is, with so much Scriptural evidence available, why have the majority of God's beloved covenant people failed to recognize the promised Messiah? My friend, I promise you that in parts one through seven of chapter fourteen, you will procure the true Biblical answer to that question. As a matter of fact, you will not only receive the answer to the question, but you will also gain insight into the contents of numerous passages of Scripture that for generations Bible scholars, ministers, theologians and laymen alike have desired and, in some cases, longed to possess.

We are, however, dealing with a subject that is vastly involved. It is a matter of such great depth that it will require your earnest participation in a lengthy study of God's Word in order for me to impart to you a tiny glimpse of the overall picture. Nevertheless, if you pay close attention to the information that is contained in all seven parts of chapter fourteen, this inspired study will provide you with more Scripturally sound and Biblically confirmed revelation than you have ever before obtained on this subject.

In addition to supplying you with the promised in-depth Scriptural knowledge, this information will totally change your viewpoint regarding the Jews' rejection of the Messiah. Although, at this time it might seem impossible, I assure you that if you keep a teachable spirit and you allow the truth in all seven parts of chapter fourteen to expose and help you to discard any misconceptions on this issue which, throughout your life, you may have ignorantly embraced, you will end up thanking God for the Jews' blind and deaf state. Yes, you will end up thanking God in spite of the fact that their spiritually blind and deaf condition caused them to fail to recognize the Messiah. Furthermore, as amazing as it might now seem, you will actually come to appreciate and value the Jewish people because of their blind and deaf spiritual infirmities. So, with all that said, let us go straight to the core of this problem.

For years, the Church has been flooded with men's ignorant and destructive wrong doctrines concerning the issue of the Jews' failure to recognize the Messiah. Sadly, for almost two thousand years, the Church's misinterpretations and distortions of certain Scriptures have brought undeserved worldwide suffering and persecution upon the Jewish people. Therefore, in order to clear God's reputation and to relieve the descendants of Abraham, Isaac and Jacob of the unfair and cruel condemnation and mistreatment that the Church has perpetrated upon them, the record must and will be set straight. I will begin to clear the record by bringing to your attention several of the previously indicated merciless, wrong church doctrines.

FALSE DOCTRINE NO. 1: The Jews' spiritual blindness and deafness, which stopped them from recognizing their Messiah, was the result of their own sinfulness.

FALSE DOCTRINE NO. 2: The Jews had every opportunity to recognize and to believe on the Messiah. However, they were unwilling to do so.

FALSE DOCTRINE NO. 3: The Jews would have been able to recognize the Messiah if their hearts had been right. Yet, they chose to deliberately harden their hearts.

FALSE DOCTRINE NO. 4: The Jews would have automatically recognized the Messiah and believed on Him if they had been willing to repent of their sins, lay aside their man-made doctrines and traditions and humbly accept the truth that Yeshua spoke. Albeit, they refused to allow themselves to understand His words or to believe on Him.

FALSE DOCTRINE NO. 5: The Jews' spiritual blindness and deafness, which consequently brought about their failure to recognize the Messiah, was a punishment from God for their past sins.

As the series progresses, you will see beyond doubt that the preceding church doctrines, doctrines which the Church applies to Jews who were alive during Yeshua's earthly visit and to Jews who are alive today, are deceptive and outright false. More than that, you will become aware that these same doctrines are an unjust blight upon God's holy character. Therefore, in order to set the record straight and to clear God's holy name in that area, I will gradually fit each individual piece of the Scriptural puzzle in its proper place. So please, give your full attention to the following information. For, you are about to obtain your first glimpse of the true overall picture regarding the Jews' failure to recognize the Messiah.

The first point that you need to be aware of is that **God and God alone** is responsible for the Jews' blind and deaf spiritual condition which is mentioned in the three verses that we will soon read. **The Scriptures clearly reveal that God deliberately closed His peoples' spiritual ears and shut their spiritual eyes so as to intentionally dull their spiritual understanding**. Yes! You understood my last statement. God Himself caused His own beloved people to be spiritually blind and deaf! Consequently, the Jews were and still are unable to recognize their long awaited Messiah. And what is more, **God did not and does not want them to recognize the Messiah**. Yes! You read the preceding sentence right! I said that God did not and does not want them to recognize the Messiah.

In Biblical terms, my last statement would read, **God did not and does not want the Jewish people to see or to hear or to understand, or to turn to Him for spiritual healing**. It was not at that time, nor is it at this time God's will that the nation of Israel as a whole be saved. We will deal with those Jews who were and are the exception to that rule later in the series. However, right now, we must stick to the issue at hand which involves God spiritually disabling His own beloved people.

In a moment, you will see the former truths for yourself in *The Living Bible*. Yes, you will see how through the prophet Isaiah, God showed aforetime that which He had already foreordained concerning the Jews' unfavorable response to the Messiah during His first visit to earth.

> *Isaiah 6:8-10 (The Living Bible.)*
>
> *[8]Then I heard the Lord asking, "Whom shall I send as a messenger to my people? Who will go?" And I said, "Lord, I'll go! Send me."*
>
> *[9]And he said, "Yes, go. But tell my people this: 'Though you hear my words repeatedly, you won't understand them. Though you watch and watch as I perform my miracles, still you won't know what they mean.'*
>
> *[10]Dull their understanding, close their ears and shut their eyes. I don't want them to see or to hear or to understand, or to turn to me to heal them."*

God makes Himself clearly understood in the preceding verses. He reveals that He is the one who gave the command that initially dulled His people's understanding, closed their ears and shut their eyes. God also distinctly states that He carried out that premeditated act because **He did not want His people to see or to hear or to understand or to turn to Him to heal them (that is, He did not want the Jews to recognize the Messiah when He came or to understand His teachings and miracles or to turn to the Messiah to spiritually heal them).**

When the Messiah arrived, God's will was carried out to the letter. Isaiah's prophecy in Isaiah 6:8-10 was completely fulfilled. As God had planned, the Jewish nation failed to recognize the Messiah or understand His teachings or turn to Him for spiritual healing. And what is more, God's original purpose for spiritually disabling His people, which you will learn about later in the series, was partially achieved.

In the following text taken from the *Holy Bible, King James Version*, the Messiah Himself provides overwhelming proof that what I just stated is absolutely true. As a matter of fact, Yeshua actually refers to Isaiah's aforementioned prediction. Quoting Isaiah, He lets the Jews know that in them Isaiah's inspired words in Isaiah 6:8-10 were fulfilled. For, their response to the Messiah was exactly as God had planned and as Isaiah had foretold. **After all, since God had aforetime rendered His people spiritually blind and deaf and therefore unable to recognize the Messiah or understand His teachings, how else could they have reacted**. Read the Messiah's words and see the previous truth for yourself.

Matthew 13:13-15 (King James Version.)

13Therefore speak I to them in parables: because they seeing see not; and hearing they hear not, neither do they understand.

14And in them is fulfilled the prophecy of Esaias, which saith, By hearing ye shall hear, and shall not understand; and seeing ye shall see, and shall not perceive:

*15For this people's heart is waxed gross, and their ears are dull of hearing, and their eyes they have closed; **lest at any time they should see with their eyes, and hear with their ears, and should understand with their heart, and should be converted, and I should heal them.***

Having access to Isaiah's original quote (Isaiah 6:8-10) that Matthew records Yeshua as citing (Matthew 13:13-15) gives you a great advantage. I say that it gives you an advantage because by referring back to Isaiah's original quote, you are made aware of the true content of Yeshua's statement that Matthew recorded in the previous verses. Yes, you know that the Jews' eyes were closed not on account of their hard hearts but rather because God closed them. Moreover, you are aware that the Jews' hard hearts were the result of their God-decreed blind and deaf spiritual disabilities.

As you saw previously in Isaiah 6:8-10, the prophet stated that God did not want His people to see. Neither did God want His people to recognize the Messiah and be spiritually healed. In order therefore to accomplish his will and purpose in the aforementioned areas, God deliberately spiritually disabled His people. Yes, God Himself dulled their understanding. As Yeshua said in Matthew 13:15 when citing Isaiah's prophecy, *"For this peoples' heart is waxed gross...."*

By substituting Greek for the English word "gross," the sentence in verse fifteen would read, He made their hearts **thick** and **stupid**. **God**

Himself made His people spiritually dense. God disabled them to the point that they lacked spiritual discernment.

Having access to all the facts really does give you an edge. It also helps you to rightly divide the Word of truth as the apostle Paul instructed in 2 Timothy 2:15.

Oh, my friend, I implore you to read again Isaiah's words in Isaiah 6:8-10 and to give serious thought to them. **For, the prophet is telling you that it was God's will that the Jews be in an intellectual spiritual stupor when the promised Messiah came. It was God's will that the Jews be so spiritually blind and deaf that they could not recognize the Messiah or understand the Messiah's teachings or the meaning of the miracles that He performed. Furthermore, it was God's will that the majority of the Jews not be permitted to turn to the Messiah to spiritually heal them.**

I say that all those things that are mentioned in the former paragraph were God's will because, as you yourself have seen in God's Word, God was the one who initially dulled His people's spiritual understanding, closed their spiritual ears and shut their spiritual eyes. God was the one who gave them a spirit of stupor. Thus, it stands to reason that if it had not been God's will for the Jews to be spiritually blind and deaf, He would not have put them in that pathetic situation in the first place.

Think about it! If you want men to perceive spiritual matters, you do not deliberately dull their spiritual understanding. If you want men to pay attention to and to comprehend your teachings, you do not stop up their ears. If you want men to recognize you, you do not blind their eyes.

My friend, God understands the preceding basic principles far better than you and I do. God is all-wise! Thus, God knew before He made the Israelites spiritually blind and deaf, that when the Messiah came, the majority of His people would not be able to recognize Him or understand His teachings. The Scriptures make it clear that God planned it that way! Yes, keeping His people from recognizing the Messiah was indeed part of God's original purpose for making His people blind and deaf. As the Lord said in Isaiah 6:10 in *The Living Bible*, "*...**I don't want them** to see or to hear or to understand, or to turn to me to heal them.*"

Surely, it is now obvious to you that under the circumstances that God predicted in Isaiah 6:8-10, the majority of the Jewish people could not possibly have done anything but fail to recognize the Messiah. And furthermore, they could not possibly have done anything but fail to believe the words that He spoke. In their foreordained spiritual stupor, the only course of action that was open to the Jewish nation was to oppose

Yeshua's teachings and to reject Him as the Messiah. Opposition to the Messiah and His teachings, upon His first visit to earth, was God's foreordained will for the nation of Israel. And by the end of your examination of every Biblical truth in all seven parts of this chapter, you will have received a mountain of Scriptural confirmation which will verify that fact.

After learning earlier in the series about God's everlasting love for the Jews, you might well ask, "What in the world did God's beloved people do that was serious enough to cause God to deafen their spiritual ears and blind their spiritual eyes, thus rendering them spiritually inept in mental agility? Was it the same sins that forced God to send His people into captivity in Babylon that also caused Him to dull their understanding so as to keep them from recognizing the Messiah?"

No, my friend! It was not the Israelites' sins that moved God to close their spiritual ears, shut their spiritual eyes and dull their understanding so as to keep them from recognizing the Messiah. The truth is that God had carried out His purpose in that area and had restricted Israel's spiritual understanding long before the prophet Isaiah made his statement in Isaiah 6:8-10. As a matter of fact, **God had blinded Israel's eyes, stopped up their ears and dulled their understanding hundreds of years before Isaiah was born.** Therefore, as a professing Christian, it is high time that you understood exactly when God did carry out His purpose in that area.

You will soon see all that I have just mentioned reaffirmed on the pages of God's Word. For, you are about to see Scriptural evidence which proves that in Isaiah 6:8-10, God's servant, Isaiah, was simply pointing out the truth that when the Messiah came, the Jews would still be in the same spiritually blind and deaf condition that they had been in during their four-hundred years of Egyptian bondage. Moses himself reveals and describes the Jews' ongoing blind and deaf spiritual condition in the book of Deuteronomy. Moses' own words in the next text should be more than enough Biblical proof to convince you that my last statement is absolutely factual.

Deuteronomy 29:2-4 (The Amplified Bible.)

2Moses called to all Israel and said to them, You have seen all that the Lord did before your eyes in the land of Egypt to Pharoah, to all his servants, and to all his land;

3The great trials which your eyes saw, the signs, and those great wonders.

4Yet the Lord has not given you a [mind and] heart to understand and eyes to see and ears to hear, to this day.

In the former verses, Moses sets forth the pure, unadulterated truth. **He makes it absolutely clear that the Israelite's spiritual blindness and deafness existed prior to their leaving Egypt**. To be precise, in verses two and three of the previous text, Moses specifies that their blind and deaf condition was present during the plagues and judgments that God poured out upon Pharoah, all his servants and all his land. **Furthermore, he lets us know that Israel's spiritual stupor still existed after the exodus**. For, it was some time after the Israelites had left Egypt that in the last verse, verse four, Moses said, *"Yet the Lord has not given you a [mind and] heart to understand and eyes to see and ears to hear, to this day."*

To take this issue a step further, I intend to present to you undeniable New Testament evidence which verifies that the Jews' spiritual blindness and deafness (that is, the blindness and deafness which Moses' previous declaration proves existed before God's people left Egypt and which was clearly evident during Yeshua's time on earth) continued even through the apostle Paul's lifetime.

In the previously mentioned New Testament documentation which you will soon read, the Jewish apostle Paul follows Isaiah's example and cites Moses' statement in Deuteronomy 29:4. He even quotes a portion of Moses' statement. Paul, as you know, was an authority on the Scriptures. He had completed his education under the famous Jewish teacher, Gamaliel. Therefore, when Paul quoted Moses in the succeeding text, he knew exactly what he was doing. He was showing the Church that the same spiritual stupor (that is, the same spiritual blindness and deafness) that, by God's design, the Israelites had experienced from the time that they became a nation in Egypt and which had persisted throughout the time of Moses has been carried over to the New Testament era and still exists.

My friend, it is the same God-decreed spiritual blindness and deafness which Moses revealed in Deuteronomy 29:4 that has kept the Israelites in a spiritual stupor from the beginning of their birth as a nation in Egypt until this very day. Yes, it was that same God-ordained spiritual blindness and deafness that Moses revealed in Deuteronomy 29:4 that Isaiah predicted in Isaiah 6:8-10 would render the Jews incapable of recognizing the Messiah when He came to earth the first time. Moreover, it is that same God decreed spiritual blindness and deafness which continues to keep the majority of the Jews from recognizing the Messiah even to this very day.

Read Paul's words for yourself in the next text, and you will then understand all that I have just stated. Pay particular attention to verse eight. For, as I said earlier, in that verse, Paul cites the written words that the prophet Moses had spoken in Deuteronomy 29:4. It is because the Jewish apostle Paul was simply repeating the contents of the recorded words of Moses that he begins verse eight with the words, *"As it is written."* Along with other crucial points, I have doubly highlighted the words, *"As it is written"* so that they will stand out as you read them in the following text.

As you read, also notice how Paul identifies the fact that it was **God** who made the Jews spiritually blind and deaf, or as Paul states, *"**God** gave them a spirit (an attitude) of stupor."*

> *Romans 11:7-8 (The Amplified Bible.)*
>
> *⁷What then [shall we conclude]? Israel failed to obtain what it sought [God's favor by obedience to the Law]. Only the elect (those chosen few) obtained it, while the rest of them became callously indifferent (blinded, hardened, **and made** insensible to it).*
>
> *⁸**As it is written, God gave them** a spirit (an attitude) of stupor, eyes that **should not see** and ears that **should not hear, [that has continued] down to this very day**.*

Where can one find the source of Paul's reiteration in the previous Scriptural reference, verse eight? Where is Paul's statement written? As I said earlier, *"it is written"* in Deuteronomy 29:4 which reads, **"Yet the Lord has not given you a [mind and] heart to understand and eyes to see and ears to hear, to this day."**

If you are fortunate enough to possess a copy of *The Amplified Bible*, you will notice that one of the additional references that the translators have inserted at the end of Romans 11:8 is Deuteronomy 29:4. And as you know, Deuteronomy 29:4 is the same reference that we studied earlier, and it is the same reference that I repeated in the former paragraph. This shows that even *The Amplified Bible* translators are aware that in Romans 11:8 Paul cited the words of the prophet Moses. Moreover, if you happen to have a *King James* reference Bible and you run down the references for Romans 11:8 that are provided in that edition of the Bible, you will again be directed to Moses' words in Deuteronomy 29:4, words which you now know were the source of Paul's previously mentioned rendition. *"Yet the Lord has not given you a [mind and] heart to understand and eyes to see and ears to hear, to this day."*

Upon careful scrutiny of the former Scriptural evidence, one is compelled to accept the truth that the Israelites were spiritually blind and deaf from the time that they became, in Egypt, the great nation that God promised Abraham, Isaac and Jacob they would become. **Thus, you might say that the Israelites' spiritual blindness and deafness were God decreed national birth defects, hereditary spiritual birth defects that both Moses and Paul inform us have been passed** *"down to this very day."*

The previous Scriptural truths are extremely important to you. They are important for the following reasons.

(1) They provide you with irrefutable Scriptural proof that, as a whole, the Jews have never been healed of their blind and deaf, God decreed, spiritual birth defects.

(2) They also provide you with irrefutable Scriptural proof that God deprived the Jews of spiritual understanding long before they committed the abominable sins that were later recorded in God's Word.

By now, it should be crystal clear to you that the Jews' God-decreed spiritual blindness and deafness was not and is not a consequence of their past sins. So, surely you do not think that the righteous God of Abraham, Isaac and Jacob would have punished His people with spiritual blindness and deafness for crimes that they did not do? No! The righteous Judge of all the earth would not have deliberately disabled His people (that is, He would not have punished them by depriving them of spiritual understanding) for sins that they did not commit. No! A thousand times no!

Do you now understand the reason why I said earlier that church doctrine, doctrine which teaches the falsehood that the Jews' previously mentioned blindness and deafness was and is the result of their past sins, is a blight upon God's uncompromisingly righteous character? Such lying doctrine as I have described is a blight upon God's character because it teaches the Church that God acts unjustly and unrighteously. It teaches the Church that God punishes innocent people for crimes that they have not committed.

My friend, truth demands a response. Therefore, in order for you to respond to truth in a righteous manner, you must first carefully consider the available Scriptural evidence that I have provided and that I will continue to present in all seven parts of this chapter. Then, after painstakingly scrutinizing all the available information, you must be willing to draw a righteous conclusion that is based entirely on the truth of God's Word rather than your own preconceived wrong ideas. If you do what I have suggested, you will eventually realize that there is only one righteous conclusion that you can possibly come to. And that conclusion is that the Jews' dull spiritual understanding, a condition that inevitably caused them to fail to recognize the Messiah, was not and is not the result of their past sins. **<u>God Himself made His beloved people spiritually blind and deaf so that they would not be able to recognize the Messiah or understand His teachings</u>**.

The religious leaders of Israel, including God's holy prophets, did not escape the previously mentioned God decreed, inherited spiritual infirmities. On the contrary, they were as equally blind and deaf as the rest of God's spiritually handicapped covenant people. Oh, yes! By the inspiration of the Holy Spirit, the prophets foretold future events and did many wondrous supernatural works. However, except upon rare occasions (a subject which I intend to shed light on in a later segment of chapter fourteen), they did not understand the deep inner meaning of the inspired future predictions that they made or the miracles that they performed any more than their fathers had understood Moses' words and miracles in Deuteronomy 29:4. For, as you saw earlier in God's Word, the Lord has not given His Abrahamic covenant people *"...a [mind and] heart to understand and eyes to see and ears to hear, <u>to this day</u>."* And furthermore, God's prophets were no exception to the rule.

See God's prophets' spiritual plight in the following verses. See just how spiritually intellectually dull the teachers of Israel really were.

Isaiah 29:10-12 (The Amplified Bible.)

[10] For the Lord has poured out on you the spirit of deep sleep. <u>And He has closed your eyes, the prophets; and your heads, the seers</u>, He has covered and muffled.

[11] And the vision of all this has become for you like the words of a book that is sealed. When men give it to one who can read, saying, Read this, I pray you, he says, I cannot, for it is sealed.

[12] And when the book is given to him who is not learned, saying, Read this, I pray you, he says, I cannot read

Further verification of my earlier statement regarding the religious leaders being as equally blind as the rest of the Israelites is seen in the next text.

Isaiah 56:9-12 (The Amplified Bible.)

⁹*All you beasts of the field, come to devour, all you beasts (hostile nations) in the forest.*

¹⁰*[Israel's] watchmen are blind, they are all without knowledge; they are all dumb dogs, they cannot bark; dreaming, lying down, they love to slumber.*

¹¹*Yes, the dogs are greedy; they never have enough. And such are the shepherds who cannot understand; they have all turned to their own way, each one to his own gain, from every quarter [one and all].*

¹²*Come, say they, We will fetch wine, and we will fill ourselves with strong drink! And tomorrow shall be as this day, a day great beyond measure.*

Isaiah makes it clear that Israel's religious leaders (that is, Israel's watchmen or shepherds) were spiritually blind. Their teachers were so spiritually blind regarding future happenings that they could not even comprehend their future fate. As Isaiah tells you in verse twelve of the previous text, catastrophe loomed ahead for Israel. Yet, in their spiritual stupor, their teachers could not perceive the danger and horror that lay ahead. To Israel's blind and deaf religious leaders, the future looked rosy.

After reading the previous verses, you will soon agree that, like all the other Israelites, the religious leaders of Israel certainly lived up to Moses' prediction in the following verses. For, since they were incapable of understanding the deep inner meaning of what God was doing right before their eyes, there was no way that they could have understood the signs of their future fate. Read Moses' prediction for yourself.

Deuteronomy 32:28-29 (The Amplified Bible.)

²⁸*For they are a nation void of counsel, and there is no understanding in them.*

²⁹*O that they were wise and would see through this [present triumph] to their ultimate fate!*

We will also read Moses' former prediction in *The Living Bible.*

Deuteronomy 32:28-29   (The Living Bible.)

<u>**28***Israel   is   a   stupid   nation;   foolish,   without   understanding.***</u>
<u>**29***Oh,   that   they   were   wise!   Oh,   that   they   could   understand!   Oh,   that   they   would   know   what   they   are   getting   into!***</u>

Later in the series, you will be provided with additional Scriptural evidence regarding the aforementioned spiritual condition of God's prophets and the religious leaders of Israel. However, right now, I do not want to get you sidetracked. So, I will keep the promise that I made earlier and with the aid of the Holy Spirit, I will continue to carefully and systematically reveal the answer to the question, "Why Did The Jews Fail To Recognize The Messiah?"

As you gradually study more and more of the enlightening information contained in parts one through seven of chapter fourteen, the Scriptural points that I touched on earlier will be continually reinforced. Those points will also be covered in much more detail. However, for now, my aim is to provide you with an orderly arrangement of numerous vital building blocks of understanding. For, I am convinced that once you possess the main pieces of this amazing Scriptural puzzle, you will be able to more easily connect together the remaining pieces of Biblical information. So, on that note, let us consider and then carefully assemble the next key piece of this incredible, soon to be revealed, mystery.

It is important to note that God did not **totally** deprive his beloved people of spiritual understanding. No! While it is true that the Israelites were void of spiritual intelligence in certain areas, they were given a generous opportunity to excel in one particular type of spiritual intelligence. **God did not dull the Israelites' understanding when it came to <u>His revealed will</u> (that is, when it came to His righteous laws which He gave to them via Moses and which later became known as "Moses' Law" or "the Law of Moses").**

Since in Deuteronomy 29:4, Moses revealed the Israelites' God-decreed spiritual handicaps, handicaps that inevitably caused their failure to understand the deep inner meaning of the wondrous works that God did in Egypt, it is no coincidence that in verse twenty-nine of that same chapter, He then directed the Israelites' attention to the one area of spiritual understanding that God had so graciously and abundantly imparted to them.

Shortly, you will see in the Scriptures that Moses actually divided the different areas of spiritual understanding into two clearly specified categories. He defined one type of spiritual intelligence as the ability to understand *"the secret things,"* and he defined the other as the ability to understand *"the things which are revealed."* **He explained to the Israelites that the first category (that is, the secret mysteries of God's Word) would not be given to them.** God intended to temporarily keep those secrets to Himself. It was so that He could keep the previously mentioned *"secret things"* hidden from His covenant people that, prior to that time, God had been forced to dull their understanding. And, as you saw previously in Deuteronomy 29:4, God accomplished that task by closing His people's spiritual ears and shutting their spiritual eyes to that particular area of understanding.

On the other hand, God always intended that the Israelites and their posterity understand the things that He revealed to them, things that they needed to understand in order for them to keep His laws (that is, the Law of Moses). You see, God would never have blinded His own people's eyes to the degree that they would be unable to recognize or understand the very commandments that He had originally created them to keep. Such an act would have deliberately forced them into sin, and our uncompromisingly righteous God would never have caused His beloved people or for that matter any people to sin by breaking His commands. God hates sin!

No! God did not spiritually disable His people to the point that they could not recognize or understand His basic laws. On the contrary, God generously revealed His will to His people in the area of Moses' Law so that to the best of their ability, if they would, they could fear Him and keep His commandments.

Yet, even though God had so graciously endowed His people with the priceless, most crucial area of understanding (that is, the understanding of His revealed laws), their eyes were blinded to the deep inner secrets of Moses' Law and also to the future predictions that Moses made. For example, their eyes were blinded to the spiritual significance of the symbology of the external rituals of the law which were a preview of the wonderful things to come. Their eyes were also blinded to the predictions that Moses made which, along with the symbology of the external rituals, foretold future events such as the Messiah's first visit to earth, the miraculous works that He would perform, His own people's foreordained rejection of Him and His eventual death for the sins of all mankind.

Later in the series, you will be given an abundance of Scriptural confirmation for all that I just said. However, in the meantime, as you read Moses' inspired words in the following verses, you will easily recognize the two distinct doubly highlighted categories of understanding that I identified earlier. I am speaking of course of *"the secret things"* and *"the things which are revealed."*

Deuteronomy 29:29 (The Amplified Bible.)

29*The secret things belong unto the Lord our God, but the things which are revealed belong to us and to our children forever, that we may do all of the words of this law.*

It is not my intention to draw you into a lengthy study on Moses' Law in the middle of this topic. Nevertheless, for a time, it is necessary for me to frequently refer you to the Law of Moses so that you might obtain a measure of insight into the area of understanding that God imparted to Israel. I will, however, do my best to keep my explanations as brief and to the point as possible.

(1) God poured out priceless wisdom and understanding of *"the things which are revealed"* upon those of His covenant people who made every effort to faithfully keep His laws. The more obedience to God's laws that the Israelites exhibited—the more wisdom and understanding of those laws they received. The Psalmist explained how it all worked in the following text.

Psalm 119:96-105 (The Amplified Bible.)

96*I have seen that everything [human] has its limits and end [no matter how extensive, noble, and excellent]; but your commandment is exceedingly broad and extends without limits [into eternity].*

97*Oh, how love I Your law! It is my meditation all the day.*

98*You, through Your commandments, make me wiser than my enemies, for [Your words] are ever before me.*

99*I have better understanding and deeper insight than all my teachers, because Your testimonies are my meditation.*

100*I understand more than the aged, because I keep Your precepts [hearing, receiving, loving, and obeying them].*

101I have restrained my feet from every evil way, that I might keep Your word [hearing, receiving, loving, and obeying it].

102I have not turned aside from Your ordinances, for You Yourself have taught me.

103How sweet are Your words to my taste, sweeter than honey to my mouth!

104Through Your precepts I get understanding; therefore I hate every false way.

105Your word is a lamp to my feet and a light to my path.

(2) The prior words of the Psalmist show us that both wisdom and understanding of God's laws were generously conferred upon those Israelites who learned and obeyed God's revealed will (that is, God's commandments). Make no mistake, wisdom is just as crucial to God's people performing the original purpose of their creation as understanding is. You see, knowledge of God's Word is a wonderful thing to possess. However, when men do not have the wisdom (that is, the sound judgment and spiritual intelligence) they need to know how to apply that truth to every area of their lives and to every situation that arises, they end up with nothing but head knowledge. And mere head knowledge (that is, the sum range of what men have learned without application) has no eternal value.

People who possess only head knowledge do not grow in righteousness. Why? Because righteousness is applied truth. Righteousness is produced when God's righteous commands are applied to men's lives (that is, when men learn and obey God's commands). Therefore, it is evident that God's covenant people needed an abundance of wisdom (that is, intelligence, or as some might say, "good old common sense") so that they would know how to apply God's laws to their lives in every given situation. You will appreciate the way *The Living Bible* translators expound that very truth in the next verse.

Psalm 119:125 (The Living Bible.)

125for I am Your servant; therefore give me common sense to apply your rules to everything I do.

(3) It should now be evident to you that when God's covenant people applied His Word (that is, His laws) to their lives including making the required ritualistic animal sacrifices, then like the Psalmist, they became knowledgeable of God's commands and wise in applying them to their lives (that is, they became spiritually intelligent in the things that

pertained to the revealed will of God). Furthermore, as you learned in an earlier chapter of this work, under the former conditions, those who applied God's Word to their lives also got to enjoy all the abundant blessings promised in the Horeb covenant while at the same time managing to avoid its curses.

The prophet Moses possessed and recognized the value of the previously mentioned wisdom and understanding. Consequently, he informed the Israelites that if they obeyed all God's commandments, the surrounding nations who witnessed the results of the application of God's commands to their lives and to every situation that arose in their nation would admire and respect them. Moses assured the Israelites that under these stipulations, the nations would declare them to be a wise and understanding people. Read Moses' declaration for yourself in the next text.

Deuteronomy 4:5-14 (The Amplified Bible.)

5Behold, I have taught you statutes and ordinances as the Lord my God commanded me, that you should do them in the land which you are entering to possess.

6So keep them and do them, for that is your wisdom and your understanding in the sight of the peoples who, when they hear all these statutes, will say, Surely this great nation is a wise and understanding people.

7For what great nation is there who has a god so near to them as the Lord our God is to us in all things for which we call upon Him?

8And what large and important nation has statutes and ordinances so upright and just as all this law which I set before you today?

9Only take heed, and guard your life diligently, lest you forget the things which your eyes have seen and lest they depart from your [mind and] heart all the days of your life. Teach them to your children and your children's children—

10Especially how on the day that you stood before the Lord your God in Horeb, the Lord said to me, Gather the people together to Me and I will make them hear My words, that they may learn [reverently] to fear Me all the days they live upon the earth and that they may teach their children.

11And you came near and stood at the foot of the mountain, and the mountain burned with fire to the heart of heaven, with darkness, cloud, and thick gloom.

12And the Lord spoke to you out of the midst of the fire. You heard the voice of the words, but saw no form; there was only a voice.

13And He declared to you His covenant, which He commanded you to perform, the Ten Commandments, and He wrote them on two tables of stone.

14And the Lord commanded me at that time to teach you the statutes and precepts, that you might do them in the land which you are going over to possess.

God's laws are the revealed will of God, **"the things which are revealed,"** that Moses referred to in Deuteronomy 29:29.

(4) God's laws (that is, God's commands) are the light, the illumination, that God gave to His people to guide them into true wisdom and understanding. They are the God-given chart which continually keeps God's people on course (that is, they are the chart that maps out the direction God's people must follow in order for them to become established in truth and righteousness). **The writer of Psalm 119 knew that God's commands were his source of wisdom and understanding. Thus, he begged God to open his eyes to the true intent of His laws.** Read the Psalmist's informative words in *The Living Bible.*

Psalm 119:1-20 (The Living Bible.)

1Happy are all who perfectly follow the laws of God.

2Happy are all who search for God, and always do his will,

3rejecting compromise with evil, and walking only in his paths.

4You have given us your laws to obey—

5oh, how I want to follow them consistently.

6Then I will not be disgraced, for I will have a clean record.

7After you have corrected me I will thank you by living as I should!

8I will obey! Oh, don't forsake me and let me slip back into sin again.

⁹How can a young man stay pure? By reading your Word and following its rules.

¹⁰I have tried my best to find you—don't let me wander off from your instructions.

¹¹I have thought much about your words, and stored them in my heart so that they would hold me back from sin.

¹²Blessed Lord, teach me your rules.

¹³I have recited your laws,

¹⁴and rejoiced in them more than in riches.

¹⁵I will meditate upon them and give them my full respect.

¹⁶I will delight in them and not forget them.

¹⁷Bless me with life so that I can continue to obey you.

¹⁸__Open my eyes to see wonderful things in your Word.__

¹⁹I am but a pilgrim here on earth: __how I need a map— and your commands are my chart and guide.__

²⁰I long for your instructions more than I can tell.

You now have a good idea of what *"the things which are revealed"* entail. You know that God gave to those Israelites who were willing to learn and obey His commands an abundance of understanding of His laws and the needed wisdom to apply those laws to their lives and to every given situation.

As of yet, you have only studied the first of seven parts of chapter fourteen, seven parts which combined provide the overall answer to the question, "Why Did The Jews Fail To Recognize The Messiah?" However, I am sure that the amazing insight contained in this one segment alone has already had a tremendous impact upon your life. Of course I am referring to the fact that you are now aware that the Church's doctrines concerning the Jews failure to recognize the Messiah are nothing but fabricated deceptions and distortions. For example, you now know that the previously mentioned spiritual blindness and deafness which caused the Jews to fail to recognize the Messiah was not, as the Church teaches, a consequence of their past sins, but rather, it was a God-ordained, God-bestowed affliction.

Most of all, even though we have at present covered only a fraction of the information contained in this seven part topic, God's reputation has already been partially cleared of the terrible damage that men have done to it. For, you now know that God did not spiritually blind His people's eyes so that they could not see and deafen their ears so that they could not hear then cruelly punish them because, in their pathetic disabled state, they did not recognize the Messiah and understand His teachings.

It is not in God's uncompromisingly righteous character to be brutally cruel, unjust or unfair. My friend, we are speaking of the same God who said in Leviticus 19:14, *"You shall not curse the deaf or put a stumbling block before the blind...."* We are speaking of the same God who said in *The Living Bible* in Deuteronomy 27:18, *"Cursed is he who takes advantage of a blind man."* If God so cares for the **physically** disabled, do you not think He cares as much for His own beloved **spiritually** disabled people, His people whom He Himself struck blind and deaf for reasons which you will learn in the next six parts of this chapter.

Wake up, Church! The God of Abraham, Isaac and Jacob is uncompromisingly righteous in all His ways. He would never commit the wrongs that the Church has so ignorantly and foolishly and wickedly accused Him of. The Church has made many serious accusations and insinuations that pertain to behavior that God is in no way guilty of exhibiting. God loves the Jews with an everlasting love. He would never hurt them simply for the sake of hurting them. Neither would He break His own word and take advantage of blind and deaf men, especially when He Himself is solely responsible for their disabilities.

Later you will learn the reason why God deliberately blinded his people's spiritual eyes and deafened their ears to *"the secret things."* Then you will shed tears of deep regret for any physical or verbal abuse that you have ever personally vented upon them. However, let me end chapter fourteen, part one, by reminding you that the question, "Why Did The Jews Fail To Recognize The Messiah?" has been partially answered and will be fully answered in the remaining six parts of this chapter.

Chapter 14
Part Two

WHY DID THE JEWS FAIL
TO RECOGNIZE THE MESSIAH?

In part one of chapter fourteen, you saw in the Scriptures that the Jews' spiritual deafness and blindness to *"the secret things,"* spiritual deafness and blindness which all along has kept them from recognizing the Messiah, are absolutely not the result of their past or present sins. On the contrary, the Jews' spiritual blindness and deafness to *"the secret things"* are instead God-ordained spiritual handicaps that have been passed down to this day.

You also saw in the Scriptures that, while on the one hand, God did impose the previously mentioned spiritual blindness and deafness upon His people in order to hide from them understanding of *"the secret things,"* He did on the other hand, give His people an abundance of understanding of *"the things which are revealed"* (that is, He gave them abundant understanding of His written laws).

The information that you will receive in part two of chapter fourteen is vital. Essentially, it will help you to Scripturally identify two additional forms of spiritual blindness and deafness that also disabled the Jewish people. You will learn that unlike the Jews' blindness and deafness to *"the secret things,"* these two other types of spiritual disabilities **were not and are not imposed by God**. Having access to the forthcoming information will also help you to categorize the cause and effect of both of these additional types of blindness and deafness.

Being informed regarding the cause and effect of the two other existing forms of spiritual blindness and deafness will prove to be extremely valuable to you. Such instruction will keep you from ever again ignorantly mislabeling, misinterpreting or misrepresenting God's Word in any of the three formerly identified separate and distinct categories of spiritual blindness and deafness. That fact alone makes the promised Scriptural insight indispensable.

Since, at present, we are entering into the second segment of a seven part topic, I do not think that a detailed review is necessary. So without further delay, we will pick up where we left off at the end of part one of this chapter, "Why Did The Jews Fail To Recognize The Messiah?"

The knowledge you acquired in part one is extremely significant. It shows you that the people's access to the Lord's promised wisdom and understanding of *"the things which are revealed"* and their ability to retain and increase in those things is totally dependent upon their learning and obeying His laws. You see, that knowledge gives you instant insight into the main reason why in the following verse **God strictly prohibited His people from adding to or detracting from His written commandments**. See God's warning in the *Holy Bible, King James Version.*

Deuteronomy 4:2 (King James Version.)

²*Ye shall not add unto the word which I command you, neither shall ye diminish ought from it, <u>that ye may keep the commandments of the Lord your God which I command you.</u>*

Does it now make sense to you why God was so adamant when it came to His laws remaining untouched by human hands and human reasoning? God was undeniably strict regarding that issue because He knew that if His people started tampering with His laws, they would end up twisting, misrepresenting and misinterpreting the true intent of His holy commandments. Consequently, they would not only be void of knowledge of *"the secret things,"* they would also suffer the loss of sight and hearing in the one area of spiritual understanding that God had so graciously allotted to them (that is, they would also be without understanding of *"the things which are revealed"*).

Sadly, God's people ignored His previous warning in Deuteronomy 4:2 and disobeyed His instructions. The scribes arrogantly attempted to improve and clarify the Creator's laws. However, rather than making God's laws clearer, they instead changed their meaning altogether. They did that by ignorantly trivializing the important points of the law while emphasizing the insignificant. Thus, they deleted from and added to the true intent of God's commandments. Consequently, the scribes' superficial, man-made additions to God's commandments, which they introduced and then zealously enforced, limited the law's power to preserve the Israelites' spiritual lives and to guide them in the correct and righteous way of the Lord. The scribes' superinduction of their own trivial man-made rules, regulations and traditions actually restricted the law's power and authority to help men accomplish the original purpose for which they had been created.

You might wonder why the Jewish people would have allowed the scribes to infringe on God's sacred laws and in so doing put Israel's future spiritual welfare in jeopardy. How could God's people have stood quietly by without lifting a finger while the scribes literally distorted God's law? Well, you must keep in mind that the scribes' act of deteriorating the meaning of the Law was not completed with one stroke of the pen. Rather, their manipulation of God's law was carried out slowly and systematically over a long period of time.

The religious leaders, who were supposed to be experts in the Mosaic Law, modified the true intent of God's commandments by making one tiny alteration, one small adjustment or change at a time. However, the scribes' subtle practice of chipping away at the very essence of the Law, gradually replacing its intrinsic properties with their own foolish opinions and ideas, persisted until God's laws became unrecognizable. The sense, quality and character of the Law was no longer distinguishable.

In the following verses, the prophet Jeremiah gives an accurate account of the scribes' previously mentioned wicked behavior. He also addresses the awful ramifications of their sinful actions. He shows you the helpless predicament into which the scribes' foolish conduct had forced God's people.

The Israelites' spiritual plight became such that they no longer knew what God required of them. You see, by then, the scribes had rendered God's people so spiritually dull, so spiritually blind and deaf regarding *"the things which are revealed"* that they were unable to distinguish between right and wrong by the standards of God's Word. They were totally void of spiritual understanding of God's laws. As the prophet explains in the following text, they did not even have the sensitivity or discernment (that is, the comprehension of God's law) that the birds of the air have who instinctively recognize the Law as far as it pertains to them.

Jeremiah 8:7-9 (The Amplified Bible.)

*7[Even the migratory birds are punctual to their seasons.] Yes, the stork [excelling in the great height of her flight] in the heavens knows her appointed times [of migration], and the turtledove, the swallow, and the crane observe the time of their return. **But My people do not know the law of the Lord [which the lower animals instinctively recognize in so far as it applies to them].***

⁸How can you say, We are wise, and we have the written law of the Lord [and are learned in its language and teachings]? Behold, the truth is, the lying pen of the scribes has made of the law a falsehood (a mere code of ceremonial observances).

Try to imagine the overall repercussions that occurred as a result of Israel's spiritual leaders changing the true intent of God's law and subsequently diminishing its power and authority. The scribes could not have done more spiritual harm to God's covenant people if they had purposely poured ink over each individual Scriptural scroll and had thus blotted out every visible trace of God's written Word. For, over the long haul, they had replaced God's righteous laws with men's deadly lies, bringing about a disastrous spiritual crisis.

The wicked conduct of Israel's religious leaders had, as Isaiah had said, reduced God's people to following *"a falsehood (a mere code of ceremonial observances)."* By eventually erasing the essence of God's commands from the minds of God's people and replacing their real meaning with falsehoods, the scribes had removed Israel's chart and guide to wisdom and understanding of *"the things which are revealed."* For, you will remember that David said in Psalm 119:104, ***"Through your precepts I get understanding; therefore I hate every false way."*** How grievous it is to think that God's people were spiritually stripped of everything except that which David said he hated. For, they were left with a whole code of falsehoods.

The religious leaders of Israel had taken away the key (that is, they had taken away God's people's access) to the one area of spiritual understanding that God had so graciously imparted to them. For, as you saw in part one of chapter fourteen, the only way the Israelites could possess and grow in knowledge *of "the things which are revealed"* was by learning and obeying God's commands.

Yes, in order to gain the wisdom and understanding of *"the things which are revealed,"* God's people had to allow the true knowledge of God's law to enter into and to remain in full control in their lives. Albeit, they could not do that since they no longer had access to true knowledge. The scribes had barricaded the entrance to true knowledge with a mountain of man-made rules, regulations and traditions. That barricade was so dense that the people could not find a way through it, around it or over it. Consequently, God's people clung to the only thing that was left. They clung to a code of ceremonial observances.

King David explains how a man gains true understanding of God's laws in the next verses. As you read David's inspired words, try to picture yourself in the same pathetic spiritually deprived state that the Jews were in.

Psalm 119:129-130 (The Amplified Bible.)

129*Your testimonies are wonderful [far exceeding anything conceived by man]; therefore my [penitent] self keeps them [hearing, receiving, loving, and obeying them].*

130*The entrance and unfolding of Your words give light; their unfolding gives understanding (discernment and comprehension) to the simple.*

Truly the Israelites were in a pathetic spiritual state. For as you now know, God had already blinded their spiritual eyes and stopped up their spiritual ears, thus depriving them of understanding of *"the secret things"* that are contained in His Word. Then, to make matters worse, their own meddling religious leaders robbed them of the true meaning of God's commands and consequently of the crucial wisdom and understanding that God's commands had once imparted to them. In doing so, the scribes extinguished the very light that God's people needed to see by. They also took away their spiritual guide, forcing God's people off course. Hence, the scribes stripped God's people of the spiritual wisdom and understanding of *"the things which are revealed."* As Jeremiah stated, the birds of the air had more recognition of God's law in so far as it applied to them than did God's people.

Can you now more fully grasp the reason why Yeshua continually cried out against the religious leaders of His day? Yeshua was not blaming those leaders for starting the problem. Rather, He was blaming them for putting their stamp of approval on the wicked practices that former scribes had established. He was also blaming them for continuing to favor those wicked practices and for furthering their advancement.

Yeshua's main concern, however, was for the spiritually impoverished people of Israel who ignorantly and trustingly followed the man-made lying doctrines and traditions that previous scribes had passed down and which the religious leaders, who were in office during His time, zealously promoted. You see, Yeshua knew that just as their predecessors had done before them—so did the religious leaders of His day. They shut the door of spiritual knowledge of *"the things which are revealed"* right in the faces of God's people. They kept God's people from advancing toward truth and righteousness by encouraging them to heed the lying rules and regulations of men rather than the righteous laws of God.

None of those religious leaders had enough courage to stand on God's written Word and refuse any longer to stray from the true intent of God's laws. Therefore, their cowardice and hypocrisy also perpetuated the destructive cycle of spiritual poverty.

An example of the man-made rules and regulations that Israel's religious leaders substituted for God's commands can be seen in the following text. The case in point took place during Yeshua's visit to earth. Yet, as you study these verses, you will quickly realize that circumstances had not changed since Isaiah's time. Yeshua's words reveal how the man-made doctrines that the religious leaders of Israel introduced to God's people and then diligently enforced severely limited the Law's power and authority.

Mark 7:6-13 (The Amplified Bible.)

6But He said to them, Excellently and truly [so that there will be no room for blame] did Isaiah prophesy of you, the pretenders and hypocrites, as it stands written: These people [constantly] honor Me with their lips, but their hearts hold off and are far distant from Me.

7In vain (fruitlessly and without profit) do they worship Me, ordering and teaching [to be obeyed] as doctrines the commandments and precepts of men.

8You disregard and give up and ask to depart from you the commandment of God and cling to the tradition of men [keeping it carefully and faithfully].

9And He said to them, You have a fine way of rejecting [thus thwarting and nullifying and doing away with] the commandment of God in order to keep your tradition (your own human regulations)!

10For Moses said, Honor (revere with tenderness of feeling and deference) your father and your mother, and, He who curses or reviles or speaks evil of or abuses or treats improperly his father or mother, let him surely die.

11But [as for you] you say, A man is exempt if he tells [his] father or [his] mother, What you would otherwise have gained from me [everything I have that would have been of use to you] is Corban, that is, is a gift [already given as an offering to God],

12 Then you no longer are permitting him to do anything for [his] father or mother [but are letting him off from helping them].

13 Thus you are nullifying and making void and of no effect [the authority of] the Word of God through your tradition, which you [in turn] hand on. And many things of this kind you are doing.

In the following text, when Yeshua reproved the spiritual leaders of Israel, He simply repeated that which was already recorded in God's written Word. He cited the words of God's prophet in Jeremiah 8:8. Nevertheless, when one reads the religious leaders' response to the truth of God's Word that Yeshua relayed, one would almost think that Yeshua had spoken unfamiliar words. I say that because the religious leaders so fiercely opposed His Biblical censure that they sought to do Him harm. As you read the next text, pay special attention to Yeshua's reprimand in the first verse, verse fifty-two.

Luke 11:52-54 (The Amplified Bible.)

52 Woe to you, lawyers (experts in the Mosaic Law)! For you have taken away the key to knowledge; you did not go in yourselves, and you hindered and prevented those who were entering.

53 As He left there, the scribes and the Pharisees [followed Him closely, and they] began to be enraged with and set themselves violently against Him and to draw Him out and provoke Him to speak of many things,

54 Secretly watching and plotting and lying in wait for Him, to seize upon something He might say [that they might accuse Him].

Let us now pick up where we left off before Yeshua's visit to earth. You will recall that the prophet Jeremiah stated that the birds of the air had more recognition of God's law in so far as it applied to them than God's people had. The Israelites were spiritually impoverished. For, since the scribes had made the written law of God a falsehood, the people had no guide, no truth of God's holy commandments to impart to them spiritual wisdom and understanding, no revelation of God's redemptive law. Consequently, God's people were spiritually destroyed for lack of knowledge of God's righteous commandments.

God knew that if His people continued to obey His laws, withholding from them understanding of *"the secret things"* in order to fulfill His future purpose would in no way spiritually harm them. However, as you will see in the next verse, Israel's religious leaders' act of keeping from them knowledge and understanding of *"the things which are revealed"* was extremely detrimental to their spiritual lives.

Proverbs 29:18 (The Amplified Bible.)

18Where there is no vision [no redemptive revelation of God], the people perish; but he who keeps the law [of God, which includes that of man]—blessed (happy, fortunate, and enviable) is he.

I like the clarity that *The Living Bible* translators bring to this verse.

Proverbs 29:18 (The Living Bible.)

18Where there is ignorance of God, the people run wild; but what a wonderful thing it is for a nation to know and keep his laws!

The scribes' action of exchanging the true intent of God's commandments for *"a falsehood"* did indeed spiritually destroy God's people. For, the man-made code of ceremonial observances that the scribes had introduced to Israel and which God's people had been deceived into accepting and obeying in the place of God's laws was grossly inadequate. It was unable to perform the function that God's commandments were intended to do. As I said earlier, in tampering with God's commandments, the religious leaders of Israel had so depreciated the essence of the Law that they limited its power and authority to impart to God's people wisdom and understanding of His commandments. They limited the Law's power and authority to guide the Israelites into truth and righteousness.

The true intent of the Law was lost to God's beloved covenant people. Consequently, because they were wholly blind and deaf, because they were void of both categories of spiritual understanding (that is, because they were void of understanding of both *"the secret things"* and *"the things which are revealed")*, God's people fell headlong into abominable sin.

It is important to note that to this point in chapter fourteen, we have touched on two totally different types of spiritual blindness and deafness.

(1)   In part one, we briefly covered **the spiritual blindness and deafness that was decreed by God** in order to keep His people from understanding *"the secret things"* and in so doing fulfill His future purpose.

(2)   In this part, part two, we considered **the blindness and deafness which resulted from the disabling spiritual injuries that were inflicted upon God's people by their own wicked religious leaders.** God's people were truly victimized. The scribes had robbed them of sight and hearing in regard to *"the things which are revealed"* and left them helplessly stumbling around in spiritual darkness.

The Jewish people were entrusted with so much, and yet they failed so miserably. As I said earlier, in their scribe-inflicted blind and deaf state, they fell headlong into sin. However, before you point an accusing finger at the Jews, Gentile Christian, maybe you should first consider the Church's failure to obey God's commands which under the circumstances is an even greater offense.

I say the Church's failure to obey God's commands is greater because from the beginning God gave the Church access to both types of spiritual understanding along with all the power men need to learn and obey His commandments. God never deprived Gentile Christians of spiritual sight and hearing. No! God did not dull their spiritual understanding in regard to *"the secret things"* as He did in the case of His Abrahamic covenant people. Furthermore, as you will learn in a subsequent part of chapter fourteen, neither does God deprive Messianic believers of spiritual sight and hearing in that area. Therefore, I can go a step further. I can proclaim that **God did not deprive the true Church of spiritual understanding of** *"the secret things."*

Secondly, every Christian knows that God did not deprive the Church of *"the things which are revealed"* (that is, God did not deprive the Church of His written laws, His commandments). On the contrary, the Church has the blood-sealed new covenant. And, in the blood-sealed new covenant, God actually promises to give believers understanding of His laws and all the power they need to obey them. So as you can see, Christians have absolutely no excuse for failing to understand or failing to obey God's written commandments.

Yet, despite the fact that the Church has the promised blood-sealed new covenant and access to both categories of understanding (that is, access to *"the secret things"* and *"the things which are revealed"*),

312

church leaders committed and still commit the same offenses as did the religious leaders of Israel. Yes, like the Jewish scribes, wicked church leaders substituted their own man-made rules, regulations and traditions for the true intent of God's commandments. And, even to this day, like the religious leaders of Christ's time, wicked church leaders put their stamp of approval on those same wicked man-made doctrines and traditions and continue to favor them and to further their advancement.

Shockingly, church leaders went even further than the religious leaders of Israel. They actually went so far as to completely discard many of God's commandments. And guess what? Even though Christians have the previously mentioned new covenant promises that provide understanding of God's laws and the power to obey them, the majority of Christians have never lifted a finger to search out the truth of God's commandments for themselves or to walk in that truth.

For the most part, Christendom has willingly followed the handed down doctrines of men rather than the laws of God. And to the Church's shame, even today, most church leaders zealously teach and promote those same passed down, man-made rules, regulations, and traditions. At the same time, they actually discourage the Christians in their charge from keeping God's laws.

Now you might say, "What in the world are you talking about? I do not know of any of God's commandments that church leaders have replaced with men's doctrines." Well my friend, maybe you should consider the Ten Commandments. For example, how many professing Christians in the Church today do you personally know who keep the fourth commandment? Do you keep it yourself? **Do you keep the seventh day Sabbath holy as God commanded? And, if you <u>do not</u> keep the seventh day Sabbath holy, why don't you?**

My friend, you do not keep the Biblical Sabbath day holy, because in AD 336, wicked leaders in the Catholic Church transferred the solemnity (sacredness, grave, impressive and serious nature) of the Sabbath from the seventh day to the first day of the week. And like most of Christendom, you have been deceived into devotedly following the Church's manmade doctrines instead of the truth that is contained in the sacred Scriptures. You can search the Bible from cover to cover and you will not find one verse of Scripture that informs you of such a change. You will not find such a change, because God never transferred the solemnity of His holy Sabbath day to the first day of the week. Neither did Yeshua change the day on which men should celebrate God's fourth commandment. **No! No! No!**

Bible scholars and historians agree that <u>it was the Church, to be precise, it was the Catholic Church, not God</u>, who substituted the observance of Sunday, the first day of the week, for the observance of Saturday, the seventh day (that is, God's holy Sabbath). Moreover, the leaders of the Catholic Church openly acknowledge their act of tampering with the fourth commandment of God. For example, the following excerpt is an actual quote from the 1913 edition of *The Catholic Encyclopedia,* Volume IV, Page 153, under the heading "Commandments of God" by John H. Stapleton. Also note that Stapleton refers to the fourth commandment as the third commandment.

> The Church on the other hand, <u>**after changing the day of rest from the Jewish Sabbath, or seventh day of the week, to the first,**</u> made the third commandment refer to Sunday as the day to be kept holy as the Lord's Day....

If you read the previous article "Commandments of God" in its entirety, you will experience overwhelming grief. For, you will immediately realize that the leaders of the Catholic Church knew the truth regarding God's Ten Commandments. They were also aware of the severe punishment that will be poured out upon all those who break them. And yet, despite those facts, they deliberately chose to disregard God's fourth commandment and cast it from them. Let me share with you a few more short excerpts out of *The Catholic Encyclopedia* article that I just quoted from. I will also repeat the previous quote in context so that you will understand all that I have stated. **Keep in mind that the writer is speaking about <u>the Ten Commandments</u>.**

> Commandments of God, called also simply The Commandments, or Decalogue...<u>**ten precepts bearing on the fundamental obligations of religion and morality and embodying the revealed expression of the Creator's will in relation to man's whole duty to God and to his fellow-creatures**</u>....Written by the finger of God on two tables of stone, this Divine code was received from the Almighty by Moses amid the thunders of Mount Sinai, and by him made the ground-

work of the Mosaic Law. **Christ resumed these commandments in the double precept of charity—love of God and of the neighbor; <u>He proclaimed them as binding under the New Law</u>"** (See Matthew 5:17-20)...."<u>**The Church on the other hand, after changing the day of rest from the Jewish Sabbath, or seventh day of the week, to the first, made the third commandment refer to Sunday as the day to be kept holy as the Lord's Day.**</u> The Council of Trent (Sess. VI, can. XIX) condemns those who deny that the Ten Commandments are binding on Christians....

Pay special attention to the next two excerpts from *The Catholic Encyclopedia* article dealing with the Ten "Commandments of God." For, the Church actually records her own guilt and condemnation. Out of her own mouth the Church will be judged and convicted.

This legislation expresses not only the Makers positive will, but the voice of nature as well—the laws which govern our being and are written more or less clearly in every human heart. The necessity of the written law is explained by the obscuring of the unwritten in men's souls by sin. <u>These Divine mandates are regarded as binding on every human creature, and their violation, with sufficient reflection and consent of the will, if the matter be grave, is considered a grievous or mortal offence against God. They have always been esteemed as the most precious rules of life and are the basis of all Christian legislation.</u>

Surely, the next quote will also shock you. For, the writer not only confirms the fact that the Catholic Church substituted the observance of Sunday for God's seventh day Sabbath, **<u>but he actually boasts that</u>**

they did so knowing that there is no Scriptural authority for such a change. *A Doctrinal Catechism*, Stephen Keenan, page 174.

> Q. *"Have you any other way of proving that the Church"* (Roman Catholic) *"has power to institute festivals of precept?"*
>
> A. Had she not such power, she could not have done that in which all modern religionists agree with her;—she could not have substituted the observance of Sunday the first day of the week, for the observance of Saturday the seventh day, **a change for which there is no Scriptural authority.**

On page 50 of *The Convert's Catechism of Catholic Doctrine*, the Reverend Peter Geiermann makes the following statement.

> Q. *Which is the Sabbath day?*
>
> A. **Saturday** is the Sabbath day.
>
> Q. *Why do we observe Sunday instead of Saturday?*
>
> A. **We observe Sunday instead of Saturday because the Catholic Church, in the council of Laodicea (AD. 336), transferred the solemnity from Saturday to Sunday.**

Could these church scholars have stated the previous appalling facts any clearer than they already have in the preceding quotes? I do not think so. **For, they clearly proclaim that Catholic Church leaders, not God, changed the Ten Commandments**. Catholic Church leaders dared to set aside God's fourth commandment and replace His Sabbath command with their own man-made rules, regulations and traditions.

Oh my friend, consider the awful ramifications that have come about as a result of the Church's wicked act of casting from them God's holy Sabbath command. Today, almost the whole Church, worldwide, is disregarding God's fourth commandment. God's people adamantly refuse to worship on the seventh day (Saturday) as God commanded. Instead, they insist on worshipping on the day that the Catholic Church instituted (Sunday). Thus, like the Jews in Jeremiah 8:7-9, the Church is also following a mere code of man-made observances rather than God's righteous laws.

In Yeshua's day, the Jews were indeed guilty of adding their own rules and regulations to God's fourth commandment, but the Church's guilt goes much deeper. For, the Church deliberately disregards God's fourth commandment altogether. Yes, though the Church has God's new covenant promise that He will write His laws on His people's hearts and minds so that they will know them and obey them, still Christendom has deliberately trampled underfoot God's holy Sabbath day command.

God's Word is, however, extremely clear as to what will happen to all those who set aside His laws in preference for falsehoods and refuse to repent (that is, those who refuse to change their minds, attitudes and conduct). Both the following texts describe these people's terrible end. Yes, God's Word describes the end of all those who, in the language of *The Catholic Encyclopedia*, commit the "grievous or mortal offence against God" of breaking any of His Ten Commandments.

Galatians 6:7 (The Amplified Bible.)

*7Do not be deceived and deluded and misled; God will not allow Himself to be sneered at (scorned, disdained, or mocked by mere pretensions or professions, **or by His precepts being set aside**). [He inevitably deludes himself who attempts to delude God.] **For whatever a man sows, that and that only is what he will reap.***

The second reference is taken from the *Holy Bible, King James Version.*

Revelation 22:14-15 (King James Version.)

*14**Blessed are they that do his commandments, that they may have right to the tree of life, and may enter in through the gates into the city.***
*15**For without** are dogs, and sorcerers, and whoremongers, and murderers, and idolaters, **and whosoever loveth and maketh a lie.***

Church, wake up! As the religious leaders of Israel lied to those in their charge, so also, your spiritual leaders have lied to you! And if you choose to continue to love (that is, if you choose to continue to obey) the lying Sunday teachings of the Catholic Church instead of obeying God's fourth commandment, then like the Jews, you are proving to God and man that you love men's false doctrine more than you love the righteous laws that God promised to write on your heart and mind. Moreover, when the end comes, you will find yourself in a terrible plight. For, as you saw in the previous verses, the Church's lying man-made observances and traditions will not and can not deliver you or give you right to the tree of life or entrance into the Heavenly City. On the contrary, as Revelation 22:15 states, keeping (that is, loving) the Church's lying man-made observances in the place of God's commandments will actually keep you out of the Holy City.

Jeremiah 5:31 (The Amplified Bible.)

31The prophets prophesy falsely, and the priests exercise rule at their own hands and by means of the prophets. And My people love to have it so! **But what will you do when the end comes?**

I cannot get into a lengthy study on God's fourth commandment in the middle of this present topic. So, I encourage you to visit your local library and do your own research on the subject of the Sabbath day. I assure you that if you do as I have suggested, you will be both shocked and saddened by what you will learn. You will also be righteously indignant over the fact that you have been deceived into following and clinging to the man-made Sunday doctrine of the Catholic Church while, at the same time, being encouraged to totally disregard one of God's holy Ten Commandments. Yes, you will learn that you have been subtly tricked into sinning against God by disobeying His fourth commandment, *"Remember the Sabbath day to keep it holy."*

Read God's fourth commandment for yourself in the following text taken from the *Holy Bible, King James Version.* And then, muster up the courage to obey God rather than men.

Exodus 20:8-11 (King James Version.)

8Remember the sabbath day, to keep it holy.

9Six days shalt thou labor, and do all thy work:

10But the seventh day is the sabbath of the Lord thy God: in it thou shalt not do any work, thou, nor thy son, nor thy daughter, thy manservant, nor thy maidservant, nor thy cattle, nor thy stranger that is within thy gates:

11For in six days the Lord made heaven and earth, the sea, and all that in them is, and rested the seventh day: wherefore the Lord blessed the sabbath day, and hallowed it.

Do you now understand why, earlier, I suggested that you not point an accusing finger at the Jews? Do you also understand that the Church's failure to obey God's commands is without a doubt greater than the Jews' failure? It is greater because, except for a small number of Jewish believers, the Jews do not as yet enjoy the promises of the blood-sealed new covenant. They do not yet have the promised new covenant power that enables men to consistently learn and obey God's laws. Neither do they have understanding of *"the secret things."* On the other hand, the Church has access to all the previously mentioned spiritual benefits.

Sadly however, most Christians are so comfortable with the wicked, manmade Sunday doctrine of the Catholic Church and their consciences so bound to those doctrines that, despite all the new covenant promises that Yeshua shed His blood to provide, they openly and willfully refuse to acknowledge and confess their sin of breaking God's fourth commandment. They refuse to change their minds and conduct and turn back to God's Word. They refuse to keep God's fourth commandment even when undeniable Scriptural and historical proof of the Church's guilt is right before their eyes.

Like the Jews in Jeremiah's day, the Church at large does not even have the sensitivity or discernment (that is, the Church does not have the comprehension of God's laws) that the birds of the air have who instinctively recognize the laws of God in so far as they apply to them. If the prophet Jeremiah was alive today, he would be justified in rebuking the Church in the same manner that he rebuked his Jewish brethren in Jeremiah 8:8. He could truthfully say to the Church as a whole, "Church, '*How can you say, We are wise, and we have the written law of the Lord [and are learned in its language and teachings]? Behold, the truth is, the lying pen of the scribes has made of the law a falsehood (a mere code of ceremonial observances).*'"

I have presented more than enough Scriptural and historical evidence to prove to you that in comparison to the religious leaders of Israel, the spiritual leaders of the Church bear much more guilt in regard to their tampering with God's laws, spiritually impoverishing God's people and leading God's people into abominable sin by causing them to break God's holy commandments. Yes, I have proved to you that just as it was with the Jewish people, so it is with the Church—the Church has also been given much and yet, as a whole, she too has failed miserably. Therefore, hopefully, all insinuations, accusations and prejudice against the Jews that may have once stirred in your heart are now quieted, and you can view the following information with true insight and therefore in a totally different light.

Earlier, you saw the awful consequences that came about because the scribes of Israel disobeyed God's instructions in Deuteronomy 4:2 and added to and distracted from God's written commandments. You will recall that Israel's scribe-inflicted spiritually blind and deaf people fell into the darkness of sin.

Knowing that His people had been victimized by their own religious leaders, the Lord did everything possible to try to rescue them from the destructive trap that the scribes had deceptively led them into. He raised up one prophet after another, put His word in their mouths and sent them to His people. God's righteous prophets spoke the truth to His covenant people. They relayed to them the true meaning of God's laws. Over and over again, they exhorted the Israelites and pleaded with them to acknowledge the error of their ways, to repent and to return to the Lord, but they would not! **Consequently, because they deliberately refused to love the truth, the Israelites brought upon themselves the third category of spiritual blindness and deafness.**

God's people's eyes and ears became shrouded with the deadliest form of spiritual blindness and deafness that exists. **I am referring to the <u>self-imposed</u> spiritual blindness and deafness that grips the lives of all rebellious men and women who refuse to hear and see the truth of God's Word, men and women who refuse to acknowledge and repent of their sin, men and women who refuse to learn and obey God's commands.**

A moment ago, I purposely chose to use the word "shrouded." I chose that particular word since the shroud is associated with death and as you know, *"**the wages of sin**"* (that is, the wages of breaking God's commands) *"**is death**."* (Romans 6:23.)

A glimpse of just how spiritually depraved Israel eventually became can be seen by studying Jeremiah's accurate portrayal of the spiritual blind and deaf condition of the Jews in his day. For, he reveals the extent of the horrendous crimes against God that Israel committed, crimes that deserved the severest of punishments. As you will soon see, the people did indeed run wild. For, Proverbs 29:18 in *The Living Bible* reads, *"Where there is ignorance of God, the people run wild; but what a wonderful thing it is for a nation to know and keep God's laws!"*

The portion of Scripture that I just referred to reveals how **God's peoples' rebellion and wickedness became so widespread that the prophet Jeremiah was unable to find one righteous person in all the city of Jerusalem.** Jerusalem's occupants were covenant breakers. They had broken the Horeb agreement and sinned against God by disobeying His commands. The depth of their sin is made apparent by the fact that they brazenly and openly practiced idolatry.

Read the truth for yourself in the subsequent text, and you will find a people who were utterly spiritually impoverished. Yes, you will find a people who willingly chose and were willingly reduced to spiritual depravation. See what happens to people who, after being robbed of the knowledge of God's commandments and later confronted with the truth of God's Word, still refuse to repent and turn back to God. See what happens to people who deliberately choose to continue on in the foolishness of sin rather than return to the wisdom and understanding of *"the things which are revealed"* (God's laws).

Jeremiah 5:1-7 (The Amplified Bible.)

*¹RUN TO and fro through the streets of Jerusalem, and see now and take notice! Seek in her broad squares to see if you can find a man [as Abraham sought in Sodom], one who does justice, who seeks truth, sincerity, and faithfulness; **and I will pardon [Jerusalem—for one uncompromisingly righteous person].***

²And though they say, As the Lord lives, surely they swear falsely.

*³O Lord, do not your eyes look on the truth? [They have meant to please You outwardly, but You look on their hearts.] **You have stricken them, but they have not grieved; You have consumed them, but they have refused to take correction or instruction. They have made their faces harder than a rock, they have refused to repent and return to You.***

⁴Then I said, Surely these are only the poor; <u>they are [sinfully] foolish and have no understanding,</u> for they know not the way of the Lord, the judgment (the just and righteous law) of their God.

⁵I will go to the great men and will speak to them, for they must know the way of the Lord, the judgment (the just and righteous law) of their God. But [I found the very reverse to be true] these had all alike broken the yoke [of God's law] and had burst the bonds [of obedience to Him].

6Therefore a lion out of the forest shall slay them, a wolf of the desert shall destroy them, a leopard or panther shall lie in wait against their cities. Everyone who goes out of them shall be torn in pieces, because their transgressions are many, their backslidings and total desertion of faith are increased and have become great and mighty.

7Why should I and how can I pass over this and forgive you for it? Your children have forsaken Me and sworn by those that are no gods. When I had fed them to the full and bound them to Me by oath, they committed [spiritual] adultery, assembling themselves in troops at the houses of [idol] harlots.

Before we continue with this part of the series, let me make one point absolutely clear. **God did not put the last two categories of spiritual blindness and deafness upon His people**. No! God did not deprive them of understanding of His laws. **Their own religious leaders did that**. Furthermore, God did not make His people blind and deaf to the truth concerning His laws that He sent to them via the prophets. No! That type of spiritual blindness and deafness is always deliberately **self**-imposed. Yes, **self**-imposed spiritual blindness and deafness fall into the last category that I covered. These disabling spiritual side effects are the result of wicked unteachable, rebellious minds and hearts that refuse to hear and obey the truth of God's Word. These horrible symptoms are voluntarily carried by spiritually sick men and women who deliberately choose to wallow in disease-ridden pools of sin.

In order to accomplish His own future purpose, God did indeed deprive the Israelites of spiritual understanding of *"the secret things."* However, at no time did He deprive them of understanding of His laws (that is, He did not deprive them of understanding His commandments). On the contrary, as you have already seen in the Scriptures, God gave the Israelites an abundance of understanding of *"the things which are revealed."* Albeit, in the end, God's foolish, wicked people refused His generous gift of understanding of His laws. They chose instead to wallow in the vileness and filthiness of sin. They made a deliberate and conscious choice to blind their own eyes and to deafen their own ears so that they would not have to see and hear the truth of God's righteous commandments or obey them.

Accordingly, in retaliation for the Israelites' abominable idolatrous sins and their refusal to accept the truth that the prophets had spoken, the Lord punished them in more ways than one. Now, notice that I said, God punished them. **I did not say that He blinded and deafened them to His laws. No! The people did that themselves.** God punished the Israelites, because they hated His laws so much that they consciously chose to blind and deafen themselves to His commands. Furthermore, God's punishment was administered in the form of curses, curses that He had previously warned they would experience if they broke the Horeb covenant and sinned against Him by committing idolatry. As a result of the preceding curses, God's covenant people suffered such things as famine, pestilence and war.

Nevertheless, despite the Israelites' abominable crimes against Him, God never planned to totally destroy them. No! Regardless of how severely God chastised Israel, He repeatedly made it clear to them that, for His own name's sake, a remnant of His covenant people would always survive. For, as you learned in a former chapter of this series, God needed the Israelites alive to help Him keep His Word in Genesis 3:15, His other predictions and His covenant with Abraham, Isaac and Jacob.

One of God's recorded reminders that He will always remain faithful to His covenant with Abraham and will therefore never totally destroy His people is seen in the first verse of the following text.

Jeremiah 5:18-21 (The Amplified Bible.)

18But even in those days, says the Lord, I will not make a full and complete end of you.

Get it through your head my friend, God could not and cannot ever totally annihilate His Abrahamic covenant people. God swore by Himself that He would love them and be their God forever. So, for that reason, no matter what the Jews do or what happens, God will keep His word. Yes, He will keep His agreement with Abraham even to His own hurt. In chapter eight of this book, you saw a perfect example of what I just said about God keeping His word even to His own hurt. I am speaking about the time when, at Moses' request, God spared the Israelites even when they deserved to die for their abominable, idolatrous sins against Him.

The truth that God will never totally destroy the Israelites is so important that I am going to repeat verse eighteen. I have also highlighted verse twenty-one so that you will take special note of its contents also.

> *18But even in those days, says the Lord, I will not make a full and complete end of you.*
>
> *19And when your people say, Why has the Lord our God done all these things to us? then you shall answer them, As you have forsaken Me, says the Lord, and have served strange gods in your land, so shall you serve strangers (gods) in a land that is not yours.*
>
> *20Declare this in the house of Jacob and publish it in Judah:*
>
> *21Hear now this, O foolish people without understanding or heart, who have eyes and see not, who have ears and hear not:*

Read Jeremiah 5:1-31 for yourself in your own personal copy of *The Amplified Bible*, and as you do, notice the references for verse twenty-one that have been provided by the translators of that edition of the Bible. You will then understand that in verse twenty-one, Jeremiah was speaking of two different types of spiritual blindness and deafness.

(1) Jeremiah was speaking of the Israelites' **self-imposed** blindness and deafness to *"the things which are revealed"* that made them *"foolish"* and thus caused him to state in verse twenty-one, *"O foolish people."* For, you will recall how in verse four of the same chapter, Jeremiah had already revealed that it was the Israelites' sin that made them foolish. Jeremiah said, *"they are [sinfully] foolish and have no understanding, for they know not the way of the Lord, the judgment (the just and righteous law) of their God."* (Jeremiah 5:4.)

There can be no doubt that in the first part of verse twenty-one when Jeremiah says, *"Hear now this, O foolish people,"* he is referring to the Israelites' **self**-imposed blindness and deafness to the *"things which are revealed"* (that is, the **self**-imposed blindness and deafness to God's laws). The self-imposed spiritual blindness and deafness to *"the things which are revealed"* is easily identified in Jeremiah 5:21 since Israel's sin is made evident in that chapter.

(2) When in verse twenty-one, Jeremiah spoke of the Israelites as a people *"who have eyes and see not, who have ears and hear not,"* he was referring to the Israelites' **God**-imposed spiritual blindness and

deafness to *"the secret things,"* *"secret things"* that God said they would not understand, *"secret things"* to which all the references that are provided in *The Amplified Bible* for that verse point to.

Without the information contained in parts one and two of this chapter, the average reader would completely overlook the overall meaning of Jeremiah's words. You see, since it is obvious that the Israelites were in deep sin, the average reader would automatically draw the conclusion that Jeremiah was referring entirely to the Israelites' blindness and deafness to *"the things which are revealed"* which you now know were **self**-imposed spiritual handicaps. Yes, except for the previously specified enlightenment and the confirmation of the provided references for verse twenty-one, he or she would fail to recognize that God was also addressing Israel's original **God**-imposed blindness and deafness to *"the secret things."* God was pointing out the fact that His people were completely blind and deaf. They had absolutely no understanding of either *"the secret things"* or *"the things which are revealed."*

The full impact of all that I have just said will become crystal clear later when you study parts four through seven of chapter fourteen. For the present, however, I am concentrating on covering specific Biblical events in order to give you a glimpse of the overall picture of why the Jews failed to recognize the Messiah. So, with the added insight you now possess regarding the content of the prophet's statement in Jeremiah 5:21, it might be a good idea to read that verse again.

Jeremiah 5:21 (The Amplified Bible.)

²¹**Hear now this, O foolish people without understanding or heart, who have eyes and see not, who have ears and hear not:**

Eventually, the Israelites' sins became so horrendous and their spiritual thought processes so dull that when it came to spiritual matters that pertained to *"the things which are revealed"* (that is, to God's commandments), they were no longer able to reason intelligently, logically or rationally. Thus, by their own doing, they were stupid and ignorant in so far as God's laws were concerned. And, in addition, they were blinded by God when it came to *"the secret things"* that are hidden in God's Word. Subsequently, as I said earlier, they ended up with no spiritual understanding at all. God's people walked in total spiritual darkness.

An example of the utter depravity, sin and spiritually sluggish condition that the Israelites ended up in as a result of their **self**-imposed spiritual blindness and deafness to *"the things which are revealed"* (God's laws) can be seen in the following text taken from *The Living Bible*. As you read, give particular attention to verse eighteen. For in that verse, the prophet Isaiah also identifies Israel's **self**-imposed spiritual blindness and deafness to *"the things which are revealed"* as well as Israel's **God**-imposed spiritual blindness and deafness to *"the secret things."*

> Isaiah 44:14-20 (The Living Bible.)
>
> 14 *He cuts down cedars, he selects the cypress and the oak, he plants the ash in the forest to be nourished by the rain.*
>
> 15 *And after his care, he uses part of the wood to make a fire to warm himself and bake his bread, and then—he really does—he takes the rest of it and makes himself a god—a god for men to worship! An idol to fall down before and praise!*
>
> 16 *Part of the tree he burns to roast his meat and to keep him warm and fed and well content,*
>
> 17 *And with what's left he makes his god: a carved idol! He falls down before it and worships it and prays to it. "Deliver me," he says. "You are my god!"*
>
> 18 ***Such stupidity and ignorance! God has shut their eyes so that they cannot see, and closed their minds from understanding.***

Once again, you see in verse eighteen two categories of spiritual blindness and deafness. On the one hand, Isaiah speaks of the sinful *"stupidity and ignorance"* which refers to the Jews' **self**-imposed spiritual blindness and deafness insofar as God's commandments were concerned (that is, insofar as *"the things which are revealed"* were concerned). As you saw earlier, the Jews were *"[sinfully] foolish"* or exhibiting *"stupidity and ignorance."* On the other hand, the remainder of verse eighteen speaks of Israel's **God**-imposed spiritual blindness and deafness to *"the secret things."* By including both categories of blindness and deafness, God again conveys the Israelites' utter lack of spiritual understanding.

> 19 *The man never stops to think or figure out, "Why, it's just a block of wood! I've burned it for heat and used it to bake my bread and roast my meat. How can the rest of it be a god? Should I fall down before a chunk of wood?"*

20The poor, deluded fool feeds on ashes; he is trusting what can never give him any help at all. Yet he cannot bring himself to ask, "Is this thing, this idol that I'm holding in my hand, a lie?"

The Jews' persistent rebellion pushed God to the end of His patience with them. They had defiantly dismissed the warnings of God's prophets. They had brazenly broken the Horeb covenant by refusing to listen to God's word and obey His commands. What is more, they blatantly and openly continued to practice idolatry. No matter how severely God chastised His covenant people, they made no attempt to change their minds, attitudes or conduct. They consciously chose to remain spiritually ignorant and stupid (that is, they consciously chose to remain *"[sinfully] foolish"* or spiritually blind and deaf) regarding His laws, and they absolutely would not repent.

Finally, as prophesied, God made plans to punish His rebellious people for breaking His commands by sending them into captivity in Babylon. However, before God banished the Israelites, He directed the prophet Ezekiel to give them a demonstration of their soon to come departure into exile. God took that measure in the hope that the Israelites might realize that their own rebelliousness and their own sinful attitudes and actions were responsible for their future expulsion from the land of Israel.

Needless to say, in their **self**-imposed spiritually blind and deaf state, God's people refused to admit that they were rebellious. They were so *"[sinfully] foolish"* that they would not so much as acknowledge the seriousness of the foreboding spiritual message that Ezekiel was conveying to them through his inspired comparison. They absolutely refused to understand that the prophet's pantomime revealed their abominable deliberate sin and their future punishment for that sin. These people were so unteachable, rebellious and spiritually ignorant and stupid regarding God's laws that they failed to recognize or acknowledge their own spiritual poverty.

Ezekiel 12:1-3 (The Amplified Bible.)

1THE WORD of the Lord also came to me, saying,

2Son of man, you dwell in the midst of the house of the rebellious, who have eyes to see and see not, who have ears to hear and hear not, for they are a rebellious house.

3Therefore, son of man, prepare your belongings for removing and going into exile, and move out by day in their sight; and you shall remove from your place to another place in their sight. It may be they will consider and perceive that they are a rebellious house.

Whenever God speaks of Israel having eyes to see yet seeing not and ears to hear yet hearing not, the Biblical fact that the Jews were spiritually blind and deaf concerning *"the secret things"* should always be a consideration. Nevertheless, it is obvious that once again the main theme of the previous verses involved the Jews' **self**-imposed spiritual blindness and deafness in so far as God's commandments were concerned.

Despite God's everlasting love for Israel, everlasting love that we studied in a former chapter, God could not and would not tolerate deliberate sin. Moses had warned the Israelites time and time again that God would not put up with continued disobedience to His commands. He also told God's people in Deuteronomy chapter four that if they broke the Horeb covenant and persisted in their disobedience to God's commands, committing the sin of idolatry, God would drive them off the land that He had given to them.

God continued to repeat Moses' warning through numerous other prophets. However, when the Israelites refused to change their ways and instead continued to pursue evil, those countless prophetic warnings finally came to pass. Notice how in verse fourteen of the following verses, the Israelites deliberately chose not to hear the truth. They deliberately chose to be spiritually stupid and ignorant (that is, *"[sinfully] foolish"*) regarding *"the things which are revealed."*

2 Kings 17:13-23 (The Amplified Bible.)

13Yet the Lord warned Israel and Judah through all the prophets and all the seers, saying, Turn from your evil ways and keep My commandments and My statutes, according to all the Law which I commanded your fathers and which I sent to you by My servants the prophets.

14Yet they would not hear, but hardened their necks as did their fathers who did not believe (trust in, rely on, and remain steadfast to) the Lord their God.

15They despised and rejected His statutes and His covenant which He made with their fathers and His warnings to them, and they followed vanity (false gods—falsehood, emptiness, and futility) and [they themselves and their prayers] became false (empty and futile). They went after the heathen round about them, of whom the Lord had charged them that they should not do as they did.

16*And they forsook all the commandments of the Lord their God and made for themselves molten images, even two calves, and made an Asherah and worshiped all the [starry] hosts of the heavens and served Baal.*

17*They caused their sons and their daughters to pass through the fire and used divination and enchantments and sold themselves to do evil in the sight of the Lord, provoking Him to anger.*

18*Therefore the Lord was very angry with Israel and removed them out of His sight. None was left but the tribe of Judah.*

19*Judah also did not keep the commandments of the Lord their God, but walked in the customs which Israel introduced.*

20*The Lord rejected all the descendants of Israel and afflicted them and delivered them into the hands of spoilers, until He had cast them out of His sight.*

21*For He tore Israel from the house of David; and they made Jeroboam son of Nebat king. And Jeroboam drew and drove Israel away from following the Lord and made them sin a great sin.*

22*For the Israelites walked in all the sins Jeroboam committed; they departed not from them*

23*Until the Lord removed Israel from His sight, as He had foretold by all His servants the prophets. So Israel was carried away from their own land to Assyria to this day.*

God had driven the previous occupants off the land of Canaan because of their wickedness. Prior to the Canaanites' expulsion, the Lord had also been extremely patient with them. Yet, despite God's long-suffering toward the Canaanites, they had gone from bad to worse. However, after the Israelites had, by the power of God, taken possession of the Canaanites' land, God's people became more wicked than the previous inhabitants. To refresh your memory as to God's reasons for dispossessing the Canaanites and giving their land to the Israelites, we will again read the words of Moses.

Deuteronomy 9:4-5 (The Amplified Bible.)

[4]Do not say in your [mind and] heart, after the Lord your God has thrust them out from before you, It is because of my righteousness that the Lord has brought me in to possess this land—whereas it is because of the wickedness of these nations that the Lord is dispossessing them before you.

[5]Not for your righteousness or for the uprightness of your [minds and] hearts do you go to possess their land; but because of the wickedness of these nations the Lord your God is driving them out before you, and that He may fulfill the promise which the Lord swore to your fathers, Abraham, Isaac, and Jacob.

Notice in verses four and five that the Canaanites were driven off the land for two reasons. First, they were driven off the land because of their abominable wickedness. Secondly, they were removed so that God might fulfill His promise to Abraham, Isaac and Jacob in regard to their covenant descendants possessing the Promised Land. However, as I formerly stated, the Israelites possessed the Promised Land by the power of God and then became more sinful than the people who had lived on the land before them.

It stands to reason that God could not have allowed the Israelites to remain on that land in their deplorable rebellious and willfully sinful state when He had driven the Canaanites from it because of those identical sins. God is not partial in His judgments. Therefore, like the wicked Canaanites, the wicked Israelites were removed from the land. The only difference between them and the Canaanites was that the Canaanites were evicted permanently while, because of the Abrahamic covenant and God's sworn everlasting love for Israel, the Israelites' removal from the land was temporary.

The Israelites had taken advantage of God's grace (that is, God's favor). They had broken the covenant that God had made with them at Horeb. They had failed to comply with the requirements of that agreement by deliberately breaking God's commands. Then, when God's prophets had brought to them the truth of God's commands, they deliberately blinded their eyes and stopped up their ears so that they would not have to hear and obey. Consequently, the Israelites' continued deliberate disobedience to God's commands resulted in their temporary banishment from the Promised Land.

No doubt you are disturbed over the realization that the Jewish people blatantly broke the Horeb covenant by disobeying God's commandments. However, once again, Christians have no right to point an accusing finger at the Jewish people for failing in that area. For, just as Christians are more guilty than the Jews when it comes to adding to and diminishing from God's commandments, so they are also more guilty when it comes to the issue of men breaking covenant with God. To help you come to grips with that fact, I suggest you call up the information you received in chapter eleven of this work entitled "Why Did God Choose Abraham?" In case you have forgotten the contents of that chapter, you may want to read that segment again.

The comparison between the Jew's sinful behavior that I addressed in the last paragraph and those in the Church today who commit the same crime is astounding. Of course, I am comparing the way most professing Christians break the promised new covenant with the way the Jews broke the Horeb covenant. Each group is guilty of breaking a covenant between themselves and God by disobeying God's commandments. However, as you saw earlier, the Church's guilt and sin in that area is far greater than that of the Jews.

What makes the Church's crime unrivaled is the fact that Yeshua gave his life to fulfill God's Word in Genesis 3:15. You will recall that through His death, Yeshua destroyed Satan's power over mankind. Thus, He freed men to carry out the full original purpose of their creation. Men are now free to obey all God's laws (that is, they are free to obey all God's commandments). For, Yeshua sealed the promised new covenant with His own blood. And, in the blood-sealed new covenant, God promises to write His laws upon His people's minds and hearts so that they will understand them and obey them. God also promises to forgive all their past sins. To refresh your memory on that issue, read the contents of the new covenant for yourself in the next verses.

Hebrews 10:16-17 (The Amplified Bible.)

16This is the agreement (testament, covenant) that I will set up and conclude with them after those days, says the Lord: I will imprint My laws upon their

hearts, and I will inscribe them on their minds (on their inmost thoughts and understanding),
[17]He then goes on to say, And their sins and their lawbreaking I will remember no more.

In chapter eleven of this work, you briefly studied the contents of the previous text. You came to realize that through the new covenant you now have forgiveness from your past sins, and you have the God-given power and ability not only to learn but also to obey God's commands. Moreover, you learned that Satan no longer has any power over you. Therefore, since Yeshua has removed the chains of sin that once bound you and since He has endowed you with the previously mentioned overcoming power, you do not have to sin anymore (that is, you do not have to go on breaking God's commandments). The truth is that in order for you to sin, you have to deliberately volunteer to break God's laws.

After being reminded of the former information, do you now see why I said that the Church's offense of breaking the promised new covenant is greater than the Jews' offense of breaking the Horeb covenant? The Church's offense is greater because the new covenant was sealed with the blood of *"Immanuel [God with us],"* whereas, the Horeb covenant was sealed with animal blood. In addition, the blood-sealed new covenant frees men from sin and gives them all the power they need to understand and obey God's commandments. Whereas, the Horeb covenant did none of those things. Therefore, unlike the Christians, the Jews did not have the God-given power to overcome sin (that is, they did not have the God-given power to consistently stop breaking God's commandments). The Jews were enslaved in sin just as we believers were enslaved in sin before we accepted Christ and the benefits that He provided through the promised blood-sealed new covenant.

Earlier, I reminded you that Christians break the blood-sealed new agreement in the same way that the Jews broke the Horeb covenant. They break the new covenant by disobeying God's laws. They then refuse to change their minds and conduct. However, what disobedient Christians do not seem to realize is that God is no more fooled by those in the Church who break the new covenant than He was by those in Israel who broke the Horeb covenant. The following inspired words that Paul wrote to the Church in Galatia, which we read previously, confirm what I just said.

Galatians 6:7-8 (The Amplified Bible.)

<u>7Do not be deceived and deluded and misled; God will</u> <u>not allow Himself to be sneered at (scorned, disdained,</u> <u>or mocked by mere pretensions or professions, or by</u> <u>His precepts being set aside).</u> *[He inevitably deludes himself who attempts to delude God.] For whatever a man sows, that and that only is what he will reap.*

8For he who sows to his own flesh (lower nature, sensuality) will from the flesh reap decay and ruin and destruction, but he who sows to the Spirit will from the Spirit reap eternal life.

The fact remains that though most of the Church consciously chooses to ignore the truth, God's Word clearly warns that **Christians who break the blood-sealed new covenant by disobeying God's commandments and refusing to truly repent (that is, refusing to change their minds and conduct) will be punished far more severely than those Israelites who broke the Horeb covenant.** And rightly so, since the new covenant has better (that is, more sublime, more superior) promises. See for yourself in the following reference how those under the new covenant will be judged more severely.

Later, please take the time to read the verses prior to this next text. Also, remember that the writer of *The Letter To The Hebrews* is not speaking to non-believers. Without a doubt, he is addressing Christians. Moreover, by using the word *"we,"* the writer informs us that should he himself fall prey to that same evil, he too will be punished accordingly.

Hebrews 10:26-31 (The Amplified Bible.)

26For if we go on deliberately and willingly sinning after once acquiring the knowledge of the Truth, there is no longer any sacrifice left to atone for [our] sins [no further offering to which to look forward].

27[There is nothing left for us then] but a kind of awful and fearful prospect and expectation of divine judgment and the fury of burning wrath and indignation which will consume those who put themselves in opposition [to God].

28Any person who has violated and [thus] rejected and set at naught the Law of Moses is put to death without pity or mercy on the evidence of two or three witnesses.

29How much worse (sterner and heavier) punishment do you suppose he will be judged to deserve who has spurned and [thus] trampled underfoot the Son of God, and who has considered the covenant blood by which he was consecrated common and unhallowed, thus profaning it and insulting and outraging the [Holy] Spirit [Who imparts] grace (the unmerited favor and blessing of God)?

30For we know Him Who said, Vengeance is Mine [retribution and the meting out of full justice rest with Me]; I will repay [I will exact the compensation], says the Lord. And again, The Lord will judge and determine and solve and settle the cause and the cases of His people.

31It is a fearful (formidable and terrible) thing to incur the divine penalties and be cast into the hands of the living God!

As you learned in chapter eleven, there is absolutely no reason for Christians to break the blood-sealed new covenant by deliberately or persistently disobeying God's laws (that is, by deliberately or persistently sinning). For, Christ died to seal the new covenant with His own blood so that men would be completely free from sin and thus equipped to fulfill the purpose for which they were originally created.

The following verses give you a glimpse of the awesome new covenant power that is now available to every true believer. They show you that through the blood-sealed new covenant, believers receive not only the power but also the desire to truly fear God and keep His commandments. Yes, believers receive the power and desire both to will and to work for God's good pleasure and satisfaction and delight.

Philippians 2:12-13 (The Amplified Bible.)

12Therefore, my dear ones, as you have always obeyed [my suggestions], so now, not only [with the enthusiasm you would show] in my presence but much more because I am absent, work out (cultivate, carry out to the goal, and fully complete) your own salvation with reverence and awe and trembling (self-distrust, with serious caution, tenderness of conscience, watchfulness against temptation, timidly shrinking from whatever might offend God and discredit the name of Christ).

13[Not in your own strength] for it is God Who is all the while effectually at work in you [energizing and creating in you the power and desire], both to will and to work for His good pleasure and satisfaction and delight.

When Christians refuse to acknowledge or utilize the overcoming new covenant power that is accessible to them and instead of working for God's good pleasure, satisfaction and delight, they continue to break God's commands, they consciously choose to partake of that sin. Therefore, such behavior constitutes willful and deliberate sin. And that is why Christians who break the blood-sealed new covenant by disobeying God's written commands and who refuse to change their minds and conduct will be dealt with far more severely than those Jews who broke the Horeb covenant.

You see, the Jews broke a covenant that was sealed with the blood of animals and was therefore powerless to free them and keep them free from sin (that is, it was powerless to free them and keep them free from breaking God's commands). Christians, on the other hand, break a covenant that was sealed with the holy, priceless blood of the Lamb of God, *"Immanuel [God with us]."* They break a covenant that has the power to free them and keep them free from breaking God's commands. Therefore, in that such awesome overcoming power is now readily available to every believer through the blood-sealed new agreement, as I said earlier, Christians have to willfully and deliberately consent to sin.

Another point to consider is that with all the new covenant power that the Church now has access to, Christians should be examples of righteousness before the Jews. Christians should be showing non-believing Jews that the blood-sealed new covenant really can do what the Horeb covenant could not. Christians should be showing the Jews that, through the new covenant power that God has invested in them, they are unequivocally free to do what they were created to do. Yet, instead of being examples of righteousness, the majority of Christians fail to live holy lives.

The fact is that most professing Christians continue to sin by breaking God's commands as though Christ's blood had never been shed or had never sealed the promised new covenant. And what is worse, by their continued disobedient actions, these Christians deny the power of Christ's blood. By their actions they deny that the blood-sealed new covenant gives men the necessary power to do what they were created to do. Paul describes these disobedient Christians in II Timothy 3:5 when he says, *"For [although] they hold a form of piety (true religion),* **they deny and reject and are strangers to the power of it [their conduct belies the genuineness of their profession].** *Avoid [all] such people [turn away from them]."*

By their continuous sinful conduct, these Christians actually become guilty of the sins described in Hebrews 10:29. They not only try to take advantage of God's grace, but in doing so, they trample underfoot the son of God by publicly profaning His blood that sealed the new covenant, insulting and outraging the Holy Spirit. Yes, these disobedient Christians use the blood that sealed the new covenant for a purpose that God never intended. Christ's blood was shed to seal the new covenant in order to give men the power to be free from sin and to remain free from sin (that is, Christ's blood was shed to give men the power to be free from breaking God's commands and to ensure that they remain free from breaking God's commands). For, as we are told in 1 John 3:4, sin is the breaking of God's laws. However, these disobedient Christians try to use His shed blood as a tool to get by with sinning by breaking God's commands without receiving their deserved punishment. As I said earlier, they try to take advantage of God's grace (God's favor).

Once you become aware of the destructive effects of these Christians' disobedient actions, you can understand why in Hebrews 10:30-31, the writer reminds the Church of God's future judgment that will come upon all Christians who are guilty of breaking the new covenant by disobeying God's commands, all Christians who refuse to truly repent (that is, all Christians who refuse to change their minds and conduct), all Christians who profane the holy blood that sealed the new agreement.

The previous truth also puts the Jews' sins in perspective because it makes one aware that the Church's sins are far worse than those of the Jews. Through Christ's blood that sealed the new covenant, Christians can now be free from the bondage of sin and have all the overcoming power they need to enable them to understand and to obey God's commands. Whereas, under the Horeb covenant, the Jews did not have access to such mighty power. Thus, while it is true that God originally gave the Jewish people understanding of His laws, having understanding of God's laws without being free from sin and thus without possessing the power they needed to consistently obey those laws only served to magnify sin (that is, it only served to make sin seem overpowering and unconquerable) and thus remind the Jews of just how powerless they were to overcome it.

336

Christian, now that you are more informed regarding certain differences between the Horeb covenant and the new covenant, let me ask you a question. Who do you feel deserves to receive the *"worse (sterner and heavier) punishment"* for breaking God's commands, the Church or the Jews? Of course, your answer has to be **the Church**! Yes, in all fairness, you have to agree with God's warning in Hebrews chapter ten. You have to agree that all Christians who break the new covenant by disobeying God's commands, all Christians who upon hearing the truth refuse to repent (that is, all Christians who upon hearing the truth refuse to change their minds for the better and heartily amend their ways with abhorrence of their past sins) deserve to receive *"worse (sterner and heavier) punishment"* than the Jewish people.

You now have the answer as to why the writer of The Letter to the Hebrews warns the Church in Hebrews 10:26-31 that Christians who break the blood-sealed new agreement will be more severely punished than those Jews who broke the Horeb covenant. You also realize why Christians have no right to point an accusing finger at the Jewish people for breaking the Horeb covenant. Rather, the Church must look within herself. She must acknowledge and confess her own wrongdoing. For, it is a Biblical fact that she bears the greater guilt and sin. Only when the Church removes the beam that is in her own eye will she be able to see clearly enough to remove the tiny speck that is in Israel's eye.

With all the previously mentioned accusations against the Jews quieted, I can now begin to bring part two to a close by reminding you of two important points. The first point is that it was the Jews' **self**-imposed spiritual blindness and deafness to *"the things which are revealed"* that brought about their inevitable exile. The second point to be remembered is that Israel's **God**-imposed spiritual blindness and deafness to *"the secret things"* were not and are not the result of sin nor have the Jews ever been punished by God for their lack of understanding of *"the secret things."*

In the first two parts of this mini-series within a series entitled "Why Did The Jews Fail To Recognize The Messiah?" I identified three types of spiritual blindness and deafness that God's people experienced.

(1) The **God** decreed spiritual blindness and deafness in so far as *"the secret things"* (that is, insofar as the deep inner meaning of God's miracles, future events and Biblical revelation) were concerned.

(2) The blindness and deafness that the **religious leaders inflicted upon them** regarding *"the things which are revealed"* (that is, God's laws).

(3) The deadly **self**-imposed blindness and deafness that also involved *"the things which are revealed."*

Keep the knowledge of all three separate categories of spiritual blindness and deafness uppermost in your mind as you study the remaining five parts of chapter fourteen. For, you will soon gain even more marvelous insight into the Jews' spiritual disabilities. You will also acquire vital pieces of the overall puzzle which when completed will eventually give you the correct answer to the question, "Why Did The Jews Fail To Recognize The Messiah?"

Chapter 14
Part Three

WHY DID THE JEWS FAIL
TO RECOGNIZE THE MESSIAH?

In this, the third part of chapter fourteen, I intend to illustrate the truth that God did, upon occasion, open the spiritually blind eyes and unstop the spiritually deaf ears of certain Old Testament Jews to enable them to understand *"the secret things."* Such instances were nevertheless extremely rare and always temporary. They were designed solely to advance God's will and purpose upon the earth. However, before I begin to expound on this truth, we must first pick up where we left off in part two of chapter fourteen. There is still valuable insight to be gleaned from that period in history, insight which will shed further light on the present subject.

It was during the period of history mentioned in the former paragraph that God finally brought to pass His word that He had spoken through all His holy prophets. He drove His rebellious, disobedient people off the Promised Land and sent them into captivity in Babylon. However, God never intended to leave His people in Babylon indefinitely. The truth is that He could not have left them there permanently. Why? Because He had promised Abraham many things. Therefore, in order to protect His own reputation, God had to remain faithful to His covenant with Abraham and keep the solemn promises that He had made to him. In addition, God had to fulfill His predictions in Genesis 3:15. And, as you learned earlier in the series, God had chosen to use the Israelite nation to help him accomplish His purpose in that area also.

Even before Israel's captivity, God was aware that for Him to keep the previously indicated predictions and promises, He would eventually have to allow Abraham's descendants to return to the land that He had solemnly sworn would be theirs forever. Therefore, through the prophet Jeremiah, God had wisely and righteously stipulated in advance that the Israelites would remain in exile for a fixed period of seventy years. God planned that when their specified period of punishment ended, He would return His people to the Promised Land so that they might help Him accomplish His future will and purpose for all mankind.

Jeremiah 29:10-11 (The Amplified Bible.)

[10]*For thus says the Lord, When <u>seventy years</u> are completed for Babylon, I will visit you and keep My good promise to you, causing you to return to this place.*

[11]*For I know the thoughts and plans that I have for you, says the Lord, thoughts and plans for welfare and peace and not for evil, to give you hope in your final outcome.*

When the foretold seventy years of exile were near completion, Daniel, having knowledge of the book of Jeremiah which contained the prophet's predicted timetable of events, sought the Lord and interceded for the Israelites. **Daniel put the Lord in remembrance of His Abrahamic covenant which included God's everlasting love for His people.**

On behalf of Israel, Daniel also acknowledged and confessed that God's people had reneged on their obligation that was stipulated in the Horeb contract and had sinned by breaking God's commands. At the same time, Daniel was quick to let God know that despite Israel's appalling past sins and their deserved exile, he still expected God to remain faithful to His covenant with Abraham, Isaac, Jacob.

Daniel had a perfect right to expect God to remain faithful to the covenant since, as you learned in a former chapter of this work, Abraham never broke his binding contract with God. Therefore, it was because Daniel knew that the Abrahamic covenant remained valid that he completely trusted God to keep his end of that agreement. Yes, he knew that since the predicted seventy year interval had almost expired, God would, for His own reputation's sake, faithfully extend to the Israelites His promised mercy and loving-kindness.

For generations men have misunderstood the power that Daniel had with God. The Church surmised that it was because Daniel was righteous or because he was a great prayer warrior or because he fasted that God heard his prayers. However, you now know that though all those admirable qualities were instrumental in God answering Daniel's prayers, they were by no means the main reason why he did. The truth is that God heard Daniel's prayers for His own name's sake. **God heard Daniel's prayers because, like Moses before him, Daniel had put the Lord in remembrance of His sacred Abrahamic promises**.

Throughout most of this series, I have repeatedly emphasized how in the Abrahamic covenant God solemnly swore that the Promised Land would be the Israelites' possession forever. He also swore to love the Israelites with an everlasting love, a love that includes mercy and loving-kindness. Therefore, since Jeremiah's predicted seventy years of exile were almost over, Daniel knew that in order to fulfill that prediction and to keep the covenant and steadfast love which He swore to Abraham, Isaac and Jacob, God was compelled to answer His prayers on behalf of their descendants.

> *Daniel 9:1-7, 9, 17-19 (The Amplified Bible.)*
>
> *1IN THE first year of Darius son of Ahasuerus, of the offspring of the Medes, who was made king over the realm of the Chaldeans—*
>
> *2In the first year of his reign, I, Daniel, understood from the books the number of years which, according to the word of the Lord to Jeremiah the prophet, must pass by before the desolations [which had been] pronounced on Jerusalem should end; and it was seventy years.*
>
> *3And I set my face to the Lord God to seek Him by prayer and supplications, with fasting and sackcloth and ashes;*
>
> *4And I prayed to the Lord my God and made confession and said, O Lord, the great and dreadful God, Who keeps covenant, mercy, and loving-kindness with those who love Him and keep His commandments.*

Again, I remind you that Abraham fully completed his part of the sacred contract between himself and God. All the days of his life, he had loved God and had faithfully kept His commandments. Therefore, it was because Abraham had fully met God's covenant requirements and also because it was time for God to fulfill the prophet's prediction in Jeremiah 29:10 that in the previous verse, verse four, Daniel was able to summon forth the courage to boldly remind God of Moses' statement in Deuteronomy 7:9 regarding God keeping covenant, mercy and loving-kindness with those who keep His commandments.

In verse four, Daniel brought to God's attention the fact that even though He was not obligated to keep covenant with disobedient Israel, He was under obligation to keep covenant with Abraham, since Abraham had loved Him and kept His commandments. Yes, God was obliged to keep covenant with Abraham even though the recipients of that particular covenant, the descendants of Abraham, Isaac and Jacob, did not deserve His covenant mercy and loving-kindness.

In the next verses, Daniel acknowledged Israel's past sin. However, he acknowledged Israel's sin knowing that God was compelled to extend to them His promised mercy and loving-kindness in order to keep His unbreakable covenant with Abraham. You see, as I have repeatedly stated, Daniel was fully aware that his uncompromisingly righteous God would do right. He knew that for His own name's sake, God would faithfully keep covenant with Abraham, Isaac and Jacob.

5We have sinned and dealt perversely and done wickedly and have rebelled, turning aside from Your commandments and ordinances.

6Neither have we listened to and heeded Your servants the prophets, who spoke in Your name to our kings, our princes and our fathers, and to all the people of the land.

7O Lord, righteousness belongs to You, but to us confusion and shame of face, as at this day—to the men of Judah, to the inhabitants of Jerusalem, and to all Israel, to those who are near and those who are far off, through all the countries to which You have driven them because of the [treacherous] trespass which they have committed against You

9To the Lord our God belong mercy and loving-kindness and forgiveness, for we have rebelled against Him;

17Now therefore, O our God, listen to and heed the prayer of Your servant [Daniel] and his supplications, and for Your own sake cause Your face to shine upon Your sanctuary which is desolate.

18O my God, incline Your ear and hear; open Your eyes and look at our desolations and the city which is called by Your name; for we do not present our supplications before You for our own righteousness and justice, but for Your great mercy and loving-kindness.

19O Lord, hear! O Lord, forgive! O Lord, give heed and act! Do not delay, for Your own sake, O my God, because Your city and Your people are called by Your name.

God answered Daniel's prayers in order to fulfill His Word in Genesis 3:15, to keep His binding covenant promises to Abraham, Isaac and Jacob and to bring to pass Jeremiah's seventy year prediction. In so doing, God also protected His own reputation. Yes, for His name's sake, God extended to Israel His covenant mercy and loving-kindness and led the Jews back to the Promised Land.

Proof of God's faithfulness to His predictions and to His covenant and steadfast love which He swore to Abraham, Isaac and Jacob is seen throughout the Word of God. However, never was His faithfulness more gloriously manifested than in the Jews' return from Babylonian exile. God did indeed preserve His holy reputation by publicly fulfilling His written Word.

God's covenant mercy, loving-kindness and steadfast love are made evident in the books of Ezra and Nehemiah. For, through Israel's return to their covenant homeland and through all that took place when they arrived there, God openly and repeatedly exhibited His absolute faithfulness to His word. For instance, when His people showed forth true repentance during that period, God in turn showed forth His covenant mercy and loving-kindness.

You will recall that in chapter nine of this series, you saw in the Scriptures that God's Abrahamic covenant mercy and loving-kindness includes forgiveness for sins upon true repentance. One of the examples I used to confirm that truth was David's words in Psalm 51:1-2 in the *Holy Bible, King James Version*, which reads, *"HAVE mercy upon me, O God, __according to thy loving-kindness: according unto the multitude of thy tender mercies__ blot out my transgressions. Wash me thoroughly from mine iniquity, and cleanse me from my sin."*

To see an example of the Jews' repentance, read Ezra chapter eight. In that chapter, God's Word reveals that upon returning to the Promised Land, the Israelites brought forth fruits of true repentance. By fruits of repentance, I mean that after they had confessed their sins, their immediate response and future conduct were proof of their changed hearts and minds.

Once the Jewish people had truly repented of breaking the Horeb covenant by disobeying God's commands (that is, once they had changed their minds and attitudes and heartily amended their ways), they were able to shed their **self**-imposed spiritual blindness and deafness. The majority of God's people were once again desirous and willing to learn, understand and obey *"the things which are revealed"* (that is, they were desirous and willing to learn, understand and obey God's laws).

The following two texts combined vividly bring out the previously mentioned truths regarding the Jew's repentance, their willingness to once again learn and obey God's word and their gaining back their relinquished ability to understand God's laws. As you read both texts, pay particular attention to the highlighted portions since they emphasize important facts that you might otherwise overlook. Also note that though Ezra was himself a scribe, he neither referred to nor read from the writings of former scribes. Rather, righteous Ezra read from the sacred Scriptures.

Nehemiah 8:1-12 (The Amplified Bible.)

*¹THEN ALL the people gathered together as one man in the broad place before the Water Gate; **and they asked Ezra the scribe to bring the <u>Book of the Law of Moses</u>, which the Lord had given to Israel.***

²And Ezra the priest brought the Law before the assembly of both men and women and all who could hear with understanding, on the first of the seventh month.

³<u>He read from it,</u> facing the broad place before the Water Gate, from early morning until noon, in the presence of the men and women and those who could understand; and all the people were attentive to the Book of the Law.

The *Living Bible* translators clarify the portions of Nehemiah's statement in verses two and three which read, *"...all who could hear with understanding..."* and *"...those who could understand...."* These translators do that by simply saying, *"...all who were old enough to understand paid close attention...."* We will now continue reading from *The Amplified Bible.*

⁴Ezra the scribe stood on a wooden pulpit which they had made for the purpose. And beside him stood Mattithiah, Shema, Anaiah, Uriah, Hilkiah, and Maaseiah on his right hand; and on his left hand, Pedaiah, Mishael, Malchijah, Hashum, Hashbaddana, Zechariah. and Meshullam.

*5*Ezra opened the book in sight of all the people, for he was standing above them; and when he opened it, all the people stood up.

*6*And Ezra blessed the Lord, the Great God. And all the people answered, Amen, Amen, lifting up their hands; and they bowed their heads and worshiped the Lord with faces to the ground.

*7*Also Jeshua, Bani, Sherebiah, Jamin, Akkub, Shabbethai, Hodiah, Maaseiah, Kelita, Azariah, Jozabad, Hanan, Peliaih—*the Levites—helped the people to understand the Law, and the people [remained] in their place.*

*8*So they read from the Book of the Law of God distinctly, faithfully amplifying and giving the sense so that [the people] understood the reading.

*9*And Nehemiah, who was the governor, and Ezra the priest and scribe, and the Levites who taught the people said to all of them, This day is holy to the Lord your God; mourn not nor weep. For all the people wept when they heard the words of the Law.

*10*Then [Ezra] told, them, Go your way, eat the fat, drink the sweet drink, and send portions to him for whom nothing is prepared; for this day is holy to our Lord. And be not grieved and depressed, for the joy of the Lord is your strength and stronghold.

*11*So the Levites quieted all the people, saying, Be still, for the day is holy. And do not be grieved and sad.

*12*And all the people went their way to eat, drink, send portions, and make great rejoicing, *for they had understood the words that were declared to them.*

Nehemiah 9:1-3 (The Amplified Bible.)

*1*NOW ON the twenty-fourth day of this month, the Israelites were assembled with fasting and in sackcloth and with earth upon their heads.

*2*And the Israelites separated themselves from all foreigners and stood and confessed their sins and the iniquities of their fathers.

*3*And they stood in their place and read from the Book of the Law of the Lord their God for a fourth of the *day, __and for another fourth of it they confessed and worshiped the Lord their God.__*

You have been made aware of the fact that in the previously specified situation, God remained incredibly faithful to His predictions and to His Abrahamic covenant promises. You also know that the Israelites did repent and that they did eventually regain the ability to understand God's laws (that is, they did eventually regain the ability to understand *"the things which are revealed")*. However, in order for us to proceed to the next phase of our study we must return to the period of Israel's captivity in Babylon.

Earlier, I shared with you that within this part of the current chapter, part three, I intend to show you in the Scriptures that upon occasion God did open the spiritually blind eyes and unstop the spiritually deaf ears of certain Old Testament Jews to enable them to understand *"the secret things."* I also said that such instances were extremely rare and always temporary. They were designed solely to advance God's will and purpose upon the earth.

The prophet Daniel is a perfect example of an Old Testament Jew who was miraculously given temporary ability to understand *"the secret things."* Therefore, as you study that particular area of Daniel's life, you will have the opportunity to gain an awesome amount of spiritual enlightenment on that subject. You will also gain insight into the man himself.

While studying the previously indicated material concerning Daniel, it will help you immensely if you continue to draw upon the information that I presented in parts one and two of chapter fourteen. I am referring to the information regarding God withholding understanding of *"the secret things"* from the Israelites, which of course would have included His withholding that same understanding from righteous Daniel. With all that said, let us now turn our thoughts to the man, Daniel.

When it came to sharing Israel's punishment for sin, Daniel was no exception to the rule. He was uprooted from the Promised Land and carried into Babylonian exile along with most of His Jewish brethren. However, when it came to receiving understanding of *"the secret things,"* Daniel was very definitely an exception to the rule.

Soon, you will see in the Scriptures that upon a number of occasions Daniel was endowed with **limited** understanding of *"the secret things"* (that is, he was miraculously endowed with **limited** understanding of the meaning of future events). Daniel's understanding had its limitations in the sense that, during each of these instances, God gave to Daniel only enough understanding of *"the secret things"* to enable him to record his prophetic dream and visions and their meaning for the benefit of future generations.

Upon reading the following excerpts from chapter seven of *The Book of Daniel*, you will quickly become aware that as a spiritually blind and deaf covenant descendant of Abraham, Isaac and Jacob, Daniel had, at the time of his experience and immediately afterward, been totally unable to comprehend the meaning of his own visions. Yes, His God-imposed spiritual handicaps had kept him from understanding the deep inner meaning of *"the secret things"* that he had witnessed with his own eyes.

As a result of his spiritual disabilities, Daniel had found it necessary to ask an angel to explain to him the truth of the apparitions that he had previously seen. And since at that time it was God's will that Daniel temporarily understand *"the secret things"* in order that he might record His dream and visions and their actual meaning, the angel granted Daniel's request and interpreted for him the meaning of the amazing sights and sounds that he had seen and heard, but had not understood.

I have not included the full content of Daniel's dream and visions since that information does not pertain to our present subject matter. However, I trust that you will take the time to study those Scriptures for yourself. In the meantime, I will concentrate on providing you with the previously promised information so that when you later study the remaining four parts of chapter fourteen, you will come to truly understand why the Jews failed to recognize the Messiah.

REVELATION NO. 1

In the first reference, taken from the *Holy Bible, King James Version*, you are told that Daniel had a dream and visions. You are also informed that he later recorded all that he had seen, heard and learned throughout that entire experience.

Daniel 7:1 (King James Version.)

[1]*IN the first year of Belshazzar king of Babylon **Daniel had a dream and visions** of his head upon his bed: **then he wrote the dream, and told the sum of the matters.***

In Daniel 7:2-14, Daniel described the awesome sights and sounds that he had seen and heard in his former dream and visions, **sights and sounds which he had not understood**. You may want to take the time to read those verses and to study Daniel's detailed description of the event. As for me, I will skip over Daniel's description of his actual vision and concentrate instead on certain vital portions of **the angel's interpretation** of that vision.

The subsequent excerpts are segments of **the angel's interpretation** of the dream and visions which Daniel had already seen and which he later described in verses two through thirteen of Daniel chapter seven.

As you read the information in the next two verses, Daniel 7:15-16, The *Holy Bible, King James Version*, pay careful attention to the fact that while Daniel had actually been viewing the former futuristic sights, his being spiritually blind and deaf to *"the secret things"* had rendered him totally unable to comprehend their significance.

The truth regarding Daniel being unable to comprehend the significance of all that he had seen is made evident in the following verses. For in those verses, we are informed that after Daniel had seen the vision, he had to ask someone else to explain to him the meaning of what he had witnessed. It was not until an angel of God interpreted Daniel's visions for him and gave spiritually deaf Daniel the power to understand the meaning of his interpretation that Daniel was finally able to appreciate and understand the incredible sights and sounds (the secret things) that he had previously seen and heard.

Daniel 7:15-16 (King James Version.)

15I Daniel was grieved in my spirit in the midst of my body, and the visions of my head troubled me.

*16**I came near unto one of them that stood by, and asked him the truth of all this. So he told me, and made me know the interpretation of the things.***

Daniel 7:17-18 contains **the angel's interpretation** of a part of Daniel's dream and visions. Should you read those verses, remember that Daniel himself tells you in verse sixteen that the angel granted his request and told him the truth of the things which he had seen. However, Daniel also lets you know that he was so spiritually blind and deaf to *"the secret things"* that the angel even had to make him understand the meaning of the interpretation itself. In verse sixteen, Daniel states, *"So **he told me**, and **made me know the interpretation.**"* It is one thing to be told something. It is quite another thing to be so spiritually deaf regarding *"the secret things"* that one has to be made to understand what was said.

Despite his spiritual handicaps, Daniel was extremely zealous to know the truth. He was not satisfied with the angel's partial interpretation. He wanted more information. Daniel wanted to know all about the fourth beast that, in verse seven, he had described as being different from the other three. He also wanted to know about the ten horns and the other horn which came up later. So again, the angel granted Daniel's petition and interpreted for him the remainder of his vision.

Having access to the insight in the former paragraph forces us to conclude that the angel once again made spiritually deaf Daniel understand the meaning of the interpretation. We will read Daniel's second inquiry and a portion of the angel's interpretation of Daniel's vision from *The Amplified Bible* since the translators of that work did an excellent job of translating the following verses.

Daniel 7:19-23 (The Amplified Bible.)

19Then I wished to know the truth about the fourth beast—which was different from all the others, exceedingly terrible and shocking, whose teeth were of iron and its nails of bronze, which devoured, broke and crushed, and trampled what was left with its feet—

20And about the ten horns [representing kings] that were on its head, and the other horn which came up later and before which three of [the horns] fell, the horn which had eyes and a mouth that spoke great things and which looked greater than the others.

21As I looked, this horn made war with the saints and prevailed over them

22Until the Ancient of Days came, and judgment was given to the saints of the Most High [God], and the time came when the saints possessed the kingdom.

23Thus [the angel] said, The fourth beast shall be a fourth kingdom on earth, which shall be different from all other kingdoms and shall devour the whole earth, tread it down, and break it in pieces and crush it.

Should you desire to finish reading **the angel's interpretation** of Daniel's dream and visions, read Daniel 7:24-27. However, to help you keep your train of thought and remain on track, I myself will bypass the remainder of **the angel's interpretation.**

When the interpreting angel had finished speaking, Daniel was extremely disturbed, alarmed and grieved because of all *"the secret things"* that the angel had told him and made him understand regarding the sights and sounds that he had seen and heard in his dream and visions. Yet, despite his distressed state, Daniel made a special point of remembering every detail of **the angel's interpretation** of the meaning of his dream and visions so that he could later record them.

Keep in mind that it was the angel's interpretation of his dream and visions that Daniel understood, remembered and later recorded, not his own interpretation. Daniel had no interpretation of his own. With the angel's help, Daniel's job was simply to understand, to remember and to later record the words of God's messenger.

> *Daniel 7:28 (The Amplified Bible.)*
>
> [28] *Here is the end of the matter. As for me, Daniel, my [waking] thoughts troubled and alarmed me much and my cheerfulness of countenance was changed in me;* **but I kept the matter [of the interpreting angel's information] in my heart and mind.**

REVELATION NO. 2

Approximately two years later, Daniel had another vision. (See Daniel 8:1-14.) After his second supernatural experience, Daniel again diligently sought to understand the meaning of his vision. However, because Daniel was still blind and deaf to *"the secret things,"* he was once more unable to make any sense of what he had seen and heard. The fact that Daniel was unable to comprehend the meaning of his second vision forces one to conclude that the understanding which had been imparted to him after his first vision had been limited to that one single episode.

The next five verses confirm the truth that I shared in the former paragraph. Those verses confirm that truth by showing you that once Daniel had received and had been made to understand the angel's interpretation of his original vision, he remained spiritually blind and deaf to *"the secret things."* Proof that his spiritual blindness and deafness to *"the secret things"* remained even after he had been made to understand the meaning of the angel's interpretation of his first vision is seen by the fact that in verse sixteen, the angel was later commanded to make Daniel understand the second vision.

The angel's statement in verse sixteen makes obvious the fact that the initial ability to understand *"the secret things"* which the angel had previously bestowed on Daniel had not been a perpetual benefit. For, had Daniel's ability to understand *"the secret things"* been permanent, there would not have been any need for the angel to have commanded Daniel to understand his second vision.

Remember, like all the other Israelites, Daniel's spiritual eyes and ears had been stitched closed by divine fingers. However, in order that Daniel might further accomplish God's purpose and record the meaning of the second vision that he had seen but had not understood, God once again commanded that those stitches be temporarily extracted. As I stated earlier, **He commanded the angel Gabriel to make Daniel understand** *"the secret things"* that he had seen and heard in his second vision.

Daniel learned from the angel that *"the secret things"* which he had been permitted to physically see and hear in his second vision, things which he had not spiritually understood, were actual future events that would occur in the end of time.

As you read the five verses that I mentioned earlier, take special note of the fact that the angel commanded spiritually disabled Daniel to understand the truth that he was about to convey to him.

Daniel 8:15-19, 26-27 (The Amplified Bible.)

15When I, even I, Daniel, had seen the vision, <u>I sought to understand it;</u> then behold, there stood before me one [Gabriel] with the appearance of a man.

16And I heard a man's voice between the banks of the [river] Ulai which called and said, <u>Gabriel, make this man [Daniel] understand the vision.</u>

17So he came near where I stood, and when he came, I was frightened and fell on my face. <u>But he said to me, Understand, O son of man,</u> for the [fulfillment of the] vision belongs to [events that shall occur in] the time of the end.

18Now as he [Gabriel] was speaking with me, I fell stunned and in deep unconsciousness with my face to the ground; but he touched me and set me upright [where I had stood].

19And he said, <u>Behold, I will make you know what will be in the latter time of the indignation [of God upon the ungodly], for it has to do with the time of the end.</u>

Daniel 8:20-25 contains **the angel's interpretation** of Daniel's second vision. However, in order to keep you from getting sidetracked from the issue at hand, I have chosen to include only those Scriptures that are relevant to the present topic. One such Scripture is Daniel 8:26-27.

*26The vision of the evenings and the mornings which has been told you is true. <u>**But seal up the vision**</u>, for it has to do with and belongs to the [now] distant future.*

27And I, Daniel, fainted and was sick [for several] days. Afterward I rose up and did the king's business; and I wondered at the vision, <u>but there was no one who understood it or could make it understood.</u>

Fix your attention on the content of the following brief review. For, viewing each happening in context and arranged in sequence will help you to keep things in perspective. Insight into the content of the previous two verses, verses twenty-six and twenty-seven, will also be provided in the succeeding summary.

In verse fifteen, though he was spiritually blind and deaf to *"the secret things,"* Daniel still sought to understand the deep inner meaning of what he had seen and heard in his second vision.

In verse sixteen, God commanded the angel, Gabriel, to make Daniel understand the meaning of the vision that he had already seen, but did not comprehend.

In verse seventeen, the angel obeyed God and commanded Daniel to understand.

In verse nineteen, Gabriel told Daniel that he would make him know (that is, he would make him apprehend with clarity and certainty) what would take place in the end of time.

Gabriel kept his word in verses twenty through twenty-five. In those verses, the angel told Daniel the truth of all the future things that he had seen and heard in the vision. And most importantly, he made Daniel understand the interpretation of those things.

In verse twenty-six, the awesome things which the angel had made known to Daniel in verses twenty through twenty-five were meant for the distant future. Therefore, the angel instructed Daniel to keep the meaning of the interpretation of the vision to himself. His actual words were, *"But seal up the vision...."*

In verse twenty-seven, righteous Daniel would of course have obeyed the angel's command since he would have known that, as God's messengers, angels do God's bidding. Therefore, we must conclude from the contents of verse twenty-seven that though Daniel did tell his spiritually blind and deaf brethren what he had seen in his vision, he did not share with them the deep inner meaning of the angel's interpretation which he had himself been made to understand. Thus, without knowing the meaning of the angel's interpretation, Daniel makes it clear that none of his brethren understood the vision nor could they help anyone else to understand it.

The truth is, however, that even if Daniel had shared with his brethren the meaning of the interpreting angel's words, they still would not have been able to understand what the angel had conveyed to Daniel. For, you will recall that the angel had commanded Daniel to understand the meaning of his interpretation, whereas, the angel never bestowed that ability on Daniel's brethren. Additional Scriptural proof of that fact will be presented in a later segment of chapter fourteen.

REVELATION NO. 3

In the first year of the reign of Darius, Daniel sought the Lord with prayer and fasting. While he was praying, the angel Gabriel again appeared to him. **He shared with Daniel the reason for his visit.** <u>**Gabriel explained that he had come to give Daniel skill, wisdom and understanding.**</u>

In order for Daniel to have ever comprehended the meaning of these extraordinary futuristic disclosures, it was crucial that before or after each vision, God allowed him temporary relief from his spiritual disabilities. Such intervention was essential since Daniel was spiritually blind and deaf regarding *"the secret things."* Daniel not only needed help to understand the visions but he also had to be made to understand the meaning of the angel's interpretation of those visions. Otherwise, each one of his experiences would have been futile, and God does not deal in futility.

God certainly would not have displayed such great futuristic sights and sounds before a man whose spiritual blindness made him unable to perceive or hear them, that is of course, unless, God planned to temporarily allow that spiritually blind and deaf man to see and hear.

Along those same lines, God would not have given the interpretation of such profound secret truths to a man whose spiritual deafness would not have permitted him to understand the meaning of the angel's interpretation, that is, unless, God planned to make that deaf man understand the interpreting angel's words.

I repeat, God does not deal in futility! Thus, it makes sense that the angel did indeed equip Daniel with all the ability he needed to fully carry out God's purpose. For example, in the following verses, you are shown how, after his third vision, an angel once again temporarily bestowed on Daniel **the ability to understand the meaning of his words.**

Daniel 9: 21-23 (The Amplified Bible.)

21Yes, while I was speaking in prayer, the man Gabriel, whom I had seen in the former vision, being caused to fly swiftly, came near to me and touched me about the time of the evening sacrifice.

22He instructed me and made me understand; he talked with me and said, O Daniel, I am now come forth to give you skill and wisdom and understanding.

23At the beginning of your prayers, the word [giving an answer] went forth, and I have come to tell you, for you are greatly beloved. Therefore consider the matter and understand the vision.

The vision that Gabriel speaks of in verse twenty-three consists wholly of his own appearance and the words that he came to relay to Daniel. Therefore, when in that verse Gabriel commanded Daniel to *"consider the matter and understand the vision,"* he was instructing Daniel to consider and comprehend his words. In addition, the skill, wisdom and understanding that in verse twenty-two Gabriel told Daniel he had come to give him were obviously given for a two-fold purpose. They were given to enable Daniel to understand the meaning of the angel's words and to remember and record every detail of what he had seen in his vision and every word that the angel had spoken.

Should you desire to study **the angel's words** that I mentioned in the former paragraph, you will find them in Daniel 9:24-27. Yes, those verses contain the revelation of future events that the angel shared with Daniel after he had made Daniel to understand the meaning of his (the angel's) words. Albeit, my present aim does not include amplifying and making sense of the angel's words. Rather, at this time, my aim is to continue to provide you with an abundance of Biblical confirmation regarding the fact that God did upon occasion temporarily open the spiritually blind eyes and unstop the spiritually deaf ears of certain Old Testament Jews to enable them to hear and to understand *"the secret things."* My present goal is also to provide you with Scriptural evidence regarding the prophet Daniel's God-ordained spiritual disabilities and his subsequent need for God's intervention which gave him temporary relief from those handicaps while he accomplished God's will and purpose.

As I said earlier, God had to continually make spiritually blind and deaf Daniel understand the meaning of the things which he had either seen and heard or would see and hear in his dream and visions. God also had to make Daniel understand the meaning of each one of the angel's individual interpretations. For as I have repeatedly stated, it was necessary that the prophet Daniel understand so that he could in turn accurately record for future generations not only what he had physically seen and heard in the visions but also the true meaning of the angel's interpretation of those visions. On that note, let us consider the similar circumstances of Daniel's next vision.

REVELATION NO. 4

In the following verse, we are told that in the third year of the reign of King Cyrus, Daniel, who was by then ninety years old, had witnessed yet another vision. In that fourth and final vision, the writer explains how a messenger of God had again revealed to Daniel many future truths which referred to tribulation, conflict and wretchedness, truths which made known great tragedy and heartache that would befall the Israelites in the latter days.

The writer concludes verse one by assuring the reader that Daniel had fully understood the meaning of all that **the messenger of God had imparted to him** and therefore possessed an accurate understanding of the vision.

Daniel 10:1 (The Amplified Bible.)

*[1] IN THE third year of Cyrus king of Persia a word was revealed to Daniel, who was called Belteshazzar. And the word was true and it referred to great tribulation (conflict and wretchedness). **And he understood the word and had understanding of the vision**.*

Daniel himself goes on to explain how for three weeks before he had seen his fourth vision, he had diligently sought the Lord.

Daniel 10:2-3 (The Amplified Bible.)

*2In those days I, Daniel, was mourning for **three whole weeks.***

3I ate no pleasant or desirable food, nor did any meat or wine come into my mouth; and I did not anoint myself at all for the full three weeks.

Beginning with verse four of the same chapter and continuing through verse nine, Daniel gives a full account of the vision that he had seen after those three weeks had ended. We will pick up in verse ten where **for the final time an angel of God commands Daniel to understand the meaning of his prophetic words.**

Daniel 10:10-14 (The Amplified Bible.)

10And behold, a hand touched me, which set me [unsteadily] upon my knees and upon the palms of my hands.

11And [the angel] said to me, O Daniel, you greatly beloved man, <u>understand the words that I speak to you</u> and stand upright, for to you I am now sent. And while he was saying this word to me, I stood up trembling.

Could God have made the angel's statement in the previous verse, verse eleven, any clearer? I do not think so. My friend, in verse eleven, the angel informs you that in order for spiritually blind and deaf Daniel to truly hear and understand the meaning of his (the angel's) words, Daniel had to be made to do so. And so, once more, Daniel received a heavenly command. That command was, *"<u>understand the words that I speak to you</u>."* The angel did not request that Daniel merely pay attention. Rather, he commanded that Daniel's understanding be supernaturally awakened. This event is no less supernatural than when the angels physically blinded the eyes of the men of Sodom. It is no less miraculous than when an angel of the Lord troubled the waters of the Pool of Bethesda and people were supernaturally healed. (John 5:1-9.)

Let us now resume reading from our present text.

12Then he said to me, Fear not, Daniel, for from the first day that you set your mind and heart to understand and to humble yourself before your God, your words were heard, and I have come as a consequence of [and in response to] your words.

13But the prince of the kingdom of Persia withstood me for twenty-one days. Then Michael, one of the chief [of the celestial] princes, came to help me, for I remained there with the kings of Persia.

14<u>Now I have come to make you understand what is to befall your people in the latter days</u>, for the vision is for [many] days yet to come.

Not only do I want you to be aware that the angel once again commanded spiritually blind and deaf Daniel to understand the meaning of the words that he spoke, but I also want you to notice in verse twelve that **prior to the angel's appearance, the prophet Daniel had set his heart to understand.** In part four of chapter fourteen, we will begin to deal with certain men in Yeshua's time who likewise set their hearts to understand. So, please store that last tidbit of information for future reference.

Daniel 10:15 through Daniel 12:13 contains the future truths that the angel relayed to the prophet Daniel, truths which the angel made spiritually blind and deaf Daniel understand. Those truths reveal what will happen to the Israelites in the latter days.

Before you continue reading, I want to make something very clear. I want you to understand that the accumulation of information about Daniel that I divulged in part three was in no way intended to take away from the prophet Daniel. Daniel was a great man, full of faith and righteousness. However, he was still just a man and a spiritually disabled man at that. Furthermore, Daniel's power with God did not rest on anything that Daniel had done. Rather, as it was in the case of Moses, the power that Daniel had with God rested entirely on God's need to fulfill His own will and purpose on the earth and His unbreakable covenant with Abraham.

No, my friend, revealing the previous truth was not intended to lessen your admiration or respect for the righteous man, Daniel. Rather, my purpose and hope is that each of those facets of truth be exposed so that from this moment on your admiration, respect and awe will be mainly focused where it always should have been focused, **<u>on God</u>**. For God is the only one who is really deserving. The Lord went to unfathomable extremes to faithfully keep covenant with Abraham, Isaac and Jacob. He equipped spiritually blind and deaf Daniel with wisdom, skill and understanding so that he could comprehend and record for you and me (that is, for future generations) the meaning of all *"the secret* *things"* that he had seen and heard in his dream and visions as well as **the angel's interpretation** of those things.

There is one more important point that I feel I must shed light on. You will recall that on more than one occasion, the angel referred to Daniel as *"greatly beloved."* Hopefully with the information you now possess regarding God's everlasting love for the Israelites, you have already realized why the angel spoke those words. The angel called Daniel *"greatly beloved man"* because Daniel was a lineal covenant descendant of Abraham who kept God's commandments. And, you will recall that God promised Israel that if they obeyed His commands, He would keep with them the covenant and **steadfast love** that He swore to their forefathers. Thus, as promised, God expressed His covenant love for Daniel.

Earlier, I told you that in part three of chapter fourteen of this series, I intended to illustrate the irrefutable truth that God did upon occasion open the spiritually blind eyes and unstop the spiritually deaf ears of certain Old Testament Jews to enable them to understand *"the secret things."* I am sure you will agree that by using Daniel as my example, I have kept my word.

I also shared with you that the ability to understand *"the secret things"* which was on occasion bestowed upon certain Old Testament men was given on a temporary and limited basis only. Again, through the life of Daniel, I provided undeniable proof of that fact.

Last but not least, I assured you that in part three of chapter fourteen, you would also gain insight into the man, Daniel, which of course you have. You saw that like all the other blind and deaf Israelites, Daniel was also spiritually disabled regarding *"the secret things"* and that without the angel's intervention, he would never have been able to comprehend his visions or even the angel's various interpretations of those visions.

With the enlightenment you have received in the first three parts of chapter fourteen, you are now equipped with all the background information you need to fully understand the contents of the following four parts of chapter fourteen and to finally learn the truth to the question, "Why Did The Jews Fail To Recognize The Messiah?"

Chapter 14
Part Four

WHY DID THE JEWS FAIL
TO RECOGNIZE THE MESSIAH?

After studying parts one, two and three of chapter fourteen, you should have already come to the conclusion that it was the Jews' God-ordained spiritual blindness and deafness to *"the secret things"* that kept them from recognizing the Messiah. Nevertheless, I am sure that as you examined the enlightening information in each of the previous segments, your brain was bombarded with questions. A few of the questions that probably paraded through your mind were, "Since God is ultimately responsible for the Jews' blind and deaf plight, will He ever heal their spiritual condition? Will He ever allow them as a nation to see and to hear *'the secret things'* as His friends among the Gentiles have for so long been permitted to do? And, if at some future time God does allow their blind eyes to see and their deaf ears to hear, when will that be?"

My friend, I am glad to be able to tell you that God's Word provides answers to the preceding questions. For example, through the prophet Isaiah, God communicates to you the truth that the Jews as a nation will indeed be healed of their spiritual condition. However, He also lets you know that they will remain in their God-imposed blind and deaf state until a specified future point in time. **To be precise, they will in no wise gain spiritual understanding of *"the secret things"* until a certain period in the last days.**

The fact that the nation of Israel was spiritually blind and deaf to *"the secret things"* during the Messiah's visit to earth and the fact that Israel is still in that same spiritually disabled state today proves beyond doubt that Isaiah's prophecy, which I spoke of in the former paragraph, has not yet come to pass. I mentioned the previous point because I want you to read the Lord's prediction in verses eleven through thirteen of the following text knowing that it will be fulfilled at a future date. I have even highlighted those three verses so that when you read them from *The Living Bible*, you will remember to give them your undivided attention.

Isaiah 6:8-13 (The Living Bible.)

⁸Then I heard the Lord asking, "Whom shall I send as a messenger to my people? Who will go?" And I said, "Lord, I'll go! Send me."

⁹And he said, "Yes, go. But tell my people this: 'Though you hear my words repeatedly, you won't understand them. Though you watch and watch as I perform my miracles, still you won't know what they mean.'

¹⁰Dull their understanding, close their ears, and shut their eyes. I don't want them to see or to hear or to understand, or to turn to me to heal them."

¹¹Then I said, "Lord, how long will it be before they are ready to listen?" And he replied, "Not until their cities are destroyed—without a person left—and the whole country is an utter wasteland,

¹²And they are all taken away as slaves to other countries far away, and all the land of Israel lies deserted.

¹³Yet a tenth—a remnant—will survive; and though Israel is invaded again and again and destroyed, yet Israel will be like a tree cut down, whose stump still lives to grow again."

God makes it clear in verses eleven through thirteen of the former text that the Israelites will be kept in their invariable God-decreed spiritually blind and deaf state until a certain point in the last days. And that my friend is why the Jewish people are still blind and deaf to *"the secret things."* God is not yet ready to heal their spiritual disabilities. God tells you Himself in Isaiah 6:10, *"I don't want them to see or to hear or to understand, or to turn to Me to heal them."*

Get it through your head Christian! Yes! At some future date, Israel's blind eyes will be opened and her deaf ears will be unplugged. However, at this time in history, it is God's will that **as a nation** the Jews remain spiritually blind and deaf to *"the secret things."* And, as you saw in a previous segment of chapter fourteen, it is also God's will that Israel's religious leaders remain spiritually blind and deaf in that area.

Remember, God closed the minds of the entire Israelite population from understanding *"the secret things."* And, it is obvious why God included Israel's religious leaders in that act. I say it is obvious because Israel's teachers being unable to comprehend the deep inner meaning of God's sayings and His future Biblical predictions ensured that they would not be in a position to impart true understanding of those things to others.

The long and the short of it is that even today, God does not want the nation of Israel, including the Jews' spiritual leaders, to understand the deep spiritual matters that are recorded in His Word. Neither does He want them to understand His future predictions, or the meaning of His miracles or to recognize the Messiah. God has a plan, and the Scriptures make it clear that keeping Israel spiritually blind and deaf to *"the secret things"* is a big part of that plan.

In the subsequent text in *The Living Bible,* Isaiah illustrates the inability of Israel's religious leaders to recognize future happenings or the signs of the times. He gives you a glimpse of the utter darkness that veils their spiritual intellect in so far as Biblical predictions of the future are concerned. You studied this text in an earlier part of chapter fourteen. However, in order to refresh your memory, I suggest that you take the time to read it again.

Isaiah 29:10-12 *(The Living Bible.)*

10For the Lord has poured out upon you a spirit of deep sleep. <u>He has closed the eyes of your prophets and seers,</u>

11<u>so all of these future events are a sealed book to them</u>. When you give it to one who can read, he says, "I can't, for it's sealed."

12When you give it to another, he says, "Sorry, I can't read."

The Jews' spiritual eyesight is so impaired that they absolutely cannot interpret the signs of the times. In addition, since their teachers are also spiritually disabled insofar as *"the secret things"* are concerned, God's blind and deaf people have no one who is able to interpret the signs of the times for them. As the preceding verses inform you, future events are a closed book to the Jews and their religious leaders. Consequently, as you learned in chapter thirteen of this series, though the promised Messiah was born right under their noses, God's spiritually inept people failed to recognize Him or understand His teachings.

"Immanuel [God with us]" grew to manhood and walked among His own possession (that is, He walked among His own beloved, covenant people). Yet, in their God-ordained spiritually unintelligible blind and deaf state, they knew Him not. However, Yeshua definitely knew them. Yeshua knew that the Jews were unable to recognize Him. Furthermore, He understood why they could not identify Him. Yeshua also knew that they were unable to comprehend *"the secret things"* that are recorded in the Scriptures. Yes, the Lord was fully aware that His people and their spiritual leaders were void of spiritual discernment in the previously specified areas. And, because He knew they lacked the capacity to perceive certain spiritual matters, matters such as the meaning of the prophets' predictions, the signs of the times and even the day of the Messiah's visit among them, He made many affirmations to that effect. The following text records one of those statements.

> *Matthew 16:1-4 (The Amplified Bible.)*
>
> *¹NOW THE Pharisees and Sadducees came up to Jesus, and they asked Him to show them a sign (spectacular miracle) from heaven [attesting His divine authority].*
>
> *²He replied to them, When it is evening you say, It will be fair weather, for the sky is red.*
>
> *³And in the morning, It will be stormy today, for the sky is red and has a gloomy and threatening look.* <u>*You know how to interpret the appearance of the sky, but you cannot interpret the signs of the times.*</u>
>
> *⁴A wicked and morally unfaithful generation craves a sign, but no sign shall be given to it except the sign of the prophet Jonah. Then He left them and went away.*

Did you notice in verse three that The Amplified Bible translators twice use the word "interpret"? Yeshua said, "You know how to **interpret** the appearance of the sky, but you cannot **interpret** the signs of the times." I purposely drew your attention to the word "interpret" because in part three of chapter fourteen, you saw how righteous Daniel had also been unable to interpret "the secret things." Another reason why I drew your attention to the word "interpret" is because that word will be frequently mentioned later in the series. Therefore, each time you read the word "interpret," I want you to be able to recall how and why Yeshua used that term in verse three. For now however, you need to center your thoughts on the situation that occurred in Matthew 16:1-4.

In verse four, the Messiah reprimanded the religious leaders. He reprimanded them because they did wickedly by demanding miracles as proof of His divine authority. They broke God's command in Deuteronomy 6:16 which states in the *King James Version, "Ye shall not tempt the Lord your God, as you tempted Him in Massah."* The religious leaders tempted the Lord their God by putting Yeshua to the test just as their fathers had put Moses to the test as recorded in Exodus chapter seventeen. Yeshua did however assure the religious leaders that they would indeed be given a sign. Albeit, it would not be the miracle that they had wickedly called for. Rather, it would be the sign of the prophet Jonah. Of course, the Messiah was referring to the Biblically prophesied sign of His own future resurrection from the grave.

It is important that you understand that Yeshua's anger was directed toward the religious leaders for the Scriptural reasons that I just specified. Yeshua was upset with the religious leaders because of their blatant disregard of God's commands. He absolutely was not angry with them because they were unable to interpret the signs of the times. No! Yeshua knew that they were genuinely spiritually handicapped in that area. He would never have displayed such displeasure toward them for something that they could not help.

Yeshua was keenly aware that just as the prophet Daniel had been unable to interpret his own dream and visions, the religious leaders were unable to interpret the signs of the times. Like Daniel, all the religious leaders of Israel were spiritually blind and deaf. Consequently, again like Daniel, not one of them was, in himself, able to interpret *"the secret things."* You will recall that the angel had to command Daniel to understand the future sights and sounds that he had seen and heard in his dream and visions.

Another point to consider is the utter frustration that Yeshua must have experienced over the unreasonable, wicked demands of the religious leaders. Prior to the incident that is recorded in the previous text, He had publicly performed enough wondrous works to have proved to the whole world that He was the Messiah. However, as it had been in the time of Moses and as Isaiah predicted it would be in the Messiah's time, the Israelites' spiritual disabilities kept them from understanding the meaning of those supernatural signs. To refresh your memory as to how it was in Moses' time, read again the following verses.

Deuteronomy 29:2-4 (The Amplified Bible.)

²*Moses called to all Israel and said to them, You have seen all that the Lord did before your eyes in the land of*

Egypt to Pharaoh, to all his servants, and to all his land;

3The great trials which your eyes saw, <u>the signs, and those great wonders.</u>

4Yet the Lord has not given you a [mind and] heart to understand and eyes to see and ears to hear, to this day.

Miracles like none that had ever been seen before in Israel were wrought by the hand of Yeshua, the Anointed One. The physically blind received their sight. The deaf were made to hear. Men and women were literally raised from the dead. Yeshua healed the sick, walked on water, turned water into wine and fed five thousand people with a handful of fish and a few loaves of bread. He even stilled a raging storm with a verbal command. Yet, it was as though Yeshua had not performed those awesome miracles at all. His wondrous signs had absolutely no effect on the spiritual lives of the majority of Israel's Jewish population, especially Israel's religious leaders.

God had closed the spiritual eyes and ears of the religious leaders' so tightly that no matter how many great signs from heaven Yeshua would have provided attesting to His divine authority, they still would not have understood the meaning of His miracles or His teachings or recognized Him as the Messiah. And, since God had already predicted their response, no degree of spectacular supernatural splendor would have changed that fact. God said it all in the following verses in *The Living Bible*, and God's Word is truth.

Isaiah 6:9-10 (The Living Bible.)

9And he said, "Yes, go. But tell my people this: <u>'Though you hear my words repeatedly, you won't understand them. Though you watch and watch as I perform my miracles, still you won't know what they mean.'</u>

10Dull their understanding, close their ears and shut their eyes. <u>I don't want them to see or to hear or to understand, or to turn to me to heal them.</u>"

While Yeshua lived on the earth as a man, He taught the Jews in parables. Incredibly, the Messiah's Biblically foretold method of relaying instruction via parables was directly associated with the Jews'

God-ordained spiritual blindness and deafness to *"the secret things."* You see, Yeshua purposely taught in parables in order to fulfill God's Word in that area. God had foretold in Isaiah 6:9-10 that the Jews would not be able to understand the Messiah's teaching or His miracles. God had also made it clear that He did not want them to understand those things because He did not want them to believe on the Messiah or to be spiritually healed (that is, saved) at that time.

When in the former paragraph, I mentioned that Yeshua purposely taught in parables in order to fulfill God's Word, I was referring to Him not only fulfilling such recorded prophesies as Isaiah 6:9, *"Though you hear My words repeatedly, you won't understand them,"* but also the Psalmist's Messianic prediction in Psalm 78:1-2 and Isaiah's prediction in Isaiah 6:8-13. Yes, the Messiah taught in parables to make sure that God's Word was fulfilled and that the majority of the Jews remained spiritually blind and deaf to *"the secret things"* until God's foretold future appointed time.

Since earlier, you studied Isaiah 6:9 and Isaiah 6:8-13, I will not repeat those texts at this time. However, because the following two verses contain the Psalmist's previously mentioned Messianic prediction, I have included them.

Psalm 78:1-2 *(The Amplified Bible.)*

1GIVE EAR, O my people, to my teaching; incline your ears to the words of my mouth.

2I will open my mouth in a parable (in instruction by numerous examples); I will utter dark sayings of old [that hide important truth].

In the preceding two verses, the prophet spoke of the Messiah. **He foretold the actual method of teaching that the Messiah would use when He came.** He predicted that the Anointed One would instruct men by means of parables (that is, by means of simple stories which illustrate the lessons to be conveyed). However, the Psalmist also clearly foretold the fact that important truth would be **hidden** in the Messiah's parables.

The writer of the Gospel according to Matthew amplifies the prophet's words in Psalm 78:2. In the following verses, Matthew gives you an idea of the antiquity of the awesome secrets contained in the Messiah's parables.

Matthew 13:34-35 (The Amplified Bible.)

34These things all taken together Jesus said to the crowds in parables; indeed, without a parable He said nothing to them.

35This was in fulfillment of what was spoken by the prophet: I will open My mouth in parables; I will utter things that have been hidden since the foundation of the world.

The secrets and mysteries that Yeshua taught had already been recorded in the Jews' own Scriptures. However, because the Jews were spiritually blind and deaf, those mysteries went undetected generation after generation. Even when the Messiah verbally uttered those secret truths in parable form, His sayings of old still remained hidden to God's spiritually beloved but disabled covenant people.

Identifying and understanding the aforementioned profound mysteries that are hidden in Yeshua's Biblically prophesied parables demands concentration, perception, and spiritual intelligence and discernment in regard to *"the secret things."* However, as you are now aware, the Jews' spiritual thought processes did not encompass those intellectual qualities as far as *"the secret things"* were concerned. On the contrary, their spiritual thought processes in that particular area of understanding were completely clogged. Their minds were and in most cases still are unable to comprehend the mysteries and secrets that are hidden in Yeshua's parables.

God Himself had closed His people's minds from understanding *"the secret things"* thus inhibiting their spiritual intellectual potential in that dimension. Furthermore, as you saw previously so far as that particular level of spiritual intelligence is concerned, as a nation, the Israelites' minds will stay closed until God chooses to open them. And as you now know, God does not plan to open their minds to understanding of *"the secret things"* until His predicted appointed time in the last days. (Isaiah 6:11-13.)

It was because Yeshua was acutely aware of the Jews' God-imposed spiritual blindness and deafness to *"the secret things"* that He often ended or began His parables with a particular closing statement. He would call out, *"He that hath ears to hear, let him hear."* Sadly, for generations, the correct interpretation of the Lord's charge has eluded the Church. However, with the detailed Biblical insight that you have received to this point in the series, you are finally equipped with enough Scriptural evidence to be able to comprehend what Yeshua really meant by His previously mentioned maxim and why He said what He did. No longer does Yeshua's expression, *"He that hath ears to hear, let him hear,"* have to remain an enigma. So let us read and then examine Yeshua's declaration from the *Holy Bible, King James Version.*

Mark 4:9 (King James Version.)

⁹*And he said unto them, He that hath ears to hear, let him hear.*

In *The Amplified Bible*, the previous verse reads, *"And He said, He who has ears to hear, let him be hearing [and let him consider, and comprehend]."*

Prior to your reading Mark 4:9, *"And he said unto them, He that hath ears to hear, let him hear,"* you were enlightened as to the Jews' spiritually blind and deaf condition. Therefore, since in advance I carefully plotted out for you the Biblical cause of events regarding their disabled plight, it is very possible that you have already solved a portion of the previously mentioned mystery, a mystery that the Church has overlooked for too long. Even so, to make sure that you acquire the whole picture as to the content of Yeshua's words in Mark 4:9, I will briefly share with you the answer to that query.

First, however, you must recognize that when Yeshua made the statement in Mark 4:9, *"He that hath ears to hear, let him hear,"* He absolutely was not addressing the Gentiles. <u>Rather, He was speaking directly to His spiritually blind and deaf covenant people, the Jews</u>. We Gentile Christians can certainly benefit from and are expected to apply to our lives all that Yeshua said. However, if we are going to understand what the Lord really meant in each instance and why He said what He did, then, it is imperative that we comprehend exactly who His words were directed toward.

If you do your own research, you will inevitably come to the same conclusion as I did regarding the Lord addressing the Jewish people in Mark 4:9. Furthermore, you will be made aware that every credible Bible scholar agrees that, except on rare occasions, the words of Yeshua contained in the gospels were specifically directed toward His covenant people, the Jews. This information should come as no surprise to you since Yeshua tells you Himself in Matthew 15:24, *"I was sent __only__ to the lost sheep of the house of Israel."*

Of course, it goes without saying that if Gentiles chose to believe in Him, Yeshua did not turn them away. Nevertheless, during His time on earth, His kindness toward a few Gentiles did not change the fact that He came *"only"* to the Jews. Thus, His words in Mark 4:9, *"He that hath ears to hear, let him hear,"* were directed toward His spiritually blind and deaf covenant people.

Since, Yeshua knew that the Israelites were stone deaf regarding *"the secret things,"* you might wonder why He would say to them what He did in Mark 4:9. Why would He say to spiritually deaf people, *"He that hath ears to hear, let him hear"* (that is, he that has ears to hear; let him consider and comprehend the secret truth that is hidden in the parable that I just shared)? Was Yeshua taunting His disabled people when He made that remark? No! Of course not! The Messiah would never have mocked His spiritually handicapped people. Rather, Yeshua made the former statement for a number of reasons, two of which I will share with you.

(1) **The Messiah made the former statement in Mark 4:9 in order to fulfill that which was spoken of Him by the prophet in Psalm 78:1.** Yeshua repeated the actual contents of the statement that the prophet had predicted He would speak. You will recall that in Psalm 78:1, the prophet had foretold that the Messiah would say, *"GIVE EAR, O My people, to My teaching; incline your ears to the words of My mouth."* Thus, in fulfillment of the prophet's prediction, Yeshua stated, *"He that hath ears to hear, let him hear"* (that is, *"Let him consider and comprehend"*).

(2) The reason why Yeshua said, *"He that hath ears to hear, let him hear,"* was because He knew what you will learn later in parts five and six of chapter fourteen. He knew that a number of those Jews who were listening to His voice would by sheer mental and emotional force gradually lift the veil of spiritual blindness from their eyes and unplug their spiritual ears in order to fulfill God's Word during that particular period in history.

Yeshua's statement in Mark 4:9, *"He that hath ears to hear, let him hear"* was absolutely necessary. You see, He was actually challenging those Jews who fell into the category that I mentioned in the former paragraph to force themselves to pay attention to and to carefully and seriously consider the words that He spoke. Yeshua was instructing those Jews to forcibly bind themselves to that cause of action until their ardent zeal and the intense exertion that they continued to put forth paid off (that is, until bit by bit, their invisible yet existing spiritual earplugs were shattered by the sheer force and pressure that they applied to those unseen devices in their persistent efforts to hear the truth), and they were finally able to consistently understand the secrets and mysteries that He constantly divulged.

As you will learn in the next two consecutive parts of chapter fourteen, not many Jews possessed the essential quality or degree of spiritual zeal and vitality needed to perform the overwhelming feat that I spoke of in the preceding paragraph. However, Yeshua knew that some did. He knew that those Jews who possessed sufficient intellectual stamina would force themselves to concentrate on His words and would persevere until they gradually overcame their spiritual handicaps. Yes, He knew that some would by force persistently seize understanding of all the secret truths contained in His parables.

As surely as God commanded, *"Let there be light; and there was light,"* so the Messiah commanded, *"He that hath ears to hear, let him hear,"* and spiritual illumination came to those Jews who had ears to hear. For, they considered and progressively came to comprehend *"the secret things"* that He revealed to them.

You will also learn in parts five and six of chapter fourteen that aside from the tiny minority of Jews who would forcefully persist until step-by-step they at long last managed to gain spiritual sight and hearing (that is, until in the course of time, they managed to gain spiritual understanding of *"the secret things"* that are hidden in the Messiah's parables), Yeshua knew that what the prophets had foretold would come to pass. The Jewish people as a whole would remain spiritually blind and deaf in that God-ordained area of understanding until God's Biblically predicted future appointed time.

Being *"Immanuel [God with us],"* Yeshua also knew that at that moment, as a result of their spiritual disabilities, all the Jews who stood within the range of the sound of His voice would be unable to grasp the deep inner meaning of the parable that He taught. Furthermore, He was aware that only a small group of them would show enough interest in or concern for the truth of God's Word to put forth the degree of effort necessary to overcome their God-imposed spiritual handicaps in order to seek and to find the hidden meaning of His teachings.

God foretold in Isaiah 6:9, *The Living Bible, "Though you hear My words repeatedly, you won't understand them,"* and God's Word had to be fulfilled. Thus, great and wonderful important spiritual truth rolled off the Jewish people like water off a duck's back. God had closed the Israelites' spiritual ears, and He was not ready to open them. As you will see in the Scriptures in the next segment of chapter fourteen of this work, only those Jews who intellectually exerted themselves in order to comply with the Messiah's invitation, *"He that hath ears to hear, let him hear,"* would gradually come to understand *"the secret things"* that are hidden in His parables.

You are now aware of the extent of the Jews' spiritually disabling blindness and deafness. **You know that the Jews as a whole were unable to recognize the Messiah, they were unable to recognize the signs of the times and they were unable to understand the secret truth contained in Yeshua's parables**. Moreover, you also understand what Yeshua really meant when He made the statement, *"He that hath ears to hear, let him hear."*

The fact that a small number of Jews forced themselves to recognize the Messiah and understand the secrets that are hidden in His parables will be made crystal clear in parts five and six of chapter fourteen. Therefore, it is imperative that you retain the knowledge that you have just gained in part four since you will need to call up pieces of that information as you continue to study the remaining segments of the present chapter entitled, "Why Did The Jews Fail To Recognize The Messiah?"

Chapter 14
Part Five

WHY DID THE JEWS FAIL
TO RECOGNIZE THE MESSIAH?

As you study chapter fourteen, part five, it will become crystal clear to you why only those Jews who intellectually exerted themselves came to understand *"the secret things."* Furthermore, I will present overwhelming Scriptural evidence which will prove beyond doubt that the insight that I imparted to you in part four, insight regarding the necessity that the Jews intelligently exert themselves in order to gain spiritual understanding of the secret truth that is hidden in the Messiah's parables, is absolutely correct.

Since I have already shown you why Yeshua stated in Mark 4:9, *"He that hath ears to hear, let him hear,"* I am now in a position to keep the promise I made in chapter fourteen, part four. Of course, I am referring to my promise to provide for you Scriptural confirmation pertaining to a small minority of Jews who were gradually gaining spiritual sight and hearing regarding *"the secret things"* while the rest of the Jewish nation remained totally blind and deaf in that area of understanding.

Among many other marvelous truths, you are about to see in God's Word that the twelve apostles of Yeshua were included in that blessed minority of Jews who, by sheer determination, forced themselves to progressively overcome their spiritual handicaps insofar as understanding *"the secret things"* that are hidden in Yeshua's parables. However, as I have repeatedly reminded you, the majority of the Jewish people remained wholly blind and deaf to *"the secret things"* so that they too could fulfill their God-given mission upon the earth. Keep both these points in mind as you study the following text from the *Holy Bible, King James Version.*

Mark 4:1-34 (King James Version.)

¹AND he began again to teach by the sea side: and there was gathered unto him a great multitude, so that he entered into a ship, and sat in the sea; and the whole multitude was by the sea on the land.

2And he taught them many things <u>by parables</u>, and said unto them in his doctrine,

3Hearken; Behold, there went out a sower to sow:

4And it came to pass, as he sowed, some fell by the way side, and the fowls of the air came and devoured it up.

5And some fell on stony ground, where it had not much earth; and immediately it sprang up, because it had no depth of earth:

6But when the sun was up, it was scorched; and because it had no root, it withered away.

7And some fell among thorns, and the thorns grew up, and choked it, and it yielded no fruit.

8And other fell on good ground, and did yield fruit that sprang up and increased; and brought forth, some thirty, and some sixty, and some an hundred.

9And he said unto them, <u>He that hath ears to hear, let him hear.</u>

The next verses tell you what happened when Yeshua was alone with those who had responded to His challenge in verse nine *"He that hath ears to hear, let him hear."* In this case, those whose actions revealed that they had heeded the Messiah's order to consider and comprehend His parable were the Messiah's twelve disciples and a few other faithful followers. These Jews proved that they were equal to the Lord's challenge, *"He that hath ears to hear, let him hear,"* when despite their spiritual handicaps they still showed an interest in finding out the meaning of the parable and put forth the effort to do so. Fix your attention on the next four verses of the present text, verses ten through thirteen because each one of them holds vital information.

10And when he was alone, they that were about him with the twelve <u>asked of him the parable</u>.

In verse ten, you are informed that when the episode which is recorded in verses ten through thirty-four occurred, Yeshua was alone with the twelve and some of His other disciples. It is therefore obvious that Yeshua and His followers were separated from the great multitude of Jewish people mentioned in Mark 4:1-2 with whom Yeshua had previously shared the parable of the sower.

The fact that the writer tells you in verse ten that this small group of devoted Jews found it necessary to ask Yeshua the meaning of the parable proves beyond doubt that though they had been present when Yeshua had given His illustration, they had not grasped its secret content anymore than the great multitude had. However, after Yeshua had called out, *"He that hath ears to hear, let him hear,"* inviting those Jews who were zealous of truth to adhere to His challenge to defy their handicaps and seek and find the hidden truth in His illustration, His disciples sought for the answer to the parable of the sower just as the prophet Daniel had sought for an answer to the meaning of his vision. (Daniel 8:15, Daniel 7:15-16.) The writer says in the previous verse, verse ten, that Yeshua's disciples *"asked of Him the parable."* The next verse holds a part of Yeshua's reply.

> *11And he said unto them, Unto you it is given to know the mystery of the kingdom of God: but unto them that are without, all these things are done in parables:*

In *Strong's Exhaustive Concordance of the Bible*, Greek Dictionary of the New Testament, Strong informs you that the word, *"given,"* that the Messiah used in verse eleven is used in Greek in a very wide application. If you take the time to study Strong's definition of this word, *"given,"* in your personal concordance along with the eye-opening Scriptural information that you will receive in this segment of chapter fourteen, you will quickly become aware that in this instance Yeshua did not use this particular word, *"given,"* in the sense that we would ordinarily use it today. Some of the numerous terms that Strong provides such as "have power, smite, strike, suffer, take, utter and yield" alert the reader to that fact.

Before this chapter is ended, you will be convinced that any one or all of Strong's definitive words mentioned in the former paragraph convey the real intent of Yeshua's declaration in the highlighted portion of verse eleven. For example, the words, "smite, strike, have power" and "take" lend evidence to the fact that Yeshua was telling His disciples that, if they would, it was within their power to take by force the knowledge of the mysteries and secrets of the kingdom of God. Yeshua said, *"Unto you it is given to know the mystery of the kingdom of God."*

In the first part of verse eleven, Yeshua assured His little band of Jewish disciples that it was God's will for them to forcibly overcome their spiritual handicaps and come to know the secret truth that is hidden in His parables (that is, it was God's will for them to forcibly gain understanding of *"the secret things"* that pertain to the kingdom of God). Of course, it was God's will! After all, *"Immanuel [God with us],"* had previously called out, *"He that hath* *ears to hear, __let him hear__,"* and this small group of Jewish disciples obviously fell into the aforementioned category. Albeit, in that same verse, verse eleven, Yeshua also informed His disciples that at that time it was not God's will that those Jews outside of their circle should come to know the deep inner meaning of any of the parables.

To help you to keep verse twelve in context, I am going to repeat the portion of verse eleven that belongs with it.

> *11...but unto them that àre without, all these things are done in parables:*
>
> *12That seeing they may see, and not perceive; and hearing they may hear, and not understand; __lest at any time they should be converted, and their sins should be forgiven them.__*

The Lord communicated to His disciples in the last portion of verse eleven through verse twelve why it was not God's will at that time for most of the Israelites to understand the mysteries that are hidden in His parables. Contrary to the popular belief that Yeshua taught in parables in order to simplify the truth that He spoke and in so doing make it easier for the Jews to comprehend His teachings and be saved, Yeshua tells you Himself in the preceding verses, verses eleven and twelve, that the parables were intended to bring about the exact opposite effect.

Yeshua explained to His disciples in Mark 4:11-12 that God wanted the nation of Israel as a whole to remain blind and deaf to the secrets that were concealed in His parables because if they were allowed to comprehend those truths, they would recognize their spiritual need and repent, and God would be forced to keep His covenant and extend to them His loving-kindness, mercy and forgiveness. And, as you learned in the preceding four segments of chapter fourteen, it was not God's desire or part of His overall plan for mankind that the nation of Israel be spiritually healed or that they recognize the Messiah at that time.

Do you remember what God had predicted in Isaiah 6:10 in *The Living Bible* regarding those Jews who would be alive during the Messiah's time? He said, *"...I don't want them to see or to hear or to understand, or to turn to Me to heal them."* Therefore, Yeshua tells you Himself in Mark 4:11-12 that He deliberately taught in parables so that the majority of the Jewish people would not recognize Him or understand the parables' deep inner meaning and so that they would continue to be unable to interpret the signs of the times. To put it bluntly, the contents of His parables were intended to remain inexplicable stories to the majority of God's Abrahamic covenant people, the Jews.

13And he said unto them, Know ye not this parable? and how then will ye know all parables?

The contents of the previous verse, verse thirteen, have baffled many Christians. Throughout the years, Bible scholars and laymen alike have mentally wrestled with Yeshua's statement in that verse. They have desired and still do desire to know what Yeshua really meant when He said, *"Know ye not this parable? and how then will ye know all parables?"*

One of the keys to fully comprehending the Lord's adage in verse thirteen lies in your willingness to keep all the information in Mark 4:1-34 in context. For you see, all thirty-four verses of that text make up the whole truth that Yeshua conveyed to His followers that day. I assure you that by the time I have finished covering this entire text, you will finally know why Yeshua made the statement that He did in verse thirteen, *"Know ye not this parable? and how then will ye know all parables?"* So on that note, let us continue with our study of Mark 4:1-34.

After Yeshua had assured His disciples that it was given to them to understand the mystery of the kingdom of God that is hidden in His parables and after He had warned them that if they failed to understand the contents of the parable of the sower, they would inevitably be unable to understand the other parables, He went on to interpret the parable of the sower for them. He interpreted the parable in order to ensure that they would be given every chance to force themselves to consider and comprehend its deep inner meaning. Moreover, by sharing the interpretation of the meaning of the parable with His disciples and not with the multitude, Yeshua proved that He had told them the truth when in verse eleven He had assured them, *"Unto you it is given to know the mystery of the kingdom of God; but unto them that are without, all these things are done in parables."*

Yeshua's warning in verse thirteen, *"Know ye not this parable? and how then will ye know all parables?"* also had immediate spiritual value. Think about it! If you were told that if you did not understand the meaning of the parable of the sower, your attempts to understand other vital spiritual illustrations would be unsuccessful, then wouldn't you give your full attention to what was said from then on? If you are smart you would! And by that same token, you can be sure that Yeshua's disciples did too. Yes, after being cautioned about the serious consequences that would result from their failure to comprehend that one illustration, His disciples would most certainly have given their full attention to the Messiah's interpretation of the meaning of the parable of the sower.

Later, I will share with you more Scriptural confirmation as to why it was absolutely crucial that Yeshua's disciples fix their full attention on the words that He spoke. However, for now, let us continue to examine the verses of the present text in sequence.

Since verses ten through thirteen are part of the overall truth that Yeshua was relaying to His disciples in Mark chapter four, I have chosen to repeat them. However, Yeshua's actual interpretation of the parable, which we will study shortly, begins in verse fourteen. So as you read, keep in mind that after Yeshua had taught the parable and after He had called out, *"He that hath ears to hear, let him hear,"* He did grant His disciples' request that He explain to them the meaning of the parable. Yes, Yeshua interpreted for them the meaning of the parable of the sower just as the angel of the Lord had granted Daniel's request and had interpreted for him the meaning of his dream and visions.

> *10And when he was alone, **they that were about him with the twelve <u>asked of him the parable</u>.***
>
> *11And he said unto them, <u>**Unto you it is given to know the mystery of the kingdom of God**</u>: but unto them that are without, all these things are done in parables:*
>
> *12That seeing they may see, and not perceive; and hearing they may hear, and not understand; lest at any time they should be converted, and their sins should be forgiven them.*
>
> *13And he said unto them, Know ye not this parable? and how then will ye know all parables?*

Yeshua kept His promise in Mark 4:11 when in verses fourteen through twenty of the same chapter, He revealed to His disciples the secrets and mysteries of the kingdom of God that are concealed in the parable of the sower. However, since the whole content of the parable of the sower deals explicitly with the subject of the kingdom of God in that it contains the mystery of the kingdom of God, it makes sense that before you study Yeshua's interpretation of that parable you first learn exactly what the kingdom of God consists in.

The best and simplest Biblical description of the kingdom of God that I have found is provided by the Jewish apostle, Paul. Paul's inspired statement, though brief, is extremely eye opening. Read his description of the kingdom of God for yourself in the *Holy Bible, King James Version*. And, as you read, understand that according to 1 John 5:6 in *The Amplified Bible*, *"...The [Holy] Spirit is the Truth."*

Romans 14:17 (King James Version.)

17 For the kingdom of God is not meat and drink; but righteousness, and peace, and joy in the Holy Ghost.

If you keep in mind that **the kingdom of God is righteousness** (that is, right thinking, right speaking and right acting by the standards of God's Word) and peace and joy in the Holy Spirit (that is, peace and joy in the Spirit which belongs to those who have applied the truth to their lives and who are therefore uncompromisingly righteous), you will have no difficulty understanding Yeshua's interpretation of the parables. So on that note, I will briefly cover Yeshua's revelation of the kingdom of God contained in the parable of the sower and recorded in Mark chapter four.

14 The sower soweth the word.

15 And these are they by the way side, where the word is sown; but when they have heard, Satan cometh immediately, and taketh away the word that was sown in their hearts.

The word that the sower sowed in verse fourteen is *"the word of the kingdom."* Matthew made that fact very clear when he too recorded Yeshua's interpretation of the parable of the sower. You may want to take time and read Matthew's entire account of the parable of the sower in chapter 13. I will share only a portion of one verse that is relevant to the point I am making so that you will be convinced that the word which the sower sowed is the word of the kingdom of God. According to Matthew, part of Yeshua's words read, *"When any one heareth the word of the kingdom...."* (Matthew 13:19.)

My friend, what have you learned about the kingdom of God to this point? You have learned that the kingdom of God is righteousness (that is, right thinking, right speaking and right acting by the standards of God's Word). You have also learned that the word of righteousness (that is, the word of the kingdom) is what was sown by the sower.

Those by the wayside, people whom I will henceforth refer to as "wayside people", are those who hear *"the word of the kingdom"* (that is, those who hear someone teaching the truth of God's Word); however, they fail to understand the truth that they heard. Lack of understanding inevitably causes "wayside people" to respond unfavorably or inappropriately to the truth that they heard. Their attitudes and actions reveal total indifference, ignorance and sometimes even hostility.

If, after failing to understand God's righteous Word, "wayside people" become hostile toward the truth that they heard, then instead of applying the truth to their lives and continuing to pursue more truth, they often get offended by the word of righteousness and refuse to accept it. They turn away from the sound, righteous teaching that they heard simply because they did not correctly perceive it. Consequently, they go on clinging to the same wrong ideas that they held before they heard the truth.

A good example of the hostile conduct that "wayside people" often exhibit is seen in the following text taken from the *Holy Bible, King James Version.* I trust that you will take the time later to personally read the recorded details of this entire episode. I will cover only the information necessary to make my point regarding:

(1) What often happens when "wayside people" hear the word of the kingdom but fail to understand it.

(2) How Satan manages to take the word that was sown right out of their hearts.

In this particular case, Yeshua was the Sower and some of His own disciples were those by the wayside.

John 6:47-63, 66 (King James Version.)

47 Verily, verily, I say unto you, He that believeth on me hath everlasting life.

48 I am that bread of life.

49 Your fathers did eat manna in the wilderness, and are dead.

50 This is the bread which cometh down from heaven, that a man may eat thereof, and not die.

*51 I am the living bread which came down from heaven: if any man eat of this bread, he shall live for ever: **and the bread that I will give is my flesh, which I will give for the life of the world.***

⁵²The Jews therefore strove among themselves, saying, How can this man give us his flesh to eat?

The Jews murmured and complained throughout Yeshua's entire teaching. Right from the beginning, their God-imposed spiritual handicaps kept them from recognizing who He was and from understanding and believing His message about the kingdom of God. You see, because they were spiritually ignorant of *"the secret things,"* they mistakenly thought He was teaching false doctrine. As you read verses forty-one and forty-two of this same chapter, you will get an idea of the type of reception that the word of the kingdom received when it was sown in the hearts of the majority of the Jewish people..

In John 6:41-42, you will see how through their lack of understanding Satan managed to take the word out of the hearts of these Jewish people. You will also catch a glimpse of how Satan used the rebellious comments of these blind and deaf Jews to influence and deceive others and to thus make it possible for him to take the word from both categories of people.

In this case, Satan used the ignorant arguments and questionings of one group of Jews to distract the minds of other Jews and to stir up doubt and unbelief in their hearts. However, I am sure you are aware that Satan also uses the same evil tactic in the Church. Yes, even today, Satan uses some Christians to stir up doubt and unbelief in the hearts of other Christians. Therefore, you can imagine how the Jew's spiritual handicaps (that is, their inability to recognize the Messiah or to understand the secret truths that He spoke) made them especially vulnerable to Satan's deception.

> *John 6:41-42 (The Amplified Bible.)*
>
> *⁴¹Now the Jews murmured and found fault with and grumbled about Jesus because He said, I am [Myself] the Bread that came down from heaven.*
>
> *⁴²They kept asking, Is not this Jesus, the Son of Joseph, Whose father and mother we know? How then can He say, I have come down from heaven?*

In the previous verses, you are given a glimpse of one of the methods that Satan employs to immediately take the word of righteousness out of men's hearts. He uses **murmuring, complaining, questionings, faultfinding, unfounded verbally expressed doubts, grumbling, strife,** and so forth.

While men are hearing the Word, if they get keyed into one or two points that they have failed to understand, they will either wait until the teaching is over and ask the teacher to further explain those points (as Yeshua's disciples did in Mark chapter four) or more commonly, they will become hostile and difficult. If they fall into Satan's trap as those Jews in the previous verses did and they allow themselves to be distracted by their own questionings or by other peoples' arguments and doubts then, from that point on, everything the teacher of righteousness relays to them will fall on deaf ears. Consequently, Satan will steal from them the truth that was sown in their hearts.

With Satan's continual prodding, men who fail to understand the truth about the kingdom of God (that is, men who fail to understand what God considers to be right) will often oppose God's Word and will strive in controversy among themselves. They will make unfavorable comments about the word of righteousness that was taught. Sometimes they will even speak derogatorily about the one who taught what God considers to be right. Consequently, others who also failed to understand that same righteous teaching will allow themselves to be affected and influenced by the innuendoes, insinuations and false accusations of those ignorant faultfinders.

Because neither group of "wayside people" mentioned in John chapter six understood the kingdom truth that they heard, in their ignorance, one group grumbled and complained and spread doubt and discontent while the other group paid attention to and believed their rebellious and ignorant comments and arguments. Both types of "wayside people" failed to understand the word of the kingdom and therefore both types of "wayside people" became victims of Satan. Satan took from them the word of righteousness that was sown. In this case, as I said earlier, Satan used one group of spiritually blind and deaf Jews to stir up controversy, doubt and unbelief in the hearts of other spiritually blind and deaf Jews.

In a few moments, you will see how a great many of Yeshua's own disciples fell into the two previously mentioned categories. They failed to understand His teaching, they allowed themselves to be influenced by the wicked comments, arguments, questionings and attitudes of ignorant men, and they too ended up grumbling and complaining and spreading doubt and discontent. Yes, they too strove in controversy among themselves and consequently they too fell victim to Satan. The evil one quickly took from them the word that was sown in their hearts.

Let us backtrack and again read John 6:52 in the *King James Version*. For, that verse contains an example of men who failed to understand *"the secret things"* that Yeshua taught and who therefore found the word of the kingdom offensive.

> <u>*52The Jews therefore strove among themselves,*</u> *saying, How can this man give us his flesh to eat?*
>
> *53Then Jesus said unto them, Verily, verily, I say unto you, Except ye eat the flesh of the Son of man, and drink his blood, ye have no life in you.*
>
> *54Whoso eateth my flesh, and drinketh my blood, hath eternal life; and I will raise him up at the last day.*
>
> *55For my flesh is meat indeed, and my blood is drink indeed.*
>
> *56He that eateth my flesh, and drinketh my blood, dwelleth in me, and I in him.*
>
> *57As the living Father hath sent me, and I live by the Father: so he that eateth me, even he shall live by me.*
>
> *58This is that bread which came down from heaven:* **not as your fathers did eat manna,** *and are dead: he that eateth of this bread shall live for ever.*
>
> *59These things said he in the synagogue, as he taught in Capernaum.*
>
> **<u>*60Many therefore of his disciples,*</u> *when they had heard this, said, This is an hard saying; who can hear it?***

Verse sixty in *The Amplified Bible* reads:

> *60When* **<u>His disciples</u>** *heard this, many of them said, This is a hard and difficult and strange saying* <u>**(an offensive and unbearable message). Who can stand to hear it? [Who can be expected to listen to such teaching?]**</u>

I want you to also read John 6:60 from *The Living Bible*. Moreover, since you will already be using that particular translation, we will finish reading the remaining verses of the main text from that edition. Pay special attention to the highlighted portions, for they hold vital information. For example, verse sixty-six shows you that not just a few but **many** of Yeshua's own disciples actually turned back from following Him.

> *60Even* **<u>his disciples</u>** *said, "This is very hard to understand. Who can tell what he means?"*

61Jesus knew within himself that his disciples were complaining and said unto them, "Does this offend you?

62Then what will you think if you see me, the Messiah, return to heaven again?

63 Only the Holy Spirit gives eternal life. Those born only once, with physical birth, will never receive this gift. But now I have told you how to get this true spiritual life.

66*At this point many of his disciples turned away and deserted him.*

In their ignorance, these "wayside disciples" of Yeshua totally misconstrued the teachings of true righteousness that Yeshua had taught. They foolishly allowed themselves to be swayed by the rebellious comments, arguments and questioning of the unbelieving, blind and deaf multitude. In their intellectually unreceptive, spiritual state, among numerous other charges, they as much as accused Yeshua of teaching false doctrine. Some Bible scholars feel that they actually accused Yeshua of teaching and promoting cannibalism. However, the whole time, Yeshua had instead been revealing *"the secret things."* He had been revealing the mystery of the kingdom of God. He had been speaking about the promised new covenant which, in the near future, He would willingly lay down His body of flesh in death to provide, the new covenant that would give men deeper insight into God's righteous laws and power to obey them. He had been speaking about His blood that would soon be shed to seal the promised new covenant.

Oh, if only the Lord's disciples had paid closer attention to what Yeshua had really said instead of listening to the arguments of ignorant men and grumbling among themselves! If only these "wayside disciples" of Yeshua had been more vigilant in their search for truth and righteousness! If only they had taken the time to objectively evaluate Yeshua's teaching so that they could have thoughtfully formed a proper and righteous judgment and conclusion! For, had they carefully scrutinized His teaching, had they compared His teaching with Old Testament Scripture that pertained to the promised new covenant, they most certainly would have realized that Yeshua was simply using comparisons to make His righteous and perfect points and to reveal secrets *"that have been hidden since the foundation of the world."* (Matthew 13:35.)

In John 6:51, the Messiah made it clear that He would give them the bread (His flesh) by giving His life for the salvation of the world. He also let them know in verse fifty-eight of that same chapter that He **was not** referring to them eating His literal body as their fathers had eaten the manna. Yeshua even stated in John 6:63 that the flesh profits nothing. He assured them that He was referring to spiritual matters. He was speaking of truth (that is, He was speaking of spirit).

Oh that those shallow minded "wayside disciples" of Yeshua had cared enough about truth and righteousness to have questioned Yeshua until they received adequate enlightenment and came to fully understand His teaching! However, they did not. They had been too preoccupied with their own previously held misconceptions of what was right, misconceptions that were reinforced by ignorant, unbelieving people in the crowd, to have given the proper consideration to seeking the answer to the aforementioned mystery of the righteousness of God. Consequently, they became repulsed by the mystery of the kingdom of God of which Yeshua spoke. Imagine it! Their lack of understanding actually caused them to be repulsed by true revelation of the mystery of the very righteousness of God.

Since these people had not fully understood and applied to their lives the truth and righteousness contained in the parable of the sower, they were unable to understand Yeshua's other parables. Yeshua's words in Mark 4:13 had actually come to pass in their lives. *"Know ye not this parable? and how then will ye know all parables?"* Proof that these disciples of Yeshua were unable to understand the other parables is seen in their inability to comprehend Yeshua's illustration in the previous text. (John 6:47-63, 66.)

Because these disciples of Yeshua did not know the parable of the sower, because they had not applied to their lives the truth contained in that parable, they did not understand the deceptive practice that Satan was using on them at that very moment. They were not aware that it was absolutely necessary that men be continually on their guard against Satan's treachery. They did not understand that the very thing that Yeshua had foretold in the parable of the sower had actually come to pass in their own lives. No! They did not realize that they had become the "wayside people" that Yeshua had described in His illustration. They did not know that Satan had just taken from them the word of the kingdom that had been sown in their hearts.

Satan had deceptively used ignorant, unbelieving men (the fowls of the air, Mark 4:4) to aid him in devouring the seed (that is, in devouring the word of the kingdom) that was sown in the hearts of Yeshua's own disciples. Thus, Yeshua's words in Mark 4:13 came to pass in the lives of these "wayside disciples." *"Know ye not this parable? and how then will you know all parables?"*

Give careful thought to the question that I am about to ask you as well as the answer that I will provide.

Question: Why is it not possible for Yeshua's disciples to come to know the mysteries of the kingdom of God that are contained in all His parables if they do not first learn the secret that is hidden in the parable of the sower?

Answer: My friend, the reason why it is not possible for men to understand all the parables if they do not understand the parable of the sower is because the parable of the sower contains God's secret defense formula which when used keeps Satan at bay when the word is sown in men's hearts. Men cannot possibly come to know all the secrets contained in Yeshua's other parables if they do not first learn how to keep Satan from continually taking the word out of their hearts as fast as it is sown in them. The parable of the sower provides the Biblical solution to the former problem. You might say that it provides the secret kingdom formula. It gives men a glimpse of Satan's strategy and it educates them regarding the defense measures they must take in order to defeat his cunning strategy and deceptive tricks and hold on to the word that is sown in their hearts.

Without a doubt, these spiritually insensible, simple (that is, easily seduced) disciples of Yeshua mentioned in John 6:66 turned out to be "wayside people." And, as you now know, those by the wayside are they who hear *"the word of the kingdom";* however, they are indifferent to such teaching. They have little or no intellectual interest in pursuing or in truly understanding the righteousness of God. Consequently, these people do not diligently seek to understand the truth that they heard or exert themselves enough to apply it to their lives. They do not persistently and consistently force themselves to come to know the mystery of the kingdom of God. The prophet spoke of these foolish people in verse five of the following verses.

Proverbs 8:1-9 (The Amplified Bible.)

¹DOES NOT skillful and godly Wisdom cry out, and understanding raise her voice [in contrast to the loose woman]?

²On the top of the heights beside the way, where the paths meet, stands Wisdom [skillful and godly];

3At the gates at the entrance of the town, at the coming in at the doors, she cries out:

4To you, O men, I call, and my voice is directed to the sons of men.

5O you simple and thoughtless ones, understand prudence; you [self-confident] fools, be of an understanding heart.

6Hear, for I will speak excellent and princely things; and the opening of my lips shall be for right things.

7For my mouth shall utter truth, and wrongdoing is detestable and loathsome to my lips.

8All the words of my mouth are righteous (upright and in right standing with God); there is nothing contrary to truth or crooked in them.

9They are all plain to him who understands [and opens his heart], and right to those who find knowledge [and live by it].

"Wayside people" usually think they already understand what is right by the standards of God's Word. They are blinded by a false sense of security. Therefore, they do not feel the urgency or need to intellectually exert themselves to comprehend the truth that was sown. Neither do they feel the necessity to force themselves to stay alert when they are hearing teachings on righteousness. However, the truth is that these people really do not understand or possess the word of righteousness at all. No! Despite the fact that many "wayside people" consider themselves to be disciples of Yeshua, they neither understand nor retain the word of righteousness. Rather, they fall victim to Satan who immediately comes and by using these people's own lack of understanding or the negative, ignorant, unbelieving comments and arguments of others takes away the word of righteousness that was sown in their hearts.

As I have repeatedly stated, "wayside people" do not put forth enough effort to really comprehend the word of righteousness, never mind apply it to their lives. And of course, Satan tries to make sure that they never will. He does that by immediately taking from them the word that was sown.

"Wayside people" make themselves easy targets of prey. Sadly, they usually choose to give their attention, time and energy to the man-made doctrines of their day rather than devote themselves to the study of the righteousness of God. They do not find pleasure or excitement or joy in down-to-earth, practical teachings regarding those things which God considers to be right or those things that pertain to a man thinking right, speaking right and acting right by the standards of God's Word. They do not recognize the priceless, eternal value of the precious word of righteousness that they have heard. Sadly, as far as they are concerned, teachings on righteousness are hardly significant enough to even arouse their curiosity.

The majority of Jewish people in Yeshua's day fell into the wayside category in that their being spiritually blind and deaf to *"the secret things"* made them especially susceptible to the wayside syndrome. However, since God did not make the Gentiles spiritually blind and deaf to *"the secret things,"* Gentile Christians today who through their indifference to the truth also fall prey to Satan's thieving practices are without excuse. Furthermore, by their neglect (that is, by their failure to learn God's righteous commands and apply them to their lives in all their revealed fullness by the power provided in the new covenant), Gentile Christians publicly exhibit the fact that they have **deliberately** chosen to remain ignorant and insensible to the mystery of the kingdom of God contained in the parable of the sower.

As you again focus your attention on our main text in Mark chapter four, please keep in mind the truth that you have learned to this point in the series.

> *16And these are they likewise which are sown on stony ground; who, when they have heard the word, immediately receive it with gladness;*
>
> *17And have no root in themselves, and so endure but for a time: afterward, when affliction or persecution ariseth for the word's sake, immediately they are offended.*

Verses sixteen and seventeen describe a second group of people who with gladness immediately receive the word of the kingdom. However, when believing on the Messiah (Yeshua) or doing what is right by the standards of God's Word brings hardship, affliction, ostracism or persecution into their lives, these people cast from them the word of righteousness as quickly as they received it. I will refer to these people as "stony ground people." "Stony ground disciples" of Yeshua refuse to undergo discomfort or suffering in order to think right, speak right and act right by the standards of God's Word. Having the acceptance and approval of family members, friends, people in a particular organization, and so on means more to them than possessing understanding of *"the things which are revealed"* and *"the secret things."* Consequently, they also fall prey to Satan's deceptive practices, and they allow Satan to take out of their hearts the word of the kingdom (that is, the word of righteousness) that was sown.

For example, John 9:22 informs you that the religious leaders of Israel had threatened that anyone who confessed Yeshua to be the Christ would be expelled from the synagogue. As a result of that threat, many leading men in Israel who believed Yeshua to be the Messiah and who also believed His teachings would not confess Him. They cared more about their credibility and standing with men than they cared about pleasing God.

> *John 12:42-43 (The Amplified Bible.)*
>
> *42And yet [in spite of all this] many even of the leading men (the authorities and the nobles) believed and trusted in Him. But because of the Pharisees they did not confess it, for fear that [if they should acknowledge Him] they would be expelled from the synagogue;*
>
> *43For they loved the approval and the praise and the glory that come from men [instead of and] more than the glory that comes from God. [They valued their credit with men more than their credit with God.]*

In the next two verses, Mark 4:18-19, Yeshua continues His interpretation of the parable of the sower.

> *18And these are they which are sown among thorns; such as hear the word,*
>
> *19And the cares of this world, and the deceitfulness of riches, and the lusts of other things entering in, choke the word, and it becometh unfruitful.*

Verses eighteen and nineteen, identify a third group of people that I will call "thorn people." These "thorn people" are not willing to make the necessary sacrifices to apply the truth to their lives or to set their priorities in the proper order. They allow the cares and anxieties of the world or the distractions of the age or pleasure or material possessions or money or business activities or other worldly things or pursuits to fill their thoughts, hearts and time and to consume their energy. Thus they permit the word of righteousness to be crowded out of their lives. There is no room in the hearts of "thorn people" for truth that demands that they totally devote their lives to learning and obeying what is right by the standards of God's Word. Consequently they are unfruitful (that is, they do not produce or exhibit righteousness). They do not consistently think right, speak right or act right by the standards of God's Word. Thorn disciples value the things of the world more than they value truth or the righteousness that is imparted to men when they apply truth to their lives.

The word does not have a chance to take root in the hearts of "thorn people." The temporal things that they love so much actually become the tools that Satan uses to loot the eternal riches that could have been theirs if only their priorities had been in the proper order. A good example of "thorn people" can be seen in the following verses.

> *Luke 16:13-14 (The Amplified Bible.)*
>
> *13No servant is able to serve two masters; for either he will hate the one and love the other, or he will stand by and be devoted to the one and despise the other. You cannot serve God and mammon (riches, or anything in which you trust and on which you rely).*
>
> *14Now the Pharasees, who were covetous and lovers of money, heard all these things [taken together], and they began to sneer at and ridicule and scoff at Him.*

The Pharisees memorized and quoted the words of the prophets. Yet, it is obvious that they did not understand at all what those words mean. Read the next verses, and you will see what I mean.

> *Proverbs 8:10-14, 18-21 (The Amplified Bible.)*
>
> *10Receive my instruction in preference to [striving for] silver, and knowledge rather than choice gold,*
>
> *11For skillful and godly Wisdom is better than rubies or pearls, and all the things that may be desired are not to be compared to it.*
>
> *12I, Wisdom [from God], make prudence my dwelling, and I find out knowledge and discretion.*
>
> *13The reverent fear and worshipful awe of the Lord [includes] the hatred of evil; pride, arrogance, the evil way, and perverted and twisted speech I hate.*
>
> *14I have counsel and sound knowledge, I have understanding, I have might and power.*

18Riches and honor are with me, enduring wealth and righteousness (uprightness in every area and relation, and right standing with God).

19My fruit is better than gold, yes, than refined gold, and my increase than choice silver.

20I [Wisdom] walk in the way of righteousness (moral and spiritual rectitude in every area and relation), in the midst of the paths of justice,

21That I may cause those who love me to inherit [true] riches and that I may fill their treasuries.

The next verse of Yeshua's parable in Mark chapter four categorizes a fourth group of people that I will refer to as "good ground people."

20And these are they which are sown on good ground; such as hear the word, and receive it, and bring forth fruit, some thirtyfold, some sixty, and some an hundred.

Verse twenty describes the final category of people who hear the word of the kingdom, the word of righteousness. They are "good ground people." "Good ground people" are easily identified in that they are extremely teachable people who have an intellectual interest in the word of the kingdom and recognize the importance of learning what is right in God's sight. "Good ground disciples" of Yeshua have no interest in the latest spiritual fads or in man-made doctrines or traditions. Rather, they give strict attention to and force themselves to fully comprehend the word of the kingdom (that is, the word of righteousness). Moreover, they do not allow the fowls of the air to devour the word that was sown in their hearts (that is, they do not allow doubting, complaining, critical, ignorant men to influence or affect them in anyway). They recognize the truth and hold onto it with everything in them.

Proverbs 8:33-35 (The Amplified Bible.)

33Hear instruction and be wise, and do not refuse or neglect it.

34Blessed (happy, fortunate, to be envied) is the man who listens to me, watching daily at my gates, waiting at the posts of my doors.

35For whoever finds me [Wisdom] finds life and draws forth and obtains favor from the Lord.

"Good ground people" do not turn coward and stop doing right when they fall into difficult circumstances or when they are persecuted or afflicted on account of the truth. They do not seek the approval of men at the cost of displeasing God. Instead, they persevere during all tests and trials. They continue to make every effort to learn what is right in God's Word and to put it into practice in their lives.

Furthermore, "good ground disciples" refuse to be distracted from learning God's Word or to be enticed to sell the word of righteousness for material possessions or money or worldly pleasure. No! No! No! They will not stop confessing their belief in Yeshua or learning and obeying God's righteous Word for anything or anyone. Instead, they keep pressing forward no matter what the cost. They force themselves to pay attention to the truth that they hear. They strive to apply the truth to their lives by learning and obeying God's commands and increasing in spiritual knowledge. Thus, as Yeshua promised in Mark 4:20, they consistently produce and exhibit fruits of righteousness (that is, they produce and exhibit fruits of right thinking, right speaking and right acting by the standards of God's Word), *"some thirtyfold, some sixty, and some an hundred."*

"Good ground people" possess knowledge of both *"the things which are revealed"* and *"the secret things."* They understand the mystery of God's Word that is recorded in the parable of the sower. Thus, they are able to retain and increase in the knowledge of God's Word that they have received and applied to their lives. Yes, they know what measures to take in order to hold onto the word of the kingdom that was sown in their hearts.

When Yeshua had finished interpreting the parable of the sower, He continued to instruct His disciples without deviating one iota from His original topic. For example, you will recall that in Mark 4:11, Yeshua had assured His disciples, *"Unto you it is given to know the mystery of the kingdom of God."* Then afterward, so that His disciples would realize that His previous statement was indeed true, Yeshua interpreted for them the deep inner meaning of the parable. Thus, He actually revealed to them *"the secret things."* He revealed to them the mystery of the kingdom of God. He revealed to them how they could retain and increase in knowledge and righteousness of God's Word. He explained to them who those Jews are who forcibly overcome their spiritual handicaps, retain the truth and make righteousness (the kingdom) theirs. He also revealed to them who those Jews are who fail to retain truth and righteousness (that is, those Jewish people who fail to obtain the kingdom of God) and why they fail to obtain the kingdom.

When you read the next two verses from Mark chapter four, you will see how they correlate Yeshua's former statement in Mark 4:11 and His disclosure of the secrets of the parable that had aforetime remained hidden. You will see that while Yeshua was still referring to His disciples striving to come to understand and retain *"the secret things"* contained in the parables, one of which He had just interpreted for them, Yeshua let them know that those marvelous truths which He had relayed to them via His interpretation of the parable of the sower had been previously kept secret in order that they should eventually be revealed by Him.

The Scriptures confirm that God had always intended that the aforementioned secret truths be made manifest by the Messiah during His promised visit to earth. Earlier, you saw that Matthew, when referring to the prophet's words regarding the teachings of the promised Messiah in Psalm 78:2, had written in Matthew 13:35, *"I will utter things that have been hidden since the foundation of the world."*

The promised Messiah had come. Thus, it was time for Him to make known the mystery of the kingdom of God (that is, it was time for Him to reveal those hidden truths regarding righteousness that aforetime had been deliberately kept secret). And, as God had always planned that it should be, those truths were revealed to the Jews to whom it had been given to know *"the secret things"* that were hidden in the Messiah's parables. Yes, those Jews who heeded and fulfilled the Messiah's call, *"He that has ears to hear, let him hear,"* diligently and relentlessly sought to know and retain the secrets of the kingdom of God (that is, they diligently and relentlessly sought to know the mystery of the righteousness of God) contained in His parables.

Read now the aforementioned verses in Mark 4:21-23 in which Yeshua reveals that the time had come for all *"the secret things"* to be made known.

> *21And he said unto them, Is a candle brought to be put under a bushel, or under a bed? and not to be set on a candlestick?*
>
> *22For there is nothing hid, which shall not be manifested; neither was any thing kept secret, but that it should come abroad.*
>
> *23If any man have ears to hear, let him hear.*

What secrets other than the prophesied spiritual secrets contained in His parables would the Messiah have been speaking about in verses twenty-one and twenty-two? After all, prior to making His statement in those verses, He had told His disciples in verse eleven, *"Unto you it is given to know the mystery of the kingdom of God."* He had also just finished interpreting for His disciples the hidden meaning of the parable of the sower. He had shown them the secret to **retaining and increasing** in the knowledge and righteousness of the kingdom of God. Consequently, by doing so, He had already proven His statement in verse twenty-two, *"For there is nothing hid, which shall not be manifested; neither was any thing kept secret, but that it should come abroad."* Yes, the Messiah had revealed truth about the kingdom of God that had previously been kept secret so that it might be revealed by Him at the appropriate time in order to fulfill God's Word and best accomplish God's will upon the earth. And as you know, the Messiah eventually disclosed to His disciples the deep inner secrets that are contained in His other parables also.

In the last verse of our main text that you read a few moments ago, Mark 4:23, Yeshua repeated His command, *"If any man have ears to hear, let him hear."* Now, you might wonder why Yeshua would have felt the necessity to reiterate His former command at that particular moment since He was alone with the twelve and some of His other disciples whom He had already assured, *"Unto you it is given to know the mystery of the kingdom of God: but unto them that are without, all these things are done in parables."*

The question in the preceding paragraph is certainly legitimate. So, I will take the time to briefly explain why it was crucial that, while in the presence of His disciples, Yeshua repeat His statement, *"If any man have ears to hear, let him hear."*

It is true that Yeshua did tell His disciples previously in Mark 4:11, *"Unto you it is given to know the mystery of the kingdom of God."* However, His statement in verse eleven was an invitation. It was not a guarantee that His disciples would receive instant or permanent knowledge of all *"the secret things."* Neither was Yeshua's statement a guarantee that His disciples would overcome their blind and deaf spiritual handicaps enough to comprehend and apply to their lives the secrets that He shared with them even though He knew that some of them would. Rather, Yeshua's statement in verse eleven simply called on His followers to strive to **gradually** come to know *"the secret things."*

The following verses of our present text confirm the truth that I have just relayed to you. For, had the disciples actually possessed a guarantee that from that time forth, they would always understand and apply to their lives the truth of God's Word and subsequently gain permanently the righteousness of God, Yeshua would not have found it necessary a few moments later to have given them the severe warning that He did in Mark 4:24-25.

I have chosen to return to my main Bible source, *The Amplified Bible*, since, the translators of that edition did an exceptional job of translating the verses that I just spoke of.

Mark 4:23-25 (The Amplified Bible.)

23If any man has ears to hear, let him be listening and let him perceive and comprehend.

24And He said to them, Be careful what you are hearing. The measure [of thought and study] you give [to the truth you hear] will be the measure [of virtue and knowledge] that comes back to you—and more [besides] will be given to you who hear.

25For to him who has will more be given; and from him who has nothing, even what he has will be taken away [by force],

In verse twenty-three of the former text, Yeshua again challenged His disciples. He said, *"If any man has ears to hear, let him be listening and let him perceive and comprehend."* Then, in verses twenty-four and twenty-five, He immediately proceeded to sternly warn His still spiritually handicapped Jewish disciples regarding what it would take for them to meet all the requirements of His challenge.

Yeshua made it clear to His disciples that in order for them to gradually overcome their spiritual handicaps and be able to retain and increase in understanding and righteousness, they had to intellectually exert themselves. They had to make acquiring knowledge of God's Word and the righteousness it imparts their number one priority. They had to consistently force themselves to pay strict attention to the truth that He taught so that each time they heard the word of the kingdom, they would comprehend His teaching and immediately put the truth they heard into practice in their own lives. For as you have already seen in God's Word, only by consistently learning and obeying the truth of God's Word at any cost would His disciples be able to keep Satan from taking it from them.

Yeshua warned His disciples that the degree of thought and study that they were willing to extend in their search for truth would be the degree of virtue (moral excellence, righteousness) and knowledge (understanding) that they could expect to receive in return. Furthermore, the knowledge of the kingdom of God that they managed to retain and apply by force to their lives in order to bring forth fruits of righteousness would automatically make available to them additional truth and righteousness since being informed would prepare them to receive more truth, and righteousness is applied truth.

As any good teacher would instruct his pupils, so, Yeshua informed His disciples that they must first get the basics down pat and then build on them. For, it is a known fact that possessing understanding of one truth inevitably gives one insight into other areas of truth.

On the other hand, Yeshua made it equally clear that if His disciples neglected to give their full attention to His words, if they failed to put forth enough effort to acquire the truth, if the degree of thought and study that they gave to the truth they heard was not adequate, if they did not diligently pursue knowledge of the righteousness of God (that is, knowledge of the kingdom of God) with ardent zeal and intense exertion, if they were unsuccessful in their attempt to understand and retain the word that was sown in their hearts, if they did not seize and apply to their lives the righteousness of God that the truth imparts, **they would end up with nothing. In addition, even what they had would be taken away**. You will recall that is exactly what happened to many of Yeshua's disciples in John 6:47-66. And of course, you now know how and why knowledge and righteousness will be taken from men and by whom it will be taken.

If Yeshua's former challenge, *"if any man has ears to hear, let him hear,"* or His former invitation, *"unto you it is given to know the mystery of the kingdom of God,"* had already guaranteed them uninterrupted knowledge and righteousness of God's Word from that moment on, Yeshua would never have given His disciples the severe warning that He did in verses twenty-four and twenty-five. Neither would Yeshua have continually repeated His challenge. No! My friend, the disciples were just as disabled regarding *"the secret things"* as the other Jews were. Furthermore, they were equally vulnerable to Satan's treachery. Therefore, the Lord expected them to abide by the same rules that the rest of the Israelites were required to abide by. That is, of course, if they expected to hold onto and consistently increase in knowledge and righteousness of God.

Yeshua's teaching in Mark 4:24-25 may have evoked yet another question in your mind. You may be wondering what Yeshua meant in verse twenty-five when He said, *"For to him who has will more be given; **and from him who has nothing, even what he has will be taken away.**"* How can understanding of God's Word and righteousness be taken away from a man who does not possess either of those qualities in the first place, a man whom Yeshua Himself says, *"has nothing"*? The best way I know to answer this question is to refer you to the writings of the Jewish man who wrote *The Gospel According to Luke*. For, Luke's brief rendering of Yeshua's previous statement taken from the *Holy Bible, King James Version* sheds a great deal of light on the present subject.

> *Luke 8:18 (King James Version.)*
>
> *18Take heed therefore how ye hear: for whosoever hath, to him shall be given; **and whosoever hath not, from him shall be taken even that which he seemeth to have.***

As you can see with your own eyes, the man in question has nothing. Satan had already cleaned him out. He only **seems** to have knowledge and righteousness. However, he really does not possess those qualities at all. Thus, he loses even what he thinks and supposes that he has. He loses what he **seems** to have but really does not have at all.

Let me give you a Biblical example of men in Yeshua's day who gave the appearance of possessing knowledge and righteousness of God's Word but who really had nothing. Yeshua Himself clearly defines the character of such men in the following verses.

> *Matthew 23:27-28 (The Amplified Bible.)*
>
> *27Woe to you, scribes and Pharisees, pretenders (hypocrites)! For you are like tombs that have been whitewashed, which look beautiful on the outside but inside are full of dead men's bones and everything impure.*
> *28Just so, you also outwardly **seem** to people to be just and upright but inside you are full of pretense and lawlessness and iniquity.*

In the previous verses, Yeshua was speaking against the wicked, ignorant practices of the scribes and Pharisees of His day. He was speaking about men who appeared to be knowledgeable of God's Word, men who appeared to be devoted to God, men who seemed to be righteous but were not. The scribes and Pharisees did not practice what they preached. They spoke of men keeping God's commands while they themselves neglected and discarded God's commands in preference for man-made traditions. The scribes and Pharisees were absolutely void of knowledge of God's Word and the righteousness that God's Word imparts when it is applied to men's lives. Satan had managed to steal the word from them each time they had heard it. Thus, they did not possess understanding of *"the secret things."* And moreover, they did not even possess understanding of *"the things which are revealed."*

I could continue to focus on the hypocritical lives of the religious leaders of Yeshua's day who seemed to possess knowledge and righteousness, yet they had nothing, but it might help you to also see an example of that same problem in the Church.

Some years back, I watched a portion of a Christian Television Program. When I tuned into the show, the host, who was by the way also a Christian minister, was in the process of interviewing his guest for that day. His guest was an older man. He was a missionary, a man who had spent most of his adult life working for the Lord on foreign mission fields.

During the interview, the host made it known that the missionary was also an author. I do not recall the title of the missionary's literary work or the names of either of these men, neither do I remember the exact words that were spoken. However, I vividly recall the incident and the content of what transpired.

The host made a special point of mentioning the missionary's book, commenting on its wonderful content. He proceeded to tell his nationwide television audience how he had himself read the missionary's book and had been amazed and blessed by the profound truths that it contained. Then, to the host's shame, he boasted how he had relayed those same profound truths to his friends, acquaintances, and congregants without telling them that he was really quoting from another man's work. The host then said something to this effect, "People were astounded by the profound truths that I shared with them from your book. They thought that I had suddenly become extremely smart. They commented on how blessed I was that God had seen fit to reveal such marvelous things to me. I have thoroughly enjoyed all the praise and attention that I have received by relaying to others excerpts from your book. I was made to feel very wise and important."

Looking straight at the missionary, the host then said, "I never did tell those people that I was quoting truths that God had really revealed to you. Their praises and admiration made me feel so good that I wanted people to keep on thinking that your words were mine. I didn't share my copy of your book with them either, since they would then have discovered the source from which I had suddenly acquired all my new found wisdom."

After the host had finished speaking, he chuckled, acting as though his sinful behavior had been a big joke. However, I did not notice the missionary laughing with him, and personally, I did not think his comments were at all humorous. I was not in the least amused by that wicked man's insensibility and indifference to God's laws and man's laws or by watching the missionary quietly listening to a fellow Christian minister bragging about how he had dishonestly taken credit, praise and gratitude for information that was not his, credit that actually belonged to the missionary No! No! No! A thousand times no! Sin is no laughing matter. *"For the wages of sin is death."* (Romans 6:23.)

Any informed, righteous person who happened to have been watching that show should have been outraged by the wicked behavior of that host. Think about it! When writing his book, the missionary had probably experienced many days when his work had brought him to the point of weariness or maybe even exhaustion. He may have made tremendous sacrifices so that he could accomplish that work, sacrifices such as giving up precious time with his family and Christian friends in order to seek God for truth. Furthermore, for him to have remained set aside with God, it is entirely probable that he likewise had chosen not to participate in numerous activities that he might ordinarily have enjoyed. Yes, to record that information, he probably made tremendous sacrifices and labored until he was physically and mentally fatigued.

Keeping in mind the points I made in the former paragraph, and the fact that if that man is like most missionaries, he has most likely made monumental sacrifices in order to fulfill God's missionary call on his life, let me ask you a question. How do you think that he must have felt when after he had finally finished writing his book and it had been published, he learned that this dishonest, unrighteous Christian teacher and host had repeatedly stolen from him the deserved credit, gratitude and respect that was due to him for all his sacrifices and wearisome labor?

Now, just in case you might be tempted to reason, "Well, if the missionary really wrote the book for God's glory and since the wisdom he imparted in his book came from God's Word, he should not have felt cheated nor should he have expected anything in return," I think it would be appropriate for me to set the record straight and help you to put things in perspective. So, let us briefly consider the sin against God that is involved in the previous case. Let us also consider the sin that the host (a Christian minister) committed against his Christian brother and fellow minister.

(1) The host broke God's commandment, *"Thou shalt not steal."* Thus, he sinned against God and man. For as 1 John 3:4 in *The Amplified Bible* tells us, sin is the breaking of God's commands, the breaking of God's law. And as you know, *"Thou shalt not steal"* is one of those sacred laws. (Exodus 20:15.)

> *1 John 3:4 (The Amplified Bible.)*
>
> *4Everyone who commits (practices) sin is guilty of lawlessness; for [that is what] sin is, lawlessness (the breaking, violating of God's law by transgression or neglect—being unrestrained and unregulated by His commands and His will).*

a. The host plagiarized another man's work, committing the sin of theft and breaking the law of God and man. Plagiarism is a serious offense. You will recall that in September 1987, it came to light that U.S. Senator Joe Biden had plagiarized another man's speech. Biden was portrayed as a thief on the front page of most U. S. Newspapers. Even U.S. Senators are not exempt from the consequences of plagiarism. Fortunately for Biden, the man whose speech he plagiarized did not press charges, but if he had chosen to do so, he could have.

b. The undeserving host stole the admiration, respect and credit that belonged to another.

(2) The host failed to display God's righteous character. Instead, he proved that he himself was unrighteous by exhibiting insensitivity to and by ignoring his missionary brother's sacrifices and tedious labor so that he could himself selfishly receive undeserved praises, respect and credit from men for work that he had not done and for wisdom that he did not possess. The apostle Paul makes it clear that God would never behave in such a manner. God is not unrighteous. God would never overlook another man's labor and He certainly would not plagiarize another man's written work. Paul said in Hebrews 6:10:

Hebrews 6:10 (The Amplified Bible.)

¹⁰<u>**For God is not unrighteous to forget or overlook your labor**</u> and the love which you have shown for His name's sake in ministering to the needs of the saints (His own consecrated people), as you still do.

The point I am making is that because that TV personality is a professing Christian, a minister, a Bible teacher and the host of a Christian television show, a host who interviews many well-known people in the Christian world, like the scribes and Pharisees in Yeshua's day, he gives the impression that he is a knowledgeable and righteous man. However, also like the scribes and Pharisees, he only **appears** to have understanding of God's Word. He only **seems** to possess righteousness.

The truth is that while the man outwardly appears to be knowledgeable and righteous, he does not even keep the eighth commandment, *"Thou shalt not steal."* The bottom line is that the man is a thief and therefore according to 1 Corinthians 6:9-10, he does not possess the kingdom of God (that is, he does not possess the righteousness of God). He only thinks and supposes that he is a man of understanding and righteousness. He only seems to men to be knowledgeable and righteous while all the time he is not. No! He loves the approval and the praise and the glory that comes from men instead of and more than the glory (the righteousness) that comes from God.

You might feel that I am being unusually hard on that Christian host by saying that because he committed the sin of theft (plagiarism), he does not possess the kingdom of God. However, I am only repeating the truth that Yeshua Himself taught in the verses that we studied earlier in Mark chapter four. Moreover, I am only repeating what the apostle Paul said in the following verses.

1 Corinthians 6:9-10 (King James Version.)

⁹<u>**Know ye not that the unrighteous shall not inherit the kingdom of God? Be not deceived:**</u> neither fornicators, nor idolaters, nor adulterers, nor effeminate, nor abusers of themselves with mankind,

¹⁰<u>**Nor thieves**</u>, nor covetous, nor drunkards, nor revilers, nor extortioners, shall inherit the kingdom of God.

Now you might ask, "But what if the host lived a truly righteous life before he sinned by breaking God's command of *'Thou shalt not steal'*?

Will he still lose the knowledge and righteousness that he acquired throughout his life? And again, should he still be classed as a man who only seems to be righteous but who really is not?"

God's Word clearly answers all three of the questions that I presented in the former paragraph. You will see that under the same conditions (that is, the conditions of stealing and then failing to repent), a man does indeed lose every bit of truth and righteousness that he gained throughout his life. And yes, he does still fall into the category of a man who only seems to be righteous. In the next text, the prophet explains exactly how God views such a man.

Ezekiel 33:12-13 (The Amplified Bible.)

12*And you, son of man, say to your people,* **The uprightness and justice of the [uncompromisingly] righteous shall not deliver him in the day of his transgression;** *and as for the wicked lawlessness of the wicked lawless, he shall not fall because of it in the day that he turns from his wickedness,* **neither shall the rigidly upright and just be able to live because of his past righteousness in the day that he sins and misses the mark [in keeping in harmony and right standing with God].**

13*When I shall say to the [uncompromisingly] righteous that he shall surely live, and he trusts to his own righteousness [to save him] and commits iniquity (heinous sin), all his righteous deeds shall not be [seriously] remembered; but for his perversity and iniquity that he has committed he shall die.*

Because the truth you have just received is so very important, I will briefly sum up the main points to be remembered.

(1) If you commit sin by breaking one of God's commandments and you think that your past righteousness entitles you to preferential treatment, you are deluded. Your past righteousness will not save you from the consequences of your sin. Unless you *"Repent (think differently; change your mind, regretting your sins and changing your conduct),"* you shall die. *"For the wages of sin is death."* Your past righteousness will not be remembered. It will be blotted out of the records. From that point on, the only deeds that will show up on your record will be the sin that you committed for which you failed to repent.

(2) If you commit sin and fail to repent, from that time on you might continue to think and suppose that you are righteous, but according to God's Word you are not righteous at all. Satan stole the word of the kingdom (righteousness) right out of your heart and left you with nothing.

(3) When those who are acquainted with you come to know the truth of God's Word and recognize that you have sinned and failed to truly repent, they immediately become aware that though you appear to men to be righteous, you are not righteous by the standards of God's Word. You do not abide by the new covenant that Yeshua sealed with His own blood. Consequently, once your facade is exposed even the knowledge and righteousness that you seem to have will be taken from you. Men will finally see you through the eyes of God's righteous Word and know that you are not a knowledgeable or a righteous person.

My friend, with the Scriptural insight that you now possess, I am sure you will agree that one way or another, the example of the wicked television host that I shared with you earlier shows a man who gives the appearance of possessing knowledge and righteousness of God's Word but who really has nothing. For, as you have seen in the Scriptures, a man does not have knowledge of God's Word or the righteousness of God (that is, he does not possess the kingdom of God) until he understands and applies to his life the truth that he has heard. According to God's Word, any professing Christian who thinks, speaks and acts as wickedly as that host did is void of the kingdom of God. He is void of the knowledge and righteousness of God. He has broken the blood-sealed new covenant by disobeying God's commands and failing to repent. Satan took the word of the kingdom right out of his heart and left him spiritually impoverished.

After studying Yeshua's warning, Mark 4:24-25, that if His disciples did not pay strict attention to the truth they heard, they would not comprehend God's Word or gain the righteousness that the application of the truth imparts to one's life, nor would they gain additional knowledge and virtue, nor hold onto even what they had or seemed to have, you should now have a better idea of why I emphasized earlier that the disciples were not guaranteed instant knowledge of the secrets of God's Word nor the assurance that they would comprehend them at all. You will recall that even one of the twelve apostles (Judas Iscariot) showed by his conduct that he had not continued to learn the truth nor apply the truth which imparts righteousness to his life. Consequently, he lost everything. Yes, Judas lost even the knowledge and righteousness that he **seemed** to have.

You should now also understand more clearly why I have repeatedly used the terms "force" and "forced." I have continually and deliberately specified that the disciples were required to take and apply to their lives the truth regarding righteousness **by force** (that is, the truth of God's Word which when applied to a man's life produces righteousness). I have continually and deliberately specified those points because as well as the Scriptural evidence that I presented prior to your studying Mark 4:24-25, Yeshua clearly stated in Mark 4:24-25 that the more effort His disciples exerted in their pursuit of spiritual knowledge and righteousness, the more knowledge and righteousness they would be able to acquire.

Furthermore, Yeshua told His disciples that if they failed to put forth an appropriate amount of intellectual interest and effort, they would immediately lose the knowledge and righteousness that they mistakenly thought they had acquired. Why? Because as Yeshua shared in His parable and as He reiterates in verse twenty-five, Satan will immediately come and snatch the word of the kingdom that was sown right out of their hearts. Moreover, what Satan did not take by deception would be either crowded out by worldly pursuits and possessions and so forth or voluntarily relinquished in order to prevent persecution, abuse or discomfort of any kind. Furthermore, they would also lose even what they seemed to have. Yeshua leaves no doubt that if His disciples expected to retain and increase in spiritual knowledge and righteousness, they had to be willing to continually exert themselves in their search for and application of the truth of God's Word (that is, the word of the kingdom).

It should already be apparent to you that Yeshua's disciples did not instantly gain spiritual sight and hearing in regard to *"the secret things."* Rather, their gaining spiritual sight and hearing in that area was a gradual, step-by-step process. In the following verses in *The Amplified Bible*, the writer of *The Gospel According to Luke* provides further verification of that fact.

Luke 8:9-10 (The Amplified Bible.)

9And when His disciples asked Him the meaning of this parable,

10He said to them, To you it has been given to [come progressively to] know (to recognize and understand more strongly and clearly) the mysteries and secrets of the kingdom of God, but for others they are in parables, so that, [though] looking, they may not see; and hearing, they may not comprehend.

Over and over again, Yeshua made it clear that His disciples would not obtain instant knowledge of *"the secret things."* Rather, he plainly states in the previous verses that they would come **progressively** to understand the secrets and mysteries of the kingdom of God (that is, they would **gradually** acquire understanding of the secrets and mysteries of the righteousness of God). Yes, Yeshua continually reinforced the fact that His disciples must consistently, intellectually, physically and emotionally exert themselves so that they could eventually overcome their blind and deaf spiritual disabilities. They must exert themselves in order to understand the truth that He spoke, and they must also exert themselves in order to apply that truth to their lives and thereby retain it. They had to uninterruptedly strive to bring forth the righteous fruit that He spoke of in His parable in Mark 4:20. And, the only way that they could possibly bring forth true righteous fruit was by diligently learning and obeying God's Word (that is, by retaining and by increasing in knowledge and righteousness of the kingdom of God).

We will now pick up where we left off in Mark chapter four where Yeshua relays to His disciples two more parables. As you read both these parables, it is imperative that you keep in mind all that you have learned to this point during your study of Mark 4:1-14. Moreover, so that you will not continue to permit Satan to take from you the word that is sown in your own heart, it is especially important that you remember Yeshua's words in verse thirteen of that text which reads, *"And he said unto them, **Know ye not this parable? and how then will ye know all parables?"***

If you give adequate thought to Yeshua's statement that I cited and expounded on in the former paragraph, His words will begin to make absolute sense to you. Think about it! If you fail to learn and apply to your life the truth that is provided in the parable of the sower, truth that shows you how to defeat Satan, you will never be able to retain and increase in the knowledge and righteousness of God's Word that is found in the other parables. For, you will remain vulnerable to Satan's evil tricks. Under such circumstances, you will not have a chance. You will not realize how or when Satan took from you the truth that was sown in your heart. You will not even be aware that you ever lost that truth or the righteousness that could have been yours if only you had applied the truth to your life.

On the other hand, if you truly understand and have applied to your life *"the secret truth"* contained in the parable of the sower, you will be fully aware of and be continually on guard against Satan's tactics. Therefore, you will strive to understand the truth that you hear. You will not allow Satan to use the disbelief, grumbling, doubt, criticism and so forth of others to deter you from holding on to the truth that was sown in your heart. Neither will you allow yourself to put anything or anyone before learning and obeying God's Word.

In Mark 4:13, Yeshua was explaining to His spiritually disabled disciples that if they failed to understand and apply to their lives the truth that is contained in the parable of the sower, they would never understand His other parables. Of course, included in His other parables were the two illustrations which He later taught them in verses twenty-six through thirty-two of the same chapter.

Yeshua also told His spiritually disabled disciples in Mark 4:24-25 that if they took by force (that is, if they paid strict attention to the word of the kingdom and seized understanding of the truth that they heard and immediately applied it to their lives), more understanding and righteousness would be given to them. In other words, if upon intellectually exerting themselves, they truly received, understood and applied by force the truth about the kingdom of God that they had learned in the parable of the sower to their lives by obeying it, they would then be in a position to exert themselves even further and to gradually seize by force understanding of Yeshua's other parables. They would retain and increase in knowledge and righteousness. For they would understand the secret to holding on to the word that was sown in their hearts. Of course, it goes without saying that the aforementioned understanding would include their understanding the two parables that He was about to share with them.

Remember now, the whole thrust of Yeshua's teachings, including the parable of the sower, was specifically channeled toward encouraging His disciples to exert themselves in their search for and application of the truth contained in God's righteous Word. You will recall that the application of the truth of God's Word to a man's life is what produces the fruit of the kingdom of God that is spoken of in Mark 4:20 (that is, it produces in a man's life the righteousness of God). Thus, the more knowledge and righteousness Yeshua's disciples gain by understanding and applying to their lives the truth of God's Word the more knowledge and righteousness they will be able to acquire. Consequently, they will produce more fruit of the kingdom (righteousness). Thus, with the new covenant power that Yeshua won for mankind, the Lord's true disciples will understand and obey *"the things which are revealed"* (God's laws), and they will also gradually come to understand and align their lives to *"the secret things."*

My friend, did you seize understanding of the parable of the sower and apply the truth you learned to your own life? If you did, then assuming you keep the next two parables in the context in which Yeshua intended they remain and, if when necessary, you call up the information you learned in the parable of the sower and provided you pay strict attention to what Yeshua is teaching you in the two previously mentioned illustrations, you cannot help but understand those two parables.

You must not, however, forget the rest of Yeshua's warning in chapter four of Mark's gospel. For, you will recall that Yeshua also explained to His disciples that if they did not **continue** to exert themselves in their pursuit of the knowledge and righteousness of God, they would lose the knowledge and righteousness that they had.

In the following parables, Yeshua is simply reiterating those things which He had already taught in verses ten through twenty-five of our present text. **He is emphasizing retainment and increase. He is speaking about His "good ground Jewish disciples" holding on to the word by force that was sown in their hearts, gradually overcoming their spiritual handicaps and increasing in the knowledge and righteousness of God (that is, the knowledge and righteousness of the kingdom of God).** He is speaking about His "good ground Jewish disciples" continually growing in understanding and consistently applying to their lives the truth of God's Word that they have zealously seized until they actually develop the same righteous character as their Creator and are fulfilling the full original purpose for their existence. (Ecclesiastes 12:13.) Yeshua is speaking about His "good ground Jewish disciples" exhibiting the righteousness of God (that is, exhibiting the kingdom of God) in every aspect of their lives and in every situation. See these truths for yourself in Yeshua's parable in the following verses taken from the *Holy Bible, King James Version.*

Mark 4:26-32 (King James Version.)

26And he said, So is the kingdom of God, as if a man should cast seed into the ground;

27And should sleep, and rise night and day, and the seed should spring and grow up, he knoweth not how.

28For the earth bringeth forth fruit of herself; first the blade, then the ear, after that the full corn in the ear.

29But when the fruit is brought forth, immediately he putteth in the sickle, because the harvest is come.

The seed is the word of the kingdom (that is, the word of righteousness) which is sown in the hearts of men. The word in this case is sown on good ground, and therefore it sprouts and slowly grows to maturity (that is, once established the seed sprouts, and the sprouts force their way up through the darkness of the soil into the light where they continue to gradually develop, increasing in size until they produce the full fruit).

"Good ground Jewish disciples" come progressively to understand what being righteous really entails and how they can obtain and hold onto the righteousness of God. Once they grasp the fact that they must force themselves to comprehend and apply the truth they have heard to their lives, and they do it, they soon excel in that area. They force their way through the intellectual darkness of their blind and deaf spiritual handicaps as the seed forces its way through the soil. They push and push until they eventually break through into the light and can see clearly. They will not allow Satan to take the word from them.

In time, these "good ground Jewish disciples" produce ripe (that is, mature) fruit. They think right, speak right and act right by the standards of God's Word in every area of their life and in every situation that arises. Yet, as you can see in Mark 4:27, the man who sowed that seed has no idea how it is possible for God's spiritually blind and deaf covenant people to overcome their severe spiritual disabilities, make themselves comprehend the secrets and mysteries of Yeshua's parables and recognize Him as the Messiah. But it is possible. For as Yeshua said in verse twenty-eight, *"the earth bringeth forth fruit of herself"* (that is, the life into which the word was sown and zealously retained produces fruit of itself). Thus, when it is time for the reaping, these amazing Jewish disciples stand ready to be harvested and gathered into the Lord's storehouse. They gradually develop in holiness of character until they are finally performing the full function for which they were created. They consistently fear God and obey all His commandments. Their righteous lives reveal the fact that they are indeed true children of the kingdom of God. Yes, they show to all that they are indeed true children of the righteousness of God. For, through the blood-sealed new covenant that Yeshua gave His life to provide, they perform the full original purpose for their existence.

Concentrate now on the Lord's next parable and with the insight you have received to this point in the series, see if you yourself can interpret its meaning. We will read the next mystery from the *Holy Bible, King James Version.*

> *Mark 4:30-34 (King James Version.)*
>
> *[30]And he said, whereunto shall we liken the kingdom of God? Or with what comparison shall we compare it?*
>
> *[31]It is like a grain of mustard seed, which, when it is sown in the earth, is less than all the seeds that be in the earth:*
>
> *[32]But when it is sown, it groweth up, and becometh greater than all herbs, and shooteth out great branches; so that the fowls of the air may lodge under the shadow of it.*
>
> *[33]And with many such parables spake he the word unto them, as they were able to hear it.*
>
> *[34]But without a parable spake he not unto them: and when they were alone, he expounded all things to his disciples.*

Yeshua compares the kingdom of God (the righteousness of God) to a mustard seed for numerous reasons, two of which I will share with you.

(1) Yeshua symbolically compared the kingdom of God to a tree-like mustard plant which according to some sources can reach up to fifteen feet in height. Yeshua made that comparison because God had already decreed through His prophets that the Israelites would one day be called *"trees of righteousness."* Notice the doubly highlighted portion of the following verse from the *Holy Bible, King James Version.*

> *Isaiah 61:3 (King James Version.)*
>
> *[3]To appoint unto them that mourn __in Zion__, to give unto them beauty for ashes, the oil of joy for mourning, the garment of praise for the spirit of heaviness; __that they might be called trees of righteousness, the planting of the Lord__, that he might be glorified.*

(2) Yeshua made that particular comparison because when planted in good ground both the word of the kingdom (that is, the word of righteousness) and the mustard seed are extremely tiny. However, each of them slowly increases in size until, upon reaching full maturity, both

are exceptionally great in stature. Moreover, in both cases, others derive enormous benefit from the extensiveness of their overall development.

The word of the kingdom of God is sown on good ground in the heart of a man. In the beginning, to the natural eye, the man's limited degree of knowledge and righteousness seems relatively insignificant. Like the tiny mustard seed, it often goes unnoticed by those around him. Even the man himself may not be aware of the changes that are slowly taking place in his own character as he continues to hold onto more and more of God's Word by understanding the truth and applying it to his life. Thus, for a time, he has very little, if any, influence or effect on the lives of others.

The day comes, however, when like the mustard seed, the "good ground disciple" forces his way through the darkness that handicaps his development. He fights with everything in him to hold onto the Word of God that was sown in his heart. Thus, the light of God's Word shines brightly in his heart, and he starts to grow spiritually. Just as the earth brings forth fruit of herself so does the man produce fruit of himself. As the man increases in knowledge of God's Word and consistently applies to his life the truth that he has learned (that is, as he allows God's Word to grow and take control of his life), the sheer magnitude of his righteousness can no longer be overlooked. The significance, the greatness, the extent of the righteousness that he possesses through applying the truth to his life soon becomes evident to all. It cannot be hidden. Furthermore, his truly righteous life towers above the lives of those who beforehand seemed to be great in righteousness, but who never did learn to hold onto the word that was sown in their hearts and consistently think right, speak right and do right by the standards of God's Word.

Before the "good ground disciple" realizes what has happened, he emerges a fully mature son of the kingdom of God. He is great in the kingdom of God, great in righteousness. He has developed the righteous character of God (that is, he consistently thinks right, speaks right and does right by the standards of God's Word). In every area of his life and in every situation that arises, the man exhibits righteousness and glorifies God by obeying God's commands. As Ephesians 4:13 in *The Amplified Bible* puts it, he has arrived *"at really mature manhood [the completeness of personality which is nothing less than the standard height of Christ's own perfection], the measure of the stature of the fullness of the Christ and the completeness found in Him."*

Rather than allowing ignorant, contentious, unbelieving men to influence him for evil or to be detrimental to his spiritual growth as many of Yeshua's "wayside disciples" did in John 6:47-63, 66, this spiritually mature, uncompromisingly righteous man influences others to continue to do right. Furthermore, his brethren derive spiritual benefit from his righteous life. During their own pilgrimage to maturity of character, they know they can safely lodge temporarily in the branches of this righteous tree. They know from reading God's Word and from personal experience that a truly righteous man will only do them good since he will always do what is right by the standards of God's Word.

As the Jewish apostle Paul did in Ephesians 4:13, so will the righteous man encourage others to keep learning and obeying God's commands until they too reach *"the standard height of Christ's own perfection."* Yes, the man who is great in righteousness always encourages others to continue to pursue and to seize more and more knowledge and righteousness of God. Furthermore, he provides for others the kind of righteous example that will help them to also attain greatness in the kingdom of God.

To be sure, this righteous man's brethren find temporary spiritual shelter under his shadow. To put it plainly, his brethren are deeply affected by the truly righteous example that this man projects. They are influenced by the way his righteous thought process works and by His knowledge of *"the things which are revealed"* and of *"the secret things"* and by the truth that he speaks and by the exemplary righteous manner in which he conducts every aspect of his life. They are influenced by the fact that this uncompromisingly righteous man fears God and consistently keeps all God's commandments.

How beautiful is the truth contained in Yeshua's parables! And, how sad it is that most of God's precious spiritually blind and deaf Jewish people were and still are unable to comprehend the incredible secrets that are hidden in these revealing illustrations of the kingdom of God. For example, because the Jews' lack of understanding allowed Satan to take from them the word that was sown regarding the parable of the sower, they did not and do not know how to defend themselves from his future attacks. They were and are unable to understand the secret truth that Yeshua taught in the text that we will read shortly.

What is even worse is that neither does the Church as a whole fully understand the true meaning of the parable of the sower or the words of Yeshua in the following verses. For, if the Church really understood the secrets and mysteries of the kingdom of God contained in Yeshua's teachings, they would understand and abide by the blood-sealed new covenant and utilize the power it provides to keep all God's commandments. Yet, by her disobedient actions, it is evident that the

Church does not understand what the new covenant entails, nor does the Church keep all of God's commandments.

The Church does not even keep all the Ten Commandments. For, as you know, most Christians refuse to keep the fourth commandment. They also refuse to repent (that is, they refuse to think differently; changing their mind, regretting their sins and changing their conduct). Like the Jews in the following text, the Church has allowed Satan to rob them of understanding of *"the things which are revealed."* So, how can they retain and increase in knowledge and righteousness of the kingdom of God or its mysteries and secrets when Satan has taken the word of the kingdom out of their hearts, and they are too ignorant to even realize that it is gone. It is all so heartbreaking. To think that the Church has access to so much and yet has nothing.

Read Yeshua's words for yourself in the succeeding verses, and you will see that all that I said in the former paragraph is true. Of course, as you read, you must keep in mind that the kingdom of God is righteousness and that knowledge and righteousness only becomes yours (that is, knowledge and righteousness is only retained and increases in your life) when you learn the truth and consistently think right, speak right and do right by the standards of God's Word (that is, when you learn and obey all God's written commandments and hold onto the word of the kingdom with all your might).

Matthew 5:17-20 (King James Version.)

17Think not that I am come to destroy the law, or the prophets: I am not come to destroy, but to fulfil.

18For verily I say unto you, Till heaven and earth pass, one jot or one tittle shall in no wise pass from the law, till all be fulfilled.

19Whosoever therefore shall break one of these least commandments, and shall teach men so, <u>he shall be called the least in the kingdom of heaven</u>: but whosoever shall do and teach them, <u>the same shall be called great in the kingdom of heaven</u>.

20For I say unto you, that <u>except your righteousness shall exceed the righteousness of the scribes and Pharisees, ye shall in no case enter into the kingdom of heaven.</u>

In *Smith's Bible Dictionary* under the heading "Ten Commandments," speaking of the Law of the Ten Commandments, the Bible scholar Smith says,

> (5) It was complete, being one finished whole, to which nothing was to be added, from which nothing was ever taken away.

> (6) The Law of the Ten Commandments was honored by Jesus Christ as embodying the substance of the law of God enjoined upon man.

> (7) It can scarcely be doubted that Jesus had His eye especially if not exclusively on this law, Matt. 5:18, as *one never to be repealed,* from which not one jot or tittle should ever pass away.

It is clear that in the former text, Matthew 5:17-20, Yeshua is speaking mainly about the Ten Commandments of God. In verse nineteen, he warns the Jewish people that if they break what they consider to be the least one of God's sacred Ten Commandments and they teach others that they do not have to keep it either, that commandment will not be called least in the kingdom of God, **but they will**. Men and angels will proclaim that they are lacking in the righteousness of God. To put it Scripturally, **they are least in the kingdom of God! They are least in righteousness!**

On the other hand, Yeshua also tells the Jews in verse nineteen that if they obey all ten of *"them"* (plural) and teach others to obey *"them,"* they will be called great in the kingdom of God, great in righteousness. As you learned earlier, they will be as the tree-like mustard plant in Yeshua's parable. They will be great in spiritual stature, and men will lodge temporarily in their branches and under their shadow.

In verse twenty, Yeshua sternly warns that if their righteousness (that is, if their right thinking, right speaking and right acting by the standards of God's Word) does not exceed the righteousness of the scribes and the Pharisees, they will never enter the kingdom of God. This makes perfect sense, since you saw earlier that the scribes and Pharisees only seemed to be righteous, but they were not. Do you remember Paul's warning in 1 Corinthians 6:9? He said, *"Know ye not that the unrighteous"* (that is, know ye not that those who break God's commandments, those who refuse to do right by the standards of God's Word) *"shall not inherit the kingdom of God."*

Think about what Yeshua is saying to the Jews in the former verses, Matthew 5:17-20. You will recall that when it came to His laws (commandments), God did not spiritually handicap His people or the scribes and the Pharisees. On the contrary, God gave the Jewish people ample spiritual understanding in the area of His laws. However, the religious leaders in Yeshua's day, had fallen into the same trap that their ancestors before them had fallen into. While trying to improve on the clarity of God's law, they too had changed the true intent of His commandments. They were no longer keeping God's Ten Commandments. Man-made rules and regulations and the traditions of the elders had replaced God's righteous Ten Commandments. Consequently, the scribes and the Pharisees relaxed God's commandments, and by word and deed, they taught others to do the same.

Since the scribes and Pharisees refused to obey God's commandments themselves or teach their Jewish brethren to obey them, since they refused to think right, speak right or do right by the standards of God's Word, how could they enter the kingdom of God (that is, how could they enter the righteousness of God)? One who is unrighteous cannot be a component or part of the righteousness of God. How can unrighteous people who absolutely refuse to acknowledge true righteousness even begin to embark on the journey toward righteousness, never mind be a part of it? See for yourself in the *Holy Bible, King James Version*, how the religious leaders of Israel cast God's righteous laws (God's Ten Commandments) from them and replaced them with man-made traditions. Notice specifically the highlighted portions of the following verses.

Matthew 15:1-9 (King James Version.)

[1]*THEN came to Jesus scribes and Pharisees, which were of Jerusalem, saying,*

[2]*Why do thy disciples transgress__ the tradition of the elders__? for they wash not their hands when they eat bread.*

[3]*But he answered and said unto them, __Why do ye also transgress the commandment of God by your tradition?__*

4For God commanded, saying, Honour thy father and mother: and, He that curseth father or mother, let him die the death.

5But ye say, Whosoever shall say to his father or his mother, It is a gift, by whatsoever thou mightest be profited by me;

*6And honour not his father or his mother, he shall be free. **Thus have ye made the commandment of God of none effect by your tradition.***

7Ye hypocrites, well did Esaias prophesy of you, saying,

8This people draweth nigh unto me with their mouth, and honoureth me with their lips; but their heart is far from me.

9But in vain they do worship me, teaching for doctrines the commandments of men.

As you saw earlier, God had given the Jewish people abundant understanding of *"the things which are revealed"* (that is, God's righteous commandments). However, the scribes and the Pharisees consciously chose to obey the traditions and commandments of men rather than God's righteous Ten Commandments even as many Christians today choose to obey the man-made traditions of the Church rather than God's commandments. Consequently, as you learned in Ezekiel 33:12-13, the scribes and Pharisees were void of understanding and righteousness. They were void of the kingdom of God. They were those who appeared to possess knowledge of God's Word and righteousness, but they really had nothing. They did not even possess understanding of *"the things which are revealed,"* never mind knowledge of *"the secret things."* They were hypocrites (pretenders). Therefore, unless the scribes and the Pharisees repented and began to truly seek to do right by the standards of God's Word, they would never enter the kingdom of God (that is, they would never enter into the righteousness of God). For as I said earlier, unrighteousness cannot be a component or part of righteousness. Furthermore, as the Jewish apostle John said in 1 John 3:7 in the *Holy Bible, King James Version,* **"...*let no man deceive you: he that doeth righteousness is righteous, even as he"* (God) *"is righteous."*** Like all Jews, the scribes and Pharisees were not held accountable for their inability to understand *"the secret things."* But rightly so, they were most certainly accountable for learning and obeying *"the things which are revealed."*

My friend, you should now comprehend what Yeshua was really saying in Matthew 5:20. You should be fully aware that Yeshua was warning His people that if their righteousness, their knowledge of and obedience to God's commandments, did not exceed the righteousness of the religious leaders in Matthew chapter five, they would never enter the kingdom of God. They would never enter the kingdom of God because like those scribes and Pharisees, they too would be totally void of righteousness. Also, like the scribes and Pharisees, they would have chosen men's traditions over true knowledge and righteousness of God that is clearly described on the pages of God's holy Word. So, in their unrighteous condition, how in the world could they possibly have entered the kingdom of God (that is, how could they possibly have entered the righteousness of God)?

After studying chapter fourteen of this book, that is of course if you paid strict attention to God's Word and applied the truth you learned to your life, you will appreciate and understand more clearly the urgency and importance of Yeshua's next statement from *The Amplified Bible*.

Matthew 6:33 (The Amplified Bible.)

33 But seek (aim at and strive after) first of all His kingdom and His righteousness (His way of doing and being right), and then all these things taken together will be given you besides.

Over and over again, Yeshua described in His teachings and parables the righteousness of God. He described God's way of doing and being right (that is, Yeshua described the kingdom of God). Furthermore, Yeshua repeatedly showed His Jewish brethren the only way that they could ever truly possess the kingdom of God. First, they must seek as their necessity of life the righteousness that comes from understanding and applying *"the things which are revealed"* (that is, God's laws). Secondly, they must continuously intellectually exert themselves. They must force themselves to overcome their God-ordained spiritual handicaps. They must desire the truth of God's Word insofar as *"the secret things"* are concerned and the righteousness that would become theirs if they forcibly learned and applied that truth to their lives, truth such as the Scriptural method of keeping Satan from taking away the word that is sown in their hearts. They must *"[come progressively to] know (to recognize and understand more strongly and*

clearly) the mysteries and secrets of the kingdom of God." (Luke 8:10, *The Amplified Bible.*)

In chapter fourteen, part five, among many other marvelous truths, you have seen why only those Jews who intellectually exerted themselves came to understand *"the secret things."* You have also received overwhelming Scriptural confirmation as to the criteria that has to be met in order for a Jew to retain and increase in spiritual understanding of the secret truth that is hidden in the Messiah's parables. He must learn and obey the truth contained in the parable of the sower so that he can defeat Satan's attempts to take out of his heart the word contained in all the other parables. Thus, you now know beyond doubt why only a small percentage of Jews have managed to gain spiritual sight and hearing while the rest of the Jewish nation has remained totally blind and deaf to *"the secret things."*

You now know the answer to the question "Why Did The Jews Fail To Recognize The Messiah?" It was their God-ordained spiritual handicaps that kept them from recognizing the Messiah and from understanding *"the secret things"* that He taught. Most of the Jews were too spiritually blind and deaf to understand Yeshua's parables, and thus, they were unable to learn how to keep Satan from stealing the word out of their hearts as fast as it was sown.

In parts six and seven of chapter fourteen, you will receive even more marvelous insight on the present subject. And if you have managed to retain the word of the kingdom that has already been sown in your heart during this series, I know that you will want to continue to increase in the previously mentioned available Scriptural knowledge.

Chapter 14
Part Six

WHY DID THE JEWS FAIL
TO RECOGNIZE THE MESSIAH?

The information contained in part six of chapter fourteen is very important to our present topic. It is important because it reveals the depth of the Jews' God-imposed handicaps and provides added confirmation regarding the extremely slow progress that Yeshua's disciples made in understanding the mystery of the kingdom of God.

As you now know, Yeshua was fully aware of the extent of His disciples' spiritual handicaps. Therefore, He knew that any future advancement that they made toward overcoming their comprehensive disabilities would be accomplished slowly and with great difficulty on their part. Yet, despite His awareness of their spiritual learning disabilities, He still did not want them to give Satan any opportunity to take out of their hearts the word that was sown.

At times, Yeshua became exasperated with His disciples' inability to understand the things that He had told them and the meaning of His miracles. In the following Scriptural text which you will soon read, you will catch a glimpse of the extent of the disciples' slow progression in grasping and discerning the truth that Yeshua taught and in understanding the meaning of His miracles. You will also see an example of Yeshua's frustration with His disciples' still sluggish spiritual thought processes.

We are informed in Mark 8:1-9 that Yeshua performed an amazing feat. He miraculously fed four thousand people with seven loaves of bread and a few small fish. Astoundingly, after those four thousand people had eaten from that tiny food supply, there were seven very large baskets of scraps left over.

Soon after Yeshua had miraculously multiplied the loaves and fish, a group of Jewish religious leaders approached Him. The following verses describe what transpired next. As you read the subsequent verses from *The Living Bible*, keep in mind what I said earlier about the disciples' slow and difficult progression in perceiving the truth that Yeshua taught and their equally slow progression in understanding the meaning of the miracles that He performed.

Mark 8:10-21 (The Living Bible.)

10Immediately after this he got into a boat with his disciples and came to the region of Dalmanutha.

11When the local Jewish leaders learned of his arrival they came to argue with him. "Do a miracle for us," they said. "Make something happen in the sky. Then we will believe in you."

12He sighed deeply when he heard this and he said, "Certainly not. How many more miracles do you people need?"

13So he got back into the boat and left them, and crossed to the other side of the lake.

14But the disciples had forgotten to stock up on food before they left, and had only one loaf of bread in the boat.

15As they were crossing, <u>Jesus said to them very solemnly, "Beware of the yeast of King Herod and of the Pharisees."</u>

16"What does he mean?" the disciples asked each other. They finally decided that he must be talking about their forgetting to bring bread.

17Jesus realized what they were discussing and said, <u>"No, that isn't it at all! Can't you understand? Are your hearts too hard to take it in?</u>

18<u>'Your eyes are to see with—why don't you look? Why don't you open your ears and listen?' Don't you remember anything at all?"</u>

19"What about the 5,000 men I fed with five loaves of bread? How many basketfuls of scraps did you pick up afterwards?" "Twelve," they said.

20"And when I fed the 4,000 with seven loaves, how much was left?" "Seven basketfuls," they said.

21"And yet you think I'm worried that we have no bread?"

Verse twenty-one in *The Amplified Bible* reads,

21<u>And He kept repeating, Do you not yet understand?</u>

The reason why Yeshua got so frustrated with His disciples and kept repeating *"Do you not yet understand"* was because He knew that if they did not understand the word of the kingdom that was sown in their hearts, Satan would quickly take it from them.

By now, it should be clear to you that the disciples' comprehensive progress did not come easily or quickly. Rather, it was an extremely slow and exacting process. You might say that for some time, the disciples' spiritual eyesight remained **partially** distorted. However, we do know that in God's perfect timing the disciples' diminished clarity in perception cleared up, leaving them with 20/20 spiritual vision.

In the meantime however, can you imagine what it must have been like for Yeshua to have had to deal with the spiritually dull minds of His own disciples? Coping with their spiritual learning disabilities and their cognitive sluggishness had to have been an immensely trying and difficult chore for Him. Yet, Yeshua knew that His disciples had real spiritual learning disabilities and that they had to learn how to gradually completely overcome those handicaps. He also knew that it would be some time before they would finally develop 20/20 spiritual vision and A-1 spiritual hearing.

In the meantime, as you learned in an earlier segment of chapter fourteen and as I mentioned a few moments ago, whenever Yeshua's disciples failed to comprehend His sayings or the meaning of the miracles that He performed, any secrets, mysteries and Biblical predictions that He voiced or exhibited remained hidden from them. Therefore, in order to help His disciples to eventually fully correct this problem, Yeshua continued to exhort them and to repetitiously drum home to them the necessity of their paying close attention to all that He said and did.

You may want to read another Biblical account of the Jews' spiritual blindness and the disciples slow cognitive progress. If you do, read Mark 7:6-23.

When in the next verses Yeshua spoke to His disciples regarding His future death by crucifixion, they were totally unable to grasp the magnitude of the secret truth about the kingdom of God that He had communicated to them. For as you now know, at that time, their mental capacity to understand spiritual matters concerning *"the secret things"* was still impaired. They had not yet come to comprehend the deep inner meaning of the prophets' predictions regarding the Messiah's future death and resurrection. However, on this particular occasion, Yeshua's disciples were afraid to let Him know that they had not understood His words. Obviously they were afraid to ask Yeshua the meaning of His statement because they did not want to risk another of His stern rebukes for once again failing to pay close enough attention to His teachings. Nor did they want to appear to be stupid.

After Yeshua's death and resurrection, His disciples finally did recall and fully understand the content of Yeshua's prediction regarding His death. However, by that time, they were viewing those events with hindsight, but most of all, the promised blood-sealed new covenant knowledge, understanding, and power was at last available to them. Look now to the Scriptures and see for yourself an in-depth glimpse of the disciples' inability to comprehend the Lord's words on that occasion.

> *Luke 9:43-45 (The Amplified Bible.)*
>
> *[43]And all were astounded at the evidence of God's mighty power and His majesty and magnificence. But [while] they were all marveling at everything Jesus was doing, He said to His disciples,*
>
> *[44]Let these words sink into your ears: the Son of Man is about to be delivered into the hands of men [whose conduct is opposed to God].*
>
> *[45]However, they did not comprehend this saying; and it was kept hidden from them, so that they should not grasp it and understand, and they were afraid to ask Him about the statement.*

Notice in Luke 9:45 that what Yeshua had previously told His disciples would happen, if they failed to comprehend His words, did happen. In this instance, the secrets that He revealed to them remained hidden so that they should not understand them. Those who insist that Yeshua did not want His disciples to understand His statement in the previous verses have obviously not paid close enough attention to Yeshua's words. **For, in verse forty-four, Yeshua clearly instructed His disciples to pay attention to what He was about to say so that they would understand His words. His exact statement was,** *"Let these words sink into your ears."*

Imagine the problem that the rest of the Jews must have faced when Yeshua's own disciples continued to have difficulty understanding His parables, teachings, predictions and miracles even after He had instructed them to pay attention to His words. The Jews as a whole were completely blind and deaf regarding the mysteries and secrets of God's Word, including the prophets' predictions of the Messiah's inevitable death by crucifixion. Therefore, it was especially hard for them to comprehend the fact that the Messiah would be put to death.

Let me give you an example of what I mean. We will read from *The Living Bible*. As we do, notice that I have inserted an additional reference for your benefit at the end of verse thirty-one.

> *John 12:12-41 (The Living Bible.)*
>
> *12The next day, the news that Jesus was on the way to Jerusalem swept through the city, and a huge crowd of Passover visitors*
>
> *13took palm branches and went down the road to meet him, shouting, "The Savior! God bless the King of Israel! Hail to God's Ambassador!"*
>
> *14Jesus rode along on a young donkey, fulfilling the prophecy that said:*
>
> *15"Don't be afraid of your King, people of Israel, for he will come to you meekly, sitting on a donkey's colt!" [Zech.9:9]*
>
> *16(His disciples didn't realize at the time that this was a fulfillment of prophecy; but after Jesus returned to his glory in heaven, then they noticed how many prophecies of Scripture had come true before their eyes.)*

Notice in verse sixteen that despite the fact that Yeshua was literally fulfilling the prophet's exact words in Zechariah 9:9, the disciples still did not recognize that Zechariah's prophesy had come to pass right in front of them. Consider the degree of spiritual blindness and deafness that the disciples still must have been dealing with at that time for them to have actually witnessed Zechariah's prediction being fulfilled before their eyes and still not have perceived its meaning. Moreover, you will soon see that the rest of the Jews were in an even worse blind and deaf spiritual state than the disciples were.

> *17And those in the crowd who had seen Jesus call Lazarus back to life were telling all about it.*
>
> *18That was the main reason why so many went out to meet him—because they had heard about this mighty miracle.*
>
> *19Then the Pharisees said to each other, "We've lost. Look—the whole world has gone after him!"*

²⁰*Some Greeks who had come to Jerusalem to attend the Passover*

²¹*paid a visit to Philip, who was from Bethsaida, and said, "Sir, we want to meet Jesus."*

²²*Philip told Andrew about it, and they went together to ask Jesus.*

^{23,24}*Jesus replied that the time had come for him to return to his glory in heaven, and that "I must fall and die like a kernel of wheat that falls into the furrows of the earth. Unless I die I will be alone—a single seed. But my death will produce many new wheat kernels—a plentiful harvest of new lives.*

²⁵*If you love your life down here—you will lose it. If you despise your life down here—you will exchange it for eternal glory.*

²⁶*"If these Greeks want to be my disciples, tell them to come and follow me, for my servants must be where I am. And if they follow me, the Father will honor them.*

²⁷*Now my soul is deeply troubled. Shall I pray, 'Father, save me from what lies ahead'? But that is the very reason why I came!*

²⁸*Father, bring glory and honor to your name." Then a voice spoke from heaven saying, "I have already done this, and I will do it again."*

²⁹*When the crowd heard the voice, some of them thought it was thunder, while others declared an angel had spoken to him.*

³⁰*Then Jesus told them, "The voice was for your benefit, not mine.*

³¹*The time of judgment for the world has come — and the time when Satan, the prince of this world, shall be cast out.* [Genesis 3:15]

³²*And when I am lifted up [on the cross], I will draw everyone to me."*

³³*He said this to indicate how he was going to die.*

³⁴*"Die?" asked the crowd. "We understood that the Messiah would live forever and never die. Why are you saying he will die? What Messiah are you talking about?"*

35Jesus replied, "My light will shine out for you just a little while longer. Walk in it while you can, and go where you want to go before the darkness falls, for then it will be too late for you to find your way.

36Make use of the Light while there is still time; then you will become light bearers." After saying these things, Jesus went away and was hidden from them.

37But despite all the miracles he had done, most of the people would not believe he was the Messiah.

38This is exactly what Isaiah the prophet had predicted: "Lord, who will believe us? Who will accept God's mighty miracles as proof?"

39But they couldn't believe, for as Isaiah also said:

40"God has blinded their eyes and hardened their hearts so that they can neither see nor understand nor turn to me to heal them."

41Isaiah was referring to Jesus when he made this prediction, for he had seen a vision of the Messiah's glory.

Let me repeat a segment of the previous text that is most relevant to the point that I am making at this time. Also, to remind you of what you learned earlier in the series, I will again add the same Scripture reference at the end of verse thirty-one.

31The time of judgment for the world has come—and the time when Satan, the prince of this world, shall be cast out. [Genesis 3:15]

32And when I am lifted up [on the cross], I will draw everyone to me."

33He said this to indicate how he was going to die.

34"Die?" asked the crowd. "We understood that the Messiah would live forever and never die. Why are you saying he will die? What Messiah are you talking about?"

Consider the spiritual dilemma of God's chosen covenant people. God had already struck them spiritually blind and deaf insofar as *"the secret things"* were concerned. Then, to ensure that they remained blind and deaf until God's appointed time, the Messiah, *"Immanuel [God with us],"* taught them in parables so that they should not grasp and understand the secrets and mysteries of the kingdom of God. On top of all that, as the prophets had foretold, the Jews were unable to recognize the Messiah or comprehend God's Biblical future predictions or the signs of the times.

Even the conditions surrounding Yeshua's birth were designed by God to keep the Jews from recognizing Him as the Messiah. For generations men have wondered why the King of Kings, *"Immanuel [God with us],"* was born in such humble circumstances. Why was our King not born in a palace or at least into a wealthy, influential family. Over the years Christian teachers have done their best to explain this phenomenon. Their explanations have ranged from reasonable to totally outrageous.

We know that Yeshua had to fulfill the prophet's predictions. We also know that in II Corinthians 8:9, Paul told the Church in Corinth that though Yeshua was so very rich, <u>to help us, He became poor so that by being poor He could make us rich</u>. Of course, Paul is referring to Yeshua making us rich spiritually, rich in faith, rich in the true riches. Yet, neither of these truths reveal why it was necessary for Yeshua to be born poor in order to extend those blessings to us. Why could He not be born wealthy and still bestow such rich spiritual blessings upon us?

In a nutshell, it was necessary that Yeshua be born in such humble circumstances so that the Jews as a nation would not recognize Him as the promised Messiah.

If Yeshua had been born into the royal household, many Jews would have been encouraged to venerate Him solely for the position He held. He would have had instant popularity and a huge following simply because He was a member of the ruling family. Under such circumstances as these, it would have been easy for the Jewish nation to believe that He was the promised Messiah who would deliver them from their enemies. To the natural eye, He would have been in a perfect position to do so. Thus, to ensure that the Jewish nation remained blind and deaf to *"the secret things"* and unable to recognize Him as the Messiah, Yeshua was born into a poor, inconspicuous, insignificant family. In those humble surroundings He grew to manhood, while at the same time, His presence remained relatively unknown by the majority of the Jewish people. In His hometown, Nazareth, He was known simply as Yeshua, the carpenter's son. As Isaiah predicted in the following verse, there would be nothing about the Messiah that would cause the Jews to desire Him. This was God's plan, and it worked. The Messiah's birth went unnoticed by the nation of Israel.

By being born poor, He was more easily able to carry out God's salvation plan (that is, He was able to fulfill God's predictions and the

Abrahamic covenant promises). He managed to accomplish all that the Scriptures required of Him and at the same time do nothing that would cause the Jews **as a nation** to see *"the secret things"* or to recognize Him as the Messiah. As you will learn in chapter fourteen, part seven, the Jews must remain spiritually handicapped until the full number of the ingathering of the Gentiles have come in. (Romans 11:25.) Thus, Paul tells the Gentiles in the Corinthian Church that Yeshua deliberately became poor so that they could become rich, rich in such priceless things as salvation, faith, and the character qualities of God.

I think you will agree with me that insofar as *"the secret things"* were concerned, the deck was stacked against the nation of Israel. No matter which way they turned, as a nation, they were deliberately restricted from acquiring spiritual insight and understanding in those areas. And yet, despite Israel's debilitating blind and deaf spiritual condition, some individuals displayed extraordinary fortitude. Yeshua reveals how from the time John the Baptist first began to preach, certain Jews were so consistently desirous of truth and righteousness that through pure mental and emotional exertion and against all the odds they gradually overcame their spiritual learning disabilities in order to fulfill those longings.

Incredibly, these amazing Jews forced themselves to give their absolute attention to the truth they heard until their persistence finally paid off. They intellectually strained and struggled every step of the way until they gradually came to understand the spiritual mysteries and secrets of the kingdom of God. Yes, they gradually came to understand the truth and apply to their lives the righteousness that the truth imparts.

I stand amazed at the incredible zeal and resolution of these courageous Jews, Jews that I mentioned in the preceding paragraphs and whom Yeshua identifies in the following verse. I stand amazed because these Jews were so completely intent on seeking and finding truth and righteousness that even their God-imposed blindness and deafness could not restrict their pursuit of or deprive them from acquiring *"the secret things."*

For generations, men have been trying to figure out what Yeshua really meant in the following verse. But thanks be to God, with the insight that you have received in this chapter, you are now fully equipped with the knowledge you need to understand exactly what Yeshua meant. You will know that Yeshua was referring to a specific group of Jews who zealously forced themselves to overcome their spiritual handicaps, Jews who forced themselves to understand the truth that was sown in their hearts and who forcibly seized and applied to their lives the righteousness that the truth imparted to them.

> *Matthew 11:12 (The Amplified Bible.)*
>
> *12And from the days of John the Baptist until the present time, **the kingdom of heaven has endured violent assault, and violent men seize it by force [as a precious prize—a share in the heavenly kingdom is sought with most ardent zeal and intense exertion].***

The degree of mental effort that these courageous spiritually handicapped Jews exhibited as they barreled forward toward truth and righteousness is absolutely phenomenal. Their story is clearly told in the previous verse, Matthew 11:12. Their pursuit of truth and righteousness was so intense, so forceful, that Yeshua actually describes them as *"violent men."* Yes, these Jewish men's quest for truth and righteousness was unequivocally difficult and extremely exacting. It was a task that demanded intense cognitive exertion and mental and emotional stamina. The truth is that in order for these men to have gradually overcome their severe spiritual learning disabilities insofar as *"the secret things"* were concerned and to have held on to the word of the kingdom that was sown in their hearts, they had to have sought the kingdom of God (righteousness) above all else.

By now, you are probably wondering how these Jews managed to overcome their God-ordained handicaps. How, since God Himself had made them blind and deaf to *"the secret things,"* was it possible for them to override their God-imposed disabilities? Could it have had something to do with the fact that Yeshua deliberately gave the interpretation of His parables to some Jews and not to others?

While it is true that Yeshua only shared the interpretation of His parables with a small group and not with the majority of the Jewish people, this fact must still be eliminated from the list of possible answers to the previously mentioned query. I say that it must be eliminated from that list because Yeshua's own words prove that His divulging the interpretation of the parables could not possibly be the answer. For, you see, Yeshua reveals that men began seizing the kingdom of God before He ever shared His first parable or its interpretation. Remember that in Matthew 11:12, Yeshua makes it clear that these violent men seized the kingdom of God from the time that John the Baptist first started preaching and baptizing.

Another point to remember is that not all those who heard the interpretation of the parables managed to overcome their blind and deaf spiritual condition. Even though they came to believe the teachings of Yeshua, some still did not have what it takes to hold onto the truth they heard or to continue to seek more truth. Consequently, they turned back from following Him. Therefore, it is obvious that possessing the interpretation did not guarantee a man a share in the kingdom of God. No! It was instead the **consistent** zeal and intellectual exertion that a man expended that procured for him a share in the kingdom of God. It was the fact that certain individuals continually held on to the truth they heard with all their might by immediately applying it to their lives that enabled them to override their spiritual disabilities and seize by force the kingdom of God.

So, how, you may ask, were these Jews able to override their God-ordained blind and deaf disabilities? The correct answer is that for His own name's sake, God forced His own hand. Yes, God deliberately placed Himself in a position in which He had no other choice but to allow these zealous individuals to overcome the handicaps that He had previously imposed on them. God had to do this in order to keep His Biblical promises and fulfill His predictions.

For a moment, let us consider how God forced His own hand. You learned in a previous chapter of this work that God is bound by an unbreakable oath to extend forgiveness, mercy and loving-kindness toward His covenant people when they pursue it. That was why during His ministry, Yeshua hid the interpretation of His parables from the majority of God's people. He did not want to do anything at that time to encourage the Jewish nation as a whole to understand *"the secret things,"* recognize Him and turn to Him for spiritual healing. You see, God still needed the Jewish nation to remain in their spiritually blind and deaf state so that they could help Him accomplish His overall plan and aid Him in fulfilling numerous Biblical predictions and promises. If, at that time, the whole nation of Israel had been allowed to zealously pursue truth and righteousness to the degree that they recognized the Messiah, understood His teachings and turned to Him for salvation, God would have been forced to keep His promise of everlasting love. Yes, God would have been forced to extend mercy, forgiveness and loving-kindness to the entire nation of Israel. And my friend, at that time it was not God's will that His entire covenant nation recognize the Messiah and be saved. For, if that had happened, how then could God have continued to use His covenant nation to help Him fulfill His predictions and keep His sacred promises. It was absolutely necessary that the nation of Israel remain blind and deaf to *"the secret things"* so that they could complete their divine mission. So, Yeshua deliberately avoided causing a stampede (that is, He avoided sending a nation of violent men rushing toward the kingdom of God).

It was, however, essential that some Jews recognize the Messiah, understand His teachings and turn to Him for spiritual healing so they could help God fulfill other predictions and keep other Biblical promises concerning the Gentiles. Their role was to help God extend salvation to the Gentile nations. Consequently, the Lord allowed some Jews to override their God-imposed disabilities. For, how could all the nations believe on Yeshua and be saved if the Jewish messengers whom God sent to them did not believe that Yeshua was the Messiah? Moreover, how could those same Jews carry the message of salvation to the Gentiles, teach the Gentiles to obey all that the Lord had commanded and make disciples of them if they themselves neither recognized the Messiah nor understood His teachings?

It stands to reason that without special help, only a few Jewish people would have had enough stamina to have enabled them to overcome their blindness and deafness to *"the secret things"* even if they had received the same teachings that the Lord's followers received. Therefore, as God had always intended, the Jewish nation as a whole remained spiritually disabled. Only a small percentage were allowed to forcibly override their blind and deaf condition in order to carry out God's will concerning the Gentiles. Notice that I said, they were <u>allowed</u> to forcibly override their blind and deaf condition. I carefully chose the term <u>allowed</u> because, while God did not instantly heal this group of Jews, **neither did He defeat their gallant efforts to escape their disabilities.**

Yeshua said in Mark 4:28, *"For the earth bringeth forth fruit of herself."* My friend, the earth did bring forth fruit of herself. As in the case of the earth and the fruit it brings forth, God had already put His plan into progress, but these zealous men forced themselves to carry out God's plan. These Jewish disciples overcame their spiritually crippling cognitive disabilities. They themselves persistently pushed toward the kingdom of God until they freed themselves from the spiritual restrictions that had previously barred their access to understanding *"the secret things."* Thus, by sheer zeal and intellectual exertion, they seized by force a share in the heavenly kingdom (that is, they seized by force the truth and the righteousness that the truth imparts when it is applied to a man's life). For, as Paul tells us in Romans 14:17, **the kingdom of God is righteousness**. And, God's Word proclaims that righteousness is applied truth.

For His name's sake, God forced His own hand in allowing a minority of zealous men to force Him to extend to them His promised loving-kindness. Thus, He once again accomplished His will. The Jewish nation as a whole remained blind and deaf to *"the secret things"* while, in order to help God keep specific promises, a group of Jews triumphed over their spiritual handicaps and eventually went forth to proclaim salvation to the nations. Yes, these Jews became the children of light or as John 12:35-36 in *The Living Bible* says, they became *"light bearers."*

Now that you have an abundance of insight into what it takes for a Jew to comprehend *"the secret things,"* now that you understand what it takes for a Jew to comprehend the future predictions contained in God's Word, now that you understand what it takes for a Jew to comprehend the prophetic signs which point to the Messiah's first and second coming, now that you understand what it takes for a Jew to recognize and to believe on Yeshua, don't you have a new admiration and respect for Jewish believers? And you most certainly should have admiration and respect for them. If for nothing else, you should greatly admire and respect all Jewish believers for the ardent zeal, the intense exertion and the incredible perseverance that they had to have exhibited in order to be followers of Yeshua. For in spite of the fact that they had to overcome severe spiritual intellectual disabilities, they zealously forced themselves to pay attention to God's Word and to believe it. They violently forced their minds to recognize and acknowledge the truth, the truth that Yeshua is indeed the prophet like Moses (Deuteronomy 18:15), the promised Messiah, whose coming was foretold by all the prophets of old. These incredible, wonderful, Abrahamic covenant people of God held on to the word that was sown in their hearts so tightly that Satan could not pry it from them.

Oh, my friend, do you realize the magnitude of the truth that the Holy Spirit has just transmitted to you? For years, the Church has struggled with the contents of Matthew 11:12. Yet, men's explanations of that verse have boiled down to mere assumptions, presumptions, and opinions. However, since you are now finally equipped with all the necessary Biblical background information regarding the Jews' God-imposed handicaps and know how some of them managed to forcefully seize the kingdom of God, it is easy for you to understand the true intent of the Lord's words in Matthew 11:12. So on that note, read again Yeshua's words. Yes, drink in the truth and be refreshed.

430

Matthew 11:12 (The Amplified Bible.)

*12And from the days of John the Baptist until the present time, **the kingdom of heaven has endured violent assault, and violent men seize it by force [as a precious prize—a share in the heavenly kingdom is sought with most ardent zeal and intense exertion]**.*

Praise be to God! For the great mystery of the criteria which God uses for allowing some Jews to gain spiritual sight and hearing in the area of *"the secret things"* while others remain spiritually blind and deaf is also unveiled through the preceding correct interpretation of Matthew 11:12 and numerous other secrets that have been revealed in this chapter. Oh, my friend, don't you see? From this time on, men will no longer ignorantly misunderstand God's intentions in this area. They will no longer falsely accuse Him of being unfair or of showing partiality to some Jews over others.

Blind and deaf Israel as a whole and the small percentage of Jews who manage to force their way into the kingdom of God **are equally accomplishing God's will and purpose**. Furthermore, the nation of Israel will not be penalized for being unable to recognize Yeshua as the Messiah or for failing to understand His teachings. The nation of Israel will simply be judged by the standards of the old covenant (the Horeb covenant) while those Jews who violently seize the kingdom of God will be judged by the standards of the new covenant. Thus, if they obey God's commands, neither group can possibly lose out just because their divine calling happens to be different.

God's name is vindicated through this correct interpretation of the contents of Matthew 11:12 and through numerous other verses of Scripture contained in this entire chapter. From the day that this work was published, men throughout the world were made aware that those Jews who because of their disabilities do not recognize the Messiah or understand His teachings are used by God to accomplish His will and purpose while those Jews who do gain spiritual eyesight and hearing and are thus able to recognize and believe on the Messiah do so, not because God shows them favoritism over other Jews, but because, they themselves wholeheartedly and diligently exert their spiritual intellect in the pursuit of truth and righteousness. For His own name's sake, God does not defeat their efforts. Rather, He allows them to do so in order that they too might help Him accomplish His will and purpose. The bottom line is that each group has a special God-ordained task to perform and each mission is equally important.

We also need to consider God's amazing wisdom in this matter. Think about it. If you were going to send men to proclaim the message of salvation to the Gentile nations knowing that their mission would bring upon them tremendous spiritual and physical hardships, wouldn't you want to know prior to their embarking on that mission that they had enough stamina and zeal to accomplish the job? Don't you see, God knew what He was doing. It was all part of His wonderful plan. He made sure that those Jews whom He sent were so intent on pursuing righteousness that they would push on through the most difficult circumstances until they had accomplished their God-given task. And my friend, these Jews had already proved to God that they did possess the qualities needed to finish their God-ordained mission.

When one contemplates the Jews' spiritual disabilities and the different methods God used to ensure that they stayed disabled, one cannot overlook God's Biblical arrangement of His prophets inspired predictions. I say that because the Scriptural layout of prophetic future events has always been a problem, even for Christians. So, it has obviously posed an even greater obstacle for spiritually handicapped Jews. The fact is that spiritually blind and deaf Jews had about as much chance of understanding the prophets' inspired predictions as a physically blind man would have reading a road map or a physically deaf man would have following the verbal directions of a woman who turned her face away while instructing him on the best way to reach his destination.

As you know, the Messiah's first and second coming are often mentioned in the very same verse. In other texts, we are provided with an assortment of individual verses dealing with the Messiah's birth, death, resurrection, second coming, and His future judgments and eternal reign. To compound the problem even further, such verses of Scripture are not always sequential.

Of course, the Biblical format of the prophets' predictions has a lot to do with God not wanting the Jews to comprehend the signs of the times and other hidden truths. However, the arrangement of the prophets' predictions does have another logical aspect to it. Let me explain. As you know, men are allotted a certain amount of time on this earth. Therefore, when God's prophets spoke of a particular man, they often predicted his birth, the fulfillment of God's purpose for his life, and sometimes even his death.

In the Messiah's case however, prophecy has to be viewed in an entirely different light. The reason prophecy must be viewed differently in the Messiah's case is because, as Isaiah told us, the Messiah is actually *"Immanuel [God with us]."* The Messiah is the *"everlasting Father [of eternity]."* (Isaiah 9:6.) God's prophet tells us in Micah 5:2 that the Messiah has been alive from everlasting ages past. To put it bluntly, the Messiah, Yeshua, is God Himself. Furthermore, when He lived on earth as a man, He was God incarnate.

When, in order to fulfill God's Word, the Messiah was crucified by the Romans and placed in a burial tomb, life for Him did not end at that point in time. No! God is not like man. God is eternal. He cannot be destroyed by death. King David prophesied that very fact in Psalm 16:10 when speaking of the Messiah, he said, *"For you will not abandon me in Sheol (the place of the dead), **neither will you suffer Your holy One [Holy One] to see corruption."***

The bottom line is that the Messiah's death and His past and future visits to earth should be classed as simply events in His **eternal existence**. It might help you to more fully understand my last statement if you momentarily consider some of the main Biblical predictions that pertain to Christ's first and future second coming in the **past tense**. You would then say:

- He, the Messiah, was born a human being, a Jew.

- He fully carried out His Biblically predicted mission.

- He fulfilled Genesis 3:15.

- He was crucified.

- He gave His life to seal the promised new covenant with His own blood.

- He crushed Satan's head and removed Satan's power over mankind.

- He freed men from sin.

- He gave men the power to once again do what they were created to do (that is, to fear God and keep His commandments).

- He fulfilled the segment of the Abrahamic covenant that pertained to the salvation of the Gentile nations.

- He was buried.

- He was resurrected.

- He went back to heaven.

- He became a priest forever.

- He waited there until the predicted time for His return to earth.

- He returned to earth.

- He literally sat upon David's throne.

- He healed Israel's spiritual eyesight, so that they were able to recognize Him, believe on Him and be saved.

- He judged and punished the nations.

- He restored to Israel every inch of the land that He promised would be theirs forever.

- He reigned from Jerusalem (the capital of the world) over all the earth forever and ever.

When viewed in the past tense, it all sounds so simple, doesn't it? However, the problem is that in their spiritually blind and deaf state the Jews were and are unable to correctly separate one prophetic utterance from another, never mind understand their meaning. Consequently, as you saw in John 12:34, the Jews overlooked the prophesies that foretold how the Messiah would first come as a human being, a servant, and would die a horrible death at the hands of men. They clung instead to the predictions that pertain to His second coming which proclaim how the Messiah will sit upon the literal throne of David, punish Israel's enemies and rule forever. Moreover, if they did happen to arrange a particular Biblical prophesy in the correct order or time period, in their spiritually blind and deaf state, they were still unable to comprehend the correct meaning of the prophecy itself.

Let me give you a glimpse of the type of difficulties that God's spiritually blind and deaf people faced when it came to their sorting out and understanding the prophets' inspired predictions.

Psalm 110:1-7 (The Amplified Bible.)

1THE LORD (God) says to my Lord (the Messiah), Sit at My right hand, until I make Your adversaries Your footstool.

2The Lord will send forth from Zion the scepter of Your strength; rule, then, in the midst of Your foes.

3Your people will offer themselves willingly in the day of Your power, in the beauty of holiness and in holy array out of the womb of the morning; to You [will spring forth] Your young men, who are as the dew.

⁴*The Lord has sworn and will not revoke or change it: You are a priest forever, after the manner and order of Melchizadek.*

⁵*The Lord at Your right hand will shatter kings in the day of His indignation.*

⁶*He will execute judgment [in overwhelming punishment] upon the nations; He will fill the valleys with the dead bodies, He will crush the [chief] heads over lands many and far extended.*

⁷*He will drink of the brook by the way; therefore will He lift up His head [triumphantly].*

I am unable to present an in-depth teaching on Psalm 110 in the middle of this present series. So, rather than a lengthy study, I will provide a brief outline of its contents. You will then have a better idea of just how scattered the information is in Psalm 110 and how difficult a time God's spiritually blind and deaf people must have had, and for that matter still do have, trying to cipher its content and understand the gist of it.

(Verses 1-3)

In verses one through three of the previous text, you find the already crucified and **resurrected** Messiah sitting at God's right hand while waiting for God to deal with all His enemies. He then returns to earth for the second time to reign forever in Jerusalem and to extend salvation to His covenant people, the Jews.

(Verse 4)

Today, since Yeshua's blood has already been shed and has sealed the new covenant, verse four reflects on the past, present and future. However, when the Messiah walked the earth, that same verse spoke only of the future. It spoke of the Messiah being a priest **forever**. Verse four was one of the very Scriptures that the spiritually blind and deaf crowd referred to in John 12:34 when they refused to accept the truth that the Messiah would die. You see, the Jews could not comprehend how the Messiah could die and still be a priest forever.

The Jews had absolutely no concept of the meaning of the prophesies that pertained to Christ's death or His resurrection or His prophesied spiritual priestly function that would last forever. They expected a priest who would forever offer the external ritualistic animal sacrifices that were required under the former order (that is, under the Horeb covenant) rather than a high priest officiating in a spiritual capacity under the rules of the promised new order (that is, under the promised blood-sealed new covenant). The Jews disregarded all the prophesies which spoke of the Messiah's death and how and why He became a priest forever. They were unable to understand the secret truths that were hidden in their own Scriptures.

(Verses 5-7)

Verses five through seven again refer to the Messiah's future second coming when He will save all Israel and punish the Gentile nations.

The truth is that even a person with A-1 spiritual comprehension has to study hard and long and diligently seek the Lord when piecing together such difficult problems and placing them in the correct order and time period. So I ask you, how in the world can people who are spiritually blind and deaf to *"the secret things"* be expected to fathom such intermingled, perplexing Biblical enigma?

Except for a small minority of Jewish believers, no people on the face of the earth were and are as spiritually blind and deaf to *"the secret things"* as God's own Abrahamic covenant people. As Isaiah had foretold, they reached a point where they could sit all day long listening to God's Word spoken by the promised Messiah Himself, including the unfolding of all the prophets' future predictions of His death, and yet, they still could not understand what those parables and predictions meant.

They actually watched Yeshua (the Messiah) perform awesome miracles. Yet, they were unable to grasp the message that those miracles conveyed. They were unable to see the truth that those miracles were a sign that the promised Messiah, whom God had previously described to them through Moses, was actually walking among them. Moreover, they could not perceive any of those things because the Lord had stricken them with spiritual blindness and deafness. He had deliberately handicapped them. God made that fact clear in Isaiah 6:9 in *The Living Bible* when He said, *"Though you hear my words repeatedly, __you won't understand them__. Though you watch and watch as I perform my miracles, __still you won't know what they mean__."*

God had performed many marvelous miracles by the hand of Moses. Also through Moses, God had told His people what they should expect of the Messiah when He came to earth the first time. **Yet, when the promised Messiah, the prophet like Moses, arrived doing exactly what Moses had predicted He would do, God's people could not** comprehend that those words of Moses had literally come to pass. The Jews, like their teachers, were truly blind and deaf. They could not discern the signs of the times. Think about it! In order to have failed to recognize the Messiah after reading Moses' description of Him in the following text, the Lord's people had to have been totally spiritually blind and deaf to *"the secret things."*

> *Deuteronomy 18:15-18 (The Amplified Bible.)*
>
> *15 The Lord your God will raise up for you a prophet (Prophet) from the midst of your brethren like me [Moses]; to him you shall listen.*
>
> *16 This is what you desired [and asked] of the Lord your God at Horeb on the day of the assembly when you said, Let me not hear again the voice of the Lord my God or see this great fire any more, lest I die.*
>
> *17 And the Lord said to me, They have well said all that they have spoken.*
>
> *18 I will raise up for them a prophet (Prophet) from among their brethren <u>like you</u>, and will put My words in his mouth; and he shall speak to them all that I command him.*

As I said earlier, no people lacked spiritual understanding and discernment more than God's own people, the Jews. For God Himself had struck them blind and deaf. And blind and deaf most of them will stay, until the appointed time arrives for them to receive their complete spiritual healing.

As informed as you now are regarding the Jews' God-ordained spiritual disabilities, it should not surprise you that Yeshua responded as He did in the following verse. I am speaking about the well known incident when Yeshua's disciples informed Him that the religious leaders of Israel had been displeased, offended and indignant when they had heard His teachings. Yeshua's reply was not, however, intended to be rude or mean or to put down the religious leaders of Israel. On the contrary, under the circumstances when He directed His disciples to disregard the religious leaders, His advice was extremely wise and His statement absolutely factual. The understanding you now have (that is, understanding concerning Israel's religious leaders being unable to perceive the secret truths that Yeshua taught) will give you deeper insight into Yeshua's warning in the following verse.

Matthew 15:14 (The Amplified Bible.)

14Let them alone and disregard them; they are blind guides and teachers. And if a blind man leads a blind man, both will fall into a ditch.

Since I again mentioned the point regarding Israel's religious leaders being spiritually blind and deaf, this is an excellent opportunity for you to allow the Holy Spirit to impart to you yet another wonderful Biblical revelation. However, so that you will remember that the prophets (teachers) of Israel were indeed as equally handicapped as the rest of the Jewish people and so that you will also keep in mind the extent of their spiritual disabilities, I will repeat the following text.

Isaiah 29:10-12 (The Living Bible.)

*10For the Lord has poured out upon you a spirit of deep sleep. **He has closed the eyes of your prophets and seers,***

*11**so all of these future events are a sealed book to them.** When you give it to one who can read, he says, "I can't, for it's sealed."*

12When you give it to another, he says, "Sorry, I can't read."

The knowledge you now possess, knowledge concerning Israel's prophets being as equally spiritually handicapped as the rest of the Jews, prepares you to comprehend the marvelous disclosure that I previously mentioned. So read carefully the following verses giving special attention to verse seventeen. For, if you stay alert and you pay close attention to the contents of that verse, you may yourself be able to discern the true meaning of Yeshua's words.

Matthew 13:10-17 (The Amplified Bible.)

10Then the disciples came to Him and said, Why do You speak to them in parables?

11And He replied to them, To you it has been given to know the secrets and mysteries of the kingdom of heaven, but to them it has not been given.

12For whoever has [spiritual knowledge], to him will more be given and he will be furnished richly so that he will have abundance; but from him who has not, even what he has will be taken away.

13This is the reason that I speak to them in parables: because having the power of seeing, they do not see; and having the power of hearing, they do not hear, nor do they grasp and understand.

14In them indeed is the process of fulfillment of the prophecy of Isaiah, which says: You shall indeed hear and hear but never grasp and understand; and you shall indeed look and look but never see and perceive.

15For this nation's heart has grown gross (fat and dull), and their ears heavy and difficult of hearing, and their eyes they have tightly closed, lest they see and perceive with their eyes, and hear and comprehend the sense with their ears, and grasp and understand with their heart, and turn and I should heal them.

16But blessed (happy, fortunate, and to be envied) are your eyes because they do see, and your ears because they do hear.

17Truly I tell you, many prophets and righteous men [men who were upright and in right standing with God] yearned to see what you see, and did not see it, and to hear what you hear, and did not hear it.

Verse seventeen in *The Living Bible* reads as follows,

17Many a prophet and godly man has longed to see what you have seen, and hear what you have heard, but couldn't.

Bible scholars and teachers have taught the Church that the reason the prophets and righteous men in verse seventeen had longed to see and hear what the disciples had seen and heard *"but couldn't"* was because they lived before the Messiah came to earth. However, these teachers' account of Matthew 13:17 is extremely shallow. It does not contain the correct interpretation of the meaning of Yeshua's words in that verse.

In verse seventeen, Yeshua was telling His disciples that many prophets of Israel and other righteous Jews had in their time longed to be able to understand the secrets and mysteries of the kingdom of God. They longed to be able to realize the meaning of all the future predictions about the promised Messiah which some of them had personally relayed to God's Abrahamic covenant people yet did not perceive themselves. The prophets and other righteous men longed to understand the deep, inner meaning of the miracles which the Bible foretold that the Messiah would perform. All these things they longed to see and hear *"but couldn't."* And why couldn't those prophets and righteous people understand the mysteries and secrets of God's Word? Why couldn't they understand God's miracles and future predictions? **They could not understand those things (that is, they could not see and hear those things) because, like the rest of the Jews, they were spiritually handicapped. They were spiritually blind and deaf in regard to** *"the secret things."*

Since Yeshua describes the men in verse seventeen as being "righteous men," they obviously had kept the Horeb covenant and therefore had made every effort to learn and obey *"the things which are revealed,"* God's commands. They had also made the necessary external sacrifices whenever they had unintentionally or ignorantly broken God's laws and sinned. However, the problem was that like all the other spiritually blind and deaf Jews, they had not been able to unravel the prophetic secrets and mysteries that had been purposely hidden from their blind eyes. Most of all, they had never been able to understand the mystery of the kingdom of God. For again like all the other spiritually blind and deaf Jews, these otherwise extremely intelligent prophets and other righteous men had absolutely no inkling that the kingdom of God is righteousness or what the righteousness of God is really all about. They mistakenly saw the kingdom of God only in a literal sense (that is, as a future literal kingdom on earth).

As God's spokesmen, the prophets prophesied in the name of the Lord. However, it is evident that except on rare occasions, they had made their inspired predictions without ever really understanding the true meaning of the future events that they had foretold. According to Isaiah 29:10-12, to them, all future events were a sealed book, a book whose secrets no man, not even God's righteous prophets, could unlock until it suited God's purpose for them to do so.

It is vital that you understand that the hidden mysteries and secrets contained in Yeshua's parables were all recorded beforehand in Old Testament Scripture. Therefore, the prophets and righteous men mentioned in Matthew 13:17 actually had access to them. However, having access to the secrets and mysteries of the kingdom of God was of no great advantage to them since they could not comprehend their deep, inner meaning. They had been in the same predicament as were the majority of Jews who lived during the Messiah's visit to earth, Jews who had access to Yeshua's parables but did not understand their meaning.

Scriptural verification for my previous statement, a statement regarding the secret contents of Yeshua's parables being recorded beforehand in Old Testament Scripture, can be found in the Psalmists'

440

prophetic words which I shared with you in an earlier part of chapter fourteen. At that time, we studied the first two verses of the previously mentioned text. However, we will now include verse three. Moreover, we will read the Psalmist's inspired prediction from the *Holy Bible, King James Version.*

> *Psalm 78:1-3 (King James Version.)*
>
> [1]*GIVE ear, O my people, to my law: incline your ears to the words of my mouth.*
>
> [2]***I will open my mouth in a parable: I will utter dark sayings of old:***
>
> [3]***Which we have heard and known, and our fathers have told us.***

How sad it is, to think that the righteous men of old mentioned in Matthew 11:12 longed to understand the deep inner meaning of the inspired predictions and secret truths regarding the kingdom of God that were recorded in Old Testament Scripture, **but they could not**. On the other hand, in order to aid them in their zealous pursuit of truth and righteousness, Yeshua's disciples were provided with the actual interpretation of the meaning of those secret things. Furthermore, they forced themselves to progressively come to understand the previously mentioned secrets and mysteries. They refused to allow Satan to steal the word of the kingdom out of their hearts. Thus, they gradually seized by force the truth and righteousness of God. As you read earlier in Matthew 11:12 in *The Amplified Bible*, from the days of John the Baptist, violent men seized by force the kingdom of God (that is, they seized by force the knowledge and righteousness of God).

> *Matthew 11:12 (The Amplified Bible.)*
>
> [12]*And from the days of John the Baptist until the present time, **the kingdom of heaven has endured violent assault, and violent men seize it by force [as a precious prize—a share in the heavenly kingdom is sought with most ardent zeal and intense exertion].***

As I promised that I would at the beginning of part six, among many other truths, I have shown you in the Scriptures the depth of the Jews' God-imposed handicaps. I have also provided added Scriptural confirmation regarding the slow progress that Yeshua's own disciples made in understanding the mystery of the kingdom of God. I must add, however, that Jewish people do not lack intelligence. Jews are not handicapped when it comes to God's laws and secular learning. For example, men such as Albert Einstein and Sigmund Freud were Jews, and their intellectual genius as well as their contribution to society is acclaimed to this day. Moreover, you seldom meet a Jew that is not well educated. This fact makes their spiritual dilemma even more amazing.

Since the next and final segment of chapter fourteen, part seven holds even more insight into the present topic, I do not feel the need to summarize any further at this point. So prepare yourself to receive more marvelous enlightenment on the present subject.

Chapter 14
Part Seven

WHY DID THE JEWS FAIL
TO RECOGNIZE THE MESSIAH?

When one looks at the Jews' prolonged spiritually blind and deaf intellectual plight, at first glance, it is hard to imagine how any good could possibly be derived from their being kept in that pathetic condition generation after generation. However, upon closer scrutiny, one realizes that on God's part disabling His beloved people was an act of great kindness and mercy which was extended not only toward the Jews **but to all mankind**.

It will take a little time, but I will now explain my statement in the former paragraph. I will begin by reminding you that it was essential that the Messiah come to earth and allow His blood to be shed. It was essential in order to fulfill God's prediction in Genesis 3:15 to keep God's promises to Abraham regarding the salvation of the nations and to bring into being the promised new covenant mentioned in Jeremiah 31:31-34.

God never intended for the Horeb covenant, a covenant He made with Israel when He brought them out of Egypt, to be a permanent contract. For, as you will soon see in the Scriptures, the external ritualistic requirements of the Horeb covenant were not designed to bring to completion God's predictions and promises or to entirely fulfill God's will and purpose on the earth. Rather, they were designed to act as an indication of what was to come in the future. Likewise, God writing His Ten Commandments on tablets of stone was designed to act as an indication of that future time when He would write those same laws on men's hearts and minds.

You will soon be viewing a statement in *The Letter to the Hebrews* in which the writer refers to the Horeb covenant as being defective (that is, inadequate). However, as you study those verses, it is important to remember that God's commandments, commandments which the Horeb agreement required that Israel keep, were not in anyway flawed (that is, **God's laws were not inadequate**). On the contrary, David states in Psalm 19:7 that *"The law of the Lord is perfect...."* Also, Yeshua Himself tells you in John 12:50 that God's commandments are eternal life. Moreover, if God's laws were defective (inadequate), I do not think Yeshua would have allowed His blood to be shed to seal a new covenant that would give men power to understand and obey those same laws of God, do you? Of course you do not. So I repeat, God's commandments (God's laws) were not in anyway inadequate (defective). No! No! No! A thousand times, no! God's commands were positively not the problem.

The problem lay with the first covenant (the agreement), not with the commandments of God. Yes, the covenant that God made with the Israelites at Horeb was defective. While the first agreement was good enough to do the temporary symbolic job for which it was intended, it was inadequate to fully equip men to do what they were originally intended to do. The very fact that God promised the Israelites that He would make another agreement with them is proof that the Horeb covenant was unable to fully accomplish God's will for the future. (Jeremiah 31:31-34.)

My friend, it is a fact that the writer of *The Letter to The Hebrews* clearly states that the first covenant between God and the Israelites was not faultless. In other words, the covenant was defective. It was defective in that it was inadequate. The Horeb agreement was unable to fully accomplish God's future purpose for mankind. It was never God's intention that the first covenant (the Horeb covenant) should remain operative for all time. As I shared with you earlier, God made that fact obvious when He found fault with the Israelites' inability to keep the old covenant by promising a future new covenant. (Jeremiah 31:31-34.) The truth is that the Horeb covenant was simply an indicator of the future benefits that the new covenant would one day bestow upon mankind. It was not designed nor was it ever intended to provide those benefits. For example, the Horeb covenant did not provide the power that men needed to keep the agreement that they had entered into, whereas the new covenant which it signified would indeed provide men with such power.

The Horeb covenant most certainly was a holy contract. Therefore, it is important to remember that God faithfully kept His end of that agreement. He gave his commandments to the Israelites as He had promised. However, since the contract did not provide the Israelites with the needed power to keep their end of the bargain (that is, it did not provide them with the power they needed to consistently keep the commandments that they had agreed in that same contract to obey), the Israelites became the weak link in the Horeb contract. Moreover, the Israelites' inability to consistently keep the commands that they had promised to obey showed the inadequacy of the covenant that they had entered into. And that, my friend, is why the writer informs you that God finding fault with the Israelites actually proved that the Horeb agreement was not adequate to fully accomplish God's future purpose. It lacked the essential power to cause men to once again perform the full original purpose of their creation.

In order to abide by the righteous and just requirements of the Horeb covenant, it was necessary that the Israelites do what they had agreed to do in that contract. In other words, they had to keep God's holy commandments. They also had to observe all the external rituals of the Law. However, as you now know, men were unable to do what they had been created to do. They did not have the necessary power to keep their agreement with God by consistently keeping His commandments. For, as I have repeatedly stated, the Horeb covenant did not provide such power.

Sin held men captive. Moreover, the external ritualistic animal sacrifices that were required under the Horeb agreement did not take away sin. **They simply covered over sin**. Neither did offering those animal sacrifices provide the power men needed to consistently obey God's laws and thus stop sinning. If the external ritualistic animal sacrifices had taken away sin, there would have been no need for the Israelites to have kept on offering them year after year.

God always intended that each future event and blessing that the external sacrifices symbolically represented would one day come into glorious existence. He also intended that the Ten Commandments He had written on stone would one day be written on men's hearts and minds. However, until that day arrived, men remained trapped in their powerless, sinful state. Sin towered like a monumental, impenetrable wall around their hearts and minds, guarding its dark domain while at the same time imprisoning mankind.

The Messiah, therefore, came to earth to purchase for mankind the new covenant that God had promised in Jeremiah 31:31-34. He came to purchase a covenant that would give men all the power they needed to completely overcome sin and consistently obey God's laws (that is, to consistently keep God's commandments), a feat that they had not been able to do under the first covenant. The bottom line is that through the Messiah's death, men were freed from sin and were provided with all the power they would ever need to keep their end of the promised blood-sealed new contract. For, through the Messiah's death, all that the external sacrifices foreshadowed was fulfilled. In addition, God's commandments that were once written on stone are now written on the hearts and minds of true believers.

"Immanuel [God with us]," the Anointed One, gave His life in order to seal the promised new covenant with His own blood. Moreover, the blood-sealed new covenant is better than the Horeb agreement. The thing that makes the promised new covenant a better agreement is that it contains more excellent promises than the former covenant did. For, in the new covenant, God promises to completely forgive men's sins. Men's sins are no longer covered over, they are actually taken away. God also promises to give men all the power they need to not only understand His laws but to obey them. Yes, unlike the Horeb covenant, the promised new agreement fully equips men with the will and desire to do what they were originally created to do. It equips men with all the power they need to fear God and keep all His commandments. It equips men with the needed power to consistently keep the agreement that they have entered into. Thus, men are no longer the weak link. There is no weak link in the new covenant. The new covenant is perfect. Earlier, in this series, you saw abundant Scriptural proof for all that I just stated.

As you read the next Scriptures, try to keep in mind the information in the previous paragraph. Also remember that when the writer speaks of the Horeb covenant as being defective, he is referring to the fact that since the first covenant was simply a beautiful picture of what was to come, it did not provide all that the new covenant provides. It stands to reason that the previous temporary, symbolic agreement was inferior (that is, the previous temporary symbolic agreement was lacking) in comparison with the extraordinary completed perfection of the promised permanent new covenant.

Hebrews 8:1-13 (The Amplified Bible.)

1NOW THE main point of what we have to say is this: We have such a High Priest, One Who is seated at the right hand of the majestic [God] in heaven,

2As officiating Priest, a Minister in the holy places and in the true tabernacle which is erected not by man but by the Lord.

3For every high priest is appointed to offer up gifts and sacrifices; so it is essential for this [High Priest] to have some offering to make also.

4If then He were still living on earth, He would not be a priest at all, for there are [already priests] who offer the gifts in accordance with the Law.

5[But these offer] service [merely] as a pattern and as a foreshadowing of [what has its true existence and reality in] the heavenly sanctuary. For when Moses was about to erect the tabernacle, he was warned by God, saying, See to it that you make it all [exactly] according to the copy (the model) which was shown to you on the mountain.

6But as it now is, He [Christ] has acquired a [priestly] ministry which is as much superior and more excellent [than the old] <u>as the covenant (the agreement) of which He is the Mediator (the Arbiter, Agent) is superior and more excellent, [because] it is enacted and rests upon more important (sublimer, higher, and nobler) promises.</u>

7For if that first covenant had been without defect, there would have been no room for another one or an attempt to institute another one.

8However, <u>He finds fault with them [showing its inadequacy]</u> when He says, Behold, the days will come, says the Lord, when I will make and ratify a new covenant or agreement with the house of Israel and with the house of Judah.

As a temporary measure and indicator of that which was to come, the Horeb covenant was certainly sufficient. However, since God's people were enslaved by sin, and since the required external sacrifices of the Horeb covenant did not free men from sin or provide them with overcoming power to stop sinning, they continually broke that covenant by disobeying the commands of God which they had previously agreed to keep. Truly, men were the weak link in the first covenant. Men's inability to keep the Horeb agreement made it defective (inadequate). Study the following verses carefully and you will see what I mean.

*8However, <u>**He finds fault with them**</u> [showing its inadequacy] when He says, Behold, the days will come, says the Lord, when **I** will make and ratify a new covenant or agreement with the house of Israel and with the house of Judah.*

9It will not be like the covenant that I made with their forefathers on the day when I grasped them by the hand to help and relieve them and to lead them out from the land of Egypt, <u>for they did not abide in My agreement</u>

> *__with them__, and so I withdrew My favor and disregarded them, says the Lord.*
>
> *10For this is the covenant that I will make with the house of Israel after those days, says the Lord: __I will imprint My laws upon their minds, even upon their innermost thoughts and understanding, and engrave them upon their hearts__; and I will be their God, and they shall be My people.*

Earlier in the series in a former part of chapter fourteen, you saw in the Scriptures that God had already given the Israelites understanding of His laws (that is, He gave them understanding of *"the things which are revealed"*). Therefore, you might wonder what added advantage God's new covenant promise to give the Israelites understanding of His laws would offer them. Well, one phenomenal advantage would be that under the new covenant, the Israelites would have the commandments of God actually written in their hearts and minds instead of on tablets of stone. Think about it! God writing His laws on each individual believer's heart and mind instead of on one set of stone tablets.

A second advantage would be that God's people would finally know how to obtain and retain the righteousness that applied truth imparts. They would know how to keep Satan from stealing from their hearts not only the secrets of God's Word but also the truth regarding God's laws.

A third advantage would be the overcoming power that the new covenant provides, power to not only understand but to actually consistently keep God's laws, God's commandments.

A fourth advantage would be that God's people would come to understand *"the secret things"* that pertain to the external matters of the Law. For example, they would gain in-depth understanding of the secret truths concerning those things that the ritualistic animal sacrifices represented, truths which previously had been hidden from them. They would come to realize that the animal offerings were simply a pattern and a foreshadowing of the things that in reality had their true existence in the one time sacrifice that the Messiah made when He gave His life to seal the promised new covenant with His own blood.

A fifth advantage would be the fact that they would be free from sin, free to finally obey the laws that they had previously promised to keep, laws which they would more fully understand under the new covenant.

I could go on and on, but I think I have already made my point that the new covenant promise of understanding is indeed profound. So, let us read verse ten again and then continue studying our present text.

> *10For this is the covenant that I will make with the house of Israel after those days, says the Lord: **I will imprint My laws upon their minds, even upon their innermost thoughts and understanding, and engrave them upon their hearts**; and I will be their God, and they shall be My people.*
>
> *11And it will nevermore be necessary for each one to teach his neighbor and his fellow citizen or each one his brother, saying, Know (perceive, have knowledge of, and get acquainted by experience with) the Lord, for all will know Me, from the smallest to the greatest of them.*
>
> *12**For I will be merciful and gracious toward their sins and I will remember their deeds of unrighteousness no more.***
>
> *13**When God speaks of a new [covenant or agreement], He makes the first one obsolete (out of use). And what is obsolete (out of use and annulled because of age) is ripe for disappearance and to be dispensed with altogether.***

If God had not deprived the Israelite nation of understanding of *"the secret things,"* if He had not spiritually disabled His beloved people, then from the start, they would have perceived that the first agreement was simply a symbolic picture of all the true blessings and benefits that were to come. They would have understood that the Horeb agreement, an agreement that demanded external ritualistic animal sacrifices as a means of expiating sin, was only a temporary contract. Yes, from the beginning, they would have known that it was a contract that would last only until God made with men a permanent and better new covenant.

If God had not deprived the Israelite nation of understanding of *"the secret things,"* they would also have known that the Messiah (the Lamb of God) would come to earth the first time to lay down His life in order to seal with His own blood that permanent and better new covenant. They would have known that in offering Himself as a sacrifice, once for all time, the Messiah would take away men's sins. And in so doing, He would completely remove any need for the animal sacrifices to ever again be offered as a means of atonement for sin.

However, as you now know, for His own name's sake and for the sake of all mankind, God did deprive the Israelite nation of understanding of *"the secret things."* God did disable His beloved people by spiritually blinding and deafening them. Moreover, God did not allow anything or anyone to interfere with His keeping the nation of Israel spiritually blind and deaf or to change His well laid future plans for His spiritually handicapped people. He deliberately blocked every speck of illuminating light that might have broken through the barrier of the spiritual intellectual darkness that closed them in.

For example, when God made the first covenant with Israel (that is, the Horeb agreement), you will recall that Moses covered himself with a veil in order to hide from the Israelites the beams of light that shone from his face. That veil was absolutely necessary. For though it is true that in part Moses wore the veil because the people were afraid to come near him, there was a much more significant and profound reason for him donning that covering.

Let me share with you another marvelous revelation which will enlighten you as to the main reason why Moses put a veil over his face.

In his letter to the Corinthians, Paul provides you with an additional piece of the overall Scriptural puzzle regarding the Jews' God-ordained spiritual blindness. **Paul lets you know that the veil's main purpose was to keep the Israelites from catching a glimpse of** *"the secret things"* **regarding the future abolishment of the Horeb covenant (agreement).**

The veil was not only used to calm the people, it was also used to keep the Israelites blinded insofar as *"the secret things"* were concerned regarding the future disappearance of the temporary Horeb covenant and the ministration of the permanent new covenant. For, had the people watched as the glory of the ministration of the first covenant vanished, they might have recognized the fact that the Horeb covenant with all its external rituals, animal sacrifices and legalism was not a permanent or completed agreement. It was instead a temporary agreement that when fulfilled would disappear as surely as the glory of its ministration had disappeared from Moses' face.

For a moment, put yourself in Israel's shoes. Try to imagine how you would have felt and responded if, under the same circumstances, you had been allowed to see *"the secret things"* regarding the eventual abolishment of the Horeb covenant. Suppose you had just entered into a binding contract with God. Afterward, you found out that the agreement which you had entered into was destined to become obsolete, and that it would one day actually be abolished. You also learned that the animal sacrifices that you were required to offer under the Horeb agreement did not take away your sins. They instead only covered them over. Furthermore, you came to understand that those required animal sacrifices were a continual fresh reminder of the sins that you had committed. Worst of all, you realized that you did not have the power to consistently obey the laws that earlier you had agreed by contract to keep. You were faced with the awful truth that you were a slave to sin. Moreover, you knew that the contract that you had entered into would never change that fact.

Under the circumstances described in the former paragraph, would you agree that lack of stimulus would probably erode your determination and motivation to do right by the standards of God's Word? For instance, in such a seemingly hopeless situation, might you be tempted to throw up your hands and say, "What's the use? I'm trapped! I can't stop sinning anyway, and the animal sacrifices don't take away my sins, so why should I continue trying to please God? I might as well give up."

In the example that I just offered, did you catch a glimpse of why it was an act of great wisdom and mercy on God's part to hide with a veil the beams of light (that is, the illumination, the glory of the ministration of the Horeb covenant) that shone from Moses' face? Can you see why God did not want His beloved people to see the glory of the Horeb agreement disappear? God had to make sure that the nation of Israel remained blind to *"the secret things"* regarding the future abolishment of the Horeb covenant, for they were a chosen people. As you learned in a former chapter of this series, they had been chosen to help God fulfill Genesis 3:15 and many other predictions. They had also been chosen to help God keep His sacred covenant promises to Abraham.

The crux of the matter is that the Israelites not being allowed to watch the disappearance of the glory of the ministration of the old covenant was for the purpose of helping them fulfill their holy call. In that particular case, the cliché that says, "What you don't know won't hurt you" fits to a tee.

Pay strict attention as you read from the *Holy Bible, King James Version* the Jewish apostle's explanation of why Moses wore a veil. Also keep in mind that Paul is referring to the **first agreement** being done away with. He is absolutely not inferring that the righteous commandments of God are done away with. My friend, that would be ridiculous since as you know, under the new covenant (agreement), men are still required to keep those same laws. As a matter of fact, Yeshua died to seal with His own blood the new covenant in order to give men the power to learn and obey those same commandments. For, in the new covenant, God actually promises to write those laws on men's hearts and minds. (Hebrews 10:16-17.) Hence, the new covenant gives men the power to meet all the righteous and just requirements of the Horeb covenant without its external rituals, animal sacrifices and legalism.

In order for you to get the gist of Paul's explanation of Moses' veil, it is necessary that you start reading at the beginning of the following chapter. To help you to stay on track, I will periodically expound on the content of those verses.

> *II Corinthians 3:1-16 (King James Version.)*
>
> *1DO we begin again to commend ourselves? or need we, as some others, epistles of commendation to you, or letters of commendation from you?*
>
> *2Ye are our epistle written in our hearts, known and read of all men:*
>
> *3Forasmuch as ye are manifestly declared to be the epistle of Christ ministered by us, **written not with ink, but with the Spirit of the living God; not in tables of stone, but in fleshy tables of the heart.***

II Corinthians 3:1-16 is a segment of a letter that was written by Paul in defense of his apostleship and to make known his God-given right to minister to the Corinthian Church. Fortunately for us, the Jewish apostle, Paul, also inserts in his letter numerous other eye opening truths.

For example, in verse three, Paul is referring to both the Horeb and the new covenants. Remember, God promised in Jeremiah 31:31-34 (see also Hebrews 10:15-17) that He would write His laws on men's hearts and minds. Under the first covenant, God's Ten Commandments were written in stone. Under the promised new, more excellent covenant, God's commandments are engraved in men's hearts and minds by the spirit of God.

> *3Forasmuch as ye are manifestly declared to be the epistle of Christ ministered by us, **written not with ink, but with the Spirit of the living God; not in tables of stone, but in fleshy tables of the heart.***
>
> *4And such trust have we through Christ to God-ward.*

5Not that we are sufficient of ourselves to think any thing as of ourselves; but our sufficiency is of God;

*6Who also hath made us able ministers of **the new testament**; not of the letter, but of the spirit: for the letter killeth, but the spirit giveth life.*

The Jewish apostle, Paul, informs you in the previous verses that true ministers of the gospel, himself included, are ministers of **the new covenant**. The term **"new testament"** is simply another way of saying **"new covenant."** Paul says in verse six, ***"Who also hath made us able ministers of the new testament."***

In those same verses, Paul also describes some of the differences between the requirements of the first and second agreements. So I will briefly touch on those differences.

Under the Horeb testament (agreement), the Ten Commandments were written by God in tablets of stone. In Deuteronomy 10:5, God commanded Moses to put the tablets of stone containing the Ten Commandments **into the ark** of the covenant. The ark was a special container that had been made specifically to hold them. On the other hand, God's laws concerning the external rituals, animal sacrifices and all other legalistic matters of the Law were written with ink by Moses in the *"Book of the Law."* Moses later directed the Levites in Deuteronomy 31:26 to put the *"Book of the Law"* **by the side of the ark** which contained the Ten Commandments.

Under the new testament (covenant, agreement), God's Ten Commandments and the secret truths concerning the external ritualistic and legalistic requirements of the Horeb covenant are all written on the hearts and minds of men. Of course, the secret truths concerning the external ritualistic and legalistic requirements of the Horeb covenant that I just mentioned involve men understanding the deep inner meaning and symbology of such things as the temporary Old Testament animal sacrifices which, after being completely fulfilled, were inevitably abolished as a means of atonement.

For example, under the new covenant, men are made to understand that the animal sacrifices were simply a pattern and a foreshadowing of that which now has its true existence in the one time sacrifice that Yeshua, the Anointed One, the Lamb of God, made by offering up His own life in order to take away men's sins. He did that by allowing His blood to be shed in order to seal the promised new covenant, the new covenant in which God also promises to forgive men's sins.

So what blessings do we have in the new covenant that we did not have under the old covenant? We have God's promise to write on our hearts and minds His everlasting Ten Commandments and the truth concerning the symbology of the now fulfilled and thus abolished external rituals, animal sacrifices and legalistic matters of the Law. We also have forgiveness for our past sins and the power to obey God's commandments so that we will not continue to sin by breaking God's laws. Consequently, since Christ's death has freed us from sin, we are free (that is, we have the power) to meet all the righteous and just requirements of the Law without any longer having to comply with the Law's demands regarding the external rituals, animal sacrifices and legalism. We are free to do what we were originally created to do. We are free to fear God and keep all His commandments.

In verse six, Paul describes the external ritualistic and legalistic requirements of the Horeb covenant (that is, legalistic requirements such as the animal sacrifices) as *"the letter."* Furthermore, he goes on to say that *"the letter killeth."*

You already know why *"the letter"* (that is, why the external ritualistic and legalistic demands of the first covenant) *"killeth."* The letter kills because it exposes men's sin and is a continual reminder of men's sin, but it does not take away sin, nor does it free men from sin or provide men with the power to stop sinning. Consequently, since the wages of sin is death, *"the letter killeth."*

On the other hand, Paul describes the new covenant that is sealed with the sacrificial blood of Jewish Yeshua, the Christ, as being *"of the spirit."* He describes the new covenant as being *"of the Spirit,"* because **the spirit is the truth**, God's Word. (I John 5:7, John 6:63.) Moreover, the spirit, God's Word, gives life. (Psalm 119:50.) Take a moment to look up the word "spirit" in *Strong's Exhaustive Concordance of the Bible,* Greek Dictionary of the New Testament, and you will find that in Greek the word "spirit" "pneuma" means "life." The spirit, God's Word, is truth and life. For those reasons, Yeshua said in John 12:50, *"I know that His commandment is life everlasting."* Thus, Paul describes the new covenant that is sealed with the sacrificial blood of Yeshua, the Christ, as being *"of the spirit."*

God promised that He would write His life-giving laws on men's hearts and minds in order that they might obey them and live. So you can see that in this instance, Paul's statement in II Corinthians 3:6 is absolutely applicable. Indeed, the new covenant is *"of the spirit."* Men are now free from sin. Men are under the law of liberty (that is, men are free to obey God in everything). They are free to meet all the righteous and just requirements of the Law. They are free to keep God's laws. Men are free to walk in the Spirit (that is, men are free to walk in the truth) and live.

In the following verses, verses seven through eleven, Paul goes on to speak about the glory that was and is attributed to both covenants. He actually compares the first covenant (the ministration of death) with the more excellent new covenant (the ministration of life). And as you can guess, there really is no comparison. For, the first covenant only represented the real thing (that is, the first covenant only represented the more excellent, more sublime new covenant). The first covenant only gave men God's commandments written in stone while the new covenant gave men God's promise to write His laws on their hearts and minds.

With the insight you have already received during your study of this series, you should have no difficulty understanding Paul's teaching in the next verses of II Corinthians chapter three.

> 7*But if the ministration of death, written and engraven in stones, was glorious, so that the children of Israel could not stedfastly behold the face of Moses for the glory of his countenance;* **which glory was to be done away:**
>
> 8*How shall not the ministration of the spirit be rather glorious?*
>
> 9*For if the ministration of condemnation be glory, much more doth the ministration of righteousness exceed in glory.*
>
> 10*For even that which was made glorious had no glory in this respect, by reason of the glory that excelleth.*
>
> 11*For if that which is done away was glorious, much more that which remaineth is glorious.*

In verses ten and eleven, the apostle explains that when compared to the glory of the new covenant, the glory of the Horeb covenant which was temporarily seen in the face of Moses has come to have no splendor at all. For, the brighter, permanent glory of the new covenant with its *"more important (sublimer, higher and nobler) promises"* (Hebrews 8:6) so outshines and excels beyond measure the temporary glory of the ministration of the first covenant that was seen in Moses' face so as to make it seem like nothing in comparison.

What comparison is there between commandments written in stone which you **do not** have the power to keep and commandments written on your heart and mind which **you do** have power to keep? What comparison is there between animal sacrifices that atone for sin but never take sin away and the one time sacrifice that Yeshua made which actually frees you from sin and gives you the power to overcome sin, the one time sacrifice which gives you the power to do what you were created to do? My friend, there is no comparison.

If you visited an art gallery, and there you viewed a painting of a fireworks display with a finale of five thousand fireworks, you would think that the artist's picture was spectacular. However, if sometime later you got to be an actual spectator of the real thing, you would proclaim that the display was in reality a much more spectacular sight than the picture had conveyed. In comparison to the real thing, the picture would seem as nothing. Likewise, in comparison to the new covenant the picture of the old covenant (that is, the Horeb covenant) seems as nothing.

Pay close attention to the following verses of II Corinthians chapter three, for in them, the Jewish apostle Paul unravels the mystery that I mentioned earlier. Paul relays to you the main reason for Moses' veil.

> *12Seeing then that we have such hope, we use great plainness of speech:*
>
> *13And not as Moses, which put a vail over his face, that the children of Israel could not stedfastly look to the end of that which is abolished:*

Paul could not have explained the enigma of Moses' veil any clearer than he did in verse thirteen. He came right out and told the Corinthian Church that the main reason for Moses' veil was to keep the Israelites from seeing the future end of the Horeb covenant. Why? Because God did not want them to understand *"the secret things"* concerning the eventual abolishment of the Horeb covenant and all its external rituals, animal sacrifices and legalistic requirements. God wanted the Israelites to remain blind and deaf to *"the secret things"* in order to help Him fulfill His prediction in Genesis 3:15 and His Abrahamic promises concerning the salvation of all the peoples of the earth.

Paul goes on to explain how to this day, God has kept the majority of his Jewish brethren blinded to the fact that the external requirements of the Horeb testament (covenant) have been abolished. The Jews still do not perceive that the external requirements outlived their usefulness in that all they once represented and foreshadowed is now a reality.

Moses' face was not the only thing that was covered with a veil that day. No! The hearts and minds of God's beloved Abrahamic covenant people were also veiled. Hence, to this very day whenever the Scriptures that pertain to the external requirements of Old Testament (that is, the Horeb covenant) are read, that same veil, that God-ordained spiritual blindness, remains on their hearts. The Jews cannot understand that the old covenant has been abolished and has disappeared and that the better promised new covenant has taken its place. The Jews can only see the glory of the Horeb covenant because like those Israelites in Moses' day, they too are not allowed to see the end of the first covenant.

> *14But their minds were blinded: for until this day remaineth the same vail untaken away in the reading of the old testament; which vail is done away in Christ.*
>
> *15But even unto this day, when Moses is read, the vail is upon their heart.*
>
> *16Nevertheless when it shall turn to the Lord, the vail shall be taken away.*

In verse sixteen, Paul lets you know that the day will come when the veil of spiritual blindness will be lifted. I will go into more detail on that subject later on. At this time, however, we will continue with our present topic since there is still much to learn.

Now that you understand the mystery of Moses' veil, you will appreciate the following Scriptural confirmation concerning information that I shared with you earlier regarding the differences in the first and second covenants. I also want you to catch a glimpse of exactly what the God-imposed veil of blindness hides from the Jewish people. For you must be knowledgeable of those things if you are to appreciate and understand God's wisdom, mercy and kindness in keeping the Jews spiritually blind and deaf to *"the secret things"* generation after generation.

Under the former Horeb agreement, men could not consistently keep God's law. Thus, men's sin weakened the power (that is, men's sin weakened the effectiveness) of the Horeb covenant. However, as you learned earlier in this series, when Yeshua shed His blood and irrevocably sealed the new covenant with it, He freed men from sin and equipped them with all the power they would ever need to keep the promised new contract (that is, to consistently obey all God's laws). **Thus, under the promised blood-sealed new covenant, all the**

righteous and just requirements of the Horeb covenant can now be fully met in true believers. Yes, under the promised new covenant, men are finally free to perform the full function for which they were originally created. Men are free to fear God and keep His commandments. (Ecclesiastes 12:13.)

As you read, keep in mind what the Jewish apostle John said in 1 John 5:7 in *The Amplified Bible.* He said, *"**the (Holy) Spirit is the truth.**"* Also, remember all that you learned regarding how *"the letter killeth."*

> *Romans 8:2-4 (The Amplified Bible.)*
>
> *2For the law of the Spirit of life [which is] in Christ Jesus [the law of our new being] has freed me from the law of sin and of death.*
>
> *3For God has done what the Law could not do, [its power] being weakened by the flesh [the entire nature of man without the Holy Spirit]. Sending His own Son in the guise of sinful flesh and as an offering for sin, [God] condemned sin in the flesh [subdued, overcame, deprived it of its power over all who accept that sacrifice],*
>
> *4So that the righteous and just requirement of the Law might be fully met in us who live and move not in the ways of the flesh but in the ways of the Spirit [our lives governed not by the standards and according to the dictates of the flesh, but controlled by the Holy Spirit].*

The writer of *The Letter to the Hebrews* explains exactly what the shedding of the Messiah's blood, blood which sealed the new covenant, accomplished that the blood of the ritualistic sacrificial animals that sealed the Horeb covenant never could. As you read this writer's inspired words, keep in mind these three points:

(1) According to 1 John 3:4, sin is the violating, the breaking of God's law (that is, sin is the breaking of God's commandments). Through the blood that sealed the promised new covenant, God freed men from sin so that they could permanently stop sinning and thus accomplish what they were created to do.

(2) This whole segment of Scripture is referring to the promised new covenant and Christ's shed blood which sealed it. It is referring to the promised new covenant that provides cleansing from sin. It is

referring to the blood-sealed new covenant that gives men all the power they will ever need to understand and consistently keep God's laws.

(3) The portion of Moses' Law that the writer refers to in these verses pertains to the external rituals of the law (that is, the ritualistic animal sacrifices) **and not**, I repeat, **and not** God's everlasting commandments. The ritualistic animal sacrifices which were offered under the Horeb covenant were merely *"a rude outline of the good things to come"* (that is, a rude outline of the new covenant promises). For in the new covenant, God promises absolute forgiveness for past sins. He also promises to write His laws (that is, His commandments) upon His peoples' hearts and minds so that they will understand them and consistently obey them.

Hebrews 10:1-17 (The Amplified Bible.)

1FOR SINCE the Law has merely a rude outline (foreshadowing) of the good things to come—instead of fully expressing those things—it can never by offering the same sacrifices continually year after year make perfect those who approach [its altars].

2For if it were otherwise, would [these sacrifices] not have stopped being offered? Since the worshipers had once for all been cleansed, they would no longer have any guilt or consciousness of sin.

3But [as it is] these sacrifices annually bring a fresh remembrance of sins [to be atoned for],

4Because the blood of bulls and goats is powerless to take sins away.

5Hence, when He [Christ] entered into the world, He said, Sacrifices and offerings You have not desired, but instead You have made ready a body for Me [to offer];

6In burnt offerings and sin offerings You have taken no delight.

7Then I said, Behold, here I am, coming to do Your will, O God—[to fulfill] what is written of Me in the volume of the Book. [Ps. 40:6-8.]

8When He said just before, You have neither desired, nor have You taken delight in sacrifices and offerings and burnt offerings and sin offerings—all of which are offered according to the Law—

Earlier, I asked you to keep in mind that this whole segment of Scripture is referring to the promised new covenant and to Christ's blood which sealed it. The next verses will confirm that statement. For they will show you that the first covenant (that is, the Horeb covenant) has been done away with in order to make way for the promised blood-sealed new covenant. Notice that it was not God's laws (that is, God's commandments) that were done away with. God forbid! Rather, that which was done away with was **the former means of expiating sin** (that is, the external ritualistic animal sacrifices that were offered as a requirement of the former Horeb agreement).

> *9He then went on to say, Behold, [here] I am, coming to do Your will. **Thus He does away with and annuls the first (former) order [as a means of expiating sin] so that He might inaugurate and establish the second (latter) order. [Ps. 40:6-8.]***

Note that *The Amplified Bible* translator inserted a Scripture reference after the previous verse, verse nine. That reference is Psalm 40:6-8. I think it will be beneficial to you if you take the time and read that text before you resume your study of Hebrews chapter ten, so I have included it.

> *Psalm 40:6-8 (The Amplified Bible.)*

> *6Sacrifice and offering You do not desire, nor have You delight in them; **You have given me the capacity to hear and obey [Your law, a more valuable service than] burnt offerings and sin offerings [which] You do not require.***

> *7Then said I, Behold, I come; in the volume of the book it is written of me;*

> *8I delight to do Your will, O my God; yes, Your law is within my heart.*

King David spoke the preceding inspired words in Psalm forty. However, because he did not have understanding of *"the secret things,"* he did not comprehend the mystery of the kingdom of God that he uttered. He did not understand that he was actually predicting the future annulment of the Horeb covenant with its required animal sacrifices as a means of expiating sin. He did not realize that he was voicing the fact that God never desired or delighted in those Horeb covenant animal sacrifices because they did not take away sin. They only covered over sin. If they had taken sin away there would not have been any need to keep making sin offerings year after year. The animal sacrifices were only a temporary indicator of the real thing that was to come. David did not realize that when He spoke those words, God had the future new covenant in mind with its *"more important (sublimer, higher, and nobler) promises."* (Hebrews 8:6.)

In Psalm 40:6, David spoke of the future promised new covenant and the capacity (power) to obey God's commands that God's people would be endowed with under the new agreement. *"Behold, to obey is better than sacrifice...."* (I Samuel 15:22.) Obedience to God's commandments is what God has always wanted from men, and under the new covenant, men can now offer to God obedience rather than the sacrificial burnt offerings, sacrificial burnt offerings in which He never delighted nor desired in the first place. The Messiah's shed blood which sealed the new covenant made the new covenant a legally binding agreement and thus made the new covenant promises possible.

We will now resume reading our previous text in Hebrews chapter ten, beginning with verse nine.

Hebrews 10:9-17 (The Amplified Bible.)

9He then went on to say, Behold, [here] I am, coming to do Your will. Thus He does away with and annuls the first (former) order [as a means of expiating sin] so that He might inaugurate and establish the second (latter) order. [Ps. 40:6-8.]

10And in accordance with this will [of God], we have been made holy (consecrated and sanctified) through the offering made once for all of the body of Jesus Christ (the Anointed One),

11Furthermore, every [human] priest stands [at his altar of service] ministering daily, offering the same sacrifices over and over again, which never are able to strip [from every side of us] the sins [that envelop us] and take them away—

12Whereas this One [Christ], after He had offered a single sacrifice for our sins [that shall avail] for all time, sat down at the right hand of God,

13Then to wait until His enemies should be made a stool beneath His feet.[Ps. 110:1.]

462

14For by a single offering He has forever completely cleansed and perfected those who are consecrated and made holy.

15And also the Holy Spirit adds His testimony to us [in confirmation of this]. For having said,

16This is the agreement (testament, covenant) that I will set up and conclude with them after those days, says the Lord: I will imprint My laws upon their hearts, and I will inscribe them on their minds (on their inmost thoughts and understanding),

17He then goes on to say, And their sins and their lawbreaking I will remember no more. [Jer. 31:33,34]

Yeshua, the Anointed One, had to die in order to make God's prediction in Genesis 3:15 come true. He had to die in order to fulfill the Abrahamic covenant regarding the salvation of all the nations and many other Biblical promises and predictions. The shedding of His blood which would seal the promised new covenant would give men an opportunity to be completely free from their past sins and from the devil's power. It would free men to again do what they were originally created to do (that is, it would free men to fear God and keep His commandments). Yes, the Messiah's death was necessary. However, God had to make sure that His death was carried out exactly as the prophets had predicted.

God's own people were chosen to fulfill the prophets' words which involved their failing to recognize the promised Messiah, rejecting Him and turning Him over to the Gentiles to be crucified so that the new covenant could be legally ratified (that is, so that the new covenant could be made valid or sealed with His blood). Under such circumstances, don't you agree with my earlier comment regarding God showing great kindness and mercy toward His people, Israel, by making and keeping their eyes spiritually blind and their ears spiritually deaf?

Do you really believe that if the Jews' spiritual eyesight and hearing had been intact that they would have handed over the promised Messiah, *"Immanuel [God with us],"* to their Gentile enemies, the Romans, for crucifixion? No! A thousand times No! They would have fought to the death rather than turn over the Messiah to their oppressors. Again I ask you! If the Jews had understood what was taking place at that time, do you really believe they would have been a party to or even stood by and watched as the Messiah suffered at the hands of their enemies? No! Of course not. Yet, without the Jews' participation in God's salvation plan, the prophesies that pertained to the Messiah's death could never have been fulfilled.

Without the Jews' foreordained participation in God's salvation plan, no human being would have had a chance to be free from sin, no human being would have had an opportunity to be free from Satan's evil control. Thus, no human being would have had the power to do what they were originally created to do. The bottom line is that were it not for the Jews' God-decreed spiritual blindness and deafness and their God-ordained participation in the crucifixion of the Messiah, mankind would not today be enjoying the benefits of the promised blood-sealed new covenant. The Jews' God-appointed mission was not a pleasant one, but it was absolutely essential for the salvation of all mankind.

Earlier, I told you that I would fully explain what I meant when I said that God kept the Jews in spiritual darkness for His own purpose. I am sure you will agree that I have kept my word.

(1) God would not have disabled His beloved covenant people in the first place if He had not had a legitimate and merciful reason for doing so.

(2) God could have healed His people's spiritually blind eyes and deaf ears long ago. However, to this day, He has deliberately allowed them to remain in their blind and deaf state so that they might help Him to fully accomplish His will and purpose upon the earth.

My friend, there can be no doubt that the Jews continued blindness and deafness was an instrument of mercy to aid them in fulfilling the Bible prophecies that pertained to the Messiah's suffering and death and the promised new covenant. Furthermore, their continued spiritual blindness and deafness is a merciful tool that God has used and that He still uses to extend His promised Abrahamic blessings (salvation) to all the nations.

Do you recall how the Jews were kept in bondage in Egypt so that God's promises to Abraham would be fulfilled? God left His beloved people in that harsh and abusive situation until they became the great nation that He had promised to Abraham, Isaac and Jacob, the nation through whom the promised Messiah would eventually come. Think about it! The Jews underwent four-hundred years of severe hardship and cruelty in order to help God fulfill His Word in Genesis 3:15 and His covenant with Abraham. Well! Along those same lines, the Jews have been kept in their spiritually blind and deaf state so that through them God's promises to Abraham, Isaac and Jacob concerning the salvation of all the peoples of the earth might also be accomplished.

Oh my friend, don't you see? God made His prediction in Genesis 3:15 **before** the Jews ever sinned against Him. As a matter of fact, God gave that warning to Satan before Abraham, Isaac, Jacob, or the Jews even existed. However, since God's prediction in Genesis 3:15 had to be fulfilled, God chose the Israelites to help Him bring to pass all that He had spoken in that verse. Likewise, the covenant promises that God had made to Abraham, Isaac and Jacob had to be fulfilled. Thus, God chose His blessed people, the Israelites, to help Him keep those promises also.

Amazingly, once one is able to view the whole scenario, one is compelled to thank God for spiritually disabling the Jewish people and for extending their blind and deaf condition. I said that one is compelled to thank God for disabling the Jewish people and for extending their blind and deaf condition because the Jews' continued spiritual handicaps have been and still are greatly used by God in advancing His Abrahamic promise to bless (that is, to save) the nations through the seed of Abraham, Isaac and Jacob. Moreover, as a follower of Yeshua, I am myself a recipient of that particular promised Abrahamic blessing.

By extending His peoples' spiritually blind and deaf condition, God ultimately showed mercy to both the Jews and the Gentiles. On the one hand, the Jews were shown mercy in that their disabilities enabled them to more easily carry out the awful God-ordained bloody task that they were destined to accomplish for the glory of their God and the salvation of all mankind (that is, the task of rejecting the promised Messiah and turning Him over to the Gentiles for crucifixion). The Gentiles, on the other hand, were shown mercy in that the awful task, that by God's own design the Jews were compelled to perform, enabled Christ to ratify (that is, to seal) the new covenant with His own blood and to thus bring to pass the Abrahamic covenant promise concerning the nations' salvation. For God had told Abraham, *"In you will all the families and kindred of the earth be blessed."* Furthermore, in the following verses, Isaiah also prophesied concerning the Gentiles receiving salvation through the Jewish Messiah.

Isaiah 11:1, 9-10 (The Amplified Bible.)

1AND THERE shall come forth a Shoot out of the stock of Jesse [David's father], and a Branch out of his roots shall grow and bear fruit.

*⁹They shall not hurt or destroy in all My holy mountain,
for the earth shall be full of the knowledge of the Lord
as the waters cover the sea.*

*¹⁰**And it shall be in that day that the Root of Jesse
shall stand as a signal for the peoples; of Him shall the
nations inquire and seek knowledge, and His dwelling
shall be glory [His rest glorious]!***

It is hard to imagine how the nation of Israel will respond when God lifts the present blindness from their eyes and they are finally able to see that Yeshua is indeed the promised Messiah, the Christ, the Anointed One. It goes without saying that when that day comes, the Israelites will be devastated over their past conduct. They will be heartsick because, as Isaiah foretold, their God-ordained spiritual disabilities caused them to blindly reject and disown their Messiah. Oh, the sorrow that they will experience! Oh, how they will grievously weep and mourn! God Himself describes the Jews' extraordinary emotional pain in the following text.

Zechariah 12:10-14 (The Amplified Bible.)

*¹⁰And I will pour out upon the house of David and upon
the inhabitants of Jerusalem the Spirit of grace or
unmerited favor and supplication. **And they shall look
[earnestly] upon Me Whom they have pierced, and they
shall mourn for Him as one mourns for his only son,
and shall be in bitterness for Him as one who is in
bitterness for his firstborn.***

*¹¹In that day shall there be a great mourning in
Jerusalem, as the mourning of [the city of]
Hadadrimmon in the Valley of Megiddo [over beloved
King Josiah].*

The Amplified Bible translators provide a footnote for the previous verse, Zechariah 12:11. The contents of that footnote give the reader a glimpse of the deep grief that Israel experienced when righteous King Josiah died. God compares Israel's grief over Josiah to the future sadness that they will feel when their eyes are finally opened. You see, even the knowledge that they were spiritually blind and deaf when they carried out their God-ordained mission will not ease the degree of emotional pain and grief that the Jews will experience upon realizing the

God-decreed devastating role that they were forced to play in the Messiah's crucifixion.

> King Josiah was mortally wounded at the age of thirty-nine. His death sparked an extraordinarily deep sense of grief among the people. **That same kind of deep grief will characterize the mourning of Israel when they recognize as their once-crucified Messiah Him Who has come to reign.**

12 And the land shall mourn, every family apart: the [kingly] family of the house of David apart and their wives apart; the family of the house of Nathan [David's son] apart and their wives apart;

13 The [priestly] family of the house of Levi apart and their wives apart; the family of Shimei [grandson of Levi] apart and their wives apart;

14 All the families that are left, each by itself, and their wives by themselves [each with an overwhelming individual sorrow over having _blindly_ rejected their unrecognized Messiah].

Oh, my heart breaks and tears pour down my face when I consider the future heart-wrenching mourning that the nation of Israel will experience. The Israelites' anguish will be so great that Zechariah could only compare it to their mourning over righteous King Josiah. Their hearts will be broken. They will grieve as though they had just lost their first-born son. God's beloved Abrahamic covenant people will lament and bewail with agonizing regret. Their souls will be tortured by grief over the fact that in their God-ordained blindness they failed to recognize their Messiah when He came the first time. Thus, upon His return, the Jews' spiritual eyes will be opened, and they will look upon Him Whom they indirectly pierced.

"Pierced" is a perfect word to describe what the Jews indirectly and blindly did to their Messiah. For, as you know, in their blind and deaf spiritual state, the Jews turned Him over to the Gentiles (the Romans) who actually pierced His hands and His feet with nails when they crucified Him. King David prophesied about Christ's crucifixion. He described exactly the way it would take place. Yes, David foretold how God's own beloved people would turn the Anointed One over to the Gentiles for crucifixion.

Everything that was forecast to happen to the Anointed One was recorded in the Jews own Scriptures. Yet, as you saw earlier, God mercifully kept the Jews spiritually handicapped so that they could not understand the meaning of the prophets' future predictions or the signs of the times. For example, the prophesy that I will share with you next was written by King David. Some Bible scholars believe this to be the actual Psalm that Christ quoted as He hung suffering and dying on the cross, fulfilling this very prediction.

Psalm 22:1-19 (The Amplified Bible.)

[1]MY GOD, my God, why have You forsaken me? Why are You so far from helping me, and from the words of my groaning?

[2]O my God, I cry in the daytime, but You answer not; and by night I am not silent or find no rest.

[3]But You are holy, O You Who dwell in [the holy place where] the praises of Israel [are offered].

[4]Our fathers trusted in You; they trusted (leaned on, relied on You, and were confident) and You delivered them.

[5]They cried to You and were delivered; they trusted in, leaned on, and confidently relied on You, and were not ashamed or confounded or disappointed.

David's prophecy in the following verses was completely fulfilled at the crucifixion of the Messiah. Yet, the Jews did not recognize that it was their long awaited Messiah who hung on that Roman cross. In verse six, God's Word describes how the Anointed One was made to feel during that awful period of humiliation and suffering.

[6]But I am a worm, and no man; I am the scorn of men, and despised by the people.

[7]All who see me laugh at me and mock me; they shoot out the lip, they shake the head, saying,

[8]He trusted and rolled himself on the Lord, that He would deliver him. Let Him deliver him, seeing that He delights in him!

If you take time to read Matthew 27:43, you will see that the previous verse, verse eight, contains the exact words that God's spiritually blind and deaf beloved covenant people railed at the promised Messiah, *"Immanuel [God with us],"* during His crucifixion.

Let us continue reading David's prediction of the crucifixion of the Messiah.

> *9Yet You are He Who took me out of the womb; You made me hope and trust when I was on my mother's breasts.*
>
> *10I was cast upon You from my very birth; from my mother's womb You have been my God.*
>
> *11Be not far from me, for trouble is near and there is none to help.*
>
> *12Many [foes like] bulls have surrounded me; strong bulls of Bashan have hedged me in.*
>
> *13Against me they opened their mouths wide, like a ravening and roaring lion.*
>
> *14I am poured out like water, and all my bones are out of joint. My heart is like wax; it is softened [with anguish] and melted down within me.*
>
> *15My strength is dried up like a fragment of clay pottery; [with thirst] my tongue cleaves to my jaws; and You have brought me into the dust of death.*

Give careful attention to the next verse.

> *16For [like a pack of] dogs they have encompassed me; a company of evildoers has encircled me, **they pierced my hands and my feet.***

No one ever pierced David's hands and feet, did they? No! Of course they didn't. David is not prophesying about his own hands and feet being pierced. He is foretelling the Messiah's crucifixion. He is foretelling how upon the Jews' urging, the *"evildoers"* (the Romans) pierced the Messiah's hands and feet with nails when they crucified Him. Remember what Zechariah said in Zechariah 12:10? He prophesied, *"And they shall look [earnestly] upon Me Whom they have pierced...."* Zechariah's prediction will be fully realized upon Christ's future return to earth. For then, the Jews shall indeed look upon the Messiah whom they indirectly pierced. However, unlike the first time when in unbelief they looked upon Him whom they had pierced as He hung on a cross dying for the sins of all mankind, they will recognize the Messiah and believe on Him when He returns. Moreover, as you saw earlier, they will grieve for their past treatment of Him.

In a moment, you will read verse seventeen. However, before you do, I want you to consider what you read previously in verse fourteen—*"all my bones are out of joint."* By combining those inspired words with what is written in the following verse, you have David's prophetic description of a man being crucified. David's writing depicts a man being stretched out on a cross. Jewish Yeshua, the Anointed One, was stretched out on a cross. He was crucified.

17I can count all my bones; [the evildoers] gaze at me.

The fulfillment of the next verse is recorded in John 19:23-24. It happened exactly as David prophesied. After Yeshua, the Messiah, had been crucified, Roman soldiers cast lots for His seamless tunic.

*18**They part my clothing among them and cast lots for my raiment (a long, shirtlike garment, a seamless undertunic).***
19But be not far from me, O Lord: O my Help, hasten to aid me!

What David described in the preceding Psalm, Psalm twenty-two, is what the prophet Zachariah said the Jews would mourn for. God's people will grieve over the fact that their Messiah came and they did not recognize Him or believe on Him. Though David warned God's people in those verses that the Anointed One would be put to death and even described the manner in which He would die, they were too spiritually blind and deaf to grasp the meaning of those prophesied events. As the prophet Isaiah had said regarding the Jews and their religious leaders, *"so all of these future events are a sealed book to them...."* (Isaiah 29:11, *The Living Bible*.)

Over and over again, God told His beloved people what would happen when the promised Messiah came. He warned them that the Messiah would suffer at the hands of men. He warned them that men would kill the Messiah. However, because God's people had been stricken with spiritual blindness and deafness, they did not understand what God was telling them. No matter how often they heard or read the Biblical prophesies that contain the mystery of the kingdom of God concerning the Christ's death, they were incapable of comprehending the deep inner meaning of God's Word in that area. As the prophets had foretold, the Lord's covenant people were truly blind and truly deaf. Moreover, God wanted His blessed people to remain that way until they unwittingly had the privilege of helping Him accomplish His purpose and completely fulfilled His prophesies and promises.

Isaiah predicted the suffering that the Anointed One would undergo. He also forecast the Messiah's eventual death. He even described the Jews' God-ordained blind and deaf indifference and callousness to the Messiah's pain and torment. See Isaiah's prophecy for yourself in *The Living Bible.*

Isaiah 53:1-12 (The Living Bible.)

¹*But, oh, how few believe it! Who will listen? To whom will God reveal his saving power?*

²*In God's eyes he was like a tender green shoot, sprouting from a root in dry and sterile ground. But in our eyes there was no attractiveness at all, nothing to make us want him.*

³*We despised him and rejected him—a man of sorrows, acquainted with bitterest grief. We turned our backs on him and looked the other way when he went by. He was despised and we didn't care.*

⁴*Yet it was our grief he bore, our sorrows that weighed him down. And we thought his troubles were a punishment from God, for his own sins!*

⁵*But he was wounded and bruised for our sins. He was chastised that we might have peace; he was lashed—and we were healed!.*

⁶*We are the ones who strayed away like sheep! We, who left God's paths to follow our own. Yet God laid on him the guilt and sins of every one of us!*

⁷*He was oppressed and he was afflicted, yet he never said a word. He was brought as a lamb to the slaughter; and as a sheep before her shearers is dumb, so he stood silent before the ones condemning him.*

⁸*From prison and trial they led him away to his death. But who among the people of that day realized it was their sins that he was dying for—that he was suffering their punishment?*

⁹*He was buried like a criminal in a rich man's grave; but he had done no wrong, and had never spoken an evil word.*

¹⁰*Yet it was the Lord's good plan to bruise him and fill him with grief. But when his soul has been made an offering for sin, then he shall have a multitude of*

children, many heirs. He shall live again and God's program shall prosper in his hands.

11And when he sees all that is accomplished by the anguish of his soul, he shall be satisfied; and because of what he has experienced, my righteous Servant shall make many to be counted righteous before God, for he shall bear all their sins.

12Therefore I will give him the honors of one who is mighty and great, because he has poured out his soul unto death. He was counted as a sinner, and he bore the sins of many, and he pled with God for sinners.

If beforehand God had not mercifully stricken the Jews with spiritual blindness and deafness, they would most certainly have understood the prophet's predictions in Isaiah chapter fifty-three. They would have known that the Messiah would come to earth the first time in order to die for the sins of men (that is, in order to shed His blood to seal the promised new covenant). They would also have known that after His death, He would be resurrected. For as you know, all the circumstances surrounding the Messiah's death were recorded beforehand in detail in the Scriptures. Yes, if God had not stricken His people spiritually blind, they would have seen very quickly that Jewish Yeshua was indeed the promised Messiah whom they had waited for and longed for throughout the generations. But, oh, my friend! Had they not been made spiritually blind and deaf, they would also have seen their own God-ordained role in the Messiah's future suffering and death, and such knowledge would surely have proved to be too much for them to bear.

In the following text, taken from *The Living Bible*, the prophet Isaiah again foretold the suffering that the Messiah would undergo in order to fulfill God's prediction in Genesis 3:15 and to bring about the segment of the Abrahamic covenant that promised blessing (salvation) for all the nations. Of course, the Messiah's predicted suffering was for the purpose of sealing the promised new covenant with His own blood. Read the next verses, and you will agree with me that on God's part, keeping His beloved people spiritually blind and deaf was truly an act of great mercy, compassion and kindness.

Isaiah 52:13-15 (The Living Bible.)

13See, my Servant shall prosper; he shall be highly exalted.

> *14,15 Yet many shall be amazed when they see him—yes,
> even far-off foreign nations and their kings; they shall
> stand dumbfounded, speechless in his presence. For
> they shall see and understand what they had not been
> told before. **They shall see my Servant beaten and
> bloodied, so disfigured one would scarcely know it was
> a person standing there. <u>So shall he cleanse many
> nations.</u>**

Who else, outside of Jewish Yeshua, has ever fulfilled these prophetic Scriptures? The nations have been and continue to be cleansed from sin because of Jewish Yeshua! The nations have turned and continue to turn to the God of Abraham, Isaac and Jacob because of Jewish Yeshua! I myself personally love the Jews and I am saved and keeping God's commandments today because of Jewish Yeshua.

Rulers of nations and their subjects stand in awe of Yeshua's suffering so that mankind might be saved. This is because, as you have seen repeatedly, all the nations are included in the particular segment of the Abrahamic covenant in which God promised Abraham that in him all the nations of the earth would be blessed (that is, saved). And God is faithful to His word even when it hurts Him personally. Yes, God was faithful to His word even when keeping it meant giving His own life and shedding His own blood to seal the promised new covenant that would free mankind from sin and Satan's power and equip them to do what they were originally created to do. God was faithful to His word even when it meant deliberately disabling His own chosen people. God was faithful to His word even when it meant forcing His beloved covenant people into a position of service that He knew would break their hearts when in the future their eyes would be opened, and they would realize what they had done.

God remembered His covenant with Abraham. Through the seed of Abraham, Isaac and Jacob, the Messiah was born. Thus, through Abraham's covenant offspring, all the peoples of the earth have been given an opportunity to be cleansed from their sins. They have been given an opportunity to serve God in truth and righteousness. Yes, the nations now have the power to do what they were originally created to do. Through the promised new covenant that Yeshua sealed with His own blood, the nations have an opportunity to fear God and keep all His commandments.

Oh, praise God! For, just as He planned, He has turned the Jews' God-ordained spiritual blindness and deafness into blessings for all mankind. Praise God! For, He has purposely prolonged the Jews' inability to see and hear *"the secret things"* in order to give us Gentiles an opportunity to serve the God of Abraham, Isaac and Jacob.

Knowing these truths, how can anyone in good conscience fail to love the Jews? How can anyone fail to have compassion for God's beloved spiritually disabled people? I weep as I write these words. My heart aches for God and for His precious Abrahamic covenant people whom He loves so dearly. In grief my heart cries out, "When will we Gentiles in the Church come to appreciate what the Jews have suffered for us? When will we Gentiles in the Church acknowledge that God still loves the Jews with an everlasting love? And, when will we Gentiles realize that God still loves the Jews so completely that when we Gentiles hurt them, we automatically hurt God? Oh, when will we Gentiles in the Church stop cruelly beating down helpless, blind and deaf men and women, blind and deaf men and women who cannot comprehend why they are being so unmercifully abused."

When will we Gentiles come to understand that the Jews' failure to believe on Yeshua as the Christ was not and is not intentional? After reading John 12:37-41, we should know better than to even entertain the lying thought that the Jews' failure to believe on the promised Messiah was and is deliberate or intentional or the result of their own sins. Nevertheless, just to make sure that you do know better, maybe you should read those verses again from *The Living Bible*.

As you read the following verses, allow the truth of God's Word to sink into your brain. I am referring to the truth that shows you that **the reason why the Jews, as a nation, did not and do not believe on their promised Messiah was and is because they could not and cannot believe on Him.** Their God-imposed spiritual disabilities would not and will not permit them to believe on Him. For His own sake **and for our sake**, God has blinded their eyes and deafened their ears so that **as a nation** the Jews cannot believe on their promised Messiah. Once more, see this fact for yourself in God's own Word.

John 12:37-41 (The Living Bible.)

37But despite all the miracles he had done, most of the people would not believe he was the Messiah.

38This is exactly what Isaiah the prophet had predicted: "Lord, who will believe us? Who will accept God's mighty miracles as proof?"

*39**But they couldn't believe**, for as Isaiah also said:*

474

40"God has blinded their eyes and hardened their hearts so that they can neither see nor understand nor turn to me to heal them."

41Isaiah was referring to Jesus when he made this prediction, for he had seen a vision of the Messiah's glory.

Do you see with your own eyes what God's Word says? **The Jews "couldn't believe."** Let me repeat John's rendition of Isaiah's words. **"They couldn't believe."**

The Jews have suffered and are suffering for your benefit and advantage Gentile! They were stricken spiritually blind and deaf for you! Their failure to recognize the Messiah and their inability to understand future predictions, God's miracles, the signs of the times, the secrets in Yeshua's parables and the mystery of the kingdom of God **was not and is not the result of sin.** No! No! No! Rather, it was and is the result of their God-imposed spiritual disabilities. They were and are spiritually blind and deaf. Furthermore, they were made that way and left that way for the Lord's name's sake and **for you**. As the Jewish apostle John said in verses thirty-nine and forty of the previous text, *"they couldn't believe...,"* for *"God had blinded their eyes and hardened their hearts...."*

Listen Gentile Christian, those in the Church who would teach you that God has permanently rejected the Jews and that the Jews are no longer special to Him are telling you lies. God has not rejected His chosen covenant people. **The Abrahamic contract is still valid. Therefore, God cannot permanently reject the Jews. He promised Abraham, Isaac and Jacob that He would love their covenant descendants (the Jews) and be their God forever, and for His own name's sake, He must and will keep His word. What is more, if God had wanted His people to see and hear** *"the secret things,"* **He would have already removed the scales from their blind eyes and unplugged their deaf ears. However, as you have repeatedly seen in the Scriptures, God is not yet ready to heal them. He has purposely left them spiritually blind and deaf so that you, Gentile, might have an opportunity to be saved.**

Paul, the Jewish apostle to the Gentiles, makes it clear that the time is near when God will keep His word and will lift the dark veil from Israel's spiritual eyes. Yes, God will eventually cause His spiritually blind and deaf people to see and to hear. Paul also confirms the truth that I am teaching regarding why the Jews' blind and deaf condition has lasted for so long. He confirms that it is for the purpose of fulfilling the Abrahamic covenant and thus giving us Gentiles an opportunity to be saved.

Read the Jewish apostle's words for yourself, paying special attention to the highlighted portions. And Christian Gentile, as you read, for the Lord's name's sake, may you repent with tears if in your ignorance you have ever done harm to the Jews or spoken evil of them or harbored bad feelings toward them because they have not believed on or accepted Yeshua as their Savior.

Romans 11:1-36 (The Amplified Bible.)

1I ASK then: Has God totally rejected and disowned His people? Of course not! Why, I myself am an Israelite, a descendant of Abraham, a member of the tribe of Benjamin!

2No, God has not rejected and disowned His people [whose destiny] He had marked out and appointed and foreknown from the beginning. Do you not know what the Scripture says of Elijah, how he pleads with God against Israel?

3Lord, they have killed Your prophets; they have demolished Your altars, and I alone am left, and they seek my life.

4But what is God's reply to him? I have kept for Myself seven thousand men who have not bowed the knee to Baal!

5So too at the present time there is a remnant (a small believing minority), selected (chosen) by grace (by God's unmerited favor and graciousness).

6But if it is by grace (His unmerited favor and graciousness), it is no longer conditioned on works or anything men have done. Otherwise, grace would no longer be grace [it would be meaningless].

7What then [shall we conclude]? Israel failed to obtain what it sought [God's favor by obedience to the Law]. Only the elect (those chosen few) obtained it, while the rest of them became callously indifferent (blinded, hardened and made insensible to it).

8As it is written, God gave them a spirit (an attitude) of stupor, eyes that should not see and ears that should not hear, [that has continued] down to this very day.

9And David says, Let their table (their feasting, banqueting) become a snare and a trap, a pitfall and a just retribution [rebounding like a boomerang upon them];

10Let their eyes be darkened (dimmed) so that they cannot see, and make them bend their back [stooping beneath their burden] forever.

11So I ask, Have they stumbled so as to fall [to their utter spiritual ruin, irretrievably]? By no means! But through their false step and transgression salvation [has come] to the Gentiles, so as to arouse Israel [to see and feel what they forfeited] and so to make them jealous.

12Now if their stumbling (their lapse, their transgression) has so enriched the world [at large], and if [Israel's] failure means such riches for the Gentiles, think what an enrichment and greater advantage will follow their full reinstatement!

13But now I am speaking to you who are Gentiles. Inasmuch then as I am an apostle to the Gentiles, I lay great stress on my ministry and magnify my office,

14In the hope of making my fellow Jews jealous [in order to stir them up to imitate, copy, and appropriate], and thus managing to save some of them.

15For if their rejection and exclusion from the benefits of salvation were [overruled] for the reconciliation of a world to God, what will their acceptance and admission mean? [It will be nothing short of] life from the dead!

16Now if the first handful of dough offered as the firstfruits [Abraham and the patriarchs] is consecrated (holy), so is the whole mass [the nation of Israel]; and if the root [Abraham] is consecrated (holy), so are the branches.

17But if some of the branches were broken off, while you, a wild olive shoot, were grafted in among them to share the richness [of the root and sap] of the olive tree,

18Do not boast over the branches and pride yourself at their expense. If you do boast and feel superior, remember it is not you that support the root, but the root [that supports] you.

19You will say then, Branches were broken (pruned) off so that I might be grafted in!

20That is true. But they were broken (pruned) off because of their unbelief (their lack of real faith), and you are established through faith [because you do believe]. So do not become proud and conceited, but rather stand in awe and be reverently afraid.

21For if God did not spare the natural branches [because of unbelief], neither will He spare you [if you are guilty of the same offense].

22Then note and appreciate the gracious kindness and severity of God: severity toward those who have fallen, but God's gracious kindness to you—provided you continue in His grace and abide in His kindness; otherwise you too will be cut off (pruned away).

23And even those others [the fallen branches, Jews], if they do not persist in [clinging to] their unbelief, will be grafted in, for God has the power to graft them in again.

24For if you have been cut from what is by nature a wild olive tree, and against nature grafted into a cultivated olive tree, how much easier will it be to graft these natural [branches] back on [the original parent stock of] their own olive tree.

25Lest you be self-opinionated (wise in your own conceits), I do not want you to miss this hidden truth and mystery, brethren: *a hardening (insensibility) has [temporarily] befallen a part of Israel [to last] until the full number of the ingathering of the Gentiles has come in.*

26And so all Israel will be saved. As it is written, The Deliverer will come from Zion, He will banish ungodliness from Jacob.

27And this will be My covenant (My agreement) with them when I shall take away their sins.

28From the point of view of the Gospel (good news), they [the Jews, at present] are enemies [of God], which is for your advantage and benefit. But from the point of view of God's choice (of election, of divine selection), they are still the beloved (dear to Him) for the sake of their forefathers.

29For God's gifts and His call are irrevocable. [He never withdraws them when once they are given, and He does not change His mind about those to whom He gives His grace or to whom He sends His call.]

30Just as you were once disobedient and rebellious toward God but now have obtained [His] mercy, through their disobedience,

31So they also now are being disobedient [when you are receiving mercy], that they in turn may one day, through the mercy you are enjoying, also receive mercy [that they may share the mercy which has been shown to you—through you as messengers of the Gospel to them].

I cannot continue this study of Romans 11:1-36 without informing you that the Jews' unbelief, unbelief which the Jewish apostle Paul repeatedly refers to in this Bible chapter, is the result of their God-imposed blindness and deafness that you learned about earlier. It is not the result of sin. Remember, you saw in the Scriptures that the Jews were and are unable to believe that Yeshua is the Messiah. To refresh your memory, read those verses again from *The Living Bible.*

John 12:37-41 (The Living Bible.)

37But despite all the miracles he had done, most of the people would not believe he was the Messiah.

38This is exactly what Isaiah the prophet had predicted: "Lord, who will believe us? Who will accept God's mighty miracles as proof?"

39But they couldn't believe, for as Isaiah also said:

40"God has blinded their eyes and hardened their hearts so that they can neither see nor understand nor turn to me to heal them."

41Isaiah was referring to Jesus when he made this prediction, for he had seen a vision of the Messiah's glory.

Paul's words in the remaining five verses of our main text, Romans 11:32-36, verify all that I just said regarding the Jews' unbelief being the result of their God-imposed spiritual blindness and deafness and not the consequence of sin. I have chosen to take these last five verses of our text from the *Holy Bible, King James Version* since there is an important footnote for verse thirty-two provided in that edition which holds crucial information.

Romans 11:32-36 (King James Version.)

32 For God hath concluded them all in unbelief, that he might have mercy upon all.

Look carefully at the apostle's inspired words in the former verse, verse thirty-two. Paul clearly informs you that **God concluded all the Jews in unbelief** so that He might have mercy upon all mankind.

In Greek, the word *"concluded"* means "shut in." Remember I told you earlier that the *King James Version* provided an important footnote for verse thirty-two? Well, that footnote actually gives an alternative for the word *"concluded."* It informs you that you can say either *"God hath concluded them all in unbelief"* or you can say *"**God hath shut them all up together in unbelief.**"*

So Christian, *"**God,**"* **not their sin**, is responsible for the Jews' unbelief. *"God hath concluded them all in unbelief."* God shut up all His beloved people in unbelief so that He could extend mercy toward the Gentiles. And how did God shut up all the Jews in unbelief? He shut them all up in unbelief by disabling them. He made them spiritually blind and deaf to *"the secret things"* so that they could not and cannot believe that Yeshua is the Messiah.

Oh, what a God! And Oh, what a blessed people are the Jews! For they are unknowingly the instruments of God's promised blessing (salvation) to all the nations. They continue to suffer the effects of their God-ordained spiritual handicaps so that God might have mercy upon all mankind.

32 For God hath concluded them all in unbelief, that he might have mercy upon all.

33O the depth of the riches both of the wisdom and knowledge of God! how unsearchable are his judgments, and his ways past finding out!

34For who hath known the mind of the Lord? or who hath been his counsellor?

35Or who had first given to him, and it shall be recompensed unto him again?

36For of him, and through him, and to him, are all things: to whom be glory for ever. Amen.

Now that you understand that it has always been the Jews' God-imposed spiritual blindness and deafness to *"the secret things"* that has kept them from believing that Yeshua is the Messiah, you will appreciate reading a segment of Paul's statement in Romans chapter eleven from the *Holy Bible, King James Version.* For, as you read those verses, you will be aware that the translators of the *King James Version* certainly chose to use the better words in verse thirty when they used *"not believed"* rather than "disobedience" and "disobedient." I say that *"not believed"* is the better term, because in this particular instance, the only disobedience that the Jews were and are guilty of was and is their failure to believe that Yeshua is the Messiah. And as you know, God Himself kept and keeps them from believing in Yeshua. *"**God** hath shut them all up in unbelief"* by spiritually blinding them in order that He might show mercy to the Gentiles.

As you read the following verses from the *Holy Bible, King James Version,* I will continue to remind you of the Jews' God-imposed spiritually disabled plight.

Romans 11:19-32 (King James Version.)

19Thou wilt say then, The branches were broken off, that I might be graffed in.

*20Well; because of **unbelief** they were broken off, and thou standest by faith. Be not highminded, but fear:*

Paul makes it quite clear in verse twenty that the reason why the Jews (that is, the branches) were temporarily broken off was because of their *"**unbelief.**"* And my friend, you now know that God Himself shut the Jews up in unbelief by spiritually disabling them so that His Abrahamic covenant would be fulfilled, and the Gentiles would have an opportunity to receive God's mercy and be saved.

21For if God spared not the natural branches, take heed lest he also spare not thee.

22Behold therefore the goodness and severity of God: on them which fell, severity; but toward thee, goodness, if thou continue in his goodness: otherwise thou also shalt be cut off.

The words *"severity of God"* describe well the Jews' God-ordained disabled plight. For God shut them all up in unbelief in order to show mercy to us Gentiles.

23And they also, if they abide not still in unbelief, shall be graffed in: for God is able to graff them in again.

In verse twenty-three, Paul is telling you that when God eventually heals the Jews spiritual disabilities and they too are able to recognize and believe on the true Messiah, Yeshua, **if they do not then blind their own eyes,** they will be graffed into their own olive tree.

24For if thou wert cut out of the olive tree which is wild by nature, and wert graffed contrary to nature into a good olive tree: how much more shall these, which be the natural branches, be graffed into their own olive tree?

25For I would not, brethren, that ye should be ignorant of this mystery, lest ye should be wise in your own conceits; that blindness in part is happened to Israel, until the fulness of the Gentiles be come in.

26And so all Israel shall be saved: as it is written, There shall come out of Sion the Deliverer, and shall turn away ungodliness from Jacob:

27For this is my covenant unto them, when I shall take away their sins.

28As concerning the gospel, they are enemies for your sakes: but as touching the election, they are beloved for the fathers' sakes.

The Jews are classed as enemies of the gospel only in the sense that they do not believe the message that it proclaims. However, they do not believe the message of the gospel because they cannot believe it. For His own name's sake and for your sake, God has shut them all up in unbelief. God has blinded their eyes and deafened their ears so that they cannot recognize or believe that Yeshua is the Messiah.

28As concerning the gospel, they are enemies for your sakes: but as touching the election, they are beloved for the fathers' sakes.

29For the gifts and calling of God are without repentance.

30For as ye in times past have not believed God, yet have now obtained mercy through their unbelief:

*31Even so have these also now **not believed**, that through your mercy they also may obtain mercy.*

A small group of Jews will continue to seize by force the word of the kingdom of God that is sown. However, the majority of the Jewish people will remain spiritually blind and deaf until the Messiah's return to earth. At that time, they will recognize and believe on the Messiah, Yeshua. In the meantime, as verse thirty says, **enlightened righteous Christian Gentiles will extend mercy to the Jews**, knowing that the Jews have been shut up in unbelief partly for their sake *"...that through your mercy they also may obtain mercy."*

32For God hath concluded them all in unbelief, that he might have mercy upon all.

Oh, my friend, God has not rejected His Abrahamic covenant people. As you saw earlier, Paul clearly states in Romans 11:1-2 that God has not cast away the Jews. In verse twenty-eight of the same chapter, Paul proclaims that because of the covenant which the Lord made with Abraham, Isaac and Jacob, the Jews are still God's beloved people. God is faithful to His promises. He swore by Himself that He would love the Jews and be their God forever, and He will keep His word no matter what.

As Romans 11:15 in *The Amplified Bible* confirms, yes, the Jews have suffered temporary rejection and exclusion from the benefits of salvation so that the world may be reconciled to God, but they have not been rejected by or cast away from God Himself. No! Paul continues in that same verse by saying, *"...what will their acceptance and admittance mean? [It will be nothing short of] life from the dead!"* Thus God states in Romans 11:26, *"**And so all Israel will be saved**. As it is written, The Deliverer will come from Zion, He will banish ungodliness from Jacob."*

Church leaders have misconstrued and misinterpreted the content of yet another verse of Scripture. The verse I am speaking about is a part of the text that we just studied, Romans 11:29. For years Christian ministers and teachers have quoted Paul's words, *"For God's gifts and His call are irrevocable,"* without comprehending themselves or teaching others their true meaning. In order to understand Paul's statement in the previous verse, one must correctly analyze His words. For only then can one accurately teach the truth that Paul wrote in his letter to the Church in Rome. However, as I said earlier, in this instance, men have miserably failed to rightly handle and skillfully teach the Word of truth.

In their ignorance, and in some cases their efforts to promote their own manmade doctrines, Christian teachers have taken Paul's words in Romans 11:29 completely out of context. They insist on trying to make Paul's words in that verse apply to Gentile Christians rather than applying them to those for whom they were originally intended, **the Jews**. However, in a moment, you will be given an opportunity to consider and know the true content and intent of Paul's statement. Let us also keep Paul's words in context. For only then will you really come to know truth and righteousness in that area (that is, only then will you come to know the secrets and mysteries of the kingdom of God in that area). To refresh your memory, I will repeat Paul's words in Romans 11:28-31. Remember now, **Paul is addressing Gentiles, but he is speaking about the Jews.**

> *Romans 11:28-31 (The Amplified Bible.)*
>
> *28From the point of view of the gospel (good news),* ***they [the Jews**, at present] are enemies [of God], **which is for your advantage and benefit. But from the point of view of God's choice (of election, of divine selection), they are still the beloved (dear to Him) for the sake of their forefathers.***
>
> *29**For God's gifts and His call are irrevocable.***
>
> *30Just as you were once disobedient and rebellious toward God but now have obtained [His] mercy, through their disobedience,*
>
> *31So they also now are being disobedient [when you are receiving mercy], that they in turn may one day, through the mercy you are enjoying, also receive mercy [that they may share the mercy which has been shown to you—through you as messengers of the Gospel to them].*

It is crystal clear that throughout the previous verses, Paul is addressing Gentiles on matters concerning the Jewish people. He is absolutely not referring to the Gentiles as Church leaders have suggested. After reading Paul's words, any intelligent person has to agree with what I just said. For example, in verse twenty-eight, Paul is referring to the Jews' disabled plight. **He brings out the point that the Jews are enemies of the gospel for the Gentiles' advantage and benefit.** Verse twenty-eight in the *Holy Bible, King James Version* reads, *"As concerning the gospel, they are enemies for your sakes."* Oh my Gentile friend, the Jews are not at this time enemies of the gospel because they are a hardhearted, sinful people. No! The apostle Paul tells you in Romans 11:28 that they are enemies of the gospel **for your sake**.

In that same verse, verse twenty-eight, Paul also mentions God's unbreakable Abrahamic covenant choice (selection, election). And, as you know, the Jews are God's Abrahamic covenant choice, **the Gentiles are not!**

The apostle Paul is informing you that because of the covenant that God made with Abraham, Isaac and Jacob, God chose the Jews. Furthermore, since they are God's chosen covenant people, they are still the beloved because of the covenant that God made with their forefathers. For, God promised Abraham, Isaac and Jacob that He would love their covenant descendants and be the God of their covenant descendants forever. Thus, the Jews are God's chosen Abrahamic covenant people whom He still dearly loves. And, as you are now aware, His covenant love will never change. It is everlasting.

In verse twenty-nine, **Paul is simply informing the Church that God's Abrahamic covenant choice and the gifts He gave to the Jews because of His unbreakable covenant with Abraham, Isaac and Jacob are irrevocable.** My friend, they are irrevocable because God cannot break the Abrahamic covenant. He swore by Himself that He would always love the Jews and be their God, and He cannot take back His choice or the covenant gifts that He gave to them, gifts such as His everlasting love and the Promised Land.

God will never desert, disown or totally reject His covenant people. He loves them with an everlasting love. For example, when the Jews became so wicked that He sent them into captivity in Babylon, He loved them so much that once the predicted seventy years of punishment were over, He actually exchanged Gentile nations in order to acquire their release. So, I ask you Christian Gentile, why would God reject His people now when they are only in their present pathetic spiritual plight in order to accomplish His purpose and for **your** advantage and benefit.

See for yourself how precious God considers the Jewish people. See how He traded Gentile nations and Gentile men in order to acquire their release. See this truth for yourself in the subsequent verses.

Isaiah 43:1-4 (The Amplified Bible.)

1BUT NOW [in spite of past judgments for Israel's sins], thus says the Lord, He Who created you, O Jacob, and He Who formed you, O Israel: Fear not, for I have redeemed you [ransomed you by paying a price instead of leaving you captives]; I have called you by your name; you are Mine.

2When you pass through the waters, I will be with you, and through the rivers, they will not overwhelm you. When you walk through the fire, you will not be burned or scorched, nor will the flame kindle upon you.

3For I am the Lord your God, the Holy One of Israel, your Savior; I give Egypt [to the Babylonians] for your ransom, Ethiopia and Seba [a province of Ethiopia] in exchange [for your release].

4Because you are precious in My sight and honored, and because I love you, I will give men in return for you and peoples in exchange for your life.

If God paid such a great price to get His beloved blind and deaf people out of Babylon, imagine what He will resort to in order to acquire their full release from the Gentile nations in the end of time. No matter what it costs Him, God will remain faithful to the Abrahamic covenant. For, as you have learned throughout this series, **His Abrahamic covenant gifts and His covenant call are** *"irrevocable"* **(that is, His Abrahamic covenant gifts and His covenant choice can never, ever be annulled or made void by the act of recalling, withdrawing or reversing).**

Isaiah 43:5-8 (The Amplified Bible.)

5Fear not, for I am with you; I will bring your offspring from the east [where they are dispersed] and gather you from the west.

⁶I will say to the north, Give up! and to the south, Keep not back. Bring My sons from afar and My daughters from the ends of the earth—

*⁷Even everyone who is called by My name, **whom I have created for My glory**, whom I have formed, whom I have made.*

*⁸**Bring forth the blind people who have eyes and the deaf who have ears.***

God brought into being the nation of Israel. He created it, and He formed the spiritually blind and deaf Israelites for His own glory. He brought forth the nation of Israel to aid Him in fulfilling His word and carrying out His purpose upon the earth. The Israelites were created to suffer and in some cases even to die for God and the rest of mankind. But woe be to those who do the abusing and refuse to repent. Egypt abused and killed God's people, and as you saw in an earlier chapter of this book, Egypt paid dearly for her severe and cruel treatment of God's covenant people. Woe be to those nations who follow in Egypt's wicked footsteps, those nations who hurt God's blind and deaf Abrahamic covenant people. Woe be to the nations who abuse the very people who are shut up in unbelief for the sake of those nations.

Isaiah gives us a glimpse of the measures God will take in order to bring His beloved spiritually blind and deaf people out of the Gentile nations in the end of time. For, I am ashamed to say that the nations have unmercifully abused God's spiritually blind and deaf people. I ask you Gentile, how can we Gentiles feel badly toward the Egyptians for afflicting, oppressing and murdering God's covenant people for four hundred years when we have afflicted, oppressed and murdered them for thousands of years? Even the Church has the blood of God's beloved spiritually blind and deaf people on her hands. Yes, the Church's hands drip with the blood of God's beloved spiritually handicapped people. However, God will continue to remove His precious Abrahamic covenant people from the nations' oppressive bloody and cruel grip, and He will return them to their own land.

Isaiah 42:14-16 (The Amplified Bible.)

¹⁴[Thus says the Lord] I have for a long time held My peace, I have been still and restrained Myself. Now I will cry out like a woman in travail, I will gasp and pant together.

15I will lay waste the mountains and hills and dry up all their herbage; I will turn the rivers into islands, and I will dry up the pools.

*16**And I will bring the blind by a way that they know not; I will lead them in paths that they have not known. I will make darkness into light before them and make uneven places into a plain. These things I have determined to do [for them]; and I will not leave them forsaken.***

Gentile Christian, for the Lord's name's sake and for the sake of your own eternal welfare, repent of any wrong deed that you have ever done or any ill thought that you have ever harbored against God's dearly beloved people. Change your mind and attitude concerning the Jews. For, if Yeshua could look down from the cross at His pathetic spiritually blind and deaf people knowing that they truly did not know what they were doing, and cry out, *"Father, forgive them; **for they know not what they do,"*** can we Gentile Christians not find it in our hearts to exhibit the same attitude as our Lord? Can we not also show compassion and mercy toward God's beloved spiritually blind and deaf people, God's people who absolutely do not know what they did or what they are doing even today, God's people who are in that situation for our sake?

Yeshua, *"Immanuel [God with us],"* showed His people mercy because He knew that they were truly blind and truly deaf. He also knew that He Himself had kept them that way for His own name's sake and for the sake of us Gentiles. Oh Gentile Christian, you have not been struck spiritually blind and deaf by God. Therefore, open your own eyes and ears so that you might hear and perceive the truth! Open up your heart to God's beloved blind and deaf people! **For, as you now know, they were made blind and deaf and left blind and deaf for your sake! They have continued to be abused and afflicted and killed for you.**

Come! Let us finally reach out arms of love and compassion and appreciation to God's covenant people. Let us do all we can to repay them for the severe suffering that God has allowed them to undergo for our sake. We Gentiles owe the Jews an indescribable debt of gratitude.

Let us also appreciate God's faithfulness to His covenant with Abraham. For, He made His beloved people spiritually blind and deaf to *"the secret things"* in order to fulfill His prediction in Genesis 3:15 and the segment of His covenant with Abraham, Isaac and Jacob that promises blessing (salvation) to the Gentile nations. Most of all, He made His people blind and deaf from their birth as a nation in Egypt so

488

that they could help Him fulfill His word and thus protect His holy name. Praise be to our faithful God!

Throughout this series, God has imparted to you much insight into numerous Biblical secrets and mysteries of the kingdom of God. Therefore, because you now truly understand **why the Jews failed to recognize their Messiah,** I pray that from now on, you will view God's beloved Abrahamic covenant people in a totally different light. Yes, instead of being judgmental, I pray that you will be merciful. Instead of being uncaring and indifferent toward them, I pray that you will express warmth and appreciation. Instead of being impatient with them over what you once wrongly perceived as their deliberate, willful rejection of the Messiah, I pray that you will reach out in gentleness and patience, knowing that they are genuinely spiritually disabled. Most of all, I pray that every day of your life, you will be aware that God has temporarily kept them in that pathetic spiritual situation for the sake of His holy name, His Biblical predictions, His covenant with Abraham **and for you! For you! For you, Gentile!**

Praise be to the Lord, for among many other truths, you now know the answer to the question, "Why Did The Jews Fail To Recognize The Messiah?"

Chapter 15
Part One

WHY SHOULD THE
CHURCH SUPPORT ISRAEL?

If you carefully review the extensive information that you have received to this point in the series entitled *Why Should Every Christian Pray For And Support Israel?* you will quickly agree that you have already acquired sufficient Scriptural evidence to prove that it is God's will that the Church vigorously support the nation of Israel. However, in order to make sure that you are one hundred percent convinced of that fact and to ensure that you do not lose sight of the most important reason why every Christian should support Israel, I am going to elaborate upon that topic.

Of course, the most important reason why you should support Israel involves God's holy name. In chapter twelve, you were given insight into a large part of the role that God intended that Israel fulfill in His restoration plan. You will recall that even Israel's deliverance from the bondage of Egypt was designed by God to exalt His name and prepare the way for its acknowledgment by the other nations. God's prophet announced in Isaiah 63:14, "*...So did You lead Your people [Lord] to make for Yourself a beautiful and glorious name [to prepare the way for the acknowledgment of Your name by all nations]."*

As you learned, Israel was called to be a priestly nation. Israel was to be a prophet to the nations, a spokesman for God. The surrounding Gentile nations should have been able to look at Israel and stand in awe as they witnessed the joy, peace and contentment experienced by a righteous nation living under God's laws.

I have just given you a brief reminder of the type of righteous characteristics that God intended that His beloved Israel demonstrate before the Gentile nations. Had the prophet Israel done what he had been called to do, throughout history, he would have automatically continued to pave the way for the acknowledgment of God's name by the other nations. Yes, if the prophet Israel had consistently kept the Horeb covenant by obeying God's commandments and by making the appropriate animal sacrifices whenever he sinned by breaking those commandments, he would have fulfilled his God-given mission. He would have led the surrounding nations to the truth and righteousness of *"the things which are revealed,"* God's laws.

However, instead of exalting and honoring God's name before the nations, the prophet nation, Israel, disgraced and discredited God's reputation. Imagine the terrible stigma that was attached to God's name when that prophet, the very spokesman of God, became corrupt, when that prophet projected darkness instead of light, when his justice became perverted and his life exhibited everything that was evil. The following text confirms all that I have just stated.

Hosea 9:8-9 (The Amplified Bible.)

*8Ephraim was [intended to be] a watchman with my God [and a prophet to the surrounding nations]; **but he, that prophet, has become a fowler's snare in all his ways. There is enmity, hostility, and persecution in the house of his God.***

9They have deeply corrupted themselves as in the days of Gibeah. The Lord will [earnestly] remember their iniquity; He will punish their sins.

Israel (Ephraim) was called to lead a holy life and to exhibit God's revealed truth and righteousness before the surrounding nations. However, instead of fulfilling God's purpose, the nation of Israel rebelliously turned in the opposite direction. Rather than teaching the nations righteousness, the prophet Israel taught them wickedness. The awful truth is that much of Israel's depravity, filthiness and depth of sin was unknown to those surrounding Gentile nations until the corrupt prophet, Israel, taught them to dabble in and to copy his abominations. Consequently, instead of projecting light to the nations, the prophet Israel, actually became darkness. Instead of being a refuge of righteousness, Israel became a horrible trap to lead others into sin. As Hosea said in the previous verses, the prophet Israel became a fowler's snare in all his ways.

After God had kept His promises to their forefathers and had shed His love upon their descendants, after He had set the Israelites apart for Himself, commissioned them, blessed them and given them the Promised Land, they foolishly threw it all away and walked after the evil desires of their own sinful hearts and minds. Yes, instead of following God's instructions and setting a righteous example for the neighboring nations, the Israelites deliberately broke the Horeb covenant by breaking God's commands. God's people cast His laws from them as though they were insignificant and worthless.

Worst of all, by disregarding the Lord's commands, the Israelites displayed irreverence and disrespect for God's holy name before all the nations. Their behavior was especially wicked since **Moses had warned God's people prior to that time that their deliberate disobedience to God's commands would be classed as a refusal to reverently fear God's glorious name**. You see, in order for men to show reverence to God's name, they have to obey God's commands. See this for yourself in the following verse.

Deuteronomy 28:58-59 (The Amplified Bible.)

[58]If you will not be watchful to do all the words of this law that are written in this book, that you may [reverently] fear this glorious and fearful name [and presence]—THE LORD YOUR GOD—

[59]Then the Lord will bring upon you and your descendants extraordinary strokes and blows, great plagues of long continuance, and grievous sicknesses of long duration.

Regardless of Moses' foreboding warning in Deuteronomy 28:15-68, Israel turned back from following the Lord. She rejected God's call to holiness and consecration. She refused to obey His word. The ramification of Israel's sinful behavior was that God's glorious name was brought low in the estimation of the heathen. After all, how could the heathen have been expected to reverence and respect God's name when God's own people continuously showed contempt for it by refusing to keep the Horeb covenant and obey God's commands?

After reading the previous Scriptural texts, you might well ask me, "Is this an appropriate time for you to elaborate on the Jews' past sins? Is it not counter-productive to do so? After all, in the previous chapter, you just got through sharing with us how indebted to Israel we Gentiles really are. The truth that you shared touched my heart so much that I was actually starting to develop an appreciation for the Jews. So, it would seem to me that if you want Christian Gentiles to support the Jews, you would be wiser to pursue that same avenue of thought. Otherwise, might you not defeat your own purpose by reminding us Gentiles of how the Jews failed and hurt the Lord? And even worse, since the nation of Israel has been guilty of such abominable sins against God, are you not concerned that upon being reminded of Israel's past sins, the Gentiles might say, 'Since the Jews have committed such abominable sin, why should we Gentile Christians be expected to support the nation of Israel? And why are you encouraging us to give assistance to Israel while at the same time informing us of the Israelites' past crimes against God?' "

Let me take a moment to answer the former question regarding whether this is or is not an appropriate time for me to elaborate on Israel's past sins.

(1) I am encouraging you to stand by the nation of Israel despite her past sins because supporting her is the only right and Biblical course of action for you to take.

(2) Israel's past sins are no secret. Any person who can read can open their Bible and see Israel's past sins recorded on the pages of God's Word.

(3) Though it is true that I never want you to forget that Israel has suffered much so that we Gentiles might be saved, my main reason for encouraging you to lend assistance to Israel is not because Israel deserves your help. **Rather, I am encouraging you to help Israel <u>for God's name's sake</u>. For, you will soon see in God's own Word that support for Israel is really support for God. The bottom line is that God's name, God's reputation is at stake in this issue.**

(4) For God's name's sake, it is absolutely necessary that I mention Israel's abominable sins while at the same time trying to enlist your support for Israel. You see, it is a Biblical fact that when the Jews were scattered among the nations, they actually profaned God's name. They profaned God's name by being so corrupt, so disobedient to God's laws that they forced God to drive them off the land that He had promised would be their possession forever.

God had no choice but to carry out His former warning and **<u>temporarily</u>** expel His people from the Promised Land. For as you saw earlier, instead of keeping the Horeb covenant which they had made with God and thus showing the nations the righteousness of God by obeying His laws, the Israelites showed them every sort of wickedness and abominable, sinful practice imaginable. The Scriptures reveal that God's beloved people exhibited depths of darkness that even the Gentiles were not involved in until Israel flaunted her wicked idolatrous practices in front of them. To put it bluntly, Israel became more depraved and filthy than the heathen (that is, Israel became more depraved and filthy than the Gentiles). (Ezekiel 16:27.)

Finally, the Jews' idolatrous sins and their unwillingness to repent became so utterly unbearable to God that He was forced to drive them off the Promised Land. From that point on, the Gentile nations were hindered from trusting God's word. You see, they had been told that the Israelites were God's covenant people whom God had miraculously delivered from the bondage of Egypt. They had also been informed that God had solemnly pledged to Abraham, Isaac and Jacob that the Israelites would possess the Holy Land forever. Yet, with their own eyes, they had witnessed the heathen drive the Jews from the Promised Land.

When you consider all the previously mentioned facts, it is easy to see why the Gentiles' confidence in the only true God and His word was shaken. The surrounding nations no longer believed that the Israelites and the land of Israel were special to God. Why? Because, God's own people had already profaned His name before them. Yes, the Israelites had tarnished God's beautiful and glorious reputation and had made His name a laughingstock before all the nations. Furthermore, they had caused the nations to falsely accuse God of breaking His covenant with Abraham by failing to fulfill His sacred promises.

Wicked, heathen Gentiles actually made sport of God's name. They mockingly said, "What a weak and pathetic God is the God of the Jews. He could not even keep the promises He made to their forefathers in regard to them. He could not protect His own people from their enemies on the land that He was supposed to have given them forever. Some God they serve!"

The Gentiles did not understand that God is so righteous that He cannot tolerate sin. They did not know that God forewarned His people of the consequences of sinful, idolatrous behavior. Neither did the Gentiles realize that God Himself had sent those invading foes to conquer the nation of Israel and temporarily drive His unrepentant people off the Promised Land as punishment for their idolatrous sins.

When God saw the disrespect and insults that the Gentile nations heaped upon His name, He became extremely concerned about His reputation. God Himself proclaims that He had compassion and regard for His holy name—His name which deserved glory and honor—His name which His own beloved covenant people had profaned before the nations. See these facts for yourself on the pages of God's Word.

Ezekiel 36:16-32 (The Amplified Bible.)

16Moreover, the word of the Lord came to me, saying,

17Son of man, when the house of Israel dwelt in their own land, they defiled it by [doing] their [own] way and by their [idolatrous] doings. Their conduct before Me was like the uncleanness of a woman during her [physical] impurity.

[18]So I poured out My wrath upon them for the blood that they had shed upon the land and for their idols with which they had defiled it.

[19]And I scattered them among the nations, and they were dispersed through the countries; according to their conduct and their [idolatrous] deeds I judged and punished them.

[20]And when they came to the nations to which they went, they profaned My holy name in that men said of them, These are the people of the Lord, and yet they had to go forth out of His land.

[21]But I had regard, concern, and compassion for My holy name, which the house of Israel had profaned among the nations to which they went.

I want you to see how the translators of *The Living Bible* convey the contents of the last two verses, verses twenty and twenty-one. In a little while, we will also be reading verse twenty-two from that same translation.

Ezekiel 36:20-22 (The Living Bible.)

[20]But when they were scattered out among the nations, then they were a blight upon my holy name because the nations said, 'These are the people of God and he couldn't protect them from harm!'

[21]I am concerned about my reputation that was ruined by my people throughout the world.

God's reputation was unfairly and wrongfully tarnished by His own people. The nations were convinced that the God of Israel could no longer be trusted to keep His promises or that He was not able to keep them. You see, they did not know that God's intention was that the Israelites' separation from their land would only be **temporary**. They thought the Jews' loss of their land was permanent.

From that time forth, the protection of His own name became God's first priority. He realized that to save face before the Gentile nations, He had to get the Jews back to the Promised Land and fulfill all the covenant promises that He had made to their forefathers. However, God wanted the Jews to know that He was not going to bring them back to the land that He promised would be theirs forever because they deserved

His intervention. No! He was going to bring them back in order to keep His sacred covenant with Abraham, Isaac and Jacob and thus protect His own holy name.

Look now at the next verse and see with your own eyes why God is blessing the Jews even today. See why in this generation, God brought and will continue to bring His people back to the Promised Land. See why God will spare a remnant of the line of Abraham, Isaac and Jacob. And most of all, see why God must keep His promises to Israel's forefathers, no matter what.

> *22Therefore say to the people of Israel:* *"**The Lord God says, I am bringing you back again, but not because you deserve it; I am doing it to protect my holy name which you tarnished among the nations.**"*

Gentile Christian, do you now understand that it is your duty to support the nation of Israel? You must show kindness to and support Israel for the sake of God's reputation. God tells you Himself that the Jews do not deserve what He has done or what He is doing or what He will do for them. However, God certainly does deserve to have His good and glorious name restored in the eyes of the nations. Remember what God said in Ezekiel 36:21 in *The Amplified Bible.* He said, *"But I had regard, concern, and compassion for My holy name...."*

Beginning with verse twenty-two, we will study the remaining portion of our original text, Ezekiel 36:16-32, from *The Amplified Bible.*

> *Ezekiel 36:22-32 (The Amplified Bible.)*
>
> *22Therefore say to the house of Israel, **thus says the Lord God:** **I do not do this for your sakes, O house of Israel, but for My holy name's sake,** which you have profaned among the nations to which you went.*

My friend, could God have made it any clearer as to why every Christian should support the nation of Israel? I do not think so. You now know that you are not expected to support Israel because of the Jews themselves. Rather, you are expected and even required to support Israel because of God's reputation. For in supporting Israel, you are helping to protect and to clear God's holy name.

In verse twenty-two, God says, *"Therefore **say to the house of Israel.**"* So I say to you, Israel, it is not for you that God is doing these things. It is not for you that He has allowed you to return home. It is not for you that He will eventually return to you all your land. It is not for you that in the future He will help you to conquer all your enemies.

It is not for you, Israel, that God will pour out His Spirit and salvation upon you in the end of time and spare a remnant of Abraham's, Isaac's, and Jacob's seed. It is not for you that He will build the Lord's places and populate your cities and give you an opportunity to accept the Messiah upon His second coming.

No, it is not for you, Israel! Rather, it is for the protection of God's own name that He will do all those things. It is to keep His Word in Genesis 3:15 and all His covenant promises to Abraham, Isaac and Jacob and to show His power to the nations. And most of all, it is to vindicate (that is, to clear from harm) His own holy name which, in your wickedness, you profaned. God Himself tells us in the following verses why He will perform the previously mentioned wonders.

> *23And I will vindicate the holiness of My great name and separate it for its holy purpose from all that defiles it—My name, which has been profaned among the nations, which you have profaned among them—and the nations will know, understand, and realize that I am the Lord [the Sovereign Ruler, who calls forth loyalty and obedient service],when I shall be set apart by you and My holiness vindicated in you before their eyes and yours.*

God declares in verse twenty-three that in the end of time, He will vindicate His holy name. Furthermore, in that same verse, God states that He will vindicate His name through the very race of people who profaned it before the nations. The whole earth will be looking on as God uses the Jews to clear His name of all the harm that they have done to it. And just how will God vindicate His name before the nations? He will vindicate His name by keeping all the promises He made to Abraham, Isaac and Jacob regarding their covenant descendants, the Jews. God will vindicate His name by showing the world that, no matter what happens, He can be trusted to keep His predictions and promises. Yes, all the nations of the earth shall witness firsthand God's faithfulness to the sacred covenant that He made with Abraham, Isaac and Jacob.

Verse twenty-three contains insight into why God has never allowed His covenant people to be totally wiped out. No, not even during those times when the Jews deserved such judgment did God allow the Gentiles to annihilate them. **The fact is that God has never allowed the** nations to completely destroy His people because God needs the Jews to help Him vindicate His name. The only way that God's name can be truly justified before the nations is by God keeping all the covenant promises which He made to the Jews' forefathers regarding them.

If God had, at any given time, allowed the nations to utterly destroy (that is, to annihilate) the Jews, with that one act, God would have destroyed the only chance He has to fully vindicate His holy name. Consequently, God would then have been partly responsible for the nations' continued distrust and abuse of His name, the distrust and abuse that the Jews had previously brought upon it. For, God would then have given the nations just cause to accuse Him of being a covenant breaker. Furthermore, the nations would have taken credit for the destruction of God's chosen people. So as you can see, for His own name's sake, God could not and can not allow the nations to permanently triumph over His people, the Jews. God tells you this Himself on the pages of His Word.

Isaiah 48:11 (The Amplified Bible.)

11 For My own sake, for My own sake, I do it [I refrain and do not utterly destroy you]; for why should I permit My name to be polluted and profaned [which it would be if the Lord completely destroyed His chosen people]? And I will not give My glory to another [by permitting the worshipers of idols to triumph over you].

Now that you more fully understand the necessity of God preserving the Jewish nation and keeping His Abrahamic covenant, we will return to our former text.

Ezekiel 36:23-32 (The Amplified Bible.)

23 And I will vindicate the holiness of My great name and separate it for its holy purpose from all that defiles it—My name, which has been profaned among the nations, which you have profaned among them—and the nations will know, understand, and realize that I am the Lord [the Sovereign Ruler, who calls forth loyalty and obedient service], when I shall be set apart by you and My holiness vindicated in you before their eyes and yours.

24For I will take you from among the nations and gather you out of all countries and bring you into your own land.

25Then will I sprinkle clean water upon you, and you shall be clean from all your uncleanness; and from all your idols will I cleanse you.

26A new heart will I give you and a new spirit will I put within you, and I will take away the stony heart out of your flesh and give you a heart of flesh.

27And I will put My Spirit within you and cause you to walk in My statutes, and you shall heed My ordinances and do them.

28And you shall dwell in the land that I gave to your fathers; and you shall be My people, and I will be your God.

29I will also save you from all your uncleannesses, and I will call forth the grain and make it abundant and lay no famine on you.

30And I will multiply the fruit of the tree and the increase of the field, that you may no more suffer the reproach and disgrace of famine among the nations.

31Then you shall [earnestly] remember your own evil ways and your doings that were not good, and shall loathe yourselves in your own sight for your iniquities and for your abominable deeds.

32Not for your sake do I do this, says the Lord God; let that be known to you. Be ashamed and confounded for your [own] wicked ways, O house of Israel!

As God said He would do in the previous text, He has gathered and is continuing to gather the Jews out of all the countries of the world. Yes, God is gradually bringing the descendants of Abraham, Isaac and Jacob back to their own God-given land. Moreover, as He said He would do, God is also causing Israel's agriculture to flourish. Before the eyes of the whole Gentile world, God multiplies the fruit of the tree and the increase of the field.

But remember Gentile Christian, God is not pouring out these Abrahamic covenant blessings upon His people because they have faithfully kept the Horeb covenant and obeyed His commands. Nor is He pouring them out because His Abrahamic covenant people deserve

His bountiful blessings. No! The truth is that God is not performing these marvelous wonders for Israel at all. Rather, as you have just learned, He is accomplishing them to protect and vindicate His own holy name before all the world through the Jewish people.

God's covenant with Abraham, Isaac and Jacob demands that God love the Jews with an everlasting love. The Abrahamic covenant also demands that He remain their God and they His people forever. However, God makes it known in the previous verses that, like all the rest of the contract, He will not fulfill those sections of the Abrahamic agreement because Israel deserves it. No! Everything that God does for Israel in these last days will be done to vindicate His own beautiful and glorious holy name which the Israelites disgraced before all the nations. Yes, He will love the Jews forever. Yes, He will be their God forever. But He will not keep those covenant promises for them. No! He will keep them strictly to protect His own reputation.

As verses twenty-five through twenty-eight reveal, the day will come when Israel will accept the Messiah (Yeshua). Upon the Lord's second coming, the Jews will be cleansed from their past idolatrous sins. They will embrace the promised blood-sealed new covenant (that is, their past sins will be forgiven, and God's laws shall be written on their hearts and minds so that they will fully understand them and obey them). God's Word says in verse twenty-eight, *"And you shall dwell in the land that I gave to your fathers; and you shall be My people, and I will be your God."* Nevertheless, God also says in verse thirty-two, *"Not for your sake do I do this, says the Lord God; let that be known to you. Be ashamed and confounded for your [own] wicked ways, O house of Israel!"*

Earlier, I told you that I would explain why it was necessary that I mention Israel's abominable past sins while at the same time continuing to enlist your support for the nation of Israel. I feel that I have kept my promise. **I have explained to you how it was Israel's wicked behavior that was responsible for God's name being profaned in the first place, and how, despite Israel's wickedness, God will still keep His promises and thus abundantly bless them. Furthermore, I have shown you that He will not do those things for the sake of Israel, rather, He will do those things in order to protect His own name which, as a result of their abominable idolatrous sins and their being justly driven from the land of Israel, the Jews profaned before the nations.**

Christian Gentile, it should now be clear to you that you do not have to like what the Jews are. Neither do you have to condone what the Jews have done or in some cases still do. You simply have to want to see God's name cleared through His people, Israel. For the sake of God's reputation, you must be willing to give your all in order to see God's will accomplished in this area.

God has put a love in my own heart for Israel that no man nor worldly circumstance can remove. I love the Jews. I love Israel. Moreover, so do all God's laborers at The Living Word Church of Niceville. We have been led by God Himself to love and support Israel. However, we do not love them blindly. No! We know why God has put this love and burden for Israel in our hearts.

We are aware that God did not plant this special love for Israel in our hearts because the Jews deserve it. Rather, He planted this love for Israel in our hearts for His own name's sake. Furthermore, our love is not superficial or conditional. Therefore, we express our love in the only way that true love for God and man can be expressed. We express our love for God's Abrahamic covenant people by obeying God's commands and by carrying out His written will in regard to Israel.

Our love for Israel asks for nothing other than to see God's reputation cleared of all the harm that the Israelites have done to it, to see God's name exalted throughout all the earth and to see men doing what they were originally created to do (that is, to see men keeping all God's laws, all God's commandments). However, we know that we will only see God's will accomplished in those areas when God fully keeps His promises to Abraham, Isaac and Jacob regarding their covenant descendants, the Israelites.

For God's name's sake, each individual segment of the Abrahamic covenant that pertains to the Jews must and will be fulfilled in its entirety. Therefore, it is imperative that every Gentile Christian beneficiary of the Abrahamic promise of salvation set aside his or her selfish, petty differences and be concerned instead about God's purpose being accomplished on the earth regarding Israel and most of all, His name being vindicated.

Since you now comprehend that God's first priority in this whole matter is the vindication of His holy name, I think it might help you to see the dictionary definition of the word "vindicate." *The American Heritage Dictionary* defines the word "vindicate" as such:

> To clear of accusation, blame, suspicion, or doubt with supporting arguments or proof....To justify or

> prove the worth of, esp. in light of later developments.

In Latin the word "vindicate" can also mean to avenge or defend.

God will eventually shut the mouths of all who wrongly criticize His past actions. He will clear His name of all false accusations, blame, suspicion and doubt, and He will do it with supporting argument and proof. He will prove that His beautiful and glorious holy name is worthy of respect. Yes, He will defend His righteous actions against all who oppose His dealings.

God has already brought to pass many of His Abrahamic covenant promises. His actions of being born a human being and giving His life to fulfill Genesis 3:15 and the Abrahamic covenant will completely justify His name in the end. **However, until that time, He will continue to show proof that He is faithful to His word. That proof will be the complete fulfillment of Genesis 3:15 and His sacred promises to Abraham, Isaac and Jacob.**

In the end, God's own righteous character and His faithfulness to His word will vindicate His holy name. Yes, God's name will be cleared of all the insults, blame and false accusations that men have heaped upon it. However, until that time arrives and God's Abrahamic promises are finally fulfilled in their entirety, is it right for the Church of Christ to sit back in her rocking chair of indifference and refuse to lift a finger to help the Lord clear His name? God forbid!

The Church must wake up and come to God's aid. For God's name's sake, the Church must start wholeheartedly supporting the nation of Israel. In all good conscience, she must help God carry out His program for Israel. Furthermore, the Church must not stop with moral support. She must offer Israel financial support.

This is the Church's historical opportunity to exalt God's name instead of profaning it. It is an opportunity for the Church to rally to God's side and to experience the blessed privilege of aiding God in lifting up His holy name before the world rather than beating it down by neglecting or hurting Israel through word or deed.

This is the Church's chance to exhibit the character of King David—David, who wanted above all else to see God's will done—David, who desired more than anything in life to see God's purpose fulfilled and

502

God's plan for Israel carried out. This is the Church's opportunity to be men and women after God's own heart.

God originally said the following words in I Samuel 13:14. However, we will read them as they were repeated in the book of Acts.

Acts 13:22 (The Amplified Bible.)

²²*And when He had deposed him, He raised up David to be their king;* **of him He bore witness and said, I have found David son of Jesse a man after My own heart, who will do all My will and carry out My program fully.**

By this time, I am sure that there are a number of questions that you would like to ask me personally. Two of those questions might be, "Since you shared earlier about the love you and your church fellowship have for the Jews and since you are encouraging the Church as a whole to love and to financially support Israel, is the Living Word Church of Niceville practicing what she preaches? And if she is, how is the Living Word Church of Niceville financially supporting Israel?" My friend, both the previous questions deserve a response. So I will do my best to answer them.

When in 1982 God first revealed to the members of the Living Word Church of Niceville the truth regarding Israel and His holy name, we were sorely grieved over His sad plight. We wept, we prayed and we asked God to direct us in ways that would help Him vindicate His name and carry out His purpose for Israel.

We were not satisfied to offer Israel words alone. We realized that if we were going to be of real service to the Lord we had to do more than speak kind, caring and supportive words to Israel. We had to put actions behind our prayers.

When I had finished presenting the original lesson entitled *Why Should Every Christian Pray For And Support Israel?* God's laborers at the Living Word Church of Niceville decided that from that time forth, ten percent of all the tithe that comes into the Church would be set aside for Israel. We then went a step further. We ended up donating not just ten percent of the tithe to that cause but ten percent of all the finances that came into the Church.

Because at first, we were not sure of the best way to financially help Israel, we eventually contacted a representative of The Jewish National Fund (JNF) in Tampa, Florida, a wonderful Jewish man named Larry Wasser. The first JNF project that we became a part of involved planting trees in Israel. We had read God's words in the following text along with numerous other Scriptures, and we wanted to help God accomplish His will in the area of replanting the desolate places in Israel. So we rushed to God's aid.

Ezekiel 36:33-36 (The Amplified Bible.)

33Thus says the Lord God: In the day that I cleanse you from all your iniquities I will [also] cause [Israel's] cities to be inhabited, and the waste places shall be rebuilt.

34And the desolate land shall be tilled, that which had lain desolate in the sight of all who passed by.

35And they shall say, This land that was desolate has become like the garden of Eden, and the waste and desolate and ruined cities are fortified and inhabited.

36Then the nations that are left round about you shall know that I the Lord have rebuilt the ruined places and replanted that which was desolate. I the Lord have spoken it, and I will do it.

In the previous verse, Ezekiel 36:36, God promised to replant the desolate places in Israel. However, when God says He will do something, He often works through human vessels. Of course, we are aware that God is the one who is ultimately responsible for all that is accomplished through those chosen instruments. God is the planter, but we willingly became the spade. Pretty soon we were involved in planting one grove of trees after another in the land of Israel. We have even had the honor of planting trees in the Holy City of God, Jerusalem.

From the planting of trees we progressed to sending finances to help Israel build water reservoirs. Water, as I am sure you already know, is a priority item in Israel.

While our JNF tree planting and other projects in Israel were flourishing, we became aware of the plight of the Ethiopian Jews. Through yet another Jewish organization, we had the privilege to financially help the Ethiopian Jews get back to Israel.

The world is aware how plagues and famine swallowed up the Ethiopian people and their land. But most of the world did not and still does not know why that particular famine received so much publicity for a limited time. Neither do they know why they were so touched by that singular famine when at the same time there were famine victims literally dying of hunger in many parts of the world.

To this day, the people of the world do not understand that they actually became vessels that were used by God to get the Ethiopian Jews back to the land of Israel. They do not realize that through them, God accomplished His purpose and fulfilled His promises to Abraham. God stirred up the emotions of the whole world in order to air lift a few thousand Ethiopian Jews back to the Land of Promise.

How fulfilling it was for us to have been aware of the spiritual aspect of what was taking place during that time. How rewarding it was to have known from the day we sent our first contribution to aid the Ethiopian Jews that we were helping God fulfill His word and vindicate His holy name. We were helping Him gather His people from the nations and deliver them safely to the Promised Land.

While most of the world thought that the success of the American airlift rescue mission in Ethiopia was due to men's skill or lady luck, we knew different. We knew that the deliverance of those Ethiopian Jews came about as a result of God keeping His promises to Abraham, Isaac and Jacob in order to vindicate His own name. And you can be sure that we gave our faithful God all the glory, praise and honor that was due Him for His miraculous intervention and the success of that mission.

We continued our support of the Ethiopian Jews for many years after they had arrived safely in Israel. The reason why we extended our financial gifts was because the Ethiopian Jews still needed aid until they became established in their ancient homeland. During that same period, we also sent financial gifts to an organization that was providing aid to persecuted Jews in Russia.

Recently, we began sending financial gifts to a Jewish organization in Tampa, Florida, the **Florida Action for Jews in the former Soviet Union**. Through **Florida Action**, we are now helping Russian Jews immigrate to Israel. We are also providing food, medicines and other necessities to those Jews who are too old or sick to make such a trip. Last but not least, we are providing financial aid to those Russian Jews who are persecuted, those Jews

From the first time we contacted JNF, we have continued sending financial contributions to that organization. At present, we are involved in two JNF projects. One of those projects is in Jerusalem and it is called "Jerusalem 3000." Throughout the years, we have cheerfully and willingly continued to contribute ten percent of all the church's monthly finances to financially support numerous projects in Israel.

Many people have asked us, "How can such a small group as yours afford to do all the things you do? Right off the top, you give ten percent of all your church fellowship's income to finance projects that aid Israel. In addition to that, from the beginning of your ministry, the Living Word Church of Niceville has sent free and postpaid taped teachings upon request all over the world. And now, you send free and postpaid books to anyone throughout the world who requests them. All this, and you never ask for donations from anyone. How in the world do you manage to do so much while organizations considerably larger than yours have trouble making ends meet and are always begging for money?"

My friend, I can only answer your questions by saying, "This is God's work, and He makes sure that we have all we need to accomplish what He has called us to do. However, I have to confess that we do have an edge. Our edge is that we have no ulterior motives. We look for nothing but to please God and to help Him vindicate His glorious name. Because we sincerely desire to please God, and because we bless Israel, God keeps blessing us. As I shared with you earlier, God faithfully keeps His word. He promised to bless those who bless Israel, and He does."

We do not, however, turn God's promised blessings into a formula to acquire our own selfish desires. Neither do we demand that God give us things He never intended that we have. Our motives are pure and unselfish, and God knows that they are. So He prospers the Living Word Church of Niceville in order that we might advance the cause of righteousness throughout the world by financially supporting Israel and by teaching the truth of God's Word regarding Israel and God's commandments. In so doing, we can help to vindicate His name.

We simply wait on God for everything that the ministry of the Living Word Church of Niceville needs. **Now, notice that I said, we wait for everything the ministry needs, not everything we want. We wait on God to provide everything we need to do His will**. After all, when we see God righteously keeping His promises to Abraham, Isaac and Jacob and their descendants, the Jews, how can we fail to trust Him? His name is beautiful and glorious, and He is certainly deserving of our trust.

God is marvelous! He is truly faithful! Without a doubt, He can be trusted to provide for His own work. However, when He does provide, we do not spend His provision for the ministry on such foolish things as luxurious church buildings. God forbid! We use God's financial blessings as God intended.

We use God's financial blessings to support Israel and to spread the truth of God's Word throughout the whole world so that all men will be aware that God's name must be vindicated and so that all men will come to understand exactly how God intends to accomplish the vindication of His name. For, only when men are informed on the present topic can they make a conscious decision and a righteous commitment to help God vindicate His name by supporting Israel.

We use God's financial provision to feed God's spiritually hungry people with the meat of God's Word. We use it to spread truth, truth such as you have received and are receiving in this literary work, truth about God's commands, truth about righteousness, truth about Israel, truth about God's holy name.

Oh, my friend, God wants you to know the truth so that you can apply it to your life. What country are you in as God imparts the truth in this series to you? Are you in America or Canada? Are you across the sea or ocean? Are you in Africa, Korea, India, England, Germany or even Israel?

Wherever you are, purpose in your heart right now that you will make every effort to support Israel. Make up your mind to support Israel no matter what others do or say. Do not let ignorant men cause you to fail to help God carry out His purpose upon the earth. Do not let Satan steal the word of the kingdom that has been and will be sown in your heart during this series. Turn your eyes and heart toward Israel, and humble yourself to do God's will. Not for the sake of the Jews but for the sake of God's holy name, for the sake of God's reputation.

God's plan will proceed and be accomplished with or without your help, Gentile Christian. God's name will be vindicated with or without your help. But oh, my friend, surely you do not want to stand in opposition to God's covenant promises being kept and His holy name being vindicated, do you? Have you so easily forgotten why you were called, Christian Gentile? **You were called to bear and bring honor to God's holy name!** So, isn't it about time you fulfilled your God-given call which is described in the following verse.

Acts 15:14 (The Amplified Bible.)

14Simeon [Peter] has rehearsed how <u>God first visited</u>
<u>the Gentiles, to take out of them a people [to bear and</u>
<u>honor] His name.</u>

How much clearer can it be? God wants to use you, Christian
Gentile. He wants you to begin to do what He has called you to do. He
has raised you up to bear and honor His name. But you cannot honor
His name with words alone. I tell you Christian, actions speak louder
than words. You now know what you are called to do. So go and obey
God's Word. Go and bear and honor God's beautiful and glorious holy
name by loving and supporting the nation of Israel, the nation through
whom God will eventually vindicate His name and completely fulfill His
sacred promises to Abraham, Isaac and Jacob.

James 1:22 (The Amplified Bible.)

22But be doers of the Word [obey the message], and not
merely listeners to it, betraying yourselves [into
deception by reasoning contrary to the Truth].

After reading in Acts 15:14 *"...how God first visited the Gentiles, to*
take out of them a people [to bear and honor] His name," are you
beginning to see how all the pieces of the Scriptural puzzle fit together
perfectly? In fulfillment of Genesis 3:15 and God's promise to
Abraham, the Messiah was born. In fulfillment of Genesis 3:15 and
God's promise to Abraham, the Gentile nations were given an
opportunity to be saved. Now, we Gentiles who have received salvation
are called to bear and honor God's name, the name that has for so long
remained vulnerable to insults and blame and false accusations in order
to give us Gentiles a chance to be saved. And now, we actually have an
opportunity to honor that holy name by helping God keep His promises
to Abraham, Isaac and Jacob in regard to the Jews and the land of Israel.

As you now know, everything, even the vindication of God's holy
name revolves around God keeping His sacred promises to Abraham,
Isaac and Jacob. So, what better way could we Gentiles have of
fulfilling our God-given call than to help God clear the very name that
we are called to bear and honor?

Christian Gentile, you must not profane the name you bear by using
it for a purpose that God did not intend. You must not, in the name of
the Lord, abuse the very people whom God desires to use to bring about
His promises to Abraham, Isaac and Jacob. You must not hinder and
delay the vindication of God's name by ignorantly slowing down the

vindication process. Rather, you must do everything in your power to pave the way for God's covenant promises to be fulfilled in Israel.

The Jewish people must survive. Furthermore, they must be preserved on the land that God promised their forefathers would remain theirs forever. So Christian Gentile, go to your church fellowship, go to your church leaders, go to the leaders of your prayer and Bible study groups. Let them read for themselves the truth of God's Word that is recorded in this inspired book entitled, *Why Should Every Christian Pray For And Support Israel?* For God's name's sake, try to persuade those with whom you worship to stop raising money for church buildings that will quickly decay and crumble into pieces and, instead, do something with those finances that will have eternal value.

Nowhere in the New Testament are we Christians told that we are called to erect church or ministry buildings. However, we are informed that we are called to bear and honor God's name. So, for the sake of God's reputation, search out avenues through which your church group can financially support Israel.

God's laborers at the Living Word Church of Niceville are not asking you to send money to us. We do not solicit funds. Neither do we gain funds by pretentious means as some ministries do (that is, we do not offer materials free-of-charge and then deceptively request donations or love gifts in return). Nor do we ask people to send to us their prayer requests so that we can gain addresses for the purpose of soliciting funds. **Such practices are deceptive and we do not participate in them.**

I made the previous statement because I want you to be aware of a specific fact. **I want you to understand that we at the Living Word Church of Niceville have nothing to gain financially by encouraging you to financially support Israel.** If Christians send offerings to the Living Word of Church of Niceville, it is because they see a worthy ministry, a ministry that is promoting God's will and purpose on the earth. And, it is always because the Holy Spirit has personally dealt with them. It is not because we have ever asked them to send offerings. **On the other hand, we do ask that for God's name's sake, like us, you seek out ways to financially support the nation of Israel. We ask that you do all you can to help God vindicate His holy name.**

There is one more very important point that I must make before I close chapter fifteen, part one. Your support for Israel must not depend on feelings alone. The reason why your support for Israel must not be governed by feelings is because you might not feel compassionate or generous toward Israel all the time. Neither must your support for Israel depend on decisions that the Israeli government might make day-to-day. For you might not always agree with Israel's decisions or policies.

For instance, in August 1982 Israel decided to try to put a halt to Palestinian Liberation Organization (PLO) terrorist attacks by invading Lebanon. Consequently, world opinion was split on that issue. Then, shortly after that invasion, there was world uproar when the Lebanese Christian militia put to death six hundred suspected PLO terrorists. During that incident many hard and often false accusations were made against Israel even though the Israelis did not perform those executions. On the contrary, the Lebanese Christian militia was totally responsible for putting to death those PLO terrorists.

So, as you can see, not everyone in the world is in agreement with certain actions of Israel's government or, in some cases, their failure to act. Furthermore, the news media is noticeably biased in its reporting of Israeli and Palestinian matters. The news media unfairly criticizes Israel while at the same time promoting Palestinian causes even when the PLO continues to practice terrorism and blatantly insists that they will not stop their terrorist acts until they have taken from Israel every inch of the land that God promised would belong only to Israel forever. That is why I tell you that if your support for Israel hangs on whether the Israelis react or do not react to situations as you think they should, then I am afraid your support will not endure the test.

The day might come when you are so upset with an action that the Israelis may have taken or a judgment they may have made which conflicts with your own ideas of how things should be handled that you will change your mind and stop supporting Israel. Your excuse for removing your support or turning on Israel might be, "This is wrong! God would not want me to side with Israel in this matter!"

You might be influenced by the anti-Israeli propaganda with which the news media daily bombards its listeners, readers and viewers. As a result, you might become disillusioned. You might even go so far as to want the Israelis punished for what you perceive to be their lack of discretion. Moreover, because you may have had a bad day yourself, you might feel that their punishment should be severe. You would then be making your judgments dependent on how you feel or what you think rather than basing your decisions on and drawing your conclusion from God's Word alone.

You might even go so far as to want your own government to put a stop to any aid or financial support earmarked for Israel. Then what will happen? You will play right into the hands of Israel's enemies.

And again, though God promises in His Word that He will bless those who bless Israel and curse those who curse her, you must not support Israel for those blessings alone, especially not for financial gain. I emphasize that point because if you support Israel solely for the purpose of benefiting from the previously mentioned Biblical promise, the day may come when your desire to see Israel punished might be greater than your desire for personal gain. You might even convince yourself that since the Israeli's are doing something that you consider to be a mistake or even evil, God's warning that He will curse those who curse Israel might not apply in that particular situation. In the heat of the moment, in your estimation, you might feel that the Israeli's deserve to be punished.

Christian Gentile, if you are a true follower of God, your support for Israel will no longer be conditional. Neither will your support for Israel depend on your likes or dislikes or any personal convictions that you might have. Your support for Israel will not even depend on whether you like the Jewish people or not. Rather, your love and support for Israel will rest solely on your obedience to God's Word and your desire to see God's holy name vindicated through Israel before all the world.

In chapter fifteen, part two, you will see in the Scriptures that the early Church showed preferential treatment toward God's beloved people, Israel. Yes, you will be presented with undeniable Scriptural proof that early Church Christians willingly and eagerly financially supported God's Abrahamic covenant nation. Moreover, the truth you will receive in part two will give you added incentive to financially support the nation of Israel.

Chapter 15
Part Two

WHY SHOULD THE
CHURCH SUPPORT ISRAEL?

In chapter fifteen, part one, I promised that in part two I would provide you with Scriptural proof that the early Church Christians willingly and eagerly financially supported the nation of Israel. I will now keep my word.

Amazingly, every Biblically recorded instance of money being collected by the early Church gives evidence of the fact that those church collections were designated exclusively for Israel. My last statement may have surprised you. However, once you have examined all the evidence that I will gradually present to you, I am convinced that you will wholeheartedly agree with me that the Scriptural evidence is conclusive. For you to acquire an overall view of the aforementioned proof, it is necessary that we briefly scan a particular area of the apostle Paul's ministry beginning with the first documented prediction of the Jewish prophet, Agabus.

In "The Acts of the Apostles," we are informed that the prophet Agabus traveled from Jerusalem to Antioch in Syria, the very place where Barnabas and Paul were instructing the Church. When the prophet, Agabus, arrived in Antioch, he prophesied through the Holy Spirit that a severe famine would come upon Israel. I must add that Agabus's prophecy was fulfilled during the reign of the Roman Emperor Claudius.

Recognizing that the New Testament prophet, Agabus, had spoken by the power of the Holy Spirit, the Church in Antioch resolved to send relief to their brethren in Judea. Each man purposed to give in proportion as he had prospered. Moreover, because of their impeccable characters, Barnabas and Paul were chosen to deliver that God-ordained offering to the elders of the Church in Jerusalem.

See these facts for yourself in the following text in *The Living Bible*.

Acts 11:25-30 (The Living Bible.)

25*Then Barnabas went on to Tarsus to hunt for Paul.*

26When he found him, he brought him back to Antioch; and both of them stayed there for a full year, teaching the many new converts. (It was there at Antioch that the believers were first called "Christians".)

27During this time some prophets came down from Jerusalem to Antioch,

28<u>and one of them, named Agabus, stood up in one of the meetings to predict by the Spirit that a great famine was coming upon the land of Israel.</u> (This was fulfilled during the reign of Claudius.)

29<u>So the believers decided to send relief to the Christians in Judea, each giving as much as he could.</u>

30<u>This they did, consigning their gifts to Barnabas and Paul to take to the elders of the church in Jerusalem.</u>

Verses twenty-nine and thirty in the *Holy Bible, King James Version* read,

29Then the disciples, every man according to his ability, determined to send relief unto <u>the brethren</u> which dwelt in Judea.

30Which also they did, and sent it to the elders by the hands of <u>Barnabas</u> and <u>Saul</u>.

Barnabas and Paul completed their God decreed mission. They safely delivered the Church's alms and offerings to the elders in Jerusalem. Then, according to the subsequent verse, they returned to Antioch in Syria.

Acts 12:25 (The Living Bible.)

25Barnabas and Paul now visited Jerusalem and, as soon as they had finished their business, returned to Antioch, taking John Mark with them.

As one continues to study the Scriptures, it becomes evident that the Lord had not finished using the apostle Paul in the capacity of fund raiser for the nation of Israel. For His name's sake, God had to ensure that His Abrahamic covenant people who dwelt in Israel survived the famine in order to help Him carry out His Biblical predictions and His promises to Abraham, including His promise concerning the salvation of the whole world. Thus, in Acts 12:25, Paul delivered to Jerusalem the first of many gifts that the Church eventually sent by his hand to Israel.

Another important point to keep in mind is that Christian Gentiles as well as Jewish believers were eventually called to send generous offerings to the land of Israel. An example of the Gentiles' generosity toward those in Jerusalem is seen in the following text. For in those verses, you will see that the offerings Paul delivered to God's needy people in Jerusalem included gifts from the Churches in Macedonia and Achaia.

The Zondervan Pictorial Bible Dictionary under the heading "Achaia" informs us that Macedonia and Achaia generally mean all of Greece. Remembering that fact, we will read the next information from *The Amplified Bible.*

Romans 15:24-33 (The Amplified Bible.)

24I hope to see you in passing [through Rome] as I go [on my intended trip] to Spain, and to be aided on my journey there by you, after I have enjoyed your company for a little while.

25For the present, however, I am going to Jerusalem to bring aid (relief) for the saints (God's people there).

*26For it has been the good pleasure of **Macedonia** and **Achaia** to make some contribution for the poor among the saints of Jerusalem.*

*27They were pleased to do it; and surely they are in debt to them, **for if these Gentiles have come to share in their [the Jerusalem Jews') spiritual blessings, then they ought also to be of service to them in material blessings.***
*28**When therefore I have completed this mission and have delivered to them [at Jerusalem] what has been raised**, I shall go on by way of you to Spain.*

29And I know that when I do come to you, I shall come in the abundant blessing of the Gospel of Christ.

30I appeal to you [I entreat you], brethren, for the sake of our Lord Jesus Christ and by the love [given by] the Spirit, to unite with me in earnest wrestling in prayer to God in my behalf.

*31**[Pray] that I may be delivered (rescued) from the unbelievers in Judea and that my mission of relief to Jerusalem may be acceptable and graciously received by the saints (God's people there),***

32So that by God's will I may subsequently come to you with joy (with a happy heart) and be refreshed [by the interval of rest] in your company.

33May [our] peace-giving God be with you all! Amen (so be it).

Romans 15:31 reveals that in this case, in order to carry out his God-ordained mission and deliver the Gentile Christians' contributions to the nation of Israel, Paul was even willing to place himself at risk. He was forced to ask for special prayer for his safety so that he could fulfill his *"mission of relief to Jerusalem."*

The list of recorded donors who gave of their material blessings to Paul's God-ordained cause goes on and on. For instance, the Corinthian Church also contributed money for the needs of God's Abrahamic covenant people in Jerusalem. See these facts for yourself in the following verses. Keep in mind that in New Testament times Corinth was the capital of Greece.

I Corinthians 16:1-4 (The Amplified Bible.)

1NOW CONCERNING the money contributed for [the relief of] the saints (God's people): you are to do the same as I directed the churches of Galatia to do.

2On the first [day] of each week, let each one of you [personally] put aside something and save it up as he has prospered [in proportion to what he is given], so that no collections will need to be taken after I come.

3And when I arrive, I will send on those whom you approve and authorize with credentials to carry your gift [of charity] to Jerusalem.

4If it seems worthwhile that I should go too, they will accompany me.

Notice that in verse one of the previous text, Paul mentions **the churches of Galatia**. He says, *"you are to do the same as I directed the churches of Galatia to do."* The New Testament writings do not reveal the exact number of Galatian churches that were involved in raising money for Israel. However, under the heading "Galatia," *The Zondervan Pictorial Bible Dictionary* informs us that Galatia in New Testament times was of a territory in north-central Asia Minor and was also a Roman province in Central Asia Minor. The province included parts of Phrygia, Pisdia, Lycaonia and Isauria. Politically the term Galatia denoted the entire Roman province. According to the previous source, scholars now recognize that the cities of Antioch, Iconium, Lystra and Derbe were also in the province of Galatia. Having understanding of the many cities incorporated under the name "The Churches of Galatia" gives one an idea of how vast was the number of Gentile churches who financially supported the nation of Israel.

Later we will touch on the actual offerings that were raised. In the meantime, we see that the Corinthian Church's generous financial gifts for Israel are again mentioned in chapters eight and nine of Second Corinthians. As a matter of fact, Paul devoted two whole chapters to that subject. As you read the previously mentioned two chapters in their entirety, remember that though many church leaders take Paul's words out of context in order to raise money for their own church projects and ministries, the truth is that both chapters deal solely with the Church's financial support for Israel. No other type of fund raising whatsoever is mentioned by Paul in either chapter.

II Corinthians Chapters 8 and 9

CHAPTER 8 (The Amplified Bible.)

1 WE WANT to tell you further, brethren, about the grace (the favor and spiritual blessing) of God which has been evident in the churches of Macedonia [arousing in them the desire to give alms];

2 For in the midst of an ordeal of severe tribulation, their abundance of joy and their depth of poverty [together] have overflowed in wealth of lavish generosity on their part.

3 For, as I can bear witness, [they gave] according to their ability, yes, and beyond their ability; and [they did it] voluntarily,

4 Begging us most insistently for the favor and the fellowship of contributing in this ministration for [the relief and support of] the saints [in Jerusalem].

5 Nor [was this gift of theirs merely the contribution] that we expected, but first they gave themselves to the Lord and to us [as His agents] by the will of God [entirely disregarding their personal interests, they gave as much as they possibly could, having put themselves at our disposal to be directed by the will of God]—

According to *Smith's Bible Dictionary* under the heading "Macedonia," Macedonia was the first part of Europe to receive Christianity. The Macedonians were extremely close to Paul since he had delivered the gospel to them.

In these verses, Paul brags on the Macedonians for their generosity to Israel. The Macedonian Christians gave until it hurt them financially. Yet, they still counted it a joy to be able to contribute. Paul did not have to wring aid for Israel out of these Gentile Christians. No! The Christians in Macedonia begged for the privilege of contributing to such a worthy, God-ordained cause. They possessed the type of attitude that God desires that all Gentile Christians express regarding financial support for the nation of Israel.

Let us now continue reading in the present chapter, picking up where Paul encourages the Corinthian Church to exhibit the same generous attitude toward Israel as the Christians in Macedonia had demonstrated.

> *5Nor [was this gift of theirs merely the contribution] that we expected, but first they gave themselves to the Lord and to us [as His agents] by the will of God [entirely disregarding their personal interests, they gave as much as they possibly could, having put themselves at our disposal to be directed by the will of God]—*

> *6So much so that we have urged Titus that as he began it, he should also complete this beneficent and gracious contribution among you [the church at Corinth].*

> *7Now as you abound and excel and are at the front in everything—in faith, in expressing yourselves, in knowledge, in all zeal, and in your love for us—[see to it that you come to the front now and] abound and excel in this gracious work [of almsgiving] also.*

> *8I give this not as a order [to dictate to you], but to prove, by [pointing out] the zeal of others, the sincerity of your [own] love also.*

> *9For you are becoming progressively acquainted with and recognizing more strongly and clearly the grace of our Lord Jesus Christ (His kindness, His gracious generosity, His undeserved favor and spiritual blessing), [in] that though He was [so very] rich, yet for your sakes He became [so very] poor, in order that by His*

poverty you might become enriched (abundantly supplied).

10[It is then] my counsel and my opinion in this matter that I give [you when I say]: It is profitable and fitting for you [now to complete the enterprise] which more than a year ago you not only began, but were the first to wish to do anything [about contributions for the relief of the saints at Jerusalem].

As you read verses eleven through fifteen, note that Paul is telling the Christians in the Corinthian Church that each one of them is only expected to give to Israel in proportion to what he has. Paul emphasizes that what really counts is that they have a willing generous heart and that they do their best to give to Israel as much as they can.

11So now finish doing it, that your [enthusiastic] readiness in desiring it may be equaled by your completion of it according to your ability and means.

12For if the [eager] readiness to give is there, then it is acceptable and welcomed in proportion to what a person has, not according to what he does not have.

13For it is not [intended] that other people be eased and relieved [of their responsibility] and you be burdened and suffer [unfairly],

14But to have equality [share and share alike], your surplus over necessity at the present time going to meet their want and to equalize the difference created by it, so that [at some other time] their surplus in turn may be given to supply your want. Thus there may be equality.

15As it is written, He who gathered much had nothing over, and he who gathered little did not lack.

16But thanks be to God Who planted the same earnest zeal and care for you in the heart of Titus.

17For he not only welcomed and responded to our appeal, but was himself so keen in his enthusiasm and interest in you that he is going to you of his own accord.

18But we are sending along with him that brother [Luke?] whose praise in the Gospel ministry [is spread] throughout all the churches;

19And more than that, he has been appointed by the churches to travel as our companion in regard to this bountiful contribution which we are administering for the glory of the Lord Himself and [to show] our eager readiness [as Christians to help one another].

20[For] we are on our guard, intending that no one should find anything for which to blame us in regard to **our administration of this large contribution.**

21For we take thought beforehand and aim to be honest and absolutely above suspicion, not only in the sight of the Lord but also in the sight of men.

22Moreover, along with them we are sending our brother, whom we have often put to the test and have found him zealous (devoted and earnest) in many matters, but who is now more [eagerly] earnest than ever because of [his] absolute confidence in you.

23As for Titus, he is my colleague and shares my work in your service; and as for the [other two] brethren, they are the [special] messengers of the churches, a credit and glory to Christ (the Messiah).

24Show to these men, therefore, in the sight of the churches, the reality and plain truth of your love (your affection, goodwill, and benevolence) and what [good reasons] I had for boasting about and being proud of you.

CHAPTER NINE (The Amplified Bible.)

1**NOW ABOUT the offering that is [to be made] for the saints (God's people in Jerusalem**), it is quite superfluous that I should write you;

2For I am well acquainted with your willingness (your readiness and your eagerness to promote it) and I have proudly told about you to **the people of Macedonia, saying the Achaia (most of Greece)** has been prepared since last year for this contribution; and [consequently] your enthusiasm has stimulated the majority of them.

3Still, I am sending the brethren [on to you], lest our pride in you should be made an empty boast in this particular case, and so that you may be all ready, as I told them you would be;

4Lest, if [any] Macedonians should come with me and find you unprepared [for this generosity], we, to say *nothing of yourselves, be humiliated for our being so confident.*

⁵*That is why I thought it necessary to urge these brethren to go to you before I do and make arrangements in advance **for this bountiful, promised gift of yours, so that it may be ready, not as an extortion [wrung out of you] but as a generous and willing gift.***

⁶*[Remember] this: he who sows sparingly and grudgingly will also reap sparingly and grudgingly, and he who sows generously [that blessings may come to someone] will also reap generously and with blessings.*

⁷*Let each one [give] as he has made up his own mind and purposed in his heart, not reluctantly or sorrowfully or under compulsion, for God loves (He takes pleasure in, prizes above other things, and is unwilling to abandon or to do without) as cheerful (joyous, "prompt to do it") giver [whose heart is in his giving].*

⁸*And God is able to make all grace (every favor and earthly blessing) come to you in abundance, so that you may always and under all circumstances and whatever the need be self-sufficient [possessing enough to require no aid or support and furnished in abundance for every good work and charitable donation].*

⁹*As it is written, He [the benevolent person] scatters abroad; He gives to the poor; His deeds of justice and goodness and kindness and benevolence will go on and endure forever!*

¹⁰*And [God] Who provides seed for the sower and bread for eating will also provide and multiply your [resources for] sowing and increase the fruits of your righteousness [which manifests itself in active goodness, kindness, and charity].*

¹¹*Thus you will be enriched in all things and in every way, so that you can be generous, and [your generosity as it is] administered by us will bring forth thanksgiving to God.*

¹²***For the service that the ministering of this fund renders does not only fully supply what is lacking to the saints (God's people), but it also overflows in many [cries of] thanksgiving to God.***

*13Because at [your] standing of the test of this ministry, they will glorify God for your loyalty and obedience to the gospel of Christ which you confess, **as well as for your generous-hearted liberality to them and to all [the other needy ones]**.*

*14And they yearn for you while they pray for you, **because of the surpassing measure of God's grace (His favor and mercy and spiritual blessing which is shown forth) in you.***

15Now thanks be to God for His Gift, [precious] beyond telling [His indescribable, inexpressible, free Gift]!

I will not take time to cover the marvelous blessings promised in the previous two chapters. However, you can yourself study chapters eight and nine, paying particular attention to the specific area of almsgiving and offerings that bring those promised Biblical blessings upon a man's life. For, the only area of giving that is mentioned throughout either of those chapters is financial support for Israel.

How sad it is that ministers today repeatedly take the previous Scriptures out of context and use Paul's writings as a vehicle to raise money for every kind of project except the one that Paul intended when he wrote those words. Therefore, it must be repeatedly emphasized that Paul's fund raising for the financial needs of the nation of Israel is the only subject and priority contained in the previous two chapters.

Also, keep in mind that the liberal aid that was entrusted to the Jewish brethren in Judea was shared with any needy Jew, whether that Jew believed in Yeshua or not. I say that because as well as the New Testament proof that I will present in a few moments, God's Old Testament Law requires that the Jewish people exhibit kindness and mercy to the needy among their brethren. So, the fact is that though the Churches' offerings were delivered to **the Church** in Jerusalem, **all** needy Jews in Israel benefited from that relief, not just those Jews who believed in Yeshua. And rightly so since as you now know, God needs all the Jews, both believers and non-believers, to help him fulfill His Biblical predictions and His promises to Abraham, Isaac and Jacob. Furthermore, God loves the Jews with an everlasting love.

In order for you to see Scriptural confirmation of the fact that it was not only needy believers but all Jews who benefited from the financial aid that the early Church fellowships sent to the nation of Israel, you will need to read again two of the previous verses, paying special attention to the highlighted portion. This time however, we will read those verses from the *Holy Bible, King James Version.*

II Corinthians 9:12-13 (King James Version.)

12For the administration of this service not only supplieth the want of the saints, but is abundant also by many thanksgivings unto God;

*13Whiles by the experiment of this ministration they glorify God for your professed subjection unto the gospel of Christ, **and for your liberal distribution unto them, and unto all men;***

Notice that in verse thirteen, Paul says that the Church's liberal distribution is unto the Jewish Christians in Jerusalem *"**and unto all men"*** or, as *The Amplified Bible* reads, *"...and to all [the other needy ones]."* Paul's words have to refer to all needy men in Israel since these contributions had been designated solely for Israel. There, my friend, on the pages of God's Word is proof that all needy Jews in Israel benefited from the church relief that Paul delivered to Jerusalem. Thus, I repeat what I said earlier. It was not only believing Jews, but *"**all men"*** (that is, **all Jews in Israel**) who benefited from the financial support that the early Church sent to the nation of Israel. And what is more, since the Jews as a nation are God's beloved Abrahamic covenant people, it makes perfect sense that all the needy Jews in Israel should have benefited from those God-ordained offerings.

Another important truth to keep in mind is that when Peter, James and John met with Paul and Barnabas in the verses that we will soon read, after extending their right hand of fellowship, they told Paul that he and Barnabas should go to the Gentiles and they would go to the Jews. On that occasion, **Peter, James and John made only one stipulation. That stipulation was that Paul and Barnabas were to remember the poor.** Paul concludes the details of his meeting with Peter, James and John by saying that what the three elders suggested that he do, regarding the poor, was the very thing that he was already eager to do.

My friend, in the incident that I mentioned in the former paragraph, where Paul was cautioned to remember the poor, which poor people do you yourself think the Jewish apostles Peter, James and John were referring to? They were of course referring to their poor Jewish brethren in Jerusalem. For the Holy Spirit Himself had already made known to Paul the needs of his brethren in Jerusalem. Moreover, Paul had been chosen by the Church to become involved with fund raising for Israel. Prior to his previously mentioned visit with Peter, James and John, he had already delivered the Church's first financial contribution to the elders in Jerusalem. Therefore, it stands to reason that in the following verses all four men were referring to keeping up the Gentiles' side of the financial aid that, prior to that time, God had supernaturally led the Church to begin to provide through the prophet Agabus, aid for their poor Jewish brethren in Judea (Israel). And, as you have seen and will continue to see in the Scriptures, Paul kept his word to Peter, James and John regarding the Gentiles' contributions for the saints in Jerusalem.

Turn to Galatians 2:7-10 and read about Paul's meeting with Peter, James and John and their previously mentioned demand that Paul agreed to.

Galatians 2:7-10 (The Amplified Bible.)

7But on the contrary, when they [really] saw that I had been entrusted [to carry] the Gospel to the uncircumcised [Gentiles, just as definitely] as Peter had been entrusted [to proclaim] the Gospel to the circumcised [Jews, they were agreeable];

8For He Who motivated and fitted Peter and worked effectively through him for the mission to the circumcised, motivated and fitted me and worked through me also for [the mission to] the Gentiles.

9And when they knew (perceived, recognized, understood, and acknowledged) the grace (God's unmerited favor and spiritual blessing) that had been bestowed upon me, James and Cephas (Peter) and John, who were reputed to be pillars of the Jerusalem church, gave to me and Barnabas the right hand of fellowship, with the understanding that we should go to the Gentiles and they to the circumcised (Jews).

10They only [made one stipulation], that we were to remember the poor, which very thing I was also eager to do.

As I said earlier, under the existing circumstances, the only poor people that Paul could possibly have been referring to were his needy Jewish brethren in Jerusalem. Additional proof is in the fact that the reference for verse ten (that is, the reference provided by the scholars of the *Holy Bible, King James Version*, published by Thomas Nelson Inc.) is Acts 24:17. That verse quotes the apostle Paul's words which are,

*"Now after many years I came to bring alms **to my nation**, and offerings."* So, these particular Bible scholars recognize that in Galatians 2:10, Peter, James and John did indeed specify continued aid for Israel.

Paul kept his word to Peter, James and John regarding the poor in Jerusalem, even to his own hurt. We have often wondered why Paul insisted on going to Jerusalem after the prophet, Agabus, had told him that if he did, the Jews would bind his hands and feet. **Well, you will see later that his urgency in going there was to deliver more contributions for needy Jews.** First, however, I want you to read the prophet's warning to Paul in Acts 21:3-14 in *The Amplified Bible.*

> *Acts 21:3-14 (The Amplified Bible.)*
>
> *3After we had sighted Cyprus, leaving it on our left we sailed on to Syria and put in at Tyre, for there the ship was to unload her cargo.*
>
> *4And having looked up the disciples there, we remained with them for seven days. **Prompted by the [Holy] Spirit, they kept telling Paul not to set foot in Jerusalem.***
>
> *5But when our time there was ended, we left and proceeded on our journey; and all of them with their wives and children accompanied us on our way till we were outside the city. There we knelt down on the beach and prayed.*
>
> *6Then when we had told one another farewell, we went on board the ship, and they returned to their own homes.*
>
> *7When we had completed the voyage from Tyre, we landed at Ptolemais, where we paid our respects to the brethren and remained with them for one day.*
>
> *8On the morrow we left there and came to Caesarea; and we went into the house of Philip the evangelist, who was one of the Seven [first deacons], and stayed with him.*
>
> *9And he had four maiden daughters who had the gift of prophecy.*
>
> *10While we were remaining there for some time, a prophet named Agabus came down from Judea.*

11 And coming to [see] us, he took Paul's belt and with it bound his own feet and hands and said, Thus says the Holy Spirit: The Jews at Jerusalem shall bind like this the man who owns this belt, and they shall deliver him into the hands of the Gentiles (heathen).

12 When we heard this, both we and the residents of that place pleaded with him not to go up to Jerusalem.

13 Then Paul replied, What do you mean by weeping and breaking my heart like this? For I hold myself in readiness not only to be arrested and bound and imprisoned at Jerusalem, but also [even] to die for the name of the Lord Jesus.

14 And when he would not yield to [our] persuading, we stopped [urging and imploring him], saying, The Lord's will be done!

As Agabus had previously prophesied, during Paul's visit to Jerusalem, the Jews were indeed responsible for his being turned over to the Gentile authorities and for his imprisonment. The circumstances surrounding Paul's arrest are recorded in Acts chapters twenty-one through twenty-three. You may want to familiarize yourself with the content of those three chapters.

Now you might ask, "**But what Scriptural evidence can you present to prove to me that on the particular occasion in question Paul went to Jerusalem for the purpose of carrying out his promise to Peter, James and John regarding contributions for the poor?**" Before I answer the previous question, let me first provide you with some of the details that led up to Paul's own affirmation of his purpose for going to Judea.

After the Jews had fulfilled the prophet's words and brought about Paul's arrest, Paul was questioned by the commandant. However, when the commandant realized that Paul was a Roman citizen, he had Paul freed from his chains.

The next day the commandant ordered the Jewish leaders to assemble and he brought Paul before them. However, when a riot ensued, the commandant ordered his troops to rescue Paul from among the Jews and take him back to prison.

The following night, the Lord appeared to Paul and said, "*Take courage, Paul, for as you have borne faithful witness concerning me at Jerusalem, so you must also bear witness at Rome.*" (Acts 23:11.)

When daylight came, a group of Jews swore by an oath that they would neither eat nor drink until they had killed Paul. However, finding out about their wicked plot, Paul's nephew passed the information onto his uncle and Paul in turn sent his sister's son to the commandant. Once the commandant was made aware that forty men were lying in wait to ambush Paul, a Roman citizen, he put 470 of his troops on alert and they escorted Paul to Felix the governor in Caesarea, Judaea.

Upon arriving in Caesarea, the soldiers presented Paul, along with the commandant's letter of explanation, to Governor Felix. Felix told Paul that he would hear his case when his accusers arrived. Thus, five days later the high priest, some of the elders and a spokesman named Tertullus came to Caesarea to make their charges against Paul. After the Jews had offered their evidence, Felix allowed Paul to answer their charges, which he did quite well. However, the only portion of Paul's statement that we are interested in at this time is found in Acts chapter twenty-four. It involves Paul's stated reason for visiting Jerusalem in the first place. Paul himself clearly stated to Felix that **he came to Jerusalem in order to bring contributions of charity and offerings for the poor.** See this for yourself in the following text.

Acts 24:17 (The Amplified Bible.)

17Now after several years I came up [to Jerusalem] to bring to my people contributions of charity and offerings.

God's plan for allowing Paul to come to Jerusalem was twofold.

(1) He wanted Paul to bring the Church's contributions to his needy Abrahamic covenant people, those who believed on Yeshua as the Christ, as well as those who did not. (II Corinthians 9:13.) For His name's sake, God desired that His covenant people survive the severe famine that had come upon Israel.

(2) He wanted Paul to be a witness for Him in Jerusalem and in Rome. (Acts 23:11.) And, as you know, Paul was eventually taken to Rome as a prisoner.

Yet, despite the fact that God had obviously intended that Paul go to Jerusalem and Rome as a witness, Paul's verbalized purpose for traveling to Jerusalem had been to deliver the alms and offerings that the churches had collected for **the nation of Israel.** (Acts 24:17.) Notice that I said alms and offerings that the churches had collected for **the nation** of Israel. Why did I say, for **the nation** of Israel and not for the Jewish Christians or the brethren in Israel? I made that statement because that was how Paul himself described the beneficiaries of those church offerings in the *Holy Bible, King James Version*. Read the previously mentioned verse for yourself from the *King James Version*, and you will see what I mean.

Acts 24:17 (King James Version.)

17Now after many years I came to bring alms __to my nation__, and offerings.

Paul was obviously concerned about the nation of Israel as a whole, and not just the Christian minority in his nation. Moreover, you will recall that Paul had made it known to the Church in II Corinthians 9:12-13 that the offerings were intended to benefit **all** the needy Jews in Israel and not just those Jews who believed on Yeshua. God had warned Paul that a severe famine would come upon Israel, and Paul was doing his best to help all the victims of that famine. Furthermore, he had promised Peter, James and John that he would remember the poor in Jerusalem and he was adamant about keeping his agreement with them and making sure that the famine victims received relief.

To show you how severe the famine was, I will share with you a quote from *Smith's Bible Dictionary* under the heading "Agabus." Referring to the records of the historian Josephus, Smith writes:

> Josephus mentions a famine which prevailed in Judea in the reign of Claudius, **and swept away many of the inhabitants....**

After receiving the previous Scriptural and historical evidence and upon realizing that many Jews died of starvation during that prophesied famine, surely you no longer think that Paul's only concern was for the Jewish Christian minority in Israel. No, of course you don't.

My friend, now that you possess insight into the previously mentioned areas, you will suddenly find that as you study God's Word, truth pops up in the most unexpected places, for instance, Acts 20:35.

Acts 20:35 (The Amplified Bible.)

35In everything I have pointed out to you [by example] that, by working diligently in this manner, __we ought to assist the weak__, being mindful of the words of the Lord Jesus, how He Himself said, It is more blessed (makes one happier and more to be envied) to give than to receive.

When Paul spoke the previous words in Acts 20:35, he was on his way to Jerusalem to deliver the Church's alms and offerings **to his nation**. So, who else would Paul have been referring to other than his needy people in Israel for whom he was about to risk his life. Knowing that peril awaited him there, Paul was bound by the Holy Spirit to go to Jerusalem. (Acts 20:22-23.) However, as you saw in the Scriptures, Paul was obviously under the impression that he was compelled by the Holy Spirit to go there for the purpose of delivering the Church's alms and offerings to the nation of Israel. After all, Peter, James and John had insisted that they would preach to the Jews and Paul would preach to the Gentiles. So, Paul's reason for going to Jerusalem would not have been to override the apostles' orders. Rather, his reason for going to Jerusalem would have been to keep his promise to Peter, James and John and to bring the Gentile churches' alms and offerings to Jerusalem in order to assist the poor (that is, in order to assist those Jews who were weak and in desperate need of aid.

During this portion of the series, I have presented to you the Biblical evidence that I promised earlier. You have seen Scriptural proof that any Biblically recorded church collections that were taken up by the early Church Christians were designated exclusively for the nation of Israel.

I am sure that some church fellowships, as well as certain individual Christians, find great comfort and joy in the former information. I know the members of The Living Word Church of Niceville do. I say that because since 1982 we have financially supported Israel. Therefore, this segment of chapter fifteen lends added Scriptural confirmation for what the Holy Spirit led us to do all those years ago. While the majority of church fellowships and ministries were pursuing their own temporal desires (that is, while they were investing their time, energy and church finances in the pursuit of beautiful buildings, gymnasiums, Christian amusement parks and lavish fireworks displays and such), the members of The Living Word Church, like Paul and the early Church fellowships, were eagerly concentrating upon carrying out their God-ordained mission. Yes, we had our hearts and minds set on financially supporting Israel.

Oh, if only the Church today would, as a whole, follow the example of the apostle Paul and the early Church fellowships. If only church leaders today would follow Paul's example and insist that God's people's financial gifts and sacrificial offerings be designated for Israel. If the Church did this, God's beloved Abrahamic covenant nation, Israel, would not lack for anything. Moreover, the Church would finally be putting her money into something that would glorify God instead of men.

My friend, I implore you to open your spiritual eyes and see the profoundness of what the Holy Spirit has relayed to you. See the true compassion and wisdom that was expressed by the early Church. Understand that any collections for the needy that are recorded in New Testament writings, and I emphasize <u>collections</u>, were for one purpose and one purpose only. These recorded solicited funds were designated solely for Israel. As you saw with your own eyes, those offerings, those financial gifts were collected for Israel. Thus, through their generous gifts, the givers furthered God's purpose on the earth and helped God vindicate His holy name by aiding Him in fulfilling His Biblical predictions and His promises to Abraham, Isaac, and Jacob.

My prayer is that God will help Christians today exhibit the same degree of true wisdom and compassion when they give their alms, offerings and gifts that the early Church Christians exhibited. My prayer is that, for God's name's sake, each local church fellowship will take the truth in this series to heart and will put Israel at the top of their permanent donation list. My prayer is that Christian ministers and workers everywhere, including Christian radio and television hosts, will get their priorities in the correct Biblical order and that they, like the apostle Paul, will start consistently encouraging their followers to financially support Israel with their offerings.

Only when the Church is willing to follow the example that the early Church leaders set, regarding the collection and disposal of God's peoples' alms, offerings and financial gifts, will the Church be accomplishing all that God intended in that area. God does not need His Church to build for Him luxurious sanctuaries or ministry buildings. He did not ask His people for such things. However, God does need to keep His predictions and His covenant promises in order to clear His holy name. Moreover, God desires that His people among the Gentiles help Him to accomplish that feat by financially supporting the only nation through whom He can vindicate His name.

I have answered the question, "Why Should Every Christian Support Israel?" I have also kept my promise to provide you with Scriptural proof that the early Church Christians did indeed willingly and eagerly support the nation of Israel. And now, as I close this portion of the series, I beg you Gentile Christian to fulfill your God-given call to bear and honor God's name. I implore you to come to the aid of your God and Savior in these last days. Let your heavenly Father know that He has a true friend in you. Let Him know that you care about Him and His needs enough to help Him clear His name by giving your moral and financial support to the one nation that exists through whom His name can be truly justified.

Chapter 16

WHY SHOULD EVERY
CHRISTIAN PRAY FOR ISRAEL?

All over the world, God is calling Christians to pray for the nation of Israel. We at the Living Word Church of Niceville became aware of God's Biblical instructions regarding prayer for Israel and our Christian duty to obey those instructions in the early months of 1982. At that time, I was conducting a series of teachings on the subject of prayer. During that series our spiritual eyes were opened to the truth regarding the Church's Biblical obligation to pray for Israel.

Prior to that time, God had led us to send teachings of His Word on numerous subjects throughout the world. We had done our best to fulfill that God-ordained mission. However, though we were accomplishing much good throughout the world, we were not conscious of the Church's responsibility to pray for Israel. As I said earlier, it was not until later, during the previously mentioned series, that through the truth contained in the Scriptures, the Lord made us aware of our duty in that area and called us to intercessory prayer for Israel.

In blind faith, we obeyed God's Word. When I say we obeyed in blind faith, I mean that we obeyed despite the fact that we did not yet understand why God required that we pray for Israel. All we knew was that God's Word said do it, so we did.

People soon began to inquire as to why we felt we should pray for Israel every time the church doors opened and why we were suddenly so supportive of the nation of Israel. In our ignorance, we could only offer to those who inquired the same pat answers that the Church as a whole had for centuries given when referring to Israel. We would say, "We do it because the Jews are God's chosen people," or "We pray for the Israelis because God loves them," or "We do it because they are special to God," or "We do it because God said He would bless those who bless them."

Again like the rest of the Church, we were not able at that time to clarify for those who scrutinized our actions the reason why the Jews were God's chosen people. Neither could we tell them why God loves the Jews and why He has continued to love them throughout the ages. We were not able to explain why the Jews are special to God. And we certainly were not able to convey to others why God blesses people who bless them.

Sadly, as I have already made known, we were in the same unlearned state as the rest of the Church. So, since we were ignorant as to why the Church should pray for and support Israel, we handled most of men's questions by simply saying, "The Bible requires that we pray for Israel. We are simply obeying God's written instructions."

After all, how could we have adequately answered the previous barrage of questions, questions which were continually flung at us when at that point we did not possess those answers ourselves. No! At that point, we did not even know why God's Word instructed that we pray for Israel. It was enough for us that God's Word commanded that we do it. So, we willingly obeyed God's commands and began to faithfully and consistently intercede in prayer for the nation of Israel.

Then in May 1982, while we were engrossed in the series that I mentioned in the previous chapter entitled *Why Should Every Christian Pray For And Support Israel?* God generously and mercifully answered our questions. Among numerous other Biblical revelations, many of which you have already received in this series, God opened our understanding to the real reasons why He has called His Church to intercession for Israel. God entrusted us with this abundant, profound spiritual knowledge so that we could in turn send it to His beloved Church throughout the world. Yes, God showed us these truths so that we could send this marvelous information to you.

When you have finished studying this particular portion of the series, among numerous other truths, you will have learned in God's Word that if you are a true follower of God, your support and your prayer for Israel will no longer be conditional.

As you read on, you will quickly come to realize that your prayer for Israel must not be governed by your personal likes, dislikes or convictions. Neither must your prayer for Israel rest upon whether you do or do not like the Jewish people. And again, your prayer for Israel must not be dependent on whether you agree or disagree with Israel's governmental decisions or policies. For, if your prayer or lack of prayer for Israel is based on personal feelings, you will most certainly end up standing in opposition to God and His Word.

The truth is that whether you pray for Israel or not will really be determined by whether you do or do not love and know God. Moreover, whether you pray for Israel or not will ultimately determine whether you do or do not help God accomplish His will throughout the world, and especially in Israel. Why especially in Israel? Why? Because as you saw earlier in the series, Israel is special to God. God made sacred promises to Abraham, Isaac and Jacob regarding the Jews and their land, and those promises must be kept. God also loves the Jews with an everlasting love. And most importantly, God needs them. He needs them to help Him fulfill His Biblically recorded promises and predictions. Yes, God needs them to help Him carry out His purpose on the earth and vindicate His holy name before all the world.

Before we continue, I want to take a moment to briefly explain the segment of my previous statement in which I talked about your prayer for Israel being dependent on whether you do or do not love and know God. That part of my statement may have puzzled you. You may have wondered how in the world your decision to pray or not to pray for Israel could possibly have anything to do with whether you do or do not love and know God.

The following two references will fully answer the previous query. As you read the first text, keep in mind that Yeshua's commands (teachings) are God's commands. For, you will recall that Yeshua is *"Immanuel [God with us]."* Yeshua is the God of the Old and the New Testament Scriptures. Yeshua is the very Word of God. Therefore, when He refers to your obedience to His teachings, He is of course including God's written instructions regarding the nation of Israel. **He is referring to your obedience to all of God's commands.**

John 14:23-24 (The Amplified Bible.)

²³ *Jesus answered, If a person [really] loves Me, he will keep My word [obey My teachings]; and My Father will love him, and We will come to him and make Our home (abode, special dwelling place) with Him.*

²⁴ *Anyone who does not [really] love Me does not observe and obey My teaching. And the teaching which you hear and heed is not Mine, but [comes] from the Father Who sent Me.*

You now understand that God determines whether you love Him or do not love Him by your obedience or disobedience to His commands (His teachings). The next text will clearly show you that it is by that same standard that God concludes whether you do or do not know Him. John goes so far as to actually tell you that if you say you know the Lord, yet you do not obey His commands, you are a liar. The truth is that if you refuse to obey God's commands, you do not know Him at all.

I John 2:3-5 (The Amplified Bible.)

3And this is how we may discern [daily by experience] that we are coming to know Him [to perceive, recognize, understand, and become better acquainted with Him]: if we keep (bear in mind, observe, practice) His teachings (precepts, commandments).

4Whoever says, I know Him [I perceive, recognize, understand, and am acquainted with Him] but fails to keep and obey His commandments (teachings) is a liar, and the Truth [of the Gospel] is not in him.

5But he who keeps (treasures) His Word [who bears in mind His precepts, who observes His message in its entirety], truly in him has the love of and for God been perfected (completed, reached maturity). By this we may perceive (know, recognize, and be sure) that we are in Him:

It is imperative that you obey God's Biblically recorded instructions regarding prayer for Israel. For as you just saw, if you refuse to obey God's commands on that issue, you are publicly declaring that you do not love or know God. Every word that Yeshua spoke was from God. Therefore, when He declares in John 15:14, *"You are My friends if you keep on doing the things which I command you to do,"* He is referring to your obeying **God's** commands. So today, we will see if you are truly Yeshua's friend. Furthermore, we will see if you love or even know God.

"IN the beginning was the Word, and the Word was with God, and the Word was God." (John 1:1, *King James Version*.) As I said before, Yeshua is the Word of all the Scriptures, not just the New Testament Scriptures.

The Jewish apostle Paul tells you that all Scripture is inspired by God. **And, as you learned earlier in the series, when Paul spoke those words, the Old Testament Scriptures were the only Scriptures available to men.** The Bible, as we Christians know it today, was not put together until approximately 300 years after Christ's death. Keep the previous facts in mind as you read Paul's inspired words.

II Timothy 3:16-17 (The Amplified Bible.)

16Every Scripture is God-breathed (given by His inspiration) and profitable for instruction, for reproof and conviction of sin, for correction of error and discipline in obedience, [and] for training in righteousness (in holy living, in conformity to God's will in thought, purpose, and action),

¹⁷So that the man of God may be complete and proficient, well fitted and thoroughly equipped for every good work.

The apostle Paul extols the spiritual value of the Old Testament Scriptures. He proclaims that Old Testament Scripture is for the purpose of showing you what is right in God's sight so that you can fully walk in God's righteous commandments. With the truth you have already received in this series, you are conscious of what Paul is really saying in those verses. You know that Paul is telling you that the Old Testament Scriptures are for the purpose of equipping you to do what Ecclesiastes 12:13 says you were originally created to do. They equip you to fear God and to keep His commands.

With the reminder that you have just received regarding the importance of Old Testament Scripture, we can begin to carefully examine certain Old Testament texts.

As you will soon see, the following Scriptures clearly instruct God's people on the issue of praying for Israel. We will begin by reading the inspired words of King David.

Psalm 122:1-9 (The Amplified Bible.)

¹I WAS glad when they said to me, Let us go to the house of the Lord!

²Our feet are standing within your gates, O Jerusalem!—

³Jerusalem, which is built as a city that is compact together—

⁴To which the tribes go up, even the tribes of the Lord, as was decreed and as a testimony for Israel, to give thanks to the name of the Lord.

⁵For there the thrones of judgment were set, the thrones of the house of David.

⁶<u>Pray for the peace of Jerusalem! May they prosper who love you [the Holy City]!</u>

⁷May peace be within your walls and prosperity within your palaces!

⁸For my brethren and companions' sake, I will now say, Peace be within you!

⁹For the sake of the house of the Lord our God, I will seek, inquire for, and require your good.

God's Word is crystal clear on this issue. In verse six of the previous text, God's Word commands that you *"Pray for the peace of Jerusalem!"* Moreover, in that same verse, David puts a blessing on all those who express love for Jerusalem by obeying God's instructions that pertain to the Holy City, including God's commands regarding praying for the peace of Jerusalem. David's blessing reads, *"May they prosper that love you [the Holy City]!"*

When asked to define the meaning of the word "peace," the first words that usually come to an individual's mind are safety and security. However, if you look up this particular word "peace" in the "Hebrew and Chaldee Dictionary" of *Strong's Exhaustive Concordance of the Bible,* you will discover that its Hebrew meaning conveys much more enlightenment than just the benefits of safety and security. The previous source of reference provides a variety of words including "well, happy, welfare, health, prosperity, favor, rest."

Your possessing a fuller understanding of the word "peace" is very important. It will not only help you to know how and what to pray for concerning Jerusalem, but it will also give you insight into David's words in verses seven through nine of the same Psalm. In those verses, while he is showing you how to pray for Jerusalem, David actually uses one of the previous definitive words, "prosperity." He prays in verse seven, *"May peace be within your walls and prosperity within your palaces!"*

Oh, Gentile Christian, for the Lord's name's sake, I implore you to obey God's Word. *"Pray for the peace of Jerusalem!"* Pray for the welfare and happiness of Jerusalem. Pray for the health and prosperity of Jerusalem. Pray for the safety of Jerusalem. **Pray! Pray!** *"Pray for the peace of Jerusalem!"*

Jerusalem is very important to God. It is important to the Lord, because it is His habitation. Jerusalem being God's dwelling place was the reason why David said in verse nine, *"For the sake of the house of*

the Lord our God, I will seek, inquire for, and require your good."
God cares deeply about His home (Jerusalem) and the grounds that
surround it (the entire land of Israel). You will recall that in an earlier
chapter of this book, you read Moses' description of God's emotional
ties with His home and the whole land of Israel. Moses said in
Deuteronomy 11:12, *"A land for which the Lord your God cares; the
eyes of the Lord your God are always upon it from the beginning of the
year to the end of the year."*

Jerusalem is not God's temporary residence. On the contrary,
Jerusalem is God's **permanent abode**. God has promised that He will
dwell in Jerusalem **forever**. Read the next text so that there will be no
doubt in your mind as to why Zion (Jerusalem) is so very special to God.
See also why Satan continually uses wicked Gentiles to try to keep
Jerusalem in a continual state of chaotic uproar.

> *Psalm 132:13-14 (The Amplified Bible.)*
>
> *13 For the Lord has chosen Zion, He has desired it for
> His habitation:*
> *14 This is My resting-place forever [says the Lord];
> here will I dwell, for I have desired it.*

Verses thirteen and fourteen in *The Living Bible* read as such:

> *13 O Lord, you have chosen Jerusalem as your home:*
> *14 "This is my permanent home where I shall live,"
> you said, "for I have always wanted it this way."*

Knowing that Jerusalem is actually God's **eternal home** and that
God has always wanted it this way, can you now more fully comprehend
why the peace of Jerusalem is crucial to God? Can you also see why
Satan fights so hard to keep Jerusalem in a constant state of turmoil?
My friend, don't you desire peace in your own home? Don't you also
desire prosperity in your home? Then, if you desire that your home be
filled with peace and prosperity, won't you pray that God might also
enjoy those same blessings in His home?

David prayed to that end. He prayed that peace and prosperity
would be in Jerusalem (God's home). David was looking out for God's
welfare. He wanted God to experience the same rest, peace and comfort
that everyone expects to enjoy in the safety and security of their own
home.

Also, don't you set down the rules for your own home? Don't you
make the choice as to the type of environment that will be cultivated

there? Don't you decide who will and will not be allowed to stay in or to visit your home? Of course the answer to all the former questions is yes. So my friend, can you see that God must be allowed the same rights in His home as you expect in yours?

If others tried to invade your home and through either psychological or physical warfare (that is, by propaganda, political manipulation or terrorism) they attempted to take from you any part of your home or land, wouldn't you fight to the death if necessary to defend what is rightfully yours?

My friend, if you can understand and apply true justice when it pertains to your own situation or rights, won't you make every effort to ensure that God receives equal justice? Will you continue to support those who terrorize God's home, those who destroy the peace of God's home, those who invade God's home and maim and kill His beloved covenant children (the Jews), those who would divide God's home and distribute portions of it to terrorists and greedy illegal squatters, those who try to steal God's home? Will you continue to support such wicked, blasphemous people?

Any people, outside of God's Abrahamic covenant people, who attempt to claim even a tiny portion of God's home (Jerusalem), or the grounds that surround Jerusalem (that is, the entire land of Israel) are brazen, contemptible thieves. And, those who support them in such evil practices are partners in their despicable crimes against God and His Abrahamic covenant people.

Men have come up with all kinds of ridiculous reasons to justify their support of God's enemies, the Palestinians. They make such foolish comments as, "It won't hurt the Jews to give the Palestinian people some of their land. The Palestinians don't have a homeland of their own. I think the Jews should stop being so greedy. They should be kind and share the land of Israel and Jerusalem with the unfortunate Palestinian people."

I would ask anyone who has ever made such ignorant and thoughtless statements, such as those in the former paragraph, to carefully consider the following questions. Does this mean that you yourself plan to be as generous with your own home and land as you are with God's home and land? Are you going to be consistent? Are you going to practice what you preach and turn over your property to homeless people simply because they do not have a home of their own and they covet your home and property? Does this mean that you are ready to turn over the deed to your property to men who have terrorized you and the other legal occupants in your home, to men who have harassed, mocked and even killed your beloved children, to men who want to annihilate you and your family?

My friend, do you really think that the author and readers of this book are naive enough to believe that you would actually apply those same rules to your own home and to all its legal occupants? It is obvious that you have a double standard of justice. You have one set of rules for God and His Abrahamic covenant people and another standard of justice for yourself. However, double standard or not, one thing is sure, we know that you do not intend to practice what you preach. We know that you would fight to the death to protect your home, your property and your beloved children. You would not give evil, covetous, violent men one inch of one room in your home. So go and do what Yeshua told you to do. Judge fairly and righteously. Give God and His people the same justice that you and your people would expect to receive.

You saw in the Scriptures that the Lord has given **all** the land of Israel to the Jews for an **everlasting** inheritance. (Genesis 17:8, Genesis 28:10-13.) God also told you in Psalm 32:13-14 that **Jerusalem is His eternal home**. So my friend, I repeat, judge fairly and righteously. Do unto others as you would want them to do to you. Do unto God and His Abrahamic covenant people as you would have them do to you.

> John 7:24 (The Amplified Bible.)
>
> ²⁴Be honest in your judgment and do not decide at a glance (superficially and by appearances); but judge fairly and righteously.

As you again read Psalm 122:6-9, notice especially verse nine. For, with the insight and understanding that you now have regarding Jerusalem being God's eternal home, the truth contained in that verse will be so much more valuable to you. Also, remember that in this case, "the house of the Lord our God" mentioned in verse nine refers to Jerusalem itself or as Psalm 132:13-14 in The Living Bible states, God's **"permanent home."**

> Psalms 122:6-9 (The Amplified Bible.)
>
> **⁶Pray for the peace of Jerusalem! May they prosper who love you [the Holy City]!**
> **⁷May peace be within your walls and prosperity within your palaces!**

8For my brethren and companions' sake, I will now say, Peace be within you!

9<u>For the sake of the house of the Lord our God, I will seek, inquire for, and require your good.</u>

The solemn promises God made to Abraham and the promise that He made to His beloved people concerning Jerusalem also play a tremendous role in God's interest in and His concern for the Holy City. God swore that He would accomplish certain feats which involve restoring His home, Jerusalem, and blessing His elect (that is, His Abrahamic covenant children) on their own land, including the Holy City. In a few moments, you will see an example of what God's oath concerning Jerusalem entails. But in the meantime, let us keep our thoughts centered on intercessory prayer on behalf of Israel.

Carrying out the sacred covenant promises that God made to Abraham, Isaac and Jacob and the oath which He swore regarding the Holy City, Jerusalem, is paramount to God. It is so important to the Lord that He keep those sacred promises that He has raised up and continues to raise up an army of intercessors to pray for Jerusalem. These God-ordained intercessors are instructed by God Himself to barrage the gates of heaven with their prayers. They are commanded to relentlessly persist in that type of prayer until God is forced to fulfill His sacred promises to Abraham, Isaac and Jacob and keep His vow to Jerusalem. See this truth for yourself in the following verses taken from *The Living Bible.*

Isaiah 62:6-12 (The Living Bible.)

6,7<u>O Jerusalem, I have set intercessors on your walls who shall cry to God all day and all night for the fulfillment of his promises.</u> Take no rest, all you who pray, and give God no rest until he establishes Jerusalem and makes her respected and admired throughout the earth.

Among these intercessors are righteous Gentile Christians who are obedient to God's command in Psalm 122:6, *"Pray for the peace of Jerusalem!"* Among these intercessors are Christians who love and know God, Christians who are truly Yeshua's friends.

Is God calling you to intercede for Israel, Christian? Has the Holy Spirit touched your heart and soul? Above all else, do you, like King

David, want to see God's will done in Jerusalem and all Israel? Are you Yeshua's true friend? Do you love and know God? If the answer to the former questions is yes, then, obey God's Word. For God's own good, take no rest and give God no rest until He keeps His promises to Abraham, Isaac and Jacob. Take no rest and give God no rest until He keeps His vow to make Jerusalem a praise in all the earth. **Pray! Pray!** *"Pray for the peace of Jerusalem!"* **Pray for the peace of God's eternal home.**

A few moments ago, I assured you that I would provide a brief example of what God's oath to Jerusalem entails. **So, look now at verses eight and nine of our present text, and read a segment of the content of the oath which God swore to His covenant people regarding the city of Jerusalem.** Pay careful attention as you read God's words, and for God's name's sake, pray accordingly.

> *8The Lord has sworn to Jerusalem with all his integrity: "I will never again give you to your enemies; never again shall foreign soldiers come and take away your grain and wine.*
>
> *9You raised it; you shall keep it, praising God. Within the Temple courts you yourselves shall drink the wine you pressed."*

God swore with all His integrity that He would accomplish His Word in the previous verses. And, for the sake of His own name and home, God will keep His sacred vow. God will deliver His beloved Abrahamic covenant people from all their enemies and prosper them on the Land of Promise. God will bring everlasting peace and prosperity to His home, Jerusalem. And, the marvelous thing is that you, Gentile Christian, can help God accomplish all that He has promised and that which He has always desired. You can help give God the desire of His heart. You can do that great and merciful work by simply obeying God's Word, supporting Israel and praying for the peace of Jerusalem.

When you pray, you **must not** pray for the kind of peace that the nations have designed for Jerusalem. For, neither God's name nor the restoration of His eternal home is the nations' priority or goal. The nations have ulterior, selfish motives for every decision they make and every action they take. No! You must not be fooled into accepting the type of peace that the nations of the world insist on forcing on Jerusalem and God.

You will recall that during Franklin Roosevelt's presidency, the nations were responsible for wickedly dividing Jerusalem and giving portions of God's home and grounds to Israel's enemies, the Palestinians. Now those same enemies (the Palestinians) covet the whole land of Israel including the entire city of Jerusalem. They want to take complete control of God's sacred home and the entire grounds that surround it. They want to drive God's beloved covenant children out of the Holy City and make Jerusalem into their own capital. Imagine this! They want to steal the home of the Judge and Ruler of all the earth and make it into the center or seat of their own wicked government. If you have kept up with their political maneuvers, you already realize that it has always been the Palestinians' plan to first get their foot in the door and then to take over the land of Israel little by little. They had already gained control of a parcel of Israel's land which included Bethlehem. Then, in September 1999, even as Israel made plans to turn over to them yet another portion of land on the West Bank, they had the audacity to demand that Israel also hand over to them a section of Jerusalem. Moreover, as any informed person knows, Palestinian demands will not stop there. No, these Islamic intruders will not rest so long as the Israeli people possess one inch of the Promised Land. If it was within their power, they would annihilate the Israeli people and take possession of all the land of Israel this very day. Yet, the nations stand ready to help them accomplish their wicked, covetous desires.

Worst of all, I am ashamed to say that many Christian leaders and whole organizations are in agreement with the Palestinians' plan and have actually joined in their Satanic quest. Yes, many Christians are publicly backing Arafat's devious plan. To show you documented evidence of this fact, I bring to your attention a quote from an article which appeared in the *Christian Daily News* on Jan 29, 1999.

> A petition signed by over 1,000 religious figures, **including Roman Catholic and Protestant clerics,** recommends that the United States cut off all aid to both Israel and the Palestinians until they respect their people's human rights. The document, sponsored by a group called The Search for Justice and Equality in Palestine/Israel, also asks U. S. President Clinton to press for a Palestinian state, the dismantling of Jewish settlements in Palestine-controlled areas and an undivided

Jerusalem shared by both Israel and Palestine.

It was no coincidence that in January 1999, over a thousand Gentile religious figures, some of them Christian, petitioned for a Palestinian state and an undivided Jerusalem shared by both Israel and Palestine. No, it was no coincidence. For, less than five months later, Arafat himself stated that Jerusalem could be the capital of both Israel and Palestine without a need for construction of dividing walls. My friend, this man has always had a blasphemous agenda. And, his agenda has always included placing God's eternal home on the planning table. He has already taken possession of a large part of the land that God swore would belong to His covenant people, the Jews, forever. But he is still not satisfied. His covetous sights have always been focused on Jerusalem. Yes, Arafat wants to steal a part of God's eternal home (Jerusalem).

The nations were already responsible for backing Israel into a corner until she was forced to exchange Israeli land for peace. And now, the nations are supporting Arafat's plan to divide God's eternal home (Jerusalem) between the rightful heirs (the Israelis) and these impostors (the Palestinians).

In the month of April, 1999, with his own mouth, Arafat exposed his blasphemous intention to divide Jerusalem. Moreover, he fully expects the nations, including many Christians, to support his Satanic plot. It is obvious that part of his devious plan is to persuade the nations to divide Jerusalem. Oh yes, he will settle temporarily for a plan that gives control of a portion of Jerusalem to Jews and a portion to Moslems (Palestinians). However, if he gets what he is after, he intends to proclaim the Moslem section of Jerusalem to be the capital of a Palestinian state. According to *Christian Daily News*, April 11, 1999, Yasser Arafat visited the Vatican. While there, it was reported:

> Arafat stated that Jerusalem could be the capital of both Israel and Palestine without a need for construction of dividing walls. He said, "Just as both the capital of the Italian state and that of the Vatican are in Rome, so Jerusalem can contain two capitals with no barrier or wall."

My friend, Arafat's aim is to make a section of God's eternal home into the capital of a Moslem state. And, he already has the European nations siding with him in his devious endeavors

I am sure that you are already aware that Europe is not pro-Jewish. No, despite the fact that millions of Jews were slaughtered in Europe during World War II, still, the leaders of Europe refuse to do right by the nation of Israel. Of course, we are smart enough to realize that the European nations have ulterior motives for supporting the covetous desires of the Palestinians and the Moslem nations as a whole rather than supporting Israel. OIL, OIL, OIL!

The Palestinians do not possess an oil supply. They themselves have nothing to offer Europe. However, as Moslems, they have the same evil agenda as the rest of the Islamic world. The goal of Islam is the systematic destruction of the state of Israel. Therefore, the Palestinians have the complete backing of the oil-rich Islamic countries. That fact alone gives them tremendous power. Their power lies in the fact that the Europeans do not want to incur the displeasure of Arafat's numerous Moslem brothers and risk having their oil supply cut off. So, despite the fact that citizens of some of these same European countries have been terrorized and in some cases murdered by (so-called) Islamic extremists, the leaders of these countries still choose to cater to and continually reward Islamic demands. Along with many other nations, the European countries repeatedly allow Israel to be exploited by the Palestinians and the Islamic nations. They allow Israel to be continually dragged before the United Nations and left to stand alone to defend itself against charges that would be laughed at and thrown out of court if they were brought against any other country.

For example, what other country in the world would be summoned before the United Nations simply for building settlements on its own land. And again, what other country would be put through that same procedure for planning housing construction in its own capital. This is not only stupid, it is idiotic! It is a mockery of justice. From the previous reference, *Christian Daily News,* February 9, 1999, I quote:

> In an emergency United Nations session held Feb. 6, **Israel stood alone** in its defense of its settlement policies in the West Bank and Gaza, while ambassador after ambassador denounced the country's actions....the Palestinians pointed out the 6,500-unit housing project planned in the Har Homa

> neighborhood of East Jerusalem....
> Jerusalem is a hot seat of the debate
> because, although the Palestinians see
> East Jerusalem as belonging to them,
> Israelis consider all of Jerusalem to be
> part of Israel....

The Bible is clear regarding the ownership of the land of Israel, including Jerusalem. However, the ungodly, greedy European nations are not interested in God's honor or God's unbreakable covenant. They are only interested in this world's wealth which translates into the word **OIL!** Consequently, they are promoting the forming of a Palestinian state in the land that God promised would belong to Israel forever. From the previous source, March 29, 1999 we read:

> A declaration by the European Union
> Saturday supports the "right of self-
> determination" for the Palestinians. The
> statement says **the European Union
> "declares its readiness to consider the
> recognition of a Palestinian state in
> due course." One European official
> said that "despite all the diplomatic
> language, this message is crystal
> clear—Europe plans to recognize a
> Palestinian state."**

In the same article, Israel's Prime Minister protested the European Union's stand by stressing,

> The unconditional recognition of a
> Palestinian state by the European Union
> would enable the Palestinian Army "to
> establish a large military and arm itself
> without limits, draw up treaties with
> countries who want Israel's destruction
> and use their land as a base for terror
> attacks against Israel."

Once again, Europe stands in opposition to God and His written Word. Once again Europe chooses to align herself with God's enemies and a Satanic plan that can only result in her own eventual destruction.

On September 8, 1999, *The Northwest Florida Daily News* printed a disturbing article entitled, "Palestinians hope for state, Jerusalem capital." The article told how just days before the beginning of talks on a final peace agreement with Israel, the Palestinians stated that they will not accept anything less than a state encompassing all the West Bank and Gaza Strip, with East Jerusalem as its capital. And so, before the whole world, these unscrupulous braggarts finally voiced their true motives.

As I said earlier, the Palestinians and the Islamic world as a whole will never be satisfied with East Jerusalem or the other portions of Israeli land that they have already wickedly acquired. Their aim is to slowly drive God's covenant people from the Promised Land and claim God's eternal home (Jerusalem) for Islam and all the rest of land of Israel for themselves. Furthermore, in order to stay in the good graces of the oil-rich Islamic nations, the European Union is helping them carry out their dastardly plan. Yes, to get what she wants, the economy driven EU will sell out Israel without giving a second thought to either the spiritual or the temporal consequences of such an act.

The writing is on the wall, the nations have already dared to force Israel into making outrageous concessions to their enemies in order to obtain what the nations consider to be peace. I am speaking about the nations' demand that Israel turn over large portions of her land to the Palestinians and Syrians in exchange for peace. My friend, you cannot buy peace. Furthermore, God should not have to give away part of His sacred property and destroy His reputation in order to have peace in His own home.

What other nation of people in the world other than Israel would be forced to give away their land to promoters of terrorism? The whole plan is madness! This is not the kind of peace that God promised Israel. Neither is it the type of peace that will restore God's sacred home and grounds. Furthermore, this type of peace will not vindicate God's name. Rather, it will only serve to profane it since God solemnly swore that the Israelites would possess **all** the Promised Land, not just a portion of it.

The truth is that even Israel had no Biblical right to give away one inch of the land that God vowed would belong only to the covenant descendants of Abraham, Isaac and Jacob, the land that is special to God, the land that He cares for and keeps His eye on all year round, the land that He swore by Himself will belong only to the Israelites forever, the land in which His eternal home (Jerusalem) is situated.

Oh, Christian Gentile, when you pray, pray for God's idea of peace, not man's. Take no rest, and give God no rest until He keeps His promises to Abraham, Isaac and Jacob. Take no rest and give God no rest until He establishes His home and makes Jerusalem respected and admired in all the earth by fulfilling His Abrahamic promises to the Israelites and His vow to Jerusalem and by driving all wicked, thieving invaders out of His eternal home and off His Holy Land.

As a Christian, it is only natural for you to inquire whether or not Yeshua incorporated Isaiah's commands on persistent prayer for Israel into His own teachings. The answer to your inquiry is of course yes, Yeshua did incorporate Isaiah's commands on persistent prayer for Israel into His own teachings. When Yeshua walked the earth, God's instructions in Isaiah 62:6-9 were extremely important to Him. He specifically taught men to continue to diligently adhere to Isaiah's instructions and to pray that God's Abrahamic promises and His vow concerning Jerusalem be kept. Remember, Yeshua was *"Immanuel [God with us]."* So of course He was interested in God's Abrahamic promises and His vow to Jerusalem being fulfilled.

For generations, the Church has overlooked much of Yeshua's teachings on this subject. You see, most of what Yeshua taught on the topic of prayer for Israel is contained in His parables. And sadly, the Church is ignorant when it comes to the true content of most of the Lord's parables. Thus, the secrets of the Lord's parables remain hidden not only from the Jews but also from most of the Church today. Consequently, ignorant and misguided Christian teachers have twisted, misinterpreted and misrepresented the contents of those parables. Moreover, in so doing, those same misinformed teachers have the majority of the Church shamefully bombarding the gates of heaven with self-centered personal prayer requests rather than tireless intercession on behalf of Israel for God's name's sake and for the sake of God's home.

Today, however, we will keep things in perspective. We will consider only God's needs, that is, God's needs except for your need to know the truth contained in the following parable. As you read Yeshua's parable, keep in mind that Yeshua is simply reiterating the prophets' words that you studied earlier in Isaiah 62:6-7. He is referring to men observing God's instructions in regard to praying that God will keep His Abrahamic covenant promises and His vow to Jerusalem. Yeshua is repeating Isaiah's command that men not rest or give God rest until God answers their prayers on His behalf.

It is also crucial for you to understand that when Yeshua relayed this next parable, the Promised Land, including Jerusalem, was under Roman occupation. Jerusalem was not then a praise in the earth as God had promised it would be. On the contrary, Israel's enemies, who were at that time the Romans, continued to tread down Jerusalem, stripping God's people of their happiness, health and prosperity and in some cases their very lives.

Thus, in the following illustration, Yeshua is encouraging His disciples to continue to obey Isaiah's instructions that pertain to praying for the fulfillment of God's promises to Abraham, Isaac, and Jacob, His vow to make His home, Jerusalem, a praise in all the earth and His promise to restore Israel's wealth. The fact is that Isaiah's instructions on prayer for Jerusalem and God's vow to restore Israel's wealth and make Jerusalem respected and admired throughout the earth is the only topic that Yeshua dealt with in this entire parable.

Through the subsequent story, Yeshua was telling His conquered people that though they could not see immediate results from their prayers, they should not give up praying that God's Abrahamic promises and His vow to Jerusalem would be kept. He was encouraging His disciples to be persistent in their prayers on those matters. He was reaffirming Isaiah's instructions and exhorting them to do exactly what God had already told them to do in Isaiah 62:6-7. **Yeshua was telling His Jewish followers that they must continue to bombard the gates of heaven with prayers in respect to God keeping His promises to their forefathers and Jerusalem. They must take no rest nor give God rest until He fulfills His promises to Abraham, Isaac and Jacob and keeps His vow to avenge and deliver them from their enemies, restore their goods and make His home, Jerusalem, a praise in all the earth.**

Yeshua was assuring His disciples that if a wicked judge could be persuaded to do right because of the persistence of one little widow woman who refused to leave him alone until he met her request, how much more would the righteous Judge of all the earth pay attention to the urgent cries of His people who continually beat on His door pleading for justice. Yes, how much more would God keep His Abrahamic covenant promises and His vow to Jerusalem and deliver the Jews and Jerusalem from their enemies if, like the widow woman, they gave Him no rest until He did.

As I said earlier, Yeshua was simply echoing what Isaiah had already told God's people in Isaiah 62:6-7. He was telling His disciples to cry out to God in prayer all day and all night. He was instructing them to take no rest and give God no rest until He kept His Abrahamic covenant promises and His vow to Jerusalem, delivered God's people from their enemies, established Jerusalem and made Jerusalem respected and a praise in all the earth. At that time, Israel's enemies were of course the Romans. Today, Israel's main enemies are the Palestinians and most of the Islamic world.

And now, I pray, let the Lord's obedient disciples understand the mysteries and secrets of the kingdom of God that are hidden in Yeshua's parable of the unjust judge. And let them not allow Satan to steal from their hearts the word of the kingdom that is sown.

Luke 18:1-8 (The Amplified Bible.)

¹ALSO [JESUS] told them a parable to the effect that they ought always to pray and not to turn coward (faint, lose heart, and give up).

Yeshua said that God's intercessors *"ought always to pray."* He said they must not *"give up."* When Yeshua made that statement in Luke 18:1, He was reiterating Isaiah's inspired words in Isaiah 62:6-7. In that verse, Isaiah commanded that God's intercessors should *"take no rest"* until God answered their prayers.

It is important to note that the subject matter of Yeshua's parable is fervent prayer. Yeshua's profound illustration and interpretation actually holds the secret to the type of fervent prayer that He is promoting.

²He said, In a certain city there was a judge who neither reverenced and feared God nor respected or considered man.

³And there was a widow in that city who kept coming to him and saying, Protect and defend and give me justice against my adversary.

⁴And for a time he would not; but later he said to himself, Though I have neither reverence or fear for God nor respect or consideration for man,

⁵Yet because this widow continues to bother me, I will defend and protect and avenge her, lest she give me intolerable annoyance and wear me out by her continual coming or at the last she come and rail on me or assault me or strangle me.

⁶Then the Lord, said, Listen to what the unjust judge says!

⁷And will not [our just] God defend and protect and avenge His elect (His chosen ones), who cry to Him day and night? Will He defer them and delay help on their behalf?

What did the prophet Isaiah say in Isaiah 62:6-7 in *The Living Bible*? He said, "*O Jerusalem, I have set intercessors on your walls who shall cry to God all day and all night for the fulfillment of his promises. Take no rest, all you who pray, and give God no rest until he establishes Jerusalem and makes her respected and admired throughout the earth.*"

Since repetition is thought to be the best teacher, read again Yeshua's words in Luke 18:7-8.

> *7And will not [our just] God defend and protect and avenge His elect (His chosen ones), who cry to Him day and night? Will He defer them and delay help on their behalf?*
>
> *8I tell you, He will defend and protect and avenge them speedily. However, when the Son of Man comes, will He find [persistence in] faith on the earth?*

In the former illustration, Yeshua was assuring His Jewish disciples that if a wicked judge could be convinced to defend and protect and bring justice to one little widow because she wore him out with her continued demands for justice against her enemy, how much more will God hear the prayers of His Abrahamic covenant people (His elect) who give Him no rest until He fulfills His covenant promises to Abraham, Isaac and Jacob and keeps His vow to defend and protect them and to rid their land of all their enemies. Yeshua was reiterating the truth that God's prophet had spoken in Isaiah 62:6-7. He was encouraging those who had ears to hear to give God no rest until He kept His word, rid the Promised Land of all Israel's enemies and made His eternal home, Jerusalem, a praise to all the earth.

Because verse eight contains another extremely important warning, I encourage you to read it again. As you do, give special notice to the underlined portion.

> *8I tell you, He will defend and protect and avenge them speedily. However, when the Son of Man comes, will He find [persistence in] faith on the earth?*

Verse eight in *The Living Bible* reads as follows,

*8Yes! He will answer them quickly! But the question is: When I, the Messiah, return, **how many will I find who have faith [and are praying]**?*

Praying in faith for what? Praying of course that God's promises to Abraham, Isaac and Jacob will be kept, praying that God's vow to avenge Israel's enemies will be kept, praying that God will keep His promise to restore Israel's wealth, praying that the Lord will make His eternal home, Jerusalem, a praise in all the earth, praying that God's reputation will be cleared from men's harsh and false accusations, praying as God has commanded in His Word.

The faith that Yeshua is referring to in verse eight is the **living** faith that is mentioned in James 2:17-26. It is faith that has works of obedience to God's Word to back it up. Will the Lord find **living faith** when He returns to earth? Will He find the Church actively and zealously participating in prayer for Israel and especially for Jerusalem, or will He find the Church full of dead and useless faith? Will He find faith that does not have works of obedience to God's Word to back it up? Will the Lord find dead faith that does not believe that Yeshua will return to earth to entirely fulfill God's Abrahamic promises, dead faith that exhibits its lack of usefulness by failing to pray to that end, dead faith that does not believe that upon His return, Yeshua will vanquish all Israel's foes and completely deliver the Jewish people from their enemies, dead faith that is so useless that it does not encourage men to consistently pray for Israel or the peace of God's everlasting home (Jerusalem), dead faith that does not believe that God will keep His promises and answer those righteous prayers?

When the Lord returns, how many of His Abrahamic covenant people will He find praying in the manner prescribed in God's Word? And for that matter, how many Christian Gentiles will He find praying in the manner prescribed in God's Word?

Christian, when Yeshua returns, will He find you obeying His Word in Psalm 122, Isaiah 62:6-7 and Luke 18:1-8? Will the Lord find you storming the gates of heaven, consistently pleading with Him to keep His covenant with Abraham, Isaac and Jacob? Will He find you beating on His door, crying day and night, begging Him to keep His vow concerning Jerusalem for His own name's sake and for the sake of His eternal home?

When Yeshua returns, will He know that you are one of those people who never rested or gave Him rest until He was forced to keep His promise and return with deliverance for His elect (the Jews)? When the

Messiah comes the second time, will He know that He has someone in you who cared about His welfare and reputation and believed His Word enough to devote your life to helping Him vindicate His name and restore peace to His home by praying for and supporting Israel? Will He find in you a person who exhibits living faith by obeying His Word and relentlessly interceding in prayer for His covenant children (the Jews), His home (Jerusalem) and the grounds that surround His home (the entire land of Israel)? I sincerely hope so.

If you are intending to obey God's Word and start interceding for Israel, then there is something else that you should be aware of. If your prayers for Israel are going to benefit God's name, they must proceed from an obedient heart (that is, your prayers must proceed from a heart that is obedient to all God's written commands). Otherwise, Christian, you are wasting your time. For, God's Word states that if you have known, unconfessed sin in your life, God will not hear your prayers. Under such conditions as I just mentioned, your prayers will be as dead and useless as your faith. See for yourself in the following verses how futile your prayers on behalf of Israel will be if you refuse to obey God's Word and turn away from all known sin.

Psalm 66:18 (The Amplified Bible.)

18If I regard iniquity in my heart, the Lord will not hear me;

It is a fact that if you really want power with God, you must live an obedient life. Furthermore, you must pray for God's will and purpose rather than your own selfish desires. As Moses did, you too must look out for God's welfare and God's name. You must put the Lord in remembrance of His promises to Abraham, Isaac and Jacob. You must also put the Lord in remembrance of His vow to Jerusalem.

If you do all the things I just mentioned then, God's Word guarantees that the Lord will hear and answer your prayers. And my friend, what could be more in God's will than for you to pray that His unbreakable promises will be kept and His holy name cleared before all the world? What could be more in God's will than for you to pray that God's enemies be driven from His home and the holy grounds that surround it? What could be more in God's will than for you to pray that His Abrahamic covenant children regain every inch of the land that God swore by Himself would belong to them forever? What could be more in God's will than for you to ask to see true peace restored to Jerusalem and that God's home (Jerusalem) would be admired, respected and a praise in all the earth?

> *1 John 5:14-15 (The Amplified Bible.)*
>
> *14And this is the confidence (the assurance, the privilege of boldness) which we have in Him:* **[we are sure] that if we ask anything (make any request) according to His will (in agreement with His own plan), He listens to and hears us.**

Whose will? Whose plan? Not yours, not mine—God's!

> *15And if (since) we [positively] know that He listens to us in whatever we ask, we also know [with settled and absolute knowledge] that we have [granted us as our present possessions] the requests made of Him.*

Most Christians like to think that being supplied with the lust of their eyes and hearts is God's will and God's plan for them. They could care less about God's purpose, God's home or God's name. When they pray, they ask for money, cars, houses, possessions and positions. Foolish people! Their own ignorance and greed blinds them to the truth of God's Word.

Aren't there a few Christians out there who are willing to lay aside their own desires and personal prejudices in order to see **God's** will done, **God's** reputation cleared and **God's** needs met? Aren't there a few people out there who are willing to take the time to persistently intercede on **God's** behalf and for **God's** benefit?

When the Messiah returns, how many Christians will He find who have faith that He will fulfill His covenant with Abraham, Isaac and Jacob and keep His vow to Jerusalem? How many will He find that have living faith, faith that is backed up by works of obedience to God's Word in Isaiah 62:6-7? When the Lord returns, how many in the Church will He find obeying His instructions and interceding in faith for the peace of His home and grounds, for His beloved Abrahamic covenant children and most of all, for the vindication of His holy name? How many will He find interceding for Israel?

The next three verses of Isaiah chapter sixty-two are as equally important as the four verses that precede them and which you read earlier from *The Living Bible*. Why are they important? They are important because they show you that as crucial as your prayer is, prayer by itself is not enough. Yes Christian, for God's name's sake, you must intercede for Jerusalem and Israel as a whole. Albeit, in the next verses, God lets you know that your prayers must be followed by action. As the old saying goes, God expects you to "Put your money where your mouth is." God wants **living** faith.

Isaiah 62:10-12 (The Living Bible.)

10Go out! Go out! Prepare the roadway for my people to return! Build the roads, pull out the boulders, raise the flag of Israel."

11See, the Lord has sent his messengers to every land and said, "Tell my people, I, the Lord your God, am coming to save you and will bring you many gifts."

12And they shall be called "The Holy People" and "The Lord's Redeemed," and Jerusalem shall be called "The Land of Desire" and "The City God Has Blessed."

Go out! Go out Church! Help God fulfill His purpose for Jerusalem and the whole land of Israel. As I said earlier, stop spending the Church's finances on foolish, temporal things that will soon decay and perish, things such as luxurious church and ministry buildings. And Christian, stop sending your offerings to those wicked radio and television ministers who continually bring shame upon the Church of Christ. Instead, use your offerings in ways that will benefit God. Use that money to support Israel. Go out! Go out, Church of Christ!

Awake O Church! For God's name's sake, come to the aid of Israel. Build the roads, build the water reservoirs, plant the trees. Help God carry out His Word in Isaiah 62:11 in *The Living Bible*. In that verse God said that He would bring Israel gifts. Pray for and financially support Israel. For God's name's sake, pray for the peace and prosperity of Jerusalem, and then, do all you can to personally further the peace and prosperity of the Holy Land of God, Israel.

Search out Jewish organizations in your own area, such as **Jewish National Fund** and **Florida Action**, and financially support Israel and the Jewish people directly through those Jewish charitable organizations. Are the Jews in your nation persecuted and abused? If so, for God's name's sake, give them all the aid, protection and love you can. If you know of a Jewish family who desires to return to their homeland but who are not financially able to do so, offer them assistance. *"See, the Lord has sent His messengers to every land and said, 'Tell My people, I,* *the Lord your God, am coming to save you and will bring you many gifts.'"* (Isaiah 62:11, *The Living Bible.*)

I come as one of God's messengers. **I tell you, Israel, your God is coming to save you. He is going to use His righteous people among the Gentiles to help you. Through them, He will bring you many gifts.** Christian, remember what Paul said in Romans 11:31 regarding the Gentile Christians' obligation to the Jews? He said that through the mercy you are enjoying, **they may now also receive mercy.** Gentile, show Israel mercy by financially supporting her and by persistently interceding for her in her time of need.

This prophet of God cries out God's message through this literary work all over the world. Listen, Israel, your God is coming to save you. Soon all those in the Church who truly know and love God will come to your aid. For God's name's sake, and God's home's sake, they will bring you gifts. They will find ways to financially support your nation. They will help to bring your people back to Israel. They will encourage their governments to befriend you and to give you financial aid. They will also unselfishly intercede in prayer for your welfare, your happiness, your health and your prosperity.

I pray that you will voluntarily heed God's call, Gentile Christian. For, the fact remains that one way or another, the day is coming when the Gentile nations will bring their choicest goods to satisfy Jerusalem's every need. God's Word proclaims that very truth in the following verse taken from *The Living Bible,* and it will come to pass. Willingly or by force, Gentile, you will one day support Israel. For God has promised Israel that the Gentiles will provide for His home, His grounds, and His Abrahamic covenant family.

Be sure and read all of Isaiah chapter sixty. For, those verses will not only give you understanding regarding God's eternal home, but they will also give you more insight into John's references to Jerusalem in "The Revelation." Since, however, the previous topic of Jerusalem in John's Revelation is the subject matter of another entire book, and because space is limited, I will convey only a portion of Isaiah's recorded prophecy at this time.

Isaiah 60:9-18 (The Living Bible.)

⁹I have reserved the ships of many lands, the very best, to bring the sons of Israel home again from far away, bringing their wealth with them. For the Holy One of Israel, known around the world, has glorified you in the eyes of all.

10Foreigners will come and build your cities. Presidents and kings will send you aid. For though I destroyed you in my anger, I will have mercy on you through my grace.

11Your gates will stay wide open around the clock to receive the wealth of many lands. The kings of the world will cater to you.

12For the nations refusing to be your allies will perish; they shall be destroyed.

13The glory of Lebanon will be yours—the forests of firs and pines, and box trees—to beautify my sanctuary. My Temple will be glorious.

14The sons of anti-Semites will come and bow before you! They will kiss your feet! They will call Jerusalem "The City of the Lord" and "The Glorious Mountain of the Holy One of Israel."

15Though once despised and hated and rebuffed by all, you will be beautiful forever, a joy for all the generations of the world, for I will make you so.

16Powerful kings and mighty nations shall provide you with the choicest of their goods to satisfy your every need, and you will know at last and really understand that I, the Lord, am your Savior and Redeemer, the Mighty One of Israel.

17I will exchange your brass for gold, your iron for silver, your wood for brass, your stones for iron. Peace and righteousness shall be your taskmasters!

18Violence will disappear out of your land—all war will end. Your walls will be "Salvation" and your gates "Praise."

Israel needs friends! Israel needs financial aid! And God wants to use the Church to give Israel a helping hand. Therefore, may God open the Church's spiritual understanding to that which is really important. May God open the Church's spiritual eyes so that Christians might see that which has eternal value. For the sake of God's holy name, let all Christians who are called to bear and honor God's name exhibit their faith and pray for and support Israel and especially Jerusalem.

Again, I remind you that the Living Word Church of Niceville is not asking you for anything. We do not solicit funds. Rather, we are asking that, for God's name's sake and for God's home's sake, you help Israel. There are worthy Jewish organizations throughout the world, organizations such as the **Jewish National Fund** and **Florida Action**, through which you can show your financial support for Israel. So, for the Lord's name's sake, search them out for yourself. Go and help God fulfill His Word before it is too late. Christian, become a vessel through whom God can fulfill His Word and give His holy covenant nation the gifts that He has promised.

What a wonderful honor, Gentile Christian, that you should be given the privilege of helping God vindicate His holy name and helping restore peace to His eternal home by interceding in prayer for Israel. However, the following Scriptures reveal that your reward goes beyond even that privilege. You get an amazing bonus. That bonus is that you get to help God further. Through your prayer for Israel, you receive the esteemed honor of helping to bestow personal blessings on the Lord. And my friend, those blessings are not temporary, they are eternal. So you actually have the opportunity to help bestow eternal blessings upon God Almighty Himself.

As you read the truth in the next Scripture text taken from *The Living Bible,* let it penetrate into the innermost part of your being. For if you do, from this time forth whenever you pray for Israel, you will experience the wonder and satisfaction of knowing that you are helping to bestow marvelous blessings on your worthy and deserving God.

I am including verses six through eight of the next Scripture reference because I want you to see with your own eyes that your just and faithful God will eventually answer the petitions that you have made on behalf of Israel for His name's sake. After you read those verses, we will then concentrate on the previously mentioned blessings.

Jeremiah 33:6-26 (The Living Bible.)

*6Nevertheless the time will come when **I will** heal Jerusalem's damage and give her prosperity and peace.*

*7**I will** rebuild the cities of both Judah and Israel and restore their fortunes.*

*8And **I will** cleanse away all their sins against me, and pardon them.*

The following verse describes the blessings that I spoke of earlier. It shows you why you must obey Yeshua's command in Luke 8:1 and *"not turn coward (faint, lose heart, and give up)"* when it comes to praying for Israel. God explains why your prayers, prayers imploring Him to keep His Abrahamic promises and His vow to Jerusalem, are so important. He also explains why He wants you to obey His instructions and keep encouraging Him to fulfill His Abrahamic promises and make Jerusalem a praise in all the earth.

> *⁹Then this city will be an honor to me, and it will give me joy and be a source of praise and glory to me before all the nations of the earth! The people of the world will see the good I do for my people and will tremble with awe!*

Oh, Christian Gentile, the Holy City, Jerusalem, is God's eternal home. It is precious to God. As you saw in the previous verse, when His Abrahamic promises and His vow to Jerusalem are kept, Jerusalem will be an honor to Him. It will be to God a source of eternal joy, praise and glory. And God is giving you an opportunity to play a tremendous role in helping bring to pass His eternal plan for Jerusalem.

God is like any other parent. He wants to know that His children care about His needs. He wants to know that they find joy and satisfaction in looking out for His welfare. So as a parent, God asks that His children pray for those things that will supply His needs and bring Him benefit. Our Heavenly Father has given us everything we have. So, shouldn't we in turn do our part to make sure that in the future He will receive joy, honor, praise and glory before all the nations? Shouldn't we do all we can to help restore peace to God's everlasting home?

Remember also that Jerusalem is not the only part of Israel that is important to God. Moses revealed just how much the Lord cares for the whole land of Israel in Deuteronomy 11:12. The land of Israel is truly the grounds (or gardens) of God's eternal home. Also remember that God made numerous covenant promises to Abraham regarding the Jewish people and all the land of Israel. So, on that note let us continue reading our present text, for that text makes it clear that for His name's sake God will keep those promises too.

> *10,11The Lord declares that the happy voices of bridegrooms and of brides, and the joyous song of those bringing thanksgiving offerings to the Lord will be heard again in this doomed land. The people will sing: "Praise the Lord! For he is good and his mercy*

endures forever!" For I will make this land happier and more prosperous than it has ever been before.

12This land—though every man and animal and city is doomed—will once more see shepherds leading sheep and lambs.

13Once again their flocks will prosper in the mountain villages and in the cities east of the Philistine plain, in all the cities of the Negeb, in the land of Benjamin, in the vicinity of Jerusalem and in all the cities of Judah.

14Yes, the day will come, says the Lord, when I will do for Israel and Judah all the good I promised them.

In fulfillment of His promises and in answer to God's people's persistent, fervent prayers, upon the Messiah's second coming, Yeshua will conquer all Israel's enemies. He will also spiritually restore Israel. Moreover, He will restore Israel's wealth. As Jeremiah 33:11 proclaims, God's people will be happier and more prosperous than they have ever been before. That means they will enjoy more peace, happiness and financial prosperity than they did even during Solomon's rule. The land and everything on it will flourish. Furthermore, God's home, Jerusalem, will finally be respected and admired and be a praise in all the earth.

The Messiah shall sit upon the throne of David in Jerusalem forever. And that my friend is yet another important reason why God is so adamant about you praying for Israel and especially Jerusalem. You see, God also made a sacred vow to King David. He promised David in II Samuel 7:16 that his throne would be established forever. Thus, upon His return, the Messiah, whom you will recall is by birth a descendant of David, will rule forever upon the throne of David in Jerusalem.

It is fitting and correct that those for whom the Messiah gave His life should pray for the city from which He will one day rule the whole earth for eternity. It is right that we should show our concern for our Lord's future welfare and delight. However, when the Messiah returns to fulfill His vow to David and to take His seat on David's throne in Jerusalem, how many will He find who have faith and are praying that God's Abrahamic promises and His vow to Jerusalem will be kept in their entirety? How many will He find consistently praying for the peace and prosperity of Jerusalem? As Yeshua said in Luke 18:8 in *The Living Bible*, *"...When I, the Messiah, return, how many will I find who have faith [and are praying]?"*

Read now the remainder of our present text. (Jeremiah 33:15-26.)

15At that time I will bring to the throne the true Son of David, and he shall rule justly.

16In that day the people of Judah and Jerusalem shall live in safety and their motto will be, "The Lord is our righteousness!"

17For the Lord declares that from then on, David shall forever have an heir sitting on the throne of Israel.

18And there shall always be Levites to offer burnt offerings and meal offerings and sacrifices to the Lord.

My friend, I tell you again, God will answer the righteous prayers that you pray for Israel. At any cost, He will keep His covenant with Abraham, Isaac and Jacob. He will love His people, the Jews, forever. He will never totally reject them, nor will He abandon them. God will use His people to vindicate His name. Then, as He promised He would do, He will vanquish Israel's enemies, and He will save them, love them and be their God forever. PRAISE BE TO OUR FAITHFUL GOD!

19Then this message came to Jeremiah from the Lord:

20,21If you can break my covenant with the day and with the night so that day and night don't come on their usual schedule, only then will my covenant with David, my servant, be broken so that he shall not have a son to reign upon his throne; and my covenant with the Levite priests, my ministers, is non-cancelable.

22And as the stars cannot be counted nor the sand upon the seashores measured, so the descendants of David my servant and the line of the Levites who minister to me will be multiplied.

23The Lord spoke to Jeremiah again and said:

24Have you heard what people are saying?--that the Lord chose Judah and Israel and then abandoned them! They are sneering and saying that Israel isn't worthy to be counted as a nation.

25,26But this is the Lord's reply: I would no more reject my people than I would change my laws of night and day, of earth and sky. I will never abandon the Jews, or David my servant, or change the plan that his Child will someday rule these descendants of

Abraham, Isaac and Jacob. Instead I will restore their prosperity and have mercy on them.

If per chance, you still do not comprehend why God requires that you pray for Israel, Christian, then let me be blunt in my final explanation. During this series, you learned that the full original purpose of your creation was to fear God and keep His commands. (Ecclesiastes 12:13.) Well, my friend, God's Word commands, *"Pray for the peace of Jerusalem!"*

Yeshua commands in Luke 18:1 that you do not turn coward, faint, lose heart and give up praying. He commands that you remain persistent in your prayers for Israel until God answers your requests. Isaiah 62:6-7 also commands that you take no rest and that you give God no rest until He keeps His Abrahamic promises and His vow to Jerusalem and thus makes Jerusalem a praise in all the earth. So Gentile Christian, go and do what you were created to do. Go and obey God's commands. Pray for the peace of Jerusalem! Pray for Israel! Pray for God's Abrahamic covenant people!

Why is it such a puzzle to you, Christian, that God should expect you to carry out His commands regarding intercessory prayer for Israel when keeping His commands is the sole purpose for your existence. As Ecclesiastes 12:13 tells you, you were created to fear God and keep His commandments. So, as I said a moment ago, go and do what you were created to do.

What more can I say to show you the importance of your zealously praying for Israel, Gentile Christian? What more can I do to make you realize the seriousness of your ceaseless intercession for Jerusalem?

You now know why every Christian should pray for Israel. So, no matter what others do, you go and obey God's Word regarding this issue. For **God's** name's sake, for **God's** home's sake, for **God's** honor, for **God's** future joy, praise and glory, *"Pray for the peace of Jerusalem!"*

Psalm 137:5-6 (The Amplified Bible.)

5If I forget you, O Jerusalem, let my right hand forget its skill [with the harp].

6Let my tongue cleave to the roof of my mouth if I remember you not, if I prefer not Jerusalem above my chief joy!

Chapter 17

WHAT IS THE REAL MEANING OF THE PARABLE OF THE PRODIGAL SON?

As it has been with most of Yeshua's illustrations, the Church has completely overlooked the real significance of the parable of the prodigal son. For generations, the Christian world has shortsightedly used the contents of this parable as an example of God's mercy toward any backslidden Christian who desires to repent and return to God. However, Yeshua's parable contains a far greater and deeper spiritual message than the Church has realized.

In a few moments, we will begin our brief examination of the parable of the prodigal son. For, within Yeshua's story are hidden many incredible secret truths and prophesies. Much of what the Lord foretold in His parable has already come to pass while the rest will take place in God's own perfect time.

Luke 15:11-32 (The Amplified Bible.)

11And He said, There was a certain man who had two sons;

Unbeknown to many in the Church, Abraham had a total of eight sons. Hagar, Sarah's servant, was the mother of Abraham's eldest son, Ishmael. God promised Abraham in Genesis 17:20 that He would bless and multiply Ishmael. God also promised Abraham that Ishmael would be the father of twelve princes and that He would make him a great nation. However, in Genesis 17:21, God made it absolutely clear that Ishmael was not his covenant choice.

Sarah bore Abraham's second son, Isaac. He was God's Abrahamic covenant choice. Throughout this work I have repeatedly made known the contents of the sacred covenant that God made with Abraham, Isaac, and Jacob.

Abraham's other six sons were the result of Abraham's marriage to a woman named Keturah, a marriage which took place after Sarah's death. You can read the short reference to Keturah and the six sons that she bore to Abraham in Genesis 25:1-2.

Because the Bible is almost silent concerning the six sons that Keturah bore to Abraham, most Christians are not even aware that they existed. Moreover, God's Word purposely emphasizes only the two sons to whom the formerly mentioned promises pertained. For as you now know, it is crucial to God that He keep all his promises, especially His Abrahamic covenant promises. For His reputation's sake, God must show the nations of the world that He is faithful to His word.

In His parable of the prodigal son, Yeshua followed the same pattern mentioned in the former paragraph. He referred only to the two sons of Abraham to whom God's promises to Abraham applied. Those two sons were of course Ishmael and especially Abraham's covenant son, Isaac.

Pay strict attention as you study the parable of the prodigal son, for it contains profound mysteries and secrets of the kingdom of God. On that important note, let us begin to skillfully unravel those marvelous mysteries and secrets.

As I am sure you already know, Abraham's eldest son, Ishmael, was the forefather of the Arab nation. His younger son, Isaac, was the forefather of the Jewish nation, Israel. In Yeshua's parable, the elder son represents the Gentile Arab nations, while the younger son represents the Abrahamic covenant nation of Israel.

As you study Yeshua's prophetic story, think of the father as God, the older son as the Gentile Arab nations and the younger son as the nation of Israel. As I reminded you earlier, God promised both sons of Abraham blessings.

> *11And He said, There was a certain man who had two sons;*
>
> *12And the younger of them said to his father, Father, give me the part of the property that falls [to me]. And he divided the estate between them.*

Note that the Lord divided the property between both sons. According to *Smith's Bible Dictionary* under the heading "Ishmael," "The sons of Ishmael peopled the north and west of the Arabian peninsula, and eventually formed the chief element of the Arab nation...." The land of Canaan that God gave to Israel was small, but it was given with an unbreakable oath that it would remain Israel's forever.

The younger son, Israel, wanted all that God had promised but without God's watchful eye or the restraint of the father's authority. Israel did not want to keep the Horeb covenant or live by the father's laws. Rather, he wanted to do things his way. He was disobedient and rebellious. So he left God and the paths of righteousness, and he journeyed as far away from his father's restrictions as he could go. Once settled in that foreign land, he squandered the fortune that he had received from his father in loose and wicked living.

> *13And not many days after that, the younger son gathered up all that he had and journeyed into a distant country, and there he wasted his fortune in reckless and loose [from restraint] living.*

The following Old Testament text describes exactly what the younger son, Israel, did with the blessings he received from his father. To save space, I will pick out the most relevant verses. However, I trust that you will take time to read the whole chapter for yourself. In the next verses, God likens what Israel did to the wicked actions of an unfaithful, adulterous wife.

> *Ezekiel 16:10-19, 27 (The Amplified Bible.)*
>
> *10I clothed you also with embroidered cloth and shod you with [fine seal] leather; and I girded you about with fine linen and covered you with silk.*
>
> *11I decked you also with ornaments and I put bracelets on your wrists and a chain on your neck.*
>
> *12And I put a ring on your nostril and earrings in your ears and a beautiful crown upon your head!*
>
> *13Thus you were decked with gold and silver, and your raiment was of fine linen and silk and embroidered cloth; you ate fine flour and honey and oil. And you were exceedingly beautiful and you prospered into royal estate.*
>
> *14And your renown went forth among the nations for your beauty, for it was perfect through My majesty and splendor which I had put upon you, says the Lord God.*
>
> *15But you trusted in and relied on your own beauty and were unfaithful to God and played the harlot [in idolatry] because of your renown, and you poured out your fornications upon anyone who passed by [as you*

worshiped the idols of every nation which prevailed over you] and your beauty was his.

16And you took some of your garments and made for yourself gaily decorated high places or shrines and played the harlot on them—things which should not come and that which should not take place.

17You did also take your fair jewels and beautiful vessels of My gold and My silver which I had given you and made for yourself images of men, and you played the harlot with them;

18And you took your embroidered garments and covered them and set My oil and My incense before them.

19My bread also which I gave you—fine flour and oil and honey with which I fed you—you have even set it before the idols for a sweet odor. Thus it was, says the Lord God.

27<u>Behold therefore, I have stretched out My hand against you, diminished your ordinary allowance of food, and delivered you over to the will of those who hate and despise you</u>, the daughters of the Philistines, who turned away in shame from your despicable policy and lewd behavior [for they are faithful to their gods]!

Israel squandered all His blessings, breaking every command of God and even the very heart of God.

To bring us back on track, we will read again verse thirteen of our original text.

Luke 15:13 (The Amplified Bible.)

13And not many days after that, the younger son gathered up all that he had and journeyed into a distant country, and there he wasted his fortune in reckless and loose [from restraint] living.

As God said He would do if the younger son, Israel, broke the Horeb covenant and disobeyed His commands, committing idolatry, He cast Israel off the land and dispersed him among the nations. Israel lost everything. He sank as low as he could go. And while he was in that pathetic condition, no one offered a helping hand, no one befriended him.

14And when he had spent all he had, a mighty famine came upon that country, and he began to fall behind and be in want.

15So he went and forced (glued) himself upon one of the citizens of that country, who sent him into his fields to feed hogs.

16And he would gladly have fed on and filled his belly with the carob pods that the hogs were eating, but [they could not satisfy his hunger and] nobody gave him anything [better].

Remember what you read earlier in Ezekiel 16:27. God said, *"Behold therefore, I have stretched out My hand against you, diminished your ordinary allowance of food, and delivered you over to the will of those who hate and despise you...."*

To catch a glimpse of the younger son's (that is, the Jews') misery and want, all one has to do is remember what the Jews went through during World War II. The animals of this world were treated better than they were. Truly, Yeshua's parable tells their sad story. The Jews suffered things that no human should have to undergo.

And as they sat among the pigs—pigs, which represented everything that was classed as unclean to them—they finally came to their senses. As Lamentations 3:40 reveals, they said, *"Let us test and examine our ways, and let us return to the Lord!"*

Direct your thoughts once again to the contents of the parable that Yeshua taught, and compare His words to those of the prophet Jeremiah in Lamentations 3:40 that I quoted and highlighted in the former paragraph.

17Then when he came to himself, he said, How many hired servants of my father have enough food, and [even food] to spare, but I am perishing (dying) here of hunger!

18I will get up and go to my father, and I will say to him, Father, I have sinned against heaven and in your sight.

19I am no longer worthy to be called your son; [just] make me like one of your hired servants.

The Jews were broken in spirit. They desired to go back home. They were weary of the humiliation and abuse that they continued to suffer at the hands of the Gentile nations. They longed for a place of safety and warmth. By that time, they had been through so much that they felt anything would be better than what they had. So they decided to humble themselves and go back to their father's house. They desperately hoped that their father would receive them and allow them to return home.

They were truly sorry that they had broken the Horeb covenant and disobeyed God's commands, committing spiritual adultery (idolatry). In verses eighteen and nineteen they said, *"I will get up and go to my father, and I will say to him, Father, I have sinned against heaven and in your sight. I am no longer worthy to be called your son; [just] make me like one of your hired servants."*

Lamentations 3:40 (The Amplified Bible.)

40Let us test and examine our ways, and return to the Lord!

The youngest son responded to his spiritual crises as King David had responded when he sinned with Bathsheba. You will recall that David's spirit was broken down with sorrow for his adulterous sins. So David called upon God's promised steadfast loving-kindness, and God forgave him in order to keep His promise of everlasting love and mercy. The following Psalm gives you a glimpse of David's broken spirit.

Psalm 51:1-17 (The Amplified Bible.)

1HAVE MERCY upon me, O God, according to Your steadfast love; according to the multitude of Your tender mercy and loving-kindness blot out my transgressions.

2Wash me thoroughly [and repeatedly] from my iniquity and guilt and cleanse me and make me wholly pure from my sin!

3For I am conscious of my transgressions and I acknowledge them; my sin is ever before me.

4Against You, You only, have I sinned and done that which is evil in Your sight, so that You are justified in Your sentence and faultless in Your judgment.

5Behold, I was brought forth in [a state of] iniquity; my mother was sinful who conceived me [and I too am sinful].

6Behold, You desire truth in the inner being; make me therefore to know wisdom in my inmost heart.

7Purify me with hyssop, and I shall be clean [ceremonially]; wash me, and I shall [in reality] be whiter than snow.

8Make me to hear joy and gladness and be satisfied; let the bones which You have broken rejoice.

9Hide Your face from my sins and blot out all my guilt and iniquities.

10Create in me a clean heart, O God, and renew a right, persevering, and steadfast spirit within me.

11Cast me not away from Your presence and take not Your Holy Spirit from me.

12Restore to me the joy of Your salvation and uphold me with a willing spirit.

13Then will I teach transgressors Your ways, and sinners shall be converted and return to You.

14Deliver me from bloodguiltiness and death, O God, the God of my salvation, and my tongue shall sing aloud of Your righteousness (Your rightness and Your justice).

15O Lord, open my lips, and my mouth shall show forth Your praise.

16For You delight not in sacrifice, or else would I give it; You find no pleasure in burnt offering.

17My sacrifice [the sacrifice acceptable] to God is a broken spirit; a broken and a contrite heart [broken down with sorrow for sin and humbly and thoroughly penitent], such, O God, You will not despise.

The repentant prodigal son (the Jews) went back home. And wouldn't you know it? The Father ran out to meet His beloved people with open arms. In His promised mercy, compassion and loving-kindness God ran to them. He could not forget or disown His wayward Abrahamic covenant son. He could not forget His solemn promise of everlasting love for His people, Israel.

Isaiah 49:14-16 (The Amplified Bible.)

14But Zion [Jerusalem, her people as seen in captivity] said, The Lord has forsaken me, and my Lord has forgotten me.

15[And the Lord answered] Can a woman forget her nursing child, that she should not have compassion on the son of her womb? **Yes, they may forget, yet I will not forget you.**

16Behold, I have indelibly imprinted (tattooed a picture of) you on the palm of each of My hands; [O Zion] your walls are continually before Me.

God ran to meet His people with covenant love, compassion and mercy. God was ready to keep His promises to Abraham, Isaac and Jacob, and the timing was now right. For through Moses, God had told Israel that when they were in tribulation in the latter days, He would remember His covenant with their forefathers, which included bringing them back to the Land of Promise. To refresh your mind, read Moses' inspired words in the subsequent text.

Deuteronomy 4:30-31 (The Amplified Bible.)

30When you are in tribulation and all these things come upon you, in the latter days you will turn to the Lord your God and be obedient to His voice.

31For the Lord your God is a merciful God; **He will not fail you or destroy you or forget the covenant of your fathers, which He swore to them.**

Notice that Moses did not say, when you recognize and accept the Messiah, God will bring you home. No! Moses said in verse thirty, *"...you will turn to the Lord your God and be obedient to His voice."* Folks, God had to bring His spiritually blind and deaf people home so that they would be on the Promised Land to help Him carry out His end-of-time plans. For as you saw earlier in the series, the Jews must be in Israel for Christ's second coming. It will be then that their spiritually blind eyes and deaf ears will be healed, and they will finally recognize the Messiah and mourn over their past rejection of Him.

Now you might ask, but, how in the world can God keep His Abrahamic covenant promises to a nation of people who do not acknowledge Yeshua as the Messiah? My friend, you must keep in mind what you learned earlier in the series. You will recall that **as a nation**, the Jewish people cannot recognize the Messiah. For His own purpose and name's sake, God deliberately blinded their eyes and deafened their ears so that they would not recognize the Messiah or understand His teachings.

You might also ask, "But there is also the Law of Moses to be considered. How can God keep His Abrahamic covenant promises to Israel when as a nation they do not even keep the Law of Moses? There are secular Jews who absolutely refuse to obey the Law." My friend, God can and must keep His Abrahamic covenant promises despite Israel's failure **as a nation** to keep His commands.

The apostle Paul made it clear that the Abrahamic covenant is not dependent upon Moses' Law or even the new covenant that Christ sealed with His own blood. The unbreakable Abrahamic covenant stands on its own, and it must be fulfilled for God's name's sake.

Galatians 3:17-18 (The Amplified Bible.)

17This is my argument: The Law, which began 430 years after the covenant does not and cannot annul the covenant previously established (ratified) by God, so as to abolish the promise and make it void.

18For if the inheritance [of the promise depends on observing] the Law [as these false teachers would like you to believe], it no longer [depends] on the promise; however, God gave it to Abraham [as a free gift solely] by virtue of His promise.

You must also keep in mind that the youngest son, Israel, did confess and repent of his sins. Yeshua makes that fact clear in verses seventeen through nineteen of His parable. Proof of that fact is seen in the nucleus of religious Jews that exist in Israel today, Jews who have repented and who faithfully keep the Law of Moses. They just do not as yet recognize their Messiah or understand His teachings. Their God-ordained spiritual blindness and deafness will not permit them to recognize Him or understand His teachings at this time.

How exciting it is to actually get to witness God keeping His promises to Abraham, Isaac and Jacob regarding their descendants, the Jews, and the land of Israel. My friend, it was because of the Abrahamic covenant, including God's promise of everlasting love, that God welcomed the Jews home. So look again at the parable of the prodigal son, and see how every circumstance that Yeshua prophesied of the younger son's return really did come to pass.

Luke 15:20-24 (The Amplified Bible.)

20So he got up and came to his [own] father. But while he was still a long way off, his father saw him and was moved with pity and tenderness [for him]; and he ran and embraced him and kissed him [fervently].

²¹*And the son said to him, Father, I have sinned against heaven and in your sight; I am no longer worthy to be called your son [I no longer deserve to be recognized as a son of yours]!*

²²**But the father said to his bond servants, Bring quickly the best robe (the festive robe of honor) and put it on him; and give him a ring for his hand and sandals for his feet.**

²³**And bring out that [wheat-] fattened calf and kill it; and let us revel and feast and be happy and make merry,**

²⁴**Because this my son was dead and is alive again; he was lost and is found! And they began to revel and feast and make merry.**

God's heart overflowed with joy and everlasting covenant love at the return of His beloved Israel. He called for the finest clothing to be brought and put upon His beloved. And He commanded that all rejoice with Him over His son's return.

Psalm 45:13-15 (The Amplified Bible.)

¹³*The King's daughter in the inner part [of the palace] is all glorious; her clothing is inwrought with gold.*

¹⁴*She shall be brought to the King in raiment of needlework; with the virgins, her companions that follow her, she shall be brought to You.*

¹⁵<u>*With gladness and rejoicing will they be brought;*</u> *they will enter into the King's palace.*

I am unhappy to say that the older brother (the Gentile Arab nations) was not pleased with Israel's return. In the following portion of His parable, Yeshua foretells the Arabs' wicked reaction to Israel's reinstatement. (Luke 15:25-28.)

²⁵*But his older son was in the field; and as he returned and came near the house, he heard music and dancing.*

²⁶*And having called one of the servant [boys] to him, he began to ask what this meant.*

27And he said to him, Your brother has come, and your father has killed that [wheat-] fattened calf, because he has received him back safe and well.

28But [the elder brother] was angry [with deep-seated wrath] and resolved not to go in. Then his father came out and began to plead with him.

29But he answered his father, Look! These many years I have served you, and I have never disobeyed your command. Yet you never gave me [so much as] a [little] kid, that I might revel and feast and be happy and make merry with my friends;

Yeshua's prophesy in this parable is absolutely astounding. He foretold exactly what would later take place when Israel returned to his homeland. To show you why Yeshua's prophecy is so incredible, I am going to point out to you some of the most important details that are contained in His parable.

Not all nations which are today lumped into the category of "the Arab nations" are true Arabs. According to the *Encyclopedia Britannica Micropedia* under the heading "Arab,"

> Before the spread of Islam and, with it, the Arabic language, "Arab" referred to any of the largely nomadic Semitic inhabitants of the Arabian Peninsula. In modern usage, it embraces any of the Arabic-speaking peoples living in the vast region from Mauritania on the Atlantic coast of Africa, to southwestern Iran, including the entire Maghrib of North Africa, the Arabian Peninsula, and the Middle East.

Except for a tiny minority, the descendants of Ishmael have been absorbed into the Islamic world. *Smith's Bible Dictionary* under the heading "Ishmael" informs us that

> The sons of Ishmael peopled the north and west of the Arabian Peninsula, and eventually formed the chief element of the Arab nation, the wandering Bedouin tribes. They are now mostly Mohammedans....

When Yeshua relayed His parable of the prodigal son, He was totally aware of what the future held for Ishmael's descendants. He knew that they would be swallowed up by the Islamic religion. He also knew that when Israel returned home, the whole Islamic world would be passing itself off as Ishmael's descendants (the elder son).

How do we know that in His parable Yeshua was referring to the Gentile Moslem nations? Our answer is in verse twenty nine. The elder son said to the father, *"Look! These many years I have served you, and I have never disobeyed your command."*

Immediately you might respond by asking, "How can you possibly identify God's commands with the Islamic religion and its Moslem followers? They are neither Jews nor Christians. Rather, they are Mohammedans." This is true. The Moslems are not Jews nor are they Christians. Yet they profess to worship the same God that the Jews worship. They profess to worship the God of Abraham. And even though they are greatly deceived and misled, they are absolutely convinced that they are keeping God's commands.

Verse twenty-nine of Yeshua's parable is exactly the kind of statement that a Moslem would make—*"I have never disobeyed your command."* My friend, the meaning of the very word, "Islam," refers to obedience to God's commands. For example, the *Encyclopedia Britannica Micropedia* under the heading "Islam" tells us:

> The word *islam* is used repeatedly in the Quran, the Islamic scripture, in the sense of **"surrender to the will of Allah (God)."** For the Muslims, as adherents of Islam are called, the Quran is the Word of God....

> **The most important and fundamental religious concept of Islam is that of the Shariah *(q.v.)*, or the Law, which embraces the total way of life as explicitly or implicitly commanded by God.**

I repeat, verse twenty-nine of Yeshua's parable is exactly the kind of statement that a Moslem would make—"I have never disobeyed your command."

The Illustrated World Encyclopedia under the heading "Islam" informs us that as well as the Quran,

Islam also recognizes some parts of the Hebrew Torah as sacred, as well as the Psalms of the Old Testament and the teachings of Jesus.

If the previous reference is correct, then I do hope Islamic leaders will pay attention to their own teachings which incorporate parts of the Torah, the Psalms and the teachings of Yeshua. For all the previously mentioned Scriptural sources teach us to be pro-Jew and pro-Israel for God's name's sake. On that note, let us continue our study of Yeshua's parable. Pay careful attention to the angry response of the elder brother who, from now on, I will mostly refer to as the Arabs or the Arab nations.

Luke 15:28-32 (The Amplified Bible.)

28*But [the elder brother] was angry [with deep-seated wrath] and resolved not to go in. Then his father came out and began to plead with him,*

29*But he answered his father, Look! These many years I have served you, and I have never disobeyed your command. Yet you never gave me [so much as] a [little] kid, that I might revel and feast and be happy and make merry with my friends;*

30*But when this son of yours arrived, who has devoured your estate with immoral women, you have killed for him that [wheat-] fattened calf!*

31*And the father said to him, Son, you are always with me, and all that is mine is yours.*

32*But it was fitting to make merry, to revel and feast and rejoice, for this brother of yours was dead and is alive again! He was lost and is found!*

Verse twenty-eight is so extremely crucial to this part of the lesson that I want you to read it again.

28*But [the elder brother] was angry [with deep-seated wrath] and resolved not to go in. Then his father came out and began to plead with him,*

All that you see described in Yeshua's parable is exactly what happened when the Jews returned home to Israel. The Arabs (the older brother) were furious at the arrival of the Jews. Let me give you a condensed account of the circumstances that surrounded the Jews' return to the Land of Promise. You can find this information in most history books or encyclopedias. I took most of my historical facts from *The Illustrated World Encyclopedia.*

A group of Jewish leaders called Zionists purposed in their hearts to make a national homeland for the Jewish people in Palestine. The leader of the Zionists was Chaim Weizmann. Weizmann devoted most of his life to gaining an independent homeland for the Jewish people. He later became the first president of Israel. Great Britain had control of Palestine in 1917 and was in favor of making a Jewish national home in Palestine. As you can see, God was at that time working to bring about His promises to Abraham, Isaac and Jacob. The formation of God's plan to vindicate His holy name was clearly underway.

At the end of World War I, Great Britain issued a declaration called the Balfour Declaration. Many felt that the Zionists received the Balfour Declaration as a reward from the British Government for Weizmann's World War I efforts. You see, Weizmann, who taught chemistry at universities in England, invented an improved method of making acetone, a chemical which is used in explosives. When one considers the timing of Weizmann's invention, one can not help but believe that God had a hand in its success. Obviously, it was God's plan that Weismann find favor with the British in order to gain from them the Balfour agreement. This formal written statement was named for Great Britain's Foreign Secretary, the man who issued it. The declaration stated that Great Britain would support the building of a Jewish homeland.

The Arabs were, however, strictly opposed to Jewish immigration. You see, they had already settled on the land that God had given to the Jewish people, and they did not want to give the land back to its rightful owners. The greedy, covetous Arabs wanted the Promised Land for themselves. They had no regard for God's covenant with Abraham, Isaac and Jacob, nor did they show the slightest concern for God's reputation.

In an attempt to hold on to land that never belonged to them in the first place, the Arabs fought against Israel. They did not realize that they were biting off more than they could chew. They did not understand that in fighting against Israel, they were really fighting against Almighty God and His divine purpose. Israel was forced to retaliate or be annihilated. Sporadic fighting continued. It became a way of life.

Then came World War II. During that horrendous period in history, the Jews flocked to Israel in order to survive and escape persecution by the Nazis. Weizmann divided his time between the laboratory and his work for Zionism. He spent time in America where he helped to produce a synthetic rubber that was of great importance in winning the war. Thus, this great Jewish man made significant contributions towards winning both world wars.

When the end of World War II finally came, many Jewish people tried to return home to Israel. God's people wanted to return to the land on which Great Britain had promised to stand by them while they built it into a fit place to live.

Being British born, I am ashamed to say that instead of being met with the support that had been promised, the Jews, whose leader had played a major role in bringing the war to an end, were met with British warships. British soldiers actually fought with God's beloved people, refusing to allow them to disembark from the vessels which had brought them home.

The British government in power at that time did not keep its word. It failed to keep the Balfour agreement. It also conveniently forgot Weizmann's World War I contribution. The British tried to appease the Moslems at the cost of their own declaration. Finally, Great Britain turned the problem over to the United Nations. The United Nations were responsible for the appalling act of dividing Palestine, the Promised Land, into two parts—one part for Arabs, and one part for Jews.

Israel's attitude was like that of the younger son in Yeshua's parable who was willing to settle for whatever the Father would allow. He did not feel that he deserved what rightfully belonged to him. He was, therefore, even willing to relinquish his covenant rights. However, the older brother (the Arab nations) was not so humble. The Arabs swore to go to war rather than let the Jews share their own inheritance, land that God had given to the Jews only. The Arabs wanted all the land of Israel (the Jews' inheritance) for themselves.

Despite continual harassment by the Arabs, in 1948 the Jews declared themselves The Independent Republic of Israel under the United Nations Partisan Plan. That is how they fulfilled the following prophecy which was spoken thousands of years before by Isaiah the prophet. They became a nation in a day. Praise God!

Isaiah 66:8 (The Amplified Bible.)

⁸*Who has heard of such a thing? Who has seen such things? **Shall a land be born in one day? Or shall a nation be brought forth in a moment?** For as soon as Zion was in labor, she brought forth her children.*

By fulfilling His Word in Isaiah 66:8, God had performed a tremendous miracle. He had also shown how faithful He is to keep His Biblical promises. The Arabs, however, did not recognize that a great miracle had been wrought before their very eyes. They were furious with deep-seated wrath. They attacked the nation of Israel, thinking they could snuff her out while she was still young and vulnerable. But God saw what was going on, and for His name's sake, He was there to protect His beloved people, Israel.

In 1949 the United Nations arranged for an armistice, but no peace settlement was obtained. Even today, most Arab (Islamic) nations count Israel as their most hated foe. In their hostility and ignorance of what God is doing, they have harassed Israel from day one.

We will move on in history to another very important event. In 1967, Egyptian President Nasser of the United Arab Republic tried to block the Gulf of Aqaba, Israel's only water outlet to the Red Sea. Nasser convinced the Arab nations to surround Israel with tanks and all kinds of war machinery. Border skirmishes had been going on for approximately ten years. However, this action brought about full scale war.

Again, the Lord was with His Abrahamic covenant people. The tiny country of Israel, with its population of less than 3,000,000 people miraculously won that war. They completely defeated the Arab nations whose combined population was approximately 110,000,000. By the time this war was over (which only lasted six days), 15,000 Arabs had been killed, 50,000 were wounded and another 11,500 were captured. But amazingly, only 679 Israelis were killed, 2,563 were wounded and sixteen were captured. Miraculous, isn't it?

Keep in mind, it was also during the Six Day War, a war started by the Arabs, that the Jews took possession of the old city of Jerusalem. What a day! After nineteen years, the Jews could again pray at the sacred Wailing Wall. God miraculously returned old Jerusalem to its rightful owners, the descendants of Abraham, Isaac and Jacob. Praise the Lord!

The Arabs are still allowed to visit their mosque, but the land it sits on is now back in the hands of the Jews. Let us not forget, however, the reason why God gave the Jews victory over the Arab nations. He did it in order to fulfill His promises to Abraham, Isaac and Jacob, keep His vow to Jerusalem and protect His own holy name.

Oh, if only the Arab people would open their spiritual eyes and understand what God is doing! If only they would lay aside their own prejudices and evil, covetous desires and think only of God's reputation! If only every Arab who wants to see God's will done on the earth would reach out to Israel and support her for God's name's sake!

I am happy to say that there are a few Christian Arabs who pray for and support Israel. Yet as a whole, the Arab nations (the angry elder brother) certainly live up to Yeshua's prophecy in His parable of the prodigal son, don't they? But I urge any Moslem who reads this book to reconsider his or her stand regarding Israel. Oh, my Moslem friend, I implore you, do not allow your present evil attitude and conduct to continue. For God's name's sake, purpose in your heart to let go of your anger and resentment toward Israel, for it is God's desire that you rejoice with Him over Israel's return. Moreover, God clearly tells you why He wants you to rejoice with Him over Israel's reinstatement. To see the reason why all Arabs should rejoice with the Father over Israel's return, look again at Yeshua's parable. We will examine the following two verses one at a time.

Luke 15:31-32 (The Amplified Bible.)

31And the father said to him, Son, you are always with me, and all that is mine is yours.

What did Yeshua mean by His statement in verse thirty-one? Let me explain. The true lineal descendants of Ishmael were nomads. They traveled with their animals from place to place. They actually lived and grazed their sheep on the borders of all their kinsmen, including Israel. You will recall that when Yeshua was born, angels appeared to Ishmaelite shepherds informing them of the Messiah's birth. The Lord's words to Hagar also confirm the previous facts.

Genesis 16:11-12 (The Amplified Bible.)

11And the Angel of the Lord continued, See now, you are with child and shall bear a son, and shall call his name Ishmael [God hears], because the Lord has heard and paid attention to your affliction.

*12And he [Ishmael] will be as a wild ass among men; his hand will be against every man and every man's hand against him, **and he will live to the east and on the borders of all his kinsmen.***

Notice that God's Word foretold that the Arabs would live *"on the borders of all his kinsmen."* My friend, unlike the covenant nation of Israel, the Arabs were never driven from their land. Nor were they ever forbidden to graze their flocks on the borders of all their kinsmen, including the border of Israel, the land where God's eternal dwelling place (Jerusalem) is situated. Hence, the Arabs stayed in close proximity to the father during the whole time that Israel was scattered throughout the world. How much closer can one get to another than to live on the border of his land. Therefore, God could rightfully say to the Arabs, *"Son, you are always with me,"* or as *The Living Bible* states, *"you and I are very close...."*

God was simply saying to the Gentile Arabs, "Hey! You were not driven from me as your brother was. You have been close by the whole time. You have gone from place to place grazing your animals on the borders of all your kinsmen, including the border of Israel, the land where My eternal home is situated."

The last portion of Yeshua's statement in verse thirty-one, *"and all that is mine is yours,"* is also extremely important. Let me explain why those words are so important. You will recall that in verse twelve of Yeshua's illustration, the father had divided the estate between his two sons before the younger son had ever left home. Verse twelve says, *"And he divided the estate between them."* Israel, of course received the Promised Land, including Jerusalem, as his everlasting inheritance while, as you learned earlier, the elder son (the Arabs) "peopled the north and west of the Arabian peninsula." Once an estate is legally distributed, it remains the possession of the inheritor. Therefore, when the father said to the eldest son, *"all that is mine is yours,"* he was simply informing the elder son that he had already divided the property and that the elder son had in his possession everything that he had to give him. The bottom line is that since God had sworn that the land of Canaan would belong to Israel forever, that land was no longer His to give to the elder brother (the Gentile Arab nations).

God continued His exhortation to the elder son, (the Arabs) in the following verse of Yeshua's parable.

Luke 15:32 (The Amplified Bible.)

*32But it was fitting to make merry, to revel and feast and rejoice, **for this brother of yours was dead and is alive again! He was lost and is found!***

In verse 32, God explains why the Arabs should rejoice over Israel's return. He tells them that His son Israel was dead but is now alive again. Oh, my friend, God needed Israel alive so that through Israel He could fulfill His promises to Abraham, Isaac and Jacob. God needed Israel alive and well so that He could use Israel to vindicate His holy name.

Almost 3,000 years ago, the prophet Ezekiel foretold how the dead nation of Israel would live again. And God's word was miraculously fulfilled right before the eyes of the Arab nations. Yet the elder brother refused to yield to God's will. He refused to be happy for God. Look now at Ezekiel's prophecy in the vision of the dry bones. And remember, these next verses speak of the younger son, dead Israel, who came alive again.

Ezekiel 37:1-14 (The Amplified Bible.)

1THE HAND of the Lord was upon me, and He brought me out in the Spirit of the Lord and set me down in the midst of the valley; and it was full of bones.

2And He caused me to pass round about among them, and behold, there were very many [human bones] in the open valley or plain, and behold, they were very dry.

3And He said to me, Son of man, can these bones live? And I answered, O Lord God, You know!

4Again He said to me, Prophesy to these bones, and say to them, O you dry bones, hear the word of the Lord.

*5**Thus says the Lord God to these bones: Behold, I will cause breath and spirit to enter you, and you shall live;***

*6**And I will lay sinews upon you and bring up flesh upon you and cover you with skin, and I will put breath and spirit in you, and you [dry bones] shall live; and you shall know, understand, and realize that I am the Lord [the Sovereign Ruler, Who calls forth loyalty and obedient service].***

7So I prophesied as I was commanded; and as I prophesied, there was a [thundering] noise and behold, a shaking and trembling and a rattling, and the bones came together, bone to its bone.

⁸And I looked and behold, there were sinews upon [the bones] and flesh came upon them and skin covered them over, but there was no breath or spirit in them.

⁹Then said He to me, Prophesy to the breath and spirit, son of man, and say to the breath and spirit, Thus says the Lord God: Come from the four winds, O breath and spirit, and breathe upon these slain that they may live.

¹⁰So I prophesied as He commanded me, and the breath and spirit came into [the bones], and they lived and stood up upon their feet, an exceedingly great host,

¹¹Then He said to me, son of man, these bones are the whole house of Israel. Behold, they say, Our bones are dried up and our hope is lost; we are completely cut off.

Surely, in the past, the Jews must have felt like dead men, completely cut off. As Ezekiel foretold, they experienced total hopelessness and helplessness. It is easy to see why the Jews would cry out, **"We are dead men!"** However, God saw their pathetic plight. And for His name's sake, He extended to them His promised mercy and loving-kindness. **As Ezekiel prophesied in the following verses, the Lord opened their graves and caused His people to live again!**

¹²Therefore prophesy and say to them, Thus says the Lord God: Behold, I will open your graves and cause you to come up out of your graves, O My people; and I will bring you [back home] to the land of Israel.

¹³And you shall know that I am the Lord [your Sovereign Ruler], when I have opened your graves and caused you to come up out of your graves, O My people.

¹⁴And I shall put My Spirit in you and you shall live, and I shall place you in your own land. Then you shall know, understand, and realize that I the Lord have spoken it and performed it, says the Lord.

Listen folks, if you want to catch a glimpse of what it must have felt like to be in the type of horrifying and suffocating grave that the Jews were dumped in, then consider what they went through during World War II. In many European countries, they were forced into ghettos.

They were forbidden to carry food into the ghettos from outside. Through that ghastly procedure, the Nazis attempted to starve God's beloved Jewish people to death.

When the Nazis' starvation plan did not kill off God's covenant people, the Jews were shipped to concentration camps and extermination camps. I do not have to describe the kind of treatment the Jews received in those camps. You already know. Four-hundred years of affliction and oppression in Egypt was nothing compared to the horrendous treatment the Jews received at the hands of Hitler and his Nazi butchers.

The next example that I will share with you describes what it is like to be a dead nation. Hitler built a museum. In that building, he stored a collection of articles and objects that once belonged to the Jewish people. His plan was to dedicate that monstrosity of a museum to an extinct race, the Jews. Had it not been for the intervention of Almighty God, Hitler would have succeeded in accomplishing his evil, Satanic plan.

The devil tried to use Hitler and the Nazis to prevent God from keeping His prediction in Genesis 3:15 and His covenant promises to Abraham, Isaac and Jacob. Don't you see! Satan wanted to keep God from carrying out His purpose on the earth and from clearing His name by attempting to destroy the only people on the face of the earth through whom God can completely fulfill Genesis 3:15 and His Abrahamic promises and vindicate His name.

Like the Nazis before them, the Arabs are also tools of God's enemy, the devil. They think they are doing God a favor by hating, mocking, abusing and murdering the Israelites. But instead, they are harassing and desiring to destroy the very race of people that God brought up out of the grave and made alive again for the purpose of completely fulfilling His prediction in Genesis 3:15 and His Abrahamic promises and clearing His holy name.

Come on now! You do not think the Jews have been singled out for mistreatment all these years just because they are Jews, do you? No! Rather, Satan has used ignorant people and, in some cases, even whole nations to try to undermine God's plan. Satan is responsible for stirring up all the hatred and anger that men have vented upon the Jewish people. Yes, Satan has tried to use the ignorant and wicked people of this world to wipe out the descendants of Abraham, Isaac and Jacob in an attempt to keep God from fulfilling His prediction in Genesis 3:15 and His Abrahamic covenant. He has attempted to permanently ruin God's reputation and defeat God's purpose for mankind. And now, the

Arabs are willing pawns in the hands of God's enemy, the devil, just as the Nazis were.

However, Satan has lost the battle. For despite every wicked plot that he has contrived and carried out, the younger son, Israel, has come up out of the grave and is alive and back on the land of Israel as God predicted. The prophecy in Yeshua's parable has been fulfilled to the letter.

Luke 15:32 (The Amplified Bible.)

32 But it was fitting to make merry, to revel and feast and rejoice, for this brother of yours was dead and is alive again! He was lost and is found!

Can you now see what a difficult situation developed? Israel, God's lost son, returned home only to be met by his angry elder brother who resented the father's merciful and forgiving attitude towards his younger brother. The Arabs did not understand that God is bound by a sacred oath to love Israel forever. Neither did they understand that God also solemnly promised that the land of Canaan would belong to the Jews forever. The Arabs had envisioned keeping all the land for themselves. But God cannot and will not permit them to take Israel's everlasting inheritance. For the sake of His reputation, God cannot allow the Arabs to have land that has already been promised by a binding oath to the covenant descendants of Abraham, Isaac and Jacob.

By keeping this promise and showing mercy to the Jews, God is actually showing mercy to His own name. But the Arabs in their greed, blind hatred and lack of understanding do not have enough spiritual insight to be able to see the real issue.

We, Gentile Christians, also need to be very careful. We do not want to be guilty of this same offense; we do not want to fall into the same category with the Arabs, the older brother, and become angry or envious when we see God making a fuss over His beloved Israel. Rather, we need to obey God and rejoice with Him over Israel's return.

My friend, it is so important to God that you follow His instructions in this area that in His mercy God even shows you what to rejoice about! Rejoice that Israel is alive again in order to clear God's name. Rejoice that God's promises to Abraham, Isaac and Jacob are being fulfilled. And remember, God is not showing partiality to Israel. No! As you learned earlier, God is not even doing these great things for Israel. God simply wants His predictions and promises kept and His name cleared, and He deserves to have it cleared. God's holy name must come first, and you, Christian, must want it to come first.

And yet, I assure you that as you continue to support and pray for Israel, the Jewish people will become very precious to you. They will become special to you because they are the instruments through whom God's name will finally be vindicated. So, Christian, get serious about praying for Israel. Pray that Israel regains every inch of the land that was given to her by God for an everlasting inheritance.

Pray also that the elder brother (the Gentile Arab nations) will be given every opportunity to see the truth and to repent of their hatred and mistreatment of the Jews. Pray that if it is possible, along with the Gentile Christians, they will begin to support Israel and will yield to the Father's wishes and rejoice over Israel's return. For, if they do not repent and do right by the Jews, the Messiah will deal with them personally when He returns to earth. And woe be to all Israel's enemies when Yeshua, the Messiah, returns.

In the meantime, for God's name's sake, be joyful when God blesses Israel. Shout for joy when you see the Jews claiming more and more of the Promised Land, the land that God promised by a solemn oath to the descendants of Abraham, Isaac and Jacob. After all, who else should claim it? The land of Israel belongs to the Jews. It is theirs by right. It is theirs forever.

Be glad when Israel prospers; weep when she is hurting or in pain. Weep when you see Israel forced to give up one inch of her sacred eternal inheritance.

Satan, the enemy of your soul, will do anything or use anyone he can to try to stop God from keeping His predictions and promises and vindicating His righteous name. The devil will use individuals or even entire nations to try to turn the whole world against Israel. Satan will be subtle; he will carefully plan his strategy. When Israel does not react as you feel she should, he will try to manipulate you. He will use propaganda. He will use situations. He will use anything and anyone.

What will you do when the Arabs terrorize and murder the peoples of the world simply because their governments sided with Israel on a particular issue? What will you do when they take hostages and try to use them to manipulate the governments of countries that are friendly toward Israel? What will you do when Islamic extremists use terrorist tactics to try to make demands on Israel? What will you do when they try to make peoples and governments angry with Israel because she will not jump like a puppet to meet the Arabs' wicked demands? What will you do then, American Christian? What will you do then, British Christian? What will you do then, Greek, Italian, French, African Christian? I could name every country in the world, but I think I have made my point. What will you do when you are under pressure? **When Yeshua returns, how many will He find who have faith and are praying for and supporting Israel?**

Israel needs true friends. She needs friends who will stick by her when times get rough. She does not need fair weather friends. That is, she does not need Christian friends who jump on the bandwagon when everything is rosy and when it is popular to associate with Israel but quickly vanish when difficult times come.

Obey God's Word concerning Israel all the time and not just some of the time. If you know that someone wants to harm Israel and the Jews, never wish them well! Never say, "God bless you," for they are in direct opposition to God and to God's name being vindicated.

Oh Gentile Christian, for God's name's sake and for your own eternal welfare, do not side with Israel's wicked angry brother. You now know that the Arabs have absolutely no right to any part of Israel. So, do not support any measures that your government might take against the Jews or the nation of Israel. For if you do, then like all those who try to push anti-Israel policies, you will come under God's Biblical curse.

Genesis 12:3 (The Amplified Bible.)

3And I will bless those who bless you [who confer prosperity or happiness upon you] and curse him who curses or uses insolent language toward you....

Again I say, do not side with the unrighteous actions of the older brother, the Arab nations. Rather, side with God! Do God's will! The end is at hand; time is short. Do not be weighed in the balance and found wanting.

For His name's sake, God has sent His Word to you in this literary work. He has revealed to you many marvelous truths. Among those truths, He has shown you the real meaning of the parable of the prodigal son. He has given you a glimpse of His predicament and His future plans. God is warning you to be prepared for what lies ahead. Be wise. Learn and obey God's Word which He has lovingly provided for you free of charge and postpaid so that you might not sin against Him by sinning against His beloved Israel. Do not let Satan take from you the word that is sown in your heart.

Christian, rejoice with the Father over Israel's return. For praise be to God, His predictions, including His prediction in Genesis 3:15, and His promises to Abraham, Isaac and Jacob will soon be fulfilled in their entirety. God's name will be vindicated through Israel. The Messiah will return. He will save and deliver the Jews and conquer all their enemies. Jerusalem will be a praise in all the earth. And if you are faithful to obey God's Word in praying for and supporting Israel, you will hear the Lord say, *"Well done, you upright (honorable, admirable) and faithful servant! You have been faithful and trustworthy over a little; I will put you in charge of much. Enter into and share the joy (the delight, the blessedness) which your master enjoys."* (Matthew 25:21.)

Chapter 18

WILL THOSE WHO
HARM ISRAEL BE PUNISHED?

When Israel sinned, God often used the Gentile nations to punish her. However, though upon occasion God's purpose was to use the Gentiles to chastise Israel, the nations mistreated God's beloved people much more severely than He had ever intended and far beyond the appropriate time period that He had designated for their punishment. Eventually, the nations of the world came to detest the Jews simply because they were Jews. They either forgot or refused to acknowledge that God loves the Jews with an everlasting covenant love. To give you a horrific glimpse of the atrocities the nations have committed against God's covenant people (the Jewish people) and God's eternal home, we will briefly scan some of the highlights of Israel's history from 732 B.C. before tackling the question posed in the title of this chapter, "Will Those Who Harm Israel Be Punished?"

(732 B.C.) The Assyrian King Tiglath-Pilesser III forced Israel to pay high taxes to him. When war broke out, he took away from Israel the Mediterranean coast and carried many Israelite captives into exile.

(722 B.C.) The northern kingdom (Israel) fell to the Assyrians. 27,290 Israelites were carried away captive to northwestern Mesopotamia and to Media.

(586 B.C.) The Babylonians conquered the southern kingdom (Judah), stole all the Jews' treasures, ransacked the temple, burned down town after town and then burned down the city of Jerusalem. The Babylonians also executed many of Israel's leaders and carried the Jewish people into exile, leaving only a small group of people to keep the land tilled.

(445 B.C.) The Jews returned from exile, and under the leadership of Nehemiah, they rebuilt the walls of Jerusalem. During the rebuilding of the walls, Tobiah, his followers and the Samaritans were a continual source of harassment to God's chosen people, the Jews.

(332 B.C.) Jerusalem was conquered by Alexander the Great. In 320 B.C., one of Alexander's generals, Ptolemy I, took control of Jerusalem. He entered Jerusalem on the Sabbath Day and took many

captives. Ptolemy forced the Jewish captives to live in numerous foreign countries.

(175-162 B.C.) Antiochus of Syria killed the Israelites, plundered and then destroyed Jerusalem. He also destroyed copies of the Law of Moses and put a halt to the Jewish practice of circumcision. Antiochus went so far as to set up an idol of the false god Zeus in the temple. He then had his soldiers sacrifice pigs on the Lord's altar. Any Jew who refused to worship Zeus was tortured and then murdered. At the hands of the butcher, Antiochus, the Jews were in danger of total annihilation.

(63 B.C.) From this point on, Israel came under Roman rule. In 40 B.C., Herod the Great, the son of an Edomite procurator, was appointed King of Judea by the Romans. In 37 B.C., with the help of the Roman Emperor Gaius Octavian, Herod took control of all Israel. Herod's cruelty and mistreatment of the Jews is well documented.

(A.D. 70) As Yeshua had prophesied, the Romans completely destroyed Jerusalem. Thousands of Jews were killed or sold into slavery. Rather than surrender to the cruelty of Roman rule, the Jews at the Fort of Masada committed mass suicide.

(A.D. 135) The Romans again captured and destroyed Jerusalem. It was later rebuilt by the Roman Emperor Hadrian. After the completion of the Holy City, Hadrian gave an edict that no Jew be allowed to enter Jerusalem.

(A.D. 335) The Roman Emperor Constantine turned the city of Jerusalem into a Christian center.

(A.D. 636) The Muslims invaded and conquered Israel and built the Dome of the Rock in Jerusalem.

(A.D. 1095-1096) In his book *Jewish Literacy* under the heading "Crusades," Rabbi Joseph Telushkin informs the reader,

> In 1095 when Pope Urban II called for the Crusades to regain Palestine from the "infidels," tens of thousands of Christians set out for the Holy Land. Those Jews unfortunate enough to live in the cities through which the Crusaders passed were generally offered the choice of conversion or death; a few lucky communities were permitted to pay a large bribe to be left unmolested.

In May 1096, Crusaders besieged the Jewish community of Worms, Germany. The local bishop offered to save the Jews from their attackers if they converted to Christianity. Almost all of the Jews refused, and eight hundred were murdered.

Approximately twelve thousand Jews were killed in the early months of the first Crusades....

(A.D. 1099-1187) The crusaders conquered Jerusalem. In the name of Christianity, they massacred both the Jews and the Muslims. According to the same article in Rabbi Joseph Telushkin's book, *Jewish Literacy*,

In 1099, when the crusaders captured Jerusalem, they gathered all the city's Jews into a synagogue and burned them alive. Afterward, they banned all non-Christians from living in Jerusalem.

(A.D. 1290) All Jews were expelled from England. They were not re-admitted until 1656.

(A.D. 1492) All Jews were expelled from Spain. The expulsion involved approximately 200,000 people. Tens of thousands died while trying to reach safety.

(A.D. 1517) Jerusalem fell to the Ottomans. It was for a time brought under Egyptian control and was then later returned to the Ottomans.

(A.D. 1648-1649) The Jews were massacred in the Ukraine by Cossacks who were led by the Jew hater, Bogdan Chmielnitzki (Khmelnitsky). In his book *Jewish Literacy* under the heading "CHMIELNITZKI MASSACRES (1648-1649)," Rabbi Joseph Telushkin shares documented evidence taken from a Hebrew document, N. Hanover, *Yeven Mezulah* pp. 31-32.

"Some of them [the Jews] had their skins flayed off them and their flesh was flung to the dogs. The hands and feet of others were cut off and they were flung into the roadway where carts ran over them and they were trodden underfoot by horse.... And many were buried alive. Children were slaughtered in their mother's bosoms and many children were torn apart like fish. They ripped up the bellies of pregnant women, took out the unborn children, and flung them in their faces. They tore open the bellies of some of them and placed a living cat within the belly and left them alive thus, first cutting off their hands so that they should not be able to take the living cat out of the belly... and there was never an unnatural death in the world that they did not inflict upon them."

Many Jews who were not murdered during the massacres were sold as slaves, usually to Constantinople's slave markets.

...Chmielnitzki hated all Jews indiscriminately. It is estimated that his Cossack troops murdered well over 100,000 Jews at a time when world Jewry probably numbered no more than a million and a half.

(A.D. 1918) Israel came under British occupation. The Arabs made Israel's existence unbearable, a condition that exists to this day.

(1920's-1930's) The video documentary *America and the Holocaust, Deceit and Indifference* informs the viewer that in the 1920's and 1930's anti-Semitism was widespread in America. The doors of many places that were open to most Americans were closed to Jews. For example, a beach on Chesapeake Bay, Washington, D.C., displayed a sign which placed the Jews on the same level as animals. The sign read: "NO JEWS OR DOGS ALLOWED."

Job opportunities for Jews were also restricted. Arthur Hertzberg, an historian, reveals how the telephone company hired no Jews, the big three auto industry hired no Jews, the insurance company, aside from insurance agents within their structure, hired no Jews. Hertzberg also informs the viewer how Jews were systematically excluded from academic life.

Upon placing an application for employment, one woman tells how she received a reply stating that it was not their policy to accept students of Jewish nationality. After acquiring a particular position, another woman told how the same day that she was hired, she was asked by the boss what church she attended. When she informed him that she did not attend church, she went to a synagogue, he told her, "I wouldn't hire a Jew. You're fired!"

If Jews did manage to get a job, they were often told that they would receive less pay than other employees doing the same work. They were also told that they would never be able to acquire a partnership.

When a public opinion poll (the Roper Poll) was taken in July 1939, it showed how the majority of Americans felt about Jews. The poll stated: **"Jews are different and should be restricted."** 53% of Americans voted **Yes**.

This documentary also exposes the anti-Semitism that prevailed in the American government. It especially reveals the anti-Semitism that prevailed in the State Department and, in particular, the Immigration Department during World War II and the Nazi repression of the Jewish people. For those Jews who attempted to escape Europe, the State Department's anti-Semitism policies became a life threatening force. The historian, David Wyman states,

> In regard to American Consulates in Europe, anti-Semitism was widespread. There is no doubt about it. We have clear evidence. I learned in my own research that particularly it was seen in Zurich, in Oslo, in some Consulates in Vichy, France and in Lisbon. In fact, the situation was so bad in Lisbon that American Jewish Groups had to go to the Quakers and request that they send a non-Jew to Lisbon to try to persuade the American Consulate there to stop the obstruction of Jewish immigration.

While Jewish people patiently waited for the anti-Semitic American Immigration Department to issue them visa's, many of them were taken away to death camps. The anti-alien Assistant Secretary of State,

Breckenridge Long, held the Jews' fate in his hands. According to the historian, Wyman,

> To what extent anti-Semitism was involved is not clear but what we do know is that as a result immigration was sharply cut. In twenty years of research, probably the most disgraceful document that I've ever run into, is this memorandum written by Breckenridge Long in June 1940 in which he outlines the means by which consuls secretly and illegally can cut very sharply into immigration.

Long wrote,

> We can delay and effectively stop for a temporary period of indefinite length the number of immigrants into the United States. We could do this by simply advising our consuls to put every obstacle in the way and to require additional evidence and to resort to various administrative devices which would postpone and postpone and postpone the granting of the visas!

While Long's merciless anti-immigration tactics prevailed, American Jews had little influence. According to Arnold Forster, General Counsel, Anti-Defamation League, the American Jews had a hard enough time dealing with the anti-Semitic attitudes and actions of those around them. Non-Jewish Americans did not want Jews living in their neighborhoods, eating in their restaurants or even attending the same schools.

In 1939 a bill proposed **special sanctuary for 20,000 Jewish children** above the number allowed by the quota. Viola Bernard, M. D. Non-Sectarian Committee for Refugee Children said,

> The need for this kind of legislation was desperately pressing. The children being smuggled out of Austria and Germany were already separated from their parents which was traumatic enough, and it was essential to get them

into individual homes and a sense of
well being.

This merciful bill was immediately opposed. From the lips of a cousin of President Roosevelt, Laura Delano, proceeded a comment that summed up the cruel, unmerciful and indifferent attitude toward the Jewish people of the majority of Americans. She wickedly stated:

> 20,000 charming children would all too
> soon grow into 20,000 ugly adults.

Recognizing that the bill was politically unpopular, President Roosevelt chose to take no action. The bill of course died in committee. As a result of Roosevelt's heartless act, **20,000 Jewish children were denied refuge in the land of America.**

America had become almost as anti-Semitic as Germany. America's signs said, "NO JEWS OR DOGS ALLOWED," Germany's signposts read: "JEWS NOT WANTED. JEWS KEEP OUT." The only difference was that America did not insist that the Jews sit on special yellow benches, labeled "FOR JEWS."

Lying anti-Jewish propaganda was dispensed throughout America. One hundred (100) organizations campaigned against the Jews. Newspaper headlines read:

(Silver Legion Ranger)
"FREE SPEECH STOPPED BY JEW RIOT."

(Healey's Irish Weekly - Gentiles Awake!)
"TO COMBAT THE RADICAL JEWISH MINORITY INFLUENCE."

(American Gentile)
"JEWISH PRESS-CONTROL EXPOSED!"

(National American)
"JEWS DEFILE OUR CHRISTMAS!"

(American-Ranger)
"COMMUNISM IS JEWISH."

An extremely anti-Semitic radio host, Father Charles Coughlin, a Roman Catholic priest, was the most influential anti-Semitic, spokesman in America. He had a weekly radio program through which he constantly spewed his evil anti-Semitic propaganda. He had access to 3,000,000 people. Think about it! 3,000,000 people in whose minds he continually stirred up anger and hatred toward the Jewish people. On one occasion he stated:

> The system of International Finance which has crucified the world to the cross of depression was evolved by Jews for holding the peoples of the world under control.

While persecution and neglect continued to increase in America, the migration of Jews to Israel from Germany also increased. It increased because Hitler's persecution far surpassed that which the Jews experienced in any other Gentile country. The Arabs resisted the Jews' migration and with the help of the British did everything they could to keep God's people from entering the Promised Land.

> To keep peace with the Arabs who controlled the areas' vast oil reserves, in 1939 London decided to issue a white paper that strictly limited Jewish immigration.
>
> 15,000 people a year for five years, then no more. For Jews trying to escape the Reich, the door to Palestine was now virtually shut.

Christian, for a moment, consider the utter wickedness and greed of the Gentile nations. Outside of tiny Canaan, the Gentile nations of the world (that is, all non-Jewish nations) count as their property every inch of land on earth. During the Babel incident in Genesis 11:8, God scattered the people to the four corners of the earth. God also divided up the world among the nations. Each Gentile nation was given a particular portion of land and a supervising (guardian) angel. Israel was not included in this division of land nor did God give Israel a supervising angel. Israel was God's personal possession. The land that Israel was destined to inherit and take possession of was temporarily inhabited by the Canaanites.

It is interesting to note that in Genesis 9:24-26, Noah cursed the Canaanites (the descendants of Ham). Noah predicted that the Canaanites would become the servants of Shem's descendants. This curse was evidenced when the Canaanites did indeed become slaves to Israel (Shem's descendants) in Joshua 9:1-27. You will recall that God drove the Canaanites from the land of Canaan because of their wickedness and refusal to repent. God was able to disinherit the

Canaanites and drive them off the land since He never swore by a solemn oath that the nations would live forever on the land that He had allotted to them. However, God did swear by a solemn oath that the land of Canaan would belong to the Israelites forever.

> *Deuteronomy 32:8-9 (Living Bible.)*
>
> [8] *When God divided up the world among the nations, He gave each of them a supervising angel!*
> [9] *But He appointed none for Israel; for Israel was God's own personal possession!*

It is appalling that though the Gentile nations possess all the land on earth except Israel, they cannot stand for God's beloved covenant people to enjoy their tiny covenant possession. The nations will not allow the Jews to live in peace on their own God-given land. As you saw in an earlier quote, in 1939 the nations forcibly kept the Jews from entering the Promised Land. The emotional pain that the Jews must have experienced upon being denied entry into their own land is unimaginable.

Fleeing Jews were also denied entrance to other countries. So, while they were forcibly kept from returning to their own God-given land, they were at the same time refused entry to most of the other countries of the world. They were not only displaced people with nowhere to go, but they were a people for whom no country cared, a people to whom no country extended mercy or compassion.

An example of the unmerciful attitudes, the harsh treatment and the overwhelming rejection exhibited toward the Jewish people by **all** the Gentile nations of the world can be seen in yet another video cassette documentary entitled, *The Doomed Voyage of the St. Louis.*

This documentary informs the viewer that in 1938, innocent German Jews were attacked by Hitler's storm troopers. Their homes and businesses were vandalized, destroyed and burned. Jews were beaten and arrested. Jewish children were openly persecuted, degraded and ostracized. The Jews suffered all this when their only crime was that of being born Jewish.

Before Hitler began his carefully planned genocide campaign, the Jews were pressured to leave Germany. Some Jews were given actual time limits. However, since the United States of America had already refused to give refuge to **20,000 Jewish children** and President Roosevelt had sat silent during the Senate debate on that issue, in what corner of the world could those thousands of Jews still trapped in Germany have hoped to find asylum?

In the spring of 1939, stripped of all their possessions and fiscal wealth except for their passage tickets, two weeks' clothing, a tiny amount of currency and a passport stamped with a red "J," 930 Jewish refugees boarded the Hamburg-America liner, M.S. *St. Louis*. The liner was bound for Cuba, a country where many of the passengers already had family members. To escape the terrors that Germany held for them, the Jews were willing to go anywhere. They were even willing to go to Latin America or China. Like so many other Jews fleeing Germany, the passengers of the *St. Louis* could not wait around in order to follow normal immigration procedures. They knew that their departure had to be speedy. For, if they did not make a quick exit from Germany, they might not be alive when permission to enter other countries finally came. Considering America's deadly immigration policy, "postpone and postpone and postpone the granting of visas," the Jews' decision to exit Germany as fast as they could made perfect sense.

Thank God that these 930 Jewish passengers were treated well by the honorable German captain of the *St. Louis*. However, upon arriving at their destination, the Jews found that the Cuban authorities were not so kind or honorable. The Cubans refused to allow the Jewish passengers of the *St. Louis* to disembark. The Jews' relatives (that is, their husbands, fathers, and so on) already in Cuba were denied access to their families on board the *St. Louis*. Children frantically called to their fathers. Husbands and wives shouted back and forth. However, they were not allowed to so much as touch each other. Then, after three weeks of waiting in the harbor and suffering this type of heartbreaking treatment, anti-Semitic forces won. Cuban authorities turned away 907 of those 930 Jewish refugees, leaving their grieving family members mourning on the shores of Cuba.

When the Jewish passengers of the *St. Louis* were informed that they would be returned to Germany, they were panic stricken. One man became so despondent that he chose suicide rather than face such a terrifying prospect.

A Jewish organization, the Joint Distribution Center (JDC) had offered the Cuban government the enormous sum of $250,000.00 for the release of the passengers. You must keep in mind that in 1939, $250,000.00 was a fortune. It was also all the money that the JDC organization had at that time. In return for the money, the JDC had asked that the Cuban government give asylum to the remaining 907 Jewish passengers. Cuba demanded $500.00 per passenger, an amount that the Cuban authorities knew the JDC did not have. So, with the good captain's help, the JDC continued to try to get one of the other Gentile countries to accept the Jewish refugees but without success.

When the captain sailed the *St. Louis* near the coast line of Florida, the expectations of God's beloved covenant people rose immensely. In making that detour, he of course had hopes that the USA would open her arms to these terrified Jewish refugees. But to her shame, America also turned her back on God's needy, broken people. America refused to accept the desperate, frightened passengers of the *St. Louis*.

Americans all over the country did not want to rescue these destitute, homeless Jewish refugees. One newspaper displayed a sketch of the Statue of Liberty. On the base of the statue was written the words, "Give me your tired, your poor. Send those, the homeless, tempest tossed to me...." However, on Liberty's torch arm hung a foreboding sign that read, "THOU SHALT NOT ENTER!" The majority of the American people had made it absolutely clear that they did not want to take them in. Oh yes, like all the other Gentile countries, America came up with all kinds of excuses. However, by their actions, or their failure to act, Americans said, "Jews, keep out! We do not want you," while all the time, they knew that those 907 Jews, including many children, would most likely be sent back to Germany and consequently to concentration camps and probable death.

President Roosevelt refused to intervene on behalf of those 907 Jewish refugees. By their actions, the American people had said, "Jews keep out," and Roosevelt was adamant about carrying out America's desire. He did not even show the good captain the courtesy of sending a reply to his request for asylum for his desperate passengers.

When the Jewish passengers were told that the American people had refused to give them asylum, panic gripped their hearts. They clung to each other in grief and terror. As the *St. Louis* pulled away from America's coastline on that awful day, any hope the passengers once had of finding a safe refuge in a Gentile country was dashed in pieces.

Fearing that in their now hopeless state some of His Jewish passengers might take their own lives, the captain set up a suicide watch. You see, the Jews reasoned that since America, the land of the free, had rejected them, no other nation would save them from Hitler's death camps. To the shame of all the nations, the Jewish refugees were proved right. For, as the nations of the world were systematically contacted by members of the JDC, one by one, they refused to give protection to the 907 Jews. Over and over again, God's people's cries for assistance went unheeded. No country wanted God's beloved, oppressed people. No country cared about them.

After being refused entry to America, the passengers of the *St. Louis* sailed to Canada, only to be denied refuge once again. The truth is, they never stood a chance of being admitted into Canada since anti-Semitism was rampant in high places in that country also. Yes, anti-Semitism was flourishing even in the office of Mackenzie King, the prime minister of Canada. According to the book *None Is Too Many* by Irving Abella and Harold Troper, page 36,

> The government, for its part, had successfully survived Evian and wished not to be bothered with the refugee issue again—not at the behest of Jewish members of Parliament or Jewish Leaders. Indeed, if the MP's had not succeeded in moderating government policy, they had unfortunately succeeded in convincing the government that distant refugees were a Jewish problem, not a national one. And Mackenzie King himself was beyond reach. As far as he was concerned, the admission of refugees perhaps posed a greater menace to Canada in 1938 than Hitler. If accepting Jewish refugees could threaten Canada's national cohesion, could there not be merit in Hitler's fears about Jews in Germany? "The truth is," King wrote, "Hitler and Mussolini, while dictators, have really sought to give the masses of the people, some opportunity for enjoyment, taste of art and the like and, in this way, have won them to their side"; and perhaps in a veiled reference to the Jews of Germany, King went on to say that "the dictatorship method may have been necessary to wrest this opportunity from the privileged interests that have previously monopolized it."

A week after the Evian fiasco, the prime minister gave an informal party at his summer residence, Kingsmere. Sitting on the porch after dinner, he chatted for over an hour with his guests, who included the secretary of the American legation in Ottawa. Among other things, King fondly recalled his meeting with Hitler in Germany a year earlier. As the American diplomat reported back to Washington, **"He described Hitler as being, in his opinion, a very sincere man. He even described him as being 'sweet.' He said that he [Hitler] had the face, as he studied it, of a good man,** although he was clearly a dreamer and gave the impression of having an artistic temperament. During the conversation Hitler had sat with his hands folded and his only gesture was to raise and lower his hands from time to time without unfolding them. He [King] intimated that he had asked Hitler some very frank questions and that he had been satisfied with Hitler's answers."

In September 1938, less than a year before Canada declared war on Germany, King was still mixed in his attitude to Hitler—sorrowful over Hitler's methods but understanding of his motives. **"He might come to be thought of as one of the saviors of the world,"** King wrote. "He had the chance at Nuremberg, but was looking to force, to might, and to violence as means to achieving his ends, which were, **I believe, at heart, the well being of his fellow-man; not all fellow-men, but those of his own race."**

Another obstacle standing in the way of any, would-be, Jewish immigrants entering Canada was the vocally anti-Semitic Frederick Charles Blair. In 1936 Blair was promoted to director of the Immigration Branch with full deputy-minister status. From page 8 of the previous source I quote:

> **For Blair the term "refugee" was a code word for Jew. Unless "safeguards" were adopted, he warned Thomas Crerar, Canada was in danger of being "flooded with Jewish people," and his task, as he saw it, was to make sure that the "safeguards" did not fail. Indeed, he was inordinately proud of his success in keeping out Jews.** "Pressure on the part of Jewish people to get into Canada," he wrote, "has never been greater than it is now, and I am glad to be able to add, after 35 years experience here, that it was never so well controlled." **Blair expressed a strong personal distaste for Jews, especially for "certain of their habits."** He saw them as unassimilable, as people apart, as threatening people "who can organize their affairs better than other people" and so accomplish more. He complained bitterly that Jews were "utterly selfish in their attempts to force through a permit for the admission of relatives or friends." "They do not believe that 'No' means more than 'perhaps'." And Jews, he lamented, "make any kind of promise to get the door open but...never cease their agitation until they get in the whole lot." **Blair saw a conspiracy behind all Jewish attempts to get their co-religionists into the country....**

The authors of the book *None Is Too Many*, a book which I hope you will acquire and read, bring out numerous examples of Blair's anti-Semitism. On page 9 of that same revealing source we read:

Blair was of course an anti-Semite. His contempt for the Jews was boundless. In a revealing letter to a strong opponent of Jewish immigration, Blair elaborated on the reasons for his prejudice:

I suggested recently to three Jewish gentlemen with whom I am well acquainted, that it might be a very good thing if they would call a conference and have a day of humiliation and prayer, which might profitably be extended for a week or more, where they would honestly try to answer the question of why they are so unpopular almost everywhere....I often think that instead of persecution it would be far better if we more often told them frankly why many of them are unpopular. **If they would divest themselves of certain of their habits I am sure they could be just as popular in Canada as our Scandinavians....**Just because Jewish people would not understand the frank kind of statements I have made in this letter to you, I have marked it confidential.

But, though it was Blair who finally interpreted government regulations and who acted as the de facto judge and jury on individual requests for admission, to blame him alone for Canada's response to Jewish immigration would be both overly simplistic and incorrect; after all, he was, although powerful, only a civil servant whose actions reflected the wishes and values of his superiors. Not to accept refugees was a political decision, not a bureaucratic one. **It was Mackenzie King, Liberal prime minister throughout most of the 1920s**

604

and again after 1935, and his cabinet ministers who, in the final analysis, were responsible for keeping Jews out of Canada.

The preface of the literary work *None Is Too Many* sums up this tragedy and Canada's mistreatment of God's precious covenant people, the Jews. The last part of the preface reads:

> To the condemned Jews of Auschwitz, Canada had a special meaning. It was the name given to the camp barracks where the food, clothes, gold, diamonds, jewelry and other goods taken from prisoners were stored. It represented life, luxury and salvation; it was a Garden of Eden in Hell; it was also unreachable.
>
> In effect, the barracks at Auschwitz symbolized what Canada was to all the Jews of Europe throughout the 1930s and 1940s—a paradise, enormous, wealthy, overflowing and full of life; but out of bounds, a haven totally unaccessible. Why Canada was closed to the Jews of Europe is the subject of this book. It is a story summed up best in the words of an anonymous senior Canadian official who, in the midst of a rambling, off the record discussion with journalists in early 1945, was asked how many Jews would be allowed into Canada after the war. His response seems to reflect the prevailing view of a substantial number of his fellow citizens: "None," he said, "is too many."

Oh, if only King and Blair had known the truth! If only they had known that the Jews were so unpopular for God's name's sake! If only they had comprehended that the Jews were also suffering for the Gentiles' sake, including them! However, they neither understood nor cared. So, the Jewish passengers of the *St. Louis* were turned away from Jew-hating Canada.

Finally, in an effort to save the lives of these 907 Jewish refugees, the heroic captain of the *St. Louis* sailed near the coast of England with the intention of setting his ship on fire if the British people again refused asylum to the 907 Jewish passengers. He hoped that such an act would force the English to rescue the weary passengers of the *St. Louis*. The captain did not, however, have to resort to such severe measures. The JDC finally managed to persuade Britain, Belgium, Holland and France to give asylum to his Jewish passengers.

On June 17, 1939, the *St. Louis* docked in Belgium. The refugees' horrific forty days and forty nights had ended. As part of the agreement, the Jews were split up between the four countries that had been persuaded to give them refuge. However, because the Americans had refused asylum to these 907 Jews, most of them eventually suffered the very fate that they had so feared when they had begged the Americans to give them refuge. When Hitler's armies conquered Belgium, Holland and France, those Jewish refugees, along with the rest of the Jewish people, were rounded up by the Nazis and sent to interment and concentration camps. In those death camps, 600 of the 907 *St. Louis* Jewish passengers perished. The only *St. Louis* Jewry who survived the Holocaust, were those Jews who had been allotted to England.

It should be noted that before America abandoned the down trodden passengers of the *St. Louis* to their eventual tragic fate, numerous polls had been taken. Those polls showed that though the majority of Americans did not approve of Hitler's treatment of the Jews, they themselves did not want to be responsible for their welfare. They did not want those Jewish people to enter America. Thus, the Americans totally rejected the idea of giving asylum to those 907 Jewish refugees. Yes, like the rest of the Gentile world, the Americans refused to show mercy or compassion to God's beloved Abrahamic covenant people.

(1943-1945) In the video cassette documentary, *America and the Holocaust, Deceit and Indifference,* the historian, David Wayne tells viewers that since the U. S. State Department was blocking data pertaining to the systematic genocide of the Jews, and Roosevelt refused to help, and the majority of churches refused to speak out on behalf of God's helpless covenant people, and the newspapers buried what little they did print on that issue on the inner pages, Jewish activists became the only avenue left to bring such information to the attention of the American public. One of these Jewish activists was a man named Peter Bergson.

Bergson set out to make the public aware of what was transpiring in Germany. He managed to cause the newspapers to print such items on the front pages rather than hide them on the back pages. The Bergson group did this through advertisements. Bergson also solicited the aid of a U. S. Congressman (D-Ga.) Will Rogers, Jr. Congressman Rogers agreed to aid the Bergson group in their efforts to promote public awareness. It seems that Peter Bergson was a genius in the area of publicity. Thus, when the American press account stated that Romania might release 70,000 captive Jews, a member of the Bergson group, a Broadway playwright named Ben Hecht, put together a full page ad stating: "FOR SALE TO HUMANITY 70,000 JEWS GUARANTEED HUMAN BEINGS AT $50 APIECE."

I could go on and on, revealing one horrible anti-Semitic situation after another, but I think I have made the point that America was responsible for much of the misery and abuse that the Jews suffered before, and during World War II. To acquire these facts in detail, you should view both the video documentary *America and the Holocaust, Deceit and Indifference* and *The Doomed Voyage of the St. Louis.* I guarantee that if you do, your eyes will be opened in regard to America's persecution and neglect of God's precious covenant people.

(1947) On July 6, 1997 on the Public Broadcasting Station, Morley Safer narrated the documentary entitled *Exodus 1947.* This informative program chronicled the 1947 voyage to Palestine of a steamer, the *Exodus,* and its human cargo of 4,500 Holocaust survivors. The Jewish community across America had sent money to buy and to fix up the old steamer in order that it might carry those 4,500 Holocaust survivors to the Land of Promise.

The war was over, but British occupation of Palestine still existed, and a quota of Jewish immigrants to Palestine was strictly enforced. Any Jews who landed in the Promised Land illegally were arrested, deported and placed in camps in Cyprus.

From the beginning of the old steamer's voyage, the British did everything they could to try to stop these broken Holocaust victims from going home. For example, the small crew of the restored steamer consisted of brave American Jews who had very little sea experience. So, the British attempted to have their papers denied. When their attempts to sabotage the voyage failed, a British man-of-war trailed every move that the restored frail wreck of a steamer and her frightened passengers made. The British wickedly planned to board the steamer as soon as she entered the waters of Palestine, arrest the Holocaust survivors and ship them to camps in Cyprus.

Hoisting the name of their ship, "*Exodus*," and the Star of David, the shaky steamer tried to outrun the six British war ships that followed in her wake. The crew's strategy was to crash the steamer on the shores of Tel Aviv and have the Holocaust survivors disembark and run to safety. However, before the Jews could carry out their plan, the British rammed the *Exodus* and rushed on board the unarmed vessel with guns and tear gas. The crew and the terrified Holocaust survivors fought back with cans of corned beef. One unarmed Jew was shot to death in the face. He died holding a can of corned beef in his hand. Tear gassed, clubbed and shot, with 140 injured and 3 dead, the Holocaust survivors finally surrendered. God's beloved people were allowed only a glimpse of the Promised Land through tear-filled eyes. Their rickety ship was then turned away by those for whom they unknowingly suffered all these inhumane injustices, the Gentiles. For unbeknown to these Jews and the Gentiles who persecuted them, they were suffering so that the Gentiles might have an opportunity to be saved.

Not many months after the 1947 *Exodus* incident ended, the UN partitioned Israel. Since you are already aware of the United Nations act of dividing the Holy Land and of the Arabs' deadly persecution of the Israelites, I am not going to take time to repeat information that we have already covered. Rather, I will insert vital information that is not so widely known.

In his book *Jewish Literacy* under the heading "Expulsion of Jews from England, 1290," Rabbi Joseph Telushkin provides a list of the countries that throughout history banished the Jews from their land.

> Jews have been expelled at one time or another from almost every European society in which they have lived.

The following list identifies some of those countries that persecuted and eventually expelled God's beloved people. It also gives the approximate dates when those expulsions took place.

England	1290
France	1306 and 1394
Hungary	1349-1360
Austria	1421
Germany	14th-16th centuries
Lithuania	1445 and 1495

Spain	1492
Portugal	1497
Bohemia	1744-1745
Moravia	1744-1745

Between the fifteenth century and 1772, Jews were not permitted in Russia: when they were finally admitted, they were restricted to an area known as the Pale of Settlement. Between 1948 and 1967, almost all the Jews of Aden, Algeria, Egypt, Iraq, Syria, and Yemen, though not officially expelled, fled these countries, fearing for their lives.

It would take volumes of books to relay to you all the historical documentation of thousands of years of cruelty, abuse and blood shed that the nations have perpetrated upon the covenant descendants of Abraham, Isaac and Jacob. God's beloved people were often purposely portrayed in such a bad light as to make men feel almost obligated to despise them. And, to the Church's shame, professing Christians were often the ones most responsible for such devious portrayals.

Take for instance the famous Christian poet and playwright, Shakespeare. He wickedly depicted the Jews as despicable people in his work, *The Merchant of Venice*. Through this play, Shakespeare sent an anti-Semitic message throughout the whole world that is so compelling that even today there are men and women who hate the Jews because of it.

Whenever I think of Shakespeare, I am reminded of a particular letter I received from a Christian school teacher who lives in Kenya, East Africa. This Kenyan woman shared with me that when she attended public school and the university, Shakespeare's works were required reading. She told how Shakespeare's writings had greatly influenced her life. Through them she came to vehemently hate the Jews. Sadly, at that time, she had never even met a Jewish person. Yet, she had been deceived into despising all God's beloved covenant people. She perceived all Jews to actually be the despicable villains that Shakespeare portrays in his work.

When she received the tape series, *Why Should Every Christian Pray For And Support Israel?* by Norma Duncan, her eyes were opened. She knew that Shakespeare had deceived her. Immediately the woman fell on her knees and sincerely repented. After she received forgiveness from the Lord, she ran to her neighbors to share with them the good news concerning the Jews, good news that she had found through the teachings of God's Word in this tape series. I am happy to say that this woman and many others in her community now love and consistently pray for the Jews and the nation of Israel as a whole.

The works of Shakespeare are acclaimed worldwide. His supposed birthplace, Stratford-upon-Avon, England, is an absolute shrine to the memory of this man. Men flock to a church building in Stratford. There they stand or sit, gazing at a bust of Shakespeare, adoring the man whom they proclaim to be a literary genius.

Yet, I tell you that Shakespeare's work is indeed the work of a genius. It was inspired by that evil genius himself, Satan. For, only Satan could have been behind literature that promotes such hatred of God's beloved people, literature that feeds the prejudices of its audience, literature that has for centuries interfered with the vindication of God's holy name, literature that brings down God's curse upon all those who practice its evil persuasions.

If you think that I might have misunderstood Shakespeare's intentions, let me assure you that I have not. To give you documented evidence that what I have shared with you is true, I will share with you a portion of an article that confirms all that I have previously stated regarding the object of such a play. The following quote is taken from *The Illustrated World Encyclopedia* Library of the Literary Treasures under the title "The Merchant of Venice."

> This is one of Shakespeare's most popular comedies. The main plot was apparently intended to be the one based on traditional oriental stories in which the hero must solve a riddle to win the fair lady. **After starting to write a play on this theme, Shakespeare apparently found that the story of Shylock and the pound of flesh was far more suited to his genius and he made it the main theme.** *The Merchant of Venice* **has been criticized and there have been many**

> **suggestions that it be omitted from school reading and from performance because the villain Shylock is a Jew, but in Shakespeare's times Jews and the entire Jewish people were customarily cast as villains....He fashioned the ending to suit his audiences' prejudice....**

In his book *The Meaning of Shakespeare*, the author, Harold C. Goddard, lends even more insight into the evil anti-Semitic character of Shakespeare.

> The anti-Semitism of the twentieth century lends a fresh interest to *The Merchant of Venice*. It raises anew the question: How could one of the most tolerant spirits of all time have written a play that is centered around, and seems to many to accept, one of the most degraded prejudices of the ages? "About 1594," says a recent critic of high standing, "public sentiment in England was roused to an outbreak of traditional Jew baiting; and for good and evil, Shakespeare the man was like his fellows. **He planned a *Merchant of Venice* to let the Jew dog have it, and thereby to gratify his own patriotic pride of race**.
>
> "The Bond Story," says another contemporary commentator, "has an anti-Semitic edge, and in recent years many secondary schools have wisely removed the play from the curriculum...Shakespeare simply accepts the Jews as a notoriously bad lot...I do not see how a Jew can read *The Merchant of Venice* without pain and indignation." And others express themselves to the same effect.
>
> But few who vindicate Shakespeare do so in a bold or ringing tone. They are

timid, or qualified, or even apologetic. The thought of how the Elizabethan crowd at any rate must have taken Shylock makes them shudder. And beyond doubt, whatever the poet intended, most of his audience must have made the Jew an object of ridicule or contempt, or both. Is there danger that modern schoolboys will do the same?

The author of *Jewish Literacy*, Rabbi Joseph Telushkin, reveals more information on the present topic under the heading "Shylock."

One of the ugliest characters created by William Shakespeare (1564-1616) is Shylock, a Jewish moneylender who insists that a non-Jew, Antonio, repay his overdue loan in a pound of flesh drawn from near the heart. The sadistic Shylock is ultimately thwarted by a legal trick, but the damage inflicted on the Jews by *The Merchant of Venice* has been far greater than a pound of flesh. the image of Jews as a nation of moneylending Shylocks has persisted throughout the Middle Ages into the modern world. To this day, the illegal industry of high-interest loans is known as "Shylocking."

More remarkably, the odious Shylock was created out of thin air. Shakespeare had never met or seen a Jew in his life, since the Jews had been expelled from England in 1290, more than 350 years before his birth, and not readmitted until 1656, forty years after his death.

This play is certainly not the only instance of Jews being vilified in a society in which they no longer lived. A century after their expulsion, Chaucer depicted Jews as ritual murderers of young Christian children in *The*

Canterbury Tales. Even after the Jews were re-admitted to England, their image did not undergo a permanent improvement. In the nineteenth century, Charles Dickens fashioned yet another stereotypical Jewish villain, Fagin, who made his living training young boys to become pickpockets.

The previous authors, Shakespeare, Chaucer and Dickens are greatly celebrated in this world. But I tell you, I would not want to be in their shoes when they stand before God on Judgment Day and have to give account for what they have done to God's name and God's beloved people, the Jews.

I am sure that by now you are probably wondering what could possibly have caused Shakespeare, Chaucer and Dickens to display such deep disgust and hatred for the Jewish people. As a Christian myself, I am ashamed to say that these authors acquired their deplorable anti-Semitic attitudes and behavior from, of all places, the Christian Church. The truth is that the Church has been one of the Jews' staunchest persecutors, especially the Roman Catholic Church. The Catholic Church is responsible for perpetrating the worst of this abuse. The following information substantiates my statement.

After the destruction of the Jewish homeland by the Romans in AD 70, the Jews were dispersed throughout the earth. They became a people without a country. And though they posed no threat to any foreign government, the nations afflicted them beyond measure and certainly far more than God had ever intended.

As you saw earlier in this series, the nations' mistreatment of God's chosen people continued generation after generation. The Jews have been expelled from country after country. They have been lied about, humiliated, robbed, imprisoned, separated from their families, mutilated, murdered, shut away in concentration camps, starved, tortured, branded, gassed and their bodies burned in incinerators. And, as a Christian myself, I am horrified to admit that the Church is responsible for much of the previous abuse.

Most people mistakenly believe that the Nazis invented the distinguishing identity badges that the Jews were forced to wear during World War II. However, in the Middle Ages, the Roman Catholic

Church actually invented that evil system of Jewish identification. *The Catholic Encyclopedia* Volume VIII, 1910 Edition, Page 393 under the heading, "Jew," and subheading, "(8) Era of the crusades (1038-1300)," bears out that fact. Read the truth with your own eyes, and see also how the Church refuses to take responsibility for her actions. Rather than admit her sin, the Church continues to justify her evil deeds.

> The year 1204, in which closed the Fourth Crusade, marked the beginning of still heavier misfortunes for the Jews. That very year witnessed the death of Maimonides, the greatest Jewish authority of the twelfth century, and the first of the many efforts of Innocent III to prevent Christian princes from showing favor to their Jewish subjects. Soon afterwards, the Jews of southern France suffered grievously during the war against the Albigenses which ended only in 1228. In 1210, those of England were ill-treated by King John Lackland and their wealth confiscated to the Exchequer. Next, the Jews of Toledo were put to death by crusaders (1212). The conciliar legislation of the time was generally unfavourable to the Jews, and it culminated in the anti-Jewish measures of the Fourth Council of the Lateran (1215), among which may be mentioned the exclusion of Jews from all public offices, **and the decree that they should wear a Jew badge**.

From the same article under subheading, "(3) Judaism since A.D.70," I quote:

> **The obligation of wearing a distinguishing badge was of course obnoxious to the Jews. At the same time, Church authorities deemed its injunction necessary** to prevent effectively moral offences between Jews and Christian women.

Oh, the cruelty and humiliation! Oh, the persecution! Oh, the pain! The anti-Semitic Roman Catholic Church made God's beloved people, the Jews, a public exhibition and then pretended to be guiltless of promoting Christendom's hatred and abuse of God's covenant people. The Church publicly singled out innocent, spiritually blind and deaf Jewish men and women in order to make public spectacles of them. Then, the Church continually knocked about their stumbling, spiritually handicapped victims. Yes, the Church did these things to the very people, the Jews, whom God had kept blind and deaf for His own name's sake and for the Gentiles' sake.

Are you also aware that it was the Church and not the Nazis that created the ghetto system? Yes, the Church was the first to force the covenant descendants of Abraham, Isaac and Jacob into ghettos. The author of the previously mentioned source, *Jewish Literacy,* under the heading "Ghetto" informs us of this truth.

> **In Italy, where the institution originated, the ghettos were under the rule of the popes.** The virulently antiSemitic Pope Paul IV formalized the institution in a papal bull, *Cum nimis absurdum* (1555), in which **he argued that it was absurd for Christians to act lovingly to the very people who had been condemned by God for their sins. He therefore legislated that Jews residing in areas under papal rule be segregated into ghettos.** Although Jews would be permitted to leave the ghetto to go to work, they would be forbidden to be outside it at night. The ghetto gates were to be closed each evening and on Christian holidays as well. Each ghetto was to be allowed but one synagogue. **The Jews were to wear a distinctive yellow hat when they were outside the ghetto, so that Christians could immediately recognize them.** Subsequent to Paul IV's bull, ghettos spread very quickly throughout Italy, and from there to the rest of Europe. In some areas, government authorities purposely

situated brothels inside the ghetto or
alongside it.

Do you see the type of devilish acts that transpire when Christians do not have a correct understanding of the Scriptures? Do you see what happens when uninformed Christians depend on wicked, ignorant church leaders to spiritually guide them? As Yeshua said, they both fall into the ditch. God's Word proclaims that God loves the Jews with an everlasting love. Ignorant men, such as Pope Paul IV, misinterpret and misrepresent God's Word, insisting that the Church should not love them. Oh, if only that wicked Pope had realized that his very words and actions placed his own life under the curse of God Almighty. For God said, He would *"...curse him who curses or uses insolent language toward you...."* (Genesis 12:3.)

Throughout history, mob violence against the Jews has been a common occurrence. Ignorant, wicked Christians have verbally abused God's beloved, Abrahamic covenant people. Christians have shouted at the Jews such accusations and slurs as "Christ killer" and "swine." Instead of thanking them and blessing them for being the race through whom God brought salvation to the world, the Church blamed the Jews for Christ's death. Instead of showing the Jews mercy and gratitude for suffering for God's name and for the Gentiles' sake, the Church wrongly condemned and hated them.

The Church's hatred toward the Jews has not diminished with time. For example, to this day the people of Spain actually display their hatred of the Jews during a yearly fiesta.

You may have viewed the NBC November 17, 1996 news special "Dateline." If you did, you heard the heart-rending account of the English woman, Vicki Moore, in her crusade to save Spain's horribly abused animals. You also learned about the incident that triggered the whole crusade.

Vicki told how she had read a short article in a newspaper regarding a little donkey that would be purposely crushed to death during a fiesta in Spain. After reading that article, Vicki decided that she would single-handedly confront the people of Nuevo Laredo, Spain and try to rescue that little donkey.

I am ashamed to say that to the Spanish people who, as you know are predominantly Catholic, **that little, helpless soon to be crushed donkey represented the town Jew from medieval times**. Therefore, whatever abuse was perpetrated upon that pathetic creature was really intended for the Jewish people whom the Spaniards obviously still hate to this day. According to "Dateline," the donkey (representing the town Jew) is chased by the townspeople through the streets of Nuevo Laredo. During this cruel and insane chase, every kind of verbal, physical and emotional abuse is heaped upon the frightened, innocent victim. Sometimes the poor little animal collapses under the sheer weight of the screaming, angry mob.

Vicki Moore was right to show concern for that one little donkey, but God is concerned to the point of heartbreak for His beloved people whom that abused donkey only represented. For, it is obvious to all that the hatred which provoked Spain's expulsion of the Jewish people in 1492, hatred which caused the deaths of tens of thousands of those Jews who attempted to escape, has not diminished at all. Rather, Spain's despicable, wicked hatred of God's beloved people is refurbished and blatantly proclaimed and relished each year during the public abuse and sometimes murder of a frightened, helpless little donkey.

Christians need to take time and consider all the Biblical facts. They need to remember that when the Jews sinned in the wilderness, God did not punish future generations of Israelites for their father's sins. Instead, it was the children of those who had sinned who took possession of the Promised Land and experienced God's promised blessings. Again, when, because of their sins, God sent the Jews into captivity in Babylon, He did not punish future generations for their father's sins. No! Seventy years later, God delivered His beloved people from Babylon, and for His name's sake and for the sake of His everlasting covenant love, He brought them back to their own land.

Since God provides so many examples of His covenant mercy and loving-kindness toward His people, why has the Church not followed His example? I will tell you why the Church has failed to follow God's example. It is because Satan has deceived the Church. He has deceived the Church in an attempt to defeat God's purpose and keep God from clearing His holy name.

If any one nation of people is going to be blamed and persecuted for the mistreatment Christ received and for the cruel way in which He died, by rights, such blame and punishment belongs to Rome. It is true that in their God-ordained, spiritually blind and deaf state, Israel's religious leaders did hand Yeshua over to the Romans, but it was the Romans who physically, verbally and emotionally abused Him. It was the Romans who put Him to death. Furthermore, in their God-ordained, spiritually blind and deaf state, the Jews truly felt that Yeshua deserved to die. But not so with the Romans. The Romans knew that they were murdering an innocent man. Pilate actually stated, *"I find no fault in this man."* (Luke 23:4, *King James Version.*)

The Jews were forbidden under Roman law to put people to death. So, it would not have been possible for them to have executed Yeshua. Moreover, the Roman procurator of Judea, Pontius Pilate, could have refused to scourge and crucify Yeshua. He possessed the necessary power to spare Yeshua's life. For personal, political reasons, Pilate consciously chose to crucify Him. Yet, despite all these facts, we Christians do not relentlessly pursue the citizens of Rome in order to persecute them for what their ancestors did. No! We do not pursue in order to persecute them because we know that the Romans were simply unknowing vessels carrying out God's purpose for all mankind. However, since the Jews were spiritually blind and deaf vessels who were also carrying out their God-ordained mission and God's purpose for all mankind, why in the world does the Church insist on blaming and persecuting them?

Open your eyes, Church, so that you might comprehend what the Holy Spirit is relaying to you. Understand that throughout the years the devil has used the Church to carry out his evil scheme to try to keep God from fulfilling His Word. He has used the Church to try to prevent God from keeping His covenant with Abraham, Isaac and Jacob and His vow to Jerusalem.

Throughout the ages, foolish, misguided, deceived church leaders and their followers believed they were doing God a favor by abusing and murdering the Jews. Little did they know that they were actually mistreating the apple of God's eye. They were mistreating the race of people whom God loves with an everlasting (fixed, unchanging, firmly loyal or constant) love. And by their sinful actions, they grieved the heart of God. Little did they know that they were afflicting and oppressing the only race of people on the face of the earth through whom God can vindicate His name. What a mess!

Oh, the shame of it! To think that the Nazis later patterned their abuse of the Jews after the Church's mistreatment of them. Yet, despite the fact that this truth is well documented, most Christians today refuse to acknowledge the Church's past sins and confess them. They refuse to repent (that is, they refuse to think differently; change their mind, regretting their sins and changing their conduct).

The biased leaders of the Roman Catholic Church so ingrained anti-Semitism into the character of the Church that it overflowed into Protestantism like polluted, poisonous water pouring from a foul smelling, stagnant pond. An example of one of the worst cases of the Protestant Church's anti-Semitism is vividly and horribly portrayed in the life of the reformist, Martin Luther.

For generations Luther, the founder of the Lutheran Church, has been lifted up by Protestants as a brave and righteous man of God. He is considered a hero in most Protestant circles. Until I learned the truth about his appalling anti-Semitism, he was also one of my heroes. But not anymore. Now I look upon the anti-Semitic Protestant, Luther, in the same way that I look upon the unrepentant, anti-Semitic Roman Catholic Church that produced him. I look upon Martin Luther with shame, embarrassment and horror.

Luther did not however start out persecuting the Jews. When he broke away from the Catholic Church, he had high hopes of converting the Jews to Christianity and therefore treated them quite well. But when after twenty-five years he did not succeed in persuading the Jewish people to become Christians, he was furious. Like the Catholic Church that he had left, Luther did not comprehend the Biblical truth that the Jews are genuinely unable to recognize Yeshua as the Messiah or understand His teachings. He did not know that God had planned it that way partly for the Gentiles' sake, including himself. He took the Jews' refusal to convert to Christianity as a personal insult. He acted like a spoiled child who could not have his own way.

If you are a true Christian who really loves God, then the contents of the next quote will break your heart as it did mine. While writing this book, I have been so stricken with grief over the Church's past and present mistreatment of the Jews that I have not slept well. I have stayed awake weeping and repenting for the past and present sins of the whole Church. Read now the following segment taken from the source, *Jewish Literacy*, under the heading "Martin Luther and the Protestant Reformation."

> Yet, less than twenty five years later, this same man was to pen the most antiSemitic writings produced in Germany until the time of Hitler. Incensed that the Jews had not followed his brand of Christianity, **Luther outlined eight actions to be taken against them:**

Burn all synagogues.

Destroy all Jewish homes.

Confiscate all Jewish books.

Forbid Rabbis to teach, on pain of death.

Forbid Jews to travel.

Confiscate Jewish property.

Force Jews to do physical labor.

[And, in case the preceding restrictions proved insufficient] Expel all the Jews.

On one occasion, this earlier opponent of Christian love said: "I would threaten to cut their tongues out from their throats, if they refuse to acknowledge the truth that God is a Trinity and not a plain unity."

Unfortunately, these antiSemitic ravings were not peripheral jottings of Luther's; instead, they became well known throughout Germany. **Four hundred years later, Hitler proudly claimed Luther as an "ally:" [Speaking of Martin Luther, Hitler said], "He saw the Jew as we are only beginning to see him today." When the Nazis carried out the infamous Kristallnacht pogrom on November 9-10, 1938, they announced that the action was taken in honor of Luther's birthday (November 10).** <u>**At the Nuremburg trials, Nazi propagandist Julius Streicher defended himself with the claim that he had not said anything worse about the Jews than had Martin Luther.**</u>

Christian, if the previous documented information does not send you to your knees to intercede for the sins of the Church as Daniel interceded for the sins of Israel, then I do not know what will. The Roman Catholic Church and the Protestant, Luther, and his followers were absolutely wrong. They were wrong to persecute God's beloved people, and they were wrong to attempt to force Jews to convert to Christianity.

Why was the Roman Catholic Church and Martin Luther, the founder of the Protestant movement in Germany, wrong to force Jews to convert? They were wrong because, as you learned earlier, God purposely left the majority of the Jews in spiritual blindness and deafness and therefore unable to recognize the Messiah or understand His teachings for the sake of His own name and for the sake of the Gentile nations. God has kept them spiritually handicapped in order to give us Gentiles an opportunity to be saved. Furthermore, it is God's will that most of the Jews remain spiritually blind and deaf until His purpose is fully accomplished regarding the salvation of the Gentiles.

The truth is that the Gentiles are the ones who are actually holding up the spiritual healing of the Jews, not the Jews themselves. The apostle Paul makes that fact extremely clear in the following verses.

> *Romans 11:25-26 (The Amplified Bible.)*
>
> *25Lest you be self-opinionated (wise in your own conceits), I do not want you to miss this hidden truth and mystery, brethren: __a hardening (insensibility) has [temporarily] befallen a part of Israel [to last] until the full number of the ingathering of the Gentiles has come in,__*
>
> *26And so all Israel will be saved. As it is written, The Deliverer will come from Zion, He will banish ungodliness from Jacob.*

In verse twenty-five, Paul is informing you that the Jews' spiritual eyesight and hearing will not be healed until the full number of the ingathering of the Gentiles has been completed. The point is, we Gentiles are the ones responsible for prolonging the Jews' God-ordained, spiritually blind and deaf state. We are prolonging this period because only a few Gentiles will obey God's commands after making a verbal commitment to serve Christ.

As Paul told you in Romans 11:21-22, a text which you studied earlier in the series, the disobedient shoots (that is, disobedient Christian Gentiles) are being cut off continually. Thus, until the number (the quota) is filled, Israel will continue to wait in her spiritually blind and deaf state. She will wait for her turn to be grafted back into her own olive tree. Then as you saw in verse twenty-six, *"**And so all Israel will be saved**. As it is written, The Deliverer will come from Zion, He will banish ungodliness from Jacob."*

Oh, the wickedness! Oh, the nerve! How could the Church have acted so disgracefully? The Jews' suffering and their spiritual blindness and deafness has been prolonged for us. Yet we, the Church, have returned evil for good. We have abused, persecuted, robbed, expelled, tortured and even murdered God's beloved chosen people. We are guilty of biting the hand that feeds us. We are guilty of horrendous sin against God and His covenant people.

God is extremely angry with the Gentile nations, including Gentile Christians who have mistreated and in many cases still do mistreat His beloved people, the Jews. And, God's anger is absolutely justified. Furthermore, the nations, including the unrepentant Church, will not get away with this wickedness. Like those nations in Zachariah's day, so shall God punish all who have done and who are doing harm to Israel.

Zechariah 1:12-21 (The Amplified Bible.)

12 Then the Angel of the Lord said, O Lord of hosts, how long will You not have mercy and lovingkindness for Jerusalem and the cities of Judah, against which You have had indignation these seventy years [of the Babylonian captivity]?

13 And the Lord answered the angel who talked with me with gracious and comforting words.

*14 So the angel who talked with me said to me, Cry out, Thus says the Lord of hosts: **I am jealous for Jerusalem and for Zion with a great jealousy.***

*15 **And I am very angry with the nations that are at ease; for while I was but a little displeased, they helped forward the affliction and disaster.***

Look now at the remaining verses of this text, and see the punishment that awaits all the peoples of the world who mistreat Israel, professing Christians and non-Christians alike. And as you contemplate God's future punishment, I urge you to repent of any wrong doing that you yourself may be guilty of in this area. Furthermore, I implore you to purpose in your heart that from this day forward, you will do all you can to encourage your church fellowship and your country to support Israel.

> *18Then I lifted up my eyes and saw, and behold, four horns [symbols of strength].*
>
> *19And I said to the angel who talked with me, What are these? And he answered me, These are the horns or powers which have scattered Judah, Israel, and Jerusalem.*
>
> *20Then the Lord showed me four smiths or workmen [one for each enemy horn, <u>to beat it down].</u>*
>
> *21Then said I, What are these [horns and smiths] coming to do? And he said, These are the horns or powers that scattered Judah so that no man lifted up his head. <u>But these smiths or workmen have come to terrorize them and cause them to be panic-stricken, to cast out the horns or powers of the nations who lifted up their horn against the land of Judah to scatter it.</u>*

Be warned you leaders and rulers of nations. Keep your hands off Israel! God's Word makes it clear that for you to harm Israel is comparable to sticking your finger in God's own eye. See this truth for yourself in *The Living Bible.*

> *Zechariah 2:6-9 (The Living Bible.)*
>
> *6,7" 'Come, flee from the land of the north, from Babylon,' says the Lord to all his exiles there; 'I scattered you to the winds but I will bring you back again. Escape, escape to Zion now!' says the Lord.*
>
> *8<u>The Lord of Glory has sent me against the nations that oppressed you, for he who harms you sticks his finger in Jehovah's eye!</u>*

Can you imagine how it would feel if someone deliberately stuck his finger in your eye? Can you imagine the pain and personal insult of such an injury? It is beyond our comprehension to think that any people would dare to stick their finger in God's eye. But they do. Every time they hurt the Jews or turn on Israel, they are sticking their finger in God's eye. They are inflicting excruciating emotional pain, embarrassment and humiliation on God. The bottom line is that what men do to God's beloved Abrahamic covenant people, they do to God.

God will not, however, continue to put up with such abuse. Verse nine makes that fact crystal clear.

> *9" 'I will smash them with my fist and their slaves will be their rulers! Then you will know it was the Lord of Hosts who sent me.*

The end of those nations who harm Israel is written in the following verse.

Zechariah 12:9 (The Amplified Bible.)

> *9And it shall be in that day that I will make it My aim to destroy all the nations that come against Jerusalem.*

Do you see this, leaders of nations? Do you see this, Mr. President, Mr. Prime Minister, Mr. Premier? Do you see this, Your Majesty? Be warned and do not be found fighting on the wrong side. Do not be found fighting against the Lord God Almighty. God is warning you today. If you will only do what is right, you can protect yourself and the people over whom He has raised you up to rule. Read this Biblical prophecy again and be warned:

> *9And it shall be in that day that I will make it My aim to destroy all the nations that come against Jerusalem.*

Israel is God's inheritance. God loves her with an everlasting love. Therefore, woe be to those nations or their leaders who try to harm her. For what we do for or against Israel, we do for or against the Lord. The following verses taken from *The Living Bible* describe their end.

Deuteronomy 32:34-35 (The Living Bible.)

> *34But Israel is my special people, Sealed as jewels within my treasury.*
> *35Vengeance is mine And I decree the punishment of all her enemies: Their doom is sealed.*

Be warned, you rulers of nations! Repent and obey your Creator or your doom is sealed! God will gather your armies into the Valley of Jehoshaphat and there He will punish you for harming His people.

Woe be to you members of the United Nations! For you will be severely punished for partitioning the land of Israel and giving a part of God's Holy Land to the wicked Arabs. Because of his pathetic predicament at that time, the younger brother (Israel) was willing to accept anything you offered him, but God is furious over what you did.

You arrogantly dared to give away a portion of God's Holy Land, land that He swore would belong to the Jews forever. You dared to dishonor your Creator's name by dishonoring His Word. Woe be to you, Arab nations! When God comes to deal with you, like Edom, you will regret your abusive treatment of the Jews. See these facts for yourself in the following verses taken from *The Living Bible*.

> *Joel 3:1-14 (The Living Bible.)*
>
> [1] *"At that time, when I restore the prosperity of Judah and Jerusalem," says the Lord,*
>
> [2] ***"I will gather the armies of the world into the "Valley Where Jehovah Judges" and punish them there for harming my people, for scattering my inheritance among the nations and dividing up my land.***

World leader, consider God's warning! God informs you in verse two that He will punish every nation that has had a part in harming His people, scattering His people among the nations **and partitioning the land of Israel (Palestine)**. Oh, world leader, tremble in your shoes! Inquire into this situation. Was your government one of the United Nations who had a part in partitioning the Promised Land? Did the representative of your nation vote to bring about that prophesied dastardly deed? If so, woe be to you! For the Judge of all the earth will repay. As God's Word says in the former verses, He will gather all the nations into the Valley of Jehoshaphat and there He will mete out full justice for their atrocious acts against His name, His beloved people and for dividing His land and giving part of it to the wicked Arab nations.

Remember earlier when I shared with you how the Gentile nations took the Jews captive, sold them into slavery, robbed all their treasures and destroyed the city of Jerusalem? Well, see in the following verses how God will eventually punish the nations for every one of those wicked acts.

> [3] *"They divided up my people as their slaves; they traded a young lad for a prostitute, and a little girl for wine enough to get drunk.*
>
> [4] *Tyre and Sidon, don't you try to interfere! Are you trying to take revenge on me, you cities of Philistia? Beware, for I will strike back swiftly, and return the harm to your own heads.*
>
> [5] *You have taken my silver and gold and all my precious treasures and carried them off to your heathen temples.*

⁶You have sold the people of Judah and Jerusalem to the Greeks, who took them far from their own land.

⁷But I will bring them back again from all these places you have sold them to, <u>and I will pay you back for all that you have done.</u>

⁸I will sell your sons and daughters to the people of Judah and they will sell them to the Sabeans far away. This is a promise from the Lord."

⁹Announce this far and wide: Get ready for war! Conscript your best soldiers; collect all your armies.

¹⁰Melt your plowshares into swords and beat your pruning hooks into spears. Let the weak be strong.

¹¹<u>Gather together and come, all nations everywhere.</u> And now, O Lord, bring down your warriors!

¹²<u>Collect the nations; bring them to the Valley of Jehoshaphat, for there I will sit to pronounce judgment on them all.</u>

¹³Now let the sickle do its work; the harvest is ripe and waiting. Tread the winepress, for it is full to overflowing with the wickedness of these men.

¹⁴<u>Multitudes, multitudes waiting in the valley for the verdict of their doom! For the Day of the Lord is near, in the Valley of Judgment.</u>

In 1974, I was invited to a special gathering at the home of a Christian doctor and his wife in Valparaiso, Florida. At that time, this couple's friend and house guest was Corrie Ten Boom, author of *The Hiding Place*. Corrie visited this family periodically in order to recuperate from her hectic ministerial obligations. So as not to tax Corrie's strength, only a few hand-picked Christians were invited to the doctor's home that evening. Fortunately, I was one of those few, though I must confess, at the time, I did not understand why I had been given that privilege.

It was several years after meeting Corrie that God poured upon me the truth regarding the Church's obligation to pray for and support Israel and at the same time gave me an overwhelming love for the Jewish people. Only then did I come to really appreciate Corrie Ten Boom and to thank God for giving me the privilege of personally meeting a woman who had demonstrated true love and support for the Jewish people. She was a Dutch woman who had been imprisoned in a concentration camp for ten months for protecting Jews during World War II.

Corrie as you may know, is now deceased. However, recently I watched a rerun of one of her television interviews. When asked what caused her to show such kindness to the Jews, she quoted a portion of a text that I will share with you in a few moments. Since we are studying about God's future judgment of the nations for their treatment of the Jews, I felt that I wanted to interject Yeshua's illustration which includes the verse that Corrie quoted.

As you read Yeshua's words in Matthew 25:31-46 from the *Holy Bible, King James Version*, compare His words with what you read a moment ago in Joel 3:1-14. Also keep in mind that your treatment of Yeshua's Jewish brethren will be rewarded or punished. The Lord Himself said, *"I will bless those who bless you [who confer prosperity or happiness upon you] and curse him who curses or uses insolent language toward you."* Read now and understand the real meaning of the Lord's parable in Matthew chapter twenty-five. Understand that Yeshua was actually reiterating and amplifying Joel's prophecy in Joel 3:1-14.

Matthew 25:31-46 (King James Version.)

31 When the Son of man shall come in his glory, and all the holy angels with him, then shall he sit upon the throne of his glory:

32 <u>And before him shall be gathered all nations: and he shall separate them one from another, as a shepherd divideth his sheep from the goats:</u>

The content of the previous verse, verse thirty-two, is extremely important. For, it reveals exactly who all nations are that will be gathered before the Lord and judged. Verse thirty-two informs you that it is the **Gentile** nations who will be assembled before the Lord. Israel is not counted among the nations. Only **non-Jewish** nations will, at that time, be judged and separated into two groups, sheep and goats.

To verify all that I said in the former paragraph, read the following definition of the Greek word "nations" (ethnos) from *Strong's Exhaustive Concordance of the Bible.*

> foreign (non-Jewish)...Gentile, heathen, nation, people.

Every non-Jewish nation will be gathered before the Lord, judged and divided into one of two groups. Which one of the two groups they end up in will be determined by their past good or bad treatment of the Lord's brethren, the Jewish people.

Since you now know God's reasons for gathering all nations before Him, and you know who *"all nations"* are, I think it would be beneficial for you to read again the first two verses of Yeshua's parable.

Matthew 25:31-46 (King James Version.)

31 When the Son of man shall come in his glory, and all the holy angels with him, then shall he sit upon the throne of his glory:

32 And before him shall be gathered all nations: and he shall separate them one from another, as a shepherd divideth his sheep from the goats:

33 And he shall set the sheep on his right hand, but the goats on the left.

34 Then shall the King say unto them on his right hand, Come, ye blessed of my Father, inherit the kingdom prepared for you from the foundation of the world:

35 For I was an hungred, and ye gave me meat: I was thirsty, and ye gave me drink: I was a stranger, and ye took me in:

36 Naked, and ye clothed me: I was sick, and ye visited me: I was in prison, and ye came unto me.

37 Then shall the righteous answer him, saying, Lord, when saw we thee an hungred, and fed thee? or thirsty, and gave thee drink?

38 When saw we thee a stranger, and took thee in? or naked, and clothed thee?

39 Or when saw we thee sick, or in prison, and came unto thee?

40 And the King shall answer and say unto them, Verily I say unto you, Inasmuch as ye have done it unto one of the least of these my brethren, ye have done it unto me.

41 Then shall he say also unto them on the left hand, Depart from me, ye cursed, into everlasting fire, prepared for the devil and his angels:

Do you remember what the Lord said in Genesis 12:3? He said, He would bless those who blessed the covenant descendants of Abraham and curse him who cursed or used insolent language toward them. Thus, in verse forty-one, the Lord calls these Gentiles on the left hand *"ye cursed."* They are cursed because they mistreated and neglected His Jewish brethren.

> *42For I was an hungred, and ye gave me no meat: I was thirsty, and ye gave me no drink:*
>
> *43I was a stranger, and ye took me not in: naked, and ye clothed me not: sick, and in prison, and ye visited me not.*
>
> *44Then shall they also answer him, saying, Lord, when saw we thee an hungred, or athirst, or a stranger, or naked, or sick, or in prison, and did not minister unto thee?*
>
> *45Then shall he answer them, saying, Verily I say unto you, Inasmuch as ye did it not to one of the least of these, ye did it not to me.*
>
> *46And these shall go away into everlasting punishment: but the righteous into life eternal.*

The Christian Gentile, Corrie Ten Boom, will be one of those righteous sheep on the Lord's right hand. For, she fed the Lord's brethren (the Jews). She protected and hid them. She took care of their needs when they were sick. She gave them drink. But woe be to those who fail to meet the Jews' needs! Woe be to those goats who neglect or mistreat them! For, they shall be placed on the Lord's left side. They shall go away into everlasting punishment.

The Church as a whole has not understood the secret mystery that Yeshua spoke forth in His parable of the sheep and the goats. The Church has been under the mistaken impression that Yeshua was referring to the Church caring for their Christian brethren. They have not realized that Yeshua was instead referring to the Gentiles' good or bad treatment of His Abrahamic covenant brethren, the Jews. However, righteous Corrie Ten Boom obviously understood that Yeshua was speaking about His Jewish brethren. For, as I said earlier, when asked why she had shown kindness to the Jews, she quoted from Yeshua's parable of the sheep and the goats.

Christian, do not disclaim responsibility for the Church's actions or for your own. Do not plead ignorance. God looks into your innermost thoughts. He knows when or if you are covering up sin. Let me share with you a Scripture that clarifies my last statement.

Proverbs 24:11-12 (The Amplified Bible.)

11Deliver those who are drawn away to death, and those who totter to the slaughter, hold them back [from their doom].

12If you [profess ignorance and] say, Behold, we did not know this, does not He Who weighs and ponders the heart perceive and consider it? And He Who guards your life, does not He know it? And shall not He render to [you and] every man according to his works?

Repent! And then rise up true Church of God! Go forward! Start doing what you were taken from among the Gentiles to do. Honor God's holy name by praying for and supporting God's beloved Israel. Honor God's name by praying for and supporting Israel until, in the future, she is established as God intended. Help God fulfill His holy Word and protect His reputation. Be like Corrie Ten Boom. Reach out to the Jewish people with all the love and support that you can muster. Be a sheep. Do not be a goat.

As for those of you who refuse to repent, those of you who consciously choose to remain anti-Semitic, those of you who continue to mistreat the Jews just because they are Jewish, those of you who think you can beat the Jews down until you eventually destroy them, hear the Word of the Lord taken from *The Living Bible.*

Psalm 129:1-8 (The Living Bible.)

1Persecuted from my earliest youth (Israel is speaking),

2and faced with never-ending discrimination—but not destroyed! My enemies have never been able to finish me off!

3,4,Though my back is cut to ribbons with their whips, the Lord is good. For he has snapped the chains that evil men had bound me with.

5May all who hate the Jews be brought to ignominious defeat.

6,7May they be as grass in shallow soil, turning sere and yellow when half grown, ignored by the reaper, despised by the binder.

8And may those passing by refuse to bless them by saying, "Jehovah's blessings be upon you; we bless you in Jehovah's name."

Do you see God's warning? May all those who hate the Jews and discriminate against them be brought to disgrace and shame. May those who hate the Jews be looked upon as despicable. Isn't this how most people look upon those Germans who committed atrocities against the Jewish people during World War II, the Nazis? To most people, even the very thought of the Nazis is revolting. Furthermore, now that you know what the Roman Catholic Church, the Protestant Martin Luther and his followers, and Shakespeare and other authors did to the Jews and God's holy name, don't you also respond to their wickedness as God's Word instructs? Don't you despise their cruel and anti-Semitic behavior?

There may be some people or nations who, after harming the Jewish people, think they have gotten away with their evil deeds. People tend to think that because a long period of time has elapsed since they committed their crimes against the nation of Israel or against individual Jews, they must have gotten away with it. If you are one of those people, don't boast, don't gloat wicked man, wicked woman, wicked nation! It took 400 years for God's justice and punishment to be poured out upon Egypt for her mistreatment of Abraham's, Isaac's and Jacob's seed. Yet, as you know, in the end Egypt was severely punished and so will you be.

The most recent example we have of God's judgment being poured out upon a nation who hates Israel is God's punishment of the people of Kuwait. The Kuwaitis made no secret of their hatred of the Jews and the nation of Israel. They were one of the PLO's two largest financial supporters. Kuwait's wealth helped to keep terrorism against Israel alive. But in 1991 in the aftermath of the Gulf War, God's judgment upon Kuwait finally arrived. And to further her humiliation, God used another Islamic nation (Iraq) to destroy the Islamic nation of Kuwait. God said He will curse those who curse and who use insolent language toward His people, the Jews, and God will keep His word at any cost.

By the time the Iraqis had finished with Kuwait, it was hard to even recognize that land. You will recall that the Iraqis set Kuwait's oil fields on fire. The whole land of Kuwait was darkened by the thick, black clouds of smoke and filth that spewed from over 700 burning oil wells. Their land, their water and even the air the Kuwaitis breathed was polluted. That suffocating inferno raged out of control for almost a full year. The destruction the Kuwaitis desired to bring upon Israel was turned upon them instead. Psalm 129:5-7 in *The Living Bible* was fulfilled, *"May all who hate the Jews be brought to ignominious defeat. May they be as grass in shallow soil, turning sere and yellow when half grown, ignored by the reaper, despised by the binder."* And as God said in Joel 3:1-15 that He would do to those who harm His people, He paid the Kuwaitis back for harming Israel. Remember what we read earlier in *The Living Bible?*

> Deuteronomy 32:34-35 *(The Living Bible.)*
>
> *34But Israel is my special people, Sealed as jewels within my treasury.*
>
> *35Vengeance is mine, And I decree the punishment of all her enemies: <u>Their doom is sealed.</u>*

Again I say, be warned you rulers of nations! Repent of harming Israel. Change your attitude and conduct toward Israel, or your doom is sealed. What happened to Kuwait was only a warning.

You now have the answer to the question, "Will Those Who Harm Israel be Punished?" I am sure you will agree that God's Word makes perfectly clear the fact that all those who harm Israel will most definitely be punished. However, in His mercy, God has put the truth on this issue into your hands. He has put the truth into your hands so that you can personally repent of any wrongdoing in this area and receive forgiveness for your sins. You can change your wicked ways. You can begin to bless Israel so that God can bless you. You can begin to obey God's Word and to pray for and support God's covenant nation, Israel. You can help God vindicate His holy name.

I am going to end chapter eighteen on one last profound note: The insight you have received into Yeshua's parable of the sheep and goats sheds more light on God's statement, *"I will bless those who bless you [who confer prosperity or happiness upon you] and curse him who curses or uses insolent language toward you."* Men have often wondered why God would bless those who bless the Jews and curse those who curse them. The answer in part is that when you bless the Jews, you are doing that good unto the Lord. *"Verily I say unto you, Inasmuch as ye have done it unto one of the least of these my brethren, ye have done it unto me."* (Matthew 25:40.) When you curse them and mistreat or neglect them, you are doing that evil unto the Lord. Yeshua put it like this, *"Inasmuch as ye did it not to one of the least of these, ye did it not to me."* (Matthew 25:45.) Thus, God curses or blesses in proportion to what is done or not done to Him personally.

"Will Those Who Harm Israel Be Punished?" Yes, those who harm Israel will be punished (that is, they will be cursed). My prayer is that you **will not** be among the goats. My prayer is that **you will** be one of the righteous sheep that will be placed on the right hand of the Lord. **My prayer is that you will be blessed.**

Chapter 19

WHAT ELSE CAN CHRISTIANS DO TO HELP GOD VINDICATE HIS NAME?

During this series, you have received answers to questions that, until now, had remained hidden or at best were extremely vague. As you absorbed the already presented information, I am sure that you were deeply touched by its content. As a result of the insight that you now possess, you have no doubt developed concern for God's needs and an overwhelming desire to help God fulfill His Word and clear His reputation.

As a Gentile Christian, you may be wondering what you can do to help God vindicate His name other than by financially supporting and praying for Israel. Well, I am glad to be able to inform you that there is something else that you can do. **God does indeed have an additional mission for you to accomplish, Gentile Christian. To put it bluntly, He wants to use you to make the Jews jealous.**

Now someone may ask, "Why in the world would our righteous God want Gentile Christians to make the Jewish people jealous?" The answer to that question is quite simple. In the past, there were times when God's chosen people (the Jews) caused Him tremendous grief, pain and humiliation. The Lord had to look on, while His Abrahamic covenant people broke the Horeb covenant and cast aside and discarded all His commandments. He was continually exposed to the Jews' abhorrent idolatrous behavior. Yes, God watched as His beloved spiritual wife shamelessly lavished her attention and affections upon idols while deliberately ignoring and dishonoring Him.

The next two texts will give you a glimpse of the humiliation and pain that God was forced to endure as a result of Israel's lewd and idolatrous conduct. You will see in verses eleven through fourteen of the next Scripture that the Israelites had no excuse for such atrocious behavior. **God gave the Israelites everything that a people could possibly want. Yet, despite His generosity and tender care, the Israelites repeatedly provoked Him to jealousy with their idols.**

634

Deuteronomy 32:11-18 (The Amplified Bible.)

11As an eagle that stirs up her nest, that flutters over her young, He spread abroad His wings and He took them, He bore them on His pinion.

12So the Lord alone led him; there was no foreign god with Him.

13He made Israel ride on the high places of the earth, and he ate the increase of the field; and He made him suck honey out of the rock and oil out of the flinty rock.

14Butter and curds of the herd and milk of the flock, with fat of lambs, and rams of the breed of Bashan, and he-goats, with the finest of the wheat; and you drank wine of the blood of the grape.

15But Jeshurun (Israel) grew fat and kicked. You became fat, you grew thick, you were gorged and sleek! Then he forsook God Who made him and forsook and despised the Rock of his salvation.

16They provoked Him to jealousy with strange gods, with abominations they provoked Him to anger.

17They sacrificed to demons, not to God—to gods whom they knew not, to new gods lately come up, whom your fathers never knew or feared.

18Of the Rock Who bore you you were unmindful; you forgot the God Who travailed in your birth.

<u>**Verse sixteen makes it clear that the Israelites made God jealous with strange gods.**</u> It reads, *"They provoked Him to jealousy with strange gods, with abominations they provoked Him to anger."* God's people made Him fearful and wary of being supplanted in their affections by these new gods. The Lord was the one who had formed the Israelites into a great nation. He was the one who travailed in Israel's birth (that is, He suffered birth pains as He witnessed their affliction and abuse in Egypt, the place where He brought into being His promised great nation). He was also the one who had later looked out for the Israelites' every need. Yet these disloyal, ungrateful, foolish people pushed God and His laws aside for rivals of wood and stone. They deserted the one true God for gods that were not really gods at all.

Over and over again, God reminds His people how they provoked Him to jealousy and anger with their sinful practices and idolatrous behavior. God brings to their attention how they went so far as to practice the false religion of the sodomite cults which involved the abominable sin of homosexuality.

I Kings 14:22-24 (The Amplified Bible.)

²²And Judah did evil in the sight of the Lord, <u>Whom they provoked to jealousy with the sins they committed, above all that their fathers had done.</u>

²³For they also built themselves [idolatrous] high places, pillars, and Asherim [idolatrous symbols of the goddess Asherah] on every high hill and under every green tree.

²⁴<u>There were also sodomites (male cult prostitutes) in the land. They did all the abominations of the nations whom the Lord cast out before the Israelites.</u>

Can you imagine the jealousy and anger that God must have felt upon seeing the apple of His eye (His beloved, spiritual wife) lavishing her attention upon and prostrating herself before idols of wood and stone while at the same time totally neglecting Him? Can you imagine the pain, agony and embarrassment that God must have experienced upon witnessing the people whom He loved with an everlasting love worshipping, praising and dancing before idols?

The Jews made God jealous by brazenly flaunting their idolatrous sins before Him. <u>So, to teach them a lesson while He brought about His future purpose, God predicted that He would also make them jealous.</u> God justly foretold that the day would come when their roles would be reversed. He would force them to swallow a dose of their own medicine. He would cause them to experience a measure of the anguish, emotional pain, jealousy and anger that they had for generations inflicted upon Him with their sinful, idolatrous practices. Yes, as they had made Him fearful and wary of being supplanted in their affections by idols, so He would in turn make them fearful and wary of being supplanted in His affections by the Gentiles. God Himself confirms all that I just said in the following verse taken from *The Living Bible*.

Deuteronomy 32:21 (The Living Bible.)

²¹<u>They have made me very jealous of their idols, which are not gods at all. Now I, in turn, will make</u>

them jealous by giving my affections to the foolish Gentile nations of the world.

How did God bring to pass His warning in Deuteronomy 32:21? How did He make the Jews jealous? He did it by keeping His Word in Genesis 3:15 and the part of the Abrahamic covenant that says, *"...in you will all the families and kindred of the earth be blessed...."* He did it by extending His promised favor and salvation to the Gentile nations.

God always intended to fulfill His Abrahamic covenant and include the nations in His salvation plan. However, in His wisdom, He uses His planned attentiveness toward the Gentiles to accomplish a multiple purpose. He uses His attentiveness toward the Gentiles to teach the Jews a lesson for their past idolatrous sins and their deliberate neglect of Him. He also uses His attentiveness toward the Gentiles to make the Jews jealous (envious) just as they had made Him jealous. Yet, even more amazing is the way God uses His preoccupation with the Gentiles to show forth His covenant mercy and loving-kindness to the covenant descendants of Abraham, Isaac and Jacob. He actually uses His display of affection for the Gentiles as an incentive to make the Jews aware of what they are missing and thereby cause **some of them** to desire and seek His precious salvation for themselves. The Jewish apostle Paul explains this truth in the following verse.

Romans 11:11 (The Amplified Bible.)

*11So I ask, Have they stumbled so as to fall [to their utter spiritual ruin, irretrievably]? By no means! **But through their false step and transgression salvation [has come] to the Gentiles, so as to arouse Israel [to see and feel what they forfeited] and so to make them jealous.***

Let us also read the previous verse from *The Living Bible.*

Romans 11:11 (The Living Bible.)

*11Does this mean that God has rejected his Jewish people forever? Of course not! **His purpose was to make his salvation available to the Gentiles, and then the Jews would be jealous and begin to want God's salvation for themselves.***

Paul did his best to make his Jewish brethren jealous. He desperately hoped that through his ministry to the Gentiles **some of his Jewish brethren** would see what they had forfeited and, as a result of that reality, would turn to their Jewish Messiah and be saved. So, in order to help God fulfill His Word in Deuteronomy 32:21 and to teach the Jews a lesson for their past idolatrous sins and their shameful treatment of their Lord and make them jealous so as to encourage **some of them** to begin to desire God's salvation for themselves, Paul took certain measures which he describes in the next two verses.

Romans 11:13-14 (The Amplified Bible.)

13But now I am speaking to you who are Gentiles. Inasmuch then as I am an apostle to the Gentiles, I lay great stress on my ministry and magnify my office,
14In the hope of making my fellow Jews jealous [in order to stir them up to imitate, copy, and appropriate], and thus managing to save some of them.

Notice that in verse fourteen, Paul said, *"and thus managing to save some of them."* He said "**some**" because as you learned earlier in the series, at this time, only a few Jews are able to overcome their God-ordained, spiritual disabilities. However, it is obvious that at least a small segment of those Jews who have forced themselves to understand *"the secret things"* were in part driven to do so because they could not stand to see God giving His attention and affections to the Gentiles.

God warned the Jews that just as they had made Him jealous of their idols, so He would make them jealous of His relationship with the Gentiles. Prior to His statement in Deuteronomy 32:21, God had promised Abraham that He would give His salvation to the Gentile nations. So, it is reasonable to assume that the Jews are aware that the Gentile nations are mentioned in the Abrahamic covenant. That fact alone makes one realize that if the Jewish people were not stricken with spiritual blindness, they would quickly see the truth. The Jews would see that in offering salvation to the Gentiles, God is fulfilling both a section of the Abrahamic covenant and the warning in Deuteronomy 32:21 that He would make them jealous. However, since the majority of the Jewish people are still spiritually blind, they cannot see that great miracle. Consequently, as a nation, they continue to refuse God's offer of salvation while the Gentiles go on accepting God's generous invitation. See these facts for yourself in the following text.

Romans 10:18-21 (The Amplified Bible.)

18But I ask, Have they not heard? Indeed they have; [for the Scripture says] Their voice [that of nature bearing God's message] has gone out to all the earth, and their words to the far bounds of the world.

19Again I ask, Did Israel not understand? [Did the Jews have no warning that the Gospel was to go forth to the Gentiles, to all the earth?] First, there is Moses who says, I will make you jealous of those who are not a nation; with a foolish nation I will make you angry.

20Then Isaiah is so bold as to say, I have been found by those who did not seek Me; I have shown (revealed) Myself to those who did not [consciously] ask for Me.

21But of Israel He says, All day long I have stretched out My hands to a people unyielding and disobedient and self-willed [to a faultfinding, contrary, and contradicting people].

God warned that He would make the Jews jealous by giving His affections (that is, His favor and salvation) to the Gentile nations. Consequently, since Paul was himself a Jew, he could not use his own salvation experience to make his Jewish brethren jealous. **No! God had said He would make the Jews jealous by giving His affections to the Gentiles.**

So what did the wise apostle do to try to help God fulfill His Word and make his Jewish brethren jealous? As he explained in the verses that you read earlier (Romans 11:13-14), Paul laid great stress on his ministry to the Gentiles and magnified his office of apostle to the Gentiles. By adhering to his previously mentioned plan, Paul was able to keep letting the Jews know that God's promise to Abraham had come true. For He was emphasizing the fact that all the nations of the earth were indeed being blessed in the seed of Abraham, Yeshua. He also aided God in bringing about His Word in Deuteronomy 32:21. With Paul's assistance, the Gentiles were enjoying God's promised salvation while some of the Jewish people were indeed feeling the pangs of jealousy that God had predicted they would experience.

You just saw that as a Jew, insofar as his own personal salvation experience was concerned, the apostle Paul was not in a position to make his Jewish brethren jealous. However, that is not true in your case, Gentile Christian. You are in a position to make the Jews jealous. You are in a position to help God fulfill His Word in Deuteronomy 32:21. Consequently, God desires to use you as an instrument of His continued covenant mercy and loving-kindness toward His people. For, if you succeed in making the Jews jealous, **some of them** will become afraid of being supplanted in God's affections by Gentiles, and they will come to the Lord. However, as God foretold in His Word, for His name's sake, the biggest part of them will remain spiritually blind and deaf for a specified period of time.

At this point, Gentile Christian, you are probably wondering what God expects you to do in order to make the Jews jealous. Well, let me first advise you as to what you must **not** do. You will never make the Jews jealous by mistreating them as the Church has done for almost 2,000 years. The only thing you will accomplish by mistreating God's beloved Abrahamic covenant people will be to bring down God's curse upon your own head.

Ask yourself, Gentile, if you were a Jew, would you be envious of people who abuse you and your family? Would you long to have the same spiritual experience as those people who have tortured you, those who burned down your home and murdered your brethren? Would you envy those who humiliated and ostracized you, those who shut you away in a ghetto, those who made you wear a badge as a lying sign to all that you are inferior and should be shunned? Would you envy such monsters? No! Of course you would not. Rather, you would despise everything about such despicable people.

Oh, Church, our sin is exposed! Our mistreatment of the Jews is a glaring, grievous error! We have much to make up for. We have let down both God and His beloved Abrahamic covenant people. We have not made the Jews jealous of us. Instead, we have only succeeded in making them despise us. And worst of all, we have caused them to despise the name of Yeshua. Thus, we must repent and make up for lost time. We must help God fulfill His Word in Deuteronomy 32:21. We must help God make His beloved people jealous. For, if we start doing things God's way, then, like Paul, we too might manage to save some of them.

Now you may ask, "**What can we Christians do to make the Jews envious of the closeness that we enjoy with the Lord and cause them to covet that same kind of spiritual experience for themselves?**" Well, the first thing you have to remember is that the Jews are not fools. The Jews are blind and deaf to *"the secret things"* but they are very intelligent in every other area. They know what God demands from those who serve Him. They are fully aware that God demands absolute obedience to His written commands. They also comprehend what God's commands entail. For, you will recall that God gave the Jews understanding of *"the things which are revealed."* The Jews are by no means spiritually handicapped when it comes to God's written laws. Therefore, Gentile Christian, they know if you are obeying God's laws or if you are not obeying them.

Are you fulfilling God's purpose, Gentile Christian? Are you living the kind of holy life that will make the Jews jealous of your relationship with Almighty God? Are you showing the Jews that you really do love and know God? Do you prove that you love and know God by obeying His commandments as Yeshua and His Jewish apostle John said you must?

> *John 14:21 (The Amplified Bible.)*
>
> *21 The person who has My commands and keeps them is the one who [really] loves Me; and whoever [really] loves Me will be loved by My Father, and I [too] will love him and will show (reveal, manifest) Myself to him. [I will let Myself be clearly seen by him and make Myself real to him.]*
>
> *I John 2:3 (King James Version.)*
>
> *3 And hereby we do know that we know him, if we keep his commandments.*

Again I ask you, Gentile Christian, are you fulfilling your God-given mission? Are you living the type of obedient life that will cause the Jews to see that you truly do love and know God? Are you living the type of obedient life that will cause the Jews to see that the God of Abraham, Isaac and Jacob is indeed enjoying fellowship with you? Or are you so disobedient to God's Word that you are no threat to the Jews at all? Are you so disobedient to God's commands that you absolutely do not cause the Jews to envy or desire the kind of relationship with God that you profess to have?

Now you may ask, "Why don't the Jews feel threatened by or jealous of disobedient Gentile Christians?" My friend, the Jews do not feel threatened by or jealous of such people because in their hearts, the Jews know that disobedient Christians really do not love or know God. The Jews know that in their lawless condition, disobedient Christians cannot get close to God. Did not Yeshua and His Jewish apostle John make that point clear in the following verses?

John 14:24 (The Amplified Bible.)

24Anyone who does not [really] love Me does not observe and obey My teaching. And the teaching which you hear and heed is not Mine, but [comes] from the Father Who sent Me.

I John 2:4 (King James Version.)

4He that saith, I know him, and keepeth not his commandments, is a liar, and the truth is not in him.

Oh, Gentile Christian, "*Repent (think differently; change your mind, regretting your sins and changing your conduct)....*" (Matthew 3:2.) Go and "*Bring forth fruit that is consistent with repentance [let your lives prove your change of heart].*" (Matthew 3:8, *The Amplified Bible.*) Be like King David. Help God carry out His purpose on the earth. Learn and obey God's Word and treat the Jews kindly. If you do, I guarantee you that some of them will most certainly be jealous of your relationship with God. For, God said in Deuteronomy 32:21 that He would make them jealous, and God will continue to bring His Word to pass in that area until it has completely fulfilled its purpose.

In God's name, I implore you Gentile Christian to be patient and compassionate with the Jewish people. I know that you would like to see all the Jews accept Yeshua as their Savior. But how can the Jews, as a whole, recognize the prophesied Messiah when they are spiritually blind in regard to *"the secret things"*? The fact is that most of them will remain blind until God lifts the veil from their eyes. And as you learned earlier in the series, that spiritual healing will not take place until the Lord returns. Did not Yeshua Himself warn the Jews of that very truth in the subsequent verse?

Matthew 23:39 (The Amplified Bible.)

39For I declare to you, you will not see Me again until you say, Blessed (magnified in worship, adored, and exalted) is He Who comes in the name of the Lord!

In 1948, in their ignorance of the Scriptures, many Christians expected the newly founded nation of Israel to immediately recognize Yeshua as their Messiah. When that did not happen, those same Christians were deeply disappointed. But the reason why they were disappointed was because they did not understand the real issues involved in this matter. They did not comprehend the fact that the Jews are spiritually blind and deaf regarding *"the secret things."* Neither did they appreciate that the Jews' spiritual blindness and deafness has been prolonged for the Gentiles' sake. Most of all, they did not realize that God's first priority is to fulfill His Word so that He might vindicate His holy name. Everything else is secondary.

Most Christians are so totally caught up with the segment of the new covenant that promises men salvation that they are oblivious to everything else, even God's holy name. They cannot get it through their heads that God is not yet ready to open the spiritually blind eyes and unstop the spiritually deaf ears of the entire population of the nation of Israel.

You will understand even more why God is not ready to heal Israel's spiritual eyes and ears when you read the next chapter of this book. So for now, let us concentrate on our responsibility to make the Jews jealous.

While you are carrying out your God-given mission and helping God make the Jews jealous, Gentile Christian, do not forget that Jews are Jews. I say that Jews are Jews, because for some reason, many Gentiles and Jews alike have it in their minds that when a Jew becomes a Christian that Jew has converted to a Gentile religion. This is nonsense! We Gentile Christians are the ones who have converted to the Jewish religion through the promised Messiah, Jewish Yeshua. A Jew is simply completed when he or she recognizes Yeshua, the Anointed One, and accepts Him as their Savior. So, Gentile Christian, allow the Jews to be Jews because God needs the Jews in order to fulfill His Word and vindicate His name.

As you meditated on the previous information regarding God paying back the Jews for making Him jealous, I am sure that certain questions popped into your mind. **You are probably curious as to whether or not God's jealousy and anger toward His beloved Israel will ever end. The answer to this question is of course yes, God's jealousy and anger toward Israel will one day cease.** God cannot remain angry with Israel always since He made a sacred vow that He would love them forever. And, as you now know, God's everlasting love includes steadfastness, mercy and forgiveness. So, yes, God will eventually let go of His jealousy and anger. However, He will let go of it in His own good time.

You see, there are still some things that God must accomplish first. You will gain more insight into just what those things are in the next chapter of this book. However, right now, I want to share with you Scriptural evidence which proves that at a certain point in time, God's jealousy will indeed depart from Israel. However, before that can happen, the Lord intends to fully repay Israel for her past wicked idolatrous behavior. **Yes, only when Israel's chastisement is completed will God's jealousy and anger against Israel depart.** We will read God's words to Israel from *The Living Bible.*

Ezekiel 16:35-43 (The Living Bible.)

35 "O prostitute, hear the word of the Lord:

36 "The Lord God says: Because I see your filthy sins, your adultery with your lovers—your worshiping of idols—and the slaying of your children as sacrifices to your gods,

37 this is what I am going to do: I will gather together all your allies—these lovers of yours you have sinned with, both those you loved and those you hated—and I will make you naked before them, that they may see you.

38 I will punish you as a murderess is punished and as a woman breaking wedlock living with other men.

39 I will give you to your lovers—these many nations—to destroy, and they will knock down your brothels and idol altars, and strip you and take your beautiful jewels and leave you naked and ashamed.

40,41 They will burn your homes, punishing you before the eyes of many women. And I will see to it that you stop your adulteries with other gods and end your payments to your allies for their love.

Pay attention to the next two verses, for they prove beyond a doubt that God's jealousy and anger will depart from Israel. However, those same verses also reveal that before that happens, God will repay Israel in full for every abominable sin and every idolatrous act, that she has committed against Him. God loves Israel with an everlasting love. Albeit, it is a Biblical fact that God chastises those whom He loves.

42 "__Then at last my fury against you will die away; my jealousy against you will end__, and I will be quiet and not be angry with you anymore.

> *43But first, because you have not remembered your youth, but have angered me by all these evil things you do, I will fully repay you for all of your sins, says the Lord. For you are thankless in addition to all your other faults.*

The bottom line is that though God is angry with Israel because of her abominable idolatrous sins and though He must reciprocate in order to fulfill His prediction in Deuteronomy 32:21, He still loves Israel with an everlasting (that is, with a *"fixed, unchanging, firmly loyal or constant"*) love. **Therefore, the nations had better look out. For, once God has fully repaid Israel's wicked lawlessness and His jealousy and anger departs from her, guess where it will go? God's jealousy and anger will then be directed toward every Gentile nation that has ever harmed God's beloved Abrahamic covenant people, Israel.**

On that awful day, the nations will feel the brunt of God's terrible jealousy and wrath. Read this truth for yourself in *The Living Bible.* **And remember that as it was in the case of Edom, God's wrath will be poured out upon the Gentile nations as a result of their abhorrent mistreatment of Israel.**

> *Ezekiel 38:1-23 (The Living Bible.)*
>
> *1Here is another message to me from the Lord:*
>
> *2,3 "Son of dust, face northward toward the land of Magog, and prophesy against Gog king of Meshech and Tubal. Tell him that the Lord God says: I am against you, Gog.*
>
> *4I will put hooks into your jaws and pull you to your doom. I will mobilize your troops and armored cavalry, and make you a mighty host, all fully armed.*
>
> *5Peras, Cush and Put shall join you too with all their weaponry,*
>
> *6and so shall Gomer and all his hordes and the armies of Togarmah from the distant north, as well as many others.*

The Amplified Bible provides an informative footnote for Ezekiel 38:2. In that footnote, Bible scholars actually identify some of the nations mentioned in the previous verses. The footnote reads:

Gog is a symbolic name, representing the leader of the world powers antagonistic to God (see also Rev. 20:8). Meshech and Tubal are understood to have been the same as the Moschi and Tibareni of the Greeks—tribes that inhabited regions in the Caucasus. Rosh, which some would identify with Russia, must have designated a land and people somewhere in the same area. And therefore the Gog of Ezekiel must be viewed as in some sense the head of the high regions in the northwest of Asia. (Patrick Fairbairn, *The Imperial Bible-dictionary*).

A description of exactly what will happen to those nations that come against God's Abrahamic covenant people (Israel) is laid out in chapters thirty-eight and thirty-nine of *The Book of Ezekiel*. We will continue reading from *The Living Bible* but you may also want to read those same chapters from *The Amplified Bible*.

7Be prepared! Stay mobilized. You are their leader, Gog!

8"A long time from now you will be called to action. In distant years you will swoop down onto the land of Israel, that will be lying in peace after the return of its people from many lands.

9You and all your allies—a vast and awesome army—will roll down upon them like a storm and cover the land like a cloud.

10For at that time an evil thought will have come to your mind.

11You will have said, 'Israel is an unprotected land of unwalled villages! I will march against her and destroy these people living in such confidence!

12I will go to those once-desolate cities that are now filled with people again—those who have returned from all the nations—and I will capture vast booty and many slaves. For the people are rich with cattle now, and the whole earth revolves around them!'

13 *"But Sheba and Dedan and the merchant princes of Tarshish with whom she trades will ask, 'Who are you to rob them of silver and gold and drive away their cattle and seize their goods and make them poor?'*

14 *"The Lord God says to Gog: When my people are living in peace in their land, then you will rouse yourself.*

15,16 **You will come from all over the north with your vast host of cavalry and cover the land like a cloud. This will happen in the distant future—in the latter years of history. I will bring you against my land, <u>and my holiness will be vindicated in your terrible destruction before their eyes, so that all the nations will know that I am God.</u>**

17 *"The Lord God says: You are the one I spoke of long ago through the prophets of Israel, saying that after many years had passed, I would bring you against my people.*

18 <u>**But when you come to destroy the land of Israel, my fury will rise!**</u>

19 <u>**For in my jealousy and blazing wrath, I promise a mighty shaking in the land of Israel on that day.**</u>

20 **All living things shall quake in terror at my presence; mountains shall be thrown down; cliffs shall tumble; walls shall crumble to the earth.**

21 <u>**I will summon every kind of terror against you, says the Lord God, and you will fight against yourselves in mortal combat!**</u>

22 <u>**I will fight you with sword, disease, torrential floods, great hailstones, fire and brimstone!**</u>

23 **Thus will I show my greatness and bring honor upon my name, and all the nations of the world will hear what I have done, and know that I am God!**

Ezekiel 39:1-29 *(The Living Bible.)*

1 *Son of dust, prophesy this also against Gog. Tell him: I will stand against you, Gog, leader of Meshech and Tubal.*

2I will turn you and drive you toward the mountains of Israel, bringing you from the distant north. And I will destroy 85 percent of your army in the mountains.

3I will knock your weapons from your hands and leave you helpless.

4You and all your vast armies will die upon the mountains. I will give you to the vultures and wild animals to devour you.

5You will never reach the cities—you will fall upon the open fields; for I have spoken, the Lord God says.

6And I will rain down fire on Magog and on all your allies who live safely on the coasts, and they shall know I am the Lord.

7Thus I will make known my holy name among my people Israel; I will not let it be mocked at anymore. And the nations too shall know I am the Lord, the Holy One of Israel.

8That day of judgment will come; everything will happen just as I have declared it.

9The people of the cities of Israel will go out and pick up your shields and bucklers, bows and arrows, javelins and spears, to use for fuel—enough to last them seven years.

10For seven years they will need nothing else for their fires. They won't cut wood from the fields or forests, for these weapons will give them all they need. They will use the possessions of those who abused them.

11"And I will make a vast graveyard for Gog and his armies in the Valley of the Travelers, east of the Dead Sea. It will block the path of the travelers. There Gog and all his armies will be buried. And they will change the name of the place to "The Valley of Gog's Army."

12It will take seven months for the people of Israel to bury the bodies.

13Everyone in Israel will help, for it will be a glorious victory for Israel on that day when I demonstrate my glory, says the Lord.

14At the end of seven months, they will appoint men to search the land systematically for any skeletons left and bury them, so that the land will be cleansed.

15,16Whenever anyone sees some bones, he will put up a marker beside them so that the buriers will see them and take them to the Valley of Gog's Army to bury them. A city named 'Multitude' is there! And so the land will finally be cleansed.

17And now, son of dust, call all the birds and animals and say to them: Gather together for a mighty sacrificial feast. Come from far and near to the mountains of Israel. Come, eat the flesh and drink the blood!

18Eat the flesh of mighty men and drink the blood of princes—they are the rams, the lambs, the goats and the fat young bulls of Bashan for my feast!

19Gorge yourselves with flesh until you are glutted, drink blood until you are drunk; this is the sacrificial feast I have prepared for you.

20Feast at my banquet table—feast on horses, riders and valiant warriors, says the Lord God.

21Thus I will demonstrate my glory among the nations; all shall see the punishment of Gog and know that I have done it.

22And from that time onward, the people of Israel will know I am the Lord their God.

23And the nations will know why Israel was sent away to exile—it was punishment for sin, for they acted in treachery against their God. Therefore I turned my face away from them and let their enemies destroy them.

24I turned my face away and punished them in proportion to the vileness of their sins.

25But now, the Lord God says, I will end the captivity of my people and have mercy upon them and restore their fortunes, for I am concerned about my reputation!

26Their time of treachery and shame will all be in the past; they will be home again, in peace and safety in *their own land, with no one bothering them or making them afraid.*

²⁷*I will bring them home from the lands of their enemies—and my glory shall be evident to all the nations when I do it. Through them I will vindicate my holiness before the nations.*

²⁸*Then my people will know I am the Lord their God—responsible for sending them away to exile, and responsible for bringing them home. I will leave none of them remaining among the nations.*

²⁹*And I will never hide my face from them again, for I will pour out my Spirit upon them, says the Lord God."*

I inserted the previous two chapters of Scripture for a number of reasons. First, I wanted you to see the whole scenario by highlighting for you the most crucial verses of Scripture. Second, I inserted the two former chapters because I know that many of you live in third world countries and therefore you cannot afford nor do you even have access to the different Bible translations. Many of you cannot so much as afford a personal Bible. So, rather than tell you to look up Scripture verses in Bible translations that you do not possess, I have attempted to make God's Word more accessible to you in this free and postpaid work.

While paying attention to the highlighted portions of Scripture, read God's Word carefully, and take to heart what the Lord is telling you. **For, one day in the future, God's jealousy and anger will depart from Israel. In that day, the nations who have harmed or who are attempting to harm Israel will feel the terrible, full impact of God's jealousy and wrath. So, look out nations. Be warned! Tremble! Tremble! Tremble!**

Zechariah 8:1-2 (The Amplified Bible.)

¹*AND THE word of the Lord of hosts came to me, saying,*

²*Thus says the Lord of hosts: I am jealous for Zion with great jealousy, and I am jealous for her with great wrath [against her enemies].*

Gentile Christian, do not provoke the Lord to jealousy and anger against you. Do not force Him to keep His Word and to curse you because you have cursed or spoken evil toward His beloved Abrahamic covenant people, the Jews. Are you stronger than the Lord that you should defy Him? Repent! Repent! Repent before it is too late! Start carrying out your God-given task and begin to make the Jews jealous. Thus, in so doing, you will help God and His beloved, covenant people.

To help soften your heart toward the Jewish people, Christian Gentile, I am going to direct your thoughts toward another vital truth. That truth is that you personally owe the Jews more than you could ever express or repay. Had it not been for the Jews you would still be stumbling around in spiritual darkness. You would be without the truth of God's Word. Therefore, you would be without salvation through our Jewish Savior, Yeshua.

The fact is that it was the Jews who brought to us Gentiles the message of salvation. The Jews are responsible for the Gentiles turning to the God of Israel through Jewish Yeshua. The Jews were the ones who helped God fulfill His covenant promise to Abraham *"...in you will all the families and kindred of the earth be blessed...."* (Genesis 12:3.)

Since the Jews have done so much to further God's plan for all mankind, for once, cannot we Gentiles do something to help them by helping God further His plan in regard to them? For God's name's sake, cannot we show kindness and compassion to the Jews? Cannot we live our lives in such a way as to make them jealous of our relationship with God and thus fulfill God's Word in Deuteronomy 32:21? In this same manner, cannot we help God show mercy and loving-kindness to the Jews, and in so doing maybe we can manage to help save **some of them**? And most of all, cannot we help God vindicate His holy name?

It is true that God's uncompromisingly righteous character and His faithfulness in keeping His promises will one day vindicate His name. With the supporting proof of the fulfillment of all His predictions and promises, God's reputation will be cleared of all false accusations and blame. Nevertheless, we Gentile Christians should be willing to be instrumental in helping God clear His holy name by being unselfish, obedient vessels.

Oh, if only Christians would think of God's name first! If they did, they could help God glorify and exalt His name in all the earth. But instead, most Christians are so caught up with themselves that they willingly blind their eyes to the true priorities of God.

God has trusted us Gentile Christians with so much. In our hands, God has placed the tools that will help clear His reputation. He has given us the ability to pray for and support Israel. Yes, He has given us the ability to pray for and support the very people that He loves with an everlasting covenant love. In our hands, God has placed the truth. He has given us the truth because He trusts us to apply it to our lives and carry out His will and purpose upon the earth by praying for and financially supporting Israel.

Last but not least, Christian, in these last days, the Lord has mercifully placed into your hands the inspired information and warning contained in this book. God loves you so much that He has given you an opportunity to see the truth regarding His everlasting relationship with the Jews. He has shown you a glimpse of what the future holds so that you will not do anything that you will later regret.

Go forward in the power of the Lord, Gentile Christian! Help God accomplish His purpose on the earth. Help God clear His holy name. Help God fulfill His Word in Deuteronomy 32:21. Help God make the Jews fearful of being supplanted in His affections by the Gentiles. Help God make the Jews realize what they have forfeited so that **some of them** might get saved. Help God make the Jews jealous by treating them kindly and by living the sort of uncompromisingly righteous life that will make them desire to possess the peace, joy and closeness with the Lord that you have.

Church, do not waste your time, energy or money proselyting Judaism. You can not convert to Christianity a nation that God purposely blinded to *"the secret things."* As you have already seen in God's Word, it is a Biblical fact that other than an occasional exception the Jews are not able to recognize the Messiah. And furthermore, God needs them to remain that way in order to enable Him to clear His name and to safely gather in the remaining Gentiles who should be saved.

Church, do not stand in opposition to God's Word. Rather, use your time, energy and church finances to aid Israel and God's needy individual covenant people in some way. Get involved with such Jewish programs as **Jewish National Fund** or **Florida Action**. Help God bring His persecuted covenant people out of Russia. Help Him bring them back home to Israel. Help God provide for those Jews in Russia who need food and clothing and who are too old or sick to travel to Israel. Help God beautify His home (Jerusalem) and the holy grounds that surround it (that is, the land of Israel). Israel needs financial aid to provide such things as water reservoirs, forests and so forth, and God has financially blessed the Church so that the Church, if it will, can try to make amends for all the past injustices and damage that it did to

God's home, the holy grounds that surround His home and His precious Abrahamic covenant people.

Church, an apology alone is not enough. The Church must bring forth fruits of repentance. The Church must show by her generous deeds that she is truly repentant for her past crimes against God and His Abrahamic covenant people. The Church must prove by merciful actions that she has had a change of heart. In some cases the Church must make restitution and in other cases she must show forth mercy, kindness, compassion and generosity.

Church leaders can not apologize publicly or privately and then fail to show their sincerity. We must not follow the present example of the double minded Roman Catholic Church. For on the one hand, the Pope made a public apology for Christians' past mistreatment of the Jewish people while at the same time the news media informs us that just a month before His apology the Vatican had publicly condemned Israel and signed an agreement with Israel's enemies (the Palestinians) that is detrimental to Israel. Worst of all, this agreement opposes God's eternal purpose.

In a February 16, 2000 *Northwest Florida Daily News* article entitled "Vatican, Palestinians Condemn Actions", we read:

> VATICAN CITY—The Vatican joined the Palestinians on Tuesday in condemning Israel's hold over all of Jerusalem as "morally and legally unacceptable," aggravating the Israelis just a month before the Pope's visit to the Holy Land.
>
> An agreement signed by the Vatican and Palestinian officials called for an internationally guaranteed statute to preserve "the proper identity and sacred character" of the city, which is holy to Jews, Christians and Muslims.

This wicked action does not show fruits of repentance. Rather, it shows that these religious leaders of the Catholic Church are misguided and ignorant of God's Word. For God's Word leaves no doubt that the true character of Jerusalem is totally Jewish and it will remain Jewish forever. The Jews alone have a moral and legal right to Jerusalem. The Jews alone have a moral and legal right to make rules for Jerusalem. Think about it! Why does the Catholic Church not let Islam make rules for the Vatican. For that matter, why not give to Islam part of the land that the Vatican stands on. Would men condemn the Catholic Church for her hold on Rome and the Vatican?

Can you see why the Church must show **true** repentance? If the Jews are to begin to trust the Church, they must see true repentance. They must see a change in the Church's attitude and conduct. The Church must prove its change of heart. The Church can not be double minded on this crucial issue. For in this case, the Catholic Church still stands in opposition to God's Word regarding Jerusalem and God's name being vindicated through His promises being kept.

Church, do not be concerned about preserving Christian sites in Israel and Jerusalem. Rather be concerned about preserving God's reputation. If you do some research into those holy Christian sites, you will learn that most of them are not holy sites at all. For example, the streets that Yeshua walked on are many feet beneath the present streets. They have been filled in, covered over and rebuilt numerous times. Some are not even in the same location as the original streets. Yet, Christians walk on those new streets and claim that they are retracing the footsteps of Yeshua. Some Christians even kiss the ground thinking that the Lord may have walked on that particular spot. Come on, Church! Be realistic! Yeshua did not walk on those streets at all. As I said, the streets that Yeshua walked on lie many feet beneath the streets of Jerusalem that men walk on today.

If the Church wants to fight for something that is important to God, let us not fight for things that are not real. Rather, let us fight to see the land of Israel, including Jerusalem, permanently in the hands of those to whom God swore by Himself that it would belong to forever. Let us fight for the honor of God! And may God bless you and keep you as you strive to accomplish His will and purpose in all the vital, righteous areas that are revealed in this book.

Chapter 20

WHEN WILL ISRAEL FINALLY BE SAVED AND FIND TRUE AND LASTING PEACE?

As you continue to meditate upon the incredible Scriptural insight that you have received to this point in the series, I am sure that one question remains uppermost in your mind. **When will the nation of Israel finally be saved and find true and lasting peace?**

In prior chapters of this work, you learned that the Lord has His reasons for deferring His return and Israel's deliverance. At the top of God's list of reasons for delaying His return is His need **to fulfill His Biblical predictions and to keep His covenant** with Abraham, Isaac and Jacob. Also, although the Jews blindness to *"the secret things"* is not a consequence of their sins, they must remain in their God-ordained spiritually handicapped state **until God's hand of judgment is removed,** judgment that is the result of their past disobedience to *"the things which are revealed"* (God's written commandments). They must also remain in their spiritually handicapped state **until the full number of the ingathering of the Gentiles has come in.**

I am sure that you are in total agreement with me when I say that the previous list of reasons is enough in and of itself to necessitate Yeshua temporarily postponing His return to earth. However, you are about to gain insight into yet another reason why the Lord is forced to prolong His inevitable return.

Let me explain. Before the Lord returns to earth, Israel must once again be rigorously tested as she was tested in the wilderness. God still loves Israel with an everlasting love. Nevertheless, He cannot take back a disloyal, adulterous (idolatrous) wife. Therefore, the Lord must carefully and thoroughly examine the nation of Israel. Israel must undergo God's exhaustive examination until He is completely satisfied that, this time, she will remain faithful and obedient to Him forever. **Yes, God must be sure that His Abrahamic covenant people will accept and remain faithful to the promised new covenant.** He must be sure that Israel will diligently keep the laws (commandments) that He promised to write on His peoples' hearts and minds. (Jeremiah 31:31-34, Hebrews 10:16-17.)

The Lord is adamant about His adulterous wife being brought under subjection to His commandments (laws). And that is why, before Israel finally comes submissively trembling before her Messiah and King, God's proving process must be meticulously executed and completed.

The prophet Hosea not only predicts the outcome of Israel's previously mentioned trial period, but he also gives you a glimpse of the overall picture. Hosea shows you by word and deed what happened to necessitate Israel's predicted proving time. He also shows you the eventual outcome of that difficult examination.

I say Hosea shows you by word and deed because God actually had His prophet publicly demonstrate Israel's past sinful behavior and future deliverance. In His wisdom, the Lord knew the best way to get His point across to His people was to illustrate those truths in a simple, real life demonstration. So, that is exactly what God did. As part of the previously mentioned exhibition, God told His prophet Hosea to marry a harlot.

Hosea 1:2 (The Amplified Bible.)

2 *When the Lord first spoke with and through Hosea, the Lord said to him,* **Go, take to yourself a wife of harlotry and have children of [her] harlotry, for the land commits great whoredom by departing from the Lord.**

Please take time to read Hosea chapters one and two in their entirety. To save space, I will only touch on some of the highlights contained in those chapters.

(1) God compared His own marriage to Israel with Hosea's marriage to Gomer. The prophet Hosea took the prostitute Gomer to be his wife while being fully aware that she would eventually return to whoredom. Likewise, God had taken the idolatrous harlot, Israel, to be His wife, knowing that she would one day return to her old ways of spiritual whoredom (idolatry). Both God and Hosea entered into marriages with disloyal, unfaithful wives.

(2) During her marriage to Hosea, Gomer conceived and bore children. The names given to those children showed God's displeasure with His unfaithful wife, Israel.

(3) Gomer eventually deserted Hosea for other lovers as God's wife, Israel, had deserted Him for idols.

(4) God punished His idolatrous wife (Israel) on numerous occasions. He held back His blessings and finally sent her into captivity

in Babylon. However, as He promised He would do, seventy years later, God allowed her to return home.

(5) Sadly, it was not long after her return that Israel again broke the Horeb covenant by disobeying God's commands. She spiritually prostituted herself with idols. God used numerous methods of discipline but without success. So in 70 AD, God cast His unfaithful wife off the land that He had given to her and scattered her children throughout the whole earth.

We will pick up where God told the prophet Hosea to go and get his adulterous wife, Gomer, and bring her back into his house.

Hosea 3:1-5 (The Amplified Bible.)

¹THEN SAID the Lord to me, Go again, love [the same] woman [Gomer] who is beloved of a paramour and is an adulteress, even as the Lord loves the children of Israel, though they turn to other gods and love cakes of raisins [used in the sacrificial feasts in idol worship].

²So I bought her for fifteen pieces of silver and a homer and a half of barley [the price of a slave].

Keep in mind that you are dealing with a real life happening. Through the prophet's literal illustration, God makes a comparison between Hosea's humiliating circumstances and His own hurtful predicament. The Lord reveals how His heart was broken over Israel's idolatrous behavior. He lets you know that He has experienced the same depth of pain and anguish that any other loving husband would feel upon being betrayed, humiliated, rejected and deserted by his shameless, adulterous wife.

This time, however, Israel's return home will be handled differently. God will not immediately yield as He did when Israel returned from her Babylonian exile. No! This time, Israel will be required to prove herself. She must show beyond doubt that she has completely changed. God said He would bring her back home to the land of Israel, and He has. He also said that she would be His betrothed (that is, she would be engaged to Him). Albeit, He made it very clear that He will not resume marital relations with the nation of Israel until she has proved that she can be trusted. See this truth for yourself in the following verses.

³And I said to her, You shall be [betrothed] to me for many days; you shall not play the harlot and you shall not belong to another man. So will I also be to you [until you have proved your loyalty to me and our marital relations may be resumed].

⁴*For the children of Israel shall dwell and sit deprived many days, without king or prince, without sacrifice or [idolatrous] pillar, and without ephod [a garment worn by priests when seeking divine counsel] or teraphim (household gods).*

Only when Israel convinces her husband (God) that she can be trusted, only when He is sure that she has permanently given up all forms of idolatry, only when God is absolutely assured that Israel will abide by the blood-sealed new covenant and consistently keep the laws that He has promised to write on her heart and mind will He return to earth, heal Israel's spiritual eyesight and hearing, save her, completely deliver her from all her enemies and give her true and lasting internal and external peace.

⁵*Afterward shall the children of Israel return and seek the Lord their God, [inquiring of and requiring Him] and [from the line of] David, their King [of kings]; and they shall come in [anxious] fear to the Lord and to His goodness and His good things in the latter days.*

Verse five in *The Living Bible* reads as such:

⁵*Afterward they will return to the Lord their God, and to the Messiah, their King, and they shall come trembling, submissive to the Lord and to his blessings, in the end times.*

As you saw in the previous verses, before the nation of Israel can come to the Lord and enjoy the Lord's goodness and His blessings in the end times, she must prove herself worthy (that is, she must prove herself worthy in the sense of being suitable and safe). This time, God must find out if she will keep the blood-sealed new covenant, obey His commands and stay completely away from idols. God must be one hundred percent convinced that she will remain faithful to Him forever. Thus, it is for the previous reasons that He will first put Israel through these predicted fiery tests.

Only after this testing period will the blinders fall from Israel's spiritual eyes and her ears be unstopped. Only then will the Lord return and wipe away Israel's sins. Then, and only then, will all Israel at last be saved and enter into the promised blood-sealed new covenant with the Lord.

Romans 11:26-27 (The Amplified Bible.)

26And so all Israel will be saved. As it is written, The Deliverer will come from Zion, He will banish ungodliness from Jacob.

27And this will be My covenant (My agreement) with them when I shall take away their sins.

The prophets of old foretold that in the end, God would spare and save all Israel. However, we Gentile Christians must not forget why God intends to show such great mercy, compassion and lovingkindness toward Israel. He is not going to do it because the Jews deserve His mercy, compassion and kindness. No! **God is going to pour those blessings upon the nation of Israel in order to fulfill His Biblical predictions and keep His sacred promises to Abraham, Isaac and Jacob, including His covenant promise of everlasting love. God is going to fulfill all His promises in their entirety in order to vindicate His own holy name.**

Ezekiel 36:23-25 (The Amplified Bible.)

23And I will vindicate the holiness of My great name and separate it for its holy purpose from all that defiles it—My name, which has been profaned among the nations, which you have profaned among them—and the nations will know, understand, and realize that I am the Lord [the Sovereign Ruler, Who calls forth loyalty and obedient service], when I shall be set apart by you and My holiness vindicated in you before their eyes and yours.

24For I will take you from among the nations and gather you out of all countries and bring you into your own land.

25Then will I sprinkle clean water upon you, and you shall be clean from all your uncleanness; and from all your idols will I cleanse you.

The content of verse twenty-five which speaks of Israel being cleansed from all her idols, is extremely important. It is important because God's Word is emphatic about the specific condition that Israel must meet before she will be allowed to recognize the Messiah, Yeshua, and take hold of the promised new covenant. Read the following verse and you will understand my last statement.

Isaiah 27:9 (The Amplified Bible.)

⁹*Only on this condition shall the iniquity of Jacob (Israel) be forgiven and purged, and this shall be the full fruit [God requires] for taking away his sin: that [Israel] should make all the stones of the [idol] altars like chalk stones crushed to pieces, so that the Asherim and the sun-images shall not remain standing or rise again.*

Any Jew who, after witnessing God's Word being fulfilled in Israel, still insists on worshipping false gods or involving himself with the occult is spiritually blind to *"the secret things."* He is therefore unable to recognize the miracle that is taking place before his very eyes. However, he is not only blind to *"the secret things,"* he is also wicked and stupid. I say he is wicked and stupid because he refuses to obey God's law *("the things which are revealed")* or meet the condition laid out in the previous verse, verse nine. Consequently, if he persists in his wickedness (that is, if he refuses to completely disassociate himself from all forms of idolatry), he most certainly will not be included in Israel's end time salvation.

Yet, despite those individual Jews who persist in dabbling in idolatry, the day looms ahead when, as a nation, the Jews shall meet the condition laid out in Isaiah 27:9. Israel will serve only the one true God, the God of Abraham, Isaac and Jacob, the God who said, *"I am the Alpha and the Omega, the First and the Last (the Before all and the End of all). [Isa. 44:6; 48:12.]"* (Revelation 22:13.) Moreover, **as a nation,** Israel will permanently remove all traces of idolatry from the Holy Land. Yes, throughout the Scriptures, God's Word proclaims the day when, **as a nation,** Israel will come to know and obey *"the things which are revealed"* (God's laws).

Ezekiel 36:26-30 (The Amplified Bible.)

²⁶*A new heart will I give you and a new spirit will I put within you, and I will take away the stony heart out of your flesh and give you a heart of flesh.*
²⁷*And I will put my Spirit within you and cause you to walk in My statutes, and you shall heed My ordinances and do them.*

28And you shall dwell in the land that I gave to your fathers; and you shall be My people, and I will be your God.

29I will also save you from all your uncleannesses, and I will call forth the grain and make it abundant and lay no famine on you.

30And I will multiply the fruit of the tree and the increase of the field, that you may no more suffer the reproach and disgrace of famine among the nations.

If you are wondering how God will go about accomplishing His promises in the previous verses, the answer is that He will give the Jews' spiritual eyesight so that they can finally understand *"the secret things"* and recognize their Messiah when He returns. God will save His Abrahamic covenant people. They will gladly and willingly accept and abide by His promised new covenant. Yes, the day will come when the nation of Israel will accept and abide by the blood-sealed new covenant which provides forgiveness for sin and true understanding of God's laws. They will accept and abide by the new covenant which also provides the power to keep God's laws, the new covenant which God Himself describes in the following text.

Jeremiah 31:31-34 (The Amplified Bible.)

31Behold, the days are coming, says the Lord, when I will make a new covenant with the house of Israel and with the house of Judah,

32Not according to the covenant which I made with their fathers in the day when I took them by the hand to bring them out of the land of Egypt, My covenant which they broke, although I was their Husband, says the Lord.

33But this is the covenant which I will make with the house of Israel: After those days, says the Lord, I will put My law within them, and on their hearts will I write it; and I will be their God, and they will be My people.

34And they will no more teach each man his neighbor and each man his brother, saying, Know the Lord, for they will all know Me [recognize, understand, and be acquainted with Me], from the least of them to the greatest, says the Lord. For I will forgive their iniquity, and I will [seriously] remember their sin no more.

Israel sinned against the Lord. She deserted the Lord her husband. Nevertheless, as you saw earlier, even though Israel forsook the Lord and broke His heart by giving her attention and affections to idols, God still loves His wayward Abrahamic covenant nation with an everlasting love. Thus, the day will come when for His own name's sake, He will again betroth Israel to Himself. Yes, God will keep His covenant promise to love the descendants of Abraham, Isaac and Jacob forever. He will also keep His promise to be their God forever. **Israel shall again experience God's mercy, pity and lovingkindness along with His spiritual and temporal blessings and peace.**

Hosea 2:16-23 (The Amplified Bible.)

16And it shall be in that day, says the Lord, that you will call Me Ishi [my Husband], and you shall no more call Me Baali [my Baal].

17For I will take away the names of Baalim [the Baals] out of her mouth, and they shall no more be mentioned or seriously remembered by their name.

18And in that day will I make a covenant for Israel with the living creatures of the open country and with the birds of the heavens and with the creeping things of the ground. And I will break the bow and the sword and [abolish battle equipment and] conflict out of the land and will make you lie down safely.

19And I will betroth you to Me forever; yes, I will betroth you to Me in righteousness and justice, in steadfast love, and in mercy.

20I will even betroth you to Me in stability and in faithfulness, and you shall know (recognize, be acquainted with, appreciate, give heed to, and cherish) the Lord.

21And in that day I will respond, says the Lord; I will respond to the heavens [which ask for rain to pour on the earth], and they shall respond to the earth [which begs for the rain it needs],

22And the earth shall respond to the grain and the wine and the oil [which beseech it to bring them forth], and these shall respond to Jezreel [restored Israel, who prays for a supply of them].

23And I will sow her for Myself anew in the land, and I will have love, pity, and mercy for her who had not obtained love, pity, and mercy; and I will say to those who were not My people, You are My people, and they shall say, You are my God!

In the past, God was rightfully angry with Israel because of her abominable idolatrous sins. He informed **certain generations** of Israelites that He had rejected them because they had rejected Him. But as you saw earlier in the series, that did not mean that God had failed to keep His promise of everlasting love to future generations. On the contrary, in the following text, the prophet Isaiah once again reveals God's everlasting love for Israel. He also describes what will take place between God and Israel (His betrothed) in the last days.

Isaiah 54:1-17 (The Amplified Bible.)

1 SING, O barren one, you who did not bear; break forth into singing and cry aloud, you who did not travail with child! For the [spiritual] children of the desolate one will be more than the children of the married wife, says the Lord.

2 Enlarge the place of your tent, and let the curtains of your habitations be stretched out; spare not; lengthen your cords and strengthen your stakes,

3 For you will spread abroad to the right hand and to the left; and your offspring will possess the nations and make the desolate cities to be inhabited.

4 Fear not, for you shall not be ashamed; neither be confounded and depressed, for you shall not be put to shame. For you shall forget the shame of your youth, and you shall not [seriously] remember the reproach of your widowhood any more.

5 For your Maker is your Husband—the Lord of hosts is His name—and the Holy One of Israel is your Redeemer; the God of the whole earth He is called.

6 For the Lord has called you like a woman forsaken, grieved in spirit, and heartsore—even a wife [wooed and won] in youth, when she is [later] refused and scorned, says your God.

7 For a brief moment I forsook you, but with great compassion and mercy I will gather you [to Me] again.

8In a little burst of wrath I hid My face from you for a moment, but with age-enduring love and kindness I will have compassion and mercy on you, says the Lord, your Redeemer.

9For this is like the days of Noah to Me; as I swore that the waters of Noah should no more go over the earth, so have I sworn that I will not be angry with you or rebuke you.

10For though the mountains should depart and the hills be shaken or removed, yet My love and kindness shall not depart from you, nor shall My covenant of peace and completeness be removed, says the Lord, Who has compassion on you.

11O you afflicted [city], storm-tossed and not comforted, behold, I will set your stones in fair colors [in antimony to enhance their brilliance] and lay your foundations with sapphires.

12And I will make your windows and pinnacles of [sparkling] agates or rubies, and your gates of [shining] carbuncles, and all your walls [of your enclosures] of precious stones.

13And all your [spiritual] children shall be disciples [taught by the Lord and obedient to His will], and great shall be the peace and undisturbed composure of your children.

14You shall establish yourself in righteousness (rightness, in conformity with God's will and order): you shall be far from even the thought of oppression or destruction, for you shall not fear, and from terror, for it shall not come near you.

15Behold, they may gather together and stir up strife, but it is not from Me. Whoever stirs up strife against you shall fall and surrender to you.

16Behold, I have created the smith who blows on the fire of coals and who produces a weapon for its purpose; and I have created the devastator to destroy.

17But no weapon that is formed against you shall prosper, and every tongue that shall rise against you in judgment you shall show to be in the wrong. This [peace, righteousness, security, triumph over opposition] is the heritage of the servants of the Lord [those in whom the ideal Servant of the Lord is reproduced]; this is the righteousness or the vindication which they obtain from Me [this is that which I impart to them as their justification], says the Lord.

My friend, if you still cannot realize God's everlasting love toward Israel and Israel's eventual cleansing and reinstatement, I do not know what it will take to help you to comprehend those Scriptural facts. Israel will accept the Messiah upon His return to earth. She will also accept and abide by the blood-sealed new covenant. Yes, Israel will be spiritually healed and saved. She will obtain true and lasting peace. God will keep His unbreakable Abrahamic oath to His beloved covenant people.

Israel will be exuberant when God again reaches out to her in covenant mercy, pity and forgiveness. The prophet Jeremiah describes the joy that Israel will experience as a result of God keeping with her His solemn covenant promise of everlasting love. So, let us read the prophet's prediction of Israel's return and her full reinstatement.

Jeremiah 31:1-14 (The Amplified Bible.)

¹AT THAT time, says the Lord, will I be the God of all the families of Israel, and they will be My people.

²Thus says the Lord: The people who survived the sword found favor in the wilderness [place of exile]— when Israel sought to find rest.

³The Lord appeared from of old to me [Israel], saying, Yes, I have loved you with an everlasting love; therefore with lovingkindness have I drawn you and continued My faithfulness to you.

⁴Again I will build you and you will be built, O Virgin Israel! You will again be adorned with your timbrels [small one headed drums] and go forth in the dancing [chorus] of those who make merry.

⁵Again you shall plant vineyards upon the mountains of Samaria; the planters shall plant and make the fruit common and enjoy it [undisturbed].

^{6}*For there shall be a day when the watchmen on the hills of Ephraim shall cry out, Arise, and let us go up to Zion, to the Lord our God.*

^{7}**For thus says the Lord: Sing aloud with gladness for Jacob, and shout for the head of the nations [on account of the chosen people, Israel]. Proclaim, praise, and say, The Lord has saved His people, the remnant of Israel!**

^{8}*Behold, I will bring them from the north country and gather them from the uttermost parts of the earth, and among them will be the blind and the lame, the woman with child and she who labors in childbirth together; a great company, they will return here to Jerusalem.*

^{9}**They will come with weeping [in penitence and for joy], pouring out prayers [for the future].** *I will lead them back; I will cause them to walk by streams of water and bring them in a straight way in which they will not stumble, for I am a Father to Israel, and Ephraim [Israel] is My firstborn.*

^{10}**Hear the word of the Lord, O you nations, and declare it in the isles and coastlands far away, and say, He Who scattered Israel will gather him and will keep him as a shepherd keeps his flock.**

^{11}*For the Lord has ransomed Jacob and has redeemed him from the hand of him who was too strong for him.*

^{12}**They shall come and sing aloud on the height of Zion and shall flow together and be radiant with joy over the goodness of the Lord**—*for the corn, for the juice [of the grape], for the oil, and for the young of the flock and the herd. And their life shall be like a watered garden,* **and they shall not sorrow or languish any more at all.**

^{13}**Then will the maidens rejoice in the dance, and the young men and old together. For I will turn their mourning into joy and will comfort them and make them rejoice after their sorrow.**

^{14}*I will satisfy fully the life of the priests with abundance [of offerings shared with them], and My people will be satisfied with My goodness, says the Lord.*

Eternal salvation and eternal spiritual and temporal peace and prosperity shall soon belong to Israel. However, the Israelis will not be the only ones to rejoice. **Zephaniah informs us that God Himself will be so elated at the very thought of Israel's imminent reinstatement, the deserved punishment of Israel's Gentile enemies and the peace that will inevitably follow, <u>He will actually sing for joy.</u>** Think of it! God Almighty Himself loudly singing for joy! See this truth for yourself in *The Living Bible*.

Zephaniah 3:8-20 (The Living Bible.)

⁸<u>But the Lord says, "Be patient; the time is coming soon when I will stand up and accuse these evil nations. For it is my decision to gather together the kingdoms of the earth, and pour out my fiercest anger and wrath upon them. All the earth shall be devoured with the fire of my jealousy.</u>

⁹"At that time I will change the speech of my returning people to pure Hebrew so that all can worship the Lord together.

¹⁰Those who live far beyond the rivers of Ethiopia will come with their offerings, asking me to be their God again.

¹¹And then you will no longer need to be ashamed of yourselves, for you will no longer be rebels against me. I will remove all your proud and arrogant men from among you; there will be no pride or haughtiness on my holy mountain.

¹²Those who are left will be the poor and the humble, and they will trust in the name of the Lord.

¹³They will not be sinners, full of lies and deceit. They will live quietly, in peace, and lie down in safety, and no one will make them afraid."

¹⁴Sing, O daughter of Zion; shout, O Israel; be glad and rejoice with all your heart, O daughter of Jerusalem.

¹⁵<u>For the Lord will remove his hand of judgment, and disperse the armies of your enemy.</u> And the Lord himself, the King of Israel, will live among you! At last your troubles will be over—you need fear no more.

16On that day the announcement to Jerusalem will be, "Cheer up, don't be afraid.

17,18for the Lord your God has arrived to live among you. He is a mighty Savior. He will give you victory. He will rejoice over you in great gladness; he will love you and not accuse you." IS THAT A JOYOUS CHOIR I HEAR? NO, IT IS THE LORD HIMSELF EXULTING OVER YOU IN HAPPY SONG:

It is absolutely thrilling to know that the Lord will one day break forth in happy song. It is also exciting to be aware of the reasons behind His future vocal display of joy. However, as He usually does, God generously provides additional, inspiring information on that subject. In this same chapter, the Lord shares with you the very content of the wondrous song that He intends to sing. Read the actual words of the Almighty's song for yourself in the remaining doubly highlighted portion of our present text.

16On that day the announcement to Jerusalem will be, "Cheer up, don't be afraid.

17,18for the Lord your God has arrived to live among you. He is a mighty Savior. He will give you victory. He will rejoice over you in great gladness; he will love you and not accuse you." Is that a joyous choir I hear? No, it is the Lord himself exulting over you in happy song: "I have gathered your wounded and taken away your reproach.

19And I will deal severely with all who have oppressed you. I will save the weak and helpless ones, and bring together those who were chased away. I will give glory to my former exiles, mocked and shamed.

20"At that time, I will gather you together and bring you home again, and give you a good name, a name of distinction among all the peoples of the earth, and they will praise you when I restore your fortunes before your very eyes," says the Lord

Oh, Gentile Christian, are you now convinced as to just how much Israel's salvation and peace means to the Lord? In case any doubt remains, I will repeat verses sixteen through eighteen of the previous text. As you again read Zephaniah's amazing words, let your own heart rejoice, knowing the joy that Israel's blessed future holds for your Lord.

*16On that day the announcement to Jerusalem will be,
"Cheer up, don't be afraid.*

*17,18For the Lord your God has arrived to live among
you. He is a mighty Savior. He will give you victory.
He will rejoice over you in great gladness; He will love
you and not accuse you." Is that a joyous choir I
hear? No, it is the Lord himself exulting over you in
happy song: "I have gathered your wounded and
taken away your reproach.*

Nowhere else in Scripture are we informed that God actually sings.
However, in these verses, we are not only told that God will sing but we
are also told why He will sing. He will sing for joy. Moreover, we are
given the actual content of the song that He will sing. Consider the
quality of God's everlasting covenant love for Israel. To think that His
love for His Abrahamic covenant people is so great that He will exult
over them in happy song. But most of all, imagine the joy that God will
experience when all His promises are kept and His holy name is finally
vindicated before all the world.

My friend, by now it should be crystal clear to you that God did not
call the prophet nation, Israel, to a useless mission. No! The Israelites
were not intended to serve God in vain. The day will come when God's
covenant people will be greatly rewarded for all the God-ordained duties
which they have knowingly and in many cases unknowingly performed.
They will also be rewarded for the wrongful physical, verbal, mental and
emotional suffering and undeserved abuse that they have endured
throughout the ages. Yes, Israel shall soon receive great, eternal
rewards. For instance, Israel's salvation and peace shall endure
throughout eternity. Never again will God's beloved nation be put to
shame.

Isaiah 45:17-19 (The Amplified Bible.)

*17But Israel shall be saved by the Lord with an
everlasting salvation; you shall not be put to shame or
confounded to all eternity.*

*18For thus says the Lord—Who created the heavens,
God Himself, Who formed the earth and made it, Who
established it and did not create it to be a worthless
waste; He formed it to be inhabited—I am the Lord, and
there is no one else.*

*19I have not spoken in secret, in a corner of the land of darkness; **I did not call the descendants of Jacob [to a fruitless service], saying, Seek Me for nothing [but I promised them a just reward].** I, the Lord, speak righteousness (the truth—trustworthy, straightforward correspondence between deeds and words); I declare things that are right.*

Guess who else will benefit when the Jews finally accept the Messiah and partake of God's eternal salvation? If your answer was the Gentiles, you are right! **Righteous** Gentiles will be extremely blessed when the Jews are fully reinstated to their rightful position. Paul makes that fact extremely clear in the following verse.

Romans 11:12 (The Amplified Bible.)

*12Now if their stumbling (their lapse, their transgression) has so enriched the world [at large], **and if [Israel's] failure means such riches for the Gentiles, think what an enrichment and greater advantage will follow their full reinstatement!***

The Living Bible reads as such:

*12Now if the whole world became rich as a result of God's offer of salvation, when the Jews stumbled over it and turned it down, **think how much greater a blessing the world will share in later on when the Jews, too, come to Christ.***

Once the Jews are spiritually restored, great blessings will be bestowed upon faithful, righteous Gentiles (that is, righteous Gentiles who have treated God's Abrahamic covenant people well). Your being aware of that fact should give you added incentive to aid God in restoring them. Yes, Gentile Christian, for your own welfare, you should be bending over backwards to pray for the nation of Israel and to emotionally and financially support her.

It will, however, be an entirely different situation for those Gentiles (professing Gentile Christians and non-Christians alike) who have mistreated God's beloved Abrahamic covenant people. In Zephaniah chapter three, God goes so far as to mention the punishment that awaits such wicked Gentiles. As a matter of fact, He mentions the Gentiles' punishment in the very song that He will sing. God sings, *"And I will deal severely with all who have oppressed you...."* (Zephaniah 3:19, *The Living Bible.*)

Gentile Christian, it behooves you to start treating the Jews in a manner that is pleasing to God and in accordance with His Word and His will. So, pull yourself together! Make up your mind that you will not be among those Gentiles mentioned in Zephaniah 3:19 whom God said He will one day punish severely.

Israel has suffered greatly throughout the years. And, though some of her suffering has been the result of her own sins, the majority of it has been for God's name's sake and for the Gentiles' sake. God's people were scattered to the four corners of the earth. The land that is their inheritance lay forsaken and deserted, a home for wild animals. But my friend, God's people are now back on the Promised Land, and God's Spirit, truth, (that is, the fulfillment of God's Biblical predictions and sacred promises) is now being poured upon Israel in this the end of time. Thus, as God foretold, the land which had reverted back to wilderness has miraculously become fruitful once again.

Isaiah 32:14-18 (The Amplified Bible.)

14For the palace shall be forsaken, the populous city shall be deserted; the hill and the watchtower shall become dens [for wild animals] endlessly, a joy for wild donkeys, a pasture for flocks,

15Until the Spirit is poured upon us from on high, and the wilderness becomes a fruitful field, and the fruitful field is valued as a forest.

Study the next verses carefully, for in them you are told that soon God's justice and righteousness (that is, righteousness that comes through salvation, righteousness that comes through applying the truth of God's Word to one's life, righteousness that brings lasting internal and external peace) will dwell in the previously mentioned fruitful land of Israel. You are also shown what the effect of righteousness will be and what it will mean to God's beloved, Abrahamic covenant people as a nation.

16Then justice will dwell in the wilderness, and righteousness (moral and spiritual rectitude in every area and relation) will abide in the fruitful field.

17And the effect of righteousness will be peace [internal and external], and the result of righteousness will be quietness and confident trust forever.

^{18}My people shall dwell in a peaceable habitation, in safe dwellings, and in quiet resting places.

When Israel's proving time is over, salvation and true and lasting peace will come to Israel. Then, as you saw earlier in the series, faithful, righteous men, both Jews and Gentiles alike, shall exalt God's name. We will fully accomplish what we were originally created to do. We will fear God and keep His commandments as it is written in Ecclesiastes 12:13. Then, we Gentiles will understand what the prophet meant in Jeremiah 31:7. We will recognize and agree that Israel is indeed **the chief nation (that is, the head or highest in rank) of all the nations in the earth**. *"For thus says the Lord: Sing aloud with gladness for Jacob, **and shout for the head of the nations** [on account of the chosen people, Israel]. Proclaim, praise, and say, The Lord has saved His people, the remnant of Israel!"* (Jeremiah 31:7.) Thus, we shall all live forever in peace and righteousness under the rule of Christ.

When Will The Nation Of Israel Be Saved And Finally Find True And Lasting Peace?

(1) When God has fulfilled His Biblical predictions and promises.

(2) When God has kept every part of His sacred covenant with Abraham, Isaac and Jacob.

(3) When the Jews' punishment for making God jealous with their idols is complete.

(4) When the full number of the ingathering of the Gentiles has come in.

(5) When Israel has truly repented of her idolatry and has proved her faithfulness and loyalty to her Betrothed.

Then and only then will Israel finally be saved, healed and find true and lasting internal and external peace and prosperity.

Oh, let the Lord God Almighty sing for joy! Let the beauty of His song ring out all over the world! While Israel undergoes her period of purification, let the Church meditate upon the contents of the Lord's victorious song in Zephaniah 3:18-20. And, for God's name's sake and for our own eternal welfare, let Gentile Christians everywhere take the warning in God's song to heart!

Chapter 21

TRUTH DEMANDS A RESPONSE.
WHAT WILL YOUR ANSWER BE?

At this very moment, the stage is being set for God to fulfill His end of time predictions regarding Israel and to complete His sacred covenant with Abraham, Isaac and Jacob. Soon, all the world will be looking on as God culminates that which He swore He would do regarding Jacob's descendants and the land of Israel.

In the meantime, however, there are questions that you must consider and then answer honestly. Now that God has opened your spiritual eyes by providing you with the amazing insight contained in this literary work, what do you plan to do with all this inspired information? God has placed an abundance of truth in your hands. Can He now trust you to apply that truth to your life? Can He depend on you? Will you be diligent in carrying out His will and purpose regarding Israel? Can He rely on you to pray for Israel? Can He count on you to emotionally and financially support Israel? Are you willing to help God clear His holy name?

According to Acts 15:14, God has called certain men and women from among the Gentiles **to bear and honor His name**. In Malachi 1:11, God's prophet foretold that God's name would be great (exalted) among the Gentile nations. However, only when Christian Gentiles care enough about God's name to help Him vindicate it (that is, only when Christian Gentiles are concerned enough about God's reputation to help Him fulfill His word to Abraham, Isaac and Jacob) will Malachi's prophecy fully come to pass. Yes, only then will God's name be truly exalted among the Gentile nations.

Malachi 1:11 (The Amplified Bible.)

11 For from the rising of the sun to its setting __My name__ shall be great among the nations, and in every place incense shall be offered to __My name__, and indeed a pure offering; __for My name shall be great among the nations, says the Lord of hosts__.

Space does not permit me to enter into an in-depth study on the Biblical meaning of *"incense"* mentioned in Malachi 1:11. However, because Malachi's use of the word *"incense"* is not only relative, but is also important to the present series, I will very briefly touch on that subject.

In the literal sense, incense was used in Old Testament worship ceremonies. However, the term *"incense"* is associated with and is symbolic of prayer. For example in Psalm 141:2, King David prayed, *"Let my prayer be set forth as incense before you...."* There is also a New Testament reference in which we are informed that incense is mingled with the prayers of God's people upon the altar before the throne.

> *Revelation 8:1-3 (The Amplified Bible.)*
>
> *1 WHEN HE [the Lamb] broke open the seventh seal, there was silence for about half an hour in heaven.*
>
> *2 Then I saw the seven angels who stand before God, and to them were given seven trumpets.*
>
> *3 And another angel came and stood over the altar. He had a golden censer, and he was given very much incense (fragrant spices and gums which exhale perfume when burned), that he might mingle it with the prayers of all the people of God (the saints) upon the golden altar before the throne.*

Add the truth that pertains to God's name (that is, truth that you acquired throughout this series) with the former information regarding incense being associated with and symbolic of prayer, and you have true insight into Malachi's prophecy. Malachi foretold that the day would come when Gentiles everywhere would be so deeply concerned about God's name (God's reputation) that they would offer to Him pure and righteous prayers. They would offer to God prayers that would bring Him benefit and joy. They would offer prayers to God that would exalt His name, prayers that would be as sweet and pleasurable to God as the fragrance of incense offered on the alter before the throne.

With the understanding you now possess, pay attention to God's Word as you again read Malachi's prophecy.

> *Malachi 1:11 (The Amplified Bible.)*
>
> *11 For from the rising of the sun to its setting My name shall be great among the nations, and in every place*

incense shall be offered to <u>My name</u>, and indeed a pure offering; <u>for My name shall be great among the nations, says the Lord of hosts</u>.

The Living Bible translators also shed light on Malachi's prophecy.

Malachi 1:11 (The Living Bible.)

[11] But <u>my name</u> will be honored by the Gentiles <u>from morning till night</u>. All around the world they will offer sweet incense and pure offerings <u>in honor of my name</u>. For <u>my name</u> shall be great among the nations," says the Lord of Hosts.

Christian Gentile, can you see how Malachi's prophecy corresponds with everything that you have already learned in this series? For instance, Malachi is letting you know that all around the world, from the rising of the sun to its setting, those uncompromisingly righteous Gentiles who are called to bear and honor God's name will be offering pure prayers. Now, what kind of prayers can possibly be identified with a sweet smelling fragrance and classed as a pure offering? What type of prayers honor and exalt God's name? The prayers that Malachi is referring to are prayers that are offered by uncompromisingly righteous men and women who call upon God to fulfill His sacred promises in order to clear His holy name, prayers that seek **God's** honor.

Furthermore, in Isaiah 62:6-7, God informs us that He has raised up intercessors who will cry **day and night** (or as Malachi 1:11 states, *"from the rising of the sun to its setting... "*) for the fulfillment of God's promises. And as you now know, total fulfillment of His promises to Abraham, Isaac and Jacob is the one thing that will most certainly vindicate God's holy name.

For the sake of God's name and the fulfillment of Malachi 1:11, let all Christians intercede in prayer for Israel during every church service, every Christian gathering and especially in their individual homes. Let the Churches' most holy prayers be set forth as sweet smelling incense and a pure offering before the Lord. Let Christians everywhere pray that God's name will be cleared as He keeps His promises to Abraham, Isaac and Jacob in regard to Israel. And in so doing, let all the nations exalt and honor God's holy name *"from the rising of the sun to its setting.... "*

Christian Gentile, **now** is the time for you to bear and bring honor to God's name. **Now** is the time for you to stand up and be counted. In these last days, it is time for you to help God fulfill His word to Abraham, Isaac and Jacob by interceding in prayer for Israel. It is time for you to come to God's aid by coming to the aid of Israel. Yes, it is time for you to assist God in clearing His reputation of all blame and harm before all the world.

Pray as Yeshua prayed in Matthew 6:9-10, "*Our Father who is in heaven, hallowed (kept holy) be <u>Your</u> name. <u>Your</u> kingdom come, <u>Your</u> will be done on earth as it is in heaven.*" With the knowledge you have received in this series, you are equipped to better understand the importance of the previously mentioned portion of the Lord's prayer. So, for God's name's sake, pray that God's will and purpose will be done in all the earth, and especially in Israel. Pray that God's name will be set apart (that is, kept holy). Pray that God's name will be vindicated. And, my Christian friend, make sure that you keep free from sin so that your prayers will be heard and answered by God.

Pray! Pray! Pray that God's promises to Abraham, Isaac and Jacob will be kept in their entirety. Pray! Pray! Pray for God's people, the Jews. Pray! Pray! Pray for the peace and prosperity of God's eternal home, Jerusalem. **And always remember what the prophet Samuel said. <u>Samuel said that he would be committing sin against the Lord if he stopped praying for God's Abrahamic covenant people</u>**. If you have a problem with my last statement, then read Samuel's comments for yourself in the following verses.

> *1 Samuel 12:20-23 (The Amplified Bible.)*
>
> *20And Samuel said to the people, Fear not. You have indeed done all this evil; yet turn not aside from following the Lord, but serve Him with all your heart.*
>
> *21And turn not aside after vain and worthless things which cannot profit or deliver you, for they are empty and futile.*
>
> *22The Lord will not forsake His people <u>for His great name's sake</u>, for it has pleased Him to make you a people for Himself.*
>
> *23<u>Moreover, as for me, far be it from me that I should sin against the Lord by ceasing to pray for you</u>; but I will instruct you in the good and right way.*

God's Word specifically instructs you to pray for and support the nation of Israel. So, again I say, never, never forget the words of the prophet Samuel in 1 Samuel 12:23. **Do not sin against the Lord by**

failing to pray for His beloved Abrahamic covenant people. Pray for them without ceasing. For, when you pray for God's Abrahamic covenant people as the Bible instructs, you are really praying for God. On the other hand, if you refuse to pray in this manner, you are actually sinning against the Lord by failing to obey His commands and do the thing that will help Him clear His name and accomplish His plan for all mankind.

Christian Gentile, for God's name's sake, get serious about standing on the side of Israel. Do not let wicked or ignorant men turn you against God's Abrahamic covenant nation. Remember, a vote for Israel is a vote for God. Prayer for Israel is prayer for God. Financial support for Israel is financial support for God. Therefore, stand firmly on God's side, asking only to see His will and purpose accomplished in Israel, His sacred covenant promises kept and His holy name cleared of all harm.

God must keep covenant with Abraham, Isaac and Jacob, or His Word will never again be trusted by men. So, won't you do as Moses did and consider God's reputation first? The wrongs, mistakes and even the sins of Israel are secondary compared to God's holy name.

Won't you let God know that you now understand why He has put up with Israel's wickedness for so long? Won't you tell God how much you admire the fact that He has allowed Himself to be put through so much by both Jews and Gentiles in order to keep His solemn promises? Because you have seen His faithfulness in keeping His predictions and promises, won't you tell God how much you trust Him?

My friend, do not be like those Gentile Christians who twist God's Word in an attempt to gain for themselves. In their ignorance and greed, some Gentile Christians actually try to claim promises that God never made. Others try to claim promises that God did make but that do not pertain to Gentiles. Be unselfish! Think of God's reputation! God made those promises for Israel. Claim them for Israel. And in doing so, you will actually be helping Almighty God.

Put God in remembrance of His true promises, promises that will accomplish His will and glorify and exalt His name throughout the earth. Pray that God's promises will be kept so that all men will proclaim, "God kept His word to righteous Abraham! What a great

God He is! How faithful He is! Let all men praise the holy name of the Lord!"

Isaiah 62:6-7 (The Amplified Bible.)

*⁶I have set watchmen upon your walls, O Jerusalem, who will never hold their peace day or night; **you who [are His servants and by your prayers] put the Lord in remembrance [of His promises], keep not silence,**
⁷**And give Him no rest until He establishes Jerusalem and makes her a praise in the earth.***

I implore you, my friend, heed these inspired words of exhortation and comfort. For, if you sin against God by failing to fulfill your Biblical responsibilities regarding Israel, you will not have a leg to stand on when Yeshua returns to earth. The Jews' spiritual blindness and deafness to *"the secret things"* will be their defense. But, since you do have the ability to see and hear *"the secret things,"* what will your defense be, Christian Gentile? The truth is that you will have no excuse for failing to accomplish God's written instructions regarding praying for and supporting Israel. If, after reading the contents of this book, you are still blind to God's will in that area, you are blind because you choose to be blind.

My sincere prayer for you, Gentile Christian, is that you will be like King David, a man after God's own heart, a man who for God's name's sake desired to see God's will and purpose accomplished in Israel before anything else in life. On that note, let us review some of the Biblical steps you can follow in order to accomplish God's will and purpose in your own life.

(1) Apply to your life the marvelous Scriptural truth that you have learned in this series and become an intercessor for Israel.

(2) From an obedient life, offer up to God a pure prayer offering, an offering that will truly exalt and honor God's name.

(3) Pray for the peace and prosperity of Jerusalem.

(4) Pray that God will make His eternal home (Jerusalem) a praise in all the earth.

(5) Pray that God will punish Israel's enemies.

(6) Most of all, pray that God's predictions and promises will be kept in order that His holy name will be cleared of all harm.

(7) Urge the members of your church fellowship to obey God's Word, and encourage them to financially support Israel. For God's name's sake, try to persuade them to intercede in prayer for Israel each time you meet together.

(8) Keep an eye on the news. For in so doing, you will stay informed regarding Israel's needs. You will know the type of prayers that you should offer up to God daily on her behalf. *The Jerusalem Post, International Edition* is a good source of factual middle east news.

(9) Seek out ways to financially support Israel.

(10) Give Israel moral support. Write letters to your government officials. Let them know that you support Israel and, you are for your government befriending Israel and extending financial assistance to that nation. If you feel that your local government officials would benefit from the information contained in this book, send to us their names and addresses and (if they are not already on the Living Word Church of Niceville's mailing list), we will send to them a copy of this book free-of-charge and postpaid.

(11) If you hear anyone speaking in a derogatory manner about or toward the Jews or if you see someone doing evil or being unjust to a Jew or to the nation of Israel as a whole, do your best to set them straight.

(12) You now know how deeply God loves the Jews. So, put forth the effort to develop God's character in that area in your own life. Learn to love the Jews by obeying God's Word in regard to them. Start blessing the Jews and Israel so that God can bless you.

(13) Do your best to make the Jews jealous. You can do that by showing them kindness and by personally obeying God's written commands. The Jews will then see your closeness to God and be jealous of your relationship with the Creator. As a result of your kindness, generosity and righteousness, some of them may even desire the same experience with the Lord that you have.

(14) Be patient with God's Abrahamic covenant people and the nation of Israel as a whole. Remember Gentile, that the Jews are legitimately blind and deaf to *"the secret things"* for God's name's sake and for your sake. Furthermore, they must remain spiritually blind and deaf until God's appointed time in the last days. Therefore, you must allow God the space He needs to complete His proving process.

(15) Continue to put the Lord in remembrance of all His promises. For His name's sake, pray without ceasing for God's Abrahamic covenant people, and give the Lord no rest until He makes Jerusalem a praise in all the earth.

(16) Last but not least, never forget, Christian Gentile, what the Jews have suffered and are continuing to suffer for God's name's sake and for your sake. Furthermore, do not forget to let God know that you are aware of and appreciate the suffering that they have endured for His name's sake and on your behalf. Offer up thanks to God for His Abrahamic covenant people.

I have provided you with sixteen Biblical reminders of ways in which you can help God accomplish His will and purpose regarding Israel. However, there is something else that you can do to help Israel and in so doing help God clear His reputation.

Let me explain. If other men do not possess the truth of God's Word that you now have after reading this book, they will remain ignorant and unable to accomplish their full responsibility in the area of God's name and Israel. After all, how can men help God clear His name and accomplish His will and purpose for Israel when they do not possess accurate teaching on that subject? Therefore, I implore all Christians, ministers and laymen alike, let us work together as laborers with and for God. Let us not waste this priceless gift of inspired knowledge and insight that is contained in this book, knowledge and insight that God has given to His Church in order that His people among the Gentiles might help Him clear His holy name.

Christian, "...*all things whatsoever ye would that men should do to you, do ye even so to them....*" (Matthew 7:12.) This book was sent to you absolutely free-of-charge and postpaid, no strings attached. "...*Freely ye have received, freely give.*" (Matthew 10:8.) Share your copy of this book with others so that the Holy Spirit can minister to them in the same way that He ministered to you. Do not hoard this information for yourself and upon occasion throw out a few crumbs of truth to those around you who are spiritually hungry. Within the contents of this entire book, God has provided a scrumptious banquet for you and for them. **So, for God's name's sake, I implore you to allow men everywhere to eat their fill and be satisfied. Place a complete copy of this book into their hands.**

For many years, I have been deeply grieved over the attitudes and actions of those dishonest people who have used my work for monetary gain. I am referring to those men and women who would sell God's priceless words of righteousness to God's own people, while I, the author and teacher, do not even accept a salary from the church. Neither do I gain financially in any form from this book or from the audio taped teachings that preceded it. Moreover, this ministry that God has raised up (The Living Word Church of Niceville) distributes these inspired works worldwide at absolutely no charge.

Great sacrifices are being made so that God's people throughout the world might have an opportunity to understand God's Word and help God clear His reputation. However, we have received word that some dishonest people in certain countries, including America, are taking unfair advantage of God's peoples' desire and need to obtain the truth contained in these works. They are also taking advantage of this ministry's generosity. Let me explain. The contents of these different works (which until now had been in tape form only) is in great demand in numerous parts of the world. Due to the demand, wicked people have obtained copies of these free and postpaid works on tape at this ministry's expense, and then turned right around and made God's spiritually hungry people pay, often, exorbitant prices for them. Can you imagine any thing more wicked? Men selling the truth that is contained in works such as this one, the truth that for His name's sake, God has **freely** bestowed upon His Church?

I was even more devastated to learn that some men and women have actually dared to put my work on sale in stores. It has been reported that even some Christian ministries have put my work up for sale. Oh wicked man! Wicked woman! Are you so poor financially or so greedy for material gain that you would rob the spiritual food right out of God's people's mouths? Would you take from God's people the very knowledge that would show them how to live righteously before the Lord? Would you dare to deprive them of the knowledge that would show them how they can help God Almighty vindicate His name? This will not do! As the air we breathe is free, so the truth of God's Word must also remain free!

I have also been grieved over the fact that many Christian teachers and pastors have taken highlights and other portions of information from my work and have mixed that information with their own teachings. In their pride, they have plagiarized and taken credit for a work that is not theirs. And, in so doing, they have robbed God's people of an opportunity to enjoy this information in context and as a whole as God intended. This is disgraceful, un-Christlike behavior!

As I just stated, God intended that this information be presented as a whole, exactly the way it is. The Holy Spirit led me to carefully arrange this information in a manner that is easily understood by all. The Lord also impressed upon me to present the information as a complete series of lessons, and God's guidance was wise. For you see, highlights without the foundation of background knowledge to equip one to understand the fullness of them do not establish men and women in the truth of His Word. By themselves, highlights just do not accomplish the job.

I am sad to say that for the previously stated reasons, I have been forced to register the information in this literary work with the Library of Congress copyright division. Hopefully, this will deter future dishonest practices. For, to use all or portions of this work without written permission of the copyright holder breaks the law of God and the law of the land.

Those who refuse to adhere to the copyright stipulations are either greedy, dishonest or full of pride. What else could their motives be when, for God's name's sake, my work remains free-of-charge and available upon request to anyone in the world? What else could their motives be when someone else has made all the sacrifices and done all the work? I tell you, the love that is in me for God's name, for Israel and for the Church of Christ throughout the world cries out against such wickedness that would seek to deprive God's people of this priceless treasure.

Come Christian! Let us pull together in order to accomplish great things for God. Be unselfish! Be humble! Be teachable! For once, allow God's needs to come first. Stand with God. Become a willing vessel. Share your copy of this book with others. If that is not possible, at least give your fellow Christians the address of the Living Word Church of Niceville so that as God provides, they too can acquire a free and postpaid copy of this work, no strings attached. In this manner, you will be aiding God in vindicating His name. You will do that by informing other Christians of their duty toward God and the nation of Israel.

The Living Word Church of Niceville
144 Adams St.
P. O. Box 468
Niceville, Florida 32578
USA

Oh Christian, through the inspired teaching from God's Word that is contained in this book, God has armed you with spiritual insight that men have sought after for generations. So now, let us work together in order to spread this vital information to every person on the face of planet Earth. Already, we have reached millions of people throughout the world through audio cassettes that contain this message. But our goal is to get this revised information in book form into the hands of billions of people. For God's name's sake, we will not rest until all men have access to the truth contained in this inspired teaching of God's Word. So, for the sake of God's reputation, join with us in spreading this vital information.

My friend, so much is at stake, and time is short. If you are going to have a part in helping God clear His reputation, you must begin now! God's needs must be your first priority. For only when God's needs are displayed at the top of your priority list will you be able to prove to all men that you are truly devoted to God.

To help you understand my last statement, I want to share with you a footnote from James 1:27, *The Amplified Bible.* (Robert Jamieson, A. R. Fausset and David Brown, *A Commentary on the Old and New Testaments):*

> Religion in its rise interests us about ourselves; in its progress, about our fellow-creatures; **in its highest stage, about the honor of God**.

What stage of spiritual progress are you in Christian? Are you still concerned only about yourself? Are you caught up with your own salvation experience and your own personal needs? Or, maybe you have progressed to the second stage. Maybe you are concerning yourself with the needs of your fellow men. However, the Holy Spirit is transmitting a message of truth to you. **That message is that it is time for you to reach out a helping hand to your Creator. It is time for you to become concerned about the honor of Almighty God.**

Come, Christian! Let us work together for **God's benefit**. Let us unite for the sole purpose of meeting **God's needs**. Help your Lord by placing this free and postpaid inspired teaching from God's Word into the hands of fellow Christians in your corner of the world.

I am not asking for anything for myself or even for this ministry. I do not ask for your financial support. I have already shared with you that since I founded this ministry, twenty years ago, I have never accepted a salary. Neither am I asking that you purchase this book. For, I have also shared with you that, as the Lord provides, a copy of this book will be distributed free-of-charge and postpaid upon request to any destination in the world.

Minister, be assured that I am not attempting to proselyte the members of your church fellowship. On the contrary, the truth in this book is causing numerical growth in many individual church fellowships and ministries in diverse parts of the world. And most of all, it is bringing about spiritual growth. Tens of thousands of ministers use my works as a teaching aid in their church fellowships. For example, many fellowships have set up church libraries in order to give all their members equal access to this life changing information.

I am no threat to your church fellowship, minister. My goal does not include large followings. No! **Rather, my goal is to turn men's thoughts and hearts toward God, God's Word, God's name and God's needs.** If acquiring a large following was my aim, I would have quickly accepted the hundreds of invitations that I have received from ministers and their congregates in numerous parts of the world. For, they have pleaded with me to come to their lands and hold crusades.

Pastors, evangelists and laymen have also requested that this ministry establish church fellowships in their countries. But I have never taken advantage of these opportunities. God has not called me to those avenues of service. I am called to compile Biblical truth, subject by subject, and to offer my work to all men free-of-charge. The laborers at the Living Word Church of Niceville are called to flood the earth with the precious truth that God provides in these different series, giving all men an opportunity to become informed. In this particular case, we are called to give men an opportunity to be informed about God's relationship with the Jews and His need to keep His predictions and promises and clear His reputation.

I simply ask that you, Gentile Christian, you who are called to bear and honor God's name, put aside selfishness and pride and begin to concentrate on fulfilling your God-given call. Open your heart to Israel, not because she deserves your support and prayers, but for the sake of God's holy name!

Be joyful over the fact that through Israel God's name will soon be cleared of all the false accusations and criticism that for thousands of years men have heaped upon it. And now, with deep love, I again warn you. Do not side with the unmerciful elder brother, the Gentile Arab nations. Do not side with those who hate God's chosen people. Do not side with those who covet for themselves the land that God promised by an unbreakable oath would belong to the descendants of Abraham, Isaac and Jacob forever.

By their actions, Arabs (that is, those Arabs who hate Israel) make it clear to all that they do not love or know God. Neither do they consider God's feelings or needs or care about His will and purpose being fulfilled and His name being vindicated. For, if they truly loved God and cared about His welfare and His name, they would be siding with Israel instead of trying to destroy Israel so that they can steal her inheritance (that is, so that they can steal Israel's God-given land) for themselves.

Christian Gentile, with the information you have received during this series, you ought to be encouraged to support and pray for Israel with great zeal. **Truth demands a response. God is watching and waiting to see what your response will be**. I pray that yours will be a righteous response. I pray that you will show God and man that you have reached the highest stage of spiritual maturity and devotion to God. I pray that before anything else, you will be concerned **"about the honor of God."**

Psalms 122:6-7 (The Amplified Bible.)

⁶*Pray for the peace of Jerusalem! May they prosper who love you [the Holy City]!*

⁷*May peace be within your walls and prosperity within your palaces!*

AUTHOR'S PRAYER

O Lord, God of Israel, For many years this teaching went throughout the world on audio cassette tapes. During that time you accomplished so much. You touched the lives of millions of people. You saved hundreds of thousands of souls. You saved so many that we have lost count. But now, Lord, I ask that for Your name's sake You will allow the revised printed revision of this same teaching to minister to billions of people. Open men's eyes, Lord, so that, upon reading this book, they might see and understand Your divine plan for the nation of Israel and Your beloved people, the Jews. Put within righteous Gentile Christians an overwhelming desire to see Your will done in Israel.

You, O Lord, have provided this inspired literary work for all people who will take the time to study it. You have made this free-of-charge and postpaid textbook available to the rich and poor alike. All this you have done and are doing so that men everywhere will continue to have an opportunity to learn and obey Your Word, and so that all men might realize why we Gentile Christians must pray for and support Israel.

Lord, let this seed of truth fall on good ground. Give those who study this inspired teaching from Your Word the wisdom they need to understand it and the desire to obey it.

So that Your name will be vindicated, let the truth in this series cause every true follower of Christ, Yeshua, to start praying for and supporting Israel.

You said that Your Word would never come back void. You promised it would accomplish its intended purpose. I believe Your Word, and therefore, I look to see these prayers answered for Your name's sake.

Lord, continue to raise up intercessors to pray for Israel. Bring about Your full and complete purpose for Your eternal home, Your Holy City, Jerusalem. Make Jerusalem a praise in all the earth so that You might experience the eternal joy that You deeply desire and that You have predicted in Your Word. In Your perfect time, bring internal and external peace to Jerusalem. Let prosperity fill her palaces.

Do not allow Israel's enemies to triumph over her, Lord. For, You have sworn that You will deliver her. You love the descendants of Abraham, Isaac and Jacob with an everlasting love and soon all the world will be aware of that fact. In Your timing, Lord, come and save Your people, Israel. Deliver Israel from her enemies and pour out Your eternal salvation upon Your beloved people. Totally fulfill all your Biblical predictions and Your sacred covenant with Abraham, Isaac and Jacob. Vindicate your holy name before all the world.

Lord God of Abraham, Isaac and Jacob, I ask all these things for Your name's sake.

In Yeshua's name,

Amen

I Samuel 12:22-23 (The Amplified Bible.)

22The Lord will not forsake His people for His great name's sake, for it has pleased Him to make you a people for Himself.

23Moreover, as for me, <u>far be it from me that I should sin against the Lord by ceasing to pray for you....</u>